History of American Land Law

Volume 1

English Origins and the Colonial Experience

David A. Thomas

Rex E. Lee Endowed Chair and Professor of Law Emeritus at
Brigham Young University's J. Reuben Clark Law School

VANDEPLAS PUBLISHING, LLC

UNITED STATES OF AMERICA

History of American Land Law

Volume 1: English Origins and the Colonial Experience

Thomas, David A.

History of American Land Law is a two volume set, ISBN: 978-1-60042-204-1

Volume 1: English Origins and the Colonial Experience, ISBN: 978-1-60042-205-8

Volume 2: Land Law in the American States, ISBN: 978-1-60042-206-5

Published by:

Vandeplas Publishing, LLC – September 2013

801 International Parkway, 5th Floor
Lake Mary, FL. 32746
USA

www.vandeplaspublishing.com

ISBN Volume 1:

978-1-60042-205-8

PREFACE

As important as land has been in American history, until now no one has ever written a book on the history of American land law. Many writers have contributed to this topic through book chapters and articles in professional journals, but this book is the first complete, unified treatment. Land law is a part of "property" law, which touches more aspects of our daily lives than any other single legal subject. And this history of the land law contains compelling sagas of poignant progress in Western civilization's human history. As examples, the story of the Black Plague hastening the breakdown of medieval serfdom in Europe is as much a part of America's land law history as is the first American colonies' assuring survival by recognizing private land rights for the colonists.

To make this story complete, the book traces the emergence of land rights in earliest Western societies, including those in prehistory. Detailed discussions of landholding practices in the British Isles are a necessary foundation for understanding the land law established in the British North American colonies of the 17th century. This land law is the basis for land law in virtually all modern American states. Though much American land law is still medieval in concept and vocabulary, modern trends assert themselves, albeit only gradually. The history of this land law shows a close correlation between recognizing broad private rights in land and enabling the energy, liberty and prosperity of history's most successful nation. Lively debate continues over how the land law should reflect contemporary and competing private and public values.

This history aspires to the difficult goal of being both a definitive scholarly reference work and also a work of value and interest to the general, educated reader. Some parts are more suitable for specific research; other parts are more in the form of narrative that can inform and enlighten all readers. All readers are invited to find in this story greater appreciation for the human spirit. This history also includes several dozen photo illustrations, all taken by the author and mostly from British and American locations.

TABLE OF CONTENTS

Volume 1: English Origins and the American Colonial Experience

Volume 2: Land Law in the American States

Chapter 1

Emergence of Property Rights in Earliest Human Societies[1]

SYNOPSIS

---

[1] The content of this chapter was originally written by the author, and some content was drawn or reprinted from Vol. 1 of Thompson on Real Property.

Chapter 1. Emergence of Property Rights in Earliest Human Societies

§ 1.01. Introduction.

American law students are all required to take a course called Property Law during their first year of law school. Many approach the subject with some reluctance, expecting it to be more boring and technical than subjects covered in their other courses. Property Law is indeed technical, and may even be boring to some students, but they all soon realize that Property Law touches more aspects of daily living than all other law school study subjects combined. While "property law" is a broad enough term to encompass all things that may be owned, including items of personal property or intangible property, this book will focus mostly on the law of land and all things associated with land. This can include structures on land, water law, taxation of land, airspace, minerals under the land surface, agricultural crops, and many, many more subjects.

It is possible for beginning law students studying Property Law to step outside their law school or their residence and, by looking around from one position, to see a physical manifestation of some aspect of property law in every visible object. Indeed, any person can see most major aspects of property law from one's own home, as shown in Illustration 1.

Illustration 1: The author's residence in central Utah. This one parcel of land embodies or manifests a huge array of property law topics.

A typical American residence exhibits an astounding array of property law topics, such as estates in land, easements, property tax, land use regulation, real estate finance (real estate contracts, mortgages, real estate investments), construction law, land title records and recording systems, real estate transactions, marital property, inheritance, trusts, concurrent interests, landlord and tenant law, constitutional issues (such as search and seizure, eminent domain, and regulatory takings), private and public nuisance, trespass, waste, bankruptcy, title insurance, real estate brokers, mechanics' liens, surveys and boundaries, land descriptions, and adverse possession.

A glance toward the area around the author's residence shows another astonishing array of property law topics, as revealed in Illustration 2.

Illustration 2: This view from near the author's home in central Utah shows Mt. Timpanogos (11,750 feet above sea level). Depicted here are the major property law topics of public lands, natural resources, environmental regulation, conservation, water rights, mines and minerals, and agricultural law.

This diverse and complicated field of law called property law attained its complexity through the course of a fascinating history. This history explains not only the complexity but also the often arcane and anachronistic character of American land law. American property law has retained more of the ancient aspects of medieval property law than has the property law of any other national legal system growing out of the English common law. This leads to an exotic vocabulary and more than a few concepts that have no better justification for existence than their historical origins.

The chapters in this book will first treat the history of general, traditional subject areas of land law, and then cover modern developments in more specialized topics.

This chapter shows how peoples in emerging cultures of the past or the present have perceived ownership or property rights. Such an exercise is not wholly academic. Much can be gained in learning how people in the beginning phases of social development assigned value to the things of everyday life and how those values were institutionalized, preserved, and protected. Such inquiries sometimes reveal that certain cherished and stoutly defended contemporary notions of property rights are not necessarily natural, evolutionary offshoots of human need and instinct, and indeed, may even be modern cultural aberrations. Such inquiries also present an opportunity to re-examine and perhaps reform the values nourished in modern societies, many of which are tied to land as people's greatest traditional material resource.

Such a reassessment is beyond the scope of this chapter and this book. Here it suffices to show how people in the formative societal stages perceived and managed their material resources. The fact that the examples are somewhat disconnected in time and space helps to show the wide variety in their land customs. Also within this variety of examples may be found certain generalities about the development of land concepts as they are linked to material and cultural progress.

In the world of cultural and social anthropology, which forms the basic environment of this chapter, evidence tends to be serendipitous, and conclusions are generalizations in search of exceptions. In this discipline, experts routinely refute other experts who have generalized on favorite issues, because interpretation and speculation are so often essential for drawing conclusions. Reliance on any one set of views, therefore, is to expose o1ne's credibility to risk of easy impeachment by those holding other views, perhaps equally sound. In this chapter, principal positions and responsible opposing viewpoints are presented.

This chapter also introduces concepts of property in the state of nature, the importance of the community for early humans, and anthropologists' definitions of property. "Property" signifies ownership and is broad enough to signify ownership of both land and items of personal, movable or intangible property. The text cites specific examples and general conclusions concerning property rights recognized in emerging hunting, herding, and farming cultures.

§ 1.02. Property as Perceived in the State of Nature.

Even the earliest examples of property holding in emerging cultures cannot reveal how property concepts actually originated. With the information available, it simply is not possible to determine how humans in the "state of nature" first began to recognize some sort of property characteristics, either of possession or ownership. This lack of evidence has left the "state of nature" field wide open to the learned speculations of several disciplines, each promoting its own perceived rationality and none subject to final dismissal by the others. Whether the earliest humans were by nature peaceful or warlike, whether property was originally perceived as an individual or as a community asset, and whether both tangible and intangible items could be considered property, are still matters beyond our knowledge.

Nevertheless, one can clearly recognize that property, however defined, has played a crucial role in the progression of human society to greater complexity. Thus, nomadic hunter-gatherers were likely less interested in claiming and marking off an individual plot of ground for a season than in ensuring that their prospects for hunting success in a larger, less specifically defined territory were not threatened.[2] Later, the long-term rights in specific land attained greater importance when agriculture took over as the means of subsistence and prosperity. Further sophistication appeared out of necessity when resources became not only valued but scarce.

So, while knowledge about people and their property in the state of nature remains elusive, certain patterns of progression appear from what information is available about early or emerging cultures.

§ 1.03. The Importance of the Community in Emerging Cultures.

It requires only rudimentary knowledge of early peoples to realize that

[2] *See* William Graham Sumner and Albert Galloway Keller, *The Science of Society* 287-302 (1927).

lifestyles and survival centered around one's immediate group, usually a group based on kinship. Even the persons most physically capable of providing for themselves needed the presence of the group to perpetuate the race, to help in times of disability, and in myriad other circumstances. Both common sense and abundant evidence suggest that the integrity and survival of the group were paramount, indeed, even more important than the survival of any individual member of the group. Submerging individuality within the group identity produced several important consequences. For instance, if the group was threatened by external hostility, all members would help to meet and overcome the threat. A threat or injury to any member of the group constituted a threat to the entire group, and a group response was necessary. Even minor threats, slights, or offenses, whether to the group or to an individual member, necessarily called for a response, because to acquiesce would show weakness and vulnerability. If a group member committed an offense against a member of another group, the offender's group atoned to the victim's group, perhaps without directly involving either of the original individual parties.

Because recompense for injury was mostly a matter of satisfying group pride and demonstrating that the group could not be attacked with impunity, the rightness or wrongness of harmful conduct would seldom be at issue. Thus a perpetual feud could easily develop when one group avenged itself for an injury, and the offender's group felt compelled to respond to the vengeful conduct, followed by a response to the response, and so on. Numerous examples of such conduct abound even in relatively modern times in the United States, of which the famous feud between the Hatfields and the McCoys of the Appalachian mountains, beginning in the 1860s, is a typical and well-known example.[3] In emerging cultures, mutually acceptable arrangements for ending the perpetual and suicidal violence of the feud eventually developed.

With the group so all-important, individual identity and individual accountability with respect to those outside the group remained rudimentary. And yet norms and customs relating to individual members emerged within the group to regulate internal affairs, identifying

---

[3] *See generally,* Otis K. Rice, *The Hatfields and the McCoys* (1978).

aberrational conduct, allocating resources, and recognizing property and inheritance rights, among other matters. So, despite the group mentality so evident among emerging cultures, and despite the obvious need of early humans to share many tasks and resources in order to survive, individuality within the emerging community seems to have flourished, and this is somewhat evident even in matters of property.

§ 1.04. Anthropologists' View of "Property."

Anthropologists have generally accepted a definition or conception of property rights that blends both the property item and the relationships pertaining to the item. According to this view, "property" signifies not so much the object but rather the "network of legal relations" that affects the behavior pertaining to that object. The person possessing the property is accepted as holding certain rights and powers regarding that object.[4]

One author illustrated this view with an appropriate prehistoric scenario:

> As an illustration, a stone conveniently shaped for use as an axhead lies unnoticed and unused for years on the surface of the ground. It is not property. It is, in legal terminology, a "res nullius": a nothing. A wandering tribesman finds it, takes it, and uses it as a hand ax. This in itself makes the stone merely an object of possession. If the social practices of the possessor's tribe are such that any other person could appropriate this tool at will, it would still be a mere matter of possession. But if the custom is such that his fellow tribesmen recognize that he has special "rights" in possessing that piece of rock and that all others have a duty to desist from using or taking it, then it is an object of property. The stone has not changed, but the social pattern with respect to it has. It is the special and peculiar set of social relations which has transformed

[4] E. Adamson Hoebel, *The Law of Primitive Man: A Study in Comparative Legal Dynamics* 58 (1954).

the rock into an object of property.[5]

If, for purposes of discussion, property in emerging cultures can be generally characterized as recognized rights of possession or ownership, then property rights in both personal property and in land would seem to have been widespread in emerging cultures. As will be shown in the following sections, however, individual rights in property were less commonly recognized than in modern society; group or communal rights were more common, especially in land.

§ 1.05. Recognition of Individual Rights in Personal Property.

§ 1.05(a). Private Property Rights in Food.

§ 1.05(a)(1). Private Rights in Food Subject to a Duty to Share.

In emerging cultures, private property rights in food warrant special mention, because food was so closely identified with survival, and the right and instinct to claim food as one's own was frequently counterbalanced with a customary and reciprocal duty to share the food items with others. Some have seen this duty to share as a form of communal ownership, but others have criticized that viewpoint as overlooking the essentially private nature of the original possessory right.[6]

Societal recognition of private property rights in food probably arose from the effort expended in the hunting, gathering, or growing of food. But customs of compelled sharing may have been based on a recognized

---

[5] E. Adamson Hoebel and Everett L. Frost, *Cultural and Social Anthropology* 248 (1976).

[6] *See* Patrick J. Dubbs and Daniel D. Whitney, *Cultural Contexts: Making Anthropology Personal* 187 (1980).

interdependence. Thus, in studies of Baffin Land Eskimos[7] and of Comanche Indians of the American plains,[8] scholars have shown that the hunter who actually bagged the game was required by custom to share with other hunters in the area, or even with other tribespeople, once the hunter returned the kill to camp. This pattern was so widespread that "sharing of food, even though the food is privately owned, is the basic virtue of almost all American Indian tribes and of most of the primitive hunters of the world."[9]

Yet, some writers have pointed out that such sharing, even if dictated by custom, was not necessarily the individual person's altruistic concession to communal ownership and necessity, because the private owner who shared readily gained recognition for prowess and generosity.[10] In some cultures, food pooling occurred, again not as a form of communal ownership, but to enhance the leader's resources for impressive entertaining, for providing emergency relief when the group fell on hard times, or for aiding destitute members of the community.[11] The owner or procurer of the food in extreme hardship might decline to share.[12]

A different school of thought maintains that such sharing was

---

[7] Franz Boas, "The Eskimo of Baffin Land and Hudson Bay," 16 *Bull. Am. Museum Nat. Hist.* 116 (1907).

[8] E. Adamson Hoebel, *The Political Organization and Law-Ways of the Comanche Indians* 119 (1940).

[9] E. Adamson Hoebel and Everett L. Frost, *Cultural and Social Anthropology* 251 (1976).

[10] Elizabeth Marshall Thomas, *The Harmless People* 182 (1959); R. Lowie, *Primitive Society* 207-10 (1947).

[11] E. Adamson Hoebel and Everett L. Frost, *Cultural and Social Anthropology* 251 (1976).

[12] Mervyn J. Meggitt, *Desert People: A Study of the Walbiri Aborigines of Central Australia* 120 (1965); E. Adamson Hoebel, *The Political Organization and Law-Ways of the Comanche Indians* 119 (1940).

inconsistent with any notion of private property rights.[13] Nevertheless, the prevailing view seems to be that underlying the customary sharing and pooling of food items could usually be found a pronounced private property right.[14] This right would probably be acknowledged in recognition of the effort expended in obtaining or producing the item.[15]

§ 1.05(a)(2). Private Rights in Food Corresponding to the Effort Expended in Obtaining the Food Items.

The custom of attributing private rights to things produced by private effort may have been less compelling with respect to game and plants simply taken from the wild,[16] and more common as to cultivated food items and as to fabricated items such as tools and weapons.[17] Garden produce grown under individual effort on a plot of land subject to individual ownership or use would normally be considered private property; however, a number of cultures have been noted in which garden produce was either grown or distributed communally.[18]

---

[13] John Beattie, *Other Cultures: Aims, Methods, and Achievements in Social Anthropology* 194 (1964); William Seagle, *A History of Law* 56 (1946).

[14] As to private property rights in game, *see*, *e.g.*, Ruth Landes, "The Ojibwa of Canada," in *Cooperation and Competition Among Primitive People* 90-91 (Margaret Mead, ed., 1937).

[15] Patrick J. Dubbs and Daniel D. Whitney, *Cultural Contexts* 187 (1980).

[16] It was common, however, for a finder to mark as private property a beehive, an eagle's nest, a wild fruit tree, a hibernating bear's den, and similar discoveries. *See* E. Adamson Hoebel and Everett L. Frost, *Cultural and Social Anthropology* 252 (1976).

[17] Robert Anderson, *The Cultural Context: An Introduction to Cultural Anthropology* 220 (1976).

[18] E. Adamson Hoebel and Everett L. Frost, *Cultural and Social Anthropology* 252 (1976).

With a conspicuous exception in the state-owned llamas among the ancient Incas,[19] most domesticated animals in emerging cultures were privately owned, even if their grazing land was considered common property. This was probably stimulated in part by the ease with which relationships of genuine affection could arise between a person and an individual animal.[20] The private property attributes of livestock undoubtedly strengthened notions of private property generally and led directly to early disparities of wealth among persons in the same community, inasmuch as cattle and other livestock were widely accepted as the hallmarks of affluence in early societies.

§ 1.05(b). Private Property Rights in Non-Food Items.

Anthropologists readily acknowledge the close relationship between an object or artifact that has been made by human effort and the rights of the person who made it or uses it. But disagreement has arisen over whether this relationship is really a recognition of private property rights in the thing. Perhaps the spear or axe was not so much the property of, but only an extension of, the personality of its maker. Early humans are believed to have had an intense attachment to objects of personal use, and they widely used property "marks." Indeed, because such personal items were commonly seen as extensions of their possessor, they were often destroyed when the owner died.[21]

The question of whether private property rights were recognized in personal artifacts was highlighted by the peculiar style of canoe "ownership" among the Trobriand Islanders in the southwestern Pacific.[22]

---

[19] John Howland Rowe, "Inca Culture at the Time of the Spanish Conquest," in *Handbook of South American Indians* 219 (Julian Haynes Steward, ed., 1946-59).

[20] *See* E. Evans-Pritchard, *The Nuer: A Description of the Modes of Livelihood and Political Institutions of Nilotic People* 16-50 (1940).

[21] William Seagle, *A History of Law* 51-52 (1946).

[22] Bronislaw Malinowski, *Crime and Custom in Savage Society* 17-21 (1967).

"Ownership" of each canoe reposed in one person, but each crew-member had a right of use. At community fishing times, the canoe owner had to join the fishing with his canoe, or let someone else take it, and the crew members had to fulfill their tasks. This arrangement may have been a form of private ownership with reciprocal obligations to form the users into a team.[23] Alternatively, if the "owner" could not refuse the use of the canoe, perhaps no private right existed after all.[24] That latter viewpoint perhaps arises out of an overly rigorous and narrow conception of property rights, especially in the context of an emerging culture. Whatever the precise mix of private rights and duties customarily attributed to an "owner" of an object, it seems clear they were more than would have been recognized for merely communal possession or ownership.

§ 1.05(c). Private Property Rights in Intangibles.

Indeed, whether private ownership of an object was absolute, or was heavily burdened by rights in other members of the community, or partook of some arrangement in between, it seems clear that some pre-eminent private property or ownership rights were everywhere recognized in the person who found, captured, cultivated, made, or used the item of property.

This pattern extended even to intangible, or incorporeal, things. Rituals, songs, charms, dances, names, legends, and the rights to perform certain tasks of labor are a few of the things in which early cultures seem to have recognized private property rights. In occasionally transferring rights in such intangible items for consideration, it is apparent that both parties to the transfer acted on the premise that private proprietary rights were changing hands. Again, an alternative explanation is that such rights were held communally, rather than privately; that consideration was merely part of validating the ritual; and that private rights, if any, gained cognizance only if and when the culture progressed from its emerging stage.[25] Most

---

[23] *Id.* at 18.

[24] William Seagle, *A History of Law* 53 (1946).

[25] *Id.* at 52.

likely, both private and communal ownership of intangibles occurred, and it has been observed that, "as a rule, the more specialized the intangible, the more likely it will be individually owned."[26]

§ 1.05(d). Whether Personal Property in Emerging Cultures Was Predominantly Privately or Communally Held.

For purposes of the inquiry conducted in this chapter, the debate over whether emerging cultures commonly recognized private as opposed to communal property rights in things other than land is interesting, but not especially important. For even a right communally held by a kinship group or some other limited community implies some concept of property rights beyond the notion of common property indiscriminately available to all. Moreover, the evidence is strong that emerging cultures recognized some form of individual property rights.

To some extent, the debate over whether peoples held property privately or communally has been stimulated by the desire or need of some to show that humankind's innate or instinctive notions about property favor private rights, rather than communal or communistic rights. Somehow, goes the reasoning, if the innate property concepts in the "state of nature" can be established, that will be a guide for finding the most suitable property regimes in modern legal systems. Or, expressed even more simplistically, if humans instinctively favor notions of private property rights, even without the materialistic overlay of modern society, then the most appropriate contemporary political systems are democracies emphasizing individual agency and ownership rights in property. Conversely, if the impulse of early societies is to the shared rights in communal resources, then perhaps that defines the ideal of the future.

Several flaws in such syllogisms suggest that the debate over private versus communal property in emerging cultures really is not that important. The available evidence fails to show that either private or communal

---

[26] Patrick J. Dubbs and Daniel D. Whitney, *Cultural Contexts* 187 (1980).

systems were the exclusive expression of property rights in emerging cultures. None of the peoples studied reveal humans in the state of nature; the property notions of even the most unsophisticated cultures are shaped to some extent by time, place, and other circumstances. Even if the type of property holding in the "state of nature" could be established, or even if a primeval preference for private over communal, or vice-versa, were shown, that is no sure guide to a suitable system of property laws today, when the extremes of material excess and resource scarcity present unprecedented challenges.

Yet, the examination of property right notions in emerging cultures can be instructive. If the impulse of early humans is to accord special privileges of possession or ownership to the person who captures, finds, makes, or productively uses a thing, perhaps that is an inherently sensible philosophical foundation for modern property law. Similarly, if property rights in some emerging cultures were shared because they affected things essential to common subsistence or survival, that too, may be a good guide for modern society and law.

§ 1.06. Property Rights in Land Among Emerging Cultures.

§ 1.06(a). The Importance of Private Property Rights in Land Relative to the Economy of an Emerging Culture.

All societies are territorially based, and most draw their sustenance from the soil, either directly or indirectly.[27] While the land itself is important to people at every stage of cultural development,[28] the significance of establishing property rights in land varies profoundly with

---

[27] E. Adamson Hoebel and Everett L. Frost, *Cultural and Social Anthropology* 249 (1976). These authors note that an entirely sea-based community of Malayan sea gypsies may be an exception to this statement.

[28] Norman F. Cantor, *The Civilization of the Middle Ages* 8 (1993).

each stage of progress achieved by a particular culture or society. If a culture is at the so-called hunter-gatherer, or forager, stage of development, it is important for that society to have access to enough land to obtain an adequate supply of game and other edibles. But other rights typically associated with property or ownership, such as the right to occupy or to transfer to someone else, are less urgent. If the people are transient or nomadic, then again, only the momentary adequacy of any given territorial expanse is at issue, for the means of subsistence or survival are not dependent upon having permanent possession of a particular, specific parcel of land. When those nomadic people can no longer find the means of subsistence in that location, the particular land being occupied is abandoned and other, more fruitful land is found and just as summarily occupied. The attachment or proprietary impulse is to what can be found on the land, not to the land itself. Of course, if there is great disparity in the abundance of yield between one parcel and another, then eagerness for particular land intensifies, but when that abundance is exhausted, the people easily forsake the once desirable tract.

This casual attitude toward land as property is forever forgotten once the culture has adopted any other economy, whether pastoral, agricultural, or industrial. In a pastoral culture, the keeping of flocks and herds may require large tracts of land, but not so much as the predecessor hunter-gatherer culture. Land is desirable essentially for its browse and water only, so, from that perspective, the particular tract of land used is not especially important. However, even herders must occupy the land in order to exploit it, and some grazing lands are more conveniently located than others; hence, interest in particular tracts of land intensifies. Nevertheless, interest in particular tracts of land is mostly at the group level, because "the necessity to rove makes individual ownership impractical."[29] Herders use land resources because they are members of a group, not because they have obtained private rights to the land. Therefore, they "tend to hold pasture and water resources in common."[30]

---

[29] E. Adamson Hoebel and Everett L. Frost, *Cultural and Social Anthropology* 249 (1976).

[30] Beryl Lieff Benderly et al., *Discovering Culture: An Introduction to Anthropology* 106 (1977).

Even greater interest in land is found in the cultures characterized by the so-called "shifting horticulturalist." This type of economy has progressed from herding to farming, so smaller tracts of land are more intensively used, but not permanently.

No one plot of land will support a household permanently; the farmer clears a plot, works it for several seasons, and moves on. During the years of cultivation, however, the farmer invests considerable time and labor in it. Groups following this system tend to favor a combination of private and communal landholding. The social group as a whole formally owns the land. The individual who works it has rights to the use and produce of a plot as long as the plot is kept under cultivation. After the plot is abandoned, however, it reverts to the group as a whole, to be given to some other cultivator at a later date.[31]

Anthropologists see this so-called "usufruct tenure"—the right to enjoy the use and product of the land, but not to transfer it—as a source of frequent misunderstanding and conflict in clashes between cultures. Europeans who thought they were buying land outright from African chiefs, with rights to alienate the land, were, from the natives' perspective, only getting allotments for temporary use.[32] The same misunderstanding arose on the American frontier.[33]

Finally, in developed societies with permanent, intensive agriculture and many other valuable land uses, private ownership of land is most pronounced, but many limitations are imposed by governments in behalf of communal or "public" interests. In summary, the more intensive the agricultural or other land use, the more urgent is the impulse for individual appropriation of land.[34]

---

[31] *Id.*

[32] John Beattie, *Other Cultures: Aims, Methods, and Achievements in Social Anthropology* 193 (1964).

[33] Beryl Lieff Benderly et al., *Discovering Culture: An Introduction to Anthropology* 106 (1977).

[34] William Seagle, *A History of Law* 53-54 (1946).

In emerging cultures, when land is "owned," it is almost always owned collectively, rather than individually, and the ownership is shared by members of a kinship or territorial group, but not by strangers.[35]

§ 1.06(b). Property Rights in Land Among Hunter-Gatherer Cultures.

"In egalitarian hunting-gathering cultures, basic resources of land and water, plants and animals, and human labor are available and accessible to everyone."[36] The land is valuable only for its resources, which fluctuate with climate, seasons, and intensity of use.[37] Researchers have found a few examples of limited private land ownership in hunter-gatherer cultures, such as among the Algonkian Indians of the American Northeast[38] or the Veddas of Sri Lanka.[39] In general, however, "common ownership of hunting territories by kin groups is commonplace," and even non-owners may have a right to use the land for hunting, an accommodation accorded in anticipation of reciprocity when survival is at stake.[40] In these cultures, private rights may be recognized in certain sites, such as a water hole, or for certain uses. The Pomo Indians of California, for example, recognized private rights in certain lands for the specific purpose of gathering acorns.[41]

The territoriality practiced by hunter-gatherer groups was not necessarily exclusive. A Dobe Bushman group used a territory within about

---

[35] Carol R. Ember and Melvin Ember, *Cultural Anthropology* 99 (4th ed. 1985).

[36] Robert Anderson, *The Cultural Context: An Introduction to Cultural Anthropology* 220 (1976).

[37] *Id.*

[38] Frank G. Speck, "The Family Hunting Band As the Basis of Algonkian Social Organization," 17 *Am. Anthropologist* (n.s.) 289-305 (1915).

[39] Charles Gabriel Seligmann and Brenda Z. Seligmann, *The Veddas* 106-121 (1915).

[40] Joseph B. Aceves and H. Gill King, *Cultural Anthropology* 152 (1978).

[41] *Id.*

a six-mile radius from a water hole where it temporarily camped, but the group made no attempt to defend the territory against incursion by others.[42] The Hadza of Tanzania did not claim exclusive rights in lands where they hunted.[43] Australian aborigine clans developed emotional ties to particular land, but other clans had access to those lands.[44] However, Paiute Indians in the American Great Basin did claim and defend against others a hunting territory used by inhabitants of a particular group of villages. Possibly this was because the plant and animal resources were more abundant and predictable in certain areas.[45]

In a society such as that of the Andaman Islanders in the Indian Ocean, in which the harvesting of a particular tree or group of trees was assigned to one family, what appeared to be a form of ownership may in reality have been only a type of division of labor, especially because the family then shared the harvest produce with others.[46] And the groups themselves may fluctuate in their composition with the variation in resources accessible to the group, as among the !Kung in Africa.[47]

§ 1.06(c). Property Rights in Land Among Pastoral Cultures.

It is clear that acquiring certain defined rights in particular land is of higher importance to pastoral people, who must watch over and provide

---

[42] Richard B. Lee, "What Hunters Do for a Living, or, How to Make Out on Scarce Resources," in *Man the Hunter* 31 (Richard B. Lee and Irven DeVore, eds., 1968).

[43] James Woodburn, "An Introduction to Hadza Ecology," in *Man the Hunter* 49-55 (Richard B. Lee and Irven DeVore (eds.) 1968).

[44] L.R. Hiatt, "Ownership and Use of Land Among Australian Aborigines," in *Man the Hunter* 99-102 (Richard B. Lee and Irven DeVore, eds., 1968).

[45] Rada Dyson-Hudson and Eric Alden Smith, "Human Territoriality: An Ecological Reassessment," 80 *Am. Anthropologist* 21-41 (1978).

[46] A.R. Radcliffe-Brown, *The Andaman Islanders* 41 (1922).

[47] Lorna Marshall, *The !Kung of Nyae Nyae* 251 (1965).

feed for flocks and herds, than such land rights would be to peoples who rely only on transient hunting and foraging. Pastoral use of land is more intense and the need to obtain use of land with adequate grazing and water resources is more critical to survival. Although both hunters and herders can move on when the land no longer provides the sustenance they seek, and indeed, many pastoral peoples are nomadic, such moves are less desirable and more threatening for the herders. More commonly, pastoral peoples will locate more or less permanently in areas where the land can be relied upon to meet the needs of their animals.

In general, "among pastoral peoples stock is owned by individual families, [and] pastures are held in common."[48] Thus, the property right interests of pastoralists lie in *possession* of animals, pastures, water rights and migration rights, rather than in *ownership* of the land.[49] In pastoral cultures, because of animals' need to rove, the boundaries of the grazing land in use, whether held individually or in common, would not be rigid, and in any event, individual ownership of grazing land would be impractical under some circumstances.[50]

For some pastoralists, land rights are seasonal. Several nomadic herding groups in Persia held grazing lands in common, but actually used the pastures sequentially, according to their schedules of migration.[51] The Kirghiz in Asia recognized particular rights in pasture lands only in the winter, when good lands were scarce; in the other seasons, all was common property.[52] And some herders traditionally have agreements with farmers

---

[48] William Seagle, *A History of Law* 55 (1946).

[49] Patrick J. Dubbs and Daniel D. Whitney, *Cultural Contexts: Making Anthropology Personal* 186 (1980) (emphasis added).

[50] E. Adamson Hoebel and Everett L. Frost, *Cultural and Social Anthropology* 249 (1976).

[51] Fredrik Barth, *Nomads of South Persia: The Basseri Tribe of the Khamish Confederacy* 4-6, 54-55, 104-105 (1964).

[52] V.V. Radlov, *Aus Siberien* 414 (2d ed. 1968).

for the use of newly harvested fields.[53]

In modern times, pastoralists naturally seek to secure needed rights in land, usually by acquiring grazing rights in public lands or outright private ownership of the needed land. This is a natural development in economies where the land is recognized as a finite resource and where different users compete for the same land. Also, the communal way of life for many modern pastoralists has given way to private, individual ownership of both the animals and the land they use.

§ 1.06(d). Property Rights in Land Among Farming Cultures.

If a culture, in accordance with the traditional view, becomes more sophisticated as peoples progress from hunting and foraging to pastoral pursuits, and from herding to farming, then it may also be said that interest in individual land rights also intensifies along the way. The herder makes more intense use of the land than the hunter, but the farmer exceeds them both in the need for a more or less permanent, private plot of ground. Ancestral Puebloans in the southwestern U.S., depicted in Illustration 3, were both farmers and hunters.

Primitive farming techniques lead to soil exhaustion and require that farming peoples move on to other land from time to time. Thus, it is less likely that the form of property rights recognized will be permanent or will apply to land that is not actually occupied.[54]

---

[53] Joseph B. Aceves and H. Gill King, *Cultural Anthropology* 152 (1978).

[54] *See* generally Richard F. Salisbury, *From Stone to Steel: Economic Consequences of Technological Change in New Guinea* (1962); Jared Diamond, *Collapse: How Societies Choose to Fail or Succeed* 6 (2005).

Illustration 3. This museum exhibit from Mesa Verde National Park in Colorado depicts Ancestral Puebloan people (6th-13th centuries, A.D.) subsisting by both hunting and farming.

Land distribution among primitive farmers typically is in the form of a temporary allocation by a chieftain, but the recipient family has exclusive use of the allocated land for the duration of occupancy. Ordinarily, the occupants would have no right to sell the land or transfer its use to someone outside their group. Tacitus reported of the ancient Germanic tribes of his day that they allocated land to families or similar kinship groups, and that periodic reallocations occurred in order to maintain the land's fertility.[55]

A Truk Islander who cultivated a plot of land or planted a breadfruit tree could use the land or tree exclusively for his lifetime, and could assign those rights to his children. However, he could not sell the land or the tree, and if he had not assigned their use to his children, the use rights reverted to the larger kinship group.[56]

From the modern Anglo-American legal perspective, viewing property

---

[55] Cornelius Tacitus, *Germania* 169-171 (Loeb ed. 1963).

[56] *See generally,* Ward Hunt Goodenough, *Property, Kin, and Community on Truk* (1951).

as a varying collection of rights, several dimensions of property might be recognized in an early farming society: property rights were held by the chief who allocated the land, by the family head who held the allocated right of occupancy, and by the family member who actually cultivated the land. None of those "owners," however, assumed the right to sell the land, or to use it for other than agricultural purposes.

In some cultures, hunting, herding, and farming all occurred. Among the Tsembaga in New Guineau, the people had access for hunting, foraging, or herding anywhere in the tribal territory, but the hunter's family garden could be located only within the area assigned to the particular clan or subclan.[57] In a mixed pastoral and farming culture, similar arrangements could prevail. Among the Nuer in Africa, however, individual persons held the cattle; pastures and water were held by sections of the tribes; and garden plots could be planted wherever land was available.[58]

Another tribe, the Kofyar, assigned all land to individual owners, so that the land would be fully used and exploited, but only the lineage group could transfer the land.[59] This same tribe recognized personal property rights in movable structures, but considered permanent structures as part of the land. Anthropologists have noted various other multi-faceted systems of land ownership among emerging farming peoples.[60]

The general pattern of land tenure in farming cultures of emerging societies, allocation by collective authority for use by individual families, prevails in emerging societies all over the world, albeit with innumerable glosses. Among some Indonesian peoples, any individual clan member may claim for cultivation any of the land held communally by the clan or

---

[57] Roy A. Rappaport, *Pigs for the Ancestors: Ritual in the Ecology of a New Guinea People* 19-21 (1984).

[58] E. Evans-Pritchard, *The Nuer: A Description of the Modes of Livelihood and Political Institutions of a Nilotic People* 17, 77 (1940).

[59] Robert McC. Netting, *Hill Farmers of Nigeria: Cultural Ecology of the Kofyar of the Jos Plateau* 159 (1968).

[60] Joseph B. Aceves and H. Gill King, *Cultural Anthropology* 152 (1978).

village. The claimant may not sell the land, but may pledge it as security (although creditor foreclosure rights are limited), and the land is inheritable within the family line. If the line dies out, the land reverts to communal ownership. The clan or village may transfer use of the land to outsiders, but only for a year at a time with annual renewals. If the individual farmer later fails to cultivate the land, it either reverts to the group or it may be claimed by someone else who wishes to work it.[61]

Among the Ifugao in the Philippines, social organization was based on individual families, with no village hierarchies. A cultivator's exclusive right of use continued even after a field was abandoned following soil exhaustion. Another person could, without permission, cultivate an unused field for a period of time equal to the time the field had theretofore been unused, but then the right of the original cultivator was revived. Otherwise, abandoned land returned to the communal domain only when it fell back into the condition it was in when originally claimed for cultivation. Rice fields were held by families and were subject to inheritance rights.[62]

Among American Pueblo Indians, fallow land could not be used by another without the consent of the person to whom the land was allocated. Grazing land was communal. All rights of land use, however, were dependent upon performance of certain civic duties related to the maintenance of the community. Upon failure to meet these conditions, land use rights could be revoked.[63]

Similarly, the land allocation systems in effect among several African tribes required performance of civic duties, such as labor on public projects, payment of taxes, and military service. Land use rights could be inherited within the family.[64] This level of sophistication among emerging farming cultures bears some resemblance to the incipiently feudalistic land

---

[61] Barend ter Haar, *Adat Law in Indonesia* 81-127 (1948).

[62] Roy Franklin Barton, *Ifugao Law* 40-44 (1919).

[63] Mischa Titiev, *Old Oraibi: A Study of the Hopi Indians of Third Mesa* 181 (1944).

[64] Max Gluckman, *Custom and Conflict in Africa* 16-17 (1956).

practices among the Anglo-Saxons[65] and continental Normans.[66]

The cliff dwellings among the Ancestral Puebloans of the American Southwest, shown in Illustration 4, suggest more stable, permanent allocations of dwelling spaces, but the actual nature of these property rights is unknown.

Illustration 4. Pueblo Bonito, a complex in the Chaco Canyon National Historical Park in northwestern New Mexico, and also a World Heritage site, was built and occupied by Ancestral Puebloans between the 9th and 12th centuries, A.D. Its 650-800 rooms in structures rising to four or five stories may have been used for residential or ceremonial purposes.

§ 1.07. Summary of Property Rights Recognized in Emerging Cultures.

Despite the enormous variation in practice among the individual emerging cultures worldwide that have been studied, some general features emerge:

---

[65] David A. Thomas, "Anglo-Saxon Antecedents of the Common Law," 1985 *B.Y.U. L. Rev.* 453, 497-501.

[66] David A. Thomas, "Common Law Under the Early Normans," 1986 *B.Y.U. L. Rev.* 109, 116, 118-120.

> Practices and customs relating to property rights in land among emerging cultures were closely related to the means of survival. Because affiliation with some kind of group was essential to survival, the group ultimately held the rights to determine and allocate many forms of property, especially land.
>
> Individual rights in non-land property, such as artifacts, were recognized insofar as the items were essential to survival or were viewed as extensions of the person, such as a spear, but often the resources or goods produced by their use had to be shared within the group or even with strangers.
>
> Individual rights in land were usually only use—or usufruct —rights, with "reversionary" rights retained by the communal group. Rights of allocation could be exercised by the communal chief, perhaps through several levels of hierarchy, but the allocations, once made and properly maintained, usually could be inherited only within family lines.
>
> Rights to alienate land outside the group usually rested, if they existed at all, only with the group, and not with any individual occupant of the land.

These conclusions should discourage any attempt to find in the property practices of emerging peoples the foundation for contemporary value judgments about individual versus communal property rights. The adoption of any particular regime of communal or individual property rights by a particular people seems more closely related to economic conditions and personal convenience rather than to any primeval, intuitive notions about property in a perfect world.

A more intriguing question lies in evaluating the property practices associated with the supposed hierarchy of civilized development. If human society really does progress from hunting to herding to farming and highly commercial and technological economies, are the property right regimes recognized in the more advanced cultures superior to those of the less advanced cultures? If such regimes are indeed superior, are they inherently superior (or at least morally superior), or do they attain superiority merely because the cultures in which they arise are stronger? United States Chief Justice John Marshall briefly acknowledged this issue in affirming that, by virtue of conquest and of transmission of title from the British, the American government held title to land superior to the land rights of the native inhabitants then in occupancy: "We will not enter into the controversy, whether agriculturists, merchants, and manufacturers, have a right, on abstract principles, to expel hunters from the territory they possess, or to contract their limits."[67]

As a practical matter, of course, a system of government that asserts sovereignty over land also establishes the qualifications for and limitations upon land rights available to its individual citizens and inhabitants. Typically, the range of individual land rights is reduced as the land comes under more intense pressure from increasing population or becomes more valuable for more and diverse purposes. Value judgments about the desirability of retaining particular private rights under such circumstances may vary. On the one hand, recognizing private property rights may encourage and reward individual agency, ambition, and initiative. On the other hand, properly administering property as a common source of wealth—indeed, a commonwealth—may help eliminate the worst forms of individual deprivation and raise the welfare of society generally.

§ 1.08. Bibliography.

Books

Aceves, Joseph B. and H. Gill King, *Cultural Anthropology* (1978).

Alston, Lee J., Gary D. Libecap, and Bernardo Mueller. *Titles, Conflict, and Land Use: The Development of Property Rights and Land Reform on the Brazilian Amazon Frontier* (1999).

---

[67] Johnson v. M'Intosh, 21 U.S. (8 Wheat.) 543, 588 (1923).

Anderson, Robert, *The Cultural Context: An Introduction to Cultural Anthropology* (1976).
Barth, Fredrik, *Nomads of South Persia: The Basseri Tribe of the Khamish Confederacy* (1964).
Barton, Roy Franklin, *Ifugao Law* (1919).
Beattie, John, *Other Cultures: Aims, Methods, and Achievements in Social Anthropology* (1964).
Benderly, Beryl Lieff et al., *Discovering Culture: An Introduction to Anthropology* (1977).
Bernhardt, Kathryn, *Women and Property in China: 960-1949* (1999).
Clarke, Alison and Paul Kohler, *Property Law: Commentary and Materials* (2005).
De Laveleye, Emile, *Primitive Property* (G. R. L. Marriott trans. 1999)
Diamond, Jared M., *Collapse: How Societies Choose to Fail or Succeed* (2005).
Diamond, Jared M., *Guns, Germs, and Steel: The Fates of Human Societies* (1997).
Digby, Kenelm Edward, *An Introduction to the History of the Law of Real Property* (1897).
Diosdi, Gyorgy, *Ownership in Ancient and Preclassical Roman Law* (1970).
Dubbs, Patrick J. and Daniel D. Whitney, *Cultural Contexts: Making Anthropology Personal* (1980).
Ember, Carol R. and Melvin Ember, *Cultural Anthropology* (4th ed. 1985).
Engels, Frederick, *The Origin of the Family, Private Property, and the State In Light of the Researches of Lewis H. Morgan* (1884).
Erdenebaatar, B., *The Pastoral Environment and the Economy, Culture and Environment in Inner Asia* (1996).
Evans-Pritchard, E., *The Nuer: A Description of the Modes of Livelihood and Political Institutions of a Nilotic People* (1940).
Fales Mario, *A Survey of Neo-Assyrian Land Sales, Land Tenure and Social Transformation in the Middle East* (1984).
Finley, M.I., *Economy and Society in Ancient Greece* (1982).
Finley, M.I., *Studies in Roman Property* (1976).
Fischer, David Hackett, *Albion's Seed: Four British Folkways in America* (1989).
Foster Benjamin R., *Administration and Use of Institutional Land in Sargonic Mesopotamia* (1982).
Gelb, Ignace J. et al, *Earliest Land Tenure Systems in the Near East: Ancient Kudurrus* (1991).
Gluckman, Max, *Custom and Conflict in Africa* (1956).
Goodenough, Ward Hunt, *Property, Kin, and Community on Truk* (1951).
Hann, C. M., *Property Relations: Renewing the Anthropological Tradition* (1998).
Hoebel, E. Adamson, *The Law of Primitive Man: A Study in Comparative Legal Dynamics* (1954).
Hoebel, E. Adamson, *The Political Organization and Law-Ways of the Comanche Indians* (1940).
Hoebel, E. Adamson and Everett L. Frost, *Cultural and Social Anthropology* (1976).
Hudson, Michael and Baruch A. Levine, *Privatization in the Ancient Near East and Classical World* (1996).
Knauft, Bruce M., *From Primitive to Postcolonial in Melanesia and Anthropology* (1999).
Kuper, Adam, *The Reinvention of Primitive Society: Transformations of a Myth* (2005).
LeFevre, Robert, *The Philosophy of Ownership* (1966).
Lowie, R., *Primitive Society* (1947).
Maisels, Charles Keith, *The Emergence of Civilization: From Hunting and Gathering to Agriculture, Cities, and the State in the Near East* (1990)

Malinowski, Bronislaw, *Crime and Custom in Savage Society* (1967).
Mann, Charles C., *1491: New Revelations of the Americas Before Columbus* (2005).
Marshall, Lorna, *The !Kung of Nyae Nyae* (1965).
Mass, Jeffrey P., *Family, Law, and Property in Japan 1200-1350* (2000).
McKay, John P., Bennett D. Hill, and John Buckler, *A History of World Societies* (3d ed. 1992).
Meggitt, Mervyn J., *Desert People: A Study of the Walbiri Aborigines of Central Australia* (1965).
Miceli, Thomas J., *Economic Approach to Law* (2003).
Netting, Robert McC., *Hill Farmers of Nigeria: Cultural Ecology of the Kofyar of the Jos Plateau* (1968).
Noyes, C. Reinold, *The Institution of Property: A Study of the Development, Substance and Arrangement of the System of Property in Modern Anglo-American Law* (1936).
Pestman, P.W., "The Law of Succession in Ancient Egypt," in J. Brugman et al, eds., *Essays on Oriental Laws of Succession* (1969).
Pipes, Richard, *Property and Freedom* (1999)
Radcliffe-Brown, A.R., *The Andaman Islanders* (1922).
Radlov, V.V., *Aus Siberien* (2d ed. 1968).
Rappaport, Roy A., *Pigs for the Ancestors: Ritual in the Ecology of a New Guinea People* (1984).
Rice, Otis K., *The Hatfields and the McCoys* (1978).
Rose, Carol M., *Property and Persuasion: Essays on the History, Theory, and Rhetoric of Ownership* (1994).
Salisbury, Richard F., *From Stone to Steel: Economic Consequences of Technological Change in New Guinea* (1962).
Schrijver, Nico, *Sovereignty Over Natural Resources: Balancing Rights & Duties* (1997).
Seagle, William, *A History of Law* (1946).
Seligmann, Charles Gabriel and Brenda Z. Seligmann, *The Veddas* (1915).
Siegan, Bernard H., *Property Rights: from Magna Carta to the Fourteenth Amendment* (2001).
Sumner, William Graham and Albert Galloway Keller, *The Science of Society* (1927).
Tacitus, Cornelius, *Germania* (Loeb ed. 1963).
Ter Haar, Barend, *Adat Law in Indonesia* (1948).
Thomas, Elizabeth Marshall, *The Harmless People* (1959).
Titiev, Mischa, *Old Oraibi: A Study of the Hopi Indians of Third Mesa* (1944).
Weber, Max, *The Agrarian Sociology of Ancient Civilizations* (R.I. Frank trans., (1976) (1909)).
Westbrook, Raymond, *Property and the Family in Biblical Law* (1994).
Wickham, Chris, *Land and Power: Studies in Italian and European Social History, 400-1200* (1994).

Chapters in Books

Hiatt, L.R., Ch. 10, "Ownership and Use of Land Among Australian Aborigines," in Lee, Richard B. and Irven DeVore, eds., *Man the Hunter* (1968).
Landes, Ruth, Ch. 3, "The Ojibwa of Canada," in Mead, Margaret, ed., *Cooperation and Competition Among Primitive People* (1937).
Lee, Richard B., Ch. 4, "What Hunters Do for a Living, or, How to Make Out on Scarce Resources," in Lee, Richard B. and Irven DeVore, eds., *Man the Hunter* (1968).

Rowe, John Howland, "Inca Culture at the Time of the Spanish Conquest," in Steward, Julian Haynes, ed., *Handbook of South American Indians* (1946-59).
Ward, William A., "Some Aspects of Private Land Ownership and Inheritance in Ancient Egypt, ca. 2500-1000 B.C," in Tarif Khalidi (ed)., *Land Tenure and Social Transformation in the Middle East* (1984).
Woodburn, James., "An Introduction to Hadza Ecology," in Lee, Richard B. and Irven DeVorde, eds., *Man the Hunter* (1968).

Articles

Anaya, S. James, "Maya Aboriginal Land and Resource Rights and the Conflict Over Logging in Southern Belize," 1 *Yale H.R. & Dev. L.J.* 17 (1998).
Arrunada, Benito, "Property Enforcement as Organized Consent," 19 *J.L. Econ. & Org.* 401 (Oct. 2003).
Baer, Klaus, "The Low Price of Land in Ancient Egypt," 1 *J. Am. Res. Center in Egypt* 25 (1962).
Bailey, Martin J., "Approximate Optimality of Aboriginal Property Rights," 35 *Journal of Law and Economics* 183 (1992).
Banner, Stuart, "Two Properties, One Land: Land and Space in Nineteenth-Century New Zealand," 24 *Law and Social Inquiry* 807 (1999).
Banner, Stuart, "Why Terra Nullis? Anthropology and Early Property Law in Early Australia," 23 *Law & Hist. Rev.* 95 (Spring 2005).
Benson, Bruce L., "Property Rights in Primitive Societies: Law Without Government," 26 *Harv. J.L. & Pub. Pol'y* 923 (Summer 2003).
Boas, Franz, "The Eskimo of Baffin Land and Hudson Bay," 16 *Bull. Am. Museum Nat. Hist.* 116 (1907).
Carstens, Peter, "The Inheritance of Private Property Among the Nama of Southern Africa Reconsidered," 53 *Africa* 58, 68 (1983).
Caudill, David S., "Race, Science, History and Law," 9 *Wash. & Lee Race & Ethnic Anc. L.J.* 1 (Spring 2003).
De Obalda, Irma, "Western Intellectual Property and Indigenous Cultures: The Case of the Panamanian Indigenous Intellectual Property Law," 23 *B.U. Int'l L.J.* 337 (2005).
Demsetz, Harold, "Toward a Theory of Property Rights II: The Competition Between Private and Collective Ownership," 31 *J. Legal Stud.* 653 (June 2002).
Dyson-Hudson, Rada and Eric Alden Smith, "Human Territoriality: An Ecological Reassessment," 80 *Am. Anthropologist* 21 (1978).
Elias, Sian, "First Peoples and Human Rights, A South Seas Perspective," 39 *N.M. L. Rev.* 299 (Spring, 2009).
Epstein, Richard A., "Possession as the Root of Title," 13 *Ga. L. Rev.* 1221 (1979).
Epstein, Richard A., "Property Rights Claims of Indigenous Populations: The View from the Common Law," 31 *University of Toledo Law Review* 1 (Fall 1999).
Field, Bany C., "The Evolution of Property Rights," 42 *Kyklos* 319 (1989).
Foster, Benjamin R., "Early Mesopotamian Land Sales," 114 *J. Am. Oriental Soc'y* 440, 444 (1994).
Freyfogle, Eric T., "Ethics, Community, and Private Land," 23 *Ecology L.Q.* 631, 632-638 (1993).
Freyfogle, Eric T., "Land Use and the Study of Early American History," 91 *Yale L.J.* 717 (1985).
Fuentes, Juan Andres, "Protecting the Rights of Indigenous Cultures Under the Current Intellectual Property System: Is It a Good Idea?" 3 *J. Marshall Rev. Intell. Prop. L.* 88 (Fall, 2003).

Gambaro, Antonio, "Property Rights in Comparative Perspective: Why Property is so Ancient and Durable," 26 *Tul Eur. & Civ. L.F.* 205 (2011).

Gardner, Peter J., "Our Intellectual Property World: Charting a Course from Ancient Native Cultures to the Threshold of the Future on a Roiled Sea of Macroeconomics, Morality and Ethics," 44 *Idea: The Journal of Law and Technology* 237 (2004).

Green, Shelbey D., "Specific Relief for Ancient Deprivations of Property," 36 *Akron L. Rev.* 245 (2003).

Gunawardana, R.A.L.H., "Necessary Evil, The Growth of A System of Judicial Courts and the Response It Evoked Among the Buddhist Monastic Community in Ancient Sri Lanka," 55 *Buffalo L. Rev.* 685 (July 2007).

Huff, Andrew, "Indigenous Land Rights and the New Self-Determination," 16 *Colo. J. Int'l Envtl. L. & Pol'y* 295 (Spring 2005).

Kelley, Jill Koren, "Owning the Sun: Can Native Culture Be Protected Through Current Intellectual Property Law?" 7 *J. High Tech L.* 180 (2007).

Malagrino, Dylan Oliver, "Applying Communal Theories to Urban Property: An Anthropological Look at Using the Elaboration of Common Property Regimes to Reduce Social Exclusion from Housing Markets," 10 *U.C. Davis Bus. L.J.* 33 (Fall 2009).

Paterson, Robert K., "Resolving Material Culture Disputes: Human Rights, Property Rights and Crimes Against Humanity," 14 *Willamette J. Int'l L. & Disp. Resol.* 155 (2006).

Pruner, Jacqueline F., "Aboriginal Title and Extinguishment Not So 'Clear and Plain': A Comparison of the Current Maori and Haida Experiences," 14 *Pac. Rim L. & Pol'y J.* 253 (2005).

Renger, Johannes M., "Institutional, Communal, and Individual Ownership or Possession of Arable Land in Ancient Mesopotamia from the End of the Fourth to the End of the First Millennium B.C.," 71 *Chi.-Kent L. Rev.* 269 (1995).

Riley, Angela R., "Recovering Collectivity: Group Rights to Intellectual Property in Indigenous Communities," 18 *Cardozo Arts & Entertainment Law Journal* 175 (Spring 2000).

Sangmpam, S. N., "Sociology of 'Primitive Societies,' Evolutionism, and Africa," 10 *Sociological Forum* 609 (1995).

Schmidtz, David and Elizabeth Willott, "Reinventing the Commons: An African Case Study," 37 *U.C. Davis L. Rev.* 203 (Nov. 2003).

Seielstad, Andrea M., "The Recognition and Evolution of Tribal Sovereign Immunity under Federal Law: Legal, Historical, and Normative Reflections on a Fundamental Aspect of American Indian Sovereignty," 37 *Tulsa L. Rev.* 661 (Spring 2002).

Speck, Frank G., "The Family Hunting Band As the Basis of Algonkian Social Organization," 17 *Am. Anthropologist (n.s.)* 289 (1915).

Thomas, David A., "Anglo-Saxon Antecedents of the Common Law," 1985 *B.Y.U. L. Rev.* 453.

Thomas, David A., "Common Law Under the Early Normans," 1986 *B.Y.U. L. Rev.* 109.

Thorland, Charles D., "Ancient Land Law: Mesopotamia, Egypt, Israel," 71 *Chi-Kent L. Rev.* 321 (1995).

Tsosie, Rebecca, "Land, Culture, and Community: Reflections on Native Sovereignty and Property in America," 34 *Ind. L. Rev.* 1291 (2001).

Ward Kathleen. A., "Before and After the White Man: Indian Women, Property Progress, and Power," 6 *Conn. Pub. Int. L. J.* 245-267 (2007).

Wiersma, Lindsey, "Indigenous Lands as Cultural Property: A New Approach to Indigenous Land Claims," 54 *Duke L.J.* 1061 (February, 2005).

Chapter 2

The Beginnings of Law in Western Civilization: The Emergence of Law from Prehistory

SYNOPSIS

Chapter 2. The Beginnings of Law in Western Civilization: The Emergence of Law from Prehistory

§ 2.01. What is Law?

A history of law should begin with a clear notion of what law is, but that is a definition upon which little agreement has ever existed. The California Supreme Court once declared that "There is no word in the [English] language which, in its popular and technical application, takes a wider or more diversified signification than the word 'law.' Its use in both regards is illimitable."[68] This, however, has not stopped other American

[68] Miller v. Dunn, 14 P. 27, 28 (Cal. 1887).

courts from noting that law is "generally understood"[69] and, "as used in legislative enactments, has a well known and definite meaning."[70] American courts have also adopted Blackstone's definition of law as "A rule of civil conduct prescribed by the supreme power in a state, commanding what is right and prohibiting what is wrong."[71]

Similar formulations have appeared outside the Anglo-American legal tradition. Cicero named law "the highest reason implanted in nature, which prescribes those things which ought to be done, and forbids the contrary."[72] Grotius defined law as "a rule of moral action obliging to that which is right,"[73] and Jhering said law is "the sum of rules of constraint which obtain in a state."[74]

In its earliest Germanic or Nordic roots, the word for law ("lag") meant something that was laid or fixed or placed.[75] In its highly developed and variant modern forms, law seems to be a distinct and recognizable concept, even if difficult to define in a comprehensive statement.

This chapter and several following chapters will help explain how western civilization changed from a collection of cultures with only rudimentary law, to its present condition, which in most ways is dominated by law. In this chapter, it will be shown how the beginnings of law among the prehistoric peoples of western civilization burgeoned into many legal

---

[69] Sate v. United States Express Co., 145 N.W. 451, 455 (Iowa 1914) (stating–and paraphrasing Blackstone's definition–that law is "quite generally defined . . . as 'a rule of civil action prescribed by the supreme power in a state commanding what is right and prohibiting what is wrong.'").

[70] Rich Hill Coal Co. v. Bashore, 7 A.2d 302, 312 (Pa. 1939).

[71] 1 William Blackstone, *Commentaries* *44.

[72] Marus Tullius Cicero, *De legibus libri tres*, Leb. I, c. 6, p. 46 (Georg Olms Verlag (1973) (1824))

[73] *De jure belli ac pacis* (1625), 1. 1. 9, § 1.

[74] 1 Rudolf von Jhering, *Der Zweck im Recht*, 320 (2d ed. 1884).

[75] 6 *The Oxford English Dictionary* 113 (1970).

systems; as early cultures transformed custom into law, then law became an integral element of overall societal development. The evolution of law generated changes in the customs and rules governing rights in land and other property.

§ 2.02. "Law" and Social Organization Among Western Civilization's Prehistoric Peoples

It is a bit odd that a history of anything—especially of something like law—should begin with an examination of its prehistory, of its existence before writing. But it is obvious that even people who did not write must have organized and conducted their affairs according to generally accepted traditions, customs and rules. Eventually, these practices assumed the force of law, although exactly when and how that happened is much discussed among scholars.

Even without leaving behind written records, it is clear that prehistoric peoples adopted forms of social organization, and that they conducted their affairs within the frameworks of these social organizations in a more or less orderly way. Whether these traditions, customs and rules could be called law during prehistoric times is not a crucial determination; however, it is important to recognize that the foundations for modern legal systems were laid in prehistory.

§ 2.02(a). "Law" and Social Organization in the Prehistoric West During the Ice Ages

In the prehistory of western civilization,[76] only a cursory review need

---

[76] Western civilization and the West are referred to in this chapter as more or less synonymous with Europe, and the terms are used interchangeably. The summary and generalized statements in this chapter are based on enormous scholarly documentation and details. Many of those conclusions are the subject of ongoing academic debates, and all are subject to refinement or revision as research and discovery continue. For further reading, see, e.g., Richard Bradley, *The Prehistory of Britain and Ireland* 27-87, 226 278 (2007); Andrew Jones, ed., *Prehistoric Europe: Theory and Practice* 285-372 (2008); Sarunas Milisauskas, ed., *European Prehistory: A Survey* 143-387 (2002); T. Douglas Price, *Europe Before Rome*

be extended back before the last ice age, because it is only upon the final (or the most recent) receding of those ice sheets that Europe's period of uninterrupted human occupancy begins.

The archaeological and anthropological record also suggests that humans first entered Europe from Africa, perhaps as they learned to cope with seasonal change and the increased difficulty of getting food during the harsher seasons of the year. It is not yet possible to differentiate among these early peoples according to tribal names or other distinguishing cultural characteristics, so mostly what is known about these nameless, faceless generations is their migrations and their progress in material culture and social organization.

It is also not yet possible to make anything more than a general statement about racial characteristics of ice age Europeans. In the racial classifications that have been suggested for prehistoric humans, based generally on cranial and dental details, scholars have termed these peoples of Europe and western Asia as Caucasoid. Within this general and geographical class, many local "racial" variations developed, probably influenced somewhat by environmental conditions. Also, during the last ice age, when sea levels lowered by as much as 300 feet, human movements and migrations produced both expansion and mixing of racial groups.

After entering Europe, prehistoric people were repeatedly driven back to the south by a succession of "ice ages"—advancing and receding ice sheets over most of Europe—and, being mobile and nomadic, their habitation of Europe ebbed and flowed with the ice. Throughout most of prehistory, these peoples retained, in addition to their mobility, the other general characteristics of hunter-gatherer economies and social organizations that were—as far as we know—essentially egalitarian and not conspicuously stratified.

In those earlier millennia, the archaeological record is abundant, but limited in scope. It shows that prehistoric Europeans lived in caves, temporary campsites, and even in settlements. They were hunter-gatherers

---

15-218 (2013).

and usually moved in search of the game that was their principal source of sustenance. Living in small groups, they organized themselves in order to find and process their food.

§ 2.02(b). "Law" and Social Organization in Prehistoric Europe After the Ice Ages

§ 2.02(b)(1). Farming Comes to Europe

The end of the last ice age brought profound and unprecedented developments. As Caucasoid peoples returned to Europe on the heels of the receding ice cap, the cultural characteristics of their hunter-gatherer economy that had survived through the numerous ice ages of the preceding millennia gave way finally to an economy of growing crops and domesticating animals. And, with an agricultural economy, ranked societies appeared and became commonplace, and people imposed more control over their natural environment rather than living totally within its natural constraints. It is not known why these changes should have occurred following the most recent ice age, when they apparently had not occurred between any of the earlier ice ages.

The last major ice cap in Europe began to retreat only about 15,000, B.C. Several minor re-advances of glaciation followed, but gradually animals moved back to the land as it was released from glacial conditions, and humans followed the animals. The period of uninterrupted human resettlement in northern Europe began probably between 11,000 and 10,000, B.C. Ancient caves were re-occupied, open settlements grew up in lowland areas, and human occupation probably occurred all over Europe, including throughout a large land basin extending from Britain to Denmark. Now mostly covered by the North Sea, that area still yields prehistoric artifacts in modern fishing nets.

Farming societies established themselves in southeastern Europe as early as about 7,000, B.C., and spread to the northwest over the next three thousand years. While it is likely that some agricultural staples and domesticated animals were introduced into southeastern Europe from the near East, it is not known whether the establishment of farming itself was an indigenous parallel development, or was imported from the near East, or arose from a combination of those factors. In the very early stages of farm life, living arrangements were characterized by short term campsites, locations for specialized activities, and temporary herding bases. Eventually, however, these became more permanent habitations and were grouped into small settlements. From burial remains it seems that the household was the centrally important unit of social organization, and that the people shared a common general belief system. Both of these factors helped in achieving order in these prehistoric societies. The existence of settlements and villages during this period also suggests that the people cooperated in some of the tasks of husbandry, and this, too, would have depended on some form of social organization.

By about 5,000, B.C., copper-working had begun and, with it, increasing specialization in other crafts. Ore extraction and processing, and the development of crafts generally, indicate growing sophistication in social organization. While some villages were significantly larger than others, and may have asserted some type of social or political leadership, there is for this period still no evidence of change from the type of social organization in which the household continued to be the central unit.

Any suggestion at all of social organization raises the likelihood that the people recognized some form of law. If a settlement is created, or land is divided and assigned, or craft specialization is sponsored, some person or group possesses or is accorded the power and right to make and enforce such decisions; such a society is therefore to that extent subject to the rule of law.

This is the pattern of social organization and law that arose in central Europe, where farming did not appear until about 5,500, B.C. Thereafter farming spread rapidly to the west. Probably newcomers introduced farming into central Europe, and there is some evidence for contact with and exchanges between the arriving farmers and the native hunters. For a while, a mixed society of hunters and farmers prevailed, and, while farming had spread all over continental Europe by 4,500, B.C., it had not necessarily been yet embraced by a majority of the population. As farmers and hunters thus lived side by side, eventually the farming cultures began to dominate.

In the extreme northwest of Europe, Britain became an island by about 6,000, B.C., and farming did not appear until about 4,000, B.C.; the hunter-gatherer groups co-existed with the farmers and did not disappear from Britain until about a thousand years later.

During the two millennia it took for farming to supersede hunting as the main subsistence activity in Europe, those cultures interacted and combined in many different ways, so that distinct regional cultures emerged. In western and northern Europe, for instance, the hunting element was stronger in the combined cultures, and the overall material culture was less elaborate. Cultural emphasis in those regions shifted from houses for the living to burials for the dead; burial tombs themselves, of timber or stone, became larger, and eventually a tradition formed of building them under monumental mounds of various shapes and sizes. Widespread evidence of these monuments survives today in northern and western Europe. Indeed, the numerous stone monuments in a wide variety of configurations appearing in large areas of Europe result from remarkable social organization and something like the power of law in prehistoric European societies.

These prehistoric communities combined methods of organizing for large undertakings with the technical expertise required to move enormous quantities of earth, to clear vast woodland areas, to build complex trackways, and to transport huge stones long distances for monuments and barrows. The large stone monuments for ceremonial and burial sites are, of course, the most impressive and permanent reminders of prehistoric societies whose main features—including legal customs—still remain mysteries. However, it must be assumed that these societies needed impressive political and legal powers to marshal the human and material resources necessary for such projects. For instance, it has been estimated that the henge-like enclosure at Durrington Walls in Wiltshire, England, which covers 30 acres, required workers using antler picks, ropes and baskets for 900,000 man hours to remove 65,000 cubic yards of material. The largest monument of this era anywhere in Europe, the man-made mound called Silbury Hill, shown in Illustration 5, also in Wiltshire, covers 5.5 acres, reaches 131 feet in height, and would have required the full-time labor of 500 men working every day for ten years, about 15,000,000 man hours.

Illustration 5: Silbury Hill, in Wiltshire, England, is an artificial mound dating from the middle of the third millennium, B.C. It is the tallest prehistoric man-made mound in Europe. Marshaling the massive labor requirements for such a project would have required a powerful governing authority.

A wide variety of circular ceremonial enclosures, called henges, appear in the neolithic or stone age British topography, and range from the monumental to the humble. An example of the latter is in Illustration 6, a typical prehistoric henge on Britain's Salisbury plain.

In some parts of northern and central Europe, peopled shifted from monument building in henges and mounds to ever wider stone circles, which had some features of astronomical alignment. Stonehenge and Avebury, also in Wiltshire in southwestern England, are the best known examples of this phenomenon. Although some modern observers have raised the possibility that the prehistoric builders were engaging in more than elementary mathematics, more likely those sites simply aided in working out calendars and the timing of rituals. Elsewhere in Europe, such a strong tradition of stone monuments did not arise.

Illustration 6: Shown above is a smaller prehistoric henge. Dotting the Salisbury Plain in southern England are stone age earthworks known as henges, typically consisting of a ditch within a ring bank. Their purpose was probably ceremonial rather than defensive, and they represent a land use that spans a very long prehistoric period.

§ 2.02(b)(2). Prehistoric Trade Expands: Laws for Commerce

Throughout this period, far-reaching trading links are in evidence. Indeed, the expanding importance of commerce stimulated wealth and growth in settlements favorably sited along trade routes, and the larger communities extended and elaborated their social organizations and forms of legal regulation. Introduction of the plough, wheeled vehicles and domestic horses boosted the economic strength essential to promote widespread commerce. These peoples also conducted industrial scale mining.

Trading expanded first in southeastern Europe. Beginning about 2,000, B.C., peoples from the islands of Crete and the Aegean and from the southern Greek mainland, principally the Minoan and Mycenaean civilizations, established extensive trade links between the western and eastern Mediterranean regions, including especially Egypt. Although there is no direct evidence for how they regulated this commerce, presumably merchants made heavy use of standard weights and measures, writing, and systems of organization, administration, and accounting.

These early Mediterranean societies also formed trade links between various regions in western and northern Europe; this trade brought at least temporary prosperity to individual groups and locales, without requiring major social restructuring. In fact, the spread of goods through trade evidently did not include the spread to the European continent of economic and social patterns developed in these Aegean cultures.

§ 2.02(b)(3). Social Change and Growth of Law: Prehistoric Europe and Britain

Concurrent with such economic activity, various cultures in Europe underwent constant internal adjustment. The fairly well-developed evidence for this in Britain is generally typical for what was going on throughout Europe during the third and second millennia, B.C. In the middle of the third millennium, B.C., the archaeological artifacts reveal that prehistoric British society was changing. One change, as already mentioned, was the introduction of monumental henges, or circular enclosures surrounded by a ditch with a bank located outside the ditch. Stonehenge, the most famous of these, dates from about 3,000, B.C., and is shown in Illustration 7.

Much evidence from this period also indicates rising social unrest. About 2,500, B.C., archaeological evidence shows abandoned camps, blocked tombs and revegetation of previously cleared areas, revealing that some form of social change or even violent crisis was spreading throughout Britain. Consistent with this evidence are indications of increased use of defended enclosures and other activities of warfare. Pottery, flint-working, bone-working, and other crafts also became cruder during this time, suggesting that life had become less ordered. The responses to such crises no doubt stimulated growth of more centralized social and legal power.

Illustration 7: The Stonehenge site, like Silbury Hill, would have required pervasive customs or a powerful governing authority over both people and land, commanding massive labor forces extending periodically over several centuries.

Not all the growing social unrest was necessarily violent, but may have resulted from growing differences in personal wealth. Such differences are more apparent in the archaeological record, especially from the greater differences in the wealth and variety of grave goods in burials. Archaeologists excavating in graves and other repositories have discovered artifacts of widespread origins all over the British Isles. Many of these grave goods were either imported directly from Ireland or from across the English Channel or copied from objects originally crafted on the continent. Thus these peoples carried on an active commerce in some luxury items, and however rudimentary such commercial activity may have been, they likely governed it by a core of broadly accepted customs, rules, or laws.

Both in Britain and in Europe generally the changes from 2,500, B.C., the differences in personal wealth would have lead to society becoming more stratified. It is reasonable to conclude that accumulation of greater wealth and power by some persons spurred increased conflict; and group-oriented chiefdoms appeared and became dominant. In this style of social organization, the chief possessed personal wealth and power, and, sustained by some kinds of generally accepted ritual, probably controlled the distribution of land, goods and services and the use of skilled labor.

Because evidence for commercial activity and regulation is found at sites where evidence of residential activity is absent, those sites also may have served as locations for ordinary market activity. While it is natural to assume that itinerant traders prompted the spread of goods such as pottery and metalwork, a few sites, devoid of artifacts indicating residential use, have also been identified as possible communal meeting places or trade centers where manufacture, distribution, and exchange of goods may have occurred. These peoples would have likely governed this type of commercial or market activity by generally accepted rules, customs or even laws.

§ 2.02(b)(4). Land Distribution is Organized: A Law of Property Emerges in Prehistoric Europe and Britain

The rise of agricultural communities in prehistoric times also required formulating rules to determine how land was to be held. Little is known about how land was distributed or owned during European prehistory, especially whether ownership was communal or individual. Again, information from prehistoric Britain is probably typical of the west European continent generally and is more complete and straightforward because of Britain's island isolation.

In Britain between 3,000 and 2,000, B.C., agricultural communities were probably organized as small single farmsteads. In some areas those farmsteads were adjacent to large enclosures surrounded by ditch systems, and people may have used the enclosures as meeting places, ritual sites, cattle corrals, and especially as settlements. Researchers have found evidence of fences even in the third millennium, B.C. The inhabitants would have required considerable social organization to create, maintain and regulate these enclosed sites. Prehistoric British communities also conducted mining and manufacturing activities—particularly the manufacture of pottery—and in these pursuits, too, they would have required significant social organization and accepted rules for land use.

The settlement pattern in Britain by the early half of the second millennium, B.C., consisted of isolated farmsteads in the south of Britain, and of more populous settlements predominating in the north and along all the coasts. The people occupied many settlements only seasonally, and some of these sites were simply caves.

About 1,500, B.C., the first evidence appears for British landscape subdivisions, that is, orderly division of large territories. Farmers all over Britain began to enclose or mark their fields by hedges, ditches or stone banks, even though the characteristics of farming activity differed from area to area. The circumstances of these enclosure arrangements suggest they were the product of a one-time decision rather than of evolutionary extension. The inhabitants divided their common lands off from household or farmstead lands and larger units into individual fields, and these new boundaries overlay and superseded older monuments and land divisions. In Wessex especially, such field divisions have been called "Celtic fields," even though they pre-date known Celtic settlements in the area.

Then, early in the first millennium, B.C., the inhabitants replaced all the old British field systems and "Celtic fields" with even larger open areas bounded by linear bank or ditch earthworks, sometimes referred to as ranch boundaries. These boundary markers were generally linear, but often not straight. Varying from 10 to 20 feet in width, the boundaries sometimes extended for several miles and are believed to have created division lines between different large landholders. They, too, signify the activities of persons who wielded considerable political and "legal" power.

Developments on the European continent paralleled these changes. Beginning about 1100, B.C., early Europeans more commonly used hillforts, and defensive stockades also became much more common; field divisions, although not so well-defined as in Britain, are in evidence all over Europe. These European societies, ready to emerge from prehistory, possessed authority and organizational structures for monumental undertakings, and, judging from the richer burials, some of their wealthier leaders were powerful indeed.

§ 2.02(c). Summary of Social Organization and Landholding Characteristics in Prehistoric Europe

The state of knowledge about prehistoric European societies, including their landholding practices, does not provide any explicit information concerning the role and rule of law in those societies, and, without documentary sources, that is unlikely to change. However, archaeology has revealed enough about the activities of those societies that one may presume the active importance of some form of law. The following characteristics of prehistoric European societies strongly suggest a reliance upon law:

> People organized and maintained settlements and communities, apparently according to some standard arrangements.
>
> People carried on trade, both internally and externally.
>
> People carried on mining, manufacturing, and similar enterprises requiring large resources and cooperative efforts.
>
> People carried on monument-building, requiring enormous labor and transportation resources.
>
> People organized and distributed land according to regular, albeit occasionally changing, patterns and rules.
>
> People accumulated wealth and power, and accompanying social prominence, and would have maintained these by some forms of social order.

§ 2.02(d). The Emergence of Distinct Cultures and The Transition from Prehistory to History

The advance of cultural progress in Europe seems clearly to have proceeded from southeast to northwest, and no doubt benefitted from stimuli of nearby eastern civilizations. Out of the somewhat generic and nameless, faceless mass of prehistoric peoples throughout Europe, eventually a few distinct communities and cultures began to emerge. Beginning about 2,000, B.C., the Aegean cultures of Crete and Mycenae were the first of these to achieve a distinct identity. Although they were literate, the fragments of writing still extant are mostly undecipherable, so these people remain in the shadows of prehistory. Other peoples of southern and southeastern Europe, who are in the full light of history, succeeded them.

The first prehistoric people in northern Europe to escape anonymity were the Celts. Elements of what eventually became Celtic culture can be traced back to 1200, B.C., and even earlier; these elements were unified in the so-called Urnfield culture of central Europe, from approximately 1200 to 700, B.C. An early era of distinctly Celtic culture, known as the Hallstatt period, extended from about 700 to 500, B.C., and it was during this time that Celtic tribes, by then dominant all over Europe, entered Britain, introducing Iron Age technology. About 250, B.C., another Celtic group immigrated into Britain, bringing the more advanced La Tene culture. Finally, during the first century, B.C., a group of Celtic tribes, known collectively as Belgae, invaded Britain from Gaul, and entered the historical record as among the tribes conquered by the Romans. Other areas of northern Europe, such as parts of Scandinavia, remained in their prehistory even longer.

Despite the dearth of specific information about the development and rule of law in these transitional societies, their reliance on law seems clear from the archaeological findings and through reconstructions derived from later literary sources. Unfortunately, so little is known about the origins of these European cultures that one can only guess as to whether they were influenced by the earliest civilizations that arose in the Middle East.

Acknowledging the realistic possibility that legal traditions in Mesopotamian and Egyptian societies did indeed touch the West, in both its prehistoric and historic cultures, a review of those legal systems is in order, and is found in the next chapter.

§ 2.03. Bibliography.

Books:

Arnold, Bettina, and D. Blair Gibson, eds., *Celtic Chiefdom, Celtic State* (1995).
Bakels, Corrie C., *The Western European Loess Belt; Agrarian History, 5300 BC - AD 1000* (2009).
Blackstone, William, 1 *Commentaries on the laws of England. In four books. By William Blackstone, Esq. Solicitor General to Her Majesty* (5th ed. 1773).
Bogucki, Peter, *Forest Farmers and Stockherders: Early Agriculture and its Consequences in North-Central Europe* (1988).
Bradley, Richard, *The Past in Prehistoric Societies* (2002).
Bradley, Richard, *The Prehistory of Britain and Ireland* (2007).
Childe, V. Gordon, *The Prehistory of European Society* (2009).
Cicero, Marcus Tullius, *De legibus libri tres*.
Maine, Henry Sumner, *Ancient Law. Its Connection with the Early History of Society and its Relation to Modern Ideas* (10th ed. 1906).
Grotius, Hugo, *De jure belli ac pacis* (2d ed. 1631).
Jones, Andrew, ed., *Prehistoric Europe: Theory and Practice* (2008).
Milisauskas, Sarunas ed., *European Prehistory: A Survey* 143-387 (2002).
Piggott,Stuart, *Ancient Europe From the Beginnings of Agriculture to Classical Antiquity* (1965).
Price, T. Douglas, *Europe Before Rome* (2013).
Price, T. Douglas, ed., *Europe's First Farmers* (2000).
Stuart, Gilbert, *A View of Society in Europe* (2d ed. 1783).
Tamanaha, Brian Z., *A General Jurisprudence of Law and Society* (2001).
Von Jhering, Rudolf, *Der Zweck im Recht* (2d ed. 1884).

Chapters in Books

Bogucki, Peter, and Pam J. Crabtree, "Ancient Europe, 8000 B.C. to A.D. 1000" in *Encyclopedia of the Barbarian World* (2004).

Articles

Bogucki, Peter, "The Establishment of Agrarian Communities on the North European Plain," 8 *Current Anthropology* 1 (Feb., 1987).
Byrnes, William H., "Ancient Roman Munificence: The Development of the Practice and Law of Charity," 57 *Rutgers L. Rev*. 1043 (Spring 2005).
Gambaro, Antonio, "Property Rights in Comparative Perspective: Why Property is So Ancient and Durable," 26 *Tul. Eur. & Civ. L.F.* 205 (2011).
Gilman, Antonio, "The Development of Social Stratification in Bronze Age Europe," 22 *Current Anthropology* 1 (Feb. 1981).
Kroger, John. R., "The Philosophical Foundations of Roman Law: Aristotle, the Stoics, and Roman Theories of Natural Law," 2004 *Wis. L. Rev*. 905.

Redfield, Robert, "Maine's Ancient Law in the Light of Primitive Societies," 3 *The Western Political Quarterly* 574 (Dec. 1955).

Renfrew, Colin, "Trade and Culture Process in European Prehistory" 10 *Current Anthropology* 151 (Apr.-Jun., 1969).

Renfrew, Colin, Ian Todd, and Ruth Tringham, "Beyond a Subsistence Economy: The Evolution of Social Organization in Prehistoric Europe," *Bulletin of the American Schools of Oriental Research. Supplementary Studies No. 20, Reconstructing Complex Societies: An Archaeological Colloquium* 69 (1974).

Straumann, Benjamin, "Is Modern Liberty Ancient? Roman Remedies and Natural Rights in Hugo Grotius's Early Works on Natural Law," 27 *Law & Hist. Rev.* 55 (Spring, 2009).

Utz, Stephen G., "Maine's Ancient Law and Legal Theory," 16 *Conn. L. Rev.* 821 (1983-1984).

Cases

Miller v. Dunn, 14 P. 27 (Cal. 1887)

Rich Hill Coal Co. v. Bashore, 7 A.2d 302 (Pa. 1939)

State v. United States Express Co., 145 N.W. 451 (Iowa 1914)

Chapter 3

Law and Land Regulation in Western Civilization's Earliest Historic Societies

SYNOPSIS

Chapter 3. Law and Land Regulation in Western Civilization's Earliest Historic Societies

§ 3.01. The Development of Law and Land Regulation in Ancient Mesopotamia

As civilization progressed from hunter-gatherer to agricultural societies, the formation of settlements was a natural development. In the prehistory of western civilization, evidence of the earliest agricultural settlements comes from the plains on both sides of the Tigris River in northern Mesopotamia, where rainfall sufficed to sustain agriculture. These settlements date from about 6,000, B.C. By about 5,000, B.C., agricultural settlements had emerged in southern Mesopotamia, where rainfall was insufficient, but primitive irrigation systems using river water could produce an agricultural surplus. Irrigation and other advances—such as large urban communities, wheeled vehicles, the first system of writing, and written laws—occurred first in southern Mesopotamia. Because writing was not only developed but practiced in a medium of clay tablets that have survived millennia in a favorable climate, it is possible to trace the beginning of written law in western civilization from a cradle of that civilization, the Mesopotamian dynasties of Sumer, Akkad, Babylon, and Assyria.

§ 3.01(a). Sumer and Akkad

If, as is widely believed, some sort of surplus of life's necessities is required for progress, then it is no surprise that the earliest known advances in civilization arose out of the southern tip of the so-called Fertile Crescent, the combined valleys and deltas of the Tigris and Euphrates rivers, and usually known as ancient Mesopotamia. Though arid, the area could be made fertile through irrigation, which also helped keep the abundant river waters under some control. That the surplus in crops required for urban life occurred here is confirmed by modern calculations for grain yields here in 2,500, B.C., equaling the best grain yields of modern North America. Also, the agricultural abundance and growing populations forced expanding groups to confront one another and work out ways of coexisting and of cooperating on large projects such as irrigation and drainage.

The first identifiable government and the first agricultural settlements in the area to be known as Sumeria arose around 5,000, B.C. The early settlers in this area were among the first peoples to domesticate sheep and goats and to cultivate wheat and barley. Various Semitic emigrants later joined these early settlers, and the Semites eventually branched into Akkadians, Assyrians and Arameans. In about 3,300, B.C., non-Semitic Sumerians,[77] probably from as far north as modern Turkey, entered the area. By developing more sophisticated irrigation systems, the Sumerians and their predecessors created surplus crops, which eventually produced trade and the resources needed to support artisans and engineers. As a class of scribes arose and became the first people known to record epic poems, such as the *Epic of Gilgamesh*, the Sumerians' language became prevalent in the area, and their historical era began about 3,000, B.C., when their earliest known writings appeared. Out of these conditions, urban life coalesced into the first cities and city-states.

As researchers discovered and at least partially deciphered the numerous clay tablets of the Sumerians, a picture of city life characterized by residential and other districts, specialized industries, and political and religious activities emerged. A part of the Sumerian population carried on such urban enterprises and were supported by the produce from intensive agriculture carried on by other parts of the population. The earliest cities originally were not walled, but persistent conflict eventually led to the appearance of the first walled cities about 2700, B.C.

Eventually Sumerians divided their territory into a dozen or so city-

---

[77] One school of thought hypothesizes that Sumerians were not immigrants, but simply indigenous successors of the earlier culture.

states, and in these they anchored their political and legal structure. Leaders taught the people that a god presided over the territory of each city-state, under an allotment believed to have been made at the creation of the world. In each city, the main and subsidiary temples and their staffs at first were the heart of political as well as religious power.

The temples and their associated lands were economically self-sufficient and thus conducted the full range of agricultural and industrial enterprises, often as the dominant economic force in the city. Temple lands were inalienable (not transferable between living persons) and, if the use of temple lands was assigned to various temple personnel or other private persons, those lands were also uninheritable. The actual ruler of the city was considered the human steward of the temple deity, or if the deity was a goddess, the ruler's wife was steward. As part of the total control exercised within the temple jurisdictions, workers on the temple estates received rationed portions of all the commodities they required for subsistence.

In time, ever larger tracts of land became subject to private ownership. Records show land purchases, with the price being paid not only to the principal owner/seller, but also to other persons holding collateral or concurrent forms of ownership in the tract. Land transactions were ceremonially ratified by driving a peg into a wall and pouring oil into the ground. Through these transactions it has been surmised that much land came to be held by family organizations, subject to alienation only by action of the family head, with the purchase price divided among all the relatives in the selling family according to their proportionate interests.[78]

Intense scholarly debate has focused on whether the temple estates and related enterprises completely dominated the host city-state, or whether a robust sector of private land ownership and of non-temple economic and political activity existed alongside the temple sector. Convincing pieces of evidence support the notion that popular assemblies not governed by the temples conducted some functions of government. If later documentary

78 C. J. Gadd, "The Cities of Babylonia," in 1, pt. 2, I. E. S. Edwards, C. J. Gadd and N. G. L. Hammond, eds., *The Cambridge Ancient History* 131 (3d ed. 1971).

evidence accurately describes the earliest practices, then a political organization, in addition to the temple organization, governed a typical Sumerian city-state. The political organization included two types of popular assemblies: one consisting of a council of elders and mayor for each precinct of the city (and precincts were assigned according to the gates in the city wall), and the other a city-wide assembly attended by all free males. Both types of assemblies were almost wholly devoted to judicial functions, with the city-wide assembly deciding the more important cases. Supreme judicial power rested in the city ruler, but the ruler sometimes referred cases to the assembly.

Some textual references even suggest that the assembly might be called upon to choose the king or ruler, and—by analogy from the religious stories—it is even possible that women participated in some of these assemblies. One respected historian concludes that, "Taken together, the testimony of records, epics and mythological stories leave no doubt that the Sumerian city-states emerged into history with a dual assembly of elders and citizens."[79]

With increasing rivalry between city-states, kings eventually took over whatever elements of popular sovereignty had been practiced in early times, and some city-states gained power over others. Strong rulers temporarily united the city-states about 2,800, B.C. However, the continuing hostilities between them left them vulnerable to outside conquest, first by the Elamites about 2530, B.C., and then by the Semitic people known as Akkadians under Sargon I (to be distinguished from the 8th century, B.C., Assyrian king Sargon II). About 2334, B.C., Sargon I again united all the Sumerian city-states and created a model of government that had influence lasting well beyond his dynasty of only a century. When that dynasty ended in 2193, B.C., upon the death of the last of five Akkadian kings, the city-states became independent and once again vied for hegemony over one another. Beginning in about 2112, B.C., Ur became ascendant; Ur-Nammu, the city governor, soon spread his rule to neighboring Lagash, and styled himself "king of Sumer and Akkad."

---

[79] Jacquetta Hawkes, *The First Great Civilizations* 154 (1973).

Ur-Nammu is best known, however, for his law code, fragments of which scholars have recovered and translated. It is presently the oldest known written law code. This neo-Sumerian code of Ur-Nammu, ca. 2110, B.C., was recorded on a clay tablet found in Nippur, and first translated in 1952. The tablet was divided into four columns on the front, containing a prologue of Ur-Nammu's achievements, and four on the back, containing the provisions of the code. Only five of those provisions can be reconstructed intelligibly; these deal with trial by water ordeal, returning a slave to the master, and three rules calling for money payments in response to personal injuries.[80] A few years after these were translated, fragments of another tablet, this found in the ruins of Ur, were also positively identified as from the Ur-Nammu code; this new addition to the earliest code gave many more rules, especially regarding payments for various offenses.[81] Such provisions show that Sumerians had not adopted the so-called talionic, or retaliatory, "eye for eye, tooth for tooth" formulations favored by the Semitic people and that were still extant in Biblical texts centuries later.[82]

Other early Mesopotamian codes include a Semitic code that mentions a king named Bilalama, of Esnunna, ca. 1970, B.C.; the code of King Lipit-Ishtar,[83] 1934-1924, B.C.; and, of course, the famous code of Hammurabi, ca. 1750, B.C. Between Lipit-Ishtar and Hammurabi, Semitic Amorites invaded and settled southern Mesopotamia, and, when Hammurabi eventually unified that area into the kingdom of Babylon, a strong Semitic element appeared in the talionic (retaliatory) features of his law code.[84]

---

[80] Samuel Noah Kramer, "Ur-Nammu Law Code," 23 *Orientalia* 40 (1954).

[81] Jacob J. Finkelstein, "The Laws of Ur-Nammu," 22 *J. of Cuneiform Studies* 66 (1969).

[82] Samuel Noah Kramer, *From the Tablets of Sumer* 50 (1956).

[83] The promulgator may have been Lipit-Ishtar's son Shulgi. Norman Yoffee, "Context and Authority in Early Mesopotamian Law," in Ronald Cohen and Judith D. Toland, eds., *State Formation and Political Legitimacy* 95 (1988).

[84] Portions of Old Assyrian laws have also been found, dated between 2350 and 2100, B.C.. So fragmentary that analysis is problematic at best, they appear to govern court organization and procedure. The laws may be the work of a jurist explaining prior enactments and cases or instructive material for scribes. Some

These codes may have been a type of valedictory statements from the issuing monarchs, proclaiming rules in force and the monarch's diligence in upholding them. Other royal edicts and judgments in lawsuits were based specifically on the circumstances of the cases at hand rather than on the codes.[85]

The common elements of these codes are so strikingly similar that some scholars believe in the existence of a sort of customary "common law" throughout Mesopotamia during this era.[86] Keeping in mind that these so-called "codes" likely reflect contemporary customary law, summaries of those three law codes illustrate how easy it is to view them as simply expressions of the "common law" of the era. The subjects covered by provisions of Bilalama's code from Esnunna may be summarized as follows:

§§ 1-11:	offenses relating to prices and rates of hire, and related offenses
§§ 12-13:	trespass on a field or in a house
§ 14:	hire payable
§§ 15-16:	goods received from or entrusted to a coparcener or a slave
§§ 17-18:	acquiring a bride

Middle Assyrian laws, dated ca. 1450-1250, B.C., contain mostly provisions about women. Hittite laws from ca. 1450, B.C., describe penalties for various offenses, but their author did not pretend to possess any inherent authority of enforcement. *See generally,* Godfrey Rolles Driver and John Charles Miles, eds. & trans., *The Assyrian Laws* (1937).

[85] Jacob J. Finkelstein, "Ammisaduqa's Edict and the Babylonian Law Codes," 14 *Journal of Cuneiform Studies* 15 (1961); Raphael Sealey, *The Justice of the Greeks* 30-37 (1994).

[86] *See, generally,* Godfrey Rolles Driver and John Charles Miles, eds. and trans., *The Babylonian Law* 9, 11 (1968).

§§ 19-21: repaying loans of grain or money

§§ 22-24: seizing dependent persons in distraint [for debt]

§§ 25-26: taking a person's daughter in marriage

§§ 27-28: how a woman becomes a wife

§§ 29-30: how a husband who returns from an absence abroad recovers his wife

§ 31: dishonoring a slave girl

§§ 32-33: faithless nurses

§§ 34-35: children of slave-girls

§ 36: liability of one who accepts a pawn

§ 37: collapse of a house

§§ 38-41: sale of a family's house, land, and goods

§§ 42-48: assaults and injuries

§§ 49-52: flight by and loss of slaves

§§ 53-55: dealing with a goring ox

§§ 56-57: dealing with a savage ox

§ 58: dealing with a falling wall

§ 59: divorce.[87]

---

[87] *Id.* at 7-8.

Many of the provisions and the individual technical terms in this code are also found in Hammurabi's Babylonian code issued over two centuries later. According to one estimate, the substance of about three quarters of Bilalama's code appeared in Hammurabi's code, even though probably no direct borrowing occurred; instead, probably the customary law from which both codes were drawn was still essentially the same, even though widely separated in time and space.[88]

In the Mesopotamian code of Lipit-Ishtar, which also predates Hammurabi's Babylonian code by nearly two hundred years, further similarities are confirmed. The decipherable provisions of that code "treat a variety of civil causes—hire of boats, care of orchards, regulations concerning slaves, possession of a house, family laws concerning marriage and inheritance—nearly all of which have close analogies with the better known laws of Hammurabi . . . ."[89]

§ 3.01(b). Hammurabi's Code of Babylonian Laws

The so-called Third Dynasty of Ur that produced the code of Ur-Nammu ended with the fall of Ur in about 2004, B.C. By then, several cities farther north had become stronger and more independent, and some of their rulers, such as Lipit-Ishtar and Bililama, patterned their governments and issued law codes in imitation of Ur. Invasions and settlements by Semitic Amorites from the west made political consolidation of these south Mesopotamian city-states very difficult. This fragmentation of political power persisted until Hammurabi, based in Babylon, unified the various cities and formed them into the Old Babylonian Empire in about 1762, B.C.

By the time the code of Hammurabi appeared, ca. 1750, B.C., at least

---

[88] C. J. Gadd, Ch. XXII, "Babylonia, c. 2120-1800, B.C.," in 1, pt. 2, I. E. S. Edwards, C. J. Gadd, and N. G. L. Hammond, eds., *The Cambridge Ancient History* 635 (3d ed. 1971).

[89] *Id.*

one important change had taken place in the character and tone of the law codes. The somewhat liberal Sumerian system of using various specified money payments as punishment for personal injury and property was partially replaced in the Hammurabi code with the older, Semitic approach of "eye for eye, tooth for tooth," an approach believed to have Canaanite origins. In modern terms, such legal rules are referred to as lex talionis, a law of retaliation. Other than these more severe and retaliatory penalties, the essential subjects of earlier Mesopotamian law were perpetuated in Hammurabi's code, as indicated in the following descriptive summary:

Offenses against the administration of justice:
- false charges (§§ 1-2)
- false testimony (§§ 3-4)
- falsification of judgment (§ 5)

Offenses against property
- stealing and receiving stolen property (§§ 6-13)
- kidnapping (§ 14)
- harboring fugitive slaves (§§ 15-20)
- housebreaking and robbery (§§ 21-24)
- looting a burning house (§ 25)

Land and houses
- tenure of fiefs (§§ 26-41)
- duties of farmers (§§ 42-48)
- debts of farmers (§§ 49-52)
- offenses connected with irrigation (§§ 53-56)
- cattle trespass (§§ 57-58)
- cutting down trees (§ 59)
- care of palm groves (§ 60-A)
- offenses connected with houses (§§ 60-B to 60K)

Trade and commerce
- loans from merchants (§§ 60-L to 60-T)
- commercial agency (§§ 60-V to 107)
- innkeeping (§§ 108-111)
- fraud by a carrier (§ 112)

- distraint and pledge of persons for debt (§§ 113-119)
- safe custody or deposit (§§ 120-126)

Marriage, family and property

- slander of chief priestess or married lady (§ 127)
- definition of married lady (§ 128)
- adultery (§§ 129-132)
- remarriage in husband's absence (§§ 133-136)
- divorce (§§ 137-143)
- concubinage with slave girls (§§ 144-147)
- maintenance of diseased wife (§§ 148-149)
- gifts from husband to wife (§ 150)
- liability of spouses for debt (§§ 151-152)
- murder of husband (§ 153)
- incest (§§ 154-158)
- inchoate marriage (§§ 159-161)
- devolution of marriage gifts after wife's death (§§ 162-164)
- gift to son *inter vivos* (§ 165)
- succession among sons (§§ 166-167)
- disherison of sons (§§ 168-169)
- legitimation (§ 170)
- widow's property (§§ 171-174)
- marriage of free women to slaves (§§ 175-176)
- remarriage of widow (§ 177)
- sacral women (§§ 178-184)
- adoption and nursing of infants (§§ 185-194)

Assaults and talion

- assault on father (§ 195)
- assaults on men (§§ 196-208)
- assaults causing miscarriage (§§ 209-214)

Professional men

- surgeon (§§ 215-223)
- veterinary surgeon (§§ 224-225)
- barber or brander (§§ 226-227)

master builder (§§ 228-233)
boatbuilder and shipman (§§ 234-240)

Agriculture
oxen (§§ 241-252)
wrongful conversion of fodder by bailiff (§§ 253-256)
hire of husbandmen (§ 257-258)
wrongful conversion of agricultural implements (§§ 259-260)
hire of glazier (§ 261)
duties of shepherds (§§ 262-267)
hire of beasts and wagon (§§ 268-272)
hire of seasonal workers (§ 273)

Wages and rates of hire
wages of craftsmen (§ 274)
hire of boats (§ 275-277)

Slaves
warranties on sale of slaves (§§ 278-279)
purchase of slaves abroad (§§ 280-282).[90]

§ 3.01(c). Sumerian and Babylonian Laws Compared

Early in the modern twentieth century, before the various fragmentary Mesopotamian legal provisions had been identified with separate rulers or dynasties, a compilation of the known Sumerian provisions was compared with the 282 numbered sections of Hammurabi's later Babylonian code,

---

[90] G. R. Driver and John C. Miles, eds. and trans., *The Babylonian Laws* 43-45 (1968). *See also*, Jacquetta Hawkes, *The First Great Civilizations* 175-176 (1973), describing the laws of Hammurabi in terms of categories. The most numerous category is the family, and in these laws women were "quite fairly treated." The second largest category is laws governing land tenure. Next is the category of trade and commerce. The laws listed first deal with the administration of justice.

demonstrating extensive similarity:[91]

Fragment Provision Description	Hammurabi Code #
If one is assigned land for planting an orchard, but some is left vacant, the vacant portion shall be reassigned	61
One who takes over the garden land of another, but neglects it, shall pay a fine	65
One who cuts wood in the garden of another shall pay a fine	59
A landowner who agrees but fails to so cultivate the land as to protect adjoining land, shall indemnify the other owner for any related loss	71
If a slave escapes from one master to join another for a month, the second shall pay the first with another slave or with money	15, 16, 19
A slave who complains twice to the master shall receive a mark on the forehead	282

[91] The summary in the text is based primarily on Stephen Langdon, "The Sumerian Law Code Compared with the Code of Hammurabi," 23 *J. of the Royal Asiatic Society* 489 (1920). *See also,* Francis Rue Steele, "The Code of Lipit-Ishtar," 52 *Am. J. of Archaeology* 425 (1948).

One who unsuccessfully accuses another shall pay the penalty of the accusation	3, 4, 11, 126
One who takes a vacant house and pays taxes on it for three years shall have the house	30
The son of a second wife shall receive an equal portion of the father's property and his mother's dowry.	167
If both a wife and a handmaid have borne sons, and the handmaid's son has been freed, that son shall not receive a portion of the father's property	170, 171
A son born to his widower father's handmaid shall receive his portion of his father's property	170, 171
One who fathers a son by a public prostitute (hierodule) must support the mother, but the mother may not abide in the father's household so long as the wife is alive	144-147
One who jostles or strikes a woman and causes a miscarriage shall pay a fine	209-213
One in charge of a ship that is lost during a river crossing shall pay the loss to the owner	236-239, 240

An adopted child who rejects the adoptive parents shall be sold; adoptive parents who reject the child shall be deprived of house and goods	185-193
An oxherder who loses an ox to a lion shall pay the value to the owner	244, 266, 267
An oxherder who allows an ox to be lost shall restore an ox to the owner	245, 267
A son who rejects his father shall be branded, fettered and sold in slavery.	192, 226
A wife who rejects her husband shall be thrown into the river	142, 143
A husband who rejects his wife shall pay her a fine	137-140
A man who kills, injures or abuses his slave shall pay a fine	245-248, 199, 252[92]

§ 3.01(d). The Relationship Between the Social Organization and the Legal System in Ancient Mesopotamia

The abundant evidence of intense political and economic activity in the Mesopotamian cities compels the conclusion that both public and private law were important elements of everyday life. Huge caches of clay tablets documenting the mundane details of daily life in Mesopotamia also confirm that contracts, property conveyances and court judgments were regular

---

92 Stephen Langdon, "The Sumerian Law Code Compared with the Code of Hammurabi," *Journal of the Royal Asiatic Society* 489 (1920).

features of Sumerian, Akkadian and Babylonian urban life. The early tablets were inscribed with pictographs, and later tablets were covered with a wedge-shaped script known as cuneiform. Only a small portion of the hordes of clay tablets discovered in early Mesopotamian urban sites have been examined, and only relatively few of those have been deciphered, but in legal matters even these show intense activity in property conveyancing and commercial contracts, detailed rules governing family relationships, and an active judiciary.

Early legal proceedings took place within temple precincts; later only the oaths were taken in the temple and case records were filed in the temple. The kings issued law codes and heard final appeals, but the actual administration of law and justice was the province of the city governors. A typical litigant would be prepared with witnesses or documentary evidence, and in conducting the case might be assisted by a court official who occasionally would be paid for those services. After the oaths in the temple, a scribe writing on a clay tablet recorded the proceedings; the judgment would also be recorded on a tablet and the tablets stored in an orderly fashion.

The laws themselves show features that persisted even into the early European laws. Fines and other punishments varied according to the class of the litigant, and, in cases of irreconcilably conflicting evidence, a trial by ordeal might be ordered to resolve the conflict. The full text of one court proceeding, from about 1850, B.C., has revealed that the courts relied on the precedential value of earlier cases. In this proceeding, the wife of a murder victim had been secretly informed that her husband had been murdered, but had said nothing about that information until much later, after the prosecution had commenced. The prosecutor's attempt to condemn her, along with the murderers, for her silence was rejected because she had not actually participated in the crime. Discovery of a second clay tablet record of the same case showed that the case was noted and used as precedent in another proceeding.[93]

Outside the courts, the legal documents of the Mesopotamian societies

---

[93] Samuel Noah Kramer, *From the Tablets of Sumer* 51-55 (1956).

consisted of contracts, promissory notes, deeds, wills, and receipts, numerous examples of all of which are found in the clay tablets.

This legal system reflected the needs of developing Mesopotamian society. As the temple institutions declined in power, a class of free and wealthy private citizens arose which, when allied with the political rulers, clearly was more powerful than those in the temple sector. The rulers of several or all the city-states sometimes united in support of a national king, with recognized power and authority over the constituent city-states. This pattern of combination was frequently repeated in Western societies, notably in Mycenaean Greece of the first millennium, B.C., and in Anglo-Saxon England, beginning in the sixth century, A.D.

Mesopotamian society exhibited other characteristics that would have seemed familiar in early medieval Europe. Some of the ancient laws allude to landholders whose holdings also obligated them to perform military and other services, suggesting that a form of feudalism was in effect. Almost all persons were subject to work calls for irrigation and other public projects, although eventually more and more exemptions were recognized. Laws regarding slaves were detailed and complex. Craft and merchant guilds and other specialty associations were common and were also regulated by law. It appears that the Mesopotamians produced not only the earliest laws in western civilization, but also were the first to implement many of the familiar forms of social organization and political structure.

Although Hammurabi's empire collapsed within a decade after his death in about 1750, B.C., and a succession of regional dynasties ensued, the Sumero-Babylonian culture and laws persisted. Hittites sacked Babylon in 1595, B.C.; Kassites subsequently ruled Babylon for about 400 years. In northern Mesopotamia, Hurrians ruled until early in the 14th century, B.C.; then Assyrians expanded their power in all directions until the mid-11th century, B.C. After an Arameaen interlude Assyrian expansion continued until Nineveh was destroyed by Medes in the 7th century, B.C. A new Babylonian empire then flourished until conquered by the Persians in 539, B.C. Persia fell to the Macedonian Alexander the Great in 331, B.C., and with this Macedonian conquest the centuries-long hegemony of ancient Sumerian legal culture in Mesopotamia finally broke down.

Incredibly, this legal tradition had persisted even though Aramaic replaced the Akkadian language and cuneiform writing during the time of Persian rule. Through all of these changes of rule, the main features of the mature Mesopotamian laws and legal system remained in force, essentially unchanged for two millennia.

Did this stable, sophisticated and very ancient legal system leave any legacy for western civilization, or did it simply expire under Hellenistic influences? Perceptive readers will have already noted that even the small bits of Mesopotamian laws quoted above are remarkably similar to portions of the law of Moses, which passed into the Judeo-Christian foundation of western heritage. One could also find striking parallels with legal customs of Germanic and other early European peoples. However, no evidence of any direct influence is known. Less obvious and less well-known is the possible influence of Mesopotamian civilization and law on that other most important of the ancient historic civilizations, that of Egypt, beginning in the 4th millennium, B.C.

§ 3.02. The Development of Law and Land Regulation in Ancient Egypt

§ 3.02(a). Introduction

The possibility and plausibility of western civilization's debt to ancient Egypt, especially through the contributions of Mesopotamia, has been raised by scholars, especially by James Breasted, a great pioneer of Egyptian studies.[94]

However, in legal developments, it cannot be discerned whether the greater influence on the West came from Mesopotamia or from Egypt. In law and in most other affairs, ancient Egypt was in early and substantial contact with Mesopotamian society. Various tribes in Egypt were consolidating into northern and southern monarchies during the era when Sumerians were migrating to southern Mesopotamia, about 3,300, B.C., and

[94] *See, e.g.,* James Henry Breasted, *A History of Egypt* (1937).

commencing their historical era about 3,000, B.C. Egypt's northern kingdom enjoyed cultural superiority over the south—probably because of stronger contacts with Mesopotamia—and succeeded in conquering the southern kingdom about 3,200, B.C.

Egyptian culture and law were still developing only slowly during the first ages of unification, but once true unity was achieved, matters moved quickly, and Mesopotamian influence grew stronger. Unification did not produce real political stability in Egypt until the beginning of the so-called Old Kingdom about 2,700, B.C.[95] Partly this was because of fundamental differences in the character of the two cultures. In the south, the feudal customs of recently nomadic peoples probably held together their scattered settlements; in the north, the more prosperous and progressive urban communities relied on a more complex social organization, although huge city-states in the Mesopotamian tradition never did develop.

Once Egypt was unified, the development of its civilization then accelerated, and Egyptians probably borrowed some major cultural traits from the Mesopotamians, such as certain art motifs, monumental architecture, and writing, inasmuch as those features appeared in Egypt rather suddenly in already mature form quite soon after unification. However, it is not known whether these Mesopotamian influences in Egypt were transmitted by gradual infiltration of migrating peoples, by trade, or by conquest and rule under dynastic overlords. As remarkable as the evidence is for Mesopotamian influence, equally remarkable was the Egyptians' ability quickly to surpass their mentors and create their own unique culture from the common base.

Quite likely unifying the northern and southern kingdoms in Egypt also spurred the development of Egyptian law. Here the influence of Mesopotamian traditions of written law codes was conspicuously absent, although many substantive principles of Mesopotamian law could be found in Egyptian law. Egypt's traditional reliance on conducting legal business

[95] Dates of the various Egyptian kingdoms, and of the dynasties within those kingdoms, have been subject to widely varying estimates from Egyptologists. Dates given in this chapter represent respectable but not necessarily majority or the most recent opinions.

in oral form did not change until the 7th century, B.C., when the demotic form of their written language was popularly accepted; therefore, the early growth of Egyptian law can be described only in generality. However, once that law had matured and legal transactions were conducted in written form, Egyptian law began to have a powerful influence on Greek and Roman law. Indeed, the Egyptian view, as reported by Diodorus of Sicily in the first century, B.C., was that the Athenians were colonists from Egypt and that the political and social organization in Athens faithfully reflected that of contemporary Egypt.[96]

Development of Egyptian law followed the growth of Egyptian government. After unification, the Egyptian monarch was a more absolute ruler than the Sumerian monarchs had been, since the Egyptian ruler was venerated as a god, not merely as a servant of a god. However, in Egypt as in Mesopotamia, a large bureaucratic hierarchy was created to give enforcement to the royal decrees, and this bureaucracy was responsible for forming much of the law and legal system.

One important but as yet unanswered question is in what particulars Egyptian contacts with southern Mesopotamia may have influenced the early development and content of Egyptian law. All the evidence of contact between the two societies points toward movement only from Mesopotamia to Egypt, so that "it is necessary to conclude that the bearers of the Mesopotamian influences were Sumerians who migrated to Egypt and settled in the Nile Valley."[97]

If there was such a flow of immigrants in the era before unification of the kingdoms, the migrations probably ceased after unification, and most of ancient Egypt's cultural features probably emerged thereafter as indigenous developments.

---

[96] C. H. Oldfather (trans.), *Diodorus of Sicily* I.28.3 (Loeb Classical Library, 1946).

[97] I. E. S. Edwards, Ch. XI, "The Early Dynastic Period in Egypt," in 1, pt. 2, I. E. S. Edwards, C. J. Gadd, and N. G. L. Hammond, eds., *The Cambridge Ancient History* 1, 44 (3d ed., 1971).

§ 3.02(b). The Developmental Period of Egyptian Law

A persisting oddity of Egyptian legal history is that very little direct or circumstantial evidence exists for early Egyptian law after unification, but what evidence there is shows a legal system in mature form. The available sources give no details about the developmental period of Egyptian law. The earliest known legal document from Egypt comes from the Sixth Dynasty (ca. 2420-2294, B.C.), and so is technically later than the earliest legal documents from Mesopotamia, but possible future discoveries from the developmental period of Egyptian law may yet confirm the Egyptian system—and replace Sumerian law—as the West's oldest known legal system. Indirect evidence, such as inscriptions on stelae and in tombs, refers to legal transactions and documents from as early as the Third Dynasty (ca. 2815-2690, B.C.).

It is also possible that some characteristics of Egyptian culture contributed to the paucity of legal documentation. It has been said that the ancient Egyptians had no sense of cumulative as opposed to repetitive time, and so no sense of history. With linear progress being incomprehensible, heaven and earth differed only in degree, and the pharaoh was the earthly manifestation of the king and creator in heaven. The society in both heaven and earth was static, change was evil, impersonal law was not recognized, and law was therefore neither written nor codified.[98]

§ 3.02(c). Egyptian Law in the Old and Middle Kingdoms

During the Old and Middle Kingdoms, extending over twelve dynastic periods and about sixteen centuries, from the 32nd to the 16th centuries, B.C., the Egyptian legal system can be described only in generalities. The Egyptian government was an absolute monarchy and the pharaoh was the sole legislator. Apparently, however, private law and private ownership of both personal and real property were able to develop.

---

[98] Paul Johnson, *A History of the Jews* 30-31 (1987).

One could obtain ownership of property by purchase or by gift, but acquisition by gift had to be affirmed by a document. This extra requirement of documentation for transfer of ownership by gift would also be a characteristic of the code of Hammurabi and of Germanic codes much later, but first appeared in Egyptian law.

To affirm a gift, one wrote a document on papyrus, containing a declaration of the owner's willingness to transfer ownership, with names of three witnesses to the declaration, and an official rolled and sealed the document, so that no changes could be made thereafter. One confirmed executory or future obligations by an oath invoking divine power and sanctions. It is not known if such an oath was crucial for the validity of the obligation in ancient Egypt, as it was to become in later western legal systems.

Egyptians made payments for transactions in kind rather than currency, but a standard valuation system for barter objects eventually emerged, so that the governing law became a law of sale, rather than merely of barter.

Because of Egyptian obsession with afterlife and with securing adequate provision for comforts of the dead, they sometimes conveyed property in perpetuity to a certain class of persons who agreed to provide the necessary offerings eternally. These conveyances were similar to those in medieval Europe by which a monastery accepted land donations in return for covenants to perform rituals or prayers for the donors in perpetuity. However, the Egyptian settlements reached a surprising degree of sophistication in creating reversionary and other rights in case the conditions were not kept. Standardized forms for conveyances, contracts and other transactions were in use. In a uniquely Egyptian twist, some transactions occurred between a mortal, living personality, as one party, and the afterlife version of the same person as the other party.[99]

Similarly, since testamentary transfers in ancient Egypt were unknown, owners expected to make settlements on beneficiaries while the owners

---

[99] T. Eric Peet, Ch. IX, "Contemporary Life and Thought in Egypt," in 2, J. B. Bury, S. A. Cook, and F. E. Adcock, eds., *The Cambridge Ancient History* 212-214 (1924).

were still alive and, in some as yet unknown manner, retain a right of possession for the rest of the owner's life.

In litigation, a strict law of evidence relying on appeals to divine intervention added technicality to procedure. As in the medieval European legal tradition of oath-helpers, the key procedural decision would often concern whether and how many witnesses or oath-givers could be called to affirm the authenticity of a document or an allegation, rather than the substantive outcome. Thus a type of formalism supplanted an actual weighing of evidence.

The well-developed Egyptian bureaucracy included a sophisticated revenue law and collection system. Also, in about the 19th century, B.C., the Egyptian pharaoh managed to limit the power of the local nobility, so that there gradually arose a middle class consisting of small farmers, merchants, and artisans.

§ 3.02(d). Egyptian Law in the New Kingdom

With the advent of the New Kingdom in the 16th century, B.C., written legal documents became more numerous and their survival to the present more common. Nevertheless, even though several pharaohs were known as law-givers, no Egyptian code has been preserved. Once the demotic form of written Egyptian language became popular in the 7th century, B.C., many traditionally oral legal transactions assumed written form, and the preservation of those documents is a principal source of information about older Egyptian law.

By about the 14th century, B.C., the sealed papyrus document confirming a transaction was replaced by a different type of document, written by a scribe, witnessed, and executed in such a way that it could not be changed and thus did not need to be sealed. Evidence shows loans from this period that commonly carry 100% interest compounded annually. The security for such a loan might consist of agreeing to be flogged if the promise was broken, although even this was not so extreme as some of the penalties in contemporary and later Assyrian law.

Evidence also reveals marriage settlements, concluded at the time of the marriage. A widower who remarried was required first to provide for the children of the first marriage by conferring on them two-thirds of his estate. A husband could divorce his wife by a simple repudiation procedure.

As to marriage itself, according to Diodorus of Sicily writing in the 1st century, B.C., Egyptian law permitted men to marry their sisters;[100] and "among private persons the wife should enjoy authority over her husband, the husbands agreeing in the marriage contract that they will be obedient in all things to their wives."[101]

Because burial of the body was deemed essential for afterlife, the Egyptian law of succession required that one must have buried the decedent's body to become an heir of the decedent.

Law courts consisted of local dignitaries holding meetings and trying cases under the direction of a local administrative official. Other leading citizens had a right to administer justice and might sit in hearings with the administrative official holding court. The highest court was in Thebes.[102] In a typical proceeding, the litigants appeared and spoke; a few minutes later the magistrate pronounced a non-appealable judgment. Harder cases took longer.[103]

Rules that actually focused on the veracity and probity of the evidence eventually replaced the old ritualistic rules of evidence, although a lengthy period of return to old rituals came and went during the New Kingdom. Magistrates frequently used documentary evidence provided by the tax rolls

---

[100] This practice become common in Egypt during the Ptolemaic and Roman regimes. Adolf Erman, *Life in Ancient Egypt* 153 (1971).

[101] C. H. Oldfather (trans.), *Diodorus of Sicily* I.27.2 (Loeb Classical Library, 1946).

[102] 2 G. Maspero, *History of Egypt* 136-137 (M. L. McClure, trans., n.d.).

[103] *Id.* at 137.

to determine questions of property ownership and personal status.[104] One papyrus describes the contending parties each giving a deposition before the judge, the court giving judgment, and the losing party agreeing to carry out the judgment.[105]

Judges were noted for their prowess in leading the parties to settlement before an action had to go to judgment. Decisions of the courts were followed closely and celebrated in literature, and the leading law officials were admonished to "see that everything is done according to the rules, helping everyone to his right . . ,"[106] still suitable as a modern guide.

No such enlightenment suffused Egyptian criminal law and procedure. Corporal punishment was heavy (100 strokes compared to the usual 40 strokes under contemporary Jewish law) and torture was frequently used on both defendants and witnesses.[107] Convicted criminals were subjected to bizarre forms of execution, mutilation and other punishments. Multiple restitution, such as in the code of Hammurabi, the law of Moses, and early Roman law, was the rule.

The scraps of surviving information on criminal procedure relate mostly to prominent cases, such as those of tomb-robbers, but they reveal in a general way the procedure followed in ordinary criminal cases. After the pharaoh's officials visited the scene of the crime and reviewed the facts, they heard evidence, all under oath and all recorded. The court administered to all witnesses a preliminary beating of a stick on their hands and feet, which was repeated if false or incomplete testimony was suspected. The court rendered the decision, but the pharaoh determined the

---

[104] T. Eric Peet, Ch. IX, "Contemporary Life and Thought in Egypt," in 2, J. B. Bury, S. A. Cook, and F. E. Adcock, eds., *The Cambridge Ancient History* 214-215 (1924).

[105] *Id.* at 215.

[106] *Id.* at 207-208.

[107] Pierre Montet, *Everyday Life in Egypt* 267-269 (1981); William Graham Sumner, *Folkways* 236 (1906).

punishment.[108]

Throughout most of Egyptian history, whether in the Old, Middle or Late Kingdoms, the pharaoh acted as the supreme and usually sole legislator, while justice administration and other functions of the legal system were left to the pharaoh's chief minister, commonly referred to in the scholarly literature as the vizier. Usually one vizier was assigned for Upper Egypt, and one for Lower Egypt. Although no code of Egyptian law has yet been discovered, that such a code existed seems well-established. Some evidence suggests that an actual code of law existed at least as early as the Twelfth Dynasty (20th century, B.C.) and that leather objects shown laid out before the vizier are the rolls of the pharaoh's codified law.[109]

The administration of the legal system and judicial organization were more complex. Although judicial functions were carried on under the pharaoh's authority, the lower courts varied in composition, sometimes with all members but the vizier having only advisory authority.[110] When actually in court, the parties were not accompanied by advocates, but represented themselves, and the scribes provided procedural guidance. The courts determined most cases on the basis of the documentary evidence and the parties' testimony; occasionally witnesses also testified. A decree of Pharaoh Seti I in the fourteenth century, B.C., described punishments for magistrates who received complaints but failed to act on them.[111]

§ 3.02(e). Later Egyptian Law

Beginning in the late eighth century, B.C., and until Egypt was

---

108 T. Eric Peet, Ch. IX, "Contemporary Life and Thought in Egypt," in 2, J. B. Bury, S. A. Cook, and F. E. Adcock, eds., *The Cambridge Ancient History* 211-212 (1924).

109 William C. Hayes, Ch. IX, "Egypt: Internal Affairs from Tuthomosis I to the Death of Amenophis III," in II, pt. 1, I. E. S. Edwards, C. J. Gadd, and N. G. L. Hammond, eds., *The Cambridge Ancient History* 313, 357 (3d ed., 1971).

110 *Id.* at 358.

111 John A. Wilson, *The Culture of Ancient Egypt* 242-243 (1951).

conquered by Alexander the Great in 332, B.C., Egyptian law felt the impact of civil war and foreign invasions. These forces of change, however, also created contacts with the Egyptian legal system that may have influenced the invaders' own legal systems. Certain Egyptian practices eventually became almost universal in the legal systems of the west. Property owners in Egypt by this time were retaining all documents pertaining to their "chain of title"; standard forms were developed for common transactions; persons were permitted to sell themselves into servitude, a practice that was also common among Germanic tribes of later eras. Husbands often settled their entire present and future estates upon their wives and children at the time of the marriage, but probably retained very broad powers of use and administration, so that conveyance of the property right itself was of little disadvantage. This eliminated the need for formal succession procedures at death; however, the wife and oldest son were frequently required to join in property conveyances in order to give clear title.

Egyptians still carried on their litigation almost entirely in writing, with oral argument usually not allowed. Parties would often consult with an official who aided them in reaching settlement, before resorting to trial.

During the period of Persian rule over Egypt (525 to 332, B.C., with intermittent periods when rulership was lost), no evidence suggests that Egypt borrowed any law or legal tradition from Persia, or that Persians tried to alter any existing Egyptian law. But the immense respect held for Egyptian law is revealed in an act attributed to the Persian ruler Darius in ordering all Egyptian law to be placed in writing.

Of perhaps even more pertinence for a history of law in the West is an occurrence during the reign of the Pharaoh Amasis in the mid-sixth century, B.C. Amasis revised Egyptian laws, which revision included a law requiring each inhabitant annually to declare to the governor the inhabitant's means of sustenance. Reportedly this provision was noted by Solon while visiting Egypt from Athens, and Solon in turn had it adopted and enforced in Athens.[112] Conquest of Egypt by the Greeks, and later by

---

[112] James Henry Breasted, *A History of Egypt* 591 (1937).

the Romans, and still later by the forces of Islam and much later by the Napoleanic armies, left little of indigenous Egyptian law in force or even discernible, so any bequest to the west would have been made through Crete and Greece.

§ 3.03. Law and Land Regulation in the Aegean and Greek Civilizations

§ 3.03(a). Rise and Fall of the Early Aegean Cultures

In the preceding section, it was suggested that some aspects Egyptian law may have been carried to Athenian Greeks of the 6th century, B.C. The Greek culture and society, however, had already risen on independent developments extending back many centuries earlier into prehistoric times.

Around 2,000, B.C., in Crete, a sophisticated and literate society living in large settlements appeared out of the indigenous culture. These people were the so-called Minoans, and their cultural advances may reflect contact with or arrivals from societies in the Near East. The language of the Cretan and other Aegean cultures was a form of Greek.

The great wealth and elaborate structures of the Minoans' "urban" communities were sustained by large surrounding farm areas and abundant transportation resources relying on wagons and draft animals. The central buildings, today dubbed "palaces" even though their precise functions are unknown, held enormous facilities for food storage and manufacturing processes; the labor forces required for their construction and operation would have been huge. The written records that have been discovered, while still largely undecipherable, show detailed accounting for supplies, craft labor and other transactions.

The ethnic and cultural progenitors of this Cretan society remain unknown, although it is appealing to adopt Will Durant's view that "in its racial origins the Cretan culture was Asiatic, in many of its arts Egyptian;

in essence and total it remained unique."[113]

This assertion strengthens the belief that these Minoan progenitors of western civilization effected a transition from the early and marvelous societies of the Near East. While Cretan culture flourished, contacts abounded with all the neighboring societies, according to widespread discoveries of artifacts from Crete. Crete has also yielded the earliest positive evidence for writing in the Aegean characters, a pictographic or hieroglyphic script possibly inspired by Syria or Egypt.

When earthquakes destroyed virtually all the major Minoan structures about 1,600, B.C., Cretans promptly rebuilt them, and the surrounding village communities of Crete continued as before. Building configurations in some of the settlements suggest a central authority ruling from the "palaces," and a local ruler or governor in the villages. Fire destroyed almost all of these structures on the island about 1425, B.C.; whether the fires were from invasion or volcanic eruption is not known. This culture, though literate, is still largely inaccessible to us, because so little written information has yet been deciphered. Accordingly, only the most generalized speculations about Minoan legal customs are possible.

Meanwhile, on the Greek mainland about 1,600, B.C., indigenous communities formed the wealthy, Greek-speaking Mycenaean culture, whose affluence may have resulted in large part from trade with the Minoans in Crete. Researchers have recovered fragments of writing that give details of economic and military matters as well as reveal a tenurial system of landholding based on social ranks and resembling feudal landholding. Mycenaean settlement centers, too, featured great, massively fortified "palaces" and elaborate collections of luxury items. Water conduits for the fortified areas and other engineering works, such as roads and bridges, are evident even today. The far-flung trading activities of both the Minoans and Mycenaeans established contacts with the Near East, Egypt, and Mediterranean Europe to the west.

About 1,200, B.C., the main centers of Aegean civilization suffered a

---

[113] 2 Will Durant, *The Story of Civilization: The Life of Greece* 20 (1939).

fate similar to that of the Minoans and were destroyed; whether through civil war or by outside force is not known. The region thereafter went into an extended cultural and economic decline. Yet Cretans and some Greeks believed that Greek law derived from models in Crete. When archaeologists in the 19th century recovered the inscriptions of a law code in the city of Gortyn in southern Crete, dated between 600 and 400, B.C., this code revealed a relatively enlightened law that may indeed have influenced Greek lawgivers. But only in this Gortyn code does Crete yield a specific, known contribution to western legal history.[114]

§ 3.03(b). Law in Classical Greece

§ 3.03(b)(1). Characteristics of Law in Pre-classical Greece

The Greek societies that eventually emerged from these ancient Aegean cultures made profoundly important contributions to the development of western civilization. And, while no modern nation of the West traces its legal system directly back to Greek law, Greek systems of law and government achieved extremely important advances in establishing the rule of law as a characteristic of civilization.

One likely finds the origins of Greek law in developments typical of other people emerging into higher forms of culture. It is impossible to know exactly how human societies first formed and how they were regulated and governed. However, archaeological discoveries together with modern anthropological studies invite some educated guesses, and also permit a keener appreciation of the Greek achievement in moving from early to more advanced stages of civilization.

Prehistoric peoples everywhere probably learned very early that chances of survival were much enhanced when they lived and worked in groups, and the most natural groups were kinship groups. Indeed, the integrity of one's group, and one's ability to affiliate and identify with a

---

[114] Raphael Sealey, *The Justice of the Greeks* 37-43 (1994).

group, became much more important than asserting one's own individuality, in contrast to modern attitudes. The ultimate punishment for misconduct was typically exile or exclusion from the group.

Early common customs well illustrated the primacy of the group. Examples of such customs are (1) insisting on revenge whenever anyone from the group was injured or offended, so the group would not reveal weakness or vulnerability, and (2) exacting such revenge usually on a group to group basis, with neither the individual victim or offender necessarily having a role in the vengeance process. Naturally, if a group deemed it necessary to seek revenge each time someone from the group was injured, and this was so even if the injury was itself inflicted in vengeance, then the cycles of vengeful violence—the blood feuds—would continue endlessly.

Prehistoric people apparently realized that open-ended vengeance threatened the existence of all, so they developed devices to resolve their conflicts and compose their differences without violence but with finality. Such devices as expiatory encounters and regulated fights were succeeded in many early cultures by a regulated system of payments for various offenses, often tied to the status of the victim or offender as well as to the seriousness of the offense.[115]

Apparently this development pattern occurred in Greece at a very early time, as some passages in the earliest Greek literature infer.[116] In the 8th century, B.C., Homer penned a few brief lines in the *Iliad* describing a scene on Achilles' shield in which full payment of blood-money for a man who had been killed is at issue.[117] The 8th century Greek poet Hesiod, in his *Theogony* and *Works and Days,* also alludes to kings' roles in settling

---

[115] William Seagle, *The History of Law* 36-43 (1946).

[116] Even though the Greeks acted very early in adopting a system of money payments for personal injuries, it may be recalled that such payment arrangements appear even earlier in Mesopotamian law, such as ca. 2110, B.C., in the Sumerian code of Ur-Nammu.

[117] *Iliad* 18.497-508.

disputes.[118] Thus literary evidence suggests that by the beginning of the seventh century, B.C., Greek city-states had adopted similar procedures for settling disputes.

§ 3.03(b)(2). Influence of Greek Political Organization on Greek Law

The Greeks' procedures for settling disputes were similar to those adopted centuries earlier in the Near Eastern cultures. However, while the Greek-speaking cultures may have borrowed individual legal customs from the autocratic peoples of the Near East, they did not adopt Mesopotamian and Egyptian forms of government. Instead, prominent families or monarchs probably ruled the early the Aegean societies, and this pattern evolved in Greece to rule by elected assemblies and councils, and even to some forms of limited democracy. Eventually in classical Greece, the most literate of all ancient cultures, local leaders studied and compared forms of government, publicly confronted public issues, and produced written law codes.

Even before the classical period in Greek history, Greek-speaking peoples had clung tenaciously to their political traditions. The extinction of Mycenean society during the twelfth century, B.C., was followed by a long period of cultural darkness, during which destroying invaders settled in. Most of them were Dorians from the north, but Dorian culture never subsumed Athens, which eventually emerged as a center of a truly Greek culture, flourishing with wealth from extensive colonization and sea-borne trade. Growth of urban life and related political institutions was conspicuous during the period 750-500, B.C., and the far-flung Greek Mediterranean colonies copied the political and legal practices of their home cities.

It was during this period that written law appeared among the Greeks, albeit only in Athenian sources, so far as is known today. Even after this period the only recovered written source of Greek law outside Athens is the

---

118 Michael Gagarin, *Early Greek Law* 24-25, 46-50 (1986).

mid-fifth century Gortyn Code from Crete. Nevertheless, other evidence suggests that by the middle of the seventh century, B.C., Greek city-states began to adopt written laws.[119]

According to these sources, the *polis* or city-state gave law its shape. The city-state was by far the most common form of political organization adopted during this period, and was an independent, sovereign political unit, often including surrounding villages and territory. In northern Greece, federations of unfortified villages and their respective territories also appeared.

Typically a king, council, and assembly of adult male citizens conducted government functions within a city-state. These divisions had originally developed during the times and under the circumstances of the migrations. In a pattern that was to become familiar all over ancient Europe, even up to the Germanic and Viking invasions of the early Middle Ages, the position of war leader became one of hereditary kingship as the invaders became settlers; the leaders of individual military units or contingents became members of the council; and the able-bodied warriors became the assembly composed of adult males. In the Greek setting, the king's position was more vulnerable to change, because it was less stable; elective institutions grew up alongside the king to cover for weakness in the ruler, and councils grew stronger when the monarch was weaker. When factions within councils were unable to compose their differences, they often resorted to assemblies, and the popular assemblies became places to settle political contests. Occasionally the assemblies may have given voice to the lower classes to be heard against the ruling classes. "Tyrants" arose, persons who seized control of a city-state without any official or hereditary authority, but who kept institutions and laws in place.

In each Greek city-state, the usual institutions and powers of king, council and assembly developed along idiosyncratic lines. In Sparta, for instance, dual hereditary kings merely carried out the foreign policy and military decisions pronounced by the assembly, but the kings were also members of the council and they exercised judicial powers over public

---

[119] *Id.* at 51.

roads, marriages of heiresses and adoptions of sons. The council's special jurisdiction was to try capital cases and prepare matters for consideration by the assembly. In addition, Spartan assemblies chose five "ephors," officers who conducted much of the daily business of law and government. These officers often opposed the kings but by themselves could not coerce the kings.

By the sixth century, B.C., evidence suggests that the Spartan assemblies were issuing documentary legislative enactments, perhaps in a two-stage procedure according to which the measures were first introduced by councils for consideration and then adopted at the assemblies. Such a procedure has had many counterparts in other ancient societies, notably Roman and Germanic. Probably by means of these assembly decisions, Spartans adopted the well-known system of strict public education and discipline that helped produce their remarkable military successes in the sixth century, B.C.

Because of those military successes, the Spartan society entered into a series of bilateral treaties with neighboring city-states, eventually creating what is modernly known as the Peloponnesian League. This was the first alliance created explicitly by political power rather than relying on some fiction of common descent.

Meanwhile, in Attica, by the seventh century, B.C., Athens had succeeded in creating a unitary state by absorbing the neighboring city-states and territories. There the former monarchical system had evolved into the political institutions of an executive board (archons), a council (council of Areopagus), and an assembly.

§ 3.03(b)(3). Growth of Law in Classical Greece

The legal history of classical Greece is essentially the legal history of classical Athens. Also, it is a murky mixture of legend and legislation, but it represents the recorded beginnings of legal history in western civilization. According to Athenian tradition, in 621, B.C. a leader named Draco recorded all the laws pertaining to homicide. Parts of an inscription of these laws made in 409, B.C., have been recovered and, supplemented by other evidence, reveal criminal justice processes in evolution from ancient forms and motivations to the basic elements of modern systems. Procedural provisions forming part of Draco's law inferred the continuing use of the ancient practices of blood feud and mitigating compensation. If one accused of killing was able to convince a court that the act was unintentional, the victim's family, which traditionally had a right to exact revenge, could accept compensation in place of vengeance and then vote to pardon the accused. If the vote for pardon, which was required to be unanimous, was unsuccessful, the accused was given safe conduct to the border. A special court was established for such cases, to judge intent and consider ameliorating the penalties for unintentional acts; this suggests a shift toward modern criminal jurisprudence and increasing state involvement in matters that were traditionally left to be resolved by private actions of families and tribes. Several other courts dealing with intentional killings added further sophistication to criminal law by recognizing the lawfulness of certain kinds of killings and distinctions between killings of citizens, slaves and foreigners.

The next important figure in Athenian legal history was Solon, who was serving as an archon (chief magistrate) in 594, B.C., and whom Athens commissioned to record the law, perhaps as a means of reducing the class strife that then afflicted Athens. One probable cause of this strife was discontent among a large class of the population who held land under a type of slavery or serfdom, and who were kept in their oppressed circumstances partly by lack of access to the law. Apparently Solon succeeded in obtaining freedom, citizenship, and land ownership rights for these people and thus blunted the threat of violent revolution.

Of equal importance was Solon's effort to make a written statement of all the laws, the result of which was to brush away all of Draco's laws except those on homicide. Solon's code lacked the system and order of a modern legal code, but it was more than a mere set of new laws, because it reshaped the political entity as only a revolution or constitution could do. Class divisions of free persons based on wealth rather than heredity, and popular participation in court processes regardless of one's class, began the slow introduction of democratic elements into Athenian justice and society.

The historian Will Durant noted Aristotle's statement, "Some believe, that Solon intentionally introduced obscurity into his laws, to enable the commons to use their judicial power for their own political aggrandizement" and Plutarch's comment, "their differences could not be adjusted by the letter, they would have to bring all their causes to the judges, who were in a manner masters of the laws." Durant thought that this power of appeal to popular courts was key to Athenian democracy. [120]

Among the more important features of Solon's laws were individual ownership of property (including apportionment of property among male heirs), use of wills to transfer decedents' property, citizenship for skilled and permanently resident aliens, limitations on dowry sizes to encourage marriage for affection rather than affluence, and state supported education for sons of soldiers who died in battle. Most importantly, his laws, for which he claimed no divine origin, were reduced to writing and made available to be read by any who cared to seek them out.

Although the individual details of Greek law have had little impact on later legal systems, certain characteristics of the Greek approach to law were profoundly important. In the writing of their laws, the Greeks transformed their sacred customs and usages into laws that were secular and free of religion. Also, the seriousness of particular conduct was often made dependent upon the doer's intent. Individual accountability supplanted family or clan responsibility. Penalties imposed by public authority replaced private vendettas of vengeance.

Nevertheless, for all of its sophisticated detail, ancient Greek law, according to some, "has had a negligible influence on posterity."[121] Even Greek laws and procedures that seem to have modern counterparts were usually not the direct sources for those modern practices. Greek philosophers who may have influenced Roman jurists had little influence on Greek law itself. And the rise of Roman jurists, those who primarily wrote rather than practiced law, was an essentially and uniquely Roman

---

[120] 2 Will Durant, *The Story of Civilization: The Life of Greece* 116 (1939).

[121] S. C. Todd, *The Shape of Athenian Law* 4 (1993).

phenomenon. Roman law, not Greek law, was massive in its detail and marvelous in its systematization, exerting a profound influence on the legal developments of western civilization. Greek law, so far as is now known, was never given a systematic statement. And not only was Greek law lacking in system, but it also produced few sources that could impress or influence successor societies. An active jurisdiction such as Athens had no case reports, as in common law jurisdictions, nor juristic writings, as in civil law jurisdictions, and the few Greek philosophers who interested themselves in questions of law had no influence on the courts.

On the other hand, Solon's laws were still in effect in Athens and well-known in Rome five centuries after he announced them. Study of individual Greek laws reveals rules that seem surprisingly familiar, reminding us that in many areas Greek legislation was the model and guide for much of that Roman law upon which the legal structure of Western civilization rests.

§ 3.04. Roman Law and Land Regulation

§ 3.04(a). Etruscan Beginnings

It is said that the Etruscans "are among the irritating obscurities of history," having "left upon Rome so varied an influence that Rome can hardly be understood without them";[122] yet Roman sources reveal little about these origins and the Etruscan language still holds most of its secrets.

Developing their urban civilization centuries before Rome, Etruscans brought their largest city-states together in a federation that remained loose in accordance with the inhabitants' desires for independence. Within the federation each city-state followed the familiar governmental evolution of monarchy changing to oligarchical rule by prominent families, which in turned changed to rule by assemblies of affluent citizens. The highest officer in each city-state was probably a type of magistrate with judicial powers and functions and who served for a limited term, perhaps one year.

---

[122] 3 Will Durant, *The Story of Civilization: Caesar and Christ* 5 (1944, 1972).

The general resemblance of these institutions of rule to later Roman public institutions and officers is probably no coincidence. No doubt the Romans borrowed heavily from their Etruscan predecessors, not only the institutions but also the substantive rules of law. The Roman symbol of ruling power, the fasces—a bundle of rods bound together with and around an ax with blade projecting—was first the Etruscan symbol of rule.

Etruria dominated early Roman history, with Etruscan kings governing Rome itself from 616 to 509, B.C. After losing control of Rome, the Etruscans were challenged by the Greeks at sea and the Celtic Gauls in the north and then ultimately were conquered by Rome. Through all of these crises the Etruscan city-states apparently remained disunited and in a mostly feudal form of social organization, unable to adapt in response to the threats from their neighbors.

Durant believed that "the marks and relics of Etruscan influence were to survive in Roman civilization to its end."[123]

§ 3.04(b). The Rule of Law in Rome

By the time native Romans succeeded in expelling the Etruscan kings the notion of monarchy had become permanently repugnant, offensive to the tradition of limited popular government that had developed even during reigns of the native Roman monarchs before the Etruscan kings. According to legend, Rome even from its founding was organized into three tribes, each with subdivisions called curiae, roughly corresponding to clan groups identified by a common ancestor. The curiae all together formed an assembly called the Comitia Curiata, which selected a king and performed other judicial and legislative functions.

Meanwhile certain clans, having achieved conspicuous wealth and prestige, gradually formed the patrician class; the heads of those clans, again according to legend, had been organized by Rome's founder Romulus into the first Senate. This Senate had been responsible for nominating the

---

[123] *Id.* at 17, citing Livy, *History of Rome,* I, 8; Strabo, *Geography,* v, 2. 2; II George Dennis, *Cities and Cemeteries of Etruria* 166 (1907).

king that was eventually chosen by the assembly, and the Senate's close association with the Roman monarch gave it increasing prestige, influence and authority.

Roman tradition originally excluded from both the early Assembly and the Senate the majority of Roman inhabitants, the poorer class known as the plebs, possessing neither religious cultic traditions nor common ancestors such as characterized the patrician clans. Initially, the plebs had virtually no political, religious or civil rights and were accordingly also not obligated to give military service or pay taxes. Apparently during the Etruscan monarchy of the sixth century, B.C., plebs were able to serve in the army, so that their exclusion from public life became an even more acute cause of deep and continuing discontent. The Senate, too, was unhappy under the unlimited monarchy of the Etruscans, because it had previously considered the king as simply the executive of the Senate. About 508, B.C., the Senate assembled an army and deposed the Etruscan king, opening the way for the birth of the Roman republic and the emergence of profoundly important legal developments.

Upon expulsion of the Etruscan kings, aristocratic citizen-soldiers formed an assembly; the assembly rejected lifetime kings and instead created a dual executive by selecting two men as consuls, with equal powers, and to rule for only a one-year term. Under the leadership of the early consuls, the assembly established the basic elements of the Roman legal system and form of government: kingship was prohibited, public office could be held only with popular consent, and imposition of capital or other severe punishment could be appealed to the assembly. The assembly represented replacement of rule by monarchy with rule by aristocracy, usually referred to as patricians. These patricians all represented various tribal clan heads that originally had achieved success in farming, and with financial power had gained political ascendancy. These clan heads and some wealthy businessmen formed the two orders that eventually made up the senate.

The senate, now consisting solely of wealthy aristocrats, relaxed the discriminatory laws only when the plebs refused to fight in the army or give service in public works at times when Rome was threatened by enemies.

Along with those minor legal reforms, the Senate created new public offices, two tribunes and three aediles, as defenders of the plebs. With these advocates, and an emerging republican form of government dividing power among the Senate, the popular assemblies and various magistrates, it was only natural that the plebs would begin to show even greater interest in the form and substance of the laws.

From earliest times patrician priests had recorded and interpreted laws, but had kept their writings hidden from public view. The law remained for most a mystery to be used only by a favored few for maintaining their prerogatives in place. In 454, B.C., the senate finally relented to plebeian pressures for written and accessible laws, and sent a delegation to Greece to study the laws of Solon and others. After they returned and reported, the Senate chose ten other senators (*decemvirs*) to prepare a new written code, which was submitted to the Assembly and passed with some changes; then the *decemvirs,* under a grant of broad governmental power, were assigned to implement the code over a period of two years. Thus the customary and current existing law of Rome—a mixture of tribal customs, and royal and priestly edicts—was codified, written on twelve bronze or wooden tablets for permanent display in the Forum, and known thereafter as the Twelve Tables.

So impressive was the influence of those who authorized, drafted and implemented the Twelve Tables, that the tablets were thereafter viewed as the source of all public and private law, and they were in fact the first written form of the law that would be Rome's most enduring contribution to western civilization. Whereas Roman law before the Twelve Tables had been both customary (mostly oral) and controlled by religious officials, after the Twelve Tables the primary source of law was public, written, and beginning to become secularized. In a general sense, popular insistence on written laws results from increasing literacy in the citizenry and democracy in government, factors that continue to be essential for the rule of law. Only fragments of the Twelve Tables have survived to the present, and these fragments are presented in Appendix 1 to reveal their elements of archaic tradition, procedural complexity, and of enlightened restraint on the absoluteness of government power.

The actual content of the legal rules set forth in the Twelve Tables was not as important for the history of western law as the institutions and procedures by which the law was formed and reformed. Early in the third century, B.C., teachers undertook the first public instruction in Roman law, leading to professional lawyers rather than priests becoming the dominant persons in both Roman law and Roman society. Virtually all magistrates of any kind under the Roman system had power to act as judges in cases, although praetors were usually the judges, and their decrees infused the laws of the Twelve Tables with a steady current of interpretations and even revisions. Such praetorial pronouncements, or edicts, in addition to formal legislation, decrees of the Senate and finally even imperial decrees, all amended and nourished the law of the Twelve Tables into the Roman law that is regarded as Rome's most important contribution to the world.

Roman law was further secularized, or separated from the authority of the priestly class, by creation of the office of *praetor*. The praetors (and to a lessor extent the officials known as *aediles curules*) were neither legislators nor judges, but would be considered today as sort of elected administrators who were charged to help parties in a legal dispute properly frame the dispute and get it presented to a judge. While the praetors did not pronounce or apply the law, their functions led to their having almost sole power over development of legal procedure. Moreover, where the law did not offer a remedy that seemed clearly needed in a particular situation, the praetor could by edict create new procedures that would in effect permit the needed remedy to be applied.

The power and influence of the praetors proved to be immense. In tempering or enlarging the effects and remedies of the formal law (the *jus civile*) the praetors often drew from the customary law (the *jus gentium*) to inject corrective elements of equity and good faith. This in fact was part of a longer process by which incorporating elements from the customary laws of the peoples who became Romans enlarged and enriched the ancient Roman law. Also, praetors acted to overcome the limitations on their ability to revise the laws. These limitations rested in the fact that they served terms of only one year, and that the edicts they announced during the term actually expired at the end of the term. In practice, the praetors thoughtfully framed the edicts, usually with a view to their lasting effect, and many were carried on from praetor to praetor. Edicts carried over for many praetorian terms came to be considered part of the established law. Some long-standing edicts became so revered that praetors were prohibited from changing them.

The Law of the Twelve Tables and the huge body of law introduced by the praetors and similar officials were part of Roman legal developments during the period of the Roman Republic (ca. 510 to 27, B.C.), developments which tended to remove law from its traditional secrecy and obscurity. One other important development during this time that had the same effect was the emergence of Roman jurists. Originally, the knowledge of the law and of the procedure used in issuing legislation reposed in the priests, because law had a religious significance. By the beginning of the third century, B.C., the priests began functioning more distinctly as lawyers, separating these tasks from their religious roles, and this led to more openness in the law. First, according to Roman legend, the legal formulas and phrases used in litigation were published by one of the priest/lawyers in 304, B.C. Then, in 252, B.C., another priest/lawyer began giving legal advice to parties in such a way that the advice became accessible to the public. In about 200, B.C., Rome issued a publication containing the Law of the Twelve Tables, an interpretation of that law, and a newer version of litigation formulas and phrases. All the persons promulgating these works were priests acting as lawyers, and their audiences were probably other lawyer priests. Gradually, these lawyers formed a separate class in Roman society, held in high esteem because they not only knew the law but practiced law, usually without remuneration and usually in behalf of less fortunate members of the community.

When the lawyers advised clients, they all went to a public place, the clients stated their problems, and the lawyers gave their advice orally and in public. Even a magistrate, such as a praetor, might appear as a client, and probably much of what praetors contributed to the development of Roman legal rules actually originated with the lawyers consulted by the praetors. Other persons came simply to listen and learn. While the lawyers gave public advice as to how to conduct litigation, they did not appear or plead in court. In applying and interpreting legal rules, Roman lawyers then–as modern lawyers now–no doubt found many creative ways to view and utilize the law, which enlarged and enriched Roman law. Probably many lawyers wrote about the law and furthered its open accessibility to the entire citizenry. Unfortunately, almost all writing about the law during the era of the Roman Republic has been lost.

When the Roman Republic came to an end and the reigns of caesars over the Roman Empire commenced, Roman lawyers performed even more important work in behalf of Roman law. The so-called classical period of Roman law extended from about the beginning of the reign of Augustus in 27, B.C., and lasted for about 250 years. The period is termed classical because during this time Roman law attained such refinement in thoughtfulness, detail and thoroughness, that some believe it has never been surpassed. Indeed, Roman law from the height of its classical development is the basis for many modern legal systems. During this classical period the Roman lawyers also laid the foundation for the later scientific approach to law that was brought to culmination by German legal scholars of the nineteenth century. These proponents of "legal science" produced a legal structure and issued systematic legal treatises based on principles and relationships they perceived in their study of the rich and sophisticated detail of classical Roman law.

Much of the lawyers' work in contributing to the development of Roman law consisted of giving responses to clients' questions. Lawyers were honored for the quality of their responses and eventually some responses became mandatory authority for the courts. Also, one of the greatest of the classical Roman lawyers, Salvius Iulianus, in about 130, A.D., prepared a code that organized and restated the perpetual edicts of the old praetors, even though praetors by this time were no longer a factor in Roman legal developments. About thirty years later, the great law teacher Gaius prepared a short textbook (the "Institutes") that concisely and clearly summarized classical Roman law and had great influence on later lawyers and legislators.

Imperial legislation (also called constitutions) and decrees deciding cases also contributed enormously to Roman law both during and after the classical period. The constitutions were later gathered, sifted and organized in a principal part of the effort to codify Roman law under the Emperor

Justinian in the sixth century, A.D.

§ 3.04(c). The Essence of Roman Law

Because the greatness of Roman law rests somewhat in the sophistication of its approach and the technicality of its detail in serving a huge and complex empire, it is of course impossible to give a simple summary of the main points of the law.[124] However, the following paragraphs may demonstrate the maturity of Roman law.

According to Gaius, "all law pertains to persons, to property, or to procedure."[125] Under the category of the law of persons, Roman law defined the distinction between and the rights pertaining to each of several classes of citizenship. Family matters were governed more by law as custom weakened, including a decline in the life-and-death powers of fathers over family members, and a gradual elevating of the status of women. The law governed with mixed success matters of family, marriage and children. Roman criminal law recognized crimes against the state, against business or social groups, and against individual persons. By a slight inconsistency, detailed and increasingly humane laws over slaves and slavery were included in the law of persons, rather than in the law of property.

Roman society was very materialistic, and the law of property dominated Roman law, especially in issues dealing with ownership, acquisition, transfer, occupancy, contract, obligation, debt, exchange, and crimes against property. Durant declared that "in its final form, the law of property was the most perfect part of the Roman code."[126] This materialism that was sustained by law and the "pax Romana" was exhibited in much of what was constructed under Roman authority, as shown in Illustration 8.

---

[124] A superbly readable summary of the main points and divisions of classical Roman law is found in 3 Will Durant, *The Story of Civilization: Caesar and Christ* 394-406 (1944).

[125] Gaius, *Institutes*, I, 8.

[126] 3 Will Durant, *The Story of Civilization: Caesar and Christ* 400 (1944).

Illustration 8: This is a model reconstruction of one of four monumental twin-arched gates in the wall of the Roman city of Verulamium, near St. Albans north of London. Verulamium was the third largest city in Roman Britain, and its splendor demonstrates the Romans' confident materialism nurtured by their laws governing property and commerce.

Romans were litigious despite the confusion and technical absurdities of their very complex procedural rules. Whereas in the Republican era the praetors as magistrates helped formulate the cases for presentation to the judges, in later times the magistrates actually decided the cases, usually by summary judgment, as Roman government became more of an absolute monarchy. The legal profession was divided into advocates, legal technicians, consultants and jurists, to aid clients in the various procedural stages of litigation. Cases might be tried before a single judge or a jury of several dozen drawn from a jury list consisting only of men from the senatorial and equestrian classes. Legal torture of slaves persisted throughout Roman history, although evidence thus derived was deemed untrustworthy. Criminal penalties were fixed by law rather than left to judicial discretion.

In its legal relations with conquered peoples Rome attempted to meld the system and order of its own law with the revered customs of the subject peoples. A special praetor was appointed to help formulate law and decisions in matters involving the alien peoples. Edicts from this office gradually created a *ius gentium*, or law of nations, which recognized and incorporated values and principles widely recognized throughout the Mediterranean world. It has been perhaps more realistically described as "local law adapted to Roman sovereignty, and designed to govern the peoples of Italy and the provinces without giving them Roman citizenship and the other rights of the [Roman law]."[127]

§ 3.04(d). Roman Law and the Dark Ages

As the classical age of Roman law drew to a close about 250, A.D., the empire itself had begun its decline. During this era more and more subject peoples were incorporated into the empire and most of them became Roman citizens after almost universal citizenship was granted in 212, A.D. The laws of these conquered peoples became somewhat romanized, and the law of Rome itself became more preoccupied and "vulgarized" with matters of practice rather than of principle. In the fourth century, A.D., with the division of imperial government into western and eastern portions, ruled from Rome and Constantinople, respectively, the West succumbed to barbarian incursions and Rome itself fell with finality in 476, A.D. In the sixth century, A.D., the eastern emperor Justinian undertook the great project to rescue, revive and perpetuate Roman law.

The objective of Justinian's commissioners was to make an authoritative written statement of Roman law which would replace all other forms and renderings of Roman law. The several stages of this project consisted of making a collection of imperial legislation or constitutions that were still considered relevant and valid (the Codex); collecting and codifying the edicts and other sources of Roman law that were found mainly in the law school books of the time and changing those laws as necessary to suit the times (the Digest); creating a textbook on Roman law (the Institutes); and gathering Justinian's own decrees (the Novels). Altogether this work is known as the Corpus Juris (or Iuris) Civilis.

The Corpus Juris Civilis became the law of the Byzantine Empire,

---

[127] *Id.* at 405.

which after the reign of Justinian entered a protracted decline. When the Empire actually disintegrated several centuries later, elements of Roman law survived in the countries of eastern Europe that arose in place of the Byzantine government, but those countries soon asserted their own national legal customs.

The earlier and more cataclysmic fall of Roman government in the west did not mean the immediate rejection of Roman law. In the areas taken over by Germanic peoples, rulers attempted to maintain a Roman-based system of laws for former Roman citizens, and the resulting "barbarian laws," discussed in the next chapter, present an interesting mix of Germanic and Roman legal customs. However, as the Dark Ages deepened, it became more difficult to maintain any coherent legal system, and Roman law virtually disappeared in western Europe. A new chapter on Roman law opened in about 1100, A.D., when scholars discovered the Corpus Juris Civilis. This opened a new chapter in the history of Roman law, which students then began again to study, interpret and revere as a treasure from an honored past. Roman law experts gradually reapplied Roman law in European societies becoming too advanced for their old traditional legal systems.

§ 3.04(e). Transmission of Roman Law to the Modern West: The Byzantines

§ 3.04(e)(1). Introduction

Greek colonists founded Byzantium a hundred years before Rome was born. While Byzantium prospered from its geographical position, and attracted the conquering attention of Alexander the Great, it made no contribution to culture or law until after it was swept into the Roman state. Reborn in 330, A.D., as Nova Roma under the Roman emperor Constantine, Byzantium preserved its Roman heritage long after Rome and the cities of the west had fallen to barbarians. Most importantly, it preserved in Justinian's Code what can be described as highlights and outlines of Roman law—long after that law had outlived the vitality of its classical prime–and managed to pass those precious fragments on to the new states of the west. The post-Justinian developments in Byzantine law exerted no further general influence on western legal history, but formed part of the legal history of several east European nations.

§ 3.04(e)(2). The Formation of Byzantine Law

From its beginning as a colony founded by ancient Greek settlers in about 657, B.C., Byzantium retained its name for a thousand years and until well after coming under Roman hegemony. The foundations of the Byzantine empire began to be laid in 330, A.D., when the Roman emperor Constantine designated the ancient Greek colony of Byzantium, on the European side of the Bosporus strait, as his new imperial and eastern capital Constantinople. With this action he also began a lavish program of municipal development. In 395, A.D., the Roman Empire, which had always been governed according to geographic sectors, was formally divided into western and eastern empires, ruled by the two sons of Theodosius I. By that time, Christianity had become the sole imperial religion, so Constantinople in the east and Rome in the west also became the Christian centers. By 500, A.D., Constantinople had grown to a population of 500,000, and was able to maintain Roman imperial traditions and culture while the western portion of the empire fell before barbarian assaults.

The early rulers of the eastern portion of the empire would not have acknowledged themselves as "Byzantine," but still considered themselves Romans; they long aspired to subdue the barbarians in the west and restore a united Roman empire. Nor did the citizens of the eastern empire refer to themselves as Byzantine: they, too, considered themselves Romans; their law was Roman imperial law, and even though they were mostly Greek-speaking, Latin was the language of government and law. Yet their society had fully imbued the hellenism of Alexander the Great, and early in the sixth century, A.D., Greek replaced Latin as the language of the law in the eastern empire.

By Justinian's time, Roman law had lost much of its greatness. As described earlier, since the end of the classical era of Roman law, about 250, A.D., Roman law in the west had slipped into decadence and vulgarization. During the classical era, the law had been enlivened by comments of important legal experts known as jurists. Three centuries later, however, the jurists were content to simply study extracts, fragments and summaries of the works of earlier jurists. This pathetic condition was not only accepted but made mandatory by the imperial Roman law known as the Lex Citationis, issued in Rome in 426, A.D., and which decreed that only the works of the five greatest jurists of the classical past (Gaius, Paulus, Ulpianus, Papinianus, and Modestinus), could be consulted in the courts. Moreover, these centuries-old sources were to be used as the sole authorities in proving the points of law at issue in individual cases. This effectively blunted whatever creative effort contemporary jurists might otherwise have brought to bear on legal problems. Thus the Roman legal profession of the fifth century, A.D., in effect conceded that it had nothing new to offer to the body and principles of Roman law, and in fact permitted no new developments.

Even the law schools contributed to this stagnation. In the eastern Empire, law schools–including the important schools at Berytos and Byzantium–continued to promote the study of and respect for the law of the classical period, but students studied and treated the law simply as dogma. The perception of law as a living system died out.

However, the existence of these law schools did facilitate the recodification of Roman law that took place early in the sixth century under the Emperor Justinian. Justinian's project was only the last and greatest of a series of attempts to capture and preserve old Roman law in a code. As early as 291, A.D., the Roman compilers of the Codex Gregorianus had attempted to assemble the emperors' cumulated legislation, called constitutions, because these pronouncements had become so prolific as to be chaotic and unusable. Others continued this effort in a project called the Codex Hermogenianus, until about 365, A.D. Another project, sponsored by the eastern emperor Theodosius II and the western emperor Valentinian III beginning in 429, A.D., was more successful. A commission of sixteen lawyers was appointed to the task in 435, A.D., and eventually produced what is know as the Theodosian Code. This code was accepted as valid law in both the eastern (438, A.D.) and the western (439, A.D.) parts of the empire.

As the grand culmination of these recodification projects, Justinian's project was consistent with his significant successes in restoring the unity of the former Roman empire, and arose out of a desire to restore the Roman law to its former greatness. His objective was to create a comprehensive written code of Roman law then in force, which code would then replace all other earlier forms and versions of Roman law.

§ 3.04(e)(3). Byzantine Law: A Late Version of Roman Law

§ 3.04(e)(3)(A). The Components of Justinian's Code

The idea of codifying Roman law (that is, gathering and organizing individual imperial decrees) was well-accepted by Justinian's time. The century-old Theodosian Code had become partially obsolete and had grown disorganized and contradictory with the addition of new laws since the original codification effort. Further, Rome's traditional laws sometimes conflicted with the indigenous laws of subject peoples, especially in the east with its Hellenistic traditions. Not least, Christian influence had tempered some aspects of imperial law. The old Theodosian Code had, in fact, lost resemblance to an organized code.

To restore order to this law, the emperor Justinian in 528, A.D., appointed as commissioners ten jurists, including one Tribonian, who was to assume a leading role. Barely one year later, using the Theodosian Code as a reference, and after assembling, reviewing, selecting, discarding, rewriting and rearranging the old imperial edicts, or constitutions, dating from since Hadrian's reign (117-138, A.D.), the jurists completed and Justinian issued the Codex Constitutionum portion of the code. The constitutions they retained and edited assumed the force of law and, from April 16, 529, A.D., all other imperial decrees were nullified.

Having thus selected and reissued imperial legislation on general principles of law, the commissioners then took the same approach to the edicts by which the emperors had resolved particular problems arising under Roman law. This was a preparatory step toward gathering the writings of the ancient, great jurists who had commented on and applied Roman law. Justinian appoint a new commission under Tribonian to sift through the rulings of these great Roman jurists. The commissioners were mostly law school teachers, and it was students in the law schools who intensely studied and discussed these old writings of the great jurists from Rome's classical period. The commissioners gathered and arranged the jurists' opinions or fragments of opinions; they also had authority to edit the writings by updating, condensing, correcting, reconciling and commenting on them. They drew about 80% of the finished work from the writings and opinions of the jurists Ulpian, Paul, Papinian, Gaius and Modestinus, all three or more centuries old. In 533, A.D., they completed this project and published it as the Digests. All statements in the Digests were made binding on the judges; all other jurists' opinions lost their legal authority; other collections of jurists' opinions were no longer copied, and eventually almost all disappeared. What few fragments of these other opinions survive indicate that "Justinian's [editors] omitted opinions favorable to freedom, and by impious fraud transformed some judgments of ancient jurists to better consonance with absolute rule."[128] Moreover, by insisting on the almost exclusive use of these great but very old authorities, the emperor assured the final ossification of Roman law.

While the Digests project was underway, Tribonian and two associates prepared the Institutes, a handbook or text of Roman civil law to accompany and facilitate use of the Digests. Remarkably, the Institutes, which mostly updated the 400-year-old Commentaries of Gaius, were themselves given the force of law when issued in 533, A.D.

By 533 it was discovered that the Codex of 529 had become obsolete as Justinian issued new laws, so Tribonian and four associates produced a second edition, which was issued in 539, A.D., replacing the first edition and acquiring the force of law.

Even though these three compilations in Justinian's Code seemed to

---

[128] 4 Will Durant, *The Story of Civilization: The Age of Faith* 112 (1950).

deny the elements of vitality and creativity in Roman law, Justinian himself considered law "a living element in society and prescribed that changes and additions to the law could be effected, but it was his intention that this would come about only by means of imperial constitutions."[129]

Justinian continued issuing new laws until his death in 565, A.D. His laws, or constitutions, issued between 534 and 565, were compiled as the Novels, the fourth component of Justinian's Code. This complete code became and is still known as the *Corpus Juris Civilis,* or the body of civil law. Justinian's Code, except for the Novels, was written in Latin, Justinian's own language, even though Greek was by then the language of the eastern empire. The Novels, compiled after Justinian's death, were written in Greek, and their publication marked the end of Latin as the language of law in the east. Official translations and condensations of the Code were subsequently published in Greek.

Together these four components—Codex, Institutes, Digest and Novels–comprise the Corpus Juris Civilis, described by one authority as "perhaps the greatest monument of legal activity the world has known. It contains a legal system that is far from perfect and that is extremely difficult to use in practice as a source of law. But it is a monumental work, the importance of which, long after the Roman Empire had passed away, cannot be stressed too strongly."[130]

§ 3.04(e)(3)(B). The Principal Themes of Law in Justinian's Code

As had the Theodosian Code before it, the Justinian Code enacted Christian orthodoxy into law. It acknowledged the church in Rome as the leading see, but the emperor was over the church and the empire made law for the church.

In social legislation, Byzantine Roman law was progressive. It

[129] Paul Van Warmelo, *An Introduction to the Principles of Roman Law* 25 (1976).

[130] *Id.*

eliminated the class of former slaves known as freedmen and assigned them to the ranks of the free. It softened slavery itself, but legalized institutions of serfdom. It moderately improved the status of women, but repealed the moral reform provisions enacted during Caesar Augustus's first century reign.

A significant shift in property rights occurred as Justinian's Code broadened agnate inheritance (to blood relatives who trace their kinship through males) to cognate inheritance (to relatives on the mother's side or through females). It declared property given to the church as inalienable.

Some aspects of justice became more humane, others more savage. Only a magistrate's order could impose imprisonment, and usually only for detention rather than punishment. Moving quickly to trial was deemed desirable, and the parties could transfer civil trials to a bishop's court. Litigants could appeal judgments to a higher court, to the Senate, and ultimately to the emperor. As befits the Byzantine stereotype, mutilation was in common use as a penalty.

§ 3.04(e)(3)(C). The Influence of Justinian's Code on Byzantine Law Generally

The Code of Justinian remained the code of the Byzantine Empire throughout its long history, indeed until the empire's demise in 1453, A.D. Jurists translated it into Greek, produced commentaries and gave abbreviated, official renderings in Greek. As the Byzantine empire shrank in space and importance, its Roman law survived for a time in the various east European states that emerged from the old empire. And even though that law was eventually replaced by new systems of law, it influences eastern Europe even today.

§ 3.04(e)(3)(D). Summary of the Influence of Byzantine Law on Land Law in Western Civilization

Roman law disappeared more quickly in the west of Europe and was lost throughout western Europe's dark age. Roman law was vulgarized; Roman citizens lived under Roman law even among their barbarian overlords, but Roman law disappeared as the Roman citizens died out. Not until 1100, A.D., did jurists teaching law in Bologna, Italy, re-discover the Digest of Justinian's Code. As they recovered the manuscripts of the *Corpus Juris Civilis,* they wrote commentaries and glosses, or explanatory notes, on the text, considering it to be a lost heritage. They began to apply Roman law in practice, seeking thereby to improve their contemporary legal systems in adapting Roman law to the needs of their more sophisticated societies. Although this process occurred throughout western Europe, it was more pronounced in the south, where the influence of the old Roman empire had survived more conspicuously. The advent of printing hastened the spread of the works of the glossators and commentators over much of Europe, so that Roman legal principles were assimilated into the laws of many European nations. Some of this influence even reached England.[131]

Thus the work of Justinian's commissioners to preserve a small and ancient part of the old Roman imperial law enabled its basic principles eventually to be transmitted into the law of most west European states. In this sense, Byzantine law is of immense importance to the history of law in western civilization.

While Roman law was the most conspicuous element in the legal traditions of the West–that is, of western European countries– it was not the sole element. Other legal traditions that were contemporary with Rome, and some of which predated Rome, persisted throughout the Roman period and European Dark Ages. Of these one of the most intriguing is Jewish Law, described in the next chapter.

---

[131] *Id.* at 26.

§ 3.05. Appendix: Provisions from the Twelve Tables of Early Roman Law.

Fragments of the Laws of the Twelve Tables[132]

TABLE I

The Summons before the Magistrate.

I. "If you summon a man before a magistrate and he refuses to go, take witnesses and arrest him."

II. "If he attempt evasion or flight, lay hands upon him."

III. "If he be prevented by sickness or old age, let him who summons him before the magistrate provide the means of transport; but not a covered vehicle unless as an act of benevolence."

IV. "For a rich man, a rich man only can be *vindex.*[133] In the case of a *proletarius,* any one may be *vindex.*"

V. "If the parties agree, that is to say, come to terms, let the suit be stopped and the matter arranged."

VI. "If no arrangement is made between the parties, let the cause be entered before midday, either in the comitium or in the forum, in the presence of both parties."

VII. "After midday let the magistrate grant judgment to the party present."

VIII. "No step shall be taken in an action after sunset."

---

[132] Paul Monroe, *Source Book of the History of Education for the Greek and Roman Period* 334-344 (1923). Fragmentary texts not enclosed in quotes are inexact versions rendered from several sources.

[133] A kind of bail or surety.

IX. . . .

TABLE II

Judicial Proceedings.

I. The provisions of the Twelve Tables upon the amount to be deposited, called *sacramentum,* by the litigants respectively.

II. ". . . A serious illness . . . an engagement with *a peregrinus*[134] . . . should either of these circumstances exist in connection with the judge, the arbiter, or one of the litigants, the cause must be adjourned."

III. "Any one who wants a witness must summon him by calling upon him in a loud voice, stating that he will require his attendance on the third day of the market."[135]

IV. The provision which permitted the compounding of a theft.

TABLE III

Execution following Confession or Judgment.

I. "In case of debt either upon confession or judgment, the debtor shall have thirty days grace."

II. "That term having expired, the plaintiff shall have the *manus infectio*[136] to bring the debtor before the magistrate."

III. "If the debt is not paid, or surety provided, the creditor shall take the debtor, put him into chains or into the stocks, the weight of the chains not

---

134 A stranger or foreigner to the city.

135 The markets took place every ninth day; the third day of the market would be the twenty-seventh day.

136 A species of execution of final process.

to exceed fifteen pounds, but less at the creditor's will."

IV. "The debtor shall be at liberty to live as he thinks fit, provided it be at his own expense. In the event of his being unable to provide his own nourishment, the creditor in whose custody he is shall supply him with at least one pound of bread daily."

V. Provision relating to —

1. The right of compromise.

2. The debtor's captivity, in default of compromise within sixty days, and of his production during this interval in the comitium on three successive market days, and the public declaration of the amount in which he was condemned.

VI. Provision allowing the creditor after the third market day, he not being paid, either to put his debtor to death or to sell him to any stranger resident beyond the Tiber; and which, in the case of there being several creditors, enacts as follows: "After the third market day, his body may be divided. Any one taking more than his just share shall be held guiltless."

TABLE IV

The Rights of the Father.

I. Provision as to the immediate destruction of monstrous or deformed offspring.

II. Provision relating to the control of the father over his children, the right existing during their whole life to imprison, scourge, keep to rustic labour in chains, to sell or slay, even though they may be in the enjoyment of high state offices.

III. "Three consecutive sales of the son by the father releases the former from the *patria potestas.*"

IV. Provision relating to the duration of gestation: no child born more than ten months after the decease of his reputed father to be held legitimate.

TABLE V

Inheritance and Tutelage.

I. Provision relating to the perpetual tutelage of women. Vestals are free both from their tutelage and from the *patria potestas.*

II. Provision prohibiting the *usucapion*[137] of *res mancipi*[138] belonging to females under the tutelage[139] of their agnates,[140] except in the case where they have been delivered by the woman herself with the authority of her tutor.

III. "The testament of the father shall be law as to all provisions concerning his property and the tutelage thereof."

IV. "In the event of his death intestate and without *suus hares,* the nearest agnate shall succeed."

V. "In default of agnates, the gentiles[141] shall succeed."

VI. In the event of no tutor being specified in the will, the agnates are the legitimate tutors.

VII. "The custody of an idiot and of his property, in case there is no curator (*custos*), belongs to the agnates; in default of agnates to his gentiles."

---

[137] Acquisition by use or by possession for a certain period.

[138] Things requiring more than mere delivery to constitute transfer of ownership.

[139] Protection exercised over those who did not have the capacity required by civil law for the accomplishment of legal acts.

[140] Blood relatives on the father's side.

[141] Belonging to the same clan or gens.

VIII. A provision by which the inheritance of an enfranchised person dying without *hares suus* was transferred to his patron.

IX. The inheritance is divided as of right among the heirs.

X. Provision from which is derived the *actio familiae ercisundae,* that is, the action which must be taken to enforce the division of an inheritance.

XI. The slave enfranchised by will, upon condition of his giving a certain sum to the heir, can, in the event of his being alienated by the heir, secure his freedom by the payment of this sum to the alienee.

TABLE VI

Dominion and Possession.

I. " The words pronounced in the ceremonies of the *nexum*[142] and the *mancipium* shall be law."

II. Provision enforcing double payment as penalty for denying the declaration of the *nexum* or *mancipium.*

III. "Possession for the period of two years in the case of land, or of one year in connection with other things, vests the property."

IV. Provision relating to the acquisition of the marital power over the woman by the fact of possession of one year, with the faculty given to the woman of preventing this effect of possession by absenting herself for three nights consecutively in each year from the house of her husband.

V. "No possession by an alien, however long, can vest in him the property of a citizen."

---

142 The general term for alienation or transfer of property, especially *per as ei libram*—by the bronze piece of balance.

VI. In the case of the *manuum consertio,*[143] let the magistrate give the provisional possession to whomsoever he may think fit. In the case, however, of a claim to liberty, the magistrate shall always give the provisional possession in favour of liberty.

VII. "Timber attached to a building or the support of a vine shall not be removed."

VIII. But an action to recover the double value lies against the user of the property of another.

IX. "If the material becomes detached, and so long as it remains so . . . (the owner can recover by *vindicatio*[144]*).*"

X. The property in a thing sold and delivered does not pass to the purchaser till payment.

XI. Provision confirming the *cessio*[145] before the magistrate, as likewise the *mancipatio*.

TABLE VII

The Law Concerning- Real Property.

I. Two feet and a half at least must be left between adjoining edifices for the purposes of proper ventilation.

II. Provisions concerning plantations and constructions or excavations upon adjoining plots of ground.

---

143 A feigned judicial combat for trying the property right in a given thing.

144 A legal process of claiming possession.

145 Alienation or surrendering of property.

III. "A garden . . . a small inheritance. . .a barn."[146]

IV. A space of five feet must be left between adjoining fields for the purposes of access and the turning of the plough. This space cannot be acquired by *usucapio*.

V. In the event of there being any dispute about the boundaries, the magistrate is to give three arbiters to the parties, who shall settle the matter.

VI. The breadth of a road is to be eight feet; at the end, where it turns, sixteen feet. If the road is impassable, the owner of a right of way may cross wherever he pleases.

VII. The proprietor whose property is threatened with damage arising from artificial works for the collection of rain-water, or from an aqueduct, has a right to demand a guarantee against this injury.

VIII. The branches of a tree overhanging adjoining property must be pruned all around up to fifteen feet from the ground.

IX. A proprietor may go on to adjoining land to pick up the fruit that has fallen from his tree.

TABLE VIII

On Torts.

I. Capital punishment is decreed against libellers and public defamers.

II. "Retaliation against him who breaks the limb of another and does not offer compensation."

III. For the fracture of the bone (or the tooth) of a freeman, the penalty is

---

[146] Not restored.

300 asses;[147] in the case of a slave, 150.

IV. "For any injury whatsoever committed upon another the penalty shall be 25 asses."

V. " . . For damage unjustly caused . . . (but if by accident) reparation."

VI. For damage caused by a quadruped, reparation or the forfeiture of the animal.

VII. An action shall lie against him who depastures his flock upon a neighbour's land.

VIII. "He who by enchantment shall blight the crops of another, or attract them from one field to another . . . "

IX. He who during the night furtively either cuts or depastures a neighbour's crops, if of the age of puberty, shall be devoted to Ceres and put to death; if under that age, he shall be scourged at the discretion of the magistrate and condemned in the penalty of double the damage done.

X. The incendiary of a house or of a haystack near a house, if acting intentionally and of sound mind, shall be bound, scourged, and put to death by fire. If by negligence, he shall repair the damage; or, if too poor, shall be chastised moderately.

XI. A penalty of 25 asses is to be inflicted upon any one who without right has felled the trees of another.

XII. "Any one committing a robbery by night may be lawfully killed."

XIII. A robber surprised during the day must not be put to death, unless heattempts to defend himself with arms.

---

[147] A small copper coin, worth in the earlier period about 16 2/3 cents; depreciated until by the time of the Second Punic War it was worth about two-thirds of a cent.

XIV. A thief taken in the act, if a free man, shall be scourged and made over by *addictio* to the person robbed; if a slave, shall be scourged and thrown from the Tarpeian rock; but those under the age of puberty shall, at the discretion of the magistrate, be scourged and condemned to repair the damage.

XV. . . .

XVI. . . .

XVII. Provision prohibiting the acquisition by *usucapio,* that is to say, by possession of stolen property.

XVIII. Interest upon money lent must not exceed an ounce. That is to say, one twelfth part of the principal per annum, which is eight and a third per cent per annum, calculating according to the solar year of twelve months, according to the calendar of Numa. The penalty for exceeding this interest is the quadruple.

XIX. For fraud in bailment a double penalty.

XX. Provision giving all citizens the right of action to remove suspected tutors, and imposing a double penalty for the abstracted property of the pupil.

XXI. "The patron who shall commit a fraud upon his client shall be devoted to the gods."

XXII. "He who has been a witness or acted as scalebearer and refuses to give testimony shall be accounted infamous; and incapable of giving or receiving testimony."

XXIII. Provision ordering false witnesses to be thrown from the Tarpeian rock.

XXIV. Capital punishment for homicide.

XXV. "(Capital punishment decreed against) any one who practices enchantments or uses poisonous drugs."

XXVI. Provision against seditious gatherings by night in the city, awarding capital punishment.

XXVII. *Sodales,* or members of the same college or corporation, are at liberty to make what rules binding upon themselves they may think fit, provided that they do not contravene the law.

TABLE IX

Public Law.

I. Provision prohibiting the passing of any law concerning a private individual.

II. The great comitia, that is to say, the comitia by centuries, have alone the right to enact laws inflicting capital punishment upon a citizen, that is to say, which could deprive him of life, liberty, or citizenship.

III. The penalty of death is awarded to the judge or arbitrator appointed by the magistrate who accepts a bribe.

IV. Provision relating to the question in the case of homicide; and the right of appeal to the people in the case of any penal sentence.

V. The penalty of death decreed against any one who should excite the enemy against the Roman people; or who should deliver a citizen to the enemy.

TABLE X

Sacred Law.

I. "The dead must not be buried nor burned within the city."

II. "Do no more than this . . . The wood of the funeral pile shall not be smoothed."

III. Restrictions against sumptuous funerals; the dead are not to be buried nor burned in more than three robes; nor in more than three fillets of purple; nor shall the funeral be attended by more than ten flute players.

IV. "Women shall not be allowed to tear their hair nor make immoderate wailings."

V. "The bones of the deceased shall not be collected for the purpose of giving him a subsequent funeral (except in the case of death in battle, or in a foreign country)."

VI. Provision prohibiting the embalming the bodies of slaves, funeral banquets, expensive libations, coronal garlands, and the erection of incense altars.

VII. "But if the deceased has either personally or by his slaves or horses obtained any public trophy, he shall be entitled to the honour it confers."

VIII. Prohibition against more than one funeral, or more than one funeral ceremony, for the same deceased.

IX. "Gold must not be buried with the dead; but if the teeth are fastened with gold, this may be either buried or burned."

X. No funeral pile or sepulchre shall be erected within sixty feet of another man's house, except with his consent.

XI. Neither a sepulchre nor its vestibule can be acquired by usucapio.

TABLE XI

Supplement to the First Five Tables.

I. Prohibiting marriage between patricians and plebeians.

TABLE XII

Supplement to the Last Five Tables.

I. Provision establishing the *pignoris capio*[148] against the debtor for the payment of the purchase-money of a victim, or the hire of a beast of burden when the hire has been expressly made in order that the sum paid should be devoted to purpose of sacrifice.

II. "If a slave has committed a theft or any other injury . . . the direct action does not lie against the master, but the *actio noxalis*[149] does."

III. "If any one wrongfully acquires the interim possession of a thing, the magistrate shall appoint three arbitrators to determine the question; and if they decide against him, he shall be mulcted in a sum equal to double the profits."

IV. It is forbidden to consecrate anything which is the subject of a suit, and a double penalty is inflicted for doing so.

V. Abrogates all previous and contradictory enactments.

§ 3.06. Bibliography.

Books

Driver, Godfrey Rolles and John Charles Miles (eds. & trans.), *The Assyrian Laws* (1937).
Driver, Godfrey Rolles and John Charles Miles (eds. & trans.), *The Babylonian Laws* (1968).
Birks, Peter Goodwin, ed., *New Perspectives in the Roman Law of Property: Essays for Barry Nicholas* (1989).
Breasted, James Henry, *A History of Egypt* (1937).
Burdick, William L., *The Principles of Roman Law and Their Relation to Modern Law* (1938).
Diamond, A. S., *Primitive Law, Past and Present* (1971).
Diodorus of Sicily, (H. Oldfather, trans.) (1946).

148 The seizure of the security.

149 An action on account of an injury.

Durant, Will, *The Story of Civilization: The Life of Greece* (1939).
Durant, Will, *The Story of Civilization: Caesar and Christ* (1944, 1972).
Durant, Will, *The Story of Civilization: The Age of Faith* (1950).
Edwards, Chilperic, *The World's Earliest Laws* (2d ed. 1934).
Erman, Adolf, *Life in Ancient Egypt* (1971).
Gagarin, Michael, *Early Greek Law* (1986).
Hawkes, Jacquetta, *The First Great Civilizations* (1973).
Johns, C. H. W., *Babylonian and Assyrian Laws, Contracts and Letters* (1904).
Johnson, Paul, *A History of the Jews* (1987).
Kramer, Samuel Noah, *From the Tablets of Sumer* (1956).
Maspero, G., *History of Egypt* (M. L. McClure (trans.) (n.d.)).
Monroe, Paul, *Source Book of the History of Education for the Greek and Roman Period* (1923).
Montet, Pierre, *Everyday Life in Egypt* (1981).
Nicholas, Barry, *An Introduction to Roman Law* (1962).
Seagle, William, *The History of Law* (1946).
Sealey, Raphael, *The Justice of the Greeks* (1994).
Sumner, William Graham, *Folkways* (1906).
Todd, S. C., *The Shape of Athenian Law* (1993).
Van Warmelo, Paul, *An Introduction to the Principles of Roman Law* (1976).
Westbrook, Raymond, et al., eds., *A History of Ancient Near Eastern Law* (2003).
Wilson, John A., *The Culture of Ancient Egypt* (1951).
Wooley, C. Leonard, *The Sumerians* (1928).

Chapters in Books

Edwards, I. E. S., Ch. 11, "The Early Dynastic Period in Egypt," in 1, pt. 2 Edwards, I. E. S., C. J. Gadd, and N. G. L. Hammond, eds., *The Cambridge Ancient History* (3rd ed., 1971).
Gadd, C.J., Ch. 13, "The Cities of Babylonia," in 1, pt. 2 Edwards, I. E. S., C. J. Gadd and N. G. L. Hammond, eds., *The Cambridge Ancient History* (3d ed. 1971).
Gadd, C.J., Ch. 22, "Babylonia, c. 2120-1800, B.C.," in 1, pt. 2 Edwards, I. E. S., C. J. Gadd, and N. G. L. Hammond, eds., *The Cambridge Ancient History* (3d ed. 1971).
Hayes, William C., Ch. 9, "Egypt: Internal Affairs from Tuthomosis I to the Death of Amenophis III," in 2, pt. 1, Edwards, I. E. S., C. J. Gadd and N. G. L. Hammond, eds., *The Cambridge Ancient History* (3d ed. 1971).
Peet, T. Eric, Ch. 9, "Contemporary Life and Thought in Egypt," in 2 J. B. Bury, S. A. Cook and F. E. Adcock, eds., *The Cambridge Ancient History* (1924).
Yoffee, Norman, Ch. 5, "Context and Authority in Early Mesopotamian Law," in Ronald Cohen and Judith D. Toland, eds., *State Formation and Political Legitimacy* (1988).

Articles

Finkelstein, Jacob J., "Ammisaduqa's Edict and the Babylonian Law Codes," 14 *J. Cuneiform Studies* 15 (1961).
Finkelstein, Jacob J., "The Laws of Ur-Nammu," 22 *J. Cuneiform Studies* 66 (1969).

Godbey, Allen H., "The Place of the Code of Hammurabi," 15 *The Monist* 199 (1905).
Kramer, Samuel Noah, "Ur-Nammu Law Code," 23 *Orientalia* 40 (1954).
Kroger, John R., "The Philosophical Foundations of Roman Law: Aristotle, the Stoics, and Roman Theories of Natural Law," 2004 *Wis. L. Rev.* 905.
Langdon, Stephen, "The Sumerian Law Code Compared with the Code of Hammurabi," 23 *J. Royal Asiatic Society* 489 (1920).
Pound, Roscoe, "The Valuation of Property in the Roman Law," 34 *Harv. L. Rev.* 229 (1921).
Steele, Francis Rue, "The Code of Lipit-Ishtar, 52 *Am. J. Archaeology* 425 (1948).

Chapter 4

The Influence of Jewish Law on the Law of Western Nations and A Concise Legal History of Jerusalem

SYNOPSIS

Chapter 4. The Influence of Jewish Law on the Law of Western Nations and a Concise Legal History of Jerusalem

§ 4.01. Legal Influences Found in the Ancient Near East

The cultural milieu out of which Jewish law arose had widely disparate elements. On the one hand was the ancient Egyptian culture, characterized, as mentioned in Chapter 3, by an archaic view that society in both heaven and earth was static, and that change was evil. Impersonal law was not recognized, and law was therefore neither written nor codified.[150] Mesopotamian cultures, on the other hand, were much more dynamic, and also held kings accountable to the gods; monarchs were not permitted to administer or issue laws arbitrarily. Placing laws in writing strengthened the force of law.

In § 4.04 of this chapter are described the various peoples, rulers and legal systems that imposed themselves on the land eventually to be known as Palestine or Israel and the city of Jerusalem. These included nomadic Semites in Canaan, Egyptians, the nomadic patriarchs of the Old Testament, Israelites, Hivites, Jebusites, Assyrians, Babylonians, Persians, Greeks and Romans, among others.

§ 4.02. The Emergence and Development of Jewish Law

Despite its similarities to other near Eastern legal traditions, the Mosaic code was still unique. It was issued as written by God, not by any person merely acting on divine instructions. Thus it was not only not subject to amendment, it also meant that no future Hebrew monarch was qualified to issue a law code. In addition, the divine source of the Mosaic law meant that all crimes were sins and all sins were crimes.

Whereas the Mesopotamian codes focused on property, and assessed money values for various offenses and injuries, the Mosaic law covered conduct that was a serious offense against God and was not subject to being expiated or pardoned. Only if the misconduct or mishap were not prompted by guilty intent would the more traditional financial penalties be assessed, although these would be strictly applied, as suggested by the well-known "eye for eye" provisions. While the Mosaic code imposed the death penalty for various serious offenses against God and against the sanctity of human life, its punishments for crimes against property were free from the physical cruelty and mutilation that often characterized the Mesopotamian codes.

At the heart of the Mosaic code were the Ten Commandments, or

---

150 Paul Johnson, *A History of the Jews* 30-31 (1987).

Decalogue. Some of the rules in the Decalogue were found in other near Eastern societies, but "for a comprehensive summary of right conduct to God and man, offered to, accepted by and graven upon the hearts of an entire people, there is nothing in antiquity remotely comparable to the Ten Commandments."[151] An enormous elaboration of rituals and rules governing every aspect of life extended out from the Ten Commandments, both as recorded in the Old Testament and later by scholarly and rabbinical interpretation and commentary.

The fundamental law is the Torah of Moses (the Pentateuch, or the first five books of the Old Testament). In this body of law, religion and law and ethics are all combined without apparent distinction. Jewish tradition holds that Moses received a written Torah, essentially as contained in the Pentateuch, and also an oral or orally transmitted or traditional Torah, the substance of which was later recorded in the *Mishnah*, *Midrash* and *Talmud*. This tradition consisted of explanations and interpretations of the Pentateuch, and other rules, norms and innovations not necessarily derived from the ancient writings.[152] Indeed, it is widely believed that even before Moses received the law, the Israelites were developing their own indigenous legal customs, applied by elders or judges in the course of dispute resolution.

Both the written and oral tradition versions of the law were transmitted. Ezra (fl. 458-444, B.C.), who came to Jerusalem from Babylon, is acknowledged as the first of the scribes, learned persons who assumed the roles of preservers and students of the law. Centuries later, at about the beginning of the common era, a new type of student of the law, called *tannaim*, arose around Hillel, and these scholars or rabbis, active mostly in Palestine, exercised great influence on the development of Jewish law for the next two centuries.

During this time, the legal experts delivered pronouncements on the application of law in particular circumstances, which authoritative

---

[151] *Id.* at 34-35.

[152] *Id.* at 9-10.

statements were called *halakah*. To illustrate or instruct on rules of conduct outside the precise limits of the law, these authorities also presented legends, moral sayings, folklore, philosophical speculation, historical notes, theological observations, scientific data, and the miscellany of traditional teaching, all of which came under the heading of *hagadah*. Under Rabbi Judah the Patriarch (170-219, A.D.), scribes collected, edited, and issued the body of *halakah* in a work called the *Mishnah*. Thereafter, the scholars, called *amoraim*, concentrated on examining, interpreting and debating the *Mishnah*. Principles of "law" are embodied in the *halakah* and the *Mishnah*, but are not set apart as distinct components. Within those legal principles arose a distinction between laws derived from Biblical text (Biblical law) and those derived from the writings of scribes and rabbis (Rabbinical law). As the scholarly work of the *amoraim* accumulated it became the content of the Babylonian and Palestinian *Talmuds*, of which the Babylonian was considered the most authoritative. It was compiled between 499 and 540, A.D., when Babylon was considered the chief center of Jewish learning.

The *Mishnah* itself is not systematically arranged, but Maimonides (1135-1204, A. D.) later gave it a semblance of order in a restatement called the *Mishneh Torah*. Also, laws were generally divided into "laws between man and God" (ceremonial and ritual observances, and duties essentially religious and spiritual) and "laws between man and man" (law and morals in the modern sense). This division of the *halakah* was set beside another, older division of the laws into money matters, penalties, capital offenses, and prohibitions religious and ceremonial.

This older arrangement of the law, along with the *Talmud* of Babylon, was taught in the Jewish schools of Babylon, and the heads of those schools were constantly asked to give interpretations and answers to questions concerning the *Talmud*. Collections of their responses are an important component of Jewish law. Those responses were similar to adjudications, especially since those school heads also exercised administrative control over the Jewish courts and judges which were permitted to function among the Babylonian Jews. As early as the 8th century, A.D., one of the school heads compiled a systematic summary of the norms of Talmudic law, and others followed. When the Babylonian school fell into decline early in the

11th century, other schools throughout Europe and north Africa rose to prominence. In all of these, judicial decisions, commentary, responsa, systematic codes and express legislation were refining and embellishing the law. Throughout their history, Jewish communities resolved most of their legal problems in their own religious courts and thus developed detailed legal rules covering every aspect of daily life.

§ 4.03. The Interaction of Jewish Law with the English Common Law of Land

The isolation and separation of Jewish communities was both cause and effect of the isolation and separation of Jewish law. Even though Jewish law developed without much interaction with other legal systems, it acquired an astounding richness. The ability of this legal system to achieve richness and maturity despite insularity is a singular characteristic of Jewish law. Nevertheless, some borrowings from the many other legal systems with which Jewish law coexisted may have occurred. As Jews lived all over the Mediterranean and Near Eastern world, the commercial practices they encountered no doubt affected the ways they did business. Jewish criminal law depended heavily on criminal law of whatever country they were in. In modern times, Jews have turned to secular law and courts for adjudication of their conflicts. In the State of Israel, the rabbinic courts have only limited jurisdiction. Jewish courts cite American and English case law for persuasive authority.[153]

One of many illustrations of this phenomenon is found in comparisons of Jewish land law with the English common law of land.

One is first struck by the procedural similarities between these two legal systems. One could liken the Anglo-Saxon local feudal customs, local court decisions, royal court decisions, and occasional legislation to the Jewish Torah, Mishnah, Talmud, Mishneh Torah, the judicial decisions, responsa and commentaries. In both systems, the law is essentially based on a limited canon, and is then further refined and expanded as a result of

---

[153] *Id.* at 437.

applying the law to specific cases.

Both Jewish law and common law are essentially case law systems; legislation within these systems usually governs specific problems rather than pronouncing general principles; codification has not been prevalent.[154] Both systems assign to the law a powerful role in society, so that even governing authorities–earthly and possibly even divine authority–are subject to law.[155]

Both systems emphasize individual liberty and accountability, and the decentralization of societal authority, and this has led both systems to address matters of legitimacy and jurisdiction. Even the highest governing authorities are subject to limitations on their powers and must often affirmatively establish legitimacy and proper jurisdiction in order to assert those powers.

As suggested in the preceding paragraph, land law under the English common law and land law under Jewish law were formed by similar systemic processes—shaped by applications in individual cases rather than by prefabricated codes—but the results are very dissimilar. Only a few isolated points of the common law of land are traceable to the influence of Jewish law in England, and virtually no evidence exists of Jewish land law borrowings from the English common law.

The Jewish law of property was first set forth with clarity in Maimonides' Mishneh Torah, completed in 1180, A.D., one of the world's greatest works of legal scholarship. In his Book XII, the Book of Property, he outlined rules for the purchase and acquisition of title to both personal and real property. However, it was not until publication of the *Encyclopedia Judaica* and the resulting textbook *Principles of Jewish Law* that a broader and systematic exposition of Jewish property law was

---

[154] "In Jewish law as in the Common Law of England, the judges and teachers, in interpreting, explaining and applying the rules of law gave effect to the needs and ideals of their own time. Thus, slowly and gradually they changed and adapted to the law of life." G. Horowitz, *The Spirit of Jewish Law* 91 (1973).

[155] Dorff, Elliott, and Arthur Rosett, *A Living Tree* 435 (1988).

created, but even that work does not present a discrete discussion of land law.

Even to state the main points of Jewish land law in only a very general sense reveals that these detailed legal rules have no obvious antecedent in the text of the Old Testament, and also suggests that they are not obviously borrowed from other legal systems. These main points may be described as follows:

> Land is more or less the same as immovable property
> Ownership of land can be proved by three years' possession; other modes of acquisition are also recognized
> Land is divided into best, median and poorest quality for the purposes of recovery under tort claims, creditors' claims, and wife's claims or recovery, respectively
> Owned and ownerless lands are acquired by different methods
> Owned land may be classed as public, private, or consecrated
> Owned land may also be classed as free (unencumbered) or encumbered and mortgaged
> Ownership of land may be limited in time, and may be severable; acquisition by sale or gift is recognized
> Rights in land may include sole ownership, shared ownership, rights in the land of others (such as servitude rights or mortgage rights)
> One may acquire owned property, ownerless property, and rights in the property of others.

By way of comparison, one notes that the legacy of feudalism lingers on in the English common law of land. According to common law rules, one may hold land according to various styles or forms of ownership ranging from full, perpetual, almost allodial rights, to mere tenancies revocable at will, to interests designed to commence in the future, all such forms corresponding to and descending directly from the Anglo-Norman feudal hierarchy of landholders.

Concurrent ownership in several forms was recognized, but always in ways that sought to identify a responsible single owner or owning entity, and all arising from the need to fulfill feudal responsibilities.

Servitudes, the rights to use another's land, were a late development in the common law, essentially in the 19th century, and even those who held no land to be benefitted could enjoy the benefits of a servitude.

To even list these common law real property interests by name sufficiently illustrates how truly arcane and esoteric these interests are:

Estates (freehold): fee simple absolute, fee tail, fee determinable, fee simple subject to condition subsequent, fee simple subject to executory interest, life estate.

Future interests: reversion, vested remainder, contingent remainder, right of entry or power of termination, possibility of reverter, executory interest.

Tenancies (non-freehold): tenancy for a term, periodic tenancy, tenancy at will, tenancy at sufferance.

Servitudes: easement (express, by implication, of necessity, by prescription), real covenant, equitable servitude (including reciprocal implied servitude).

Concurrent ownership: joint tenancy, tenancy in common, tenancy by the entirety (for married couples), tenancy in coparcenary, tenancy in partnership.

Under the common law, land may also be used as security for credit transactions; may be purchased, donated and inherited; may be subject to mortgages and other encumbrances; may be subject to various inchoate claims by those standing in close relationship to the landholder (such as dower or homestead rights); and may be transferred by adverse possession. Various fruits of the land, including mineral assets, may be subject to separate ownership. Land is subject to both public regulations and to restrictions under private covenants with other landholders. The common law implies five or six warranties in transfers of land, but at least one of them, the covenant of seisin, invokes a feudal concept no longer intelligible in Anglo-American real property legal vocabulary.

As should be clear from comparing the summaries of Jewish and common law land law described above, one can identify no specific points of resemblance between Jewish land law and traditional common law principles of real property, despite the mechanical similarities in deriving law, especially the case law system. The common law of real property, essentially a product of an Anglo-Norman feudal system that greatly exalted the value of land in a male-warrior society, sprouted marvelous distinctions and complexities that make the simpler classifications of Jewish law seem straightforward indeed. Only in the twentieth century have England and a few American states moved toward simplifying land law by statute. Examples of the continuing common law complexities may be found in the notion of ownership expressed as various estates in land and future interests and in the division of servitudes into easements (express and implied), real covenants and equitable servitudes. Nevertheless, in some details (such as acquisition of immovable property by means similar to common law adverse possession) Jewish property law is similar to common law, both having emerged from actual cases adjudicating real controversies between ordinary people.

Jews had a strong presence in medieval England during the most important early formative years of the English common law, and contemporary Jewish law was much more complex and mature. However, it is likely that few if any substantive legal doctrines were directly borrowed from Jewish law by common-law lawyers and judges. In their commercial interactions with Gentiles all over Europe, Jewish lenders and merchants developed a number of sophisticated procedural devices to protect and facilitate their activities. Over time, some of these became so completely incorporated into the common law that they assumed the status of substantive legal principles:

1. The Jewish gage, or pledge, emerging from the Jewish law of execution rather than the law of mortgages, introduced into feudal England

the then novel notions that a debtor's lands could be liable for debts even while still in the possession of the debtor, and that all the debtor's personal and real property could be liable for satisfaction of debt.[156] The early common law form of mortgage, requiring the borrower's property to be transferred to the lender and to revert to the borrower only upon satisfactory repayment of the debt, was adopted directly from the forms of such transactions between Jews and non-Jews in England. This form was in general use until early in the 15th century.[157]

2. Under Jewish law a formal declaration by a debtor, in court, acknowledging the existence of the debt, could be embodied in a court document and have the effect of a judgment sufficient to withstand the contrary testimony of any number of witnesses. Apparently the recognizance doctrine in English law emerged directly from the Jewish practice, incorporating not only the confession of debt but also the recognition that the debtor's lands thereby stood bound as security for the debt.[158]

3. When, in common law jurisdictions, litigating parties reach a settlement, the result is often expressed in a document called a release. The

---

[156] J. Rabinowitz, *Jewish Law, Its Influence on the Development of Legal Institutions* 250-257 (1956).

[157] J. Rabinowitz, *Jewish Law, Its Influence on the Development of Legal Institutions* 290-310 (1956). The evidence for this connection, too, is largely circumstantial, as explained by Rabinowitz: "The conditional conveyance by way of security had been in use by the Jews for a long time prior to their settlement in England, and was used by them in England in their transactions with Christians. The technical device by which the conditional conveyance was effected was, in every detail, identical with the classical English mortgage in its original form, namely, two separate instruments were used and a third party was employed as a depositary. A device similar in conception and design to the conditional conveyance was used by the Jews during the middle ages in England and elsewhere for the purpose of evading a certain rule of the Hebrew law which is similar to the rule against penalties in English law. The Jews introduced the business of money-lending on a large scale in England, and with it the means by which this business was carried on. When Englishmen learned the business of money-lending from the Jew they adopted his methods and devices, outstanding examples of which are the conditional conveyance by way of security and the conditional bond which have survived to our own day." *Id.* at 309-310.

[158] *Id.* at 257-263.

traditional form and wording of the English general release appear to have been borrowed directly from the Jewish "starr of acquittance," introduced by Jews in medieval England. In addition to affording release from the most recent debt, the document wording releases the debtor from all debts between the parties since the creation of the world, a distinctly Jewish formulation.[159]

4. The modern warranty clause which is part of many English and American real property transactions may have originated with wording in medieval Jewish transactions, including the principle that the warrant would be backed by all real property retained by the grantor.[160]

5. The origins of dower in Anglo-American common law are not precisely known, but surely have significant Germanic roots, and some aspects of the doctrine may have emerged from Jewish practice. The common law dower, now largely replaced by statutory formulas, conferred on a widow a life interest in one-third of the lands held in freehold by the husband at any time during the marriage. Conveyances by the husband free of dower required a release from the wife at the time of the grant, a practice possibly borrowed by the English from the Jews.[161]

6. It is not known whether the similar institutional features of the Jewish law court in England and the English trial by jury represent an instance of parallel development, or of borrowing, or of cross-influences.[162]

7. It has also been surmised that Jews influenced the "rule of law" clause (number 39) in the English Magna Carta of 1215, prohibiting deprivation of liberty or property "except . . . by the law of the land," and

---

[159] *Id.* at 263-270.

[160] *Id.* at 273-284. The evidence for this borrowing is wholly circumstantial.

[161] *Id.* at 284-289. *See also* J. Rabinowitz, "The Influence of Jewish Law on the Development of the Common Law," in L. Finkelstein, ed., *The Jews: Their History, Culture, and Religion* 837-838 (4th ed.1960).

[162] J. Rabinowitz, "The Influence of Jewish Law on the Development of the Common Law," in L. Finkelstein, ed., *The Jews: Their History, Culture, and Religion* 837-838 (4th ed.1960).

thus subjecting all governing powers in England to the "law of the land."[163]

It should also not be overlooked that the teachings of the Bible, accepted as a sacred text in common-law nations, have exerted a continuing influence over the values reflected in the common law.

As to whether common law influenced Jewish law in any particulars, including with respect to land law, there is no evidence. Jewish law was quite mature even while the common law was in its formative stages. Then the expulsion of Jews from England occurred just as the common law was undergoing its most important developmental period.

In summary, land law under the Anglo-American common law and land law under Jewish law were formed by similar systemic processes, shaped by applications in individual cases rather than by prefabricated codes, but the results are very dissimilar. Only a few isolated points of the common law of land are traceable to the influence of Jewish law in England, and no evidence exists of Jewish land law borrowings from the common law.

This comparison between Jewish law and English common law in a single doctrinal area typifies the paucity of interaction between Jewish law and other legal systems, leading to the conclusion that the richness and maturity of Jewish law was an essentially indigenous development. This in turn requires the conclusion that Jewish law was not an important factor in the developing legal traditions of western civilization.

§ 4.04. A Concise Legal History of Jerusalem.

§ 4.04(a). Jerusalem's Legal Prehistory.

For thousands of years before written histories ancient peoples and societies inhabited the land in and around Jerusalem. Almost nothing is known of their customs of law, government and social organization. Archaeological work at Jericho has unearthed artifacts from the 7th

---

[163] *Id.* at 845-847

millennium, B.C., making Jericho perhaps the earliest fortified city of which we know. From this evidence, we assume that some of these prehistoric societies were characterized by powerful leadership and coordination of labor resources. Material culture was strongly affected by immigration from other regions, and presumably so was social structure.[164]

Topography played an important role. Among the prehistoric Canaanites, the fragmented terrain led to the forming of small, independent political entities.

About the second millennium, B.C., nomadic western Semites gained control of Canaan and inevitably came under the scrutiny and influence of Egypt. From texts inscribed on pottery bowls and clay figurines of the 19th century, B.C., Egyptian-sponsored governors of Jerusalem, which by now had developed into a city, are mentioned. It appears that by the eighteenth century, B.C., "Jerusalem, like the rest of Canaan, had evolved from a tribal society with a number of chieftains to an urban settlement government by a single king."[165]

Egyptian civil and criminal legislation were apparently highly developed, and by the Egyptian Fifth Dynasty the law of private property and of bequest was detailed and precise. Court cases were presented at great length but almost always only in writing. The pharaoh was the source of law and final judge, and the vizier was the chief administrator.[166]

A dynasty of foreign rulers established themselves in Egypt at the end of the 18th century, B.C. Collectively known as Hyksos, these non-Semitic peoples entered Egypt through Canaan and profoundly affected every aspect of life in Canaan as they passed through, including creation of a sort of feudal society under a ruling class of chariot warriors.

---

[164] Emmanuel Anati, "The Prehistory of the Holy Land (Until 3200 BC)," in Michael Avi-Yonah, ed., *A History of the Holy Land* 27-28 (1969).

[165] Gosta W. Ahlstroem, *The History of Ancient Palestine* 169-172 (1993); Benjamin Mazar, *The Mountain of the Lord* 45-46 (1975).

[166] 1 Will Durant, *Story of Civilization: Our Oriental Heritage* 161-164 (1954).

§ 4.04(b). The Beginning of Jerusalem's Historical Period.

§ 4.04(b)(1). Entry of the Patriarchs into Canaan.

Entry of the Patriarchs into Canaan, as told in Genesis,[167] signaled the arrival of a nomadic society, which only hesitatingly entered into such transactions as the purchase of land, exemplified by Abraham's purchase of the cave of Machpelah for a burial place.[168] In about 1580, B.C., native Egyptian forces expelled the Hyksos and began once again establishing dominance over Canaan. Jerusalem emerged in the fourteenth century as one of the city-states of Canaan that was under Egyptian domination. And, even as Egyptian control in Canaan waned in the 14th century, B.C., Jerusalem remained completely loyal to Egypt. Nevertheless many of the internal political, administrative and legal arrangements that had been introduced into Canaan by the earlier Hyksos invaders were left in place. Thus the basic unit of a city kingdom persisted, headed by a ruler with broad powers. Citizens, merchants, artisans, landowners and others had well-defined "obligations" to the state.[169] And by this time, another group of outsiders had achieved a significant presence in Jerusalem, an Aryan people known as the Hurrians from Mitanni in northern Mesopotamia, referred to in the Bible as the Hivites or Horites.

§ 4.04(b)(2). Melchizedek and Salem.

At some moment during this long, pre-Davidic interlude occurred the Biblical account of Abraham's encounter with Melchizedek, king of

---

[167] Ch. 23, v. 9.

[168] Genesis 23:16-18.

[169] Hanoch Reviv, "The Canaanite and Israelite Periods (3200-332 BC)," in Michael Avi-Yonah, ed., *A History of the Holy Land* 40-48 (1969).

Salem,[170] a city or settlement believed by many to be identified with Jerusalem.[171] Abraham is depicted as paying a tithe to this ruler, who is credited in some sources with the founding of Jerusalem, and of receiving a divine blessing in return. Davidic kings of Judah were later considered to be priests after the order of Melchizedek,[172] and this same office is mentioned in the Epistle to the Hebrews in the Christian New Testament.[173]

§ 4.04(c). Davidic Jerusalem.

When the tribes of Israel entered Canaan, according to the Biblical account, Joshua divided the land between the tribes. Judah captured Jerusalem, but lost it to the Jebusites, a people of unknown (but possibly Hittite) origin, who then held it until the time of David in the eleventh century, B.C. David conquered Jerusalem with his own troops and made it his city, the city of David, aligned with neither Judah of the south nor Israel of the north. It is quite possible that the Jebusites were not slaughtered, and they and Israelites coexisted in the city. David probably took over the old Jebusite administration and kept the old municipal officials. The courts of David and Solomon exhibited many Egyptian characteristics, such as a grand vizier, a secretary for foreign affairs, a recorder in charge of internal matters, and a "king's friend." Virtually all of David's policies and activities ultimately reinforced Jerusalem's position of primacy as a capital or the seat of government and worship.[174]

§ 4.04(d). Jerusalem Under Judah and Israel.

As described in the Bible, Solomon's enormous building program in

---

170 Genesis 14:18-20.

171 David B. Galbraith et al, *Jerusalem, The Eternal City* 26 (1996).

172 Karen Armstrong, *Jerusalem, One City, Three Faiths* 30 (1996).

173 Hebrews 5:6, 7:1-3.

174 Karen Armstrong, *Jerusalem, One City, Three Faiths* 37-47 (1996); David B. Galbraith et al, *Jerusalem, The Eternal City* 38-50 (1996).

Jerusalem, strengthening the fortifications and erecting the temple and palace, combined with abolition of religious centers elsewhere in Israel to punctuate Jerusalem's position as the religious and political center of the country. However, the re-emergence of two kingdoms after Solomon's death diminished Jerusalem's importance. To divert religious attention from Jerusalem, Jeroboam, king of the northern ten tribes built his capital at Shechem and established shrines at Dan and Bethel, the northern and southern limits of his domain. Jerusalem, meanwhile, remained under the unpopular kingship of Rehoboam and in a few years suffered a plundering raid by the Egyptian pharaoh Shishak. For the next two hundred years, from Solomon to Hezekiah, the two Israelite kingdoms quarreled and intrigued against one another and Jerusalem lost its standing as the political and religious center for all Israel.

§ 4.04(e). Assyrian Law in Jerusalem.

Early in the 8th century, B.C., while Assyria was preoccupied with capturing Damascus, Judah under Uzziah and Israel under Jeroboam momentarily cooperated to expand Israelite territories to the extent of the old Davidic kingdom. At the same time Jerusalem itself was also expanded, adding about 150 acres to the northwest of the site it then occupied. In 722, B.C., the Assyrians captured Samaria, removed most of the northern Israelites (the so-called "lost" ten tribes) and inserted in their place other peoples from distant parts of the Assyrian empire, who eventually mixed in and became the Samaritans of later Biblical times. The southern kingdom of Judah, including Jerusalem, became a vassal kingdom of the Assyrian empire.

Assyrian law of this period was distinguished by a "martial ruthlessness." In addition to the most atrocious punishments prescribed for serious offenses, trial by ordeal was sometimes used for more ordinary misconduct. Local administration was originally in the hands of feudal barons, but eventually came under the control of governors appointed by the king, a form passed on to Persia and Rome.[175]

---

[175] 1 Will Durant, *Story of Civilization: Our Oriental Heritage* 272 (1954).

§ 4.04(f). Jerusalem Under Babylonian Law.

As described earlier in this chapter, during this period the prophet Isaiah delivered powerful condemnations of Jerusalem's society and stirring visions of a holier future. Beginning in 715, B.C., king Hezekiah reasserted Judah's independence from Assyria, responded to the call for a religious cleansing, and also fortified and prepared Jerusalem for the expected retaliatory assault. Under his direction, workers strengthened walls and created the famous water tunnel from the Gihon spring. Second Kings declares that the Assyrian siege was broken off when the army was decimated by a plague, so Jerusalem enjoyed a few more years of independence. Egypt imposed authority over Judah for a few years, 609-605, B.C., before Egypt's enemy Babylon brought Judah into its domain and destroyed Jerusalem. Babylonians attacked and deported Judean Israelites in 605, 597 and 586, B.C. In the last year mentioned, Babylonians destroyed Jerusalem and the temple and removed most of the population. The Babylonian conquerors governed from Mizpah, a few miles north of Jerusalem.

The Babylonian system of government featured central and local lords or administrators appointed by the king, and these were advised by provincial or local assemblies of elders, who maintained a measure of local self-government. Substantively, the law of Hammurabi was still revered. Priests were the early judges, and courts were in the temples, but secular personnel and settings eventually replaced them. Babylonian law included the talionic feature, related to the English word "retaliatory," simplistically summarized by the phrase "eye for eye, tooth for tooth." Eventually, even these punishments in kind were replaced by money damages. Private property rights were recognized. This Code compels respect even today.[176]

By the time the first groups of Jews began returning from exile in Babylon, now under Persian rule, about 70 years later, Samaritans had moved into Jerusalem and raised opposition both to the rebuilding of the temple and to turning over city administration to the returning Jews. Nevertheless, the Jews in Jerusalem built a new temple and dedicated it in

---

[176] *Id.* at 230-232.

515, B.C., and the city enjoyed considerable autonomy from the Persian imperial overlords. During the fifth century, B.C., Ezra and Nehemiah obtained both religious and administrative authority from the Persian government to carry out assignments in the Judean province, helping to establish religious reforms and restore the walls and some prosperity in Jerusalem. Under Nehemiah, ten percent of the province's population were moved into Jerusalem to defend it. To open the 4th century, B.C., Ezra was sent from Babylon to Judea to, among other reasons, instruct the Jews in the law of their god. In Jerusalem, he read and explained the Torah, or some part of it, and took vigorous action to implement its tenets.

§ 4.04(g). Persian Law in Jerusalem.

Persian law, meanwhile, was the will of the king (itself a reflection of divine will), and a royal decree was irrevocable. Nevertheless a complex system of courts and litigation evolved, including "speakers of the law" to assist litigants. A satrap governed each province, aided by a type of permanent civil service staff. "Each region retained its own language, laws, customs, morals, religion and coinage, and sometimes its native dynasty of kings."[177]

§ 4.04(h). Jerusalem Under Alexander the Great, the Ptolemies and the Seleucids: Hellenistic Law

Little is known of Jerusalem while it remained under the Persians. Only when Alexander the Great ended that reign does the history of Jerusalem re-emerge from obscurity. In 322, B.C., Alexander was, in fact, welcomed peacefully into the city, and he offered symbolic sacrifice in the temple. In response, Alexander allowed not only the inhabitants of Jerusalem but all other Jews in Babylon and Medea to enjoy their own unique laws and customs.[178] Thus the Torah continued to be the official

---

[177] *Id.* at 361-364.

[178] Josephus, *Antiquities* 11.8.4-5.

law, and the administration that had operated under the Persians probably remained in place.

The next year Alexander died and Jerusalem entered a period of changing fortunes under the competing Ptolemies and Seleucids, parties associated with Alexander's principal generals who took over the conquered territories. At first, the Ptolemaic rulers from Egypt prevailed, and once again Jerusalem resumed administrative and religious leadership and enjoyed broad autonomy in domestic affairs. An Aaronic high priest headed the city's administration. He was assisted by a council, called the *Soferim*, or Men of the Great Assembly, comprised of powerful teachers in the class of scribes that developed in the late Persian period. In 275, B.C., Greek Seleucids from Syria contended for hegemony in Judea, inauguarating the so-called Syrian wars of the next 75 years; during this time the *Soferim* declined and disappeared.

The Seleucid Antiochus III, the first Syrian ruler of Judea, permitted the Jews of Jerusalem to live according to their unique laws and customs, as Alexander had done, and so the Torah still continued as the official law. The old *Soferim* was revived, in the form of the *Gerousia*, or Council of Elders, and later known as the Sanhedrin. This body attended to the general administrative, political, judicial, and social affairs of Jerusalem and the surrounding area. Two teachers directed the affairs of this council, one known as prince or president, the other as father of the court. Factional strife disrupted political stability and legal privileges. The factions consisted of Jews opposed to advancing Hellenistic culture and Jews who accepted it (sentiments which tended to divide along Ptolemaic and Seleucid lines).

Hellenistic law was classical Greek law. "Greek legislation is the basis of that Roman law which in turn has provided the legal foundations of Western society."[179] At this time it still retained numerous "primitive" elements, but the rule of law, increasingly secular law, was nowhere more faithfully followed. The Seleucids observed municipal autonomy, even though the Seleucid monarchy, following Asiatic tradition, was absolute.

---

[179] 2 Will Durant, *Story of Civilization: The Life of Greece* 257-259 (1966).

The Hellenizers prevailed for a time, and Jerusalem was reorganized into a new Greek *polis* named Antiochia, a process described by one writer as the abrogation of the Torah as Jerusalem's constitution. Civil unrest between the Jews themselves invited repression by the Syrians, loss of governing privileges and an attempt to destroy the Jewish religion altogether by Antiochus IV in 168, B.C.

§ 4.04(i). Jerusalem Ruled by the Hasmoneans.

This provoked the Hasmonean, or Maccabean, revolt, to restore the true worship. In 165, B.C., the rebels succeeded in gaining control of the Temple Mount, but could make no further gains. Jerusalem remained a divided city until concluding a peace treaty guaranteeing religious liberty three years later. Revolt continued thereafter, with the rebels seeking full political independence. The Syrians appointed Jonathan Maccabeas high priest and governor in 152, B.C., enabling him to govern all Jerusalem except the Acra, which held the Syrian king's garrison. In 142, B.C., his successor Simon expelled the Syrians, won immunity from taxes, and confirmed independence for the Jews. The high priesthood of the Aaronic order was now made hereditary in the Hasmonean line and Jerusalem eventually became the capital of an independent Hasmonean kingdom. The Hasmoneans once again made Judea a theocracy, and like other Semitic societies, closely associated the spiritual and temporal powers.

Opposition to the worldly and somewhat Hellenistic ways of the Hasmoneans and the religious party known as the Sadducees led to formation of the religious party known as the Pharisees. The Pharisees increased their civil and religious powers so as to impose their positions on all Jews, from their center in Jerusalem. All of this activity, especially as it relates to law and government in Jerusalem, then came to an abrupt end in 63, B.C., when Pompey's armies imposed the rule of Rome on Judea.

§ 4.04(j). Roman Rule in Jerusalem.

§ 4.04(j)(1). Pre-Christian Roman Administration.

Pompey left Judea and other areas under Jewish rule, including the non-contiguous Galilee, but razed Jerusalem's walls to the ground. However, when Julius Caesar succeeded to power in Rome, he allowed the walls to be rebuilt. Then, in a brief but violent interlude, Parthians invested Jerusalem, which Herod then re-took by siege three years later after a horrible massacre of the inhabitants, and Romans installed Herod as king of the Jews in Palestine with virtually total control. After Herod's death, rule by his son Archelaus was so brutally disastrous that Rome took Judea and Jerusalem under direct Roman administration, with a provincial governor as chief executive. Caesarea continued as the seat of government, but in Jerusalem the

> Council of Elders and its successor, the Sanhedrin, ruled as a Jewish law court in matters of faith, manners, and law in which Roman interests were not directly affected. The Council possessed no powers of capital jurisdiction (without confirmation of the imperial magistrate), except against a pagan who trespassed into the inner courts of the Temple beyond the permitted Court of the Gentiles. The Council consisted of members of the Sadducean aristocracy and more moderate Pharisees and scribes.[180]

As is illustrated by the well-known encounters of Paul with both Jewish and Roman authorities, Roman law and civil rights applied to those holding full Roman citizenship, and the indigenous folk were governed in most matters by their own local laws and customs. Little is known about what local law was applied, because the Jews themselves were bitterly divided about which law should be applied. Pharisees hoped that all aspects of life could be governed by The Law, the Torah, and urged all

---

[180] David B. Galbraith, et al, *Jerusalem: The Eternal City* 155 (1996).

Jews to observe the purity regulations originally prescribed in the Torah only for priests officiating in the temple. With that attitude, it made little difference to the Pharisees what government was in power as long as they were free to manage their own domestic affairs. Unfortunately, persistent guerrilla violence by parties of zealots exploded in full revolt, provoking Rome to suppress that revolt with resulting horrible loss of Jewish life and freedom and the utter destruction of the temple in 70, A.D. As described by historian Will Durant:

> Judea was almost shorn of Jews, and those that remained lived on the edge of starvation . . . The high-priesthood and the Sanhedrin were abolished. Judaism took the form that it has kept till our own time: a religion without a central shrine, without a dominant priesthood, without a sacrificial service. The Sadducees disappeared, while the Pharisees and the rabbis became the leaders of a homeless people that had nothing left but its synagogue and its hope.[181]

During the siege of Jerusalem, Johanan ben Zakkai, an elderly pupil of Hillel, escaped from the city and set up an academy near the Mediterranean coast, organizing a new Sanhedrin, the *Bet Din* (law court), after the fall of Jerusalem. The new council, composed mostly of Pharisees and rabbis, chose a patriarchal leader who appointed administrative officers over the Jewish community, and who had power to excommunicate recalcitrant Jews. Under the forceful leadership of the Patriarch Gamaliel, contradictory interpretations of the Law were reviewed and resolved and made binding upon all Jews. Illustration 9 shows a graphic model of Jerusalem from this time period.

Continuing violence allegedly touched off by Jews all around the Mediterranean prompted Hadrian in 130, A.D., to order a shrine to Jupiter built on the temple site and in 182 to prohibit circumcision and public instruction in Jewish Law. After suppressing the second revolt in Palestine, the Bar Cocheba revolt, Hadrian further forbade observance of the Sabbath

---

[181] 3 Will Durant, *Story of Civilization: Caesar and Christ* 545 (1972).

or any Jewish holy day and the public performance of any Jewish ritual. Jews were allowed in Jerusalem only on one designated day each year. Romans erected the pagan city of Aelia Capitoline, with its imperial shrines on the Jewish temple site, on the ruins of Jerusalem, and its layout defines most of the old city today. Judea became Palestine.

Illustration 9. This detailed model of Jerusalem from 66, A.D., when the city was under Roman rule, is a reminder that the city at one time or another during its history was subject to almost every major legal system of the West.

§ 4.04(j)(2). Administration of Jerusalem under Christian Roman Rule.

For the next two centuries, Roman officials ruled Jerusalem as an ordinary sub-provincial municipality. Public law was Roman; private law was Roman if one was a Roman citizen; otherwise, the law applicable to one's own ethnic group applied. Even when the pagan Roman character of Aelia was suddenly swallowed up in Constantine's embracing of Christianity, early in the 4th century, A.D., when the imperial capital was no longer in Rome and the Byzantine empire was a reality, little of Jerusalem's law changed. The religious life of the city, however, began a profound transformation as Christian shrines, pilgrimages and doctrinal disputes began increasingly to focus on Jerusalem.

Law has been described as the most characteristic and lasting expression of the Roman spirit. Without a written constitution, the Roman legal system nevertheless became marvelously complex and sophisticated. Roman jurisprudence continues as a living force in many Western jurisdictions today.[182]

§ 4.04(k). Jerusalem Under the Byzantines.

Indeed, with the growing power of the Christian churches and officials in Byzantine Jerusalem, the line between municipal and ecclesiastical authority was often crossed. For example, in 438, A.D., Eudokia, wife of Emperor Theodosius II, made a pilgrimage to Jerusalem. While there, she gave permission for Jews to pray at the Temple Mount on several days in addition to the one day previously allowed. In 444, A.D., she returned as ruler of Palestine and while in Jerusalem became involved in doctrinal disputes about the person and nature of Christ. Consequently, Jerusalem became a patriarchate that outranked other Christian jurisdictions in Palestine.

Byzantine law, of course, was Roman law in its declining days, but had retained prominence through the codes of Theodosius and Justinian. Such codes were intended to absorb and reconcile the influence of Christianity, the conflicting laws of regions taken into the empire and to turn the accumulations of Roman law into a logical code. Both codes enacted orthodox Christianity into law. They effected significant changes in civil rights, laws of property and inheritance, slavery, and in the Augustinian laws for moral reformation.

Dissension weakened the Byzantine empire, and that weakness encouraged Persian attacks. Christian Byzantine Jerusalem succumbed to a Persian siege in 614, A.D., and Persian Jerusalem was left under the rule of the Jews who had been their allies in the siege. However, the Persians resumed direct control of the city two years later in 616, A.D. Persian law

[182] *Id.* at 391-406.

at this time was still based on its ancient code and was stable. Much local autonomy was still observed. Soon Byzantium and Persia reconciled and evacuated each other's territories, so that Jerusalem was returned to Christian control in 629, A.D.

§ 4.04(1). Jerusalem Under Islamic Rule.

After a siege of only a few months, Byzantine Jerusalem surrendered to Islamic forces in 638, A.D. Both Christians and Jews in the city were thereafter treated as "protected minorities," who paid a poll tax, could not bear arms, and had to surrender their means of self-defense; they were granted religious freedom, but not equality with Islam. This is best illustrated by a decree attributed to the conquering Caliph Umar, which, while perhaps not authentic, does accurately express Muslim policy in Jerusalem:

> [The caliph] grants [to the Christians in Jerusalem] security, to each person and their property: to their churches, their crosses, to the sick and the healthy, to all the people of their creed. We shall not station Muslim soldiers in their churches. We shall not destroy their churches nor impair any of their contents or their property . . . or anything that belongs to them. We shall not compel the people of Jerusalem to renounce their beliefs and we shall not do them any harm.[183]

Also, buildings of other faiths were required to be lower and smaller than Muslim religious buildings.

At first continuing the Christian ban on Jews living in Jerusalem, the Muslims later revoked the prohibition and invited Jewish families from Tiberius to live in a designated area. Jerusalem, however, did not become the capital of Muslim Palestine, a fact which retarded the city's development.

---

[183] Tabari, *Ta'rikh ar-Rusul wa'l-Muluk* I:2405.

Under the Arabs, the old order of life continued. Law was deduced from the Koran. As Muslim jurists formulated responses to new situations, their traditions, the Hadith, became a second source of Islamic law, often reflecting the principles of Roman, Byzantine and Jewish law. Minute regulation of conduct and ritual became as characteristic of Islamic law as it is for Jewish law. Under Islamic administrations, "government lands were measured, records were systematically kept, roads and canals were multiplied or maintained, rivers were banked to prevent floods; . . . Palestine . . . was fertile, wealthy and populous."[184]

However, turmoil in the Islamic world persisted. In 868, A.D., a Turkish commander took power in Egypt, also assuming control of Syria and Palestine. He restored law and order and improved trade and the economy. Both Christians and Jews were permitted to inhabit Jerusalem.

Islamic rule in Jerusalem was violently interrupted by Crusaders in 1099, and during their rule, until 1187, most of the inhabitants of Jerusalem were European. French was the official language and the Crusaders made extensive attempts to re-create continental European feudalism in the areas of Palestine they dominated.

The Crusaders' Assizes of Jerusalem set forth the structure and law of the Kingdom of Jerusalem; the document was described as "one of the most logical and ruthless codifications of feudal government." The barons assumed all ownership of land and reduced the former owners to feudal serfs with heavier burdens than European serfs.[185]

Saladin's splendid victory in 1187 reintroduced Islamic rule in Jerusalem. And just when it appeared that the Third Crusade under Richard the Lionhearted might win back Jerusalem for the Europeans, Richard was forced to return to England and deal with domestic disturbances. Christians resumed rule in Jerusalem from 1229 to 1239, largely because no other party had sufficient interest to oppose it. Then,

---

[184] 4 Will Durant, *Story of Civilization: The Age of Faith* 225-227 (New York: Simon & Schuster, 1950).

[185] *Id.* at 592-594.

from 1244 to 1517 Egyptian-based military leaders known as the Mamluks, ruled Jerusalem, and they generally neglected the city.

Transition to Ottoman Turkish rule in 1516-17 at first produced little change in the city, even with a governor appointed to administer municipal affairs. The second sultan, Suleiman ("The Magnificent") revised the legal system of the Ottoman empire and undertook grand building programs in all his domains, including Jerusalem.

Under the Ottomans church and state were one and the Koran and the traditions were the basic law. The same association of scholars that interpreted the Koran also provided the teachers, lawyers, judges and jurists of the empire. It was such scholars who compiled the definitive codes of Ottoman law. Christians and Jews enjoyed considerable religious freedom under the Ottomans and were permitted to rule themselves by their own laws in matters not involving Muslims. Tenant farming and feudalism were widespread.

In 1831 the Egyptian viceroy Muhammad Ali introduced significant improvements in the administration of Jerusalem. A centralized administrative system supervised improvements in the city, expanded religious freedoms, revitalized the town council, and for the first time in centuries, guaranteed rights to life and property to all inhabitants.

§ 4.04(m). Jerusalem Law in Modern Times.

Ottoman rule in Jerusalem ended in 1917, and the British Mandate for Palestine commenced in 1922. At that time, the law of Palestine was based to a large extent on a codification of Muslim civil jurisprudence and on Turkish adaptations of French law. The Mandate administration enacted early legislation on companies, partnerships and bills of exchange, and a steady stream of further legislation continued until 1947, all following British legislative prototypes. The land law, for instance, was Ottoman with two important legislative additions, the Land (Settlement of Title) and Land Transfer Ordinances. Also English common law and doctrines of equity penetrated into local jurisprudence, especially when there was a gap in Palestinian law.

Jerusalem was divided after the 1948 war, then unified again in 1967, and then by act of the Knesset officially declared the capital of the state of Israel in 1980.

Today, Jerusalem is the name of one of Israel's districts, and this district includes the municipality of Jerusalem, whose council bylaws are subject to approval by the Ministry of the Interior. Municipal courts generally have the jurisdiction they exercised during the Mandate.

§ 4.05. Bibliography.

Books

Ahlstroem, Goesta M., *The History of Ancient Palestine* (1993).
Armstrong, Karen, *Jerusalem: One City, Three Faiths* (1996).
Benvenisti, Eyal, *Legal Dualism: The Absorption of the Occupied Territories into Israel* (1990).
Cohn, Haim Hermann, *Jewish Law in Ancient and Modern Israel, Selected Essays* (1971).
Dorff, Elliot N., and Arthur Rosett, *A Living Tree: The Roots and Growth of Jewish Law* (1988).
Durant, Will, and Ariel Durant, *The Story of Civilization: Our Oriental Heritage* (1954), *The Life of* Greece (1966), Caesar *and Christ* (1944), *The Age of Faith* (1958).
Edwards, Chilperic. *The Oldest Laws in the World: Being an Account of the Hammurabi Code and the Sinaitic Legislation With a Complete Translation of the Great Inscription Discovered at Susa* (1906).
Elon, Menachem, *The Principles of Jewish Law* (1975).
Falk, Ze'ev, *Hebrew Law in Biblical Times* (1964).
Finkelstein, Louis, ed., *The Jews: Their History, Culture and Religion* (4th ed. 1960).
Galbraith, David B., Daniel Kelly Ogden, and Andrew C. Skinner, *Jerusalem: The Eternal City* (1996).
Hecht, N.S., et al., eds., *An Introduction to the History and Sources of Jewish Law* (1996).
Horowitz, George, *The Spirit of Jewish Law: A Brief Account of Biblical and Rabbinical Jurisprudence, With a Special Note on Jewish Law and the State of Israel* (1973).
Jackson, Bernard S., *Essays in Jewish and Comparative Legal History* (1975).
Jackson, Bernard S., ed., *Modern Research in Jewish Law* (1980).
Johns, C. H. W., *Babylonian and Assyrian Laws, Contracts, and Letters* (1904).
Johnson, Paul, *A History of the Jews* (1987).
Kretzmer, David, *The Legal Status of the Arabs in Israel* (1990).
Lankin, Doris, *Israel Today, The Legal System* (1964).
Mazar, Benjamin, *The Mountain of the Lord* (1975).
Pilter, W. T., *The Law of Hammurabi and Moses* (2009).
Pollack, Daniel, *Contrasts in American and Jewish Law* (2001).

Rabinowitz, Jacob J., *Jewish Law: Its Influence on the Development of Legal Institutions* (1956).
Smith, J. M. Powis, *The Origin and History of Hebrew Law* (1931).
Zane, John Maxcy, and James M. Beck, *The Story of Law* (1927).

Articles

Auerbach, Charles, "The Talmud-A Gateway to the Common Law." 3 *W. Res. L. Rev.* 5 (1951).
Ellickson, Robert C., and Charles Dia. Thorland, "Symposium on Ancient Law, Economics, and Society Part II: Ancient Land Law: Mesopotamia, Egypt, Israel," 71 *Chi.-Kent L. Rev.* 321 (1995).
Elon, Menachem, "The Legal System of Jewish Law," 17 *N.Y.U. J. Int'l L. & Pol.* 221 (1984-1985).
Elon, Menachem, "The Sources and Nature of Jewish Law, and its Application in the State of Israel," 4 *Isr. L. Rev. 80* (1969).
Frymer-Kensky, Tikva, "Tit for Tat: The Principle of Equal Retribution in Near Eastern and Biblical Law," 43 *The Biblical Archaeologist* 230 (Autumn, 1980).
Jackson, Bernard S., "Evolution and Foreign Influence in Ancient Law," 16 *Am. J. Comp. L.* 372 (1968).
Linfield, H.S., "The Relation of Jewish to Babylonian Law," 36 *The American Journal of Semitic Languages and Literatures* 40 (Oct. 1919).
Lobingier, Charles Sumner, "The Cradle of Western Law - A Survey of Ultimate Juridical Sources," 63 *U.S. L. Rev.* 623 (1929).
Malina, Michael, "Some Disparities and Parallels in Jewish and American Law," 61 *Conservative Judaism* 73 (Fall/Winter 2008-2009).
Pfeiffer, R.H., "An Analysis of the Hammurabi Code," 36 *The American Journal of Semitic Languages and Literatures* 310 (Jul., 1920).
Rabinowitz, Jacob J., "The Story of the Mortgage Retold," 94 *U. Pa. L. Rev.* 94 (1945-1946).
Sheinson, Ora R., "Lessons from the Jewish Law of Property Rights for the Modern American Takings Debate," 26 *Colum. J. Envtl. L.* 483 (2001).
Weisman, Joshua, "Some Fundamental Concepts of Property Law: A Critical Survey," 21 *Isr. L. Rev.* 529 (1986).

Chapter 5

Land Law in Ancient Britain[186]

SYNOPSIS

---

186 The content of this chapter was originally written by the author, and some content was drawn or reprinted from Vol. 1 of Thompson on Real Property.

Chapter 5. Land Law in Ancient Britain

§ 5.01. Introduction.

The history of American land law began in the British Isles, and in part is shared with the history of English land law. Rules or laws for landholding in the British Isles were in place long before they became part of history by taking written form. So, the history of Anglo-American land law actually begins in prehistory.

In the prehistory of the British Isles, very little is known of the earliest inhabitants. Several invasions of Celtic peoples displaced them, and the Celts were in turn harassed and displaced by Roman, Pictish, and Germanic invaders. Except for some written accounts from the Romans, only archaeological evidence remains from those centuries of habitation. And quite likely those early people left little to influence modern land law, except for some farming practices in parts of the British Isles. Still, studying those ancient cultures reveals much about how early societies organized their affairs around their land.

This chapter summarizes the property rights recognized in the mostly Celtic cultures that prevailed in Britain before the Roman invasions and conquest, and how four centuries of Roman rule in Britain changed those customs.

§ 5.02. Landholding Among Britain's Earliest Peoples.

§ 5.02(a). Hunter-Gatherer Peoples in Britain After the Last Glacial Age.

Britain's last glacial period drew to a close about 8300, B.C.[187] Despite the hardships of the long epochs of arctic and subarctic conditions, hunter-

---

[187] *See, e.g.*, J. V. S. Megaw and D. A. Simpson, *Introduction to British Prehistory* 6-8 (1979); John G. Evans, *The Environment of Early Man in the British Isles* 55 (1975).

gatherer societies lived in Britain during millennia of glacial conditions.[188]

By 6000, B.C., the meltwater from receding glaciers had made Britain an island, accessible from mainland Europe only by boat and forcing cultural change into more insular patterns. In anthropological terms, inhabitants of Britain after it became an island continued in a Mesolithic culture, with hunting and gathering of food resources as the primary means of subsistence.

§ 5.02(b). The Shift from Hunting and Gathering to Farming.

After about 4000, B.C., the Mesolithic culture gradually disappeared, replaced by a Neolithic culture introduced by settlers arriving from the mainland and who were mainly farmers. The shift to a farming economy brought with it change in customs governing both personal and real property.[189] In the hunter-gatherer societies, people accumulated few goods and traveled light. When they settled for longer times in more permanent locations, they acquired dwellings, livestock and other goods.[190]

The earliest farmers appeared in the period 3500-3000, B.C. Thereafter, farming expanded rapidly and the old hunter-gatherer groups all but disappeared.[191] Some hunter-gatherer activity continued, even at farming sites. Animal husbandry, with cattle, sheep and pigs, was also widespread.[192]

---

[188] T. C. Darvill, *Prehistoric Britain* 28-38 (1987).

[189] Lloyd Laing and Jennifer Laing, *The Origins of Britain* 77-86 (1980)

[190] Richard Bradley, *The Social Foundations of Prehistoric Britain* (1984).

[191] T. C. Darvill, *Prehistoric Britain* 50-51 (1987).

[192] Peter G. Reynolds, *Ancient Farming* 38-44 (1987).

§ 5.02(c). Landholding in the Early Farming Cultures.

In these early centuries of farming in Britain, the most common form of economic organization was the single homestead rather than a group of homesteads in a village.[193] When the so-called Beaker people began immigrating about 2500, B.C., they, too, lived in widely scattered single houses.[194]

The farmstead settlements would most likely have been surrounded by fields and pastures, but archaeologists have not yet identified any complete sites from the third millennium, B.C. They have occasionally found large, ditched enclosures, sometimes called causewayed camps or causewayed enclosures, next to single farmsteads in the southern and middle regions of England. They differ as to the possible functions of these formations, but it is likely that the formations were part of the settlement and agriculture activities of the farmsteads.[195]

This period has also generated isolated but intriguing evidence of communities fortified against aggression, and of larger structures suggesting the emergence of powerful chiefdoms.[196]

At about 1500, B.C., a dramatic re-ordering of agricultural land occurred in several large areas throughout Britain: In Wessex, for example, the inhabitants laid out very large field systems on the downland, sometimes incorporating barrows in the existing landscape. These field systems were large and complex. Whoever directed their construction evidently imposed them on the landscape in a single operation. Usually these systems conformed to clearly defined baselines, which could run across the country for several kilometers, ignoring the variations of local

---

193 I. H. Longworth, *Prehistoric Britain* 11 (1985).

194 *See* James L. Forde-Johnston, *Prehistoric Britain and Ireland* 18, 36-38 (1976).

195 T. C. Darvill, *Prehistoric Britain* 57-63 (1987).

196 Lloyd Laing and Jennifer Laing, *The Origins of Britain* 98-99 (1980).

topography.[197]

These ancient farmers laid out their field systems using stone banks, hedges or ditches, which effectively enclosed the fields. They scattered their little circular houses of stone or wood, or of both, among the fields or grouped them together, sometimes within ditched areas; they connected settlements and fields by droveways.[198] In Wessex, the field systems are sometimes referred to as Celtic fields, even though they arose long before invasions of Celtic peoples commenced. Agriculture within these small, rectangular Celtic fields was still practiced during the Roman period.[199]

The unitary structure of these large areas of the landscape is remarkably clear, and the field systems are on a scale hardly equaled before the Roman period. They may be thought of as "cohesive" systems, as distinct from "aggregate" systems which form by piecemeal addition. This terminology suggests analogies with the planning of settlements and their internal buildings. The size and shape of some of the larger land blocks suggest that they should be considered as whole "territories," and not simply as internal land divisions of particular farms.[200]

Throughout all the regional and local variations in such field systems apparently these prehistoric peoples became quite territorial. The same extended families or communities remained on the same land more or less permanently.

Shortly after 1000, B.C., for unknown reasons the inhabitants apparently abandoned these individual field systems, and in their place created large, open fields marked off by somewhat irregular earthworks,

---

[197] Richard Bradley, *The Prehistoric Settlement of Britain* 116 (1978); *see also* Collin Bowen, "Pattern and Interpretation: A View of the Wessex Landscape from Neolithic to Roman Times," in P. J. Fowler, ed., *Recent Work in Rural Archaeology* 44-55 (1975).

[198] T. C. Darvill, *Prehistoric Britain* 108 (1987).

[199] Peter Salway, *Roman Britain* 8 (1981).

[200] Richard Bradley, *The Prehistoric Settlement of Britain* 116-117 (1978).

often referred to by archaeologists as ranch boundaries.[201]

While these changes in landholding were occurring, various peoples immigrated into or invaded the British Isles and some aspects of Bronze Age culture began to appear and replace the Neolithic culture, and these were in turn replaced by Iron Age characteristics.[202] Researchers cannot determine if these technological advances were introduced by the invaders, or independently developed by the established peoples building on Bronze Age foundations, or both. Moreover, they also don't know whether the various invaders simply arrived and integrated themselves into the existing populace, or actually conquered major parts of the British island. However these events occurred, eventually, the British Isles were dominated by Celtic cultures.

§ 5.03. Landholding Among the British Celts.

§ 5.03(a). The Rise of the Celts.

Archaeologists have identified various cultural traits of prehistoric peoples in Europe that gave rise to elements of Celtic culture, but the early culture that seems to be the direct ancestor of the Celts is known as the Urnfield culture. With their vanity, their joy in eating and drinking, and their precocity in the crafting of weapons and ornaments, the Urnfield people foreshadowed many of the qualities of their Celtic descendants. The Europe they inhabited was the one in which the Celts were soon to emerge.[203]

---

[201] Susan Bowen, "Celtic Fields and Ranch Boundaries in Wessex," in Susan Limbrey and John G. Evans, *The Effect of Man on the Landscape: The Lowland Zone* 115-121 (Council for British Archaeology Research Report No. 21, 1978).

[202] Artifacts of immigrating Beaker people, as mentioned above, began appearing during the second millennium, B.C., but the Beaker people may not have been numerous or have ruled over the indigenous people. Some of the principal evidence for the waves of migration derives from the interpretation of "waves" of imported coins as representing movements of peoples. Obviously, such evidence reveals little about the motives or consequences connected with such migrations.

[203] Duncan Norton-Taylor, *The Celts* 22 (1974).

After the collapse of Minoan and Mycenaean cultures and Aegean civilization generally around 1200, B.C., the so-called Urnfield culture arose in the area of modern Hungary and spread rapidly in all directions, eventually covering most of eastern and southern Europe. Some elements of Urnfield culture, best characterized as a Late Bronze Age culture, even appeared in areas of modern Spain, France, the Low Countries, and Britain.[204]

Around 700, B.C., if not earlier, Celtic peoples and the earliest phases of the European Iron Age emerged from the Urnfield culture; researchers assign these Celtic peoples a common identity because of shared language and cultural traits, but their political allegiances almost never extended beyond their individual tribes.

§ 5.03(b). Sequence of the Celtic Hallstatt and La Tene Cultures.

Discoveries and excavations of prehistoric Celtic communities at Lake Hallstatt in Austria, beginning in 1846, and at La Tene on the banks of Lake Neuchatel in Switzerland, beginning in 1858, have produced elaborate studies and theories on the progressive development of Celtic culture. Archaeologists assign the earlier, so-called Hallstatt culture, which belongs to the Bronze Age, to the period 1100-700, B.C., while the later Hallstatt culture, an Iron Age culture, extended from the seventh century into the fifth century, B.C. The La Tene culture began in the fifth century, B.C., and continued until Germanic tribes or Romans expelled the Celts at various times and places throughout Europe, culminating with the Roman conquest of British Celts in the first century, A.D.

§ 5.03(c). Theories on the Emergence of Iron Age Culture in Britain.

The traditional Celtic invasion hypothesis for Britain is that Celts of the Hallstatt culture invaded Britain beginning in the sixth century, B.C.,

---

[204] Barry W. Cunliffe, *The Celtic World* 15 (1979).

establishing most of their settlements in the south and east. In the fourth and third centuries, B.C., more aggressive Celts of the La Tene culture invaded the south, and clashes between these immigrants and the earlier Celtic settlers probably stimulated much of the hillfort construction still so evident in England. A third wave of Celtic invasions then carried in a late La Tene culture in the second and first centuries, B.C., in the southeast of Britain.[205]

Julius Caesar identified these latest invaders as members of the Belgae tribe,[206] although evidence also exists for the presence of other tribes during this period.[207] This invasion hypothesis accounts for the occurrence of La Tene Celtic characteristics in the south and east and of Hallstatt Celtic characteristics in the north and west of Britain.

Others have challenged this invasion hypothesis by alternative explanations that the Iron Age culture traits were indigenous developments "immediately" based on Bronze Age antecedents.[208] Neither migrations nor kinship relationships fully explain the cultural changes that occurred in Britain during the Later Pre-Roman Iron Age, which have been dated by association with the movements of the Belgae. Moreover, many British hillforts predate the times assigned by the alternative invasion hypotheses. The result of this archaeological debate has been to raise questions about whether the British Celts, who opposed Roman invasions in the first centuries, B.C. and A.D., were relatively new arrivals or long-time settlers. From at least one perspective, that of language, the question is perhaps moot, because it is generally agreed that by the time of the Roman invasions, Celtic was the language spoken throughout Britain.[209] The widespread occurrence of Celtic place-names in Romanized forms and the

---

205 R. G. Collingwood and J. N. L. Myres, *Roman Britain and the English Settlements* 21-29 (2d ed. 1937).

206 Julius Caesar, 12 *De Bello Gallico* (Moses Hadas, trans., 1957).

207 Peter Salway, *Roman Britain* 9-10 (1981).

208 *Id.* at 9.

209 Kenneth Hurlstone Jackson, *Language and History in Early Britain* 76 et seq. (1953).

virtual absence of place-names deriving from another language strongly support the hypothesis that by the time of the Roman conquest most Britons were speaking Celtic.[210]

All the various British tribes with whom the Romans came into contact, and probably all the inhabitants of the British Isles, were Celtic in speech by the beginning of the Roman period. Researchers do not know when the Celtic language was introduced into Britain. One thing is clear: it was sufficiently early for pre-Celtic speech to have left no recognizable trace upon the British names of people or places which Roman authors mentioned in their writings from the time of Julius Caesar onward.[211]

§ 5.03(d). Landholding in Britain During the Time of Celtic Domination.

Despite their common language, the peoples of Britain were at different stages in development of material culture at the time of the initial Roman invasions in the first century, B.C. British Celts at this time, whether Hallstatt or La Tene, lived in a Bronze Age culture. In the landholding, the "people lived either in isolated farms or in hut-villages, situated for the most part on the gravel or river-banks or the light upland soils such as the chalk downs or oolite plateaux."[212] The farmers surrounded their settlements with fields they tilled either with a foot plough or a light plough drawn by oxen; such methods merely scratched the soil without turning the sod. Fields had been mostly cleared of their native scrub. "Thus the land was inhabited by a stable and industrious peasant population, living by agriculture and the keeping of livestock, augmented no doubt by hunting and fishing. Judging by the absence of towns and the scarcity of anything like true fortification, these people were little organized for warfare, though

---

[210] Peter Salway, *Roman Britain* 17 (1981).

[211] R. G. Collingwood and J. N. L. Myres, *Roman Britain and the English Settlements* 18-19 (2d ed. 1937).

[212] *Id.* at 20.

there was certainly a distinction between rich and poor."[213] Illustration 10 shows that the typical house of a British Celtic family was not elaborate.

Illustration 10. These replica Celtic huts in the open-air National History Museum of Wales, at St. Fagans near Cardiff, Wales, portray the living circumstances of British Celts, both before and after the Romans invaded.

Cultural development differed widely at different locations throughout Britain. This may have meant little difference in landholding patterns, except to the extent that cultural development determined the form of social organization. Differences in land settlement patterns seem to correspond to types of social organization, and, of course, to topography.[214]

By 150, B.C., several distinct zones exhibiting different settlement patterns existed in Britain. In the north, people inhabited mostly homesteads surrounded by enclosures. In the east and midlands they lived in villages and open settlements. The southeast, south, and Welsh

---

[213] *Id.*

[214] It is certain that a more detailed analysis of settlement types could define a clearer regional patterning and suggest more sensitive correlations with social organization than are possible at present. Martin Millett, *The Romanization of Britain: An Essay in Archaeological Interpretation* 16 (1990).

borderlands comprised the area dominated by hillforts and associated settlements. In Cornwall and west Wales people lived in strongly defended homesteads.[215]

In certain areas, hillforts became very prominent in the political life of the people. Some of these evolved into permanently occupied towns with pit dwellings; in general, they apparently arose in response to development of tribal organizations and tribal wars.[216] The Old Sarum hillfort in Illustration 11 was occupied for centuries before the nearby settlement at Salisbury emerged.

Illustration 11. Old Sarum was originally the site of an iron age hillfort in a strategically important location. It was subsequently occupied by Romans, Anglo-Saxons, Vikings and Normans before being abandoned in favor of the town of Salisbury.

§ 5.03(e). Changes Introduced by the Belgic Celts.

Only with the invasion of the so-called Belgae tribe of Celts, in the

---

[215] Barry W. Cunliffe, *Iron Age Communities in Britain* 332-335 (1978).

[216] R. G. Collingwood and J. N. L. Myres, *Roman Britain and the English Settlements* 23, 25 (2d ed. 1937).

decades before Julius Caesar landed in Britain in the middle of the first century, B.C., did intruders produce dramatic changes in land use patterns. Before invading Britain, the Belgae may have had significant contact with or even have become racially mixed with Germanic peoples on the mainland. In common with Germanic practice, the Belgae tribes had plows and other implements enabling them to work the heavier soils of woodland valleys and to thus spread out from the upland areas occupied by other Celts. The Belgae were the first Britons to clear forests and work the heavier forest soils. They left the hilltop locations and occupied valleys and controlled river crossings. They introduced the practice of marking their territories by a continuous rampart or ditch, which was common among Germanic tribes.[217]

§ 5.03(f). Landholding Patterns Inferred from Ancient Celtic Laws.

From such archaeological evidence it is difficult to discern the finer points of social organization and patterns of landholding. Indeed, the most reliable and detailed information seems to be that exhibited in written collections of Irish and Welsh laws, which date from several centuries later but are apparently of ancient origin. Such ancient laws of the Celts as we possess date from periods subsequent to the Roman occupation of Britain and depict a more elaborate social hierarchy than the archaeological evidence describes for the pre-Roman period, but probably some similar social organization existed in pre-Roman Celtic society.

These old Irish and Welsh laws confirm that the tribe was the main unit of social organization among the Celts, that a tribe consisted of a number of related kinship groups or families, and that a family was typically composed of a man and one or more wives and up to four generations of direct descendants. A common variant of this family unit would be an expanded version, including the father and brothers of the family head, and two generations of the brothers' direct descendants. It is this expanded family group that typically shared inherited goods or participated in the

---

[217] *Id.* at 28.

paying of fines.

The ancient laws also reveal that the kinship group held the land in common and distributed it for use among individual families.[218] If a king headed the kinship group, the king's power derived largely from the number of clients whose allegiance the king had secured. Clients were prominent members of the noble, warrior class. In return for the clients' loyalty and services, the king dispensed the use of property to the clients. More important clients could themselves have warriors of lesser social status as their own clients; a client was, in effect, a tenant farmer.[219]

According to the laws, a client who was a freeman typically held large numbers of livestock, certain essential farming implements and rights to certain grazing land. Under a contractual arrangement with the overlord for a definite period of time, usually set at seven years, the client rented livestock from the overlord. In return, the client rendered personal service in the overlord's household and paid a portion (usually about one-third) of his personal income in the form of finished goods. At the end of the rental period, the rented livestock became the client's property and the client was free to enter into another contract with any overlord.[220]

Clients who were lower on the social scale had less advantageous terms. Usually such clients performed field labor rather than personal household service, and they did not retain their livestock at the end of the contract period. Furthermore, each client received at the outset of the contract a form of loan from the overlord, in the amount of a portion of the client's honor price,[221] but was seldom able to repay the loan at the end of the contract period; thus a form of serfdom developed as the inability to

---

[218] Barry W. Cunliffe, *The Celtic World* 49 (1979).

[219] Nora K. Chadwick, *The Celts* 116-117 (1970).

[220] Duncan Norton-Taylor, *The Celts* 70-73 (1974).

[221] The honor price was very similar to the Germanic wergild, the economic value attached to a person's life, based mostly on the person's social status. *See* Nora K. Chadwick, *The Celts* 117 (1970).

repay the loan left the client in more or less permanent bondage.[222]

The tribal organizations in Celtic areas throughout Europe held their land in common. One tribe of Celts on the Iberian peninsula, the Vaccaei, reportedly divided up the land among tribesmen each year and shared the harvest among the entire tribe.[223] Julius Caesar's writings do not mention the subject of land ownership among the Celts, and there is no evidence that such ownership in the chief was recognized in native Celtic custom. Only when the Romans imposed their more sophisticated legal system upon Celtic communities were tribal chieftains registered as the owners or at least the possessors of the land.[224]

§ 5.03(g). Summary of Landholding Patterns Among the British Celts.

It appears that whether the British Celts lived in individual, isolated homesteads or in small village clusters, the farming patterns were basically the same and had indeed been established among native peoples even before the Celts came. Where farming rather than herding was practiced, the most common pattern was the cultivation of small, rectangular fields, marked off by low banks of earth or rocks or some similarly conspicuous boundary. Family groups held such land, and probably grazing land, too, so farmers who worked clusters of fields would have been connected through blood ties, and the rights to use these fields would have been passed on to groups of kinship descendants. There is no evidence, however, that such land was alienable outside the family, or that it could have been sold, exchanged, or otherwise transferred to a stranger.[225]

---

[222] Duncan Norton-Taylor, *The Celts* 72-73 (1974).

[223] *Diodorus Siculus*, 5:34.

[224] H. D. Rankin, *Celts and the Classical World* 130, 170 (1987).

[225] One emerging viewpoint among students of this topic is that the division of land by boundaries and the definition of settlements by ditched enclosures signify that "effective private control over land" had begun to be recognized even before the Roman conquest. See Martin Millett, *The Romanization of Britain: An Essay in Archaeological Interpretation* 96-97 (1990).

The property right in these farm lands was apparently a usufruct, or use right only, in addition to limited inheritability. If the rights to land were ultimately held by the tribe as communal property, then alienability of land was a right resting with the tribe or with a kinship clan of the tribe. Property rights so held would have been similar to landholding patterns among other cultures in similar stages of development.[226]

§ 5.04. Patterns of Landholding Among the Romano-Britons.

In describing how land was held in Britain before common law traditions began to develop, the period of Roman occupation presents an intriguing anomaly: despite almost four centuries of Roman domination in Britain and the sophistication of Roman property law, no lasting changes in British landholding practices occurred. This section explains why that was so and also describes the profound distinctions between the rudimentary landholding customs of British Celts and the refined property law of their Roman overlords.

§ 5.04(a). Summary of the Roman Conquest and Occupation of Britain.

§ 5.04(a)(1). The Early Course of Conquest and Pacification.

Rome's interest in Britain as a potential province culminated in conquest only after many decades spent in resolving civil disorder in Rome itself. The first Roman move toward Britain occurred in the late summer of 55, B.C.[227], when Julius Caesar led two legions across the Channel in a

---

[226] *See* Chapter 1, "Emergence of Property Rights in Earliest Human Societies."

[227] The outline of the Roman military campaigns in Britain is drawn in part from the fuller accounts found in R. G. Collingwood and J. N. L. Myres, *Roman Britain and the English Settlements 32-119* (2d ed. 1937), and sources cited therein. The only ancient account of the conquest under the emperor Claudius is in Cassius Dio, *Historia Romana*. Other helpful modern discussions of the campaigns are found in

somewhat abortive reconnaissance-in-force. Probably the main motive for this attack was to begin neutralizing Britain as a source of support for still rebellious Gauls. The legions fought only one major battle before a large part of the transport fleet was destroyed by stormy conditions while it lay at anchor. Thereafter, the Romans foraged and skirmished for time to repair the ships remaining afloat, and then returned across the Channel as soon as possible.

Almost a year later, in the early summer of 54, B.C., Caesar again invaded, with a much larger force, and again lost part of his anchored fleet because of rough weather. After a brief but sharp campaign in the area between Dover and London, the Romans obtained submission of the Belgic Britons opposing them. Caesar and his legions, with many hostages and prisoners, returned to Gaul in September of that year, leaving heads of several British tribes nominally in fealty to Rome.

The subsequent civil disorders in Rome, including Caesar's assassination, the rule by the Triumvirate, and the ascension by Octavian as Augustus Caesar, are well documented and give adequate explanation for the failure of Roman forces to return to Britain for nearly a century. Finally, in 40, A.D., Romans made preparations for another invasion, and only at the point of embarkation from Boulogne suddenly stopped the project, all at the order of the unstable and erratic emperor Gaius, better known to modern readers as Caligula.

Shortly after the demise of Gaius and the ascension of Claudius as emperor in 43, A.D., a Roman expedition actually landed in Britain, at the site presently known as Richborough, and carried out a methodical campaign to reduce the resistance of the British Celts. The substantial remaining wall of the Roman fort at Richborough is shown in Illustration 12.

Sheppard Sunderland Frere, *Britannia* (3d ed. 1987); John Peddie, *Invasion: The Roman Conquest of Britain* (1987); Peter Salway, *Roman Britain* (1981); Malcolm Todd, *Roman Britain* (1981); Graham Webster, *The Roman Invasion of Britain* (1980); H. H. Scullard, *Roman Britain: Outpost of the Empire* (1978); John Wacher, (1978); and Joan Liversidge, *Britain in the Roman Empire* (1968).

Illustration 12. Still impressive in their modern setting, the powerful walls of the first Romano-British fort, located at Richborough, Kent, England, provided a protected base for the Romans' successful campaign against the populous Celtic tribes beginning in 43, A.D.

Following a Roman victory in a sharp battle at the crossing of the River Medway near Rochester, the Celts raised no substantial opposition against their further advance. After advancing to the Thames, the legions halted to await the arrival of the emperor Claudius, who was making the six-week journey from Rome personally to participate in the now set-piece conquest and pacification of the native tribes. Undoubtedly, the Roman military commander Plautius made as many advance arrangements as possible for peaceful tribal submissions. Crossing the Thames as soon as Claudius arrived, the Roman army proceeded to Colchester, to which the Britons had retreated, and there Claudius received the fealty of eleven tribes.

Pursuing his policy of pacifying Britain through submission rather than conquest, Claudius set up several "client kings" to secure border areas: Cogidubnus at Chichester, Prasutagus in East Anglia, and shortly thereafter Cartimandua, queen of the Brigantes, who dominated a huge area of middle and northern Britain. After a sojourn of only sixteen days, Claudius returned to Rome.[228]

Under the leadership of the future emperor Vespasian, other Roman forces swiftly overcame the hillfort-based resistance of Celtic tribes in the British southwest, including the Isle of Wight. He placed these areas under the administration of native leaders who promised loyalty to Rome. The ostensibly pacified area yielded by these early Roman triumphs in Britain included the territory to the south and east of a line from Exeter in the southwest to Lincoln and north to the River Humber. Whereas a process of Romanization in such pacified areas would normally have begun immediately after the conquest, this process was seriously impeded for two decades or more as Roman administrative blunders and insensitivities continued to provoke revolt among the Britons. The most serious of these was the violent uprising led by Queen Boudicca in 60-61, A.D., the suppressing of which left much of southern Britain under some form of military rule until about 69, A.D.

On the frontier, intense military activity continued, with campaigns against Brigantes in the Midlands (71-74, A.D.), the Welsh in the West (74-78, A.D.), and the Caledonians in the North (78-85, A.D.). The northern limits of the Roman presence were never fully settled or stabilized, as best revealed by the construction of Hadrian's Wall, ca. 122-133, A.D., and of the Antonine Wall farther north, beginning ca. 138, A.D., and by the several shifts of Roman defenses back and forth between those barriers.

Illustration 13 shows graphic remains of a portion of Hadrian's Wall and one of its numerous mileforts.

---

[228] David A. Thomas, "The Disappearance of Roman Law from Dark Age Britain," 1984 *B.Y.U. L. Rev.* 563, 566-567.

Illustration 13. Impressive remains of Hadrian's Wall and one of its numerous mileforts show the Romans' prodigious efforts to protect their Romanized territories from the unpacified areas of Scotland and the northern tribes.

§ 5.04(a)(2). The Beginnings of Romanization.

Even though the intensity of military activity varied from time to time and place to place in Roman Britain, inexorably the forces intended to Romanize the British Celts were set in motion:

> Rome's early approach to pacification was to leave loyal client rulers largely in charge, presumably prompting little initial change in social organization. Nevertheless, Roman life drew its essence from towns and town life, and the impulse to create and embellish urban centers in Britain is unmistakable. The economic base for urbanization consisted of developing trade and opening up markets for surplus goods. Although tribes beyond the Roman pale were not attuned to capitalism and production of surplus goods, it appears that some areas of southern and southeastern Britain rather quickly adapted to such urban

> Roman ways. The beginnings of the main towns [however] do not appear until near the end of the first century. . . .[229]

In his caustic commentary on the decadent Roman influence upon the Britons, Tacitus reveals some of the means used to further Romanization:

> In order that a population scattered and uncivilised, and proportionately ready for war, might be habituated by comfort to peace and quiet, he [Agricola] would exhort individuals, assist communities, to erect temples, market-places, houses: he praised the energetic, rebuked the indolent, and the rivalry for his compliments took the place of coercion. Moreover he began to train the sons of the chieftains in a liberal education, and to give a preference to the native talents of the Briton as against the plodding Gaul. As a result, the nation which used to reject the Latin language began to aspire to rhetoric: further, the wearing of [Roman] dress became a distinction, and the toga came into fashion, and little by little the Britons were seduced into alluring vices: to the lounge, the bath, the well-appointed dinner table. The simple "natives" gave the name of "culture" to this factor of their slavery.[230]

Important elements of Romanization were the settling of discharged legionary veterans in communities or "coloniae" of their own, and the founding of completely Romanized municipalities, with the special status of "municipia." The Romans established legionary "coloniae" at Colchester sometime before 60, A.D., and at Lincoln and Gloucester during the reign of Domitian, 81-96, A.D.. The only known "municipium" was at Verulamium, near the modern St. Albans, north of London. The Roman town of Venta Silurum, remains of which are shown in Illustration 14, was located in what is now the modern community of Caerwent, near the legionary fort of Caerleon, both in Monmouthshire, Wales.

---

[229] *Id.* at 579-580.

[230] Cornelius Tacitus, *The Life of Julius Agricola* 21 (Loeb ed. 1963).

Illustration 14. The well-preserved remains of the Roman town of Venta Silurum are still found in the midst of the modern Welsh town of Caerwent, in Monmouthshire. The Romans brought sophisticated landholding practices to at least some parts of Britain.

§ 5.04(a)(3). Early Changes in Landholding Practices Introduced by the Romans.

Implicit in the investiture of British tribal chiefs with administrative duties, and in the establishment of legionary colonies and a Roman municipality, were important changes in landholding practices in Britain. However, throughout the following discussion of those changes, and of Roman property law in effect during the period of Roman occupancy, it should be remembered that little is known about how extensively the British Celts adopted these changes. Most likely, the emergence of Roman property practices was confined to a few highly Romanized urban areas of Britain, and the old Celtic property arrangements in most of the countryside remained unchanged.

It has been previously shown in this chapter[231] that property ownership among the British Celts was probably communal in form, with the head of a tribe or other large kinship group administering ownership and occupancy rights. The individual farmers who were the actual occupants of the land probably held only a right to use the land and possibly a privilege to extend the use right to their descendants. The notion that the actual occupant of the land also had other ownership rights, such as the right to alienate, was probably unfamiliar to pre-Roman Britons.[232]

Events interrupted these customs first in the Colchester area, when the Roman conquerors established the first colony of discharged legionaries. Ordinarily, the Romans would have given the veterans parcels of land from territory that had belonged to and been forfeited by the now deposed native leader. On this occasion, however, the veterans forcibly took much additional land, dispossessing native farmers. Once in occupancy of such land, the veterans were able, under Roman law, to exercise the full range of property rights pertaining to persons of their class of citizenship, which were much more extensive than the rights held by the native farmers.

Similarly, in the establishment of Verulamium as a Roman "municipium" with certain rights of self-government, Roman citizens within this urban center would have held much more extensive property rights than the property rights held by most Britons. In other tribal centers that the Romans turned into administrative centers, or "civitates," similar changes in property rights probably occurred. While it cannot be known whether comparisons of Roman and British property rights received much

---

[231] *See* § 5.03(g).

[232] One theory is that the Britons may have been moving to some forms of private land ownership even before the Roman conquest:

> It is more likely that effective private control over land had begun to emerge well before the conquest with the division of land by boundaries and the definitions of settlements by ditched enclosures . . . . Villas may not have been possible without the existence of private property, but this probably existed before villas emerged.

Martin Millett, *The Romanization of Britain: An Essay in Archaeological Interpretation* 96-97 (1990).

attention among the Britons, it can be assumed that the Roman presence alerted the native Britons to new ways of landholding. Critically important to Romanization was the superb network of Roman roads, most of whose routes are used in England today. As shown in Illustration 15, a few material fragments of Romano-British roads have survived nearly two millennia.

Illustration 15. An extant portion of a Roman road in west Yorkshire, England. The roads enabled military movements to maintain peace, and facilitated commerce and urban development, all of which enhanced land use and value.

A large municipality, such as Verulamium, shown in Illustration 16, brought urban amenities unknown to Celtic Britain a generation or two earlier.

Illustration 16. The ruins of an amphitheater at Verulamium, Roman Britain's third largest city, exemplify urban amenities introduced into Celtic Britain by Romanization. Verulamium is located near St. Alban's, north of London.

A summary of Roman property law in effect during the period of Roman occupation of Britain can help in understanding the changes in landholding patterns introduced by the Romans.

§ 5.04(b). The Impact of Roman Law on Britain.

The direct evidence for the presence of Roman law in Roman Britain is rather sparse. It consists of documentary references both to persons known to have been active in legal affairs and to legal procedures. Only from such evidence can one make judgments about how deeply Roman law penetrated into the British Celtic populace, the classes likely to have used or encountered Roman law, and Roman law's impact on Romano-British society as a whole.

Probably the Romans formalized the original conquest of Britain during the reign of Claudius by a practice from republican times: they gave the province a set of statutes, the *lex provinciae*.[233] There is, however, no conclusive evidence that the imposition of *lex provinciae* on stabilized provinces continued on into later imperial times.

The governor of the province assumed the office of *legati Augusti* and was directly accountable to the emperor, who was nominally and officially the governor or proconsul of all the frontier provinces.[234] As chief justice of the province, the governor headed the judicial service, heard legal petitions, and presided at trials, both in the capital and elsewhere in the province. He exercised primary jurisdiction in cases involving Roman citizens, capital punishment, condemnation to the mines or salt works, and amounts in excess of a certain sum; his appellate jurisdiction extended to all other cases arising in the province. His judgment in cases between non-citizens was final. Because the native non-citizens still lived under local laws to the extent they differed from Roman law, the governor's adjudicatory tasks were complicated by the variety of local Celtic laws that the native parties might invoke in a legal controversy.

Imposition of Roman influence and laws normally meant an increase of private litigation, and Roman legal terms have been found on tablets excavated in London, dating from the period of Roman territorial expansion late in the first century A.D.[235]

Beginning with Vespasian's reign in 69, A.D., the imperial Roman government sometimes appointed a special judicial officer, the *legatus iuridicus*, to assist the governor in legal matters. Six of these important legal officers in Britain are known, five by name. Two noted legal authorities among them were C. Salvius Liberalis Nonius Bassus, who was

---

[233] Peter Salway, *Roman Britain* 87 (1981).

[234] This arrangement pertained to the "imperial" provinces under the direct charge of the emperor, but not to the "senatorial" provinces left to the supervision of the Senate.

[235] Sheppard Sunderland Frere, *Britannia: A History of Roman Britain* 184 (3d ed. 1987).

probably appointed during Agricola's governorship in 79, A.D.,[236] and his successor L. Iavolenus Priscus.[237] The other *legati* were C. Sabucius Maior Caecilianus, who served during the reign of Marcus Aurelius,[238] M. Vettius Valens,[239] and M. Antius Crescens Calpurnianus, who served under Septimius Severus.[240] In addition, an anonymous *legatus iuridicus* in Britain set up an inscription celebrating one of Trajan's victories.[241]

Only fragments of Romano-British litigation records have survived. A case described in *Justinian's Digest* tells of a slave-woman condemned to labor at the saltworks, but who was then kidnapped and later repurchased by her original owner, and the owner sued the state to recover the purchase money.[242] In the Theodosian Code, one British case concerns tax revenues to be paid by decurions on behalf of their tenants.[243] Writing scratched on a wooden tablet found in the well of a Romano-British villa refers to the sale of real estate and uses Roman legal terms.[244]

---

[236] *Inscriptiones Latinae Selectae,* No. 1011 (Hermann Dessau, ed., 1962).

[237] *Id.* No. 1015. Priscus later became a highly respected teacher and head of one of the two principal schools of Roman jurisprudence.

[238] *Id.* No. 1125.

[239] *Corpus Inscriptionum Latinarum*, No. 11.383 (Eugen Bormann, ed., 1888). Valens was also appointed patron of the province, a post associated with the province council and an honor of high distinction.

[240] *Inscriptiones Latinae Selectae*, No. 1151 (Hermann Dessau, ed., 1962). Calpurnianus was briefly in charge of all provincial affairs during one of the governor's absences.

[241] R. G. Collingwood and R. P. Wright, *The Roman Inscriptions of Britain* Items 627, 1337, at 210, 442 (1965).

[242] Digesta Iustiniana 49.15.6, *translated and reprinted in* IX S. Scott, *Corpus Juris Civilis - The Civil Law* (1973).

[243] *The Theodosian Code* 11.7.2 (Clyde Pharr trans. 1952), dated November 20, A.D. 319. *See* C. E. Stevens, "A Possible Conflict of Laws in Roman Britain," 37 *J. Roman Stud.* 132-134 (1947).

[244] *See* Eric G. Turner, "A Roman Writing Tablet from Somerset," 46 *J. Roman Stud.* 115-118 (1956).

Other records are concerned with wills. In one case involving the *legatus iuridicus* Iavolenus Priscus, the petitioner sought approval for an alternative disposition of property set in trust for a beneficiary who did not survive minority.[245]

In another will case concerning the estate of a legionary who committed suicide, the decedent's will was held valid unless it could be shown that the suicide was to avoid punishment.[246] A will was usually written on tablets by someone with legal training.[247]

It is not known how extensively British Celts invoked or practiced Roman law, but Juvenal refers to Gauls teaching to Britons the techniques of pleading.[248]

Tacitus describes Agricola's encouragement to Britons to build courts of justice.[249] In one such court at York, the great Roman jurist Aemilius Papinian, who accompanied the emperor Septimius Severus to Britain in 208, A.D., administered justice while his emperor fought barbarian Picts and Scots on the British north border.[250]

These fragmentary references to Roman law in Britain show that Roman law was perhaps an active factor in the lives of the Romano-British elite, but it is not known whether it had any impact at all on the large

---

[245] *Digesta Iustiniana* 36.1.48, *translated and reprinted in* IX Samuel P. Scott, *Corpus Juris Civilis - The Civil Law* (1973).

[246] *Id.* at 28.3.6.7, 28.6.2.4.

[247] Romano-British examples are discussed in Joan Liversidge, *Britain in the Roman Empire* 304 (1968).

[248] Juvenal, *Satires* 15.111-15.112 (Rolfe Humphries trans. 1958).

[249] Cornelius Tacitus, *The Life of Julius Agricola* 21 (Loeb ed. 1963).

[250] IX *Dio's Roman History* 76.14 (Loeb ed. 1927). Papinian was at the time praetorian prefect, the officer with general jurisdiction over all civil and criminal cases in the empire outside of Rome itself. One rescript (a written statement of the Roman emperor on a question of law) of British origin survives from this time, dated May 5, 210, A.D., and is discussed in Eric Birley, *Roman Britain and the Roman Army* 52 (1953).

majority of the populace.

§ 5.04(c). Summary of Roman Land Law Concepts to 400, A.D.[251]

Roman law accorded to land, as something tangible that could be perceived by the senses (*res corporalis*), the right to be possessed and owned. In the early stage of Roman legal development, ownership of land fell into two categories: the land of Italy or land that enjoyed Italic rights (*res mancipi*), and all other land (*res nec mancipi*). Holders of Italic lands could transfer them by following certain formalities, whereas informal transfers sufficed for the other lands. Later, the distinction broke down and all transfers followed the less formal mode.

Also in the early stages of legal development, land in Italy was the only land that could be privately owned. All other land in the Roman provinces was deemed the property of the people or—at a later stage—of the emperor, and concerning which private parties could obtain only certain use and possession rights, for which they paid taxes in return. Eventually, the rights associated with holding such provincial land became quite extensive and included the rights to hold and enjoy the property, to transmit the holder's rights to heirs upon death, and to transfer possessory rights to others, along with protections for present possessory rights.

Although one could transfer or acquire interests in land by several different methods, the usual method was by actual physical "delivery," which meant putting the transferee in possession and control of the property. In later stages of Roman legal development, delivery could be achieved symbolically, by handing over a dirt clod or a brick for land or a building, or ownership could even be transferred merely by agreement, especially if actual possession did not change, such as in a sale-leaseback

---

[251] While there is no dearth of written descriptions of Roman law, writings that organize and summarize the points of Roman law on particular subjects are not so abundant. The discussion in this section is drawn from two sources that are appropriate for the degree of detail provided in this section: Paul Van Warmelo, *An Introduction to the Principles of Roman Civil Law* 61-120 (1976); and Alan Watson, *The Law of the Ancient Romans* 49-57 (1970).

arrangement. A form of adverse possession was recognized in permitting a good faith but mistaken possessor of land to acquire ownership of the land after two years of uninterrupted possession. Roman law also recognized leaseholds and concurrent ownership.

Land could also be burdened by servitudes. The earliest recognized servitudes included the right to cross the land of another by means of a right of way, such as for cattle, for a road, or for an aqueduct. Servitudes generally could not require affirmative action by the owner of the burdened land, but could prohibit certain activities on the burdened land or permit certain activities by the owner of the dominant land. Certain servitudes were recognized as attached to the land, and others were deemed personal, such as a right to make certain use of or take the fruits of the burdened land during one's lifetime.

Landholders could use their land as security for a debt. At first, the debtor simply transferred ownership and possession to the creditor and had to obtain a transfer back when the debt was paid. Later, security was achieved by transfer of possession without transfer of ownership. Finally, the land could be hypothecated: the debtor transferred neither ownership nor possession to the creditor, but the creditor could satisfy the default and the unpaid debt by taking possession of the pledged land.

§ 5.04(d). Extent of Roman Land Law Influence on Celtic Britain.

§ 5.04(d)(1). Private Property in Towns.

Perhaps the most remarkable form of Roman influence on British landholding practices arose out of the practice of forming Roman provincial administrative centers, called "civitates," out of tribal centers. If they followed the basic pattern established in other provinces, the Romans organized the civitatis around a senate[252] controlled by the landowning

---

[252] Such a regional senate traditionally consisted of 100 members, but it cannot be determined how consistently this practice was followed in Britain. Frank Frost Abbott and Allan Chester Johnson, *Municipal Administration in the Roman Empire*

class, which elected the council and magistrates. It is likely that the Romans consolidated several tribal areas into the territory of one civitas, or formed more than one civitas in the area of a single tribe, each perhaps conforming to the area of a major clan within the tribe. Once the tribal aristocrats were stabilized in their power, prestige, and wealth, they were expected to contribute heavily to the construction and introduction of Roman municipal amenities.[253]

§ 5.04(d)(2). Villas and Farms in the Countryside.

The elite and leading members of the tribes obtained outright ownership of what had been tribal property. This enabled them to serve in public office because of a property qualification imposed on those who would be public officials. The construction of villas in the regions around the civitas attests to the private property holdings of the native municipal leaders as well as of the Roman themselves. Archaeological evidence also shows, however, that many native farms alongside the villas continued to operate in the ways they had before the Roman invasion.[254] Indeed, most of the land use and farming practices changed little from pre-Roman times.[255]

By the middle of the third century, A.D., economic conditions in the Roman empire had worsened to the point that the local aristocracy "became less and less willing to serve their communities and endow them with gifts and buildings."[256] Also in the later Roman period, it is possible to detect

---

(1926).

[253] Martin Millett, *The Romanization of Britain: An Essay in Archaeological Interpretation* 66 (1990).

[254] *Id.*

[255] *Id.* at 120 (citing "New Approaches to Ancient Fields," in Graeme Barker, ed., *Prehistoric Communities in Northern England* 105-118 (1981); D. N. Riley, *Early Landscape from the Air* (1980)).

[256] "The Burden of Roman Grandeur: Aspects of Public Building in the Cities of Asia and Achaea," in Anthony King and Martin Henog, eds., *The Roman West in the Third Century* 189-198 (1981).

signs that occupants, including even peasant farmers, were consolidating land holdings, possibly to accommodate multiple occupancy.[257]

Another development in Romano-British landholding patterns revealed by archaeology is a form of dual residency in some of the villas. Archaeologists have found in these villas two or more self-contained residential units; possible interpretive explanations include a proprietor and heir maintaining an estate jointly, or two or more family members holding the power over the land, or a steward managing the estate during prolonged absences of the owner.[258] Other villas show structural forms which suggest housing for a single extended family, and thus a continuation of housing and social patterns from the pre-Roman era.[259]

Even with all of this information, the housing patterns and social organization for the majority of the population, who did not live in stone villas, is unknown, although more work in this area is underway.[260] With respect to rural settlements, settlement patterns were more likely to have remained unchanged from pre-Roman times in those areas where Romanization was least conspicuous. Probably less Romanization of landholding and dwelling patterns occurred in the more remote north and west of Britain, characterized by "round stone-built huts surrounded by oval, round or polygonal enclosure walls," a pattern that had persisted for centuries.[261] The walls apparently had no military function, but were "designed to keep cattle, sheep and children in, and thieves, wolves, and perhaps rodents out . . . ."[262]

---

[257] J. T. Smith, "Villas as a Key to Social Structure," in Malcolm Todd, ed., *Studies in the Romano-British Villa* 149, 170 (1978).

[258] Martin Millett, *The Romanization of Britain: An Essay in Archaeological Interpretation* 198-199 (1990); J. T. Smith, "Villas as a Key to Social Structure," in Malcolm Todd, ed., *Studies in the Romano-British Villa* 149, 170 (1978).

[259] *See, e.g.*, John Hadman, "Aisled Buildings in Roman Britain," in Malcolm Todd, ed., *Studies in the Romano-British Villa* 187-195 (1978).

[260] *See, e.g.*, Richard Hingley, *Rural Settlement in Roman Britain* 1-12 (1989).

[261] Brian K. Roberts, *Rural Settlement in Britain* 50-51 (1977).

[262] *Id.*

In the "coloniae," the towns for retired legionary veterans, land grants in place of cash gratuities were the rule,[263] especially if the settlements occupied sites of former military camps in the provinces. Roman soldiers often obtained Roman citizenship upon retirement from active duty, so undoubtedly they established a tradition of being independent farmers in the development of these communities. In the later stages of the Roman occupation, the agricultural landholding patterns of the areas surrounding the *coloniae* became indistinguishable from patterns in other nearby areas.

With the granting of universal Roman citizenship in 212, A.D., it is possible that Romano-Britons more frequently resorted to Roman law to determine property rights, and those Roman property rights thus became more widespread.[264] Scholars have found only one document relating to the sale of land from the period of Roman occupation of Britain, and that document is based on Roman law.[265] As noted in the following paragraphs, however, no evidence has yet emerged to show that landholding patterns for most of Roman Britain differed from those that prevailed in the pre-Roman time.

§ 5.04(d)(3). Changes in Agricultural Landholding.

Agricultural organization and landholding patterns in Roman Britain were not entirely unaffected by evolution within the Roman empire. As occurred elsewhere in the empire, the size of Romano-British landholdings increased, a result of the initial concession of private property rights to tribal leaders and the unprogressive system of Roman taxation with its broad exemptions for the wealthiest landowners. Throughout the empire, agricultural landholdings were consolidated as part of the "colonate"

---

263 G. R. Watson, *The Roman Soldier* 147-148 (1969).

264 For the view that local Celtic law remained very widespread even after the grant of universal citizenship, *see* A.L.F. Rivet, "Social and Economic Aspects," in A.L.F. Rivet (ed), *The Roman Villa in Britain* 173-216 (1969).

265 Eric G. Turner, "A Writing Tablet from Somerset," 46 *J. Roman Stud.* 115-118 (1956).

system, "whereby a landowner whose estate was sufficiently large to need cultivation by others used tenants rather than slaves as labourers. These tenants (*coloni*) became tied to the land, and even to particular estates, both by custom and by the law, which required them to remain on the land for taxation purposes. The system developed into a form of heredity service which became *de facto* feudal, at least in provinces where, unlike Britain, there were severe pressures on agricultural production."[266]

An entry in the Theodosian Code, dating from 319, A.D.,[267] defining the tax liability of British landowners has been interpreted to indicate that the colonate system existed in Britain,[268] but possibly some or even most of the peasant farmers remained free rather than under tenure. It is known that some *coloni* in Britain's tax jurisdiction were registered for taxation in their own villages rather than with the estates of other landowners,[269] which would indicate free rather than tenured status.

§ 5.04(e). Reversion to Celtic Tribalism in Britain After A.D. 400.

Whatever the impact of Roman property law and practice on landholding in Roman Britain, it seems to have been ground out of existence by the hard fighting against the Anglo-Saxons during the fifth and sixth centuries, A.D. Concurrent with the breakdown of Roman authority in Britain at the end of the fourth century, A.D., hostilities increased from Germanic incursions along the south and east coasts and Pictish raids along the north border. It is now accepted that the protracted British resistance to these assaults, rather than accommodations such as were reached with the

---

[266] Martin Millett, *The Romanization of Britain: An Essay in Archaeological Interpretation* 203 (1990); *see* A. H. M. Jones, *The Later Roman Empire A.D. 284-602: A Social, Economic and Administrative Survey* 769-808 (2d ed. 1973).

[267] *Theodosian Code* 11.7.2 (Clyde. Pharr trans. 1952) dated November 20, A.D. 319.

[268] F. Haverfield, *The Romanization of Roman Britain* 45 (1912).

[269] A. H. M. Jones, *The Later Roman Empire AD 284-602: A Social, Economic and Administrative Survey* 797 (2d ed. 1973).

Franks in Gaul, led to the invaders destroying rather than subsuming and integrating much of the Romano-British society. Abundant archaeological evidence attests that what was left of Romano-British society reverted rather swiftly to the old tribal ways of pre-Roman Celticism.[270] Indeed, this evidence shows that, as cities and towns declined, the inhabitants renovated many Celtic Iron Age hillforts; Celtic warlords returned to the hills to occupy those defended sites that had been abandoned when the Romans conquered Britain.

The death throes of Roman civilization were wrenching throughout the empire, and Britain did not escape the anguish, poignantly described by Collingwood and Myres:

> From 455, . . . we hear of no more cultural and spiritual contacts between Britain and the Mediterranean world. The culture of the romanized upper classes has sunk into discredit and fades away, now that its owners have confessed their inability to control the political situation, and abdicated in favour of what today would be called a dictatorship. Roman Britain is now rapidly dying, and we are reaching the "sub-Roman" period when men lived on the relics of Romanity diluted in a pervading medium of Celticism.[271]

These authors assert that "the general tone of Romano-British society became more and more barbarized. As the Saxon settlements grew in strength, the Roman civilization of the lowland zone was declining into a Celto-Roman civilization where Celtic elements were more and more prevailing over Roman. Latin must have been less and less used. Rome was becoming a memory."[272]

---

[270] *See* David A. Thomas, "The Disappearance of Roman Law from Dark Age Britain," 1984 *B.Y.U. L. Rev.* 563, 590-595.

[271] R. G. Collingwood and J. N. L. Myres, *Roman Britain and the English Settlements* 315-316 (2d ed. 1937).

[272] *Id.*

Archaeology further reveals that an almost complete interruption, or discontinuity, between Romano-Britons and Anglo-Saxons occurred among the landowning elite. No villa has yet been investigated that continued to be occupied into Saxon times.[273] Yet it is possible that, with the replacement of one elite by another, the life of the rural peasant did carry on as before, "that many Romano-British peasants remained to become Anglo-Saxon peasants."[274]

§ 5.05. Modern Vestiges of Ancient Landholding Patterns.

Strewn all over England and Wales are ghostly remains of the land's prehistoric and Romano-British past. Ceremonial sites at Stonehenge and Avebury, the West Kennet long barrow, the White Horse at Uffington, the Maiden Castle hillfort, the isolated legionary camps on wild Welsh hilltops, the baths at Bath, the theater at St. Alban's Verulamium, the deserted brick bathhouse at Roman Wroxeter (shown in Illustration 17), the Saxon Shore forts, the villas at Chichester, and a thousand other sites, all bespeak millennia of human habitation. None of it, however, seems to have had much overt impact on the attitudes and lifestyles of today.

[273] *Id.* at 317.

[274] Martin Millett, *The Romanization of Britain: An Essay in Archaeological Interpretation* 224 (1990).

Illustration 17. Shown here are some of the substantial ruins of Roman Viroconium, the fourth largest city in Roman Britain. Located near the present village of Wroxeter in Shropshire, England, this thriving community was at a commercial crossroads. The building was probably a public bathhouse with the typical hypocaust subflooring for heating.

§ 5.06. Bibliography.

Books

Abbott, Frank Frost and Allan Chester Johnson, *Municipal Administration in the Roman Empire* (1926).
Abies, Richard Phillip, *Alfred the Great: War, Kingship, and Culture in Anglo-Saxon England* (1998).
Appleby, John C., *Government, Religion, and Society in Northern England, 1000-1700* (1997).
Aslam, Jeremy, *Anglo-Saxon Towns in Southern England* (1984).
Barrell, Harry Ferdinand, *An Outline of Anglo-Saxon Law* (1999).
Birley, Eric, *Roman Britain and the Roman Army* (1953).
Blair, Peter Hunter, *An Introduction to Anglo-Saxon England* (1977).
Blair, Peter Hunter, *Roman Britain and Early England: 55 B.C. - A.D. 871* (1963).
Blair, W. John, *The Anglo-Saxon Age: a Very Short Introduction* (2000).
Bonser, W., *Anglo-Saxon and Celtic Bibliography (450-1087)* (1957).
Bowen, H.C. and P. J. Fowler, *Early Land Allotment in the British Isles* (1978).
Bradley, Richard, *The Prehistoric Settlement of Britain* (1978).
Bradley, Richard, *The Social Foundations of Prehistoric Britain* (1984).

Brower, Adrienne, *Over Countless Waves upon England's Shore: a Look at the Legal Progress from Britain's First Peoples to the Norman Conquest, and Why Anglo-Saxon Law Is the True Root of England's Common Law* (1999).
Brown, Michelle, *Mercia, An Anglo-Saxon Kingdom in Europe* (2001).
Caesar, Julius, *De Bello Gallico* (Moses Hadas, trans., 1957).
Campbell, James, *The Anglo-Saxon State* (2000).
Chadwick, Nora K., *The Celts* (1970).
Charles-Edwards, T.M., *The Distinction between Land and Moveable Wealth in Anglo-Saxon England's Medieval Settlement* (1976).
Collingwood, R. G. and J. N. L. Myres, *Roman Britain and the English Settlements* (1937).
Collingwood, R.G. and R. P. Wright, *The Roman Inscriptions of Britain* (1965).
Corpus Inscriptionum Latinarum (Eugen Bormann, ed., 1888).
Cramp, Rosemary, ed., *Corpus of Anglo-Saxon Stone Sculpture in England* (1984).
Cunliffe, Barry W., *The Celtic World* (1979).
Cunliffe, Barry W., *Iron Age Communities in Britain* (1978).
Dark, Ken R. and Petra Dark, *The Landscape of Roman Britain* (1997).
Dark, Petra, *The Environment of Britain in the First Millennium AD* (2000).
Darvill, Timothy C., *Prehistoric Britain* (1987).
Darvill, Timothy C., *Prehistoric Britain from the Air: A Study of Space, Time and Society* (1996).
Denman, D.R., *Origins of Ownership: A Brief History of Land Ownership and Tenure in England from Earliest Times to the Modern Era* (1958).
Diamond, Jared M., *Collapse: How Societies Choose to Fail or Succeed* (2005).
Diamond, Jared M., *Guns, Germs, and Steel: The Fates of Human Societies* (1997).
Dio, Cassius, *Historia Romana*.
Dos Passos, John R., *The Anglo-Saxon Century and the Unification of the English-Speaking People* (1903).
Evans, John G., *The Environment of Early Man in the British Isles* (1975).
Evans, John G., *Land and Archaeology: Histories of Human Environment in the British Isles* (1999).
Fisher, D. J. V., *The Anglo-Saxon Age, c. 400-1042* (1973).
Fleming, Andrew, *The Dartmoor Reaves: Investigating Prehistoric Land Divisions* (1988).
Fletcher, Richard A., *Bloodfeud: Murder and Revenge in Anglo-Saxon England* (2003).
Forde-Johnston, L., *Prehistoric Britain and Ireland* (1976).
Fowler, P.J., *The Farming of Prehistoric Britain* (1981).
Frantzen, Allen J., *Anglo-Saxonism and the Construction of Social Identity* (1997).
Frere, Sheppard Sunderland, *Britannia* (3d ed. 1987).
Harding, D.W., *The Iron Age In Lowland Britain* (1974).
Haselgrove, Colin, *Reconstructing Iron Age Societies: New Approaches to the British Iron Age* (1997).
Haverfield, F., *The Romanization of Roman Britain* (1912).
Hawke-Smith, C.F., *Man-Land Relations in Prehistoric Britain* (1979).
Hayashi, Hiroshi, *Essays in Anglo-Saxon Law* (1989).
Heywood, Samuel, *A Dissertation upon the Distinctions in Society, and Ranks of the People, under the Anglo-Saxon Governments* (1818).
Hill, Paul, *The Road to Hastings: The Politics of Power in Anglo-Saxon England* (2005).
Hill, S. and S. Ireland, *Roman Britain* (1996).
Hines, John, ed., *The Anglo-Saxons From the Migration Period to the Eighth Century: an Ethnographic Perspective* (1997).
Hingley, Richard, *Rural Settlement in Roman Britain* (1989).

Hooke, Delia, *Anglo-Saxon Settlements* (1988).
Hooke, Delia, *The Landscape of Anglo-Saxon England* (1998).
Inscriptiones Latinae Selectae, (Hermann Dessau, ed., 1962).
Jackson, Kenneth Hurlstone, *Language and History in Early Britain* (1953).
John, Eric, *Land Tenure in Early England, a Discussion of Some Problems* (1960).
Jones, A.H.M., *The Later Roman Empire A.D. 284-602: A Social, Economic and Administrative Survey* (2d ed. 1973).
Juvenal, *Satire* (Rolfe Humphries, trans., 1958).
Kelly, S. E., ed., *Charters of Shaftesbury Abbey* (1996).
Kerr, Mary, *Anglo-Saxon Architecture* (1983).
Kynell, Kurt von S., *Saxon and Medieval Antecedents of the English Common Law* (2000).
Laing, Lloyd Robert, *Anglo-Saxon England* (1979).
Laing, Lloyd and Jennifer Laing, *The Origins of Britain* (1980).
Lapidge, Michael, ed., *The Blackwell Encyclopedia of Anglo-Saxon England* (1999).
Lees, Clare A. and Gillian R. Overing, eds., *A Place to Believe In: Locating Medieval Landscapes* (2006).
Liversidge, Joan, *Britain in the Roman Empire* (1968).
Longworth, I. H., *Prehistoric Britain* (1985).
Loyn, H. R., *Anglo-Saxon England and the Norman Conquest* (1991).
Loyn, H. R., *The Governance of Anglo-Saxon England, 500-1087* (1984).
Loyn, H. R., *The Vikings in Britain* (1977).
Malone, Caroline, *Neolithic Britain and Ireland* (2001).
Mann, Charles C., *1491 : New Revelations of the Americas Before Columbus* (2005).
Megaw, J. V. S. and D. A. Simpson, *Introduction to British Prehistory* (1979).
Michelet, Fabienne L., *Creation, Migration, and Conquest: Imaginary Geography and Sense of Space in Old English Literature* (2006).
Millett, Martin, *The Romanization of Britain: An Essay in Archaeological Interpretation* (1990).
Norton-Taylor, Duncan, *The Celts* (1974).
Oliver, Lisa, *The Beginnings of English Law* (2002).
Pearson, Michael Parker, *Bronze Age Britain* (2005).
Peddie, John, *Invasion: The Roman Conquest of Britain* (1987).
Pipes, Richard, *Property and Freedom* (1999).
Rankin, H. D., *Celts and the Classical World* (1987).
Reed, M., ed., *"Anglo-Saxon Charter Boundaries", Discovering Past Landscapes* (1984).
Reece, R., *My Roman Britain* (1988).
Reynolds, Peter G., *Ancient Farming* (1987).
Riley, D. N., *Early Landscape from the Air* (1980).
Roberts, Brian K., *Rural Settlement in Britain* (1977).
Rumble, Alexander, ed., *Writing and Texts in Anglo-Saxon England* (2006).
Salway, Peter, *Roman Britain* (1981).
Scott, Samuel P., ed., *Corpus Juris Civilis: The Civil Law* (1973).
Scullard, H. H., *Roman Britain: Outpost of the Empire* (1978).
Seebohm, Frederic, *Tribal Custom in Anglo-Saxon Law; Being an Essay Supplemental To: (1) the English Village Community, (2) the Tribal System in Wales* (1972).
Siculus, Diodorus, *Bibliotheca Historica.*
Simon, Edith, *The Anglo-Saxon Manner: the English Contribution to Civilization* (1972).
Stenton, F. M., *Anglo-Saxon England* (1971).
Stenton, F. M., *The Latin Charters of the Anglo-Saxon Period* (1955).
Szarmach, Paul E., ed., *Sources of Anglo-Saxon Culture* (1986).

Tacitus, Cornelius, *The Life of Julius Agricola*
Tapp, Sidney Calhoun, *The Story of Anglo-Saxon Institutions; or, the Development of Constitutional Government* (1904).
Todd, Malcolm, *Roman Britain* (1981).
Van Warmelo, Paul, *An Introduction to the Principles of Roman Civil Law* (1976).
Wacher, John, *Roman Britain* (1978).
Walsh, William Francis, *A History of Anglo-American Law* (1950).
Watson, Alan, *The Law of the Ancient Romans* (1970).
Watson, G. R., *The Roman Soldier* (1969).
Webster, Graham, *The Roman Invasion of Britain* (1980).
Welch, Martin G., *Discovering Anglo-Saxon England* (1992).
Whitelock, Dorothy, *History, Law and Literature in 10th-11th Century England* (1981).
Winbolt, S. E., *Britain B.C.* (1943).

Chapters in Books

Bowen, Collin, "Pattern and Interpretation: A View of the Wessex Landscape from Neolithic to Roman Times," in P. J. Fowler, ed., *Recent Work in Rural Archaeology* (1975).
Bowen, Susan, "Celtic Fields and Ranch Boundaries in Wessex," in John G. Evans and Susan Limbrey, eds., *The Effect of Man on the Landscape: The Lowland Zone* (Council for British Archaeology Research Report No. 21, 1978).
Branigan, R., "North East England in the First Century," in P. R. Wilson, et al., eds., *Settlement and Society in the Roman North* (1984).
Hadman, John, "Aisled Buildings in Roman Britain," in Malcolm Todd, ed., *Studies in the Romano-British Villa* (1978).
Hayes, P., "New Approaches to Ancient Fields," in Graeme Barker, ed., *Prehistoric Communities in Northern England* (1981).
Rivet, A. L. F., "Social and Economic Aspects," in A. L. F. Rivet, ed., *The Roman Villa in Britain* (1969).
Scott, E., "Romano-British Villas and the Social Construction of Space," in R. Samson, ed., *The Social Archaeology of Houses* (1990).
Smith, J. T., "Villas as a Key to Social Structure," in Malcolm Todd, ed., *Studies in the Romano-British Villa* (1978).
Wormald Patrick, "Charters, Law and the Settlement of Disputes in Anglo-Saxon England," in Wendy Davies and Paul Fouracre. eds., *The Settlement of Disputes in Early Medieval Europe* (1986).

Articles

Bosselman, Fred P., "Limitations Inherent in the Tide to Wetlands at Common Law," 15 *Stan. Envtl. L. J.* 247 (June 1996).
Bowden, M. and D. McOmish, "The Required Barrier," 4 *Scottish Archaeological Rev.* 76 (1987).
Byrnes, William H., "Ancient Roman Munificence: The Development of the Practice and Law of Charity," 57 *Rutgers L. Rev.* 1043 (Spring 2005).
Coquillette, Daniel R., "The Lessons of Anglo-Saxon Justice," 2 *Green Bag* 251 (Spring 1999).
Hingley, Richard, "Boundaries Surrounding Iron Age and Romano-British Settlements," 7 *Scottish Archaeological Rev.* 96 (1990).
Johnston, Robert, "Pattern Without a Plan: Rethinking the Bronze Age Coaxial Field Systems on Dartmoor, South-West England," 24 *Oxford J. Archaeology* 1 (2005).

Kroger, John. R., "The Philosophical Foundations of Roman Law: Aristotle, the Stoics, and Roman Theories of Natural Law," 2004 *Wis. L. Rev.* 905.

Lefroy, A. H. F., "The Anglo-Saxon Period of English Law," 26 *Yale L.J.* 291 (Feb. 1917).

Lefroy, A. H. F., "The Anglo-Saxon Period of English Law," 26 *Yale L.J.* 388 (Mar. 1917).

Sanchez, Valerie A., "Towards a History of ADR: The Dispute Processing Continuum in Anglo-Saxon England and Today, "11 *Ohio St. J. on Disp. Resol.* 1 (1996).

Senn, Mark A., "Reflections on Some Forgotten Terms of Land Measurement," 16 *Probate and Property* 8 (Mar./Apr. 2002).

Smith, Henry E., "Exclusion Versus Governance: Two Strategies for Delineating Property Rights," 31 *J. Legal Stud.* 453 (June, 2002).

Spratt, D. A., "Recent British Research on Prehistoric Territorial Boundaries," 5 *J. World Prehistory* 439 (1991).

Stevens, C. E., "Possible Conflict of Laws in Roman Britain," 37 *J. Roman Stud.* 132 (1947).

Straumann, Benjamin, "Is Modern Liberty Ancient? Roman Remedies and Natural Rights in Hugo Grotius's Early Works on Natural Law," 27 *Law and Hist. Rev.* 55 (Spring, 2009).

Thomas, David A., "Anglo-American Land Law: Diverging Developments from a Shared History Part I: The Shared History, " 34 *Real Prop., Prob. and Trust J.* 143 (Spring, 1999).

Thomas, David A., "The Disappearance of Roman Law from Dark Age Britain," 1984 *B.Y.U. L. Rev.* 563.

Thomas, David A., "Why the Public Plundering of Private Property Rights Is Still a Very Bad Idea," 41 *Real Prop., Prob. and Tr. J.* 25 (Spring, 2006).

Thomas, R., "Land, Kinship, Relations, and the Rise of Enclosed Settlement in First Millennium B.C. Britain," 16 *Oxford J. Archaeology* 211 (1997).

Turner, Eric G., "Roman Writing Tablet from Somerset," 46 *J. Roman Stud.* 115 (1956).

Zaher, Claudia, "When a Woman's Marital Status Determined Her Legal Status: A Research Guide on the Common Law Doctrine of Coverture," 94 *Law Libr. J.* 459 (Summer, 2002).

Chapter 6

Land Law in Anglo-Saxon England[275]

SYNOPSIS

[275] The content of this chapter was originally written by the author, and some content was drawn or reprinted from Vol. 1 of Thompson on Real Property.

Chapter 6. Land Law in Anglo-Saxon England

§ 6.01. Introduction to the Chapter.

When William the Conqueror felt secure in his sovereignty over Anglo-Saxon England, he issued a decree assuring the English people that their English property rights remained essentially intact. "This also I command and will, that all shall have and hold the law of King Edward in respect of their lands and all their possessions, with the addition of those decrees I have ordained for the welfare of the English people."[276]

During the subsequent reigns of Norman and Angevin monarchs, many profound changes in the property law of England took place, but it was all on a foundation of the property rights developed during the period of Anglo-Saxon hegemony in England from the 5th to the 11th centuries, A.D. It is therefore instructive to consider how Anglo-Saxon property law developed and what factors in society influenced the emphasis of certain rights over others. To some extent these priorities remain imbedded in the contemporary Anglo-American common law of property.

One function of this chapter is to trace, as fully as possible, the transformation of Anglo-Saxon property rights from the purely Germanic legal customs of the invasion period to the rather complex arrangements that formed the foundation of the common law of property. To this end, the chapter describes the available information about the continental origins and legal customs of the Anglo-Saxons, the changes in their social organization that occurred following their invasion and settlement of large parts of Britain, the rise of law and legal institutions in England during six centuries of Anglo-Saxon dominance, the impact of Viking invasions and settlement, and the emergence of early forms of feudalism in late Anglo-Saxon times.

§ 6.02. Origins of the Anglo-Saxons.

§ 6.02(a). The Traditional Origins Reported by Bede.

Much uncertainty still prevails about the identities and origins of the earliest peoples to inhabit the areas now known as Denmark and north

---

[276] "The Laws of William the Conqueror", in *English Historical Documents* 399-400 (David C. Douglas, ed., 1953). The King Edward referred to was the so-called "Confessor", acknowledged by William as the last legitimate Anglo-Saxon king of England.

Germany and that were the homelands of those who invaded Britain in the 5th century, A.D..[277] Scholars generally believed that Germanic peoples moved southward from Scandinavia into central Europe and in time displaced Celtic tribes that had previously migrated into what is now middle and western Germany. By the time the various Germanic peoples had largely subdued or displaced the continental Celts in the 3rd century, B.C., they were arranged in three main tribal groups: (1) the northern tribes, who eventually became the Norse, Danes and Swedes; (2) the eastern tribes, who occupied lands between the Oder and Vistula rivers and would become known as Goths, Vandals, Burgundians and Lombards; and (3) the western tribes, who were found in areas now known as the Jutland peninsula in modern Denmark, Schleswig-Holstein in north Germany, north central Germany and the Rhine valley. The Germanic invaders of Britain would have been members of the western group of tribes.

Some of the western tribes came into armed conflict with Roman forces working their way along the Rhine River in the late 2nd century, B.C., and Roman influence along the left, or west, bank of the Rhine grew quickly after Romans pacified Gaul about 51, B.C. Still, many of the western tribes had little or no contact with the Romans throughout the period of Roman rule. The tribes that invaded Britain are among those tribes that had little or no Roman influence in their way of life.

The writings of the English monk/historian Bede in the early 8th century, A.D., provided the traditional identification of Britain's invaders as Angles, Saxons and Jutes. [278] Cloistered in a north English monastery, and dependent on visiting wayfarers for much information about ancient and distant occurrences, Bede penned an account reflecting the beliefs that prevailed at his time. He reported that the Anglo-Saxons actually consisted of three principal tribes, the Jutes from the Jutland[279] peninsula (modern

---

[277] For a summary of the various theories, *see* David A. Thomas, "Anglo-Saxon Antecedents of the Common Law, 1985 *B.Y.U. L. Rev.* 453, 455-456.

[278] Bede, *Historia Ecclesiastica Gentis Anglorum* 15.

[279] Some scholars maintain that the names for the tribe of Jutes and for the Jutland peninsula are of different origin. D.J.V. Fisher, *The Anglo-Saxon Age c. 400-1042* 25-27 (1973).

Denmark and north Germany), the Angles from the area of modern Schleswig-Holstein north of Hamburg, Germany, and the Saxons from the area south of the Angles. More modern archaeological research injected doubt into this account, because researchers found substantial evidence of other Germanic tribes in British sites of the invasion era, notably of the Frisians and Franks, and the Jutes remained a mysterious people, not subject to positive identification either in England or on the continent.

Currently, Bede's description has regained credibility, although the distinctions between the invading tribes are considered more blurred:

> The most plausible current reconciliation of all the evidence suggests that: (1) the Jutes, though obscure, were a distinct tribe inhabiting part of the Jutland peninsula; (2) by the fifth century, A.D., the populous and mobile north German tribes may have undergone considerable intermixing, so that artifacts of other tribes, such as Frisians and Franks, would be found among those of the Anglo-Saxons; (3) Angles, Saxons, and Jutes embarking for Britain would have moved down the Frisian coastline, perhaps with lengthy periods of settlement among both the Frisians and Franks, and would have brought with them objects that archaeologists would later identify as Frisian and Frankish; (4) in any event, some Frisians and Franks probably settled in Britain along with the other tribes.[280]

---

[280] David A. Thomas, "Anglo-Saxon Antecedents of the Common Law," 1985 *B.Y.U. L. Rev.* 453-457. *See* James Campbell, "The Lost Centuries: 400-600," in *The Anglo-Saxons* 30-31 (James Campbell, ed., 1982); D.P. Kirby, *The Making of Early England* 27-28 (1967); F.M. Stenton, *Anglo-Saxon England* 5-8, 56 (1943). The most authoritative statement of the modern accuracy and equivalencies of Bede's descriptions of Anglo-Saxon continental origins is by J.N.L. Myres:

> [Bede] goes on to locate the continental Saxons in the lands known in his day as those still inhabited by the Old Saxons, the Angles in a region known to him as Angulus which had been left empty by their migration, and the Jutes in a less well defined area situated somewhere beyond the Angles. . . .
>
> In deriving the Saxons from the districts occupied in his time by the Old Saxons, Bede is certainly pointing to the coastlands between the Elbe and the Weser valleys. . . .By Angulus, the

Probably the most telling evidence in support of this traditional thesis is the strong stylistic correlations between artifacts, such as brooches and pottery, found in the invaders' continental homelands and in their first areas of settlement in Britain.[281]

§ 6.02(b). Ancient Literary References to the Anglo-Saxon Tribes.

The first ancient writer to mention the Germanic tribes was Pytheas of Massilia (or Marseilles), who visited Britain and the coast of the North Sea in the 3rd or 4th century, B.C.[282] During the Gallic wars in the 1st century B.C., Julius Caesar had contact with the Germans and provided some written description.[283] Written in the 2nd century A.D., Claudius Ptolemy's *Geography* mentions Angles and Frisians briefly, and provides some description of the Saxons.[284] Procopius, a Byzantine historian writing in the 6th century, B.C., also briefly refers to the Frisians.[285] The fullest

---

> region that lay between the Saxons and the Jutes, Bede certainly meant Schleswig, where the name is still found on modern maps as the district of Angeln. There has been much difference of opinion over the location of Bede's Jutes. But if, as he implies, they lay somewhere beyond the Angles, he must have thought of them either to the north of Schleswig, in Jutland, or to the east in modern Holstein, where again there is a suggestive district name, Eutin, which may indicate the home of some part of the tribe at one time.

J.N.L. Myres, *The English Settlements* 46-47 (1986).

[281] J.N.L. Myres, *The English Settlements* 56-73 (1986).

[282] Pytheas was a navigator and also the author of a geography treatise, which is now lost. He is believed to have flourished sometime before 285, B.C. References to his work appear in the writings of the Greek geographer and traveler Strabo, who wrote during the last half of the first century, B.C. *See* 8 *The Geography of Strabo* 453 (Loeb ed. 1939) (H. Jones, trans.) (translator's description); 1 *id.* at 1.4.2-.3, 2.4.1-.2, 2.5.8 (Loeb ed. 1939); 2 *id.* at 4.2.1, 4.5.4 (Loeb ed. 1949).

[283] Julius Caesar, *DeBello Gallico* 4.1-.3; 6.21-.24 (M. Hadas trans. 1957).

[284] Claudius Ptolemy, *Geography* II .xi.7.

[285] Procopius, *The Gothic War* 4.20.7.

account of Germanic culture as it existed in the 1st century, A.D., is found in the writings of the Roman Cornelius Tacitus.[286]

Tacitus mentions only one of the invading peoples, the Angles, which he describes as one of seven small tribes who worshiped the goddess Nertha at an island sanctuary near their North Sea or Baltic Sea coastline.[287] Probably this obscure tribe is therefore included by Tacitus in the general descriptions he wrote of Germanic customs and culture. Because Tacitus was writing nearly four centuries before the invasions of Britain took place, it is possible that such a small tribe could have grown more prominent and powerful in the ensuing centuries.

§ 6.03. Germanic Legal Customs Relating to Property.

§ 6.03(a). Observations by Ancient Writers.

The only written descriptions of Germanic social and legal customs from ancient times are from Julius Caesar in the 1st century, B.C., Tacitus in the 1st century, A.D., and from some collections of Germanic laws dating from about five centuries or more later. The half millennium in between is truly the dark age of Germanic law.

In connection with his military campaigns in western Europe during the middle of the 1st century, B.C., Julius Caesar recorded a few observations about the Germanic tribes he encountered, including comments on their customs regarding property. According to his account, the Germanic people appeared to rely mostly on flocks and herds as their form of wealth. They held their flocks and herds privately, while holding their land in communal ownership. Differences in wealth between individual families were not large, and the practice of annually reallocating parcels of land to different

---

[286] Cornelius Tacitus, *The Agricola and Germany of Tacitus* (A. Church and W. Brodribb, trans., 1885).

[287] *Id.* at ch. 40.

kindreds or clans inhibited growth of those distinctions.[288]

By the time Tacitus wrote in the late 1st century, A.D., some changes in Germanic land customs had occurred, or else the particular tribes he described followed different customs.[289] He commented thus on landholding:

> Land proportioned to the number of inhabitants is occupied by the whole community in turn, and afterwards divided among them according to rank. A wide expanse of plains makes the partition easy. They till fresh fields every year, and they have still more land than enough; with the richness and extent of their soil, they do not laboriously exert themselves in planting orchards, inclosing meadows, and watering gardens.[290]

According to Tacitus, therefore, social standing influenced the amounts and locations of land distributions, and leaders made those allocations to individual persons rather than to kindred groups. Wealth disparities thus widened as certain persons were able to accumulate wealth faster. One writer believes that this change occurred after the Germanic tribes had been exposed to Roman goods and the Roman monetary system, which stimulated their desire for private property; the land allocation system then changed to favor private holdings and production.[291] Tacitus also noted an abundance of arable land, an observation at odds with modern theories that Germanic migrations were prompted, at least in part, by population pressures.

---

288 Julius Caesar, *De Bello Gallico* 6.22 (M. Hadas, trans., 1957).

289 Tacitus is the single best source of information on ancient Germanic social and legal customs, but some consider his credibility compromised by his manifest anti-Roman and pro-German moralizing. Also, it is unlikely that he ever directly observed Germanic people in their native habitat. *See* Cornelius Tacitus, *De Origine et Situ Germanorum* xix (J. Anderson, ed., 1938) (editor's introduction).

290 Cornelius Tacitus, *The Agricola and Germany of Tacitus* ch. 26 (Alfred J. Church and William J. Brodribb, trans., 1885).

291 E.A. Thompson, *The Early Germans* 7 (1965).

Within this regime of land regulation, it does not appear that any system of estates in land was recognized. Succession in ownership of personal property was also the subject of Germanic legal custom, according to Tacitus:

> [E]very man's own children are his heirs and successors, and there are no wills. Should there be no issue, the next in succession to the property are his brothers and his uncles on either side. The more relatives he has, the more numerous his connections, the more honoured is his old age; nor are there any advantages in childlessness.[292]

The Germanic social characteristics mentioned by Tacitus are relevant in a general way to the eventual recognition of private property rights and may be summarized as follows:

(a) tribal organization based on kinship relationships;

(b) governance by both kings (or perhaps chieftains) and councils; chiefs elected by councils and responsible for administering law in the settlements;

(c) blood feuds and composition by payments of fines;

(d) requirements that fines or penalties be paid to the king as well as to the victim's family;

(e) heavy powers of family regulation held by the husband;

(f) laws or legal customs governing succession in ownership of personal property; and

(g) regulated land holding, although probably no system of estates in land.

§ 6.03(b). Germanic Property Rights in the "Barbarian Laws."

Aside from the observations recorded by ancient observers of Germanic peoples, the only other literary evidence on how Germanic peoples

---

[292] Cornelius Tacitus, *The Agricola and Germany of Tacitus* ch. 20 (Alfred J. Church and William J. Brodribb, trans., 1885).

perceived property rights is in the so-called "Barbarian Laws ." These arose as the Roman Empire disintegrated and surrendered its western provinces to Germanic invaders. First, Roman officers under Theodosious gathered an official collection of imperial statutes, the Theodosian Code, which the emperor Valentinian III then issued in 438, A.D. This code seems to have influenced various continental Germanic rulers who issued their own law codes in the decades that followed.

These collections of laws exhibit varying degrees of influence from Roman and Christian sources, and some were intended to apply different legal rules to Germanic and Roman people living in the same area. Collectively these codes are known as the laws of the barbarians, or *Leges Barbarorum*. The earliest of these laws, which are contemporary with the Anglo-Saxon invasions and settlement of Britain, contain law codes from several large Germanic tribes, including the Visigoths, Franks, Burgundians, Bavarians, Lombards, and the continental Angles and Saxons of the later Carolingian age.

The Visigothic laws, and more particularly the Code of Euric, probably directly or indirectly influenced most Germanic law codes thereafter. The Code of Euric, from ca. 476, A.D., shows some Roman influence. The Visigothic king Alaric promulgated the *Lex Romana Visigothorum* in 506, A.D., to govern Romans living in Visigothic territories. This collection is also known as the *Breviarium Alaricianum* (Breviary of Alaric). Euric's successors in 654, A.D., issued the *Leges Visigothorum,* a collection of laws applying to both Gothic and Hispano-Roman subjects. This collection replaced the *Lex Romana Visigothorum.*

Euric's code seems to have been the immediate source for the early codes of both the Salian Franks[293] and the Burgundians.[294] The Bavarian[295]

---

[293] The code of the Salian Franks, or Lex Salica, is attributed to Clovis, 481-511, A.D.

[294] The Burgundian code was compiled between 483, A.D. and 532, A.D. The Lex Romana Burgundionum was issued ca 500, A.D., for application to Roman citizens living in the Burgundian kingdom.

[295] The *Lex Baiuvariorum* is dated from about 744-748, A.D.

and Lombard[296] codes also show Visigothic influence. Another early Frankish code, the *Lex Ribuaria*,[297] was based on the Salian Code , and the Salian Code in turn influenced the codes of the continental Angles and Saxons of the Carolingian age.

Thus the best known of these early Germanic codes—indeed the oldest Germanic code that is completely preserved—is the code of the Salian Franks, or the *Lex Salica*. As a Germanic code that was in its origins contemporary with the Anglo-Saxon invasions, and one that is fairly free of Roman influence, it might be expected to reveal some information about Germanic customs relating to property rights.

In fact, the *Lex Salica* and other early Germanic codes do not fulfill this expectation. Consisting of both individual "statutes" and precedential judicial sentences (*Weisthuemer*), these codes do not refer to most customs of daily living, such as occupancy of land, personal property, commercial dealings, inheritance, family relationships, and class privileges. Instead, the *Lex Salica* has been accurately described as "primarily a penal law . . . concerned with the redress of crimes (murder, theft, mutilation, exploitation of women) by monetary means."[298] The only references to land law in the *Lex Salica* are provisions requiring money payment for damage to agricultural fields,[299] blocking the way of another,[300] and improper fencing and enclosing.[301] From such provisions one may infer that real property was important and some individual possessory rights were recognized and protected, but any further enlightenment is not available in the documentary sources relating to the Anglo-Saxons or other contemporary Germanic tribes.

---

[296] The *Leges Langobardorum* were promulgated between 643 and 755, A.D.

[297] The *Lex Ribuaria* is believed to have been promulgated after 596, A.D., for the Ribuarian or western Franks.

[298] *Laws of the Alamans and Bavarians* 19 (Theodore John Rivers trans. 1977).

[299] *Lex Salica* tit. 9.

[300] *Id.* tit. 31.

[301] *Id.* tit. 34.

§ 6.04. Anglo-Saxon Landholding Practices Arising from the Invasion and Settlement of Britain.

Even if it were possible to identify the landholding practices customary among the Angles, Saxons, Jutes, Frisians and Franks who invaded Britain in the 5th century, A.D., perhaps that would not provide much insight into the landholding practices that emerged from the period of invasion and settlement. Some evidence suggests that the circumstances of invasion and settlement may have been so unprecedented and unique as to upset the traditional Germanic loyalties and relationships prevailing up to that time. This evidence, however, is so tenuous that any statements about property practices of the early Anglo-Saxon settlers must remain highly speculative. Despite that, if such evidence is used to construct even a general outline of invasion and early settlement history, it is possible to raise plausible theories about how property practices changed as Britain became Angle-land, or England.

§ 6.04(a). Reorganization of Tribal Structure for Invasion and Conquest.

§ 6.04(a)(1). Pre-Invasion Social Structure.

In this invasion period of the 5th and 6th centuries, A.D., an era of almost universal illiteracy among the Anglo-Saxons, it is impossible to know precise details about their social organization in their continental homelands, or how they reorganized for invasion. However, it is reasonable to assume that the pre-invasion Germanic tribes and sub-tribal groups were divided essentially along kinship lines and that the warrior class placed greatest value on subordination and loyalty to the leader and on valor in battle. If land arrangements were still being conducted in the 5th century as Tacitus had described them in the 1st century, A.D., then to be the successful leader of such a kinship group was also a sure means to rank and material wealth. According to Tacitus, Germanic peoples divided the land among the inhabitants according to rank.

§ 6.04(a)(2). Formation of New War Bands for Invasion and Settlement.

If, as evidence suggests, land was becoming crowded under pressures of growing population and approaching invaders from the east, changes in social organization were inevitable. The opportunity presented by the vulnerability of Britain to seaborne raids, which was surely communicated back across the channel to the crowds on the Frisian shores, was for new leaders to rise up, forsaking old loyalties and forging new ones. Ambition and adventurism undoubtedly played their parts as both established and emerging leaders formed war bands and struck out in their boats.[302]

Leaders would have recruited war bands not only for the seaborne invasions, but for new conquests by those invaders already settled. Even the earliest Germanic settlers, the mercenaries hired to protect the Romano-British centers, were possibly outcasts and fugitives, eligible and willing to form new bands and loyalties.[303]

The warbands, if successful, would have formed new settlements or taken over old ones. At first, perhaps unrelated by blood to comrades and enjoying the fruits of conquest, each surviving and successful warrior would have assumed a measure of independence as he turned from fighting to farming. Only later, as family relationships re-formed and local political authority developed, would stratification of land rights emerge and become pronounced.[304]

This absence of central authority during the period of invasion and conquest was a significant factor in the apparent absence of stratification in early Anglo-Saxon land rights. While kingship was probably not

---

[302] H.P.R. Finberg, *The Formation of England 550-1042* 18 (1974).

[303] J.N.L. Myres, *The English Settlements* 109 (1986).

[304] Stratification in this context means differentiation in land rights, with some rights being more extensive than others.

unknown to the continental Angles, Saxons, and Jutes,[305] apparently it did not play a role in the settlement of Britain. Apparently the earliest phases of the conquest were carried out by war bands that functioned independently under their own leaders. When successful war bands eventually combined, and migration and conquest in the 5th and 6th centuries, A.D., compelled resort to stronger central rule, kingship then arose. An early example of such a king was the West Saxon Cerdic, who took the title of king several years after beginning the conquest of land later known as Wessex.[306]

§ 6.04(b). How the Anglo-Saxons Organized for and Conducted the Invasion and Settlement of Britain.

Probably not later than the 3rd century, A.D., Saxons began a general southwestward movement, replacing or subduing the Chauci and crowding the Frisians along the North Sea coastline between the Elbe and Rhine estuaries. This unstable situation may have "stimulated the more adventurous elements in all these peoples to seek fame and fortune through plunder, piracy, and even perhaps through settlement overseas."[307]

In response, Roman imperial authority established a series of major naval stations on both sides of the English Channel, the bases on Britain's eastern and southern coasts being known as the forts of the "Saxon Shore."[308] One commander of the British naval force, a German from the

---

305 Tacitus, writing in the 1st century, A.D., remarked that the Germanic tribes sometimes elected kings in times of war. Anglo-Saxon literature gives evidence that kingship was known at an early time, through tales of Offa, a 4th-century king of continental Angles, Widsith lines 35-44, and of Beowulf, a Swedish prince who dealt with kings of other peoples. *Beowulf* lines 11-21.

306 *The Anglo-Saxon Chronicle* (E) 15 annal 495.

307 J.N.L. Myres, *The English Settlements* 53 (1986).

308 "[A]lready in the late third century Saxon pirates had become such a menace to the Channel and North Sea coasts that the Romans built a series of forts from the Wash to the Isle of Wight, which were known as the forts of the Saxon Shore." Dorothy Whitelock, *The Beginnings of English Society* 13 (1974). The forts were

Rhine estuary known as Carausius, himself resorted to piracy late in the 3rd century, and established a short-lived government of his own. In 367, A.D., with this disruption to its protective organization, Britain nearly fell to a combined assault of Picts, Scots, and Saxons.

As Roman authority in Britain weakened, Picts and Scots continued attacks from the north and west, and seaborne Germanic pirates, usually referred to as Saxons, came plundering from the south and east. In response, British leaders apparently hired Germanic mercenaries, and abundant archaeological evidence reveals that numerous Saxon settlements arose in southern and eastern Britain, often in areas near the Saxon shore forts. A plausible but unverifiable version of events during the mid-5th century, A.D., depicts discontented mercenaries turning on their British masters, and then shifting from rebellion to conquest. The cross-channel raiders, meanwhile, turned to invasion and settlement. The boat in Illustration 18 is an actual vessel used by Germanic families in making the risky North Sea crossing during the 4th century, A.D.

In the first stage of the Anglo-Saxon conquest, from roughly 450 to 500, A.D., the British resisted the invaders but steadily lost ground near the east coast river estuaries, where no natural obstacles impeded the barbarian thrusts. By 500, A.D., the Anglo-Saxons occupied most of the coastal areas of southeast and eastern England and far inland up some rivers, territory that encompassed, in more modern geographical designations, Kent, Sussex, southern Hampshire, Essex, East Anglia, Lindsey, the East Riding of Yorkshire, and thence to the Cambridgeshire fens.[309]

If one were to accept as generally accurate the accounts of the Anglo-Saxon Chronicle, which for this period relies only on very old traditions, and were to make allowance for much approximation in the dates, the sequence of invasion may be sketched in outline form as follows:

---

mostly built between 270 and 285, A.D.

[309] *See*, e.g., James Campbell, "The First Christian Kings," in *The Anglo-Saxons* 52 (James Campbell, ed., 1982); H. Munro Chadwick, *The Origins of the English Nation* 9-10 (1924).

Illustration 18. The Nydam boat was built in about 320, B.C., and is the oldest preserved Germanic deep-sea rowing boot. Seventy-five feet in length and carrying up to 45 persons, this is the type of vessel in which Germanic families headed for Britain would have made the North Sea crossing.

§ 6.04(b)(1). The Earliest Stages of the Anglo-Saxon Conquest.[310]

§ 6.04(b)(1)(A). Kent.

It appears that Kent[311] was the first area to come under Germanic domination, under the leadership of an early mercenary settler and warrior named Hengist. Hengist fought the Britons in 455, A.D., and again together with his son Aesc (or Oisc) in 457, A.D., after which the British fled Kent

[310] *See generally*, *The Origins of Anglo-Saxon Kingdoms* (Steven Bassett, ed., 1989); Martyn J. Whittock, *The Origins of England* 410-600 161-251 (1986).

[311] Kent, as a name, has its origin in the name of the Celtic tribe Cantiaci, conquered by the Romans in 43, A.D. Later Jutish conquerors called themselves Cantware. James Campbell, "The Lost Centuries: 400-600," in *The Anglo-Saxons* 38-39 (James Campbell, ed., 1982).

and retreated to London. Following battles in 465 and 473, A.D., Aesc became king in 488, A.D., and ruled Kent until 512, A.D.[312]

§ 6.04(b)(1)(B). Essex, Middlesex, and Surrey.

The early history of Essex (territory of the East Saxons) is locked in obscurity. The scant archaeological evidence reveals that Germanic settlement dates from early times, but no East Saxon king became important outside of Essex. Sometimes included in Essex were London and a separate area called Middlesex (territory of the Middle Saxons), although Middlesex, if not a separate kingdom, was probably autonomous for some time after the conquest. As an organized people, neither the folk of Middlesex nor of nearby Surrey (the "southern district") have an independent history.[313]

§ 6.04(b)(1)(C). Sussex.

Conquest of Sussex (the area of the South Saxons) began by seaborne invasion, rather than by rebellion of settled mercenaries. In 477, A.D., Aelle and his sons Cymen, Wlencing, and Cissa landed with three ships at a site identified as near Selsey Bill and drove the Britons into the Sussex Weald (an extensive forested tract). Aelle fought further battles in 485 and 491, A.D., and in the later conflict he and Cissa led forces that massacred all Britons gathered in the old Roman fort near Pevensey.[314] Bede identified Aelle as the first of the Anglo-Saxon *bretwaldas*, king not only of the south Saxons but of all people south of the River Humber.[315]

---

[312] F.M. Stenton, *Anglo-Saxon England* 16-17 (1943).

[313] *Id.* at 53.

[314] *The Anglo-Saxon Chronicle* (E) 13 annal 491.

[315] F.M. Stenton, *Anglo-Saxon England* 17-19 (1943).

§ 6.04(b)(1)(D). Wessex.

The area known as Wessex (land of the West Saxons) was invaded about 494, A.D., by Cerdic and his grandson Cynric with five ships. They apparently completed the conquest in six years.[316] Some portion of the conquered territory may have been left under the rule of Stuf and Wihtgar, possibly Jutish relatives of Cerdic, while Cerdic himself ruled a West Saxon kingdom located immediately south and west of the middle Thames. Cerdic came to be regarded as the founder of the West Saxon dynasty which eventually would rule all of England.[317]

§ 6.04(b)(1)(E). East Anglia, Mercia, and Northumbria.

In East Anglia (territory of the East Angles), fifth century Germanic settlements were located along the waterways and often close to Roman sites, suggesting peaceful immigration prior to the Saxon revolt. No kingdom arose in this area until well into the 6th century, A.D., when a new wave of invaders struck, possibly from the northern Jutland peninsula or Danish islands.

Evidence shows that the kingdom of Mercia (the land of the marches or border areas) arose during the same time, as people from East Anglia advanced inland. The southern part of Northumbria (the land north of the River Humber), known as the kingdom of Deira, was settled in the 5th century, A.D., probably by pre-revolt mercenaries, but Aelle, the earliest known king, has been dated later, to about 558, A.D. King Ida invaded and ruled in the northern part of Northumbria, eventually known as the kingdom of Bernicia, about the same time as Aelle ruled Deira.[318]

---

316 *The Anglo-Saxon Chronicle* (Parker) (genealogical preface).

317 F.M. Stenton, *Anglo-Saxon England* 19-27 (1943).

318 D.P. Kirby, *The Making of Early England* 21-23 (1967).

§ 6.04(b)(2). The Second Phase of the Anglo-Saxon Conquest.

§ 6.04(b)(2)(A). Wessex.

In a series of battles fought, according to the Anglo-Saxon Chronicle, in 552, 568, 571, 577, and 586, A.D., the Wiltshire Saxons and the Thames Valley Saxons united into the historic kingdom of Wessex.[319] Through the end of the 8th century, A.D., further expansion was sporadic, and British resistance at times very effective. The Saxons did not establish complete dominance until Egbert defeated the Britons of Cornwall in 838, A.D.[320]

§ 6.04(b)(2)(B). Northumbria.

In Northumbria, the separate Germanic kingdoms of Deira and Bernicia made painfully slow progress against powerful British rulers. The Germanic kingdoms were ultimately united under the Bernician King Aethelfrith about 593, A.D.[321] Despite subsequent dynastic struggles, the unified Germanic kingdom made major territorial gains through the seventh century, A.D. Then, as the kingdom met stiffer resistance from both the Picts and the neighboring Anglo-Saxon kingdoms, its territory stabilized during the middle of the 8th century, A.D.[322]

§ 6.04(b)(2)(C). Mercia.

The kingdom of Mercia originated in the thickly settled midland shires, with the Trent valley settlers overcoming other Germanic pioneers. This kingdom absorbed the lands known as Middle Anglia and the small kingdom of the Hwicce, and appeared in the middle of the 7th century as

---

[319] D.J.V. Fisher, *The Anglo-Saxon Age* c. 400-1042 32-35 (1973).

[320] *The Anglo-Saxon Chronicle* (E) 61 annal 835).

[321] *Id.* at 21 annal 593.

[322] D.J.V. Fisher, *The Anglo-Saxon Age* c. 400-1042 41-43 (1973).

a powerful force among the Anglo-Saxon kingdoms.[323]

§ 6.04(b)(2)(D). The Heptarchy.

The kingdoms of East Anglia, Essex, Kent, and Sussex were not able to extend their territories during this second phase of hostilities, because of the activities of the more powerful neighboring kingdoms, but they did consolidate their conquests.[324] All seven of the kingdoms discussed in this section have been artificially grouped together by some historians and called the Heptarchy.[325] The kingdoms of the Heptarchy never acted in concert, but were dominated in turn by Northumbria, Mercia, and Wessex. The process of absorption and amalgamation which produced these seven kingdoms continued throughout the period of the Heptarchy, and was halted only by the Viking invasions of the 9th century.[326]

§ 6.04(c). Development of Early Anglo-Saxon Landholding Practices After Invasion and Settlement.

§ 6.04(c)(1). Romano-British Influence on Early Anglo-Saxon Landholding Practices.

While central authority among the Anglo-Saxons was coalescing, the new settlers probably occupied their territories under a wide variety of property arrangements. A simplistic traditional perception of Anglo-Saxon settlers depicted land being sectioned off to individual families, eventually

---

[323] *Id.* at 43-44.

[324] *Id.* at 108-109.

[325] The Heptarchy is a modern designation and refers to the kingdoms of Wessex, Sussex, Kent, Essex, East Anglia, Mercia, and Northumbria. *See* D.J.V. Fisher, *The Anglo-Saxon Age c. 400-1042* 110 (1973).

[326] D.J.V. Fisher, *The Anglo-Saxon Age c. 400-1042* 110-112 (1973).

to be grouped into hundreds[327] and shires. Now research is revealing that few such generalizations can be sustained. In areas where the first Germanic settlers were probably invited mercenaries, earliest landholding patterns may have followed closely the forms still found in the Romano-British communities to which the mercenaries were attached. An outstanding example is the system of "lathes" in Kent, recorded in the Domesday Book survey issued in 1086, A.D., and which "may well retain the outline of the Romano-British system, within which Hengist and his Jutes were permitted by such sub-Roman rulers as Vortigern to make their federate settlements."[328]

A related but distinct pattern arose in parts of Northumbria, where the unique Northumbrian agricultural system stemmed directly from Celtic influence. These circumstances suggest that much land was left occupied by British farmers subject to Germanic overlords. This differed from those parts of England where the Germanic invaders sought land for their own farming activities.[329]

§ 6.04(c)(2). Absence of Stratification in Early Anglo-Saxon Landholding Rights.

One generalization that does appear valid is the absence of social stratification in the early Anglo-Saxon settlements and, by implication, in the land rights held by their inhabitants, described as "a striking feature of the period."[330] "Early Anglo-Saxon England is notable for the egalitarian quality of its modest farmsteads."[331] In archaeological terms, the adherence of initial Anglo-Saxon landholding practices to native traditions already in

---

[327] In the earliest Anglo-Saxon settlements a hundred may have been theoretically the land required to sustain a hundred fighting men and their families.

[328] J.N.L. Myres, *The English Settlements* 124 (1986).

[329] *Id.* at 200-201.

[330] Richard Hodges, *The Anglo-Saxon Achievement: Archaeology and the Beginnings of English Society* 34 (1989).

[331] *Id.*

place has been suggested in that "the vernacular architecture of the Early Anglo-Saxon farm may be an expression of a peasant family household unit which withstood the long depopulation of the countryside, the decline of the state and the demise of classical antiquity."[332]

Similarly, analysis of artifacts found in graves of 5th- and 6th-century Anglo-Saxon cemeteries attests to lack of social ranking and the absence of great differences in material wealth during this period.[333]

§ 6.04(c)(3). Possible Transfer of Contemporary Continental Landholding Practices.

From examination of Dark Age farmsteads of north Germany and Holland during the period of Anglo-Saxon migration, it is possible to determine forms of agricultural organization with which the Anglo-Saxons were familiar. This information, however, sheds only limited light on Anglo-Saxon social organization in England of that period.

Despite some evidence for continuity of Romano-British field systems, as suggested in § 6.04(c)(1), in most areas of Britain subject to Anglo-Saxon invasion "the Roman system of agriculture failed to survive through into the late Anglo-Saxon period."[334] Instead, the Anglo-Saxons may have brought with them the field systems best known to them from their continental homelands. These consisted of small, dispersed settlements and of mound settlements, the so-called *Wurten* or *Terpen*, man-made mounds used to cope with periodic flooding.[335] However, only limited evidence shows that Anglo-Saxon settlers introduced either of these systems into Britain. Also, if the Anglo-Saxons had traditions of both

---

[332] *Id.* at 36.

[333] *Id.* at 38-42. These conclusions are based on the assumption that grave goods more or less faithfully reflect the decedents' relative status in life.

[334] *Id.* at 85.

[335] *Id.* at 88.

individual farmsteads and small villages, it would be hard to distinguish these Germanic settlements from their previously existing Romano-British counterparts. In any event, it seems likely that most Anglo-Saxon settlement occurred before any type of communal open-field strip farming had developed on the continent or in Britain.[336]

§ 6.04(c)(4). Property Rights Probably Recognized in Early Anglo-Saxon Times.

§ 6.04(c)(4)(A). Absence of Direct Evidence.

Any statement about land tenures or systems of ownership rights in the early Anglo-Saxon period must be considered mostly speculative. Contemporary evidence of any sort is wholly absent, and even intelligent guesses can be contrived only by extension back from the first written sources, the Anglo-Saxon charters of the 7th century, A.D., or extension forward from the contemporary Romanized practices on the continent. The subject of land ownership has been addressed by almost none of the recognized Anglo-Saxon scholars.

In hypothesizing about property rights during this early Anglo-Saxon period, 400-600, A.D., it can reasonably be assumed that land was the resource of greatest importance to the Anglo-Saxons then as it continued to be into modern times. The rights associated with possession of land must have varied, and inevitably those rights attained the power to define one's personal status as free or unfree.

If the first Anglo-Saxon groups in England were indeed composed essentially of free persons, members of war bands owing allegiance to a free-booting leader, or farmers and their families coming for land, eventually individual families would have settled on fixed parcels of land.

The possession of land essentially affirmed one's status and right as a

[336] *Id.*

participant in the political and economic life of the group. Kemble believed that the Germanic aversion to city life or even to dwellings in close proximity to each other signified that "the Germanic community is in some sense . . . bound to the soil: its members share in the arable, the forest and marsh, the waters and pastures: their bond of union is a partnership in the advantages to be derived from possession of the land, and individual interest in a common benefit."[337]

§ 6.04(c)(4)(B). Communal Holdings Apportioned by Lot.

According to Kemble, who attributed to Anglo-Saxons the traits of their Germanic contemporaries on the continent, "the district occupied by a body of new settlers was divided by lot in various proportions."[338] Some land would have been held in surplus for future apportionments, and other portions "remained in undivided possession as commons" and as marches to define borders or defensive buffer lands with other settlements.[339] A share sufficient for the support of an individual family would eventually become known as a hide.[340]

§ 6.04(c)(4)(C). Holdings for Life Tenure Only.

It is also reasonable to assume that the possessory right held by the

---

[337] John Mitchell Kemble, *The Saxons in England* 89-90 (1876). As to some of what Kemble wrote on this subject, Pollock and Maitland's later assessment should be recalled: "It is now prudent rather than necessary to remind the reader that Kemble's brilliant conjectures [particularly on Anglo-Saxon folkland] were premature and largely unwarranted." Frederick Pollock and Frederic William Maitland, *The History of English Law Before the Time of Edward I* 62 (2d ed. 1909).

[338] *Id.* at 90. *See especially* examples of land division by lot set forth in note 1 on his page 90.

[339] *Id.* at 90.

[340] *Id.* at 91-92.

occupant of a hide of land could be best described in common law terms as a life estate. On the continent, such an interest arose originally out of Roman land law and survived into Europe's dark age. Known in that context as a *precarium*, this interest signified the practice of one party possessing and using another party's land, for whatever consideration seemed appropriate. The possessor of the land, which land was termed a *beneficium*, was vulnerable to the bonds of patronage, and at some time might find it necessary to seek the protection and submit to the power of the owner. Once written documentation of Anglo-Saxon land transactions began to appear in the 7th century, A.D., there is some evidence that many landholders had rights of tenants rather than of absolute owners,[341] as if the custom of the continent had carried over to England.[342]

The Domesday Book of 1086, A.D., also shows the common usage of some form of life estate as a type of landholding rights. Although the Domesday Book is subsequent to the Norman Conquest, it reflects property rights recognized in the late Anglo-Saxon period. It shows that some of the Anglo-Saxon aristocracy held land that they could not transfer without leave of their lords; others held their land with a right of alienation. Stenton believed that holdings without right of alienation had been obtained by gift from the lord; holdings with the right of alienation had come to the owner in the owner's own right. It cannot be known whether these distinctions had their antecedents in the early Anglo-Saxon period, but it seems likely that both forms of land acquisition would have occurred as soon as settlement began.

A form of life tenancy also appears from the earliest extant Anglo-Saxon charters describing transfers of rights in land, dating from the 7th century, A.D. These charters show that a three-fold division of landholding rights had already developed, discussed below as bookland, "laenland", and folkland. One of these, the so-called "laenland," consisted

---

[341] 2 William Holdsworth, *A History of English Law* 71 (reprint 1971).

[342] In cases where laenland was created by express agreement, "it may be compared with the Gallo-Frankish precarium, from which indeed it was perhaps derived." Frederick Pollock and Frederic William Maitland, *The History of English Law Before the Time of Edward I* 61 (2d ed. 1909).

of land "loaned" to individual tenants, usually by the English church, which had received many grants from kings and others. Possessory rights in these lands were sometimes lent out to members of the nobility, and sometimes even to the king, for the span of one or more lives, but never more than three successive lives.[343] The owner required lump sum payments, or rent, or services in return.[344] Even after the Norman Conquest, the life tenancy continued to be the usual form of landholding; an ordinary gift of land to a person was considered to convey only a life estate.[345]

§ 6.04(c)(4)(D). Land for Services or Payments.

Among the Anglo-Saxon tribes, a lord conferred lands on his followers when they reached about twenty-four or twenty-five years of age. These grants came not by inheritance, but by favor from the lord. It is not known if the lands thus granted were considered inheritable, but "in later times there is a certain amount of evidence which suggests that tenure of land for three generations may have constituted a claim to permanent possession. But even if so we cannot tell how far such a custom goes back."[346]

Even if we do not know by what arrangements the earliest Anglo-Saxon settlers held their land, analysis of the written charters that began to be used in the 7th century, A.D., does reveal a system of land rights beginning to develop relatively early in the Anglo-Saxon era. Apparently the spread of Christianity led to the spread of literacy, especially in transactions involving the church, and these charters show that distinctive property rights had already developed, even if their earliest form cannot be known.

---

343 Three lives did not mean the life spans of three persons living at the time of the loan, but meant the life of the borrower and "two successive heirs." Frederic Maitland, *Domesday Book and Beyond* 309 (1897).

344 Paul Vinogradoff, *English Society in the Eleventh Century* 292-332 (1925); 2 William Holdsworth, *A History of English Law* 70-71 (3d ed. 1923).

345 *Bracton*, 27; Y.B. 15 Edw. 3 (R.S.) 322.

346 H. Munroe Chadwick, *The Origin of the English Nation* 159-160 (1924).

These charters reveal that the land rights worked out after the Anglo-Saxon settlement usually had some sort of services or payment obligations attached to the holding of the land. Rights of inheritability or alienability would have been exceptional rights, but perhaps also available from time to time by the landholder agreeing to render additional services or payments.

§ 6.04(c)(4)(E). The Beginning of Stratification in Property Rights.

The charters also show the beginnings of the close correlation between one's property rights and social status, and the developing stratification in types of property rights. Stenton adopted the thesis that "the general drift of English peasant life in these centuries was from freedom towards servitude . . . From the moment when the kings of the migration age began to plant their companions upon the soil there must have existed communities in which expropriated Britons, and Englishmen too poor to be welcomed in settlements of their own people, were working for a lord in return for his protection . . . .[347]

While conceding that this thesis could not be supported fully by direct evidence, Stenton described the process in persuasive and informative terms, quoted at length below:

> There is no direct evidence to show the stages by which, within any single village, a community composed essentially of independent peasants developed into a community composed essentially of serfs. But the main features of the process seem fairly clear. In what appears to have been the normal case, it began with a grant from the king setting an ealdorman, a *gesith*, a bishop, or an abbot in his own place as the immediate lord of a village, and, in particular, as the recipient of the dues and services

[347] F.M. Stenton, *Anglo-Saxon England* 463 (1943).

which its inhabitants had been accustomed to render to the king himself. The independence of the village group was not threatened at first. But the narrowness of an average ceorl's resources, and the many forms of disaster to which he was exposed, made it almost inevitable that sooner or later the village community would find itself unable to provide the food-rent which its lord had a right to demand. It was generally easier for the head of a peasant household to supply labour than to keep up a regular contribution to a communal food-rent. Most lords had need of labour on the "demesnes" [lands held by the lords themselves, also referred to as domains] which they had been acquiring through co-operation with the village community in the extension of the cultivated area, or by the creation of home farms within a ring fence. It seems that, within most villages, the duty of supporting the lord by a communal render in kind gave way, in time, more or less completely, to a system by which each of the regular holdings in the open fields—hides, half-hides, and yardlands—supplied labour for the lord's demesnes on a definite number of days in every week. In itself, the change was merely a matter of economic reorganization, which need have had no legal consequences. But in most cases it seems to have formed part of a wider revolution in which the individual peasants surrendered their holdings to the lord of the village and received them back from his hands, acknowledging themselves to be his men, and placing themselves under this protection. When this step had been taken by the whole or the greater part of a village community, the manorial economy of the middle ages was brought within sight.[348]

[348] *Id.* at 464-465 (1943).

§ 6.04(c)(4)(F). Summary of Early Anglo-Saxon Property Rights.

If most or all of these surmises are correct, then the earliest Anglo-Saxon settlers typically would have obtained individual farmsteads assigned to them by the leader of their war band, along with rights in certain common lands with other members of the group or community. These possessory rights probably would have carried with them certain communal obligations similar to those known to be customary in later generations, such as road and bridge repairs and maintenance of defensive works. If they settled in still functioning Romano-British farmsteads or communities, they probably adopted the customary rights and duties recognized by the native inhabitants.

Improved stability in these early decades brought centralization of political power and stratification of property rights. War band leaders became kings, who assigned land to their chief warriors, who allotted portions to farmers and their families, each grantor retaining rights relative to subsequent grantees. Rights of inheritability and alienation were probably rare and probably required acquiescence of or payment to lord or community. The farmers, if failing to meet food-rent obligations, would gradually incur more extensive duties to provide labor on the lord's demesne. At the end of this process, the actual occupants of the land would have eventually suffered a nearly complete loss of economic and personal independence.

§ 6.05. Development of Anglo-Saxon Laws and Customs Relating to Property after ca. 600, A.D.

By the time the Anglo-Saxons emerged from their dark age of illiteracy early in the 7th century, A.D., their property rights had already undergone much sophisticated elaboration, complete with seeds of feudalism ready to flower when conditions became right. Historians see as a key event in this emergence the arrival of the monk Augustine and other clerics in Kent at about 597, A.D. Sent from Rome as an emissary of Pope Gregory,

Augustine had a mission to persuade the Kentish King Aethelberht to formally accept Christianity and urge his people to do likewise. Aethelberht had been married for nearly forty years to Bertha, a Christian Frankish princess who maintained a Christian spiritual adviser in her household.[349]

Aethelberht's eventual conversion, along with the Roman monks' subsequent successful proselyting in Northumbria, began the long, halting process of establishing the Roman church in England and achieving at least a partial reconciliation with the British Christians in the north and west. The other important consequence of these changes was to increase interest in literacy and to bring into governing circles churchmen and others who could read and write. Churchmen urged newly Christianized kings to order written collections of their laws, not only in imitation of great rulers of the ancient past, but also to formalize royal protections for the church and its officials; thus the laws or "dooms" of Anglo-Saxon kings began to be issued. Church officials also sought to secure rights of land tenure in some written form, and this led to the common use of written documents called charters in conveying property rights to the church; use of charters eventually spread to some purely secular conveyances.

In Illustration 19 is Whitby Abbey, a famous symbol of the attempts to reconcile the Roman and British Christian traditions, principally through the Whitby Synod of 664, A.D.

Thus, with respect to law and property rights, the emergence of the Anglo-Saxons from the dark age of illiteracy is characterized principally by the appearance of codes of written laws called "dooms," and the increasing use of written documents called "charters" to evidence conveyances of tenurial property rights. Although most of the charters deal directly with only one type of property, called "bookland" or "bocland," they provide insights into "laenland" and "folkland," the other forms of Anglo-Saxon landholding.

---

[349] Peter Hunter Blair, *The World of Bede* 49-67 (1971).

Illustration 19. This is the Whitby Abbey in Northumbria, England, where in 664, A.D., the Whitby Synod was convened to reconcile disparate practices between Roman and British Christianity. The Roman advocates prevailed.

§ 6.05(a). The "Dooms"[350] of Kings Who Ruled Over Individual Anglo-Saxon Kingdoms.

§ 6.05(a)(1). Kent.

The most conspicuous legal activity of early Anglo-Saxon kings was the issuance of written law codes, known as dooms.[351] Aethelberht, King

---

[350] While the precise derivation and contemporary meaning of "doom" cannot be ascertained, it appears that the term is of purely Germanic origin and in general refers to a thing that is set up or established. *See* 3 *Oxford English Dictionary* 600-601 (1933).

[351] A.W.B. Simpson, "The Laws of Aethelberht," in *On the Laws and Customs of England: Essays in Honor of Samuel E. Thorne* 5 (Morris S. Arnold et al., eds., 1981).

of Kent, produced the earliest of these after he accepted Christianity,[352] and, because it was written in Anglo-Saxon, his code has the distinction of being the first set of Germanic laws written in the vernacular.[353] Indeed, dating from ca. 601-605, A.D., this code is the earliest Anglo-Saxon writing of any kind.[354]

All of the Anglo-Saxon "codes" were codes only in the sense that they were organized somewhat systematically or logically, not because they were comprehensive statements of law. They probably reflected some customary law of the time, but in fact did not include the vast bulk of customary law. Most of the codes were preoccupied with schedules of

---

352 As related by Bede, Aethelberht had his code drawn up "according to the example of the Romans." Bede, *Historia Ecclesiastica Gentis Anglorum* ii.5.

> [I]t is possible to detect parallels, between his code and seventh-century Continental laws; yet it and the others are in the vernacular. They give the impression of a sophisticated and wide-ranging approach to the establishment of custom and royal right; Aethelbert's code is well-organized, and some of its gaps are filled by his successors in Kent. . . But gaps remain (for example on land tenure) . . . In the end these codes, like their Continental counterparts, seem to be attempts to civilize the image of Germanic kings by giving them a role for which Roman emperors were famous; it was thus more important to write something of a people's custom or a king's judgements down, than to organize the material in a comprehensive way.

Patrick Wormland, "The Age of Bede and Aethelbald," in *The Anglo-Saxons* 98 (James Campbell, ed., 1982).

353 *Id.* at 4. The Barbarian Laws discussed in § 6.03(b), *supra*, are known only through Latin manuscripts.

354

> The Laws of Aethelberht are of special interest as being the earliest document written in the English language. Some poems indeed, such as Beowulf , may have a longer history behind them, but it is highly improbable that they were committed to writing till a much later period. No other Teutonic language possesses any original records of equal antiquity, apart from short inscriptions. The remains of Gothic literature are indeed much older, but they consist entirely of translations, while the laws of the Continental Teutonic peoples, though they begin more than a century before Aethelberht's reign, are written in Latin down to comparatively late times.

The Laws of the Earliest English Kings 3 (F. L. Attenborough, ed. & trans., 1922).

"composition" payments for specified offenses, and only incidentally give glimpses into the kings' other legal concerns.[355]

It could be questioned why Aethelberht wrote a code at all. His people and surely most of his council were illiterate.[356] The traditional explanation that the code was prompted by his conversion to Christianity during Augustine's mission has been challenged,[357] but Christian influence is a certainty both in Aethelberht's and in all subsequent Anglo-Saxon codes.[358] The laws probably consisted of a set of judgments pronounced by the king and his *witan* (council), concerning both abstract propositions (similar to

---

355

> The greatest difficulty posed by early codes (and one on which the texts themselves lend no assistance) is to decide whether what they describe is traditional custom or governmental innovation. Historians have therefore seen them either as evidence of the persistence of the society described by Tacitus, or as evidence of increasing royal power. . .
>
> . . . Ultimately, it does seem probable that being made solemnly and permanently responsible for the statement of the law enhanced a king's power. Law was issued in the king's name and became the king's, in a way it may not have been before and was never to be in Scandinavia. If the early laws are most important as evidence for a stage in the history of English society, they are also a powerful symbol of the post-conversion transformation of English kingship.

Patrick Wormald, "The Age of Bede and Aethelbald," *The Anglo-Saxons* 98-99 (James Campbell, ed., 1982).

356 A.W.B. Simpson, "The Laws of Aethelberht," in *On the Laws and Customs of England: Essays in Honor of Samuel E. Thorne* 15 (Morris S. Arnold et al., eds., 1981).

357 H.G. Richardson and G.O. Sayles, *Law and Legislation from Aethelberht to Magna Carta* 1-13, 157-169 (1966).

358 Clause 1 of the Laws of Aethelberht, while probably a later addition to the original dooms, gives extraordinary legal status to ecclesiastical persons and property and is included in the oldest surviving text of this code. *See The Laws of the Earliest English Kings*, Aethelberht cl 10 (F.L. Attenborough, ed. & trans., 1922).

legislation) and concrete cases (similar to adjudications).[359]

A brief topical summary of these 90 dooms suffices to show some of Aethelberht's legal concerns during this period:

> One doom proclaims a compensation multiplier for offenses against the church and its clerics, curiously and quite incongruously greater even than for offenses against the king.[360]
>
> Eleven dooms proclaim a compensation multiplier and compensation amounts for offenses against the king and his servants or representatives and imply that in Kent, even at this early time, the king is the personal lord of every freeman.[361]
>
> Two dooms declare compensation amounts for certain offenses against noblemen.[362]
>
> Two dooms describe compensation amounts for certain offenses against non-noble freemen (and clauses 11 and 16 indicate that three classes of freedmen are recognized, possibly referring to manumitted slaves or other subject people, including Britons).[363]
>
> Five dooms deal with forcible entry into and theft from

---

359 A.W.B. Simpson, "The Laws of Aethelberht," in *On the Laws and Customs of England: Essays in Honor of Samuel E. Thorne* 5 (Morris S. Arnold et al., eds., 1981).

360 *The Laws of the Earliest English Kings* 5, Aethelberht cl. 1 (F.L. Attenborough, ed. & trans., 1922).

361 *Id.* at 5-7, cls. 2-12.

362 *Id.* at 7, cls. 13-14.

363 *Id.* at 7, cls. 15-16.

dwellings and fenced enclosures.[364]

Three dooms set fines for those supplying weapons by which offenses are committed.[365]

Six dooms deal with *wergilds* (the price of a person's life, varied according to social rank) for killing.[366]

One doom deals with false imprisonment.[367]

Fourteen dooms deal with women: injuries, marital and family relations, and misconduct.[368]

Forty dooms list various personal injuries and their required compensation amounts.[369]

Five dooms deal with various offenses by and against servants and slaves.[370]

The dooms of Aethelberht are not as varied in subject matter as the *Lex Salica*, the important early law code of the Salian Franks, but they are better organized.[371] If subject matter choice truly reflects the controversies

---

364 *Id.* at 7-9, cls. 17, 27-29, 32.

365 *Id.* at 7, cls. 18-20.

366 *Id.* at 7-9, cls. 21-23, 25-26, 30.

367 *Id.* at 7, cl. 24.

368 *Id.* at 9, cl. 31; at 15, cls. 73-85.

369 *Id.* at 9-15, cls. 33-72.

370 *Id.* at 17, cls. 86-90.

371 [D]espite Bede's statement that Aethelberht composed his dooms "after the Roman manner," they show no sign of Roman influence. It is unlikely that they owed anything definite to any model, and their general affinities lie, not with any law-book of the Western Empire, but with the Lex Salica, the great code

with which the king was most often engaged, then these laws reveal the most difficult social problems confronting an emerging Anglo-Saxon society. It should also be noted that only five of the ninety dooms deal with offenses against rights in land (in the nature of trespass) and that the entire subject of ownership or possessory rights in land is apparently left to be governed by unwritten custom.

A second Kentish code, usually called the Laws of Hlothhere and Eadric, appeared near the end of the 7th century, A.D. These two kings probably did not rule jointly; Hlothhere reigned ca. 673 to 685, A.D., and was succeeded by his nephew and rival Eadric, who reigned only a year and a half.[372] Their decrees are introduced thus: "Hlothhere and Eadric, Kings of Kent, extended the laws which their predecessors had made, by the decrees which are stated below."[373] A summary of the sixteen dooms in their laws follows:

> Four dooms assign additional *wergild* amounts for killings by servants.[374]
>
> One doom requires kidnapping to be adjudicated by oath.[375]
>
> One doom designates the custodian and guardian of a child

> which Clovis had issued for the Salian Franks. Even so, the affinities are in subject-matter and not in form; the Salic law is a far longer text than the ninety brief sections into which Aethelberht compressed his laws, and primitive as is the content of the Salic law, it was written in Latin. The Laws of Aethelberht were written in English, and are of unique interest as by far the earliest body of law expressed in any Germanic language.

F.M. Stenton, *Anglo-Saxon England* 60 (1943).

[372] *The Laws of the Earliest English Kings* 2 (F.L. Attenborough, ed. & trans., 1922).

[373] *Id.* at 19, Hlothhere and Eadric (introductory passage).

[374] *Id.* at 19, Hlothhere and Eadric cls. 1-4.

[375] *Id.* at 19, cl. 5.

whose father has died.[376]

One doom regulates the recovery of stolen property.[377]

Three dooms require certain accusations to be adjudicated by arbitration, compensation, or oath.[378]

One doom assigns penalties for defamation.[379]

Four dooms deal with offenses committed within the dwellings of others.[380]

One doom calls for witnesses to certify purchases of property in London (which may have been part of Kentish territory at the time).[381]

As with Aethelberht's code, these laws governed property only with respect to matters of misconduct on land and to certain conveyances, while leaving to still unwritten custom the vast subject matter of tenurial rights.

The third and final Kentish code is that of Wihtred, whose rule began about 690, A.D., during a period of considerable disturbance in southeast England. He issued these dooms in about 695, A.D., shortly after making peace with the Wessex King Ine.[382] One of his laws is identical to a

---

[376] *Id.* at 19, cl. 6.

[377] *Id.* at 19, cl. 7.

[378] *Id.* at 21, cls. 8-10.

[379] *Id.* at 21, cl. 11.

[380] *Id.* at 21, cls. 12-15.

[381] *Id.* at 21, cl. 16.

[382] *Id.* at 2-3.

contemporary doom of Ine.[383] These laws declare that they were drawn up by a council of "notables," including several church officials, and that they added to the Kentish legal usages.[384] A summary of the 28 dooms of Wihtred follows:

> Two dooms grant the church immunity from taxation and establish its penalty entitlement as equal to the king's.[385]
>
> Four dooms define the consequences for entering into or aiding illicit unions and not repenting of the same.[386]
>
> One doom limits the extent of hospitality to be granted to a wandering cleric not part of an order.[387]
>
> One doom regulates manumission of persons at the altar.[388]
>
> Three dooms prohibit work and travel on the Sabbath.[389]
>
> Two dooms penalize offerings to devils.[390]
>
> Two dooms penalize violations of fasting times.[391]

---

[383] *Id.* at 31, Wihtred cl. 28, and at 43, Ine cls. 20-21 (requiring a traveler to sound a warning when leaving the road).

[384] *Id.* at 25, Wihtred (introductory passage).

[385] *Id.* at 25, Wihtred cls. 1-2.

[386] *Id.* at 25-27, cls. 3-6.

[387] *Id.* at 27, cl. 7.

[388] *Id.* at 27, cl. 8.

[389] *Id.* at 27, cls. 9-11.

[390] *Id.* at 27, cls. 12-13.

[391] *Id.* at 27, cls. 14-15.

> Nine dooms regulate affirming by oath the statements and accusations by a bishop, king, abbot, priest, deacon, clerk, stranger at the altar, king's thegn (member of the aristocracy), commoner at the altar, servant of the bishop or king, servant of a lord's company, lay servant, and ecclesiastical servant.[392]
>
> Three dooms establish alternative penalties for thieves caught in the act.[393]
>
> One doom requires that a man who leaves the road without giving warning is assumed to be a thief, to be slain or put to ransom.[394]

Of these 28 dooms, 24 have a distinctly ecclesiastical flavor, reflecting the special interest of the important church officials on the council that drew up the decrees. Wihtred's dooms shed no light on property laws and customs of the time and added little to the customary law then being observed in the Kentish kingdom.

§ 6.05(a)(2). Wessex.

Although references exist to other codes—now lost—only one other Anglo-Saxon law code survives from the era prior to when Alfred the Great and his successors began legislating for all of England.[395] This pre-Alfredian code is from Ine, one of Alfred's predecessors on the throne of Wessex, and is contemporary with the Code of Wihtred in Kent, dating from ca. 688-694, A.D. Ine, too, exhibited strong religious impulses and

---

[392] *Id.* at 27-29, cls. 16-24.

[393] *Id.* at 29-31, cls. 25-27.

[394] *Id.* at 31, cl. 28.

[395] The most significant lost code is undoubtedly that of the great Mercian king Offa, which code Alfred included in the description of laws he relied on for his own code as among "the most just of the laws I have found . . . ." *The Laws of the Earliest English Kings* 63 (F.L. Attenborough, ed. & trans., 1922).

even abdicated in 725, A.D., to make a pilgrimage to Rome, where he died.[396] His laws proclaim that they were drawn up with the advice of his father, two of his bishops, his chief nobles, counselors, and many "servants of God."[397] A summary of its 76 dooms follows:

> One doom requires that clerics observe the rules of their respective orders.[398]
>
> One doom requires a child to be baptized within thirty days of birth.[399]
>
> One doom imposes penalties for working on the Sabbath.[400]
>
> Two dooms order payment of church dues.[401]
>
> On doom regulates the sanctuary of churches.[402]
>
> One doom penalizes fighting in the king's house, a monastery, a nobleman's house, and elsewhere.[403]
>
> Twenty-two dooms deal with theft, thieves, stolen property

---

[396] *Id.* at 34.

[397] *Id.* at 37, Ine (introductory passage).

[398] *Id.* at 37, Ine cl. 1.

[399] *Id.* at 37, cl. 2.

[400] *Id.* at 37, cl. 3.

[401] *Id.* at 37, cl. 4, at 57, cl. 61.

[402] *Id.* at 39, cl. 5.

[403] *Id.* at 39, cl. 6.

and unreturned borrowed property.[404]

Ten dooms regulate adjudicatory procedure, including pledges, oaths, obtaining justice, and false witness.[405]

One doom prohibits selling an Englishman into slavery overseas.[406]

Two dooms require a traveler to sound a warning when he leaves the road and permits him to be killed if he fails to warn.[407]

Eight dooms deal with various circumstances of killing and the *wergild* amounts therefor.[408]

Three dooms require maintenance for foundlings and for fatherless and illegitimate children.[409]

One doom requires return of double the bridal price if a man buys a wife and the marriage does not take place.[410]

Six dooms regulate moving without permission, eviction,

---

[404] *Id.* at 39-61, cls. 7, 10, 12, 14-18, 22, 24-25, 28-29, 36, 46-48, 53, 57, 72-73, 75. As if to confirm a continental genealogy for Anglo-Saxon laws, cl. 29 of Ine's Dooms, dealing with failure to return borrowed property, is very similar to cl. 52 of the Lex Salica, issued two centuries earlier. The need to issue positive law on this matter hints at the profound importance of possession in Germanic law.

[405] *Id.* at 39-57, cls. 8-9, 13, 19, 30, 35, 37, 41, 54, 62.

[406] *Id.* at 41, cl. 11.

[407] *Id.* at 43, cls. 20-21 (compare with cl. 28 of the doom of Wihtred, *id.* at 31, cl. 28).

[408] *Id.* at 43-61, cls. 23, 32-34, 70-71, 74, 76.

[409] *Id.* at 45, cls. 26-27; at 49, cl. 38.

[410] *Id.* at 47, cl. 31.

and failure to enter into possession.[411]

Three dooms impose penalties for damage by stray animals.[412]

Two dooms penalize destruction of trees.[413]

Two dooms discuss penalties for breaking into fortified premises and for depredations by a lord's men.[414]

Two dooms deal with obligations accompanying land use, including military service and rents.[415]

One doom penalizes illicit compacts.[416]

Five dooms deal with transactions in animals, animal parts, and animal labor.[417]

One doom sets a penalty for the early shearing of sheep.[418]

Inasmuch as they cast light on land tenures, the following dooms are quoted in their English translation:

If anyone moves away without permission from his lord

---

[411] *Id.* at 49, cl. 39; at 57-59, cls. 63-66, 68.

[412] *Id.* at 49, cls. 40, 42, 49.

[413] *Id.* at 51, cls. 43-44.

[414] *Id.* at 51-52, cls. 45, 50.

[415] *Id.* at 53, cl. 51; at 59, cl. 67.

[416] *The Laws of the Earliest English Kings* 53, Ine cl. 52 (F.L. Attenborough, ed. & trans., 1922).

[417] *Id.* at 55, cls. 55-56 at 57, cls. 58-60.

[418] *Id.* at 59, cl. 69.

and steals into another district, if he is discovered he shall return to where was before, and give his lord 60 shillings.

If a nobleman moves his residence he may take with him his reeve, his smith, and his children's nurse.

He who has [a holding of] 20 hides shall sow 12 hides of land under cultivation when he means to leave.

He who has [a holding of] 10 hides shall sow 6 hides of land under cultivation when he means to leave.

He who has [a holding of] 3 hides shall sow one hide and a half of land under cultivation when he means to leave.

If a nobleman is evicted, he may be expelled from his house, but not from the cultivated land.

If a nobleman who holds land neglects military service, he shall pay 120 shillings and forfeit his land; a nobleman who holds no land shall pay 60 shillings; a commoner shall pay a fine of 30 shillings for neglecting military service.

If a man takes a yard [a quarter hide] of land or more, at a fixed rent, and ploughs it, [and] if the lord requires service as well as rent, he [the tenant] need not take the land if the lord does not give him a dwelling; but [in that case he must forfeit the crops].[419]

---

[419] According to Stenton, this passage implies that the tenant is clearly a freeman, for the conditions on which he takes his holding have been determined by agreement between him and his lord:

> But the land is plainly regarded as the lord's; he has planted the tenant upon it, and expects it to yield rent or labour at his discretion. . . . The fact that the tenant must abandon the crops if he refuses the lord's claim to service strongly suggests that his yardland. . .had originally been sown with this Lord's seed. . . . In any case, the passage is of outstanding importance as the first

Ine's code represents a departure from the dreary catalogs of *wergild* arithmetic found in the earlier Kentish codes; it is instead an attempt to deal with conspicuous social problems. "It is the work of a responsible statesman, capable of bringing his clergy and nobles into deliberation on the blending of ancient custom and new enactment in an elaborate body of law. It stands for a new conception of kingship, destined in time to replace the simple motives which had satisfied the men of an earlier age."[420]

§ 6.05(b). How Consolidation of Anglo-Saxon Monarchical Power Affected Property Rights.

The earliest Anglo-Saxon kings ruled people, not territories.[421] Only by consolidating conquests and enjoying increasing stability could they identify specific areas as their kingdoms. The earliest kingdoms have been depicted as rather simple organizations with law in a primitive state. Indeed, "The principal function of kings was to lead their people in war.[422]

In the approximately 100 years from the time of the earliest Anglo-Saxon kings until Aethelberht issued his dooms, important changes occurred in the roles and conduct of these Germanic kings. What is known of Aethelberht's reign helps illustrate these changes. He was regarded as a progressive monarch, and his pattern of kingship presaged the styles of subsequent kings.

Aethelberht maintained contacts with "foreign courts" both in England and on the continent. He assumed personal responsibility for dealing with

---

> recorded example of a type of relationship between lord and man which during the next three centuries was to change the whole character of English rural society.

F.M. Stenton, *Anglo-Saxon England* 309-310.

[420] F.M. Stenton, *Anglo-Saxon England* 71 (1943).

[421] D.P. Kirby, *The Making of Early England* 163 (1967).

[422] D.J.V. Fisher, *The Anglo-Saxon Age c. 400-1042* 133 (1973).

Augustine's mission, regulating preaching and later legislating for protection of ecclesiastical interests.[423] His laws show increasing recognition for the "king's peace"; the law assigned extra penalties for offenses committed in the king's presence or in gatherings called by the king. Personal offenses normally resolved by payments to the kindred also resulted in fines paid to the king, who now assumed the role of protector of the people in civil affairs. His dooms reveal a king who accepted responsibility for the development and enforcement of customary law and who exhibited considerable interest in the internal affairs of his kingdom. One could infer from his dooms that Aethelberht even had officials to collect fines and arrange compositions between kindred groups.[424]

The king's most substantial resource was large tracts of land from which he rewarded his followers. While the land was technically the property of the entire people, the king had rights to rents, services, or other returns from occupancy of the land, which rights he could grant or release in return for faithful service.[425] He made such grants and releases by royal diploma or charter, and land subject to such written documents was called "bookland" or "bocland."[426] In Mercia, even a grant of land as "bookland" did not relieve the property of the customary duties of military service, bridge building, and fortress maintenance.[427] Elsewhere, "bookland" was exempt from the king's proprietary right to tax the land, known as *feorm*.[428]

---

[423] *See especially* cl. 1 of the laws of Aethelberht, *The Laws of the Earliest English Kings* 5, Aethelberht cl. 1 (F.L. Attenborough, ed. & trans., 1922).

[424] D.J.V. Fisher, *The Anglo-Saxon Age c. 400-1042* 134 (1973). Another example of a king's use of royal officials to aid in public affairs is found in the laws of Ine, from which it may be inferred that ealdormen preside over courts, and that their verdicts must be obtained before redress can be sought. *The Laws of the Earliest English Kings* 37, Ine. cl. 1 (F.L. Attenborough, ed. & trans., 1922).

[425] F.M. Stenton, *Anglo-Saxon England* 302-303 (1943).

[426] H.P.R. Finberg, "King Alfred's England," in *The Agrarian History of England and Wales A.D. 43-1042* 458-462 (H.P.R. Finberg, ed., 1972).

[427] *Id.* at 459.

[428] Walter de Gray Birch, *Cartularium Saxonicum* 143, no. 99 (1885) (grant by Wihtred, King of Kent, on April 8, 699, A.D.); *id.* at 157, no. 108 (grant of privileges by King Ini [or Ine] on May 6, 704, A.D.).

Kings also exacted revenue and tribute from subject territories.[429] It may be concluded that royal grants of interests in land defined and refined property interests, generally.

In later times the king could also order extraordinary national taxation, as shown by the *danegeld* and *heregeld* assessments of the Viking era,[430] and he took a percentage of the fines imposed by courts.[431] The national tax levies, in particular, show considerable administrative machinery at the king's disposal, machinery used to calculate and collect land assessments. National taxation based on land holdings anticipated the assertion of comprehensive royal power over all the lands of the kingdom.

Among the Anglo-Saxon kingdoms, ravages of the Danish Vikings during the 9th century, A.D., disrupted every aspect of Anglo-Saxon society. Only Wessex under Alfred the Great survived the invasions. Alfred was able to stop the Danish advance, unify the proud and disparate peoples of other conquered Anglo-Saxon kingdoms, and begin recovering territory and ruling power from the Danes. From the time of Alfred, English laws would be issued by kings whose rule extended over all of England.[432]

§ 6.05(c). "Dooms" Issued by Kings of England.

The laws, or "dooms," issued by Alfred and his successors are important because they applied to the entire English nation. However, in content the English dooms added little to the types of decrees found in earlier Anglo-Saxon codes.

---

[429] H.P.R. Finberg, "King Alfred's England," in *The Agrarian History of England and Wales A.D. 43-1042* 413 (H.P.R. Finberg, ed., 1972).

[430] F.M. Stenton, *Anglo-Saxon England* 406-407 (1943).

[431] John Mitchell Kemble, *The Saxons in England* 53-55 (1876).

[432] Alfred's achievement in unifying English government and law was probably aided by the earlier unification of the English church. *See* H.P.R. Finberg, *The Formation of England 550-1042* 51 (1974).

§ 6.05(c)(1). Dooms of Alfred the Great.

Alfred (Illustration 20) reigned from 871, A.D., until his death in about 899, A.D. The date of his code is uncertain, estimated at 892-893, A.D., by one scholar[433] and prior to 889, A.D., by another.[434]

A lengthy introduction contains a translation of the Ten Commandments and other passages from the book of Exodus, a brief apostolic history (quoting from the book of Acts of the Apostles), a description of the growth of church law, and a statement that schedules of compensations were decreed and written by many councils. The king then declared:

> Now, I, King Alfred, have collected these laws, and have given orders for copies to be made of many of those which our predecessors observed and which I myself approved of. But many of those I did not approve of I have annulled, by the advice of my councillors, while [in other cases] I have ordered changes to be introduced. For I have not dared to presume to set down in writing many of my own, for I cannot tell what [innovations of mine] will meet with the approval of our successors. But those which were the most just of the laws I found—whether they dated from the time of Ine my kinsman, or of Offa, king of the Mercians, or of Aethelberht, who was the first [king] to be baptized in England—these I have collected while rejecting the others.
>
> I, then, Alfred, King of the West Saxons, have shewn these to all my councillors, and they have declared that it met with the approval of all, that they should be observed.[435]

---

[433] F. Felix Liebermann, *Die Gesetze der Angelsachsen* 34 (1916).

[434] *The Laws of the Earliest English Kings* 35 (F.L. Attenborough, ed. & trans., 1922).

[435] *Id.* at 63, Alfred (introductory passage).

Illustration 20. A statute of the Wessex king Alfred, deservedly denominated the Great, located in his capital city of Winchester, in Hampshire. Alfred's forces turned back the nearly triumphant Danish Vikings and united the English kingdoms under Wessex. He issued an important law code and sparked an Anglo-Saxon cultural revolution.

Although little is known of the King Offa referred to in the introduction to Alfred's code, he was apparently a powerful and highly respected ruler. His power is represented in the famous Offa's Dyke shown in Illustration 21.

Illustration 21. The massive and sometimes gentle earthwork known as Offa's Dyke runs for almost 150 miles roughly along the border between Offa's Anglo-Saxon kingdom of Mercia and the Welsh kingdom of Powys, perhaps facilitating both defense and surveillance. Offa's reign, including his law code, were honored by Alfred.

These laws provide protection for ecclesiastical interests and assign penalties for various types of offenses, with greater punishments for misdeeds that threaten the king's peace. Thirty-four of the 77 clauses describe money penalties for various personal injuries.[436]

Alfred's dooms contain a singular reference to land held by title deed or charter, called "bookland" ("boclande" in Anglo-Saxon), which was inheritable and could be limited by the transferor to alienation only within the kindred:

> We have further established that a man who holds land by

---

[436] *Id.* at 87-93, Alfred cls. 44-77.

> title-deed ["bookland"], which his kinsmen have left him, shall not be allowed to give it out of his kindred, if there is documentary or [other] evidence that the power to do so is forbidden him by the men who first acquired it, or by those who gave it to him. [And he who contests such an alienation] shall make a declaration to this effect in the presence of his kindred, with the king and bishop as witnesses.[437]

After Alfred defeated the Danish King Guthrum in 878, A.D., the two kings drew up and agreed to the so-called "Treaty of Alfred and Guthrum" sometime between 880, A.D., and Guthrum's death in 890, A.D. The treaty set out procedures and penalties for certain offenses and also described the boundaries between the English and Danish areas.[438]

§ 6.05(c)(2). Dooms of Other English Kings.

The so-called "Laws of Edward and Guthrum" are described in their introduction as those laws enacted first by Alfred and Guthrum and other laws enacted later by Edward the Elder (son of Alfred) and Guthrum. Because Guthrum died in 890, A.D., and Edward the Elder reigned from 899-924, A.D., this co-authorship is suspect.[439] In any event, the decrees draw further distinctions between penalties imposed in English and Danish districts, respectively.[440]

Edward the Elder issued two other sets of laws. The first, consisting of only three clauses, makes reference to "folkland" ("folclande" in

---

[437] *Id.* at 83, cl. 41.

[438] *Id.* at 96-97, 99-101. Fictional but authentic accounts of Alfred's times and of his outstanding descendants who ruled the Anglo-Saxons, including Aethelflaed, the "Queen of the Mercians," may be found in Rebecca Tingle, *The Edge on the Sword* (2001) and *Far Traveler* (2005).

[439] The authenticity of the entire introduction is challenged in 3 F. Felix Liebermann, *Die Gesetze der Angelsachsen* 87 (1916).

[440] *The Laws of the Earliest English Kings* 97, 102-109 (F.L. Attenborough, ed. & trans., 1922).

Anglo-Saxon) and "bookland." "Folkland" is of uncertain meaning, but may possibly refer to the land held communally by all the people, or to land held according to customary rights and duties:

> Further, we have declared what [penalty] he is liable to, who withholds from another his rights either in "bookland" or "folkland." And with regard to the "folkland" [we have declared] that he [the plaintiff] shall appoint a day when he [the defendant] shall do him justice in the presence of the reeve.
>
> If, however, he [the plaintiff] does not obtain his rights either in "bookland" or "folkland," he [the defendant] who withholds the rights shall forfeit a fine of 30 shillings to the king, and 30 shillings also on the second occasion, and on the third occasion the fine for insubordination to the king, that is 120 shillings, unless he has already desisted [from his wrong-doing].[441]

In the second set of laws of Edward the Elder, one of the eight clauses refers to the "domboc," probably the "doombook"[442] of laws of Ine and Alfred, which indicates that those laws had not been superseded.[443]

Six series of laws, of uncertain dates, were issued by Aethelstan (son of Edward and grandson of Alfred), who reigned from ca. 924-939, A.D. Their subjects and probable order of issuance are I (ecclesiastical matters), II (administration of justice), V (administration of justice from a council at Exeter), III (reiteration of the substance of series I, II and V in the form of a letter to the king from officials and people of Kent), IV (administration of justice), and VI (an ordinance governing guilds, drawn up by bishops

---

[441] *Id.* at 117, 1 Edw. cl. 2.

[442] *Id.* at 120, 2 Edw. cl. 5.

[443] *Id.* at 112.

and reeves from London).[444] Perhaps the most interesting of these provisions is found in clause 2 of the second series: "With regard to lordless men from whom no [legal] satisfaction can be obtained, we have declared that their relatives shall be commanded to settle them in a fixed residence where they will become amenable to public law, and find them a lord at a public meeting."[445]

This statement illustrates the official distaste for "lordless men," and likely indicates that lordship had been significantly extended during the centuries of Anglo-Saxon rule.

Other aspects of Anglo-Saxon law appear in the laws of the English kings Edmund I (issued 942-946, A.D.), Edgar (issued 946-963, A.D.), and Aethelred II (issued 980-1016, A.D.); in the laws of the Anglo-Danish king Cnut (issued 1027-1034, A.D.); and in the various writings from and after the time of the Norman Conquest purporting to describe Anglo-Saxon law under Edward the Confessor and that were in effect at the time of the conquest in 1066, A.D.

§ 6.05(d). Customary Law Generally.[446]

No direct evidence has yet appeared as to matters of customary government and law observed by the early Anglo-Saxon invaders of Britain. However, much evidence suggests that the earliest invading folk-groups were identified by the name of the original successful leader, and that name attached to the leader's body of followers wherever they happened to go.[447] By the 7th century, A.D., as Anglo-Saxon society was

---

[444] *Id.* at 112-113, 122-173.

[445] *Id.* at 129, II Aethelstan cl. 2.

[446] In addition to the more general works on Anglo-Saxons and on Anglo-Saxon law cited in this chapter, the problems of Anglo-Saxon property law have been addressed in Eric John, *Land Tenure in Early England: A Discussion of Some Problems* (2d ed. 1964).

[447] J.N.L. Myres, *The English Settlements* 36-40 (1986); F.M. Stenton, *Anglo-Saxon England* 314, n. 1 (1943).

becoming more territorial, some old folk-groups had stabilized into administrative districts, sometimes called provinces, or certain localities eventually called shires and hundreds. This terminology originated in Wessex and had spread to most of the rest of England by 1016, A.D., primarily because of the West Saxon dominance during the Viking conflicts.[448]

Some shire boundaries probably conformed to the boundaries of the old folk-groups; others did not. Many shires were administered by important officials of the king, called ealdormen, some of whom were possibly the successors of the older folk-group leaders. Each of these officials had considerable legal power. Shires came to be divided into hundreds (or wapentakes in predominantly Danish areas), usually administered by an officer of the king called a reeve. The reeve's duties were to administer the king's lands and to preside over the hundred courts, as the ealdorman presided over the shire courts. Certain high reeves became the chief administrative officials over shires and were known as shire reeves, or more familiarly, sheriffs.[449]

The main responsibilities of the reeves, and ultimately of the ealdormen, were to maintain law and order, punish criminals, collect royal dues, conduct courts, supervise tolls, exchanges and mints and—especially in the case of ealdormen—conduct military operations.

There is unfortunately little information about town life under the Anglo-Saxons.[450] Possibly the free inhabitants of towns formed themselves into *gylds* of uncertain nature, and they may have corporately enjoyed certain privileges. London, in particular, seems to have enjoyed substantial

---

[448] F.M. Stenton, *Anglo-Saxon England* 289-290 (1943).

[449] D.P. Kirby, *The Making of Early England* 175-179 (1967).

[450] However, in recent years more attention has been given to Anglo-Saxon town studies generally. *See, e.g.*, David Hill, "Towns as Structures and Functioning Communities through Time: The Development of Central Places from 600 to 1066," and Tim Tatton-Brown, "The Anglo-Saxon Towns of Kent," in *Anglo-Saxon Settlements* 197-212, 213-232 (Della Hooke, ed., 1988).

independence.[451]

Cattle were probably the property most commonly exchanged, and the mode of transfer was actual delivery. Pledges and earnest money probably bound the bargain, although there is no direct evidence on any of these points. Written contracts were not in use.[452]

§ 6.05(e). Customary Law Regarding Land.

The rules for landholding at various times during the Anglo-Saxon age are best described in terms of the prevailing social structure, because the most distinctive characteristics of social classes were their respective relationships to the land. All land seems to have had impressed upon it certain public burdens: the obligations of military service, of bridge construction, and of fortress maintenance.[453]

The kings reserved for themselves great tracts of land in subjugated territories. They granted some of this land to their chief warrior companions who formed the noble class, and after Christian conversion, kings and others frequently made grants to the church. The grantees were supported by the rents and services of the humble agrarian folk who actually occupied and tilled much of the land.[454] These royal grants to private persons were probably only life interests; if a father wished to pass a holding on to a son, he probably had to seek the king's acquiescence. A younger son might serve in personal attendance on the king in anticipation of being favored with his own grant of land.[455]

---

[451] F. Felix Liebermann, *Die Gesetze der Angelsachsen* 232-237 (1903).

[452] Frederick Pollock and Frederic William Maitland, *The History of English Law Before the Time of Edward I* 57-58 (2d ed. 1909).

[453] H.P.R. Finberg, "King Alfred's England" in *The Agrarian History of England and Wales A.D. 43-1042* 458 (H.P.R. Finberg, ed., 1972).

[454] *Id.* at 446.

[455] *Id.* at 444-445.

At some time, probably beginning shortly after conversion to Christianity occurred, the need for church endowments not limited to the life of one grantee became obvious. Anglo-Saxon rulers began granting land to the church by means of royal charters, giving virtually full possessory and hereditary rights. This land was always referred to as "boclande" or bookland. Obtaining such charters was at first the exclusive privilege of the church, but transparent subterfuges arose. A lay person could secure a grant of bookland by founding a church or a monastery and then bequeathing it to his descendants, who would have to take orders or the veil. The bequest was always in jeopardy if heirs died out or wished to remain lay persons, so commonly the local bishop was named the ultimate grantee. Also widespread was a practice, condemned by Bede, whereby many important persons had themselves tonsured and called their institutions monasteries, but whose commitment to orders was superficial. So much land was consumed by this practice in Northumbria that there was allegedly not enough land left for grants to young warriors, who therefore often left the region.[456]

While all land was normally subject to certain secular burdens—taxation, military service, purveyance, labor, and judicial duties—Ine of Wessex went so far in 704, A.D., as to declare church lands perpetually exempt from taxation,[457] and Wihtred of Kent exempted churches from all secular burdens,[458] an act ratified by a church council in 742, A.D. But in 749, A.D., the powerful Mercian monarch Aethelbald declared that church lands would not be exempt from the secular burdens of bridge building and fortress work, although other exemptions would remain in effect.[459] A few years later his successor Offa added the requirement that holders of bookland, mostly ecclesiastical foundations,

---

[456] H.P.R. Finberg, *The Formation of England 550-1042* 92 (1974).

[457] Walter de Gray Birch, *Cartularium Saxonicum* 157, no. 108 (grant of May 26, 704, A.D.).

[458] *Id.* at 143, no. 99 (grant of April 8, 699, A.D.).

[459] *Id.* at 254, no. 178.

must meet quotas for military service.[460] Wessex followed, and by 842, A.D., Wessex land charters show that all three "common dues" were being imposed on bookland in Wessex.[461] This removed any barriers to extending bookland grants outright to lay persons, which in fact occurred during Offa's reign.[462]

Although the incidents or features of particular forms of landholding must have varied widely, apparently bookland usually carried the rights of alienation or devise.[463] The decree in Alfred's laws prohibiting holders of bookland from alienating it if ancestors had entailed it in the family was probably an aberration.[464] At the very least, the decree gives a glimpse into the alienability of bookland, and to a practice of limiting alienability to the landholder's lineal descendants.

An English king might even grant part of his own demesne as bookland. As bookland rights were extended, they sometimes included the right to hold court, or at least to keep part of the fines assessed by courts held within the territory of the grant.[465]

Land not granted by charter might have been held under a more precarious form of tenure called *laenland*, or, for convenience, loan land.

---

460 H.P.R. Finberg, "King Alfred's England" in *The Agrarian History of England and Wales A.D. 43-1042* 459 (H.P.R. Finberg, ed., 1972).

461 *See, e.g.,* 1 Walter de Gray Birch, *Cartularium Saxonicum* 390, no. 282 (grant by Brihtric, King of Wessex, in 801, A.D. (1885); 2 W. Birch, *Id.* at 13, no. 438 (grant by Aethelwulf, King of the West Saxons, in 842, A.D. (1887).

462 H.P.R. Finberg, "King Alfred's England," in *The Agrarian History of England and Wales A.D. 43-1042* 459 (H.P.R. Finberg, ed., 1972).

463 *Id.* at 461 (1972).

464 *The Laws of the Earliest English Kings* 83, cl. 41 (F.L. Attenborough, ed. & trans., 1922).

465 Frederic William Maitland, *Domesday Book and Beyond* 258-292 (1897); H.P.R. Finberg, "King Alfred's England," in *The Agrarian History of England and Wales A.D. 43-1042* 464 (H.P.R. Finberg, ed., 1972).

This may have been similar to the Gallo-Frankish *precarium*.[466]

Although it must be understood that any generalizations about *laenland* are derived from only isolated references in the charters, some broad characteristics of this form of landholding seem evident. *Laenland* could not be alienated or inherited without the king's permission or charter. If permission or charter were granted, the land became bookland, but would revert to the king if the holder died without heirs. Such a holding could be described as a lease for a term of lives, usually up to three lives, followed by a reversion.[467] *Laenland* was subject to normal secular dues and it, like bookland, could be forfeited for failure to fulfill those dues.

The tracts of land granted by loan or book were usually very large, and the grantees were often members of the lay nobility or higher clergy. Substantial portions of their holdings were occupied by tillers of the soil from several other classes, with the social class generally corresponding to the terms of their tenures.

Again, remembering that Anglo-Saxon society was not static, one may make some broad generalizations about social class and property tenures. Just below the nobility on the social scale was a class of free farmers, discussed at some length in the laws of Aethelberht,[468] and sometimes apparently labeled *geneats* or *radcnihts*. However, other than this source there is very little direct information about this class. Their land, even if free of rent obligation and freely alienable, would still have been subject to the secular dues owed to a lord or the king. Depictions of early Anglo-Saxon society as consisting mostly of such free farmers cannot be substantiated and, in fact, the Domesday Book shows that by the late 11th

[466] Frederick Pollock and Frederic William Maitland, *The History of English Law Before the Time of Edward I* 61 (2d ed. 1909); *see also* § 6.04(c)(4)(A), *supra*.

[467] Walter de Gray Birch, *Cartularium Saxonicum* 321, no. 1091 (1893) (grant for life made by Bishop Oswald of Worcester in A.D. 962); id. at 382, no. 1136 (letter of Oswald, Bishop of Worcester, in A.D. 964). *See also* H.P.R. Finberg, "King Alfred's England," in *The Agrarian History of England and Wales A.D. 43-1042* 521 (H.P.R. Finberg, ed., 1972).

[468] *The Laws of the Earliest English Kings* 5-9, Aethelberht cls. 4, 6, 8, 24, 27, 29, 31 (all referring to a "freeman" or friman) (F.L. Attenborough, ed. & trans., 1922).

century, A.D. the free class had become surprisingly small, except in the heavily Danish areas. By this time it is possible that some of these freemen had become mounted retainers for their lords or the king, thus receiving a holding and being expected in return to pay rent, perform labor, and attend to and ride on errands.[469] It is possible to see in this yeoman farmer-mounted servant a forerunner of the medieval knight, already in place before the Normans came.[470]

In Anglo-Saxon England a person could be economically dependent, and thus unfree, but still be personally free, especially in legal standing. Freemen are known to have been tenants in varying degrees of servitude. Other classes of free persons arose during the Anglo-Saxon age.[471] One of these classes, the so-called *geburs*, held much smaller tracts of land than the *geneats*, paid rent in kind and money, and performed labor for their lord. The lord, who had originally provided both the land and the livestock, reclaimed them when the *gebur* died. Still lower on the social scale, the class of *kotsetlan*, or cottagers, held land of the lord also, and performed heavy labor. Economically unfree, the *kotsetlan* probably could not move from their land, but were still personally free.[472] Even this nominal personal freedom would be lost if the *kotsetlan* were captured during civil strife or sold themselves into slavery during times of hardship.[473] It has been stated that "serfdom was much more of a personal bondage and less involved with the occupation of particular land before the Norman Conquest than after."[474]

---

[469] H.P.R. Finberg, "King Alfred's England," in *The Agrarian History of England and Wales A.D. 43-1042* 514-515 (H.P.R. Finberg, ed., 1972).

[470] Jack Lindsay, *The Normans and Their World* 301-311 (1974).

[471] *See generally* F.M. Stenton, *Anglo-Saxon England* 463-479 (1943).

[472] *See, e.g.*, 3 Walter de Gray Birch, *Cartularium Saxonicum* 111, no. 935 (1893) (grant by King Eadwig to Aelfwine in A.D. 956).

[473] H.P.R. Finberg, "King Alfred's England" in *The Agrarian History of England and Wales A.D. 43-1042* 509-510 (H.P.R. Finberg, ed., 1972).

[474] Frederick Pollock and Frederic William Maitland, *The History of English Law Before the Time of Edward I* 37 (2d ed. 1909).

It may also be questioned whether kindred relationships continued to influence landholding as the Anglo-Saxon age advanced through the centuries. Medieval practices lead us to believe that the Anglo-Saxon peasant divided his lands among the sons, or, if no sons, among the daughters, giving rise to the view that the holding was family land. This would not have been subject to alienation by the possessor. No Old English code sheds light on such arrangements.[475]

The overall picture of Anglo-Saxon landholding, especially as related to social status, is one with little known consistency throughout England, and one that was in constant fluctuation throughout the Anglo-Saxon age. Certainly it appears that at several levels of social status landholding rights were granted in return for commitments to render services and agricultural products. At the very lowest levels, a lord who established a peasant family on a farm, with not only the land and agricultural seed, but with livestock, implements, and furniture, was considered entitled to the return of all the peasant's possessions upon the peasant's death.[476] Free peasant classes at various levels may have been made up of persons both descending and ascending the social scale, depending upon the economic fortunes or vicissitudes they had encountered. And the presence of slaves in Anglo-Saxon England was pervasive. "At the time of the Norman conquest personal servitude was widespread in England. More than 25,000 slaves

---

[475] "Medieval practice suggests very strongly that the holding of the pre-Conquest ceorl had been partible among his sons, or among his daughters if he had no son, and that the conception of the holding as "family land" was so firmly established that its possessor had no right to alienate any part of it to the disadvantage of his expectant heirs. It seems reasonable to assume that the heirs of a ceorl whose holding was too small for profitable division remained on their father's land, and cultivated it jointly after his death. But it is clear that the house community of land-owning kinsmen to which such arrangements must often have given rise was in law a mere group of individuals which could at any time be dissolved by the action of its members. No text of Old English law ever attributes the ownership of land to a family. F.M. Stenton, *Anglo-Saxon England* 313-314 (1943).

[476] In an eleventh-century treatise for reeves on estate management called *"Rectitudines Singularum Personarum,"* it is stated that such a peasant should have received from his lord two oxen, a cow, six sheep, seven acres already sown upon his yardland, implements for his husbandry, and furniture for his house. 1 F. Felix Liebermann, *Die Gesetze der Angelsachsen* 444-453 (1903); F. M. Stenton, *Anglo-Saxon England* 467-468 (1943).

(*servi*) were enumerated in Domesday Book."[477]

These Anglo-Saxon arrangements for landholding, for the most part acknowledged only by immemorial custom, persisted through the Norman Conquest and into the period of common law development. They were the background and the foundation for the common law of property. Because bookland, laenland, and folkland are the only manifestations of a systematic approach to land law in Anglo-Saxon times, the next paragraphs will review what additional detail is known about these forms of property interests.

§ 6.05(e)(1). Bookland.

Anglo-Saxon bookland was entirely a creature of written instruments, called charters, that were eventually kept together in bound groups called books. Grantors used the earliest charters for grants of land by the king either directly to the church or to a lay person for church-related purposes.

Probably Roman missionaries sent to the pagan Anglo-Saxons introduced the practice of using charters. The earliest charters were written in the same script and in the same language (Latin) as other monastic documents, on the same type of material (vellum), with phrases threatening violators of charter covenants with religious rather than secular punishments, and whose uses were almost exclusively to convey land interests from a king to or for a religious institution. The "formulas" (standard phrasing of the operative provisions) were very similar to those used by the Roman Pope Gregory I, who sent the first Roman missionaries to the Anglo-Saxon King Aethelberht; this suggests that the very idea of using charters may have been introduced by the Italian missionaries sent to England.[478] As to the actual writing of the charters, "[u]ntil the tenth century, at least, it seems in fact that the writing of charters was the

---

[477] Marjorie Chibnall, *Anglo-Norman England 1066-1166* 187-188 (1986).

[478] "[The charters] are an ecclesiastical importation, modeled on the late Roman private deed, and they show us that the consent of the king's council was obtained for the act of creating bookland." Dorothy Whitelock, *The Beginnings of English Society* 153 (1974).

responsibility of the local bishop, the local abbot or their scribes [rather than the king's own clerks] (the important proviso being that such men were often in attendance on the king)."[479]

While several scholars have been tempted to interpret charter conveyances under a uniform and consistent set of rules, it is probably not accurate to ascribe a standard set of property rights as subject to conveyance by charter. Often the terminology in the charters is ambiguous and inconsistent. Under the assumption that by the 8th century, A.D., when the earliest extant charters are dated, all occupied lands were subject to certain types of service (such as military service, road building, and fortress maintenance), it has been theorized that charters normally gave relief or immunity from such burdens. In fact, wording conferring such immunity does appear in later charters, but is absent from the earlier charters. This suggests that the earliest charters did nothing more than affirmatively convey the food-rent of an estate, known as the *feorm*.

The tenurial characteristics of bookland also cannot be identified with certainty. Grantors may have used the charter at first to ensure the ecclesiastical grantee that the grant would not be revoked. If early Anglo-Saxon land practices conformed to traditional Germanic practices, then grantors could transfer certain lands—held by kinship groups—only by inheritance within the group, and could not alienate the land outside the group without group assent. Thus land granted to the church would have come from other, alienable lands held by the king, but there is some evidence that the royal grantor could later revoke such acquired property interests.[480] By use of the charter, the grantor could make the grantee's interest in such property perpetual, with documentary evidence against any presumed royal right to revoke. Such permanent transfers inevitably meant that kings drew upon a diminishing reserve of land with which to reward faithful followers; however, according to earlier practice, kings could revoke previous conveyances and reconvey those lands to others.

---

[479] Patrick Wormald, "The Age of Bede and Aethelbald," in *The Anglo-Saxons* 97 (James Campbell, ed., 1982).

[480] *Id.*

Even these conveyances out of the royal demesne might sometimes find their way back into the holdings of inheritable kinship property. It appears that on occasion a grantee of bookland, perhaps an abbot who obtained the land for ecclesiastical purposes, passed the land on to his son who also succeeded him as abbot, whereupon the land began to be treated as inheritable kinship property with rights of the kindred attached.[481] It may have been a common practice for a prominent family to use the charter as a means of enhancing its landholding by using bookland to found a monastery and then retain governance of the monastery within the family. In Bede's last work, he deplored the increasing incidence of such land grants, which "permitted local magnates to turn their establishments into sham monasteries and thus to evade their public liabilities."[482]

Apparently it later became acceptable to limit a conveyance by bookland to inheritability only with the kin. Thus a 9th century, A.D., law of Alfred the Great prohibits a landholder from alienating bookland that was obtained under such a limitation.[483]

Because most of the land "conveyed" by a charter would already be occupied by others, the effect of the charter might be better characterized as simply a surrender of royal rights. Benefits flowing to the lord from such conveyances are not mentioned in the charters, but were possibly left to be governed by custom.[484]

---

[481] *See, e.g.,* 1 Walter de Gray Birch, *Cartularium Saxonicum* 308, no. 220 (1885) (grant by Abbot Ceolfrith, A.D. 757).

[482] H.P.R. Finberg, *The Formation of England 550-1042* 92 (1974).

[483] *The Laws of the Earliest English Kings* 83, Alfred cl. 41 (F.L. Attenborough, ed. & trans., 1922).

[484] "[T]hese charters always take the form of a simple conveyance of land, and ignore the fact that the gifts which they record mean, in effect, the alienation of rights by a king for the benefit of a subject. The rights themselves are expressed in the vaguest of words, which often amount to nothing more than a statement that the land at issue is to be free from all earthly service, qualified by certain reservations in the king's interest. . . . For the rest, the king makes no attempt to intervene between the lord and the men who are to be under his authority. . . The exaction of the ancient food-rents and services by which a new lord will henceforward profit can safely be left to the control of a custom which is none the less valid because it has never been reduced to writing . . .

It has been stated that "nothing but a royal charter could free land from the king's dues and services, and defeat the claims of expectant heirs."[485] In one surviving charter the king grants land to himself for the express purpose of removing certain secular burdens from the land, so the king can thereafter convey the land to another free of such obligations.[486]

By the end of the eighth century, A.D., charters were beginning to be used for purely secular grants. Sometimes the terms of the charter indicate that money has been paid, and presumably money may have been paid even in many cases where payment was not mentioned in the charter. A grantee, of course, found it highly desirable if the land could be alienated at will and was free from royal duties.[487]

Keeping in mind that probably conveyancing practices involving bookland and even the incidents or characteristics of bookland changed over the centuries of the Anglo-Saxon age, it may still be helpful to make a general statement about the property rights associated with bookland.[488] Probably the estates created by bookland were allodial, which is to say that the owner did not hold the estate of any superior owner. Bookland was probably conveyed by delivery of the book and perhaps some additional ceremony signifying corporeal delivery of the land. Such a ceremony may have been similar to the later livery of seisin, during which the parties went on to the land and in the sight of witnesses exchanged possession of a dirt

---

"Charters of this type generally include a clause stating that the recipient of the estate may alienate or bequeath it in his will.

F.M. Stenton, *Anglo-Saxon England* 303-304 (1943); *see, e.g.,* 1 Walter de Gray Birch", *Cartularium Saxonicum* 314, (1885) (grant by King Cynewulf to Earl Bica, 778, A.D.

[485] F.M. Stenton, *Anglo-Saxon England* 304 (1943).

[486] 2 Walter de Gray Birch, *Cartularium Saxonicum* 33, no. 451 (1887) (grant by King Aethelwulf to himself, Dec. 26, 847, A.D.).

[487] Dorothy Whitelock, *The Beginnings of English Society* 154 (1974).

[488] A model and the sources for the convenient but somewhat speculative summary in the text are cited in William F. Walsh, *A History of Anglo-American Law* 16-17 (2d ed. 1950).

clod or similar object. No new book or deed would be required. Bookland probably carried with it the rights to alienate or devise, but subject to certain customary protections for heirs. However, if the charter specifically conferred rights of alienation and devise, as many but not all did, then transfer could occur without restraint from heirs. If a bookland owner died intestate, the bookland would pass to heirs, usually but not always to sons in equal shares. Rights of Anglo-Saxon women in land generally are discussed elsewhere.[489]

The charters and incidents of bookland continued after the Norman Conquest, but not for long. The feudalism introduced by the Norman Conquest placed heavy reliance on customary rights of landholding, and not the departures from those rights represented by the Anglo-Saxon charters.[490]

§ 6.05(e)(2). Folkland.

Folkland, or "folcland," is of uncertain status in Anglo-Saxon property law. It may have been virtually any land not considered bookland, and thus still subject to alienation restrictions and to customary obligations and dues.[491]

---

[489] *See* §§ 6.05(f).

[490] "The system of making grants by written instruments went on unchecked until, with the advent of the Normans and the system of feudal tenures, the old significance of the Anglo-Saxon book, as well as the name, almost disappeared. The importance of the book primarily lay in its opposition to the old Germanic customs and principles, and in the protection it afforded against the claims recognized by that system. When each and every estate formed but one link in the great feudal chain, there was no longer any use in the book as the Anglo-Saxons conceived it. The only characteristic it retained was as an evidence of title. Charters and deeds went on accumulating in great abundance, but the old Saxon book perished with the Conquest. In all Domesday, there is but one estate of boc-land mentioned. . . . There was but one object left for a written instrument, to evidence title; and the Norman charters fulfilled that object." H. Cabot Lodge, *"The Anglo-Saxon Land Law,"* in *Essays in Anglo-Saxon Law* 112 (1905).

[491] Dorothy Whitelock, *The Beginnings of English Society* 154 (1974).

The documentary references to folkland are few and indeterminative. The most authoritative statement on folkland is in a passage from the laws of Edward the Elder, issued ca. 900-925, A.D.:

> Further, we have declared what [penalty] he is liable to, who withholds from another his rights either in "bookland" or "folkland," And with regard to the "folkland" [we have declared] that he [the plaintiff] shall appoint a day when he [the defendant] shall do him justice in the presence of the reeve.
>
> §1. If, however, he [the plaintiff] does not obtain his rights either in "bookland" or "folkland," he [the defendant] who withholds the rights shall forfeit a fine of 30 shillings to the king, and 30 shillings also on the second occasion, and on the third occasion the fine for insubordination to the king, that is 120 shillings, unless he has already desisted [from his wrong-doing].[492]

A second reference is in the will of a 9th century, A.D., ealdorman named Alfred, who bequeathed bookland to his son, expecting that the king would make an additional grant of folkland to the son. If the king were not forthcoming, the son would receive additional bookland from the testator's wife.[493] As viewed by Stenton, this conveyance showed that one could hold both bookland and folkland, with differing powers of disposition.[494]

As related by another charter, the king of Kent in 858, A.D., gave land to his minister Wulflaf in exchange for other land. The land that the king received in exchange was turned into folkland by the king for himself,[495]

---

[492] *The Laws of the Earliest English Kings* 117, I Edward cl. 2 (F.L. Attenborough, ed. & trans. 1922).

[493] Walter de Gray Birch, *Cartularium Saxonicum* 195, no. 558 (1887) (will of Duke Alfred, A.D. 781).

[494] F.M. Stenton, *Anglo-Saxon England* 307 (1943).

[495] Walter de Gray Birch, *Cartularium Saxonicum* 100, no. 496 (1887).

and the king then obtained food-rents and services from holders of land previously exempt from such obligations.[496]

Pollock and Maitland pointed out that several gratuitous assumptions about folkland had been advanced and refuted during the 19th century, and concluded: "Folk-land, then, appears to have been, as Spelman said, land held without written title under customary law. We have no right to assume that there were not varieties of tenure within this general description, or that custom was uniform even in the same kingdom."[497]

Another historian was of the view that folkland generally was alienable but subject to rights of heirs, and speculated that at least some folkland was held as "freehold allodial estates under the customary law."[498] "We have little or no direct evidence of the rules of law which determined the incidents of ownership of folkland; but in view of what we find existing after the Conquest, the inference is unavoidable that the freeholder could convey his land subject to restrictions, concerning the details of which we know nothing definitely, to his heirs. . ."[499]

Whatever were the precise incidents of folkland, it surely made up the largest portion of occupied English lands, and was likely the direct source of the landholding rights that prevailed in most areas during the decades immediately following the Norman Conquest.

---

[496] "The whole tenor of the document shows that this transaction meant the imposition of public burdens on land which had previously been exempt from them, and that the king was compensating himself for the loss of *feorm* [food rents] and service from Wassingwell [the land given in the exchange] by imposing these burdens on the land at Mersham [the land received in the exchange]. . . . To the man who wrote this endorsement, folkland meant land from which the king drew food-rents and customary services." F.M. Stenton, *Anglo-Saxon England* 307-308 (1943).

[497] Frederick Pollock and Frederic William Maitland, *The History of English Law Before the Time of Edward I* 61-62 (2d ed. 1909).

[498] William W. Walsh, *A History of Anglo-American Law* 33-34 (2d ed. 1932).

[499] *Id.* at 14-15.

§ 6.05(e)(3). Laenland.

Late in the Anglo-Saxon era, documentary references to a type of landholding known as "laenland" occur. "Laen" is related to the modern German *Lehn*, or loan, and this type of property interest may be accurately described as "loaned" land. Laenland was a "grant of land for temporary use, made usually by the church or other holder of bookland, just as the book, or charter, creating bookland estates was usually made by the king."[500]

The most explicit reference to laenland in Anglo-Saxon charters is an account by Bishop Oswald of Worcester, explaining how the church planned to lease or lend some of its lands to private parties.[501] Another charter refers to laenland descending to the cathedrals at Canterbury and Rochester.[502] From these documents it has been generalized that grantors gave laenland in imitation of bookland charters, creating subordinate interests in prominent persons who themselves were not the actual occupants of the land. The grants varied in duration from one to three lives, and drew either periodic rent, a lump sum payment, or rendering of services.[503] It has also been theorized that the laenland device could have been widely used by all types of landholders to let out their lands on short terms under oral leases, especially since producing writings of any kind would have been difficult in that era.[504] Because these loaned lands were not always coincident with customary tenurial incidents "it must have been possible for a peasant to acknowledge one man as his lord and to rent land

---

[500] *Id.* at 18.

[501] 3 Walter de Gray Birch, *Cartularium Saxonicum* 382, no. 1136 (1893) (letter of Oswald, Bishop of Worcester, to King Eadgar, describing the leasehold tenures of certain church lands, ca. 964, A.D.).

[502] *Id.* at 328, no. 1097 (1893) (record of the descent of land to the Canterbury and Rochester cathedrals, ca. 965, A.D.).

[503] William W. Walsh, *A History of Anglo-American Law* 19 (2d ed. 1932).

[504] *Id.* at 19-20. *See* discussion of Worcester laenland grants to women, priests, deacons, and clerks, in R. Allen Brown, *Origins of English Feudalism* 55-56 (1973).

from two or three other landlords."[505]

As far as the documentary evidence is concerned, in the terminology of later medieval times, bookland could be described generally as the land received from the king by tenants-in-chief, while laenland would be the land held of tenants-in-chief by lesser lords.[506] However, there is virtually no evidence in Domesday Book or any other early post-Conquest source that laenland holding was widespread or that it carried over into post-Conquest landholding practices in some modified form. The scarcity of direct evidence and the speculative nature of theories about laenland has opened and left unresolved a scholarly debate over whether laenland represented an incipient form of Anglo-Saxon feudalism, well-entrenched in the generations before the Norman Conquest. If one limits the concept of feudal tenures to fee interests requiring military or other knightly service, then these laenland tenures were probably not feudal: they do not appear to be fee interests, and the consideration given for the grants was usually something other than a commitment for military service.[507] However, whether or not denominated as feudal, and whether commonly or rarely occurring, laenland appears clearly as a form of landholding based on services and other consideration in addition to or other than customary tenurial incidents. If laenland was not proto-feudalism, it might well have been the beginnings of landlord-tenant law.

§ 6.05(f). Rights of Women Under Anglo-Saxon Property Law.

As was true in the warrior societies of Dark Age Europe generally, Anglo-Saxon women were in most respects subordinate to men. However, as the rule of law emerged in Anglo-Saxon kingdoms, a certain evenhandedness regarding gender was a characteristic feature of the English legal codes and customs. This is perhaps no more clearly manifest

---

[505] D.P. Kirby, *The Making of Early England* 228 (1967).

[506] Frederic William Maitland, *Domesday Book and Beyond* 314 (reprint 1966).

[507] R. Allen Brown, *Origins of English Feudalism* 54-64 (1973).

than in matters of property rights.

Much information about rights of women under Anglo-Saxon property law can be gleaned from the charters. It is possible that the property rights of women apparent in these charters applied only to women of the social class that would normally use such charters. However, quite likely the rough parity of gender before the law manifest in these documents was a characteristic of Anglo-Saxon society generally.[508]

In these instruments women appear in the capacities of grantor,[509] grantee,[510] vendor,[511] vendee,[512] plaintiff,[513] defendant,[514] testatrix,[515] and devisee[516] with no apparent distinctions in substance, form or procedure made on account of gender. In Anglo-Saxon legal proceedings, a woman

---

[508] Although the discussion in the text is drawn as much as possible from primary sources, or at least the English translations of primary sources, this topic has been the subject of recent writing. *See, e.g.*, Christine E. Fell, *Women in Anglo-Saxon England* (1984); *The Women of England: From Anglo-Saxon Times to the Present: Interpretive Bibliographic Essays* (Barbara Kanner, ed., 1979).

[509] 1 Walter de Gray Birch, *Cartularium Saxonicum* 552, No. 396 (1885) (grant of land by King Egbert, A.D. 830).

[510] *Id.* Two grants of laenland to women are discussed and documented in R. Allen Brown, *Origins of English Feudalism* 55-56 (1973).

[511] 2 Walter de Gray Birch, *id.* At 54, No. 789 (1887) (grant by Kind Edmund, 943, A.D.); 4 John M. Kemble, *Codex Diplmaticus Aevi Saxonici* No. 789 (1846).

[512] *Id.*

[513] 3 John M. Kemble, *Codex Diplomaticus Aevi Saxonici* Nos. 693, 704 (1845).

[514] *Id.*

[515] 1 Walter de Gray Birch, *Cartularium Saxonicum* 575, No. 412 (1885) (will of the Reeve Abba, ca. 833, A.D.); 3 Walter de Gray Birch, *id.* at 600, No. 1288 (1893) (will of Queen Aethelflaed); *id.* At 602, No. 1289 (will of Aelflaed).

[516] *Id.*

was qualified to be a witness[517] or an oath-helper[518] in the same way as was a man.

In most respects this status of apparent equality prevailed even for married women. A husband could convey bookland to his wife.[519] Husband and wife could join as vendors,[520] grantors,[521] devisors,[522] and be joined as vendees,[523] grantees,[524] and devisees.[525]

Less, however, is known about a married woman's rights in lands received as dowry, morning-gift or in some form of marriage settlement. Germanic custom concerning the commitment for marriage is a necessary background for understanding of this subject. Several references to

---

[517] 3 John M. Kemble, *Codex Diplomaticus Aevi Saxonici* Nos. 693, 704 (1845).

[518] 2 Walter de Gray Birch, *Cartularium Saxonicum* 155, No. 537 (1887) (grant by King Athelred to Cuthulf, the thegn, 872, A.D.); 3 John M. Kemble, *Codex Diplomaticus Aevi Saxonici* No. 693 (1845).

[519] 2 Walter de Gray Birch, *Cartularium Saxonicum* 86, No. 486 (1887) (grant by King Aethelwulf to his thegn Dunn; Dunn's devise of the land to his wife).

[520] *Id.* at 119, No. 509 (grant by King Burhred and Queen Aethelswyth, July 25, 864, A.D.); *id.* at 141, No. 524 (grant by King Burgred and Queen Aethelsuith, 869, A.D.).

[521] 4 John M. Kemble, *Codex Diplomaticus Aevi Saxonici* No. 796 (1846); 6 John M. Kemble, *id.* at No. 1340 (1848).

[522] 3 Walter de Gray Birch, *Cartularium Saxonicum* 373, No. 1132 (1893) (will of Byrhtric and his wife Aelfswyth bequeathing real and personal property, 964, A.D.); 4 John M. Kemble, *Codex Diplomaticus Aevi Saxonici* No. 971 (1846).

[523] 2 Walter de Gray Birch, *Cartularium Saxonicum* 92, No. 490 (grant by Alhwine to Aethelwulf and his wife Wulfthryth, 855, A.D.).

[524] *Id.* at 465, No. 745 (grant by King Athelstan, ca. 929, A.D.); 3 John M. Kemble, *Codex Diplomaticus Aevi Saxonici* No. 637 (1845).

[525] 2 Walter de Gray Birch, *Cartularium Saxonicum* 176, No. 553 (1887) (will of King Alfred, 880, A.D.).

marriage as a *sale* appear in various Anglo-Saxon dooms,[526] but the transaction was probably not as crass as sale of a chattel; perhaps it should be viewed more as a transfer of the rights and duties of guardianship.

Guardianship in Germanic law was one respect in which women were categorically subordinated to men. It was axiomatic that a woman should be under the guardianship of a male, and the time of marriage marked the transfer of guardianship responsibilities and rights from the father to the new husband. That the references to Anglo-Saxon marriage or betrothal as a "sale" are really references to transfer of guardianship finds support in the fact that, in Germanic custom generally, the price paid was not derived from bargaining, but was simply the *wergild* of the bride, as fixed by her social status. The marriage price would be paid on the occasion of betrothal, and a woman who was untrue to her betrothal would owe a sum equal to her marriage price. Also, the guardian of the bride could not be compelled to specific performance, as it were, but only to pay damages in breach of contract[527] if he failed to complete the transaction.[528]

The betrothal customs described in the preceding paragraph, which prevailed among Germanic tribes generally, had been altered slightly among the Anglo-Saxons as early as the 8th century, A.D.[529] The Anglo-Saxon dooms show that, at least in some cases, the price was no longer paid at the betrothal, but only promised; instead a nominal sum of

---

[526] *See, e.g.*, *The Laws of the Earliest English Kings* 46-47 (F. L. Attenborough, ed. & trans., 1922), Ine cl. 31 ("If anyone buys a wife and the marriage does not take place . . . ."); *id.* at 14-15, Aethelberht cl. 83 ("If she is betrothed, at a price, to another man . . . ."); *id.* at 8-9, Aethelberht cl. 31 ("If [one] freeman lies with the wife of [another] freeman, he shall pay [the husband] his [or her] wergeld, and procure a second wife with his own money, and bring her to the other man's home.).

[527] The price plus one third.

[528] Ernest Young, "The Anglo-Saxon Family Law," in *Essays in Anglo-Saxon Law* 164-165 (1905).

[529] *See generally*, Document 51, "Concerning the Betrothal of a Woman, c. A.D. 975-1030)," in 1 *English Historical Documents* 431 (David C. Douglas, gen. ed., Dorothy Whitelock, ed., 1955).

earnest money was paid to the guardian at the time of betrothal.[530] Also, when the full price was eventually paid, it was given directly to the bride rather than to the guardian.[531] Thus, over many generations, the characteristics of a sale that had previously attached to arrangements of marriage had been transformed into the characteristics of a contract.

The price of the betrothal, which custom eventually directed to be paid at the time of marriage, was only one endowment for the bride. It became, by comparison, of little importance in relation to the other bridal endowment, the so-called *Morgengabe* or morning-gift. The morning-gift was originally a free-will gift by the husband to the bride on the morning after the bridal night.[532] Consisting at first of chattels, it later came to be considered as a form of widow's maintenance, and thus was necessarily property of sufficient value to sustain the wife if she survived her husband. The morning-gift, therefore, came to be almost always a gift of land, normally granted at the time of betrothal by means of a written document (to prove ownership after the husband's death); alternatively, if a specific morning-gift were not granted at the betrothal or beginning of the marriage, then the law assigned a certain portion of the husband's property, usually one-half, for maintenance of the bride if she became a widow.

Among the Germanic tribes on the continent, the bridal price and morning-gift, both promised at the time of betrothal, eventually merged and, on the continent, became the dower. In Anglo-Saxon kingdoms, the two gifts did not merge, but the morning-gift was clearly the more important of the endowments. By law and custom the morning-gift, usually one-half of the husband's property, was assured to the widow from a childless marriage. Approximately the same division of property was observed even if both husband and wife remained alive and married: if one or more live children were born to the marriage, then the couple held their

---

[530] *The Laws of the Earliest English Kings* 46-47 (F.L. Attenborough ed., & trans., 1922), Ine cl. 31; 72-73, Alfred cl. 18 §1 (1922).

[531] Alfred Eccl. Laws §12.

[532] 2 Walter de Gray Birch, *Cartularium Saxonicum* 255, No. 582 (1887) (settlement of land by Bishop Werferth on Eadnoth, A.D. 872); 4 John M. Kemble, *Codex Diplomaticus Aevi Saxonici* No. 867 (1846).

real property as community property. They also held their personal property in community, even if no children were born.[533]

Although the wife was considered under the guardianship of the husband, she was quite independent as to the household, as may be inferred from the following provisions of Cnut's laws regarding liability for stolen property brought into the house by the husband:

> Concerning stolen goods.
>
> If anyone carries stolen goods home to his cottage and is detected, the law is that (the owner) shall have what he has tracked.
>
> §1. And unless the goods had been put under the wife's lock and key, she shall be clear [of any danger of complicity].
>
> §1a. But it is her duty to guard the keys of the following—her storeroom and her chest and her cupboard. If the goods have been put in any of these, she shall be held guilty . . . .[534]

Upon the husband's death, the widow became the owner of all property she had obtained by inheritance or gift as well as the morning-gift, either as described by charter, or, in the absence of charter, usually one-half of the husband's property.[535] Unless the wife's ownership rights in the morning-gift had been limited when given by the husband, the wife had full

---

[533] *The Laws of the Earliest English Kings* 54-57 (F.L. Attenborough, ed. & trans., 1922), Ine cl. 57; 156-157, VI Aethelstan cl. 1, §1 (1922).

[534] *The Laws of the Kings of England from Edmund to Henry I* 213-215 (Agnes Jane Robertson, ed. & trans., 1925), II Cnut cl. 76.

[535] *The Laws of the Earliest Kings* 14-15, Aethelberht cls. 78-81 (F.L. Attenborough, ed. & trans., 1922).

ownership, with power to dispose of it by conveyance[536] or devise.[537] However, a widow was required to remain chaste and unmarried for at least a year after her husband's death, and for violation of this restriction, she would forfeit all her property to her husband's next of kin;[538] if she did not violate that restriction, the property was fully hers to take into her next marriage.[539] According to the laws of Cnut, if the wife was unfaithful to the husband, she forfeited all her property to her husband.[540] If the couple divorced by mutual consent and the children remained with the wife, she took half the property; if the children remained with the husband, the wife took only a child's portion of the property.[541]

Apart from the above minutiae of Anglo-Saxon custom and law regarding women's property rights, one may conclude generally that women enjoyed a relatively higher status and stronger property rights during the Anglo-Saxon centuries than during the high Middle Ages following the Norman Conquest in 1066, A.D.

---

[536] 2 Walter de Gray Birch, *Cartularium Saxonicum* 236, No. 591 (1887) (letter to King Edward setting forth events connected with the tenure of land, ca. 901, A.D.); 3 Walter de Gray Birch, *id.* at 653, No. 1318 (1893) (three-year lease of land); 3 John M. Kemble, *Codex Diplomaticus Aevi Saxonici* No. 704 (1845).

[537] 3 Walter de Gray Birch, *Cartularium Saxonicum* 600, No. 1288 (1893) (will of Aethelflaed, queen of Edmund I); *id.* At 602, No. 1289 (will of Aelflaed, sister of Queen Aethelflaed); 6 John M. Kemble, *Codex Diplomaticus Aevi Saxonici* No. 1290 (1848).

[538] *The Laws of the Kings of England from Edmund to Henry I* 210-213, II Cnut cls. 73 and 73a (Agnes Jane Robertson, ed. & trans., 1925).

[539] Walter de Gray Birch, *Cartularium Saxonicum* 328, No. 1097 (1893) (record of the descent of land and related litigation).

[540] *The Laws of the Kings of England from Edmund to Henry I* 202-203, II Cnut cl. 53 (Agnes Jane Robertson, ed. & trans., 1925).

[541] *The Laws of the Earliest English Kings* 14-15, Aethelberht cls. 79-80 (F.L. Attenborough, ed. & trans., 1922).

§ 6.06. Impact of the Viking Invasions on Property Rights in Anglo-Saxon England.

Raids of Vikings in Anglo-Saxon England began sporadically as early as 787, A.D.,[542] but the sack of the church foundations on the island of Lindisfarne in 793, A.D.,[543] was the most stunning announcement of the new danger. Illustration 22 shows the vulnerability of this wealthy establishment. These early raids, mostly by Norwegians, continued to be sporadic until about 835, A.D., whereafter regular accounts appear in the Anglo-Saxon Chronicle. The new raiders were mostly Danish and continued to be essentially small and highly mobile warbands, each of which was capable of ranging widely over Europe in a single season.

Illustration 22. Ruins of the monastery at Lindisfarne, or Holy Isle, a tidal island on the Northumbrian coast. The first of several Viking raids there in 793, A.D., signalled the beginning of the Viking age in England, and disrupted every aspect of English life.

---

[542] *The Anglo-Saxon Chronicle* 53 annal 787.

[543] *Id.* at 54 annal 793.

The raiding parties remained relatively small,[544] were seeking portable wealth, and did not come to settle. Not until 850-851, A.D., was a band of Danish Vikings reported as having wintered over in England.[545] Thereafter, the scale of Viking attacks increased, so that fleets of 150-250[546] ships became common, and the "great" Viking armies of 865[547] and 871, A.D.,[548] divided up the land they conquered in Northumbria,[549] Mercia,[550] and East Anglia.[551] Illustration 23 shows the site of the great Viking community of Hedeby or Haitabu, whence many raids originated.

Of the great Anglo-Saxon kingdoms, only Wessex survived, and was itself subjected to several bloody battles in 871, A.D. Then in 878, A.D., the Danish King Guthrum launched a surprise attack against Alfred's forces that drove Alfred and a few remaining supporters into hiding in the marshes of Somerset. Alfred then began a guerrilla campaign and his ultimate triumph over Guthrum is justly celebrated. Guthrum eventually withdrew to his secure eastern territories and accepted Christian baptism. Thus, during Alfred's lifetime, Wessex and part of Mercia were left intact as Anglo-Saxon domains, but Northumbria, East Anglia, and the rest of Mercia came under total Danish domination, the area thereafter known as the Danelaw. However, debate continues to this day over the density of Danish settlement in the Danelaw and the extent of Danish influence over property and other legal customs.

---

[544] The evidence suggests that the early raiding parties seldom consisted of more than fifty ships, and such ships would carry hardly more than thirty warriors, even without horses, slaves or other cargo.

[545] *The Anglo-Saxon Chronicle* 62-63 annal 850.

[546] The raid of 893, A.D., is reported to have been conducted with 330 ships.

[547] So described in *The Anglo-Saxon Chronicle* 66-67 annal 865.

[548] *See Id.* at 68-69 annal 871.

[549] *Id.* at 72-73 annal 876.

[550] *Id.* at annal 877.

[551] *Id.* at 74-75 annal 879.

Illustration 23. This pastoral scene is the site of Hedeby or Haitabu, located near the present Danish-German border and the German city of Schleswig. It was the largest Nordic city during the Viking age.

As to the Danish influence on Anglo-Saxon law, probably little change occurred. Even into the 11th century, when Cnut, a great Danish King of England, issued a law code, it was "in the full stream of English legal achievement," exhibiting no Danish idiosyncracies.[552] This phenomenon has been explained by the fact that Danish traditions of kindred organizations, *wergilds*, and public assemblies were very similar to those of the English. Moreover, when the Danes who settled in eastern and northern England accepted Christianity, they implicitly accepted the body of law associated with the church and were exposed to English clergy, who were usually responsible for written legal records.[553]

Nevertheless, a doom of Edgar declares "that secular rights be in force

---

[552] Henry Royston Loyn, *The Vikings in Britain* 125 (1977).

[553] *Id.* at 125-127.

among the Danes according to as good laws as they can best decide on,"[554] and Aethelred issued parallel codes for Englishmen and Danes.[555] Several distinctively Danish legal practices emerged in Anglo-Danish England. In land law, terminology was Danish, and there was heavy reliance on independent sureties for land transactions. Land measurement and assessment in the Danelaw were altered, and exhibited a new vocabulary.

In procedure, a public prosecutor may have functioned in Anglo-Danish areas. Twelve leading thegns (members of the aristocracy) in each borough went forth from the court and swore on relics that they would neither accuse any innocent person nor protect any guilty one. A majority of eight determined the presentments of this body, which resembled a jury. Differences in assessing fines and difficulties in reconciling disparate monetary units persisted in the Danelaw. Compensation paid to a slain man's lord was based on the victim's status, whereas in English areas that amount was determined by the lord's rank. Danish custom assigned a greater penalty for breach of the king's peace in the Danelaw, suggesting it was more highly valued (or more readily broken).

Most significantly, the Danes in England appear to have had a much greater proportion of free peasants in the areas they dominated. Historians are divided over whether this social difference was directly related to Scandinavian settlement or arose from regional peculiarities in place before the Danes arrived. It is appealing to attribute this freedom to "the infusion of large numbers of Scandinavian farmer warriors with their traditions of independence, reinforced by their nature as colonists."[556] Those farmers who came as raiders were free volunteers on their Viking ships. Danes also made significant contributions to urban growth in England, particularly in

---

[554] "Edgar's Code Issued at 'Wihtbordesstan,'" in 1 *English Historical Documents* 399, cl. 2.1 (David C. Douglas, ed., 1955); 1 F. Felix Liebermann, *Die Gesetze der Angelsachsen* 228-233 (1903).

[555] *See, e.g.,* "King Ethelred's Code Issued at Wantage," in 1 *English Historical Documents* 402-405 (David C. Douglas, ed., 1955); 1 F. Felix Liebermann, *Die Gesetze der Angelsachsen* 228-233 (1903).

[556] Henry Royston Loyn, *The Vikings in Britain* 132 (1977).

York.[557]

§ 6.07. Bibliography.

Books

Abies, Richard Phillip, *Alfred the Great: War, Kingship, and Culture in Anglo-Saxon England* (1998).
Appleby, John C., *Government, Religion, and Society in Northern England, 1000-1700* (1997).
Aslam, Jeremy, *Anglo-Saxon Towns in Southern England* (1984).
Barrell, Harry Ferdinand, *An Outline of Anglo-Saxon Law* (1999).
Birch, Walter de Gray, *Cartularium Saxonicum* (1885).
Blair, Peter Hunter. *Roman Britain and Early England: 55 B.C. - A.D. 871* (1963).
Blair, Peter Hunter, *The World of Bede* (1971).
Blair, W. John, *The Anglo-Saxon Age: a Very Short Introduction* (2000).
Bonser, W., *Anglo-Saxon and Celtic Bibliography (450-1087)* (1957).
Brown, R. Allen, *Origins of English Feudalism* (1973).
Brower, Adrienne, *Over Countless Waves upon England's Shore: a Look at the Legal Progress from Britain's First Peoples to the Norman Conquest, and Why Anglo-Saxon Law Is the True Root of England's Common Law* (1999).
Brown, Michelle, *Mercia, An Anglo-Saxon Kingdom in Europe* (2001).
Campbell, James, *The Anglo-Saxon State* (2000).
Campbell, James, *The Anglo-Saxons* (1982).
Chadwick, H. Munroe, *The Origins of the English Nation* (1924).
Chibnall, Marjorie, *Anglo-Norman England* (1986).
Collingwood, R. G., *Roman Britain and the English Settlements* (1937).
Cramp, Rosemary, ed., *Corpus of Anglo-Saxon Stone Sculpture in England* (1984).
Diamond, Jared M., *Collapse: How Societies Choose to Fail or Succeed* (2005).
Diamond, Jared M., *Guns, Germs, and Steel: The Fates of Human Societies* (1997).
Dos Passos, John R., *The Anglo-Saxon Century and the Unification of the English-Speaking People* (1903).
Fell, Christine E., *Women in Anglo-Saxon England* (1984).
Finberg, H.P.R., *The Agrarian History of England and Wales A.D. 43-1042* (1972).
Finberg, H.P.R., *The Formation of England* (1974).
Fisher, D. J. V., *The Anglo-Saxon Age, c. 400-1042* (1973).
Fletcher, Richard A., *Bloodfeud: Murder and Revenge in Anglo-Saxon England* (2003).
Frantzen, Allen J., *Anglo-Saxonism and the Construction of Social Identity* (1997).
Hayashi, Hiroshi, *Essays in Anglo-Saxon Law* (1989).
Heywood, Samuel, *A Dissertation upon the Distinctions in Society, and Ranks of the People, under the Anglo-Saxon Governments* (1818).
Hill, Paul, *The Road to Hastings: The Politics of Power in Anglo-Saxon England* (2005).
Hines, John, ed., *The Anglo-Saxons From the Migration Period to the Eighth Century: an Ethnographic Perspective* (1997).

---

[557] *Id.* at 135-137.

Hodges, Richard, *The Anglo-Saxon Achievement: Archaeology and the Beginnings of English Society* (1989).
Holdsworth, William, *A History of English Law* (1923).
Hooke, Delia, *Anglo-Saxon Settlements* (1988).
Hooke, Delia, *The Landscape of Anglo-Saxon England* (1998).
Hunter Blair, Peter, *An Introduction to Anglo-Saxon England* (1977).
John, Eric, *Land Tenure in Early England: A Discussion of Some Problems* (1964).
Jones, Gwyn, *A History of the Vikings* (2d ed., 1984).
Kelly, S. E., ed., *Charters of Shaftesbury Abbey* 1996).
Kemble, John Marshall, *Codex Diplomaticus Aevi Saxonici* (1845).
Kemble, John Mitchell, *The Saxons in England* (1876).
Kerr, Mary, *Anglo-Saxon Architecture* (1983).
Kirby, D. P., *The Making of Early England* (1967).
Kynell, Kurt von S., *Saxon and Medieval Antecedents of the English Common Law* (2000).
Laing, Lloyd Robert, *Anglo-Saxon England* (1979).
Lapidge, Michael, ed., *The Blackwell Encyclopedia of Anglo-Saxon England* (1999).
Lees, Clare A. and Gillian R. Overing, eds., *A Place to Believe In: Locating Medieval Landscapes* (2006).
Liebermann, F. Felix, *Die Gesetze der Angelsachsen* (1903).
Lindsay, Jack, *The Normans and Their World* (1974).
Loyn, H. R., *Anglo-Saxon England and the Norman Conquest* (1991).
Loyn, H. R., *The Governance of Anglo-Saxon England, 500-1087* (1984).
Loyn, H.R., *The Vikings in Britain* (1977).
Maitland, Frederic William, *Domesday Book and Beyond* (1897).
Mann, Charles C., *1491 : New Revelations of the Americas Before Columbus* (2005).
Michelet, Fabienne L., *Creation, Migration, and Conquest: Imaginary Geography and Sense of Space in Old English Literature* (2006).
Myres, J.N.L., *The English Settlements* (1986).
Oliver, Lisa, *The Beginnings of English Law* (2002).
Pipes, Richard, *Property and Freedom* (1999).
Pollock, Frederick and Frederic William Maitland, *The History of English Law Before the Time of Edward I* (1909).
Reed, M., ed., *"Anglo-Saxon Charter Boundaries", Discovering Past Landscapes* (1984).
Richardson, H.G., and G.O. Sayles, *Law and Legislation from Aethelberht to Magna Carta* (1966).
Rumble, Alexander, ed., *Writing and Texts in Anglo-Saxon England* (2006).
Seebohm, Frederic, *Tribal Custom in Anglo-Saxon Law; Being an Essay Supplemental To: (1) the English Village Community, (2) the Tribal System in Wales* (1972).
Simon, Edith, *The Anglo-Saxon Manner: the English Contribution to Civilization* (1972).
Smith, Henry E., "Exclusion Versus Governance: Two Strategies for Delineating Property Rights," 31 *J. Legal Stud.* 453 (June, 2002).
Stenton, F.M., *Anglo-Saxon England* (1971).
Stenton, F.M., *The Latin Charters of the Anglo-Saxon Period* (1955).
Szarmach, Paul E., ed., *Sources of Anglo-Saxon Culture* (1986).
Tapp, Sidney Calhoun, *The Story of Anglo-Saxon Institutions; or, the Development of Constitutional Government* (1904).
Thompson, E.A., *The Early Germans* (1965).
Tingle, Rebecca, *Far Traveler* (2005).

Tingle, Rebecca, *The Edge on the Sword* (2001).
Vinogradoff, Paul, *English Society in the Eleventh Century* (1925).
Walsh, William Francis, *A History of Anglo-American Law* (1950).
Welch, Martin G., *Discovering Anglo-Saxon England* (1992).
Whitelock, Dorothy, *History, Law and Literature in 10th-11th Century England* (1981).
Whitelock, Dorothy, *The Beginnings of English Society* (1974).
Whittock, Martyn J., *The Origins of England* (1986).

Articles

Bosselman, Fred P., "Limitations Inherent in the Title to Wetlands at Common Law,"15 *Stan. Envtl. L. J.* 247 (June 1996).
Campbell, James, "The Sale of Land and the Economics of Power in Early England: Problems and Possibilities." *The Haskins Society Journal: Studies in Medieval History* 1 (1989).
Coquillette, Daniel R., "The Lessons of Anglo-Saxon Justice," 2 *Green Bag* 251 (Spring 1999).
Lefroy, A. H. F., "The Anglo-Saxon Period of English Law," 26 *Yale L.J.* 291 (Feb. 1917).
Lefroy, A. H. F., "The Anglo-Saxon Period of English Law," 26 *Yale L.J.* 388 (Mar. 1917).
Sanchez, Valerie A., "Towards a History of ADR: The Dispute Processing Continuum in Anglo-Saxon England and Today, "11 *Ohio St. J. on Disp. Resol.* 1 (1996).
Senn, Mark A., "Reflections on Some Forgotten Terms of Land Measurement," 16 *Probate & Property* 8 (Mar./Apr. 2002).
Thomas, David A., "Anglo-American Land Law: Diverging Developments from a Shared History Part I: The Shared History," 34 *Real Prop., Prob. and Trust J.* 143 (Spring, 1999).
Thomas, David A., "Anglo-Saxon Antecedents of the Common Law", 1985 B.Y.U. L. Rev. 453.
Thomas, David A., "Why the Public Plundering of Private Property Rights Is Still a Very Bad Idea," 41 *Real Prop. Prob. & Tr. J.* 25 (Spring, 2006).
Zaher, Claudia, "When a Woman's Marital Status Determined Her Legal Status: A Research Guide on the Common Law Doctrine of Coverture," 94 *Law Libr. J.* 459 (Summer, 2002).

Chapter 7

Early English Land Law after the Norman Conquest[558]

SYNOPSIS

[558] The content of this chapter was originally written by the author, and some content was drawn or reprinted from Vol. 1 of Thompson on Real Property.

Chapter 7. Early English Land Law After the Norman Conquest

§ 7.01. Introduction to the Chapter.

This chapter demonstrates how the Norman Conquest, beginning in 1066, and all the changes that flowed from it, affected the development of land law in England. Although the Normans did not immediately displace the Anglo-Saxon landholding practices that were in effect at the time of the Conquest, the conquerors eventually brought elaboration and uniformity into English land law. The uniformity and consistency in all areas of the law eventually produced the common law—the law common to all of England.

This chapter will also show that foundational principles of English land law were Anglo-Saxon in origin and that the Normans introduced few novel substantive concepts. However, the techniques of government and administration practiced by the Normans and their Angevin successors directly stimulated the growth of the common law and enabled it eventually to dominate the huge variety of ancient local customs. In the context of rights in land, the rise of common law was at first inseparably bound up with the institutions of feudalism, but as new social conditions emerged from the feudal framework, the common law rules and institutions adjusted and also transcended many of their old feudal anachronisms.

While legal developments during the English Middle Ages were continuous and many-faceted, the 16th century represents a watershed of sorts for property law. The Statute of Uses in 1536 and Statute of Wills in 1540, worked out in brittle confrontation between King Henry VIII and Parliament, and the subsequent reinterpretation of those enactments in the common law courts, struck the last feudal shackles from the English system of property rights. In so doing they opened the way to many key developments in modern Anglo-American property law. Therefore, this chapter will conclude its discussion of property law growth with the developments in 16th century England.

§ 7.02. Summary of Property Rights in Late Anglo-Saxon England.

§ 7.02(a). Egalitarian Quality of Early Settlements and Land Rights.

As was shown in Chapter 6, "Land Law in Anglo-Saxon England," a lengthy and continuing elaboration of property rights took place during the entire period of Anglo-Saxon dominance in England. Most likely the first Germanic settlers were either raiding war bands or disgruntled mercenaries who turned on their British employers, and when they did begin to establish farms and villages, they acted probably as independent yeomen and warriors.[559] The old custom of the continental Germanic tribes by which the

---

[559] After examining the property-related provisions of the old continental Germanic law codes contemporary with the Anglo-Saxon invasions, the only conclusion that could be drawn in Chapter 6 was an inference that real property was important and some individual possessory rights were recognized and protected. However, any

tribal chief or council of leaders periodically reallocated arable land to family groups may have carried over, but would have swiftly become irrelevant as soon as settlement and stability were achieved.

Early Anglo-Saxon society apparently had a certain egalitarian quality that affected landholding practices. As long as pronounced social stratification was absent from the early Anglo-Saxon settlements, stratification was not apparent in the modest farmsteads or other forms of land holding.[560]

Perhaps it was this ancient egalitarian tradition that enabled King Alfred to exercise a form of public land use planning during the ninth century, as part of his overall defensive scheme against the Danes. Alfred created a system of fortified towns, called *burhs* , and he paid for those fortifications by an assessment system (a kind of public property tax and labor assessment) based on the amount of land associated with the *burh* . A unique record of the *burhs* and their associated lands was compiled in what is known as the "Burgal Hidage". The burhs were produced by a deliberate administrative effort of the Anglo-Saxon leaders. They had a common town plan; they were evenly distributed so that almost all people were within a day's march, about 20 miles, from the nearest *burh*.[561]

§ 7.02(b). Specialization of Property Interests.

No definite information about Anglo-Saxon landholding practices is available until a full two centuries after the age of Conquest, and then the evidence pertains only to the more prominent persons of Anglo-Saxon society who were accustomed to conducting land transactions and making written records, or charters, of what they had done. The earliest charters, dating from the 7th century, show that elaboration of property rights had

---

further enlightenment is not available in the documentary sources relating to the Anglo-Saxons or other contemporary Germanic tribes. *See* §6.03(b).

[560] § 6.03(b).

[561] Patrick Wormald, "The Burhs," in *The Anglo-Saxons* 152-153 (James Campbell, ed., 1982).

already begun, even though the common form of landholding was still what would today be termed a life estate. It is also apparent that holders of most occupied land were subject to requirements of military service, road building and fortress maintenance.

Whatever the usual form of Anglo-Saxon landholding, the charters mention several specialized property interests. One of these is "bookland," a form of landholding created only by written charter that may have been used to obtain relief from some or all of the service requirements and to permit alienation of the land without leave of the king. "Laenland" also is mentioned in some charters, apparently referring to land that was loaned or rented to another, either for a short term or for a period of up to three lives, meaning the grantee and two successive heirs. The remaining lands might have been included in the elusive term "folkland," land still subject to alienation restrictions and to customary obligations and dues.

§ 7.02(c). Stratified Society and Property Rights.

In addition to the possessory rights and restrictions recognized as pertaining to the immediate occupants of the land, a system of shared ownership rights was emerging in Anglo-Saxon England. These rights were stratified, with some rights of ownership subordinated to and derived from ownership rights of a socially superior person. These differences in property rights were possibly a direct result of emerging stratification in Anglo-Saxon society generally. Stability in Anglo-Saxon society helped centralize political power, which led to differences in property rights. "At the end of this process, the actual occupants of the land would eventually suffer a nearly complete loss of economic and personal independence."[562]

By the time of the Norman Conquest, English society had suffered enormously from what Stenton called "the general drift of English peasant life . . . from freedom towards servitude."[563] Little direct evidence exists for how this occurred, but it is the most conspicuous aspect of Anglo-Saxon

---

[562] *Id.*

[563] F. M. Stenton, *Anglo-Saxon England* 463 (1943).

property rights in the generation before the Conquest. Available evidence for the details of this process suggests that from the earliest days of the Anglo-Saxon conquests, conquered Britons and even very poor English peasants subjected themselves to a lord for protection. Gradually, communities originally composed of free peasants turned into villages of serfs. Whereas the villages were obligated to provide food-rents, hard times and narrow subsistence margins eventually led most to offer their inhabitants' labor when the food-rents could not be met. This led directly to the manorial economy.[564]

In Anglo-Saxon England it was still possible to be economically dependent but personally free in legal standing. Freemen are known to have

---

[564] "From the moment when the kings of the migration age began to plant their companions upon the soil there must have existed communities in which expropriated Britons, and Englishmen too poor to be welcomed in settlements of their own people, were working for a lord in return for his protection . . . There is no direct evidence to show the stages by which, within any single village, a community composed essentially of independent peasants developed into a community composed essentially of serfs, but the main features of the process seem fairly clear. In what appears to have been the normal case, it began with a grant from the king settling an ealdorman, a *gesith*, a bishop or an abbot in his own place as the immediate lord of a village, and, in particular, as the recipient of the dues and services which its inhabitants had been accustomed to render to the king himself. The independence of the village group was not threatened at first. But the narrowness of the average ceorl's [the lowest class of free persons, also called churls] resources, and the many forms of disaster to which he was exposed, made it almost inevitable that sooner or later the village community would find itself unable to provide the food-rent which its lord had a right to demand. It was generally easier for the head of a peasant household to supply labour than to keep up a regular contribution to a communal food-rent. Most lords had need of labour on the "demesnes" [lands held by the lords themselves, also referred to as domains] which they had been acquiring through co-operation with the village community in the extension of cultivated area, or by the creation of home farms within a ring fence. It seems that, within most villages, the duty of supporting the lord by a communal render in kind gave way, in time, more or less completely, to a system by which each of the regular holdings in the open fields (hides, half-hides, and yardlands) supplied labour for the lord's demesnes on a definite number of days in every week. In itself, the change was merely a matter of economic reorganization, which need have had no legal consequences. But in most cases it seems to have formed part of a wider revolution in which the individual peasants surrendered their holdings to the lord of the village and received them back from his hands, acknowledging themselves to be his men, and placing themselves under his protection. When this step had been taken by the whole or the greater part of a village community, the manorial economy of the middle ages was brought within sight."
F. M. Stenton, *Anglo-Saxon England* 463-465 (1943).

been tenants in varying degrees of servitude, and it has been stated that Anglo-Saxon "serfdom was much more of a personal bondage less involved with the occupation of particular land before the Norman Conquest than after."[565]

§ 7.02(d). Anglo-Saxon Property Rights as the Foundation for the Common Law of Property.

Anglo-Saxon landholding practices, and their correlation with social status, had little known consistency throughout England, and they must have been in constant fluctuation throughout the Anglo-Saxon age. For the most part, they were acknowledged only by immemorial custom, and persisted through the Norman Conquest and into the period of common law development. They were the foundation for the common law of property. At first it was the large landowners, close to the monarch and holding land as bookland, who pushed for individual ownership rights. These were the beginnings of the various tenures.[566]

---

[565] Frederick Pollock and Frederic William Maitland, *The History of English Law Before the Time of Edward I* 37 (2d ed. 1909).

[566] "It is in the greater landlords who hold by book or laen (the future lords of manors) that we can see not only the beginnings of individualistic ownership of the land, but also the germs of the idea of tenure. The grantees by book stand . . . in close relation to the crown. They are, in fact, a class of great tenants-in-chief. Under them the cultivators of the soil occupy their holdings. The rise of laenland interposed another class between the great man and the peasant. Between the peasant and the crown there might be the thegn who holds laenland of the church and the church to whom it has been booked by the king. In many cases we can see the germs of what will be in later law the various classes of tenure. The land booked to the church for the salvation of the donor's soul was an out-and-out gift; no services were reserved. But the donor will expect the donee to remember him in his prayers. This is not unlike tenure by frank-almoin. If the king books land to a thegn, he books it in consideration of past faithful services, probably of a military sort; but he will sometimes stipulate for continued faithful service; and the amount of military service required is sometimes specified. All free men are obliged to serve in the fryd; but this liability to serve in the fryd is coming to be attached to certain definite tracts of land, to certain five-hide units . . . . We have here various elements which may develop into tenure by military service . . . . [W]e can see the germs not only of military and socage tenure, but also of tenure by serjeanty and even of villein tenure . . ." 2 William Holdsworth, *A History of English Law* 73-74 (3d ed. 1923).

§ 7.03. Summary of Property Rights Among the Pre-Conquest Normans.

§ 7.03(a). Origins of the Normans.

Many school children learn that Normans were "Northmen," but most people know little else about these medieval marauders who conquered much of England and other European kingdoms. The Norman invasions fit squarely within the mainstream of Viking aggressions that afflicted Europe during the 8th through the 11th centuries; the Norman Conquest of England has been called "the last great Viking expansion."[567]

The founder of the Norman dynasty is believed to have been an adventurer named Rolf or Hrolf in the Scandinavian sagas.[568] In the later continental chronicles, this same figure is referred to as Rollo.[569] Rolf was apparently a Norwegian Viking pirate[570] who operated in the Baltic during his early years. He was outlawed by the Norwegian King when, desperate for food, he raided for cattle in Norway.[571]

Rolf was active during the early years of the 10th century, a time of violent unrest, but details are very sketchy. After a stay in the Hebrides, he

---

[567] Jack Lindsay, *The Normans and Their World* 4 (1974).

[568] Snorri Sturluson, *The Heimskringla: A History of the Norse Kings* 38-39 (Samuel Laing, trans., 1907).

[569] See Dudo, "De Moribus et Actis Primorum Normanniae Ducum," in *Historiae Normannorum Scriptores Antiqui* 70 (Andreas Duchesnius, ed., 1619). A brief but helpful discussion of the source chronicles and of Dudo's occasional unreliability is found in R. Allen Brown, *The Normans and the Norman Conquest* 24-25 and n.18 (1969).

[570] Rolf 's Norwegian origin is not certain, but seems probable. D. C. Douglas, "Rollo of Normandy," 57 *Eng. Hist. Rev.* 417, 423 (1942).

[571] Snorri Sturluson, *The Heimskringla: A History of the Norse Kings* 38-39 (Samuel Laing, trans., 1907); Jack Lindsay, *The Normans and Their World* 18 (1974).

probably took part in raids on what is now western France,[572] and he may also have visited the Danish King Guthrum in England at about this time.[573]

During the second decade of the 10th century, Rolf helped lead several attacks in the area of modern Normandy and conducted an unsuccessful siege of Paris. It was possible that he also directed colonization by Norse settlers in territories brought under his control. In 911, the Frankish King Charles III (the Simple), struggling to hold together remnants of the Carolingian Empire, entered into a pact with Rolf, even after defeating Rolf in a battle at Chartres.[574] Reportedly Rolf agreed to be baptized, to marry Charles' daughter, and to give homage to Charles; in return he obtained formal control over the areas of Rouen, Lisieux, Evreux, and some minor additional territory, all later known as Upper Normandy.[575]

With these arrangements in place, Rolf then expanded his territories with grim efficiency. By taking over the districts of Bayeux and Sees, he extended his control into the west, and after 924 his son moved into the Avranches and Coutances districts, which added Lower Normandy to the territory effectively under his dominion.[576]

The population he thereby brought within Norse control was probably Celtic, but had become considerably Romanized by the time the Saxons and Franks began invading in the fourth century. The Germanic invaders had mingled with the people, but had not imposed their language on the

---

[572] Snorri Sturluson, *The Heimskringla: A History of the Norse Kings* 39 (Samuel Laing, trans., 1907); Jack Lindsay, *The Normans and Their World* 19 (1974).

[573] Jack Lindsay, *The Normans and Their World* 18 (1974).

[574] *Id.* at 17.

[575] *Id.;* Dudo, "De Moribus et Actis Primorum Normanniae Ducum," in *Historiae Normannorum Scriptores Antiqui* 79-84 (Andreas Duchesnius, ed., 1619). The generous detail Dudo provides for the agreement and its attendant circumstances was probably partially fabricated. *See* D. C. Douglas, "Rollo of Normandy," 57 *Eng. Hist. Rev.* 417, 428-429 (1942). However, the occurrence of these events generally is not disputed.

[576] John Le Patourel, *The Norman Empire* 5-11 (1976); Jack Lindsay, *The Normans and Their World* 17 (1974).

conquered. Thus the people were speaking a form of French when the early Viking raiders struck in the area. The Viking raiding parties themselves were possibly of mixed origins. In Rolf's case, his early commanders and raiders were probably Norwegian, but most of the Scandinavians who actually settled in Normandy were Danish.[577] The Viking intruders adopted French language and customs, but remained a separate ruling class.

In their role as overlords, the Normans continued consolidating their control during the tenth century, and were generally successful in maintaining independence from the aggressive Frankish and Breton princes who surrounded Normandy.

Rolf died sometime between 925 and 927[578] and was succeeded by his son William I (Longsword). William I was murdered in 943, but in the year prior to his death had arranged for the succession of Richard I (the Fearless), his son by a Breton concubine.[579] Richard was bilingual, like his father William and his grandfather Rolf, and he maintained his Scandinavian connections and culture, but under his rule the Norman state began to play a more active role in the Frankish politics of the region.[580] When Richard I's long reign ended with his death in 996, his oldest son Richard II, also illegitimate, succeeded him and began to rule in 998. During Richard II's reign, the conflicts between Christians and pagans within his dominions generally were resolved in favor of Christians, and feudal rules and relationships were significantly refined.[581]

Richard II reigned until 1026, and was succeeded by his illegitimate

---

[577] D. C. Douglas, "Rollo of Normandy," 57 *Eng. Hist. Rev.* 417, 423-424 (1942).

[578] *Id.* at 434-35.

[579] Jack Lindsay, *The Normans and Their World* 53-55 (1974).

[580] D. C. Douglas, "The Rise of Normandy," 57 *Proc. Brit. Acad.* 101, 107-108, 112 (1971).

[581] D. C. Douglas, *The Norman Achievement: 1050-1100* 24-25 (1969); D. C. Douglas, "The Rise of Normandy," 57 *Proc. Brit. Acad.* 101, 114-115 (1971).

son Richard III, who died that same year after falling ill at a feast.[582] Richard III's brother Robert took over in 1027 and soon thereafter sired a son by a Falaise peasant girl. In 1034 Robert made his vassals do homage to this illegitimate son, who was then only six years old, and then turned Normandy over to the boy and left on a pilgrimage to Jerusalem. When Robert died during the return journey from Jerusalem, the boy became William II, seventh duke of Normandy and eventually "the Conqueror" and King of England.[583]

William II was born only little more than a century after his Viking great-great-grandfather Rolf formalized the Norman presence in France. Even his grandfather Richard I had still maintained Norse language and customs. Thus the Norman contribution to English law after the Conquest is best understood in the context of its Scandinavian origins.

§ 7.03(b). Sketch of Scandinavian Law.

As was common in all Germanic cultures, Viking society was divided into classes of nobility, freemen, and slaves.[584] In early Viking times, before feudal tendencies were manifest, land held by persons in the classes of nobility or freemen was held communally by the family, albeit under the father's control. Upon the father's death, the oldest son succeeded to the entire holding, but he had to compensate the younger brothers and sisters for their shares.[585] Thus financed, younger sons were able to colonize new areas or to strike out on voyages of trade or piracy.[586]

The land itself was free from obligations to overlords, but a landholder

---

[582] D. C. Douglas, *William the Conqueror* 31-32 (1964).

[583] *Id.* at 15, 35-37.

[584] Johannes Brondsted, *The Vikings* 238-242 (Kalle Skov, trans., 1965).

[585] Jack Lindsay, *The Normans and Their World* 26 (1974). In addition to the compensatory payments for their shares of the family estate, the younger brothers also received their shares of other assets.

[586] Johannes Brondsted, *The Vikings* 24-25 (Kalle Skov, trans., 1965).

might assume the burdens of personal dues or services in return for protection or support from a lord. Such lordship arrangements were strictly personal and could be transferred to other lords without affecting the rights in land. One could obtain land by becoming the follower of a lord or chief; the chief was responsible to administer justice, give support in disputes, and distribute shares of spoils.[587] Women also could own and inherit land.[588]

Either spouse could easily obtain a divorce, and illegitimacy was common.[589] Indeed, blurred distinctions between marriage and concubinage sometimes led to succession by illegitimate sons, as abundantly manifested in the Norman ducal genealogy. Of the seven Norman rulers between Rolf and William II (the Conqueror), three (Richard I, Richard II, and William II) are known to have been illegitimate.

Assemblies of free men were called Things and were common in all Nordic societies. These gatherings in each province pronounced judgments and administered the law in the area. Although they dominated the Things, the rulers were still bound by custom to consult their constituents thus assembled.[590]

Other traits common to Germanic societies, such as the responsibility

---

[587] Jack Lindsay, *The Normans and Their World* 26 (1974).

[588] Land inheritance and ownership by women are described in the tale told by a runic inscription found at Hillersjo, Uppland, Sweden:

> Germund married Gerlog, when she was a maiden. Later they had a son, before Germund was drowned. The son died later. Then she married Gudrik. They had children. Of these only a girl lived; she was called Inga. Ragnfast of Snottsta married her. Afterwards he died, and their son after him. And the mother inherited from her son. Inga afterwards married Erik. Then she died. Then Gerlog inherited from Inga, her daughter.

Ole Klindt-Jensen, *The World of the Vikings* 138 (1970).

[589] Johannes Brondsted, *The Vikings* 42 (Kalle Skov, trans., 1965).

[590] Ole Klindt-Jensen, *The World of the Vikings* 178-183; Johannes Brondsted, *The Vikings* 242-243 (Kalle Skov, trans., 1965).

of an entire kindred for individual offenses by its members, and compensations for such offenses based on wergild, were in full force in Scandinavia. As elsewhere in northern and western Europe, rulers attempted to restrict blood feud vengeance and to regulate assessment and payment of wergild fines for offenses. Generally, this regulation by the rules tended to fix responsibility for offenses more fully on the individual offender than on the entire kindred. This might have been achieved by requiring the offender personally to pay a portion of the wergild or by restricting the extent of family relationship included in the kindred.[591]

The environment and way of life had a natural influence on local legal customs. For example, farmers left their implements in the fields overnight to save time during the short harvest seasons, and laws imposed severe penalties for theft of implements left in the fields. Other laws firmly obligated neighbors to assist those who otherwise could not get their harvests in on time.[592]

Similarly, when crews pulled wintering ships up into sheds for storing and repairs, laws defined the rights associated with such laying-up and required neighboring farmers to help pull under some circumstances.[593] Presumably, extensive Norse trading led to many legal customs regulating mercantile activities.

§ 7.03(c). Changes in Norman Legal Customs After the Settlement in Normandy.

After Norman settlement rights in Normandy were formalized in 911, fundamental changes in Norman legal customs began to occur. At first, Rolf 's followers insisted on maintaining their egalitarian social status.

---

[591] Ole Klindt-Jensen, *The World of the Vikings* 178 (1970). A description of similar customs in contemporary England is contained in the second set of the laws of Edmund, an Anglo-Saxon king. *See* 3 F. Felix Liebermann, *Die Gesetze der Angelsachsen* 186-191 (1906).

[592] Jack Lindsay, *The Normans and Their World* 27 (1965).

[593] Haakon Shetelig and Hjalma Falk, *Scandinavian Archaeology* 352 (Eric V. Gordon, trans., 1937).

Until the early years of Richard II's reign, which began about 998, widespread non-feudal landholding, peasant independence, and loyalty to pagan creeds persisted.[594] However, the Normans' need to fit into emerging French society changed these cultural characteristics. They gradually adopted a new language and diminished their pirate activity. Constant threats from aggressive neighbors in adjacent lands, not restrained by any natural barriers of topography, created pressures to feudalize, that is, for landholders to seek security in submitting lands and lives to powerful warrior lords in return for physical protection. Many Normans, recognizing these inexorable forces, readily accepted feudal landholding, the French language, and even Christianity. This resulted in a substantial split from more traditional Normans, affecting especially peasants who were losing their independence.[595]

Richard I (942-996), apprehensive of French hostility, took the first halting steps toward feudalism. Military service began to be organized on the basis of feudal duties, replacing the traditional method of calling up all freemen. As a result, landholders began to change some allodial (non-feudal) tenures to feudal tenures, and many free peasants lost their independent status.[596] A serious but unsuccessful revolt of free peasants during the subsequent reign of Richard II was probably a protest against these changes and undoubtedly slowed the spread of feudal practices into the lower classes. The eventual result was a Norman style of feudalism with a highly organized military structure, but with servile status in the lower class less pervasive than elsewhere in France.

It is estimated that 100 to 120 feudal baronies existed in Normandy

---

[594] D. C. Douglas, "The Rise of Normandy," 57 *Proc. Brit. Acad.* 101, 111-115, 118-119 (1971).

[595] R. Allen Brown, *The Normans and the Norman Conquest* 39-40 (1969); John Le Patourel, *The Norman Empire* 286-290 (1976).

[596] R. Allen Brown, *The Normans and the Norman Conquest* 40 (1969). Douglas has cautioned against assuming a wholesale adoption of feudal tenures during this time. D. C. Douglas, "The Rise of Normandy," 57 *Proc. Brit. Acad.* 101, 118-119 (1971).

under Richard I.[597] A vassal of one of these barons would have held his land as a sort of tenant at will, a tenure known in Roman law as a *precarium*.[598] By the time of Richard II (998-1026), a vassal who swore fealty to a lord would receive an interest in land which would have been known as a *beneficium* under Roman law, and which granted the right to hold the property for life. As developments that had already taken place during the dominance of the Carolingian empire were imitated in Normandy, the vassal's interest evolved into the hereditary fief, or *feudum*, which could descend from father to son.[599] In return for giving up the right to revoke the land grant, the lord eventually gained the rights of wardship, to a succession duty upon inheritance, and to choose a husband for a vassal's heiress.[600] These changes occurred in no orderly or consistent fashion within the duchy, but were gradual and uneven.

Vassals' duties were only gradually defined or clarified,[601] but the more powerful lay magnates and churchmen, probably the most important landholders before the Conquest, held their land by some sort of military tenure, that is, subject to the duty to provide the services of a specific number of fully-equipped knights.[602] Because such military tenures are hardly evident prior to 1047, William probably developed them in large measure after he assumed power as duke in Normandy; he may have seen such arrangements as an effective response to the serious internal and

---

[597] Jack Lindsay, *The Normans and Their World* 59-60 (1974). *See generally* D. C. Douglas, "The Earliest Norman Counts," 61 *Eng. Hist. Rev.* 129-156 (1946), explaining that, despite civil unrest, the cohesion of the Norman counts greatly contributed to the Norman achievements.

[598] Frederick Pollock and Frederic William Maitland, *The History of English Law Before the Time of Edward I* 67-72 (2d ed. 1909); Jack Lindsay, *The Normans and Their World* 69 (1974).

[599] By 1075 Norman magnates were routinely inheriting their land.

[600] Frederick Pollock and Frederic William Maitland, *The History of English Law Before the Time of Edward I* 325-329 (2d ed. 1909).

[601] R. Allen Brown, *The Normans and the Norman Conquest* 39, 41 (1969).

[602] D. C. Douglas, *William the Conqueror* 101-103 (1964).

external threats against his early rule.[603]

Indeed the fief (land tenure derived from obligatory military service) played an important part in William's military resources. Under some conditions, he could summon every man holding at least a knight's fee; on less serious occasions he might call up only some men holding military tenures, and then only for forty days' service. Under the worst circumstances, he could call out all free tenants.[604] The system in Normandy was still being shaped at the time of the Conquest, although apparently William did much to spread the principle of a fixed rate of knight service.[605] Subinfeudation occurred in Normandy and further complicated the military tenures: a vassal owing the service of five knights might let his land out to others for ten; or, more commonly, a tenant might hold land from several lords or might hold a mere fraction of a knight's fee. Vassals who made grants in subinfeudation held a relationship to their tenants similar to the duke's relation to the vassals.[606]

Over all these baronies and vassals, Duke Richard I and his successors administered certain functions through viscounts. Viscounts, on behalf of the duke, exercised control over troops, revenue, administration of justice, castles, and bishoprics (especially after the church was weakened during widespread civil strife).[607] Usually only leading barons would be appointed viscounts, and the office gradually came to be considered a hereditary right of certain feudal families. Viscounts paid a form of rent for their appointments, and then, with responsibility for tax collection, kept any

---

[603] *Id.* at 98-103.

[604] F. M. Stenton, *The First Century of English Feudalism: 1066-1166* 13-14 (1961).

[605] D. C. Douglas, *William the Conqueror* 31-32 (1964).

[606] John Le Patourel, *The Norman Empire* 289-290 (1976).

[607] D. C. Douglas, "The Earliest Norman Counts, 61 *Eng. Hist. Rev.* 152-153 (1946); D. C. Douglas, *William the Conqueror* 139-144 (1964); John Le Patourel, *The Norman Empire* 258-260 (1976).

revenue they could obtain.[608]

The Norman dukes took other actions to improve order and stability within Norman society. For example, they limited private war, prohibited devastating opponents' land in a dispute, forbade assaults and ambushes in ducal forests, and required a license to build a castle.[609]

Information on other aspects of Norman law during this time is scant. The duke firmly controlled rights of barons to hold local courts, but otherwise no details are known. As there was no written law before the Conquest, the Norman dukes administered customary law. They did not issue writs or charters, as the Anglo-Saxons had been doing for four centuries, and the documents that were drawn up simply recorded gifts that had already been made. The most serious cases of misconduct (murder, assault, arson, and rape) were heard by the duke, although sometimes he appointed others to hear particular cases. By 1091 barons in Normandy had obtained jurisdiction over assault, rape, and arson, but not over murder cases. It is believed that criminal justice followed the system of compurgation by oath that was common to Germanic societies, but no firm evidence of this has appeared for Normandy. It is also not known whether the pre-Conquest Normans used juries (that is, bodies of inquest). However, they did employ the ordeal, including ordeal by battle.[610]

Ordeals were a conspicuous feature at the baronial councils convened by the dukes at festival times. Such councils, in addition to conducting trials by ordeal, resolved high-level disputes, decided whether to wage war,

---

[608] Timothy Baker, *The Normans* 25 (1966); D. C. Douglas, *William the Conqueror* 139 (1964); R. Allen Brown, *The Normans and the Norman Conquest* 54 (1969). The tax collection system described in the text is usually referred to as "farming," and had a long tradition extending back to Roman times and beyond. This arrangement obligated the viscount to pay a fixed sum to the duke, which the viscount was then entitled to collect from the people in his jurisdiction. As a rule, the amount of the viscount's collections exceeded the required payment to the duke.

[609] Jack Lindsay, *The Normans and Their World* 69 (1974).

[610] *Id.* at 136-138.

and occasionally proclaimed a ducal heir.[611] In 1047, William was instrumental in having a provincial council of ecclesiastical and lay magnates adopt the so-called "Truce of God," which restricted private warfare. This revealed William's penchant for involving the church, and controlling the church's involvement, in his administrative affairs.[612]

Despite these known features of Norman legal practices, any comprehensive picture of Norman law remains obscure; the continental Normans simply had no written laws, few charters and little about the legal system from their chroniclers.[613]

Such written laws and unwritten legal customs as had developed in Normandy were probably as much French as Scandinavian, although the French had little law to offer.[614]

Yet the question persists as to whether Norman law was mainly Frankish or Scandinavian. Certainly by the time the Normans began their conquest of England, much of their culture was French.[615]

---

611 *Id.* at 136-137; R. Allen Brown, *The Normans and the Norman Conquest* 54, 145-146 (1969).

612 D. C. Douglas, *William the Conqueror* 44, 51-52 (1964).

613 "Of the law of Normandy as it was on the eve of William's expedition, little is known for certain. To illustrate the period which had elapsed since the settlement of the Northmen in Neustria, there are no written laws, no books on law and very few charters, while the chroniclers have not much to tell about the legal structure of the duchy, and what they tell is not always trustworthy . . . Even in later days, after the duke of the Normans had become king of the English, the duchy was slow to follow the kingdom in the production of abiding memorials of its law . . . . [W]e have every reason to believe that the conquerors of England had little, if any, written law to bring with them." Frederick Pollock and Frederic William Maitland, *The History of English Law Before the Time of Edward I* 64-65 (2d ed. 1909).

614 "But not only had the Normans no written law of their own making; there was none that they could readily borrow from their French neighbors. Their invasions occurred in the very midnight of the legal history of France; indeed they brought the midnight with them." *Id.* at 65.

615 "It is now generally admitted that for at least half a century before the battle of Hastings, the Normans were Frenchmen, French in their language, French in their law, proud indeed of their past history, very ready to fight against other Frenchmen if Norman home-rule was endangered, but still Frenchmen . . . Their spoken

§ 7.04. Impact of the Norman Conquest on the Development of English Law.

§ 7.04(a). The Course of the Conquest.

Duke William II of Normandy would have angrily objected to being called the "Conqueror" of England. No one of his time gave more attention to assuring the legitimacy of his claim to the English throne and to the notion that the Norman invasion and settlement of England was simply the necessary effort to reclaim the English throne from a usurper.

§ 7.04(a)(1). Norman Influence in England Before 1066.

Norman influence in England began no later than 1002, when the Anglo-Saxon King Ethelred II of England married Emma of Normandy, daughter of Duke Richard I and therefore William's great aunt. Ethelred and Emma's son, known as Edward "the Confessor" when he was later King of England, was therefore William's second cousin. Ethnic ties with Normandy were even stronger and older, inasmuch as both Normandy and England were attacked, conquered and significantly resettled by Scandinavian Vikings during roughly the same era.

During the marriage of Ethelred II and Emma, many Normans came to England as part of Emma's household. In 1013, Edward and his brother Alfred were sent by their father to Normandy, to join their mother who had preceded them, due to the growing menace of Viking assaults on England. Ethelred joined them briefly in 1013, but returned to England in 1014. When Ethelred died in 1016, Cnut of Denmark, by a combination of negotiation and battle, became King of England, and about the same time

---

language was French, their written language was Latin, but the Latin of France; the style of their legal documents was the style of the French chancery; very few of the technical terms of their law were of Scandinavian origin." *Id.* at 66.

succeeded his own brother as King of Denmark.[616]

In the very year he obtained the English throne, Cnut married Ethelred's widow, Emma of Normandy, so that, from 1016, once again some Norman influence was felt in England. Indeed, Cnut's Danish followers and Emma's Norman retainers claimed a common homeland, culture, and ancestry less than a century in the past. Shortly after Cnut's death in about 1035, Ethelred's two sons Edward and Alfred, still in Norman exile, carried out short-lived expeditions to England, probably with Norman aid. However, the new King of England, Harold Harefoot, had Alfred murdered, with the complicity of Earl Godwin, father of the Harold who would oppose William at Hastings. King Harold Harefoot was Cnut's son by his first marriage, so Cnut's widow Emma went into exile in Flanders. After Harold Harefoot died in 1040, however, he was succeeded by Harthacnut, son of Cnut and Emma, who invited Edward, son of Emma and Ethelred, to share the English kingship. Harthacnut died only a year later, so Edward became sole King of England in 1042. In that year Edward was 37 years old and had spent 28 of those years in Normandy, succored by Norman magnates.[617]

When Edward assumed the throne of England, Norman influence grew stronger than ever. As stated by an anonymous contemporary biographer of Edward:

> When King Edward of holy memory returned from Francia, quite a number of men of that nation, and they not base born, accompanied him. And these, since he was master of the whole kingdom, he kept with him, enriched them with many honours, and made them his privy counsellors and administrators of the royal palace.[618]

---

[616] Cnut eventually conquered Norway in 1028, adding it to his Anglo-Danish empire.

[617] *See generally* Frank Barlow, *Edward the Confessor* (1970).

[618] *Vita Aedwardi Regis, The Life of King Edward* 17 (Frank Barlow, ed. and trans., 1962).

§ 7.04(a)(2). William's Claim to and Conquest of the English Throne.

Although the next events are attested only by Norman sources, there is no reason to doubt their reliability and mutual affirmation. In about 1051, Edward decreed that William of Normandy should be his successor, secured the agreement upon oath of the leading English nobility, and sent notification of the matter by messenger and hostages to William. William then came to England and was received and honored by Edward. In 1064, according to the same sources, Harold Godwin was sent to William in Normandy to confirm the succession and formally recognize William as Edward's heir.

But conflict could not be avoided. Edward died on January 5, 1066; the council, or Witan, elected Harold Godwin as king and crowned him on January 6, 1066. Thus the succession was thrown into wide open dispute. Once the news reached Normandy, massive invasion preparations began, and William had a monk deliver a formal statement of William's claim to the English throne to Harold. Meanwhile, another monarch undertook invasion preparations in Norway, where King Harald Hardrada raised a claim to the English throne. The same wind that kept William from crossing the English Channel in September 1066 enabled Harald Hardrada's forces to land near York, where they were totally defeated by Harold Godwin's Anglo-Saxons at the battle of Stamford Bridge. However, the Anglo-Saxon forces had arrived only after a forced march of 190 miles north from London and after withdrawing the fleet from guarding the southern coast against a Norman invasion. When the wind then suddenly changed and William crossed over to Pevensy and Hastings, Harold swiftly returned south, gathered what forces were available, and gave battle more or less at a time and place of William's choosing. The outcome at Hastings was in doubt during the entire day of battle, but at the end the field lay strewn with "the flower of English nobility and youth."[619] Once the English had been defeated, with their king and other principal leaders slain, they seemed incapable of regrouping and offering any more resistance than an

[619] William of Poitiers, *Gesta Guillelmi ducis Normannorum et regis Anglorum* 204 R. Foreville, ed., 1952).

occasional regional revolt. Historians have worked mightily to explain the Conquest. Declared one: "England on the eve of the Norman Conquest presents to the neutral historian plenty of internal reasons to explain a Norman victory in what was in effect one more disputed succession to the throne."[620]

The contrast between the culturally superior Anglo-Saxon state and the politically stronger Norman state has been aptly expressed by Stenton:

> The Normans who entered into the English inheritance were a harsh and violent race. They were the closest of all western peoples to the barbarian strain in the continental order. They had produced little in art or learning, and nothing in literature, that could be set beside the work of Englishmen. But politically, they were the masters of their world.[621]

§ 7.04(a)(3). Norman Settlement of England After the Conquest.

The Norman Conquest itself was not substantially finished until 1071. The Norman "settlement" of England began immediately in 1066 and was essentially completed with the Domesday Survey in 1086. William was crowned in London on Christmas day, 1066, but withdrew to Essex while three London castles were completed. These, including the White Tower (Illustration 24) that formed the central core of the Tower of London complex, afforded protection against the unruly London population.

---

[620] R. Allen Brown, *The Normans* 61-63 (1984).

[621] F. M. Stenton, *Anglo-Saxon England* 678 (1943).

Illustration 24. The White Tower was the central portion and keep of the Tower of London, begun by William the Conqueror ca. 1075-79. It was one of the largest and strongest castle keeps in Europe, and signified William's total power over England and its land..

William returned in triumph to Normandy in March 1067, but was required back in England in December 1067 to conduct a winter campaign to subdue Exeter. He brought his wife Mathilda to London to be crowned queen in the spring of 1068, but then William had to go pacify Northumbria and York, planting castles along the way. The next year, a rebellion broke out in York, and then prominent English leaders united with invading Danes to create a major uprising in Northumbria. To check simultaneous uprisings in Cheshire, Cornwall, Devon, Dorset, and Somerset, William dispatched trusted companions, and then personally led the forces to Northumbria. He rather quickly dealt with the military threat, but then, in the winter of 1069-1070, sought a permanent solution "by a deliberate attempt to ruin the population of the affected districts":[622]

> Then in his anger he commanded that all crops and herds, chattels and goods of every kind should be brought

[622] *Id.* at 596.

> together and burned to ashes with consuming fire, so that the whole region north of Humber might be stripped of all means of sustenance.[623]

The effects of this effort became legendary: "From the eleventh century onwards historians have noted the sustained ferocity with which the king set his men to destroy the means of life in northern England. Their generalities are abundantly borne out by the evidence of Domesday Book, which shows that within the country ravaged at this time vast areas were still derelict after seventeen years . . . It was the most terrible visitation that had ever fallen on any large part of England since the Danish wars of Alfred's time."[624]

Entering into legend were the resistance, escape from the Isle of Ely, and further adventures of Hereward the Wake during 1070-1071.

Regarding settlement, as opposed to conquest, William may at one time have intended to simply rule England as the legitimate heir of Edward. Redistribution of lands to his followers, however, as tenants in chief began immediately after Hastings, and continued with renewed pace after each revolt, so that by the time of the Domesday Survey in 1086 only two Anglo-Saxon lords of high rank were left in the realm: "The extinction and disappearance, in death, in exile and by social suppression, of the Old English aristocracy is one of the few non-controversial results of the Norman Conquest which, sociologically, is the imposition of a new and alien ruling class upon the land . . . The law changed in consequence, not least the land law, and so did the dispensation of justice to accommodate feudal notions of jurisdiction . . . ."[625]

---

[623] Orderic Vitalis, *The Ecclesiastical History of Orderic Vitalis* 232 (Marjorie Chibnall, ed., 1969).

[624] F. M. Stenton, *Anglo-Saxon England* 596-697 (1943).

[625] R. Allen Brown, *The Normans* 71-73 (1984).

Norman settlement, consisting of immigration from the continent, continued even after the death of William in 1087. Penetration of Scotland in the north and of Wales in the west proceeded until well into the twelfth century.

The Normans knew that the ferocity of their occupation would be returned in kind if possible. Their actual physical defenses against this were state-of-the-art for the time: the motte and bailey construction for castles (Illustration 25) and sturdy walls for cities and towns (Illustration 26). These security measures enabled the Norman overlords to maintain iron control over huge tracts of land.

It is difficult for us, viewing the Norman Conquest after the passage of nearly a millennium, to appreciate the monumentality of the Norman achievement or the disastrous consequences it held for the English. The stronger central rule that eventually arose from the Norman intrusion tends to obscure the decades of uncontrolled murder, oppression, rapine, humiliation, famine, and fear that the Norman invaders inflicted on much of England. Often, when the Norman barons could no longer find affluent Englishmen to plunder, they quarreled and fought among themselves, usually scourging the lands, manors, and peasants belonging to their opponents. Small wonder, then, that after numerous unsuccessful regional rebellions, the English, seeking relief from civil unrest, gave their allegiance to the Norman king rather than to discontented local magnates. This fitful and frightful struggle between the forces of chaos and control inexorably influenced English law and government.

Illustration 25. The Norman motte (the hill) and bailey (the structure or keep) at Cardiff Castle, Cardiff, Wales. This portion of the castle was begun in the late 11th century, and the castle withstood several assaults during the middle ages.

Illustration 26. The medieval Oxford city wall on the grounds of New College, University of Oxford. When the college was founded in 1379, the founders agreed to maintain the wall. Motte and bailey castle construction and sturdy walls for cities and towns enabled the Norman overlords to maintain their landholdings against hostile English inhabitants.

From a different and perhaps grander perspective, the Norman Conquest has been depicted as a profound renewal of Old English society and culture: "[Both] the Old English Church, [and] Old English society as a whole, . . . were old fashioned by the standards of northern France, features of a surviving Carolingian-type realm still in full working order in spite of the Danes. It is not unfair to say that in England at Hastings in 1066 the Old World went down before the New . . . [T]he most important single result of the Norman Conquest of England must be that it broke this country's close but barren ties with Scandinavia, and replaced both them and the affiliation with the increasingly obsolete German world by the closest bonds of absolute integration with northern France."[626]

§ 7.04(b). Norman Legal and Administrative Activities.

§ 7.04(b)(1). Local Government and Administration.

No more typical example of the interplay between English and Norman impulses can be found than in the changes in royal administrative practices introduced after the Conquest. William took over English governmental institutions intact, but by 1071 he had brought local administration entirely into Norman hands. He achieved this primarily by strengthening the office of sheriff, so that it functioned much like the Norman viscount, although it was much more subordinate to the king. Anglo-Norman sheriffs were less independent than Norman viscounts, because those who obtained the offices were usually from the lesser nobility, were changed often, and did not inherit their positions.

Although the Anglo-Norman sheriffs' traditional enforcement duties increased naturally with the growth of feudal dues and forest laws, the most important growth in the office's power was in the expanded scope of its judicial functions. Royal writs could command a sheriff to bring a case to the royal court or, in the days before rounds by royal justices were

[626] *Id.* at 75, 77.

common, could order the sheriff himself to hear and decide the case in its own locality.[627]

§ 7.04(b)(2). The Royal Court.

The Norman administrative practice that had the most direct effect on the common law's growth was the royal court. Although it is difficult to find precise information on this institution, it appears that in the early years the court usually consisted of servants who performed judicial, financial and other administrative functions, and who routinely witnessed royal writs.[628] Occasionally some members of the most powerful nobility, companions and confidants of the king with whom he discussed issues of the realm, joined this group. Such groups would not have been a formal court of law, but collectively, as a royal court, they did from time to time issue writs and judgments. Writs extant from this time are brief and cite no rules or guidelines, only commands. However, "we can be sure that the king often discussed with the barons such matters as the disposal of escheated fiefs, the settlement of conflicting claims to estates, and the marriage of heiresses; the decisions thus taken in the end determined the lines on which feudal practice was to develop."[629]

At the three great annual church festivals, the king also assembled his great court, consisting of all his tenants in chief. This council, a natural extension of the Anglo-Saxon *Witan*, also heard important cases and is the direct ancestor of the English Parliament.[630]

---

[627] D. C. Douglas, *William the Conqueror* 305-306 (1964).

[628] John Le Patourel, *The Norman Empire* 138 n.1, 139, 155-157 (1976).

[629] Jack Lindsay, *The Normans and Their World* 324-325 (1974).

[630] The early developments which eventually led to formation of a parliamentary body in England are described in 1 Frederick Pollock and Frederic William Maitland, *The History of English Law Before the Time of Edward I* 198-200 (2d ed. 1909).

§ 7.04(b)(3). Early Norman Judicial Activity.

Inevitably, a routine of judicial administration more methodical than the impromptu gatherings of nearby Norman nobles became necessary. At the time of the Conquest, the monarch's representative in the various localities was the sheriff, who had some judicial powers. It was in the king's interest to hold the sheriff's powers in check; the best control achieved by the Normans, albeit inadvertently, was in connection with steps taken to deal with financial matters. The king's agent or deputy over financial matters came to be called the chief justiciar, or Justiciar of All England. He often presided over the royal court gatherings at Easter and Michaelmas that accepted and audited money returns from sheriffs and other officers. The justiciar also resolved disputes arising from these accounts before the barons of the exchequer. By the time of William II (of England, 1087-1100), justiciars had been appointed over shires to perform comparable judicial and fiscal functions.[631]

In addition, because the king had to resolve disputes between tenants in chief, a judge, or justiciar (appointed as the king's agent, but still acting within the old Anglo-Saxon framework) tried such cases, which were commenced by royal writ. "The hearings were held at the full meetings of the shire courts where local men, including Englishmen, could pronounce on the custom of the country. Thus native tradition and feudal law were able to some extent to merge. There was not always time to examine the many witnesses closely. So the method used was of a sworn verdict being given by a group of men whom the court appointed."[632] Historians have found no definite precedent for such a practice in Normandy, but the idea of such a collective verdict was known among the Franks and in some parts of the Danelaw in England. "The origins of the jury are lost in obscurity, but the wide use of it certainly goes back to William; Domesday Book was

[631] Francis James West, *The Justiciarship in England 1066-1232* 10-13 (1966); John Le Patourel, *The Norman Empire* 143-145, 274 (1976); 1 Frederick Pollock and Frederic William Maitland, *The History of English Law Before the Time of Edward I* 156-159 (2d ed. 1909).

[632] Jack Lindsay, *The Normans and Their World* 328-329 (1974).

compiled from the verdicts of juries all over England."[633]

Eventually, Henry II (1154-1189) removed local justiciars and replaced them with itinerant or traveling justices, who were regular judicial officers.[634] In the 13th and 14th centuries these justices sometimes exercised a sweeping jurisdiction referred to as the General Eyre. It has been observed that "there was much important legislation effected . . . by means of instructions to the justices as they set out upon their Eyre,"[635] and it should be added that this was a crucial process in the formation of the common law. Centralization of judicial power continued, and eventually pleas concerning land were placed exclusively in royal jurisdiction.

Henry II also greatly increased the use of writs and sworn juries.[636] Writs, of course, had been a prominent feature of Anglo-Saxon administration. For the first four years of his reign in England, William retained Edward's Anglo-Saxon clerks, who assisted both the king and his justiciars. These clerks and their successors functioned under the direction of the chancellor, who was in charge of religious services and of writing activities. One of William's administrative improvements was to expand the issuance of writs, using them as a method of quickly sending commands throughout England. Officials sent writs only after the documents were authenticated by the seal of the chancellor.[637]

Except for these rather subtle changes of practice at the highest administrative levels, the Anglo-Norman kings made no significant changes in the court system or procedures that had existed under the Anglo-Saxons. Even William's most important judicial innovation, establishing separate bishop's courts to enforce canon law as he had in Normandy, was aimed at

---

[633] *Id.*

[634] John Le Patourel, *The Norman Empire* 260 (1976).

[635] Theodore F. T. Plucknett, *A Concise History of the Common Law* 145 (5th ed. 1956).

[636] Frederick Pollock and Frederic William Maitland, *The History of English Law Before the Time of Edward I* 138-153 (2d ed. 1909).

[637] D. C. Douglas, *William the Conqueror* 147-148, 292-293 (1964).

reforming the church, not at improving the secular legal system.[638]

Complaints against the aggressive and somewhat rapacious activities of the justices in Eyre led to yet another reform by Henry II: he chose five officials of his personal household to constitute a permanent court that would not depart from the King's Court,[639] and also would not have the financial functions that made the justices in Eyre so unpopular. This group of five justices was to remain with the king, and so was expected to travel with the king. Eventually known as the Court of Common Pleas, this court was eventually required by the Magna Carta to be in one place,[640] which place was naturally Westminster. Frequently the more important matters before the Court of Common Pleas were referred to the important counselors closest to the king, who eventually developed their own procedure for handling such referred matters and became a new court, the Court of King's Bench. The Court of King's Bench did not become an institution separate from the royal council until the reign of Edward I (1239-1307).

Maitland identified six ways in which the royal judicial institutions stimulated the development of the common law. These are, as summarized and paraphrased by Plucknett:[641]

> Under the Norman kings the Crown by its writ of right [remedied] the real or imaginary defects of justice in the feudal courts.
>
> Under Henry II it was established that no man need answer

---

[638] "Writ of William I concerning spiritual and temporal courts (1072-1076, and probably April 1072)," in *English Historical Documents* 604-605 (D. C. Douglas, ed., 1953).

[639] *Select Charters and Other Illustrations of English Constitutional History* 131 (William Stubbs, ed., 1881).

[640] *Magna Carta*, c. 17 (1215); c. 11 (1225).

[641] Frederic William Maitland, *The Constitutional History of England* 111-114 (1968), summarized in Theodore F. T. Plucknett, *A Concise History of the Common Law* 156 (5th ed. 1956).

for his freehold without a royal writ unless he cared to.[642]

Henry II also ordained that a defendant in certain pleas of land in the King's Court could have a jury trial (grand assize) instead of battle if he chose.

The possessory assizes established by Henry deliberately ignored the feudal courts and by their swiftness immediately became very popular.

The idea of contempt was used very effectively. The King would issue a writ ordering a subject to do right and justice, and if he refused, he was guilty of contempt of the King's writ. The defendant in a writ of debt, for example, not only denies his liability, but also denies tort and force in resisting the King's command.

The idea of the King's peace was not only the basis of criminal jurisdiction, but could also be used to enlarge the civil jurisdiction of the King's Court. This was effected through the action of trespass, which although criminal in form was constantly becoming more and more a civil action.

§ 7.04(b)(4). Early Norman Law-making Activity.

Although much of early Norman law-making activity in England is lost from history, perhaps more has been preserved than is the case for other European governments of that period. William was keenly aware of the legal issues affecting his claim to the English throne and was eager to promote the continuity of life and law that only a legitimate successor could provide. At his coronation ceremony in Westminster Abbey, he swore "he would rule justly and with kingly care the whole people placed

[642] *Glanvill*, XII, 25.

under him, that he would make and keep right law, and that he would utterly prohibit all spoliation and unrighteous judgments."[643]

Only a few charters, writs, and legal decrees are known to have been issued during William I's reign.[644] At an early date, the decrees were compiled into a single document, known as "The Laws of William the Conqueror." The decrees effected no noteworthy change in English legal tradition. Indeed, their most important provision, Clause 7, quoted in full below, secures to the people their ancient legal customs. These decrees may be summarized as follows:

> A wish for reverence for God, faith in Christ, and peace between English and Normans.
>
> All freemen will affirm by oath their loyalty to William.
>
> Special protection is given against murder of Normans, including fines to be paid by the entire hundred where the killing occurred.
>
> Normans are to pay "scot and lot" according to English law.
>
> Cattle sales are to be in towns before witnesses.
>
> Trial by battle is an available procedure in disputes between English and Normans.
>
> "This also I command and will, that all shall have and hold the law of King Edward in respect of their lands and all their possessions, with the addition of those decrees I have ordained for the welfare of the English people."

---

[643] "Select passages from the annals ascribed to Florence of Worcester," in *English Historical Documents* 204, 214 (D. C. Douglas, ed., 1953).

[644] *See* editor's introduction to "The Laws of William the Conqueror," in *English Historical Documents* 399 (D. C. Douglas, ed., 1953).

> The frankpledge system is imposed, securing court appearances when summoned.
>
> Slaves are not to be sold outside the country.
>
> Punishment is to be by blinding or mutilation rather than by execution.[645]

One other very important early Anglo-Norman legal document is the "*Coronation Charter" of Henry I*, believed to have influenced the *Magna Carta*. This document, summarized below, also preserves the old English laws, especially in Clause 13, which is quoted in full:

> The Church is to be free of certain abuses and oppressions to which it was formerly subject.
>
> Only just reliefs are to be charged for redemption of a decedent's land.
>
> The king will not require payment for his counsel in marriage matters; widows will not be given in marriage without their consent.
>
> Widows with minor children shall retain dowry and the marriage portion, and will not be given in marriage without their consent.
>
> Special taxes to compensate for depreciated coinage will no longer be levied.
>
> Many pleas and debts owed to his brother the late king are forgiven.
>
> Disposition of movable property belonging to a baron who

---

[645] "The Laws of William the Conqueror," in *English Historical Documents* 399-400 (D. C. Douglas, ed., 1953).

> dies intestate is explained.
>
> Forfeitures by barons need to be covered by movable property only to the amount of the forfeiture.
>
> All murder-fines incurred before the coronation are remitted; all future murder-fines are to be paid according to the law of King Edward.
>
> The forests of William I are retained.
>
> Men holding land in military tenure for knight service are exempted from taxes and other services, so that they may properly equip themselves.
>
> "I establish a firm peace in all my kingdom, and I order that this peace shall henceforth be kept."
>
> "I restore to you the law of King Edward together with such emendations to it as my father made with the counsel of his barons."
>
> Property seized since the death of William II shall be returned.[646]

Both of the above documents demonstrate the dearth of original Norman contribution to English law. These documents, as well as the low level of legislative activity by these Norman rulers, who were preoccupied with self-preservation, confirm that much of the legal foundation of the Old English state was the principal source of common law. The Normans excelled at adopting and adapting cultures of the people they dominated. Despite the fact that the transition from their rough Viking traditions and tongue to Gallo-Frankish ways was still relatively recent, they were able to assimilate the old English ways basically intact. This trait is well illustrated

---

[646] "The 'Coronation Charter' of Henry I (5 August 1100)," in 2 *English Historical Documents* 400-402 (D. C. Douglas, ed., 1953).

by the introduction of feudal military tenures into continental Norman landholding, the systematic use of such tenures by William to create a stable military force for Normandy, and William's further refinements of uniformity in applying these military tenures to an existing set of English tenures.

§ 7.05. English Land Tenures and Feudalism After the Conquest.

§ 7.05(a). William the Conqueror's Claim to All English Land.

> England belonged to [William] in a sense in which it had never belonged to any previous king. All landholders, lay and ecclesiastical, were his tenants and held of him; moreover, all who held land of the greater tenants were also the King's men and owed him allegiance. Thus there was nothing comparable to freehold tenure in post-Conquest England.[647]

It is clear that William assumed tenurial lordship over all English land, but it is unclear on what theory this claim was based. If William was the legitimate successor to Edward the Confessor, then he would have simply stepped into that king's prerogatives over English land, much of which (especially bookland) would perhaps have been held as freehold, without obligation to the king except for the occupants' customary duties of military service, road building and fortress repairs.[648] He also could claim ultimate ownership of lands forfeited by those English lords who had

---

[647] Ann Williams, "The Land of the Conqueror," in *Domesday: 900 Years of England's Norman Heritage* 47-48 (1986).

[648] It must be acknowledged, however, that even by his claim to "the entire range of powers that had belonged to any Old English sovereign," William held certain powers over all English land: "Private transactions in land were insecure until he had confirmed them, and he had a right to be consulted before a man of any position commended himself to a new lord." F. M. Stenton, *Anglo-Saxon England* 614 (1943).

opposed him in 1066 and after. However, any claim to ownership over all English land would more logically be based on the right and result of conquest, a position objectionable to William in his striving for the legitimacy of his rule of England. Not until 1086, twenty years after Hastings, did William require an oath of fealty from all free men, which would be consistent with his claim to ultimate ownership of all English land: "All free men will affirm by oath their loyalty to William."[649]

It appears that William's earlier intention was to rule over a genuine Anglo-Norman state, with Norman barons replacing only those English who actively opposed William. Until 1069, this was still a realistic possibility, because, despite the forfeitures resulting from Hastings, in 1069 English earls still held more than two-thirds of England, and the king's writs were still written in English and being sent to mostly English sheriffs.[650] This changed after William overcame the series of rebellions that commenced in 1069, so that by the time of the Domesday Survey in 1086, only two Englishmen held lands directly of the king: "To ten of his principal followers he gave almost one-fourth of England. To lesser barons he made grants of the smaller fiefs or holdings of English earls and thegns. Normally, the grants were not of a compact territorial unit but consisted of manors scattered through several counties."[651]

These grants to relatives and leading followers of the king were under a form of military tenure by which the recipient of the land was required to swear fealty to the king and agree to provide a specific number of

---

[649] "The Laws of William the Conqueror," in *English Historical Documents* (D. C. Douglas, ed., 1953); the *Anglo-Saxon Chronicle* (E or Laud version) confirms the requirement of the oath with this entry for 1086:

> Thereafter he journeyed around the country so that he came to Salisbury by Lammas, where he was met by his council and all the landholders who were of any account throughout England, no matter whose vassals they might be. All did him homage and became his men, and swore him oaths of allegiance that they would be faithful to him against all other men.

[650] F. M. Stenton, *Anglo-Saxon England* 616 (1943).

[651] Sheldon F. Kurtz, *Moynihan's Introduction to the Law of Real Property* 2-3 (4th ed. 2005).

battle-ready knights when required by the king. Such requirements of knight service, considered to burden the land itself, were even imposed upon holders of church lands, whose quotas of knights amounted to about 800 of the 5,000 knights' services obtained by William through military tenures. The barons on whom these requirements were imposed directly probably did not number more than 180.[652] With such heavy reliance on military tenure, William was undoubtedly reluctant to depend on Englishmen who had not yet adopted the military tactics and organization he had used with such success at Hastings.

§ 7.05(b). Feudal Relationships in the Eleventh Century.

§ 7.05(b)(1). Characteristics of Feudalism.

Land held by military tenure was known as an honor or a fief, and was the main component of a social system that would come to be described as feudal. In a very general sense, feudalism may have arisen as a necessary response to Viking aggressions throughout Europe: "Consequently in all fields of life the military expert was predominant, and for a time even overshadowed his great mediaeval rival, the religious expert. Between the two of them, the military and the clergy, there was little room for anything else."[653]

While no firm consensus on the precise meaning or elements of feudalism exists, the feudal relationships that evolved on the continent and formed part of the Norman experience can be described generally, with the cautionary reminder that change was constantly occurring and wide variations existed at any point in time: "Feudal relationships and customs were based on the mutual obligations of lord and man (vassal), obligations which go back so far into the common Germanic past of northern Europe

---

[652] F. M. Stenton, *Anglo-Saxon England* 626 (1943).

[653] Theodore F. T. Plucknett, *A Concise History of the Common Law* 508-509 (5th ed. 1956).

that their origins cannot be discerned. The tie between lord and vassal was established by the act of homage and oath of fealty. In the act of homage, the vassal knelt before his lord, offering his clasped hands which the lord enclosed in his own, and promised service and fidelity in return for protection. He then swore an oath, the oath of fealty, to the same effect, with his hands upon a relic or a gospel-book."[654]

Despite such solemnity, the feudal relationship could be dissolved and was "decidedly weak; it was only while the religious and social sanctity attaching to homage endured that a lord could have any reasonable dependence upon the armed assistance of his vassals."[655]

The attachment of feudal obligations to the land meant that, with the exception of those at the top of the "feudal pyramid," no lands in a feudal society were *owned*, they were *held*, and the holdings could be revoked for breach of feudal obligations. In societies just emerging into feudalism, the holdings extended only for the tenant's life, with regrants of the land to the landholder's descendants dependent upon the lord's discretion and favor.

The military nature of the most feudal obligations at the top of the system determined the nomenclature and organizational structure for feudal landholding. One holding a parcel of land called a knight's fee was by definition required to provide one knight. The size of the holding might differ from place to place, but, especially in Norman England, the lands and the extent of their obligations for knights, were expressed with great specificity. After knights lost their preeminence in military activities, such service was often commuted to money payments, and knights' fees continued to play an important role in the fiscal system of England.

Feudalism was also characterized by a remarkable decentralization of governing powers. Most defensive activity was carried out by local leaders exercising powers of government in their localities. Especially prominent among the non-military powers was the exercise of legal jurisdiction, and

---

[654] *Id.*

[655] *Id.* at 507.

the associated requirement of court attendance, over a lord's tenants.

§ 7.05(b)(2). Possible Sources of Feudalism.

While feudalism may have arisen in response to the Viking crises, its elements may have derived from several institutions extant in Europe even during Roman and post-Roman times. These several streams of influence are summarized in the following subsections:[656]

§ 7.05(b)(2)(A). The *Comitatus*.

The comitatus in prehistoric Germany was the warrior band that resulted from an early Germanic custom by which a chief would surround himself with warrior companions and enter into a personal bond with them. A comparable late Roman institution encountered by encroaching Germanic invaders would have been the band of soldiers retained by the emperor or general for his personal service. The leader provided each soldier with a military outfit, but upon the soldier's death, the outfit would be returned to the leader. From these arrangements feudalism may have derived the oath of fealty and the custom of returning military equipment upon the death of the knight.

§ 7.05(b)(2)(B). Patronage.

A Roman institution, albeit extra-legal, that may have contributed to feudal traits, was patronage. In the old Roman practice, clients would "commend" themselves to the "faith" of a more wealthy and powerful patron. In practical terms, the clients gave service and counsel to the patron, who in turn defended the clients in litigation and in other ways. When the 5th-century *Theodosian Code* declaimed clients' attempts to commend their lands as well as themselves, that certainly revealed that land commendation had been introduced and somewhat abused. Land commendation to a patron may have been driven somewhat by Roman taxation, which fell heaviest on smaller landholders and left in place huge exemptions for the larger and

---

[656] The summary that follows in the text is based on Theodore F. T. Plucknett, *A Concise History of the Common Law* 510-515 (5th ed. 1956).

more powerful owners. Thus, through patronage practices, smaller landholders may have gradually slipped into the status of dependant tenants.

§ 7.05(b)(2)(C). The *Precarium* and the *Precaria.*

A property interest that had only a tenuous existence in Roman property law, the *precarium*, may also have contributed to the development of feudal property interests. If a person petitioned a landowner for possession of some of the land, the petitioner might be granted a *precarium*, the right to occupy and use a parcel of land, revocable at will or at the death of either party. However fragile, this possessory interest was protected against third parties. In Roman practice, a debtor might surrender land to a creditor, receiving the land back as a *precarium*, until the debtor paid the debt, whereupon the lender restored the original property interest. When, under the patronage practices, commendation of land began to occur, the *precarium* would have facilitated the process: the client would turn over land to the patron, and receive back a possessory interest in the same land in the form of a *precarium*. By the 6th century, the Christian church had become a major landholder and very frequently granted *precaria* to its donors and others. Changes in custom occurred, so that some grants in *precarium* were for life, or for several generations, and others for a specific number of years. The grants for years would sometimes be renewable upon payment of rent, and such a grant came to be called a *precaria*, rather than a *precarium*. Little certain information about the origins and history of these interests is available, but there can be little doubt that they eventually contributed to the rise of feudal interests in land.

§ 7.05(b)(2)(D). Conditional Grants by Merovingian Monarchs.

In their attempts to establish order and a semblance of stable government during the 6th and 7th centuries, Merovingian rulers gave to their faithful followers large grants of land that were in theory allodial, or in more modern terminology, in freehold. Without other significant sources of revenue, however, these royal grantors came to expect some form of payment for their approval of succession to the lands by the donees' heirs. In any event, the grant was considered revocable, and might even be conditioned on the donee rendering future services. These developments, too, contributed to the rise of feudal practices.

§ 7.05(b)(2)(E). Use of Precariae by Carolingian Monarchs.

The Carolingian successors of the Merovingians concentrated their efforts on gaining control of the huge landholding of the church. As an alternative to outright confiscation, the church agreed to grant *precariae* to donees designated by the monarch, with the donees expected to pay nominal rents to the church and render services to the monarch. Even without royal prodding, the church extensively used *precariae* (that is, a form of *precarium* under which some rent was given in exchange for the property interest), to secure tenants to work smaller, scattered holdings. These grants came to be called "benefices."

§ 7.05(b)(2)(F). Military Service as a Condition of Grants in *Precarium*.

The grants of *precariae* given in response to royal recommendation had come, by circa 750, to be conditioned on the donee's rendering military service to the monarch (not necessarily to the grantor). By the time of Charlemagne's reign, all who held such interests, not just those who held land directly from the monarch, were required to give some type of military service. Because many who held *precarium* interests were smallholders, they were permitted to combine their efforts to meet obligations of military service. This led to more definite notions of the extent of land that would support a knight, so that on the eve of the Norman Conquest, Normandy had recognized and regularized the so-called knight's fee.

§ 7.05(b)(2)(G). Landholding and Jurisdictional Independence.

Deep in both German and Roman customs were impulses to recognize some degree of legal independence associated with landholding. The legal power of the landholder over his own household recognized by Germanic custom found its more extreme counterpart in Roman practice, which frequently accorded to the largest landowners the rights and profits of exercising legal jurisdiction in their domains. Within these rights of jurisdiction arose institutions that would eventually become feudal courts. Two streams of tradition are possible origins of the such courts. The old Germanic relationship of lord and vassal may have been the predecessor of the feudal jurisdiction and courts; on the other hand, there may have been a customary court conducted by the community of freemen, a type of public court, which came to be dominated by one or more large landholders. Some evidence suggests that French feudal courts derived from the old public courts that were taken over by private landowners. In such communal courts, judgment was given by landholders who were obligated to function in their court role because of their landholding, and whose successors in their court function were therefore sometimes hereditary. When fulfilling these judicial functions became too burdensome for individual landholders, the local lord, drawing from the other stream of tradition, could compel designated vassals to perform the obligations of court.

§ 7.05(b)(2)(H). Summary.

The rise of European feudalism was a complicated and attenuated process whose sources can only be guessed at from great distances of time and space. Moreover, devotees of the subject still disagree over feudalism's distinguishing features. Yet, the preceding paragraphs suggest several characteristics of medieval European society that evolved into a distinctive form of social organization that could be called feudal. Among these are: (1) the loyalty to a lord implicit in the comitatus and explicit in patronage; (2) the expression of that loyalty by relinquishing of land to a superior party, the lord, in return for protection and other benefits, and the return of that land with possessory rights only, and those rights much burdened by conditions and obligations increasingly denoting relatively servile and dependent status; (3) the eventual prominence of military service as the condition of greatest importance, attached to the landholding of those in the upper tiers of the social hierarchy; and (4) consistent with government decentralization compelled by the social and political disintegration in the Dark Ages, a relinquishing of judicial and other public functions to the larger feudal landholders.

§ 7.05(b)(3). Description of Typical Feudal Tenures and Incidents.

§ 7.05(b)(3)(A). Military Tenure.

As with other feudal tenures, it is impossible to take a snapshot of English military tenure that accurately portrays this form of landholding for any other period and place. Military tenure never, at any point in time, had a universal definiteness and stability."[657]

The viability of the military tenure as a tool of national defense in England extended for about a century after the Conquest. Military tenure itself had a much longer existence, however, being adapted to serve national needs in less direct ways. While military tenure had become somewhat characteristic of upper level Norman society, in fact the conquest of England afforded the Normans both the opportunity and necessity of refining military tenures to hold fast their English gains. However, this process was not commenced by command, but was evolutionary, and by the time it was fully evolved, it was becoming obsolete.[658]

In theory, at least, the tenant under obligation of military service provided the requisite number of battle-ready knights for a period of up to

---

[657] Frederick Pollock and Frederic William Maitland, *The History of English Law Before the Time of Edward I* 252 (2d ed. 1909).

[658] "Soon after the Conquest a process begins whereby the duty of service in the army becomes rooted in the tenure of the land. This goes on for a century; but before it is finished, before the system of knight's fees has been well ordered and arranged, the kings are already discovering that the force thus created is not what they want, or is not all that they want." *Id.*

forty days, and for service only within the realm. The leading lords were bound to provide knights in multiples of fives or tens, but the actual number seemed to bear no relation to the richness of the tenant's property resources; rather, "political and personal considerations seem to have been uppermost."[659] The tenants in chief remained ready to meet this requirement either by retaining the knights in their own household, or by granting parcels of land to others who would agree to supply part of the quota (the process of subinfeudation) or a combination of both methods. Not until about 1070 were the quotas for William's tenants in chief fixed, but there is some evidence that the process of subinfeudation was leaky, and that the leading lords' obligations were not fully supplied by their tenants.

As knight service became obsolete, or some of the great landholders deemed themselves ill-prepared to provide warriors, a substitute for knight service arose, called scutage, which was nothing more than a money payment in lieu of providing men. When scutage first appeared in the available historical evidence at about 1100, it was being applied to landholding of the church, but not many decades later it was being applied to all other kinds of tenants. Scutage also was paid by those who held by subinfeudation. Indeed, the obligation of scutage was typically imposed on the full hierarchy of subtenants.

Two forces combined to shorten the life of scutage. The cost of equipping a knight increased, making the burdens fixed in 1070 too great for some to bear. Apparently by negotiation some quotas were reduced, and those tenants often preferred to send the reduced number of knights rather than the scutage substitute for the original higher number of knights. At the same time, when the scutage for a particular tenant became a fixed sum, the value of that sum steadily declined in the face of inflation, and it became less attractive and effective for the monarchy to rely on scutage arrangements. By the end of the second century after the Conquest, scutage had become solely a source of revenue and in this role it served as an irritant to landowners until formally abolished in 1660.

---

[659] Theodore F. T. Plucknett, *A Concise History of the Common Law* 532 (5th ed. 1956).

§ 7.05(b)(3)(B). Incidents of Military Tenure.

§ 7.05(b)(3)(B)(i). Homage.

Besides the principal duty of military assistance, knight service carried several significant auxiliary conditions, or incidents. The most ancient of these was homage. Homage retained a vitality well beyond that of a merely traditional formality. Glanvill, in the 12th century, was concerned about the dilemma of owing homage to two lords who disputed with one another.[660] Even in the 13th century, Bracton's treatise provided a lengthy explanation of the reciprocal obligations implicit in homage and the precise wording of the oath of fealty that declared the homage relationship between lord and tenant.[661] A case from the Eyre Rolls tells of a tenant who surrendered his land and his homage to his lord, "when he felt himself aggrieved by the harsh lordship," on condition that he give it to an abbey.[662]

Though homage was an incident of knight service, it, too, had incidents of its own:

> The effect of homage is this, that if one has done homage to another, his true lord or a non-lord, he cannot withdraw from such lord or his homage without judgment, as long as he holds the tenement, either in demesne or in service, by which he is bound to homage. Because of the bond of homage the tenant may do nothing to the disherison of his lord or his severe injury, nor conversely, may the lord so act toward the tenant. If either so acts homage is completely dissolved and extinguished, and the *nexus* and obligation of homage, since they act contrary to homage and the oath of fealty, and it will be a just judgment that

---

[660] *Glanvill*, VII, 1.

[661] *Bracton*, fol. 80.

[662] *Rolls of the Justices in Eyre for Gloucestershire, Warwickshire and Staffordshire 1221-1222* 607-608, No. 1450 (Selden Society vol. 59, 1940).

> they be punished with respect to that in which they offend, that is, if it is the lord, that he lose his lordship; if the tenant, his tenement . . . .[663]

In a particular case known to Bracton, a lord lost his lordship over land by exercising undue influence over a ward and wrongfully colluding with another to deprive the ward of her land.[664]

§ 7.05(b)(3)(B)(ii). Wardship.

Apparently connected with the incident of homage was the incident of wardship, the right of the lord to custody of a minor tenant's land until the tenant came of age. In Normandy of the late twelfth century, it was declared that the wardship should not be exercised by the mother or kinsmen, because of possible conflict of interest, but only by the lord, because he was bound to the ward's late father through the tie of homage.[665]

However, recognizing the right of wardship in the lord may have been a Norman innovation following the Conquest. Apparently the Anglo-Saxon tradition had conferred the right of wardship on the widow and mother,[666]

---

[663] *Bracton*, fol. 80b.

[664] *Bracton's Note Book*, no. 1840.

[665] "A fatherless heir must be in ward to some one. Who shall be his guardian? His mother? No. Why not? She will take another husband and have sons by him, and they, greedy of the heritage, will slay their firstborn brother, or the step-father will slay his step-son. Who then shall be the guardian? The child's blood kinsmen? No. Why not? Lest, thirsting for his heritage, they destroy him. For the prevention of such faithless cruelty, it is established that the boy be in ward to one who was bound to his father by the tie of homage. And who is such an one? The lord of the land who never can inherit that land in demesne; for heirs of a noble race always have many heirs. Besides they should be brought up in good houses and honourably educated. Those who are brought up in their lords' houses are the apter to serve their lords faithfully and love them in truth; and the lords cannot look with hatred on whose whom they have reared, but will love them and faithfully guard their woods and tenements and apply the profits of their land to their advancement." Frederick Pollock and Frederic William Maitland, *The History of English Law Before the Time of Edward I* 326 (2d ed. 1909) (translating a custumal of Normandy dated c. 1200).

[666] Dorothy Whitelock, *The Beginnings of English Society* 94 (1974).

and this was still the practice at the beginning of the 12th century in England, as recognized in the so-called *Coronation Charter of Henry I.*[667] The first direct documentary evidence for a right of wardship in the lord does not appear until the Assize of Northhampton in 1176.[668]

In some of the medieval documents a distinction is drawn between the right to have possession of the ward's lands and a comparable right to have custody and care of the ward's person. That such questions should even be raised probably meant that rights of land occupants had advanced since the age when possessory prerogatives had ended upon the tenant's death, and all power over the land had reverted to the lord.

§ 7.05(b)(3)(B)(iii). Marriage.

Associated with wardship issues was the incident of marriage. If one underlying concern for proper supervision of a minor's lands was the fulfillment of feudal obligations, the same concern arose with respect to the widow of a landholder. Even in Anglo-Saxon times, remarriage of tenants' widows and daughters sometimes took place as directed by the tenants' lords. The Normans actively extended this practice. By 1100 a lord was required to consult with the king when marriage of the lord's daughter was proposed, and if the lord was dead, the king was entitled to determine the daughter's marriage and the disposition of her lands.[669] This practice persisted into the reign of Henry II in the latter part of the 12th century.[670] In 1193, however, is the first documentary evidence for the king directing

---

[667] "And the guardian of the land and the children shall be either the wife or some other relative who has a better right." "The Coronation Charter of Henry I," cl. 4, § 1, in *The Laws of the Kings of England from Edmund to Henry I* 278-79 (Agnes Jane Robertson, ed. and trans., 1925); *see also* "The 'Coronation Charter' of Henry I (5 August 1100)" cl. 4, in *English Historical Documents* 400-02 (D. C. Douglas, ed., 1953).

[668] William Stubbs, *Select Charters and Other Illustrations of English Constitutional History* 150, cl. 4 (1881).

[669] "The 'Coronation Charter' of Henry I (5 August 1100)" cl. 3, in *English Historical Documents* 400-402 (D. C. Douglas, ed., 1953).

[670] *Glanvill*, VII, 9 and 10; IX, 4.

the marriage of sons as well as daughters, and, of course, these decisions were made a matter of sale. Selling of wardships and marriages of widows and daughters by the king is shown by evidence a century older.[671] It has been observed that if the king was gradually losing prerogatives over tenants' lands as inheritability and alienability rights advanced, it was not without price, as "in England feudalism itself becomes commercial."[672]

§ 7.05(b)(3)(B)(iv). Aids.

If any incident of knight service invited unrestrained caprice, it was the incident of aids. Theoretically, the obligation of aid owed by the knight tenant to the lord could be required for any one of numerous circumstances that were neither regular nor well-defined. Custom eventually settled on just three occasions when an aid could be required: to ransom the lord, to knight the lord's oldest son, and to conclude the marriage of the lord's oldest daughter. As with scutage, the obligation to pay an aid would be passed on to the full hierarchy of subtenants.[673]

---

[671] *See* Frederick Pollock and Frederic William Maitland, *The History of English Law Before the Time of Edward I* 324-325 (2d ed. 1909). Indeed the evidence, a Pipe Roll, shows Henry I as the seller, despite the proclamation in his Coronation Charter that he would not accept consideration for granting permission to marry:

> If any of my barons or other men wishes to give his daughter, or sister, or niece, or cousin in marriage, let him speak with me; but I will neither take anything of his for the licence, nor will I forbid him to give her away, unless it be to an enemy of mine.

Pollock and Maitland simply commented, "That Henry [I] made these promises is certain, that he broke them is equally certain." *Id.* at 325. What is uncertain is whether the declaration in the *Coronation Charter* represents the old law and customs that the Normans subsequently altered, or whether the charter represents relaxation of the old law in order to gain political advantage among the barons.

[672] *Id.* at 328-329.

[673] Theodore F. T. Plucknett, *A Concise History of the Common Law* 536 (5th ed. 1956).

§ 7.05(b)(3)(B)(v). Relief.

The incident of knight tenure called relief emerged from the times when a military tenant's holding was not automatically passed to the heir. When the military tenant died, the relief was the amount the tenant's heir paid to the tenant's lord for permission to continue the tenancy. The amount of the relief payment was at first arbitrary, and thus subject to abuse, but later came to be regulated by charter[674] and statute,[675] varying in amount according to the extent of the tenant's holdings. When custom stabilized relief payments, this secured the inheritability of the knight's tenancy. If the decedent was a tenant in chief of the monarch, the monarch had the right to require relief payments for all the decedent's holdings, whether or not the decedent held directly of the king.

§ 7.05(b)(3)(B)(vi). Escheat.

Escheat, the reverting of land possession and ownership to the lord or the monarch, was another incident associated with knight tenancy, and could occur either upon the tenant's death without an heir or upon the tenant's commission of a felony. Although lands often escheated to the monarch, they would escheat to an intervening lord if the lordship could be shown.[676] Escheat could also occur when the tenant committed a felony, and the frequency with which such escheats occurred depended almost entirely on what acts were regarded as felonies. In the immediate decades after the Conquest, refusing to render services due to the lord was one of the few felonies then recognized, but even that was soon removed from the list of felonies. Another restraint on the incidence of felony escheat was that eventually the monarch claimed a right to hold such escheated land for

---

[674] "Similarly, the vassals of my barons shall pay the juste and lawful relief for their lands to the lords." "The Coronation Charter of Henry I," cl. 2, §, in *The Laws of the Kings of England from Edmund to Henry I* 276-77 (Agnes Jane Robertson, ed. and trans., 1925); *see also* "The 'Coronation Charter' of Henry I (5 August 1100)" cl. 2 in *English Historical Documents* 400-402 (D. C. Douglas, ed., 1953).

[675] *Magna Carta*, cl. 2, dating from 1215.

[676] In England, the old rules of escheat were officially abolished in 1925, and heirless property now all goes to the Crown.

a year and a day and to commit waste on it during that time, before relinquishing possession to the lord.

§ 7.05(b)(3)(B)(vii). Forfeiture.

Forfeiture was a related incident of knight tenure similarly limited in value to the lord. Forfeited land passed directly to the monarch, not to the immediate lord. If the monarch later re-granted the forfeited land the lord's rights revived.[677]

§ 7.05(b)(3)(C). Serjeanty Tenures and Their Incidents.

Serjeanty tenures apparently arose in the thirteenth century, and so were not part of the feudal characteristics introduced by the earliest Anglo-Norman monarchs. Tenants in chief typically rendered serjeanties that would be later identified as grand serjeanties. In earlier times, these serjeanties were scarcely distinguishable from knights' tenancies. The so-called "grand serjeanties" of the 13th century included such duties as carrying the banner of the king, carrying the lance of the king, leading the king's army, being the king's marshal, and carrying the king's sword at his coronation, among others.[678] It was also possible for tenants of lords other than the king to hold by serjeanty tenure, either to serve the lord or to serve the monarch.

Serjeanty tenures covered a huge variety of serving relationships, and perhaps that is why the incident of relief that applied to this tenure was still not fixed in amount even long after reliefs for other tenures were stabilized. Also, because so many of the serjeanty tenures were intended to render personal service directly to the king, royal permission to alienate such a tenure was consistently required, even after the king no longer insisted on

---

[677] Theodore F. T. Plucknett, *A Concise History of the Common Law* 536 (5th ed. 1956).

[678] Frederick Pollock and Frederic William Maitland, *The History of English Law Before the Time of Edward I* 282-283 (2d ed. 1909).

being consulted to alienate other tenures. Because of the types of service required of a serjeanty tenure, it was considered not subject to partition among co-heiresses, but instead was taken in entirety by the oldest sister, in the absence of a male heir. Incidents common to other tenures also applied to serjeanty. Regulation of wardship and marriage of tenants by serjeanty differed depending on whether the serjeanty was considered "grand" or "petty".[679]

§ 7.05(b)(3)(D). Free Socage Tenures and Their Incidents.

"Any tenure that on the one hand is free and on the other hand is not spiritual, nor military, nor 'serviential,' is called tenure in free socage."[680] Tenure in free socage eventually developed as the one great residual tenancy for almost every arrangement that was not military tenure. It also was free of the most burdensome incidents of military tenure, so that it became the tenancy of choice, even if holding it inferred a relatively lower social status.

The very wide variety of socage tenures arose from several types of circumstances. For instance, a tenant might be bound to render only nominal services or rents to the lord, either because the conveyance might be between related persons, or the grantee had actually purchased the land: "to have put the purchaser in the vendor's place might have been difficult, perhaps impossible [given the restrictions on alienability at the time]; so the purchaser is made tenant to the vendor at an insignificant rent."[681] For some socage tenures the lord might have demanded a more substantial rent in money, goods or produce, possibly the result of some bargaining by lords and tenants trying to strike the best deals that economic circumstances would allow. Other socage tenures imposed requirements of ordinary agricultural labor, even if the tenant was an important aristocrat. These

---

[679] *Id.* at 290.

[680] *Id.* at 291.

[681] *Id.*

duties would have been fulfilled by the socage tenant's undertenants and "seem to be the channel by which the term *socage* gradually spreads itself."[682] At times it might have been quite natural for a villein able to supply some needed labor services to step up into a socage tenure that was ordinarily open only to free persons. Indeed, some socage tenants were barely distinguishable from the unfree villeins.

§ 7.05(b)(3)(E). Tenure in Burgage.

Tenancy in burgage was an anomaly in the tenurial system. It was a tenure found only in the towns and boroughs and extended only to a burgess, a free member of the medieval commune or town. Burgage was similar to free socage in that the tenant, whose tenancy usually consisted of a house in the town, was required only to pay a small rent, with no other services required except for occasional light agricultural services. Burgage, like free socage, was free of the majority of tenurial incidents, including homage, aids, and marriage, although a relief was occasionally required and wardship usually applied. In place of the absent incidents, burgage was subject to the local customs pertaining to the borough or town. If a town had obtained from its lord control over its courts and profits, then burgage actions would be tried in those courts. Most questions of private law pertaining to burgage tenure, such as inheritability and dower, were determined by the customs of the town or borough, rather than by common law rules; burgage was often inheritable, devisable, and alienable. When a manor attained the status of a borough, the change could be signified by abolition of labor services, with burgage tenures in their place.

§ 7.05(b)(3)(F). Tenure in Free Alms (Frankalmoign).

Frequently landholders would give lands to the church under one of the ordinary tenures described above. At other times their gifts of land would require the donee to perform some specific spiritual service, and were called tenure by divine service. Such tenure might also carry a requirement

---

[682] *Id.* at 292.

of fealty to the lord. Still other gifts of land to the church might exact no precise spiritual service, but were given for general spiritual benefit, and for which no fealty was required; these tenures were known as frankalmoign, or free alms. Gradually, such tenures came to be recognized in perpetuity and to be free of any requirement for secular services. More importantly, frankalmoign tenures came to be free of the jurisdiction of the secular courts, being instead subject to the ecclesiastical courts, except that a secular court could decide any preliminary question of the actual existence of frankalmoign tenure. The role of church foundations as among the largest landholders in England came to an abrupt end when Henry VIII dissolved and confiscated property of monasteries and abbeys. This was part of his program to establish and control the Church of England in place of traditional Roman Catholicism. Fountains Abbey, in Illustration 27, the largest monastery in 16th century England, was dissolved in 1539.

Illustration 27. A small portion of the ruins of Fountains Abbey, in north Yorkshire, England. At the time of its dissolution in the reign of Henry VIII, it was the richest Cistercian foundation in England. Its lands and good were sold to a private party in 1540.

§ 7.05(b)(3)(G). The Unfree "Tenure" of Villeinage.

The very large majority of the English population in the eleventh century consisted of peasants who were considered unfree, and whose landholding was in the unfree tenure known as villeinage. Although there was a close correlation between personal status and land tenure, it was possible for a free man to hold a parcel of land by villein tenure. Other unfree tenures, such as tenancies at will and for years, came to be widely held by free persons. Villein tenure could be distinguished from other tenures on the basis of the services villeins were required to render, that "consist chiefly of the duty of cultivating the lord's demense."[683] While custom precisely defined the extent of such services, the particular work to be done from day to day remained uncertain under villein tenure, and this may be seen as a distinction from comparable agricultural services sometimes required of free tenures:

> This then seems to have been the test usually applied by the king's court. If the labour services are "uncertain," the tenure is unfree; and it is a test which condemns as unfree the great bulk of the tenures which obliged men to perform any considerable amount of agricultural labour for their lord, because, however minutely some particulars of those services may be defined, there is generally a spacious room left for the play of the lord's will. Thus the test roughly coincides with another: labour service is not necessarily unfree, but a service which consists of much labour, of labour to be done all year round, is almost of necessity unfree; for almost of necessity the tenant will be bound to obey, within wide limits, whatever commands the lord or the lord's bailiff may give him.[684]

Villeins, who were in effect serfs, were also distinct in that they were required to pay the merchet, a payment for the lord's leave for such activities as to give a daughter in marriage outside the manor, or to send a son to school, or to have a son ordained, or to sell livestock. Villein tenants were also subject to a tax on their persons called tallage. The details of all

---

683 *Id.* at 365.

684 *Id.* at 372.

these characteristics of villeinage differed widely from place to place and were in fact defined by diverse ancient customs. Perhaps this necessary reliance on local custom was one factor prompting the judges of the royal courts to reject any jurisdiction over villein tenure. Instead, villein tenants had to seek protection and justice in the manor courts.

It is neither possible nor appropriate in this chapter to recount the long process by which villeinage, and indeed serfdom, came to dominate English society and economy. By the time of the Conquest, the process was no longer relevant, because villeinage had become established, and the masses of villeins were perpetuated in their stations by birth. From a modern perspective it is easy to wince at the enormous restrictions on the personal liberties of villeins, but it should be acknowledged that these masses were nevertheless protected in their customary rights and not completely subject to the whims and caprice of their lords.

§ 7.05(b)(4). Early Rules on the Inheritability of Tenures.

The property law of post-Conquest England was characterized not only by a system of tenures and appurtenant incidents and burdens, but also consisted of rules for transferring these tenurial interests to others. In the period of the Conquest and ensuing settlement of England by the Normans, inheritability of free tenures had not yet been accepted and there was, in fact, much uncertainty about the duration of grants even to tenants in chief. Typically, the charters describing grants in the early post-Conquest years do not state whether the grant is for life, or whether the grantee's heirs have any claim on the tenancy. Thus the heir would usually have to obtain a regrant of the tenancy from the lord and to pay the lord a sum of money for that favor. Gradually, but in a relatively short time, the right of the heir to succeed to the tenancy came to be recognized, but the necessity to pay for the realization of that right also became a fixed custom, even if the amount of payment sometimes remained arbitrary. By 1100, the landholding of tenants in chief were recognized as heritable, if the proper relief were paid, as affirmed in a charter of Henry I:

> If any of my barons, earls or other tenants-in-chief has died, his heir shall not redeem his land as he did in the time of my brother, but he shall pay the just and lawful relief for it.
>
> Similarly, the vassals of my barons shall pay the just and lawful relief for their lands to their lords.[685]

Once the heritability of the highest tenures was recognized, it probably spread to the other tenures in the English feudal system. To the extent Anglo-Saxon bookland still influenced the customs by which land was held, such land may have been heritable, devisable, and alienable.

§ 7.05(b)(5). Early Rules on the Alienability of Tenures.

Alienation of land was a less urgent question in the 11th century, because the buying and selling of land occurred only rarely. More commonly, a donor gave land to the church, and such alienation raised questions about the residual or latent rights of the donor's prospective heirs. To secure title, the donee would obtain consents from the prospective heirs.

Quite likely the alienation of tenures occurred more frequently from and after the time William I made the major grants to his chief followers after the Conquest. Those tenants in chief were permitted to transfer certain rights pertaining to portions of their lands to others in return for services or payments that would assist the tenant in chief to carry out the main feudal dues owed to the king; the transfer process was known as subinfeudation. Land so alienated by subinfeudation could be further alienated by the subtenants in the same way. Landholders practiced subinfeudation widely until it was prohibited by the Statute Quia Emptores in 1290; although it probably required the lord's consent, the consent would not be withheld if the customary sum of money was paid. That this was fixed by custom

---

[685] "The Coronation Charter of Henry I," in *The Laws of the Kings of England from Edmund to Henry I* 276-277 (Agnes Jane Robertson, ed. and trans., 1925).

seems likely, because subinfeudation held potentially major disadvantages for the lord. While the services attached to the tenant's land could always be required, and forfeiture applied in case of default, subinfeudation threatened the potential value of the tenurial incidents to the lord. If, for instance, a tenant holding by knight service conveyed all or a part of the land to the church in frankalmoign and then died without heirs, the monetary value of the escheat to the lord would be insignificant.

Another form of alienation was substitution. This process simply replaced the old tenant with a new tenant, rather than creating a subtenancy. If subinfeudation may be likened to a sublease in modern landlord/tenant law, then substitution may be likened to an assignment. As with a modern assignment of a tenancy, the landlord could suffer some disadvantage if the new tenant was not as able or conscientious as the old, but the landlord's *rights* with respect to the tenancy were not harmed. Thus a substitution, while also subject to the customary requirement of consent and payment, was more freely permitted. Indeed, the same Statute Quia Emptores that prohibited subinfeudation in 1290, extended to all landholders but tenants in chief the right of substitution without payment of money to the overlord.

This discussion of alienation practices in the first generations after the Conquest must necessarily remain general, because there is very little direct and contemporary evidence of what actually occurred. By gathering inferences from statutes, legal writers and legal documents from later times, it is possible to make intelligent guesses about the practices of the 11th and 12th centuries. It must also be remembered that nowhere in England and at no time were such practices uniform; what was true for one locality at one point in time may not have been true for a neighboring area until 20 years later. Only with the emergence of a truly *common* law after the Conquest does it become more feasible to find principles of property law with general application.

§ 7.05(b)(6). Primogeniture.

If it is understood how a lord could object to subinfeudation because it threatened the value of tenurial incidents, or in some cases even the rendering of required services, then it is easier to understand why primogeniture had such a powerful appeal in a feudal system. Under primogeniture, the oldest son assumed the tenancy upon the death of the father, and the younger sons took nothing. As applied to military tenures at times when the actual rendering of knight service was still important, primogeniture may have been somewhat of a necessity. Nevertheless, primogeniture persisted and even spread to non-military tenures long after the rendering of actual military services had lost its early importance. This is probably explained by the other attractions of keeping tenancies intact, as well as by the simple enduring power of custom and tradition.

While it has been surmised that English primogeniture was imported from Normandy, it is not clear that by the time of the Conquest Normandy had settled on a custom of primogeniture. A competing contemporary custom in Normandy divided the tenancy among all the surviving sons, but the shares of the younger brothers were all held feudally of the oldest. That primogeniture in England evolved at first as a matter of custom is shown by the fact that it was not universal.[686] While it was consistently applied at first only to the military tenures, it spread gradually to the other tenures and even eventually to some of the villein tenures. These latter holdings most often descended in ultimogeniture, to the youngest son, as a means of keeping the holding intact, but it has also been suggested "that from a remote time many villein tenements have descended in a primogenitary course."[687]

At the same time descent by primogeniture was spreading, other customs came to prohibit a father from alienating land in ways inimical to expectant heirs. Thus, by Glanvill's time at the end of the twelfth century, conveyances typically recited that the grantor's heirs apparent had

---

[686] In 1255 Simon de Montfort imposed primogeniture upon his holdings in Leicester upon request of the people, who preferred it to the ultimogeniture (descent to the youngest son) that had prevailed until then. "XIII. Earl Simon's Charter introducing the law of Primogeniture into Leicester, instead of inheritance by the youngest son. [Oct. 22, 1255]," in *Records of the Borough of Leicester* 49-50 (Mary Bateson, ed., 1899).

[687] 2 Frederick Pollock and Frederic William Maitland, *The History of English Law Before the Time of Edward I* 279 (2d ed. 1909).

consented to the transaction.[688] Even in the preceding century it was common in some areas for presumptive heirs to join in conveyances.[689] With the rise of primogeniture, however, it was no longer necessary to protect rights of children who would not inherit in any event, so the father's right of inter vivos alienation became less restrained. In fact, the father became free to alienate land in favor of younger sons, without the consent of the oldest son as expectant heir, and the oldest son would simply inherit whatever property was left when the father died. These changes were evolutionary, but they demonstrate the way in which the spread of primogeniture helped relax family restraints on alienation of land. Indeed, a father could completely disinherit an oldest son. If the grantor gave the grant with warranty, in which the grantor for himself and heirs ensured the grantee against other claims upon the grant, the oldest son had no rights in the land, even though he still had a burden of military service.[690]

§ 7.05(b)(7). Mortmain.

Grants of land to churches and other institutional or corporate grantees effectively destroyed the value of some feudal incidents. These grants were referred to as grants in mortmain (dead hand), because the grantees were usually ecclesiastical corporations whose members, through their religious vows, were dead persons before the law.

Elimination or avoidance of feudal burdens had such a strong appeal that many landholders collusively granted lands to churches, but resumed possession as tenants of the grantee church. This abuse had reached such serious proportions by early in the thirteenth century that *Magna Carta* explicitly forbade the practice upon penalty of forfeiture.[691] The Statute of

---

[688] *Glanvill*, VII, 1.

[689] Paul Vinogradoff, "The Transfer of Land," in *Collected Papers* 148-167, esp. 157 (1928). The examples of presumptive heirs joining in conveyances come from Anglo-Danish districts, where a stronger tradition of free alienation prevailed. Paul Vinogradoff, *English Society in the Eleventh Century* 9 (1908).

[690] *Bracton's Note Book*, no. 1054 (1225).

[691] *Magna Carta*, c. 31.

Mortmain reiterated the prohibition in 1279, but by that time it was the practice to alienate in mortmain by first obtaining a license from the monarch. The king granted great numbers of licenses soon after passage of the statute, apparently for the immediate revenue they generated, and without regard for the losses in land such alienations might occasion for either the Crown or intermediate lords.

§ 7.05(c). The Domesday Survey and Its Influence.

The Domesday Survey is one of the most significant events in English and European medieval history. Representing, as it does, a record of the most thorough and methodical feudal state in medieval Europe, it is appropriate that its inception was explicitly and precisely noted in the contemporary record of The Anglo-Saxon Chronicle:

> The king spent Christmas with his councillors at Gloucester, and held his court there for five days, which was followed by a three-day synod held by the archbishop and the clergy . . . .
>
> After this the king had important deliberations and exhaustive discussions with his council about this land, how it was peopled, and with what sort of men. Then he sent his men all over England into every shire to ascertain how many hundreds or "hides" of land there were in each shire, and how much land and live-stock the king himself owned in the country, and what annual dues were lawfully his from each shire. He also had it recorded how much land his archbishops had, and his diocesan bishops, his abbots and his earls, and (though I may be going into too great detail) what or how much each man who was a landholder here in England had in land or in live-stock, and how much money it was worth. So very thoroughly did he have the inquiry carried out that there was not a single "hide," not one virgate of land, not even (it is shameful to record it, but it did not seem shameful to him to do it) one ox, nor one cow, nor one pig which escaped

notice in his survey.

And all the surveys were subsequently brought to him.[692]

The Norman officials took about 18 months to complete the project. The principal focus of interest in the survey was the system of landholding and the customary conditions and services attached to the holdings, most of which pre-dated the Conquest. From ancient times the hide designated the amount of land needed to support a family of free persons. Although the acreage varied from place to place, often depending on the quality of the agricultural land, for revenue purposes the acreage was standardized at about 120. Comparable designations were the sulung in Kent and the carucate in East Anglia, Yorkshire, and the east Midlands. A quarter of a hide was a yardland, and an eighth of a carucate was a bovate.

The main purpose of the Domesday Survey cannot be determined with certainty. Traditionally, historians believed that the survey was intended to identify the Danegeld assessments. The Danegeld had originated in Viking times as an Anglo-Saxon device for raising money to buy off marauding Danish Vikings. Anglo-Saxon monarchs imposed it as a land tax, assessed according to the number of hides in a holding. William the Conqueror had already used the Danegeld assessments even before the Domesday Survey; it was an almost annual tax, imposed at a very high rate and based on detailed taxation records already in existence. The Domesday Survey did, however, gather data that was highly relevant to the Danegeld assessments and could have been used to update tax liabilities, some of which had not been reviewed since the eighth century. Also, because of a renewed threat of Danish invasion in 1085, William maintained a large force of foreign mercenaries in England during that year and may have sensed how keenly useful an updated tax assessment schedule would be.

Another obvious purpose of the Domesday project was to create a record of who held what lands after the massive changes in manorial lordships over the two prior decades of Norman dominance. While the survey gave great detail on the terms by which most free tenancies were

---

[692] *Anglo-Saxon Chronicle* (E or Laud version) ann. 1086.

held, it did not record the terms by which tenants in chief or their principal undertenants held.

William's agents commenced the inquest in January, 1086, and completed it later that same year, probably by August 1. Probably by September, 1987, they completed compiling the information into the two-volume set, still extant today and known as the Domesday Book. With England divided into circuits, information for each circuit was compiled probably from the accumulated returns of several sources, including original returns by landholders, statements of hundreds of juries made in county courts, county geld accounts and hidage schedules. The instructions for the survey have been preserved for one of the circuits and are probably typical:

> Here follows the inquiry concerning lands which the King's barons made according to the oaths of the sheriff of the county and of all the barons and their Frenchmen, and of the whole hundred court the priest, the reeve, and six villagers from each village. They inquired what the manor was called; who held it in 1066; who holds it now; how many hides there are; how many ploughteams in demesne and how many belonging to the men; how many villagers; how many cottagers; how many slaves; how many freemen; how many sokemen; how much woodland; how much meadow; how much pasture; how many mills; how many fisheries; how much has been added to or taken away from the manor; what it was worth and what it is worth now; and how much each freeman and sokeman had and has. All this to be recorded thrice; as it was in 1066, when King William granted the manor, and now. And it was also noted whether more could be taken from the manor than is now being taken.[693]

Scholars' work using Domesday information is ongoing, and they will

[693] This passage is from the Ely Inquest, which preserves the instructions for Circuit III.

continue to mine important socio-economic data from the survey for many years to come. For casting light on the history of Anglo-American property law, the Domesday survey is most valuable as a confirmation that the landholding rights and duties of most English people remained unchanged after the Conquest; the relationship of people to property that emerged during the centuries of Anglo-Saxon society persisted through the Norman settlement and was the foundation on which the common law of property was built.[694]

§ 7.06 The Rise of the Common Law of Real Property.

The framework of feudal tenures did much to define the extent of and intricate relationships between rights held simultaneously by several persons in the same land. Within this framework, and surviving the eventual disappearance of the framework, was a system of land rights known as estates. Estates defined interests mostly in terms of duration. Because durational considerations did not exist in a vacuum, inevitably some substantive rights as to use and enjoyment of land were dependent upon the duration of one's ownership interest.

This section examines the system of estates in land that arose in England after the Conquest, and shows how the features of those estates underwent important changes before the Tudor era in English history (1485-1603). During that era, specifically in 1536 when the Statute of Uses was adopted, and 1540, when the Statute of Wills was adopted, major changes in the development of estates in land occurred, and discussion of these statutes and the ensuing changes is in the following section.

§ 7.06(a). The Fee Simple.

Students of the common law learn that the fee simple absolute is the greatest estate in land known to the common law, and that its two chief

---

[694] *See,* David A. Thomas, Chapter 4, "The Growth of the English Common Law of Real Property," in 1 David A. Thomas, ed., *Thompson on Real Property, Second Thomas Edition* § 4.05(c), p. 165) (1994, 2009). *See* Ann Williams and G.H. Martin, eds., *Domesday Book: A Complete Translation* (Penguin Classics, 2003).

characteristics are inheritability and alienability. The precise etymology of the term "fee" is uncertain, but it is ostensibly related to other terms signifying the feudal relationship, such as enfeoffment. In the medieval era, a holding in fee was a feudal holding, that is, subject to the rights and restrictions of feudal tenures; under the terms of these tenures, custom and law conditioned enjoyment of land upon rendering various services and payments to a superior owner. Thus ownership in fee could be contrasted with "allodial" ownership, by which one held free of any other owner's restrictions or concurrent rights, except the sovereignty of the state.

If the word "fee" signified property ownership within a feudal system, then the term "fee simple" came to describe a property interest, an estate, held by the grantee and the grantee's "heirs," which was actually a somewhat confusing way of stating that the interest was capable of descending by inheritance. The use of the term "fee simple" to describe an inheritable estate, i.e., an estate granted to a person "and his heirs," possibly became common at the end of the thirteenth century. Bracton's work discusses the characteristics of a fee simple in describing the operation of a charter of enfeoffment, by which land could be given to another to hold by specified services.[695] Land thus conveyed to the grantee and "heirs," and therefore inheritable, was the maximum estate known. And the fee thus conveyed was "simple," because it was free of restrictions. In contrast to the fee simple was the conditional fee, a fee interest whose heritability was limited or restricted unless certain family conditions occurred.

Heritability of some land rights had already been recognized in Anglo-Saxon times, and thus was not necessarily a product of the Norman Conquest. Indeed, heritability was not initially a part of the framework of Norman feudal tenures, and only gradually came to be accepted through an evolutionary process whose details remain completely obscure.

Some forms of Anglo-Saxon property rights, especially bookland, were both heritable by descent and devisable by will, even as early as King

---

[695] *Bracton*, fol. 17

Alfred's time in the 9th century.[696] Also, the Anglo-Saxon laenland holding (that is, land loaned or rented out for a finite time) might be extended for as much as three generations after the original conveyance. These pre-Conquest forms of landholding, along with the endlessly varied arrangements for agricultural and other services pertaining to peasants' lands, generally remained in effect after the Conquest, as was amply demonstrated by the Domesday Survey. The specific result of the Conquest was to replace the great Anglo-Saxon lords with great Norman lords and to systematize their land rights with respect to the king and to their immediate undertenants. These tenures at the top of the newly-organized Anglo-Norman feudal hierarchy were initially neither heritable by descent nor alienable to living grantees. Only with permission of the king could a landholder secure property for an heir, and the permission came only with a price, and often an arbitrary price at that. Only later would custom and then royal decree assure the availability of permission at a fixed and non-arbitrary price. Meanwhile, the rights and duties of the actual occupants of the land remained as before, and some of those holdings were likely heritable or alienable or both. Thus the combination of intact Anglo-Saxon property customs at the bottom of the feudal ladder, and constant pressure to extend heritability and alienability at the top of the feudal ladder, probably led to the emergence of the heritable estate that came to be known as the fee simple. The fee simple of the thirteenth century was unlike the modern fee simple, mostly because the medieval estate consisted only of a set of feudal dues and responsibilities (all related to and burdening the land, of course), whereas the modern fee is simply full ownership subject to a less onerous set of sovereign prerogatives.

A conveyance to a grantee and heirs sufficed to create a heritable estate, but Bracton and others apparently had doubts about whether such an estate was also alienable. To provide assurance on this point, conveyances were drawn in favor of the grantee and the grantee's heirs *and assigns.* Charters making such conveyances began to appear about 1200, at the same time the practice of having the grantor's expectant heirs join in the

[696] The laws or dooms of King Alfred contain a single reference to bookland, which was heritable but, when transferred, might be limited by the transferor to future alienation only within the kindred. *The Laws of the Earliest English Kings,* Alfred cl. 41 (F. L. Attenborough, ed. & trans., 1922).

conveyance ceased. This latter development signified advancing notions of alienability. Within the next century, the use of the word "assigns" was no longer necessary to indicate alienability.[697]

As one scholar summarized the evolution of the fee simple:

> [A] fee simple was inheritable by primogeniture since about 1200; . . . it was alienable without the consent of presumptive heirs since about the same date; and . . . nearly a century later it became freely alienable without the lord's consent as a result of the Statute Quia Emptores of 1290. The first two of these advances had already been made by the time of Bracton (early in the thirteenth century), and from his day, too, we have a large number of surviving charters which attest the frequency with which land was transferred.[698]

§ 7.06(b). Forms of Conditional Fees.

Several types of fee interests could not be classed as fee simple estates, because some condition or limitation deferred or rendered contingent the heritability of the interest. In England, once heritability of an interest was accepted, it was not limited to inheritance by descendants of the original grantee, but could also extend to inheritance by collateral heirs. Limiting heritability to direct descendants, or conditioning heritability upon the birth of children required specific expression of intent by the grantor.

Recognition of such interests was much older than Norman times, and even appears in one of Alfred's laws of the ninth century, describing bookland that was heritable but that could be limited by the transferor to

---

[697] This is the opinion expressed in Frederick Pollock and Frederic William Maitland, *The History of English Law Before the Time of Edward I* 14 (2d ed. 1909).

[698] Theodore F. T. Plucknett, *A Concise History of the Common Law* 558 (5th ed. 1956). Pollock and Maitland asserted that most alienations of that time were by way of subinfeudation, which was not prohibited until enactment of the Statute Quia Emptores in 1290.

alienation only within the kindred:

> We have further established that a man who holds land by title-deed [bookland], which his kinsmen have left him, shall not be allowed to give it out of his kindred, if there is documentary or [other] evidence that the power to do so is forbidden by the men who first acquired it, or by those who gave it to him.[699]

While there is no evidence that this Anglo-Saxon practice was widespread or survived into post-Conquest times, circumstances did arise that prompted conveyances conditioned on the perpetuation of the family. If a well-to-do landholder wished to settle land on a younger son, as an additional branch of the family, or to endow a daughter, a natural impulse would be to require a reversion of the property if the new family did not materialize or stopped short because no heirs were born. The earliest example of this to arise after the Conquest was the *maritagium*, or gift in free marriage. Allusions to this interest appear in the Domesday Book, although a provision in the *Coronation Charter of Henry I, of 1100* suggests that the widow without children would keep property received from her own family at the time of her marriage.[700] In the 12th-century form of *maritagium*, a father could give lands and his daughter to the daughter's new husband, usually by subinfeudation and free of feudal services until the third heir was born.[701] The third heir, meaning the third generation after the original grantee, would postpone the revival of feudal services for approximately 100 years, when the establishment of the new family and its

---

[699] *The Laws of the Earliest English Kings* Alfred cl. 41 (F. L. Attenborough, ed. & trans., 1922).

[700] "The 'Coronation Charter' of Henry I (5 August 1100)," c. 3, § 2, in 2 *English Historical Documents* 400-02 (D. C. Douglas, ed., 1953).

[701] It should also be noted that the father could provide this property for his daughter and her husband even without the consent of sons who were the expectant heirs, and this during a period when such consent was usually required for alienation.

ability to perform feudal obligations would be assured.[702] Also, homage would not be required until the third generation, but would be required from each heir thereafter.[703] If the third generation was not forthcoming, the tenancy would revert to the grantor.

With the *maritagium* as precedent and example, many varieties of conditional grants appeared beginning in the late twelfth century. Not only were variations of the *maritagium* spelled out in the conveyances, such as gifts to either husband or wife or to both jointly, and limitations to heirs of the body of either or both, but some landholders attempted to save reversions in conveyances for circumstances other than pending marriage. Considerable confusion enveloped the whole subject of conditional grants, and Bracton tried to draw some distinctions between the conditional grants in *maritagium* and other conditional grants. As to the *maritagium* grants, Bracton declared that the grant was a life estate until the birth of the prescribed heir; nevertheless, the grantee in *maritagium* could alienate the grant even before the heir was born, and the heir would be bound by the alienation.[704] Moreover, the alienation would also destroy the reversion held by the grantor, that would otherwise materialize if, after the alienation, in fact no heir was born. This statement upholding the alienation in direct contradiction to the grantor's intent and reversion was a serious irritant to landholders throughout the thirteenth century, and was finally addressed in 1285 in the Statute De Donis Conditionalibus, the first part of the Statute of Westminster II:

> [F]eofees have so far had the power of alienating the tenement so given and disinheriting thereof their issue against the will of the donors and against the express form of the gift; and moreover whereas on failure of issue of such feofees a tenement so given ought to revert to the donor or his heir according to the expressed form in the

---

[702] In some cases the grantor remained in possession until the reversion was removed by arrival of the third generation, although Glanvill considered this no completed gift, only the promise of a gift. *Glanvill*, VII, 1.

[703] *Glanvill*, VII, 18.

[704] *Bracton*, fol. 17b.

> charter of the gift, nevertheless donors have thus far been excluded from the reversion of their tenements on account of the deed and feoffment of the donees of the conditional gift, although the issue (if there were such) had died which was manifestly against the form of the gift.
>
> Wherefore our lord the King perceiving how necessary and useful it is to appoint a remedy in the aforesaid case, has established that the will of the donor according to the form manifestly expressed in the charter shall henceforth be observed, in such wise that those to whom a tenement is thus given upon condition shall not have power of alienating it and preventing it from remaining to their issue after their death, or else to the donor or his heir if issue shall fail, either by reason that there was no issue at all or if there were, that the heir of such issue had failed.[705]

That statute unified the rules for all conditional gifts, whether in *maritagium* or otherwise, and required that no alienation could defeat the inheritance rights of issue or the reversions of grantors if issue failed. Most importantly, it rather arbitrarily limited the meaning of "issue" to the first generation, rather than "an indefinitely long line of descendants of the prescribed class."[706] Despite this literal meaning of the statute, famous Year Book reports of 1312 reveal that the judges had reinterpreted the statute to extend protected issue to the third generation, and to do so for both *maritagium* grants and all other types of conditional grants.[707] So, the two

---

705 Statute of Westminster II (Statute De Donis Conditionalibus), 13 Edw., c. 1 (1285).

706 Theodore F. T. Plucknett, *A Concise History of the Common Law* 552 (5th ed. 1956).

707 Belyng v. Anon., Y.B. 5 Edw. 2, Easter Term, No. 2 (1312) (Year Books of Edward II, 5 Edward II 176 (Selden Society Vol. 31, Vol. 11 Year Book Series, 1915)); Anon., Y.B. 5 Edw. 2, Trinity Term, No. 25 (1312) (Year Books of Edward II, 5 Edward II 22 (Selden Society Vol. 33, Vol. 12 Year Book Series, 1916)). The explanation for the striking departure from the express wording of the statute was that the drafter had been careless and had actually intended to draft the statute to cover the third generation of issue rather than just the first.

forms of conveyance of less than a fee simple, that could now be called the *maritagium* and the fee tail, would be treated uniformly under judicial interpretation of the Statute De Donis. Ironically, this judicial reinterpretation did not stabilize the matter of how long an entail would endure. In a Year Book report of 1410, it is revealed for both the fee tail and the *maritagium* that the entail will last as long as there are heirs, the so-called indefinite failure of issue.[708]

In the fourteenth century lawyers and judges debated whether the grantee in tail had only a form of life estate and the issue had a remainder in fee, subject to some sort of reversion in the grantor.[709] Ultimately, the courts rejected this doctrine, too, so the fee tail suffered through another century of legal uncertainty.[710]

The history of the conditional fee and fee tail sheds light on the course of development for the whole common law. That grants in "marriage" and to the grantee and heirs of his or her body were both treated as conditional fees probably resulted from a pronounced bias among the royal justices in favor of free alienability. With a conditional fee, the grantee could alienate the interest as soon as a child was born, and the alienation remained valid even after issue failed, thus defeating any claims by the grantor to a reversion, or by any surviving issue to the property by descent. While this vastly enlarged alienability, it largely struck down the intentions of grantors. The Statute De Donis Conditionalibus in 1285 responded to the grantors' concerns, transforming the conditional fee of the law courts into a fee tail, a fee that had been cut down or "carved" or "tailored" to the grantor's desires; this fee tail protected interests of grantors and issue against alienation of anything more than the grantee's immediate possessory interest, and it assured descent only within the family line. Thus the large landholdings of great family dynasties could be held intact; they

---

[708] Y.B. 12 Henry 4, Michaelmas Term, No. 9 (1410).

[709] The argument was pressed most vigorously in Y.B. 20 & 21 Edw. (Rolls Series), 58 (1292); *see also* Anon., Y.B. 5 Edw. 2, No. 78 (1311) (Year Books of Edward II, 5 Edward II 269 (Selden Society Vol. 63, Vol. 10 Year Book Series, 1947)).

[710] Theodore F. T. Plucknett, *A Concise History of the Common Law* 556 (5th ed. 1956).

could not be defeated either by alienation or by forfeiture of anything more than the land occupant's present possessory interest. This state of legal affairs strengthened the ruling families against the monarch. Finally, in 1472 a royal court approved a method of overcoming the entail through a process known as common recovery, which turned the fee tail into a fee simple absolute. Even later, in the 19th century, the common recovery procedure was passed over in favor of giving power to the fee tail holder to accomplish the same thing simply by conveying a fee simple directly to another by deed.

Thus, in the struggle between the landed aristocracy seeking to perpetuate and strengthen dynastic landholding, and the monarchy and merchant class seeking to weaken the nobility by freer land alienability, the common law doctrine of fee tail suffered an ambivalent course of development until finally the entire estate became obsolete.

§ 7.06(c). The Life Tenancy.

A person who held land in fee, whether fee simple or a conditional fee, usually had possession or "seisin" of the land and had a heritable interest. That a person might hold land for his or her life only had also long been recognized in English law. The life tenancy was distinguishable from the fee, because it was not heritable; but it was a possessory interest, and if the life tenant was in possession, he or she was considered seised of a free tenement and entitled to all the legal protections connected with seisin. For all land held by life tenancy, there was also, in the background, an owner or tenant in fee. When the life tenant died, the land reverted to the fee tenant, even if no reversion was mentioned in the grant to the life tenant. Such a life tenant was considered to hold the land of the grantor, the fee tenant, and could be required to give an oath of fealty and render rent or services. If the grantor of the life tenancy directed that after the life tenant's death the land "remain" to another, then both the life tenant and the "remainderman" would hold of the grantor.

Some life estates arose by operation of law, such as the dower interest of a widow and the curtesy interest of a widower. Under curtesy, the widower held a life tenancy in the lands that his wife had held during the marriage, while her heirs held the fee. Under dower, the widow held a life tenancy in a third of her late husband's lands held during the marriage, and his heirs held the fee. As a freeholder with seisin, the life tenant was able to enjoy the land much as a tenant in fee.[711] Concerns for the rights of reversioners and remaindermen led to a series of 13th-century statutes imposing heavy penalties for waste, that is damage to the inheritance committed by a temporary occupant, such as a life tenant.[712]

The life tenancy, and its relationship to the fee, arguably prompted the concepts of estates in the common law. If estates are viewed as forms of ownership on a plane of time, the temporary ownership represented by a life estate, or even a series of many successive life estates, simply emphasizes that the ultimate and infinite ownership still rests with the owner in fee.

§ 7.06(c)(1). Dower.

The dower of English common law seems to have at least some of its antecedents in ancient Anglo-Saxon practices. Charters as early as the 8th century show that the prospective husband promised the marriage price at the time of betrothal, with perhaps a nominal sum as earnest money, and he paid the sum directly to the bride rather than to a guardian. Of more importance was the morning-gift, originally a free-will gift by the husband to the bride on the morning after the bridal night:

> Consisting at first of chattels, it later came to be considered as a form of widow's maintenance, and thus was necessarily property of sufficient value to sustain the wife if she survived her husband. The morning-gift, therefore, came to be almost always a gift of land, normally granted at the time of betrothal by means of a written document (to prove ownership after the husband's

---

711 According to Bracton, doweresses had fairly extensive rights on their lands to commit what would normally be considered waste. *Bracton*, fols. 315, 316.

712 *See* David A. Thomas, Ch. 70, "Waste," in 8 David A. Thomas, *Thompson on Real Property, Second Thomas Edition* (1994, 2005).

> death); alternatively, if a specific morning-gift were not granted at the betrothal or beginning of the marriage, then a certain portion of the husband's property, usually one-half, was assigned by law for maintenance of the bride if she became a widow.[713]

By Glanvill's time in the late 12th century, dower was theoretically a gift made by the husband to the bride at the church door and was required by both spiritual and secular law.[714] Bracton also recognized this requirement.[715]

Although the dower eventually attained a standard meaning of a life estate in one-third of the lands held by the husband during the marriage, it had not yet reached that point by the 13th century. In that period, a husband could either endow the bride with specific lands, not to exceed one-third of his holdings, or could make no specific endowment, in which case it was understood that she had an endowment of one-third of the lands of which he was then seised. There was no dower right in lands that came to the husband during the marriage. The dower right was gradually enlarged. Even in the Magna Carta, that is, the 1217 version, the dower is described as one-third of the lands held by the husband during his lifetime, unless the wife had accepted a lesser specific endowment "at the church door."[716] Later, it was possible for the wife to reject the lesser specific endowment in order to claim the legal maximum of one-third. However, in the 13th century, "a third of the husband's land is the maximum dower that can be claimed in lands held by military service, and from the frequency with which a [specific endowment] is mentioned, we should gather that many widows of high station had to be content with less."[717]

---

713 § 6.05(f), *supra*.

714 *Glanvill*, VI, 1.

715 *Bracton*, fol. 92.

716 *Magna Carta*, c. 7 (1217).

717 Frederick Pollock and Frederic William Maitland, *The History of English Law Before the Time of Edward I* 421 (2d ed. 1909).

For a time, the typical dower for socage tenure was one-half, based on the notion that a widow had fully shared ownership rights with her husband in socage land,[718] but with the emergence of a common doctrine on this point, the one-third share related to military tenures prevailed.

The widow could alienate the life tenancy of dower. However, under at least some local practices, she would forfeit her dower if she remarried or was unchaste, a rule also contained in the 11th-century pre-Conquest *Laws of Cnut*.[719] If the late husband had previously assigned specific lands of the endowment, the widow could enter into possession immediately upon her husband's death. If not, then the husband's heir or the heir's guardian was required to assign her portion within forty days after the husband's death. During that period, the widow was entitled to remain and to be maintained in the principal house.[720]

Dower obviously impeded alienation of the husband's land. If the husband alienated after the marriage, without the wife's consent, she could recover the land or a portion of the land from the grantee after the husband's death. Of course, the wife's consent to the conveyance freed it from any dower claim. In the first years after the Conquest, if the husband forfeited the lands because of treason, the dower interest sometimes survived; however, by the thirteenth century forfeiture or escheat always defeated dower.[721] Even such a development did not much dilute the strength of dower, that had progressed from a voluntary gift to an estate arising by operation of law.

But dower was an anomaly in the feudal scheme: "the widow's right in a very common case comes into conflict with the claim of a lord who is

---

[718] *Bracton*, fol. 93. Borough tenancies were also frequently one-half, and villein widows usually obtained the entire tenement in dower.

[719] *The Laws of the Kings of England from Edmund to Henry I* 202-03, II Cnut cl. 53 (Agnes Jane Robertson, ed. & trans., 1925).

[720] *Bracton*, fol. 96, 97.

[721] *Bracton's Note Book*, no. 1334 (1217).

entitled to wardship."[722] The changing law eventually operated against dower, "partly perhaps in the interest of expectant heirs, partly in the interest of a militant state, that regarded the land as a fund for the support of warriors."[723] As the Middle Ages progressed, it became easier for husbands to surmount dower interests and exclude dower from certain popular forms of landholding, such as joint estates, uses and trusts. In England, dower was no longer significant after passage of the Dower Act of 1833; however, in the American colonies dower was usually received as part of the common law.

§ 7.06(c)(2). Curtesy.

Curtesy, too, has an obscure origin, but in its full medieval development came to signify the widower's life estate in all his wife's lands held during the marriage, if issue had been born alive. Whereas dower was contrary to the feudal impulse, interfering with alienability and assuring property to women who might be incapable of carrying out the commitments of military tenure, curtesy was consistent with feudal concepts. The surviving husband could render the military service; also, the widower with curtesy retained the guardianship of his children, whereas the dowager lost the guardianship right to the lord. Perhaps the factor of guardianship is one of the reasons for the rise of curtesy rights, which were wholly dependent upon the birth of live issue. Another tradition concerning the origin of curtesy suggests that it was a rule created to help poor Normans who married English heiresses, and were left with nothing when the wife died and her lands descended to her heirs under English law.

The customs of Kent departed from this discrimination, and there the right of "free bench" conferred on either surviving spouse, as long as he or she remained single, a life estate in one-half of the land of the decedent spouse, whether or not a child was born. Furthermore, in Kent the surviving spouse could possibly obtain a guardianship over the other half of the land, and so could ultimately enjoy possession of the decedent's entire holdings.

---

[722] 2 Frederick Pollock and Frederic William Maitland, *The History of English Law Before the Time of Edward I* 426 (2d ed. 1909).

[723] *Id.*

In general, however, not only did the surviving husbands have the stronger right, as compared with dower, and fewer difficulties in integrating the curtesy rights into the feudal system, but they also often grasped for greater rights than those already accorded them. Two thirteenth-century statutes sought to curb abuses of curtesy rights,[724] but Year Book cases also show husbands trying to deal with the lands of their late wives in ways beyond the life estate granted them by curtesy. Curtesy, like dower, was eventually abolished.

§ 7.06(d). The Term of Years.

The term of years, although ostensibly similar to the life estate in many ways, did not play an important role in English landholding until several generations after the Conquest, and was accorded vastly different treatment under the common law. Only a few documents from Anglo-Saxon time refer to "laenland," land that was loaned out in return for lump sum or periodic rent payments. These interests more resembled a life estate than a term of years, because the duration of the laenland conveyance was measured usually by one or more lives. Leases for shorter terms were known, but rare, possibly because they are naturally reflective of vigorous commercial activity that hardly existed in Dark Ages economies. The more common motive for seeking out land would have been to create a home and farm, and for those purposes, brief terms would not do. Thus the few leases for term that do appear in the records soon after the Conquest are almost never used for establishing households.[725] Instead, such leases were part of the process of raising revenue, especially by means of the gage. In the surviving records, forty years was usually the maximum duration of a term of years, possibly because after that time it would be difficult to find witnesses to the conveyance; leases for much longer terms, even exceeding a lifetime, were acceptable.[726]

---

[724] The Statutes of Gloucester, 6 Edw., c. 3 (1278); Statute of Westminster II, 13 Edw., c. 3 (1285).

[725] The discussion of early tenancies for term is based on 2 Frederick Pollock and Frederic William Maitland, *The History of English Law Before the Time of Edward I* 106-117 (2d ed. 1909).

[726] *See, e.g., Bracton*, fol. 27.

The key historical question regarding the term for years is why it had so little legal protection when compared with tenancies in fee or for life. In the twelfth century some regarded the term of years as not even an interest in land; the tenant, or termor, threatened in occupancy had only a personal action against the lessor for breach of covenant.[727] If the termor also had a warranty and was ejected by a third person, an action could be brought against the lessor for compensatory relief. Otherwise, the termor had little or no protection against intrusion from third parties, until the trespass action became available about the middle of the 13th century.

Because the termor was not considered to have a right in the land, persons bringing actions against the land brought such actions against the lessor. If the lessor wanted to destroy the termor's occupancy, the lessor could collude with another to default in an action against the land that was directed against the lessor and bypassed the termor. In 1278, the Statute of Gloucester gave the termor the right to intervene in such action.[728]

All of these disabilities in legal remedies resulted from the position taken by common law judges that the tenancy for a term was not a "free" tenancy. This meant that the most important legal remedy for recovery and protection of the tenancy, the petty assize, was not available. The decision to consider the tenancy for a term as unfree appears to have been arbitrary, although different explanations or rationales have been offered. Ironically, the term for years had some of the most important feudal attributes: it was considered a tenement; the termor was ostensibly seised of the land (although the termor was considered to have "possession" rather than seisin); the termor even did fealty in some instances. Also, termors were grouped together with tenants for life, all of whom were called "farmers," people who pay full rent.

Yet Pollock and Maitland theorized that in crucial decisions certain English judges were momentarily enamored of Roman law doctrine that the termor had only a servitude to enjoy the fruits of possession, which was

---

[727] The termor's occupancy could be disturbed, for example, by a guardian in chivalry, by a doweress, or by an assignee of the lessor.

[728] The Statutes of Gloucester, 6 Edw., c. 11 (1278).

merely a usufruct, or a quasi-possession.[729] Another theory reminds the modern reader that the tenancy for a term was at first most often used to obtain loans of money and avoid the ecclesiastical prohibitions against usury. The borrower simply turned over to the lender a parcel of land for a long enough time that the principal and some profit could be recovered from the revenues of the land (keeping in mind that the land was already occupied by peasants and others owing various rents and services). By comparison, then, with other forms of landholding considered to be free tenements, the tenancy for a term was usually not a form of fairly permanent family property used to produce revenue for livelihood.[730]

However accurate this picture of leases for usurious money-lending may have been in the earlier feudal times, it gradually gave way to another scene, in which the so-called husbandry leases, leases for agricultural purposes, became more prominent. Not until after the Black Death did husbandry leases become common, and by then other devices for using land as debt security had been created, so such disparagement of the term as there may have been in the fourteenth century was unjustified.

It is also not accurate to ascribe the unfree nature of the term to its being held by persons of unfree status, because persons from all social classes held tenancies for terms. However, the classification of a tenancy for a term as an unfree tenure was permanently cast, so new means of legal protection also had to be devised. Eventually the very serviceable trespass action, with a specialized writ for termors, gave the termor rights against anyone who came onto the property, at first for damages, and then later for possession, too. In these developments it seemed necessary to distinguish between the seisen of a freeholder and the possession of the unfree tenancy for a term; courts concluded that the freeholder lessor was seised, while the

---

[729] "In an evil hour the English judges, who were controlling a new possessory action, which had been suggested by foreign models, adopted this theory at the expense of the termor. He must be the *conductor* who does not possess, or he must be the usufructary who does not possess the land but has 'quasi-possession' of a servitude." Frederick Pollock and Frederic William Maitland, *The History of English Law Before the Time of Edward I* 114-15 (2d ed. 1909).

[730] Theodore F. T. Plucknett, *A Concise History of the Common Law* 573 (5th ed. 1956).

termor was possessed, of the leased land. This gratuitous distinction between possession and seisin is a persistent irritant to modern students of the law, who often can think of no better synonym for seisin than possession.

§ 7.06(e). Reversions.

From the very beginning of its history in the common law, the term "reversion" carried technical and popular meanings that have been somewhat at odds with each other. On the one hand, reversion connoted the land coming back to the grantor. Even in Anglo-Saxon times, a form of the term reversion described how the land "came back" to the grantor upon the expiration of the lease. The "coming back" contrasted pointedly to the remainder, by which the land "remained out" from the grantor and eventually reposed with some third person.

On the other hand, the reversion clearly never left the grantor, but was rather the residue the estate left in the grantor after a conveyance of less than the fee simple. Later, courts heavily emphasized this characteristic in connection with protecting the reversion against invalidation under the rule against perpetuities. For feudal purposes, a reversion was a present estate, seised in service if not in occupancy, and the reversioner had the relationship of lord over tenants for life and in tail. This permitted the reversioner to invoke the protective remedies of the common law, so that the reversion was virtually indestructible. Moreover, the Statute De Donis Conditionalibus assured the reversioner that alienation by the grantee would not affect the reversion.

§ 7.06(f). Remainders.

§ 7.06(f)(1). In General.

In modern understanding, a grantor who grants an estate less than a fee simple to one grantee, and the balance of the interest to another grantee, has created a remainder in the second grantee. The remainder is similar to the reversion, but is granted to a third party rather than being retained by the grantor. It was possible to give a remainder for life, or remainders for successive lives, as well as a remainder in fee.

By the thirteenth century, lawyers and judges used terminology for both reversions and remainders, although with occasional confusion.[731] Grants in *maritagium* provided the earliest examples of remainders. Bracton's Note Book recorded a grant in *maritagium* to Beatrice and Reginald, but if Beatrice died without issue, or if her issue died without issue, the land would go to Beatrice's sister Matilda and Matilda's heirs.[732] According to Bracton, a remainderman took by substitution rather than subinfeudation.[733] The remainder, from the beginning, was a less secure interest than the reversion, because it was not possible to show that the remainderman had ever been seised. Therefore, some of the remedies derived from seisin were not available to protect the remainder interest. Several cases show vigorous challenges to the enforcement of a remainder.[734] Consequently, it was more secure to obtain the remainder through a judicial process known as a fine, than by deed. Through the fine process, the parties would appear in court with a prearranged settlement of their controversy, called a fine or final approval, and then obtain court approval for the settlement. The three-part written document containing the terms of the settlement, including one part for the public records, was regarded as an especially solemn form of conveyance and virtually unimpeachable.[735]

§ 7.06(f)(2). Contingent Remainders.

Conveyancers used the fine process with success even to create

---

[731] *See, e.g., Bracton*, fol. 18.

[732] *Bracton's Note Book*, no. 86 (1220).

[733] *Bracton*, fol. 68b.

[734] *See, e.g.*, Neuton v. Staynford, Y.B. 5 Edw. 2, Michaelmas Term, No. 24 (1311) (Year Books of Edward II, 5 Edward 2, 98 (Selden Society, Vol. 63, Vol. 10 Year Book Series, 1947)); Y.B. 18 & 19 Edw. 2 (Rolls Series), 378 (1345).

[735] In Y.B. 18 & 19 Edw. 2 (Rolls Series), 378 (1345), reference is made to the practices of two prominent royal judges who accepted as parties before them remaindermen who held by fine, but not remaindermen who held by deed.

contingent remainders, despite the real difficulties such interests caused in feudal arrangements. In a 1304 case, a tenement created by fine granted an estate to a man and his wife and "to the heirs of their bodies begotten," further granting to the man's heirs in remainder if the couple should die without heirs of their bodies. With only the mildest skepticism, the court observed, "This, however, is strange seeing that the remainder was not granted to any certain person."[736] A few years later, another grant by fine conveyed an estate to Robert for life, and upon Robert's death to C and the heirs of his body, but if C died without such heirs, to the heirs of Robert. All grantees were to hold their interests "of the chief lord of the fee," but Justice Bereford was compelled to ask who was to do homage.[737] Both cases illustrate the danger that a contingent remainder in fee could leave a lord uncertain about who was to perform feudal services. If a remainder was contingent at the time it was granted, but had vested by the time it was subject to litigation, it could be upheld.[738]

As for seisin, sometimes it was attributed to the life tenant, but held to benefit the remainderman. However, if the life estate terminated prematurely, the remainder, being dependent upon the life estate, also terminated.

Common law contingent remainders were subject to destruction if the supporting freehold estate were forfeited through tortious alienation. If the holder of the life estate attempted to convey a fee simple, the attempted alienation would be deemed tortious and the life estate would be forfeited before the contingent remainder vested; this destroyed the contingent remainder.[739]

---

[736] Y.B. 32 & 33 Edw. (Rolls Series), 328 (1304).

[737] Y.B. 2 Edw. 2, 4 (1309).

[738] Y.B. 10 Edw. 3, Michaelmas Term, No. 8 (1336); Y.B. 11 Rich. 2, 283-288 (1388).

[739] *See, e.g.*, Archer's Case, 1 Co.Rep. 66b, 76 Eng.Rep. 146 (1597).

§ 7.06(g). Concurrent Estates.

§ 7.06(g)(1). Tenancy in Coparcenary.

When two or more heirs obtained a tenancy by descent, rather than by inter vivos conveyance, they obtained a tenancy in coparcenary. Coparcenary was thus distinguishable from the other concurrent estates of joint tenancy and tenancy in common, which could be created only by inter vivos conveyance, before the Statute of Wills was enacted in 1540. Coparcenary was, like a joint tenancy, characterized by the "unities" of time, title, interest, and possession; however, like the tenancy in common, it carried no right of survivorship.[740] Coparcenary was further distinct from the other co-ownerships in that each coparcener had the right to compel partition of the estate.[741] The right of partition was not conferred upon joint and common tenants until 1539 and 1540.[742]

The origins of the tenancy in coparcenary are very obscure, but it was probably a useful and needed form of landholding in a society that had adopted primogeniture, either for when no son existed to inherit, or the local custom did not follow primogeniture. Most likely coparcenary would arise in the former circumstance, and coparceners would usually be sisters. The most direct early source about coparcenary is Bracton, who, in addition to the relatively succinct statement quoted below, wrote at great length about the process of partition, a serious event in feudal times:

> *Where partition ought to be made among co-heirs*
>
> When there are several heirs having one right and the inheritance ought to be divided among them, either because of the nature of the thing inherited or of the

[740] Some dispute existed about whether coparceners had a right of survivorship, but the courts ultimately and consistently held that they did not. Y.B. 14 & 15 Edw. 3 (Rolls Series), 34 (1341); Y.B. 17 & 18 Edw. 3 (Rolls Series), 174 (1343).

[741] *Bracton*, fol. 72-77b.

[742] 31 Hen. 8, c. 1 (1539); 32 Hen. 8, c. 32 (1540).

> persons inheriting, let a division [or] partition of the inheritance be made among them immediately after homage has been taken. In the writ *de partitione facienda* there ought to be no action between co-heirs acknowledged as heirs, even though there is disagreement among them, [for example], that one of them has a greater share than he ought to have, because the writ provides nothing except that (an extent having been made) each have his rightful portion. But if before such disagreement is settled he who has the larger portion dies seised, his heir, whether of age or a minor, shall not answer without writ, because of his ancestor's seisin, right or wrongful . . . But since a partition cannot be made among co-heirs without an extent and valuation, and an extent and valuation cannot be made without knights who, with the sheriff, make the extent, who sometimes are called justices, when they are appointed by the king, sometimes chosen by the parties by common consent, we must first see who they are appointed by the king and by what writ . . .[743]

Although isolated references to coparceners or parceners occur in the statutes of several American states, it is a property interest of almost complete obscurity and obsolescence in modern times. Thus it is interesting to see how much detail Bracton devoted to it, not only in the introductory comments quoted above, but in the very elaborate procedural instructions, occupying almost 20 printed pages in modern editions. A sampling of these issues, and an intriguing insight into the kinds of property issues that preoccupied the medieval landholder, is contained in headings for the rest of the material on parceners' partition found in Bracton:

> Writ for appointing justices to make a partition.
>
> Writ appointing justices to be present at a partition.

[743] *Bracton*, fol. 72.

Writ when the parties by common consent choose others to make the partition.

Writs in another form but of the same kind, where partition was improperly made by others.

Writ to deliver seisin to co-heirs when they have agreed among themselves as to the partition.

Another writ of the same kind: where a tenant parcener has acknowledged his share to his parcener; that an extent be made.

Writ that one be present to take the oath of the extenders if the extent is to be made outside the county.

Writ where the extenders have done nothing in response to the first order.

Writ where the knights appear but the sheriff is negligent.

Writ where an extent has been improperly made.

Forms of interlaced writs, where knights of two counties must come together to make an extent.

Writ on the complaint of an eldest daughter and parcener who does not have her rightful share nor her seniority; of making a reasonable partition by knights.

Writ to produce bodies of extenders so they may certify.

The duty of extenders.

Writ to the sheriff for giving seisin to co-heirs after

partition.[744]

§ 7.06(g)(2). Joint Tenancy.

During Bracton's time, the only form of concurrent ownership other than tenancy in coparcenary was joint tenancy. The joint tenancy is a property interest held by two or more persons simultaneously, with the survivor of them to retain the entire interest. The right of survivorship distinguishes the joint tenancy from the tenancy in common. The right of each joint tenant to compel partition, secured by statute in 1539,[745] distinguishes the joint tenancy from the tenancy by the entirety. The joint tenancy is also distinct from the tenancy by the entirety because of the dual nature of the joint tenancy, expressed by Bracton with the famous phrase "per my et per tout": each joint tenant possesses the entire tenancy ("per tout"), and each also possesses an equal fractional undivided share of the tenancy ("per my"). The fractional shares are called moieties. A tenancy by the entirety, on the other hand, is considered to be only a single ownership of the entire tenancy, with ownership held by both spouses considered as one person.

The singular ownership characteristic of a joint tenancy was especially compatible with feudal values, which discouraged any splitting of tenancies that threatened performance of feudal obligations. This unified ownership was promoted by the doctrine that joint tenants took their respective interests all together under identical circumstances, the so-called "unities" of time, title, interest, and possession. At first, the requirement of maintaining the unities meant that a joint tenancy could be created only by inter vivos conveyance. Courts held that heirs could not take a joint estate by descent, because the individuality of their status as heirs was inconsistent with the unity theoretically required for a joint tenancy. This was usually not a problem, because under primogeniture usually only the oldest son would inherit the property. When only daughters survived the landholder, they obtained the property by descent in a form of joint

[744] *Bracton*, fols. 72-77b.

[745] 31 Hen. 8, c. 1 (1539).

ownership called tenancy in coparcenary. However, the impact of heirs' individuality was shown in the rule that no right of survivorship applied to tenancies in coparcenary.

Inasmuch as Bracton is the only early documentary source for the common law origin of joint tenancies, his cryptic comments are quoted as follows:

> We have explained in the preceding portion who may give [a gift of land] and who may not. Now we must show to whom a gift may be made. It is clear that it may be made . . . to a woman or to a man, a wife as well as a husband, to them together or separately to each . . . Also not only to one but to several, to all together and at the same time or successively, by the *modus* of gift, as will be explained below . . . Since all were enfeoffed together and hold in common, the children do not succeed one the other, and if one of them dies without heirs his portion will accrue by the *jus accrescendi* to the survivors and their heirs, from several such to one, and will not revert to the donor as long as one survivor remains or one has heirs. But if all die without heirs, the whole will revert to the donor.[746]

The aspects of survivorship rules that smack of tenancy in common in the above passage from Bracton are somewhat accounted for by feudal tenurial relationships: if the children in Bracton's illustration were considered tenants in common and then died without heirs, their portions would escheat. Instead, Bracton described a rudimentary form of survivorship that not only avoided the escheat, but postponed any reversion to the grantor until all of the joint tenants had died without heirs.

Although joint tenancy enjoyed early favor in the Middle Ages, because it inhibited the splitting of tenures, it could also be used to avoid some feudal incidents and obligations. For instance, if one granted land in joint tenancy to a father, a mother, a son, and the son's heirs, it could defeat

[746] *Bracton*, fol. 13.

a lord's claim to wardship of a minor heir or a relief from an adult heir, because the estate had already passed at the time of the original conveyance. A statutory response to the conveyancers' creativity was soon forthcoming:

> As touching them that use to infeoff their eldest sons and heirs, being within age, of their heritage, for to defraud the lords of the fee of their wardships, it is provided, accorded, and agreed, that by occasion of any such feoffment no chief lord shall lose his ward.[747]

Even a joint tenancy to a husband and wife could cost the lord a wardship. If a man, married and with an infant son, conveyed in fee to another, then took back a conveyance in fee to himself and his wife, as joint tenants, the estate would belong to the wife if he predeceased her, and the lord would not have an occasion to claim a wardship. Despite these occasional problems, joint tenancies had much appeal, and during the Middle Ages any conveyance in fee or for life to two or more persons was presumed to create a joint tenancy.

Medieval joint tenants could partition their land, but only with the consent of all the cotenants; in this respect it differed from tenancy in coparcenary, under which any one coparcener could compel partition.[748]

§ 7.06(g)(3). Tenancy in Common.

Even though the early common law evinced a strong preference for construing joint conveyances as joint tenancies, alternative constructions became necessary, because one of the four unities might be missing. In that event, during the fourteenth century courts began to recognize a concurrent conveyance to separate persons as a tenancy in common, and royal courts of that era were able to distinguish between tenancies in common and joint

---

[747] Statutes of Marlborough, 52 Hen. 3, c. 6 (1267).

[748] *Bracton*, fol. 72.

tenancies.[749] The tenancy in common had no right of survivorship and, until 1540, could be created only by inter vivos conveyance; after 1540 the Statute of Wills permitted a tenancy in common to be devised by will. Without a right of survivorship, tenants in common were not able to enter into collusive conveyances designed to cut off feudal incidents. As with early joint tenancies, tenants in common during medieval times could partition only upon the consent of all the cotenants.

§ 7.06(g)(4). Tenancy by the Entirety.

The tenancy by the entirety resembles a joint tenancy as between husband and wife, because it can exist only if the four unities are present and also holds the right of survivorship. However, it is distinct in also requiring the condition of a valid marriage between the tenants and in not recognizing a right in either individual tenant to compel partition.

The origin of tenancy by the entirety is unknown, but Bracton acknowledged some form of concurrent ownership between husband and wife:

> Some tenements are privately owned, the property of an individual by himself, without a parcener or one joined to him, others are not held alone but with another joined to him or a parcener: with one conjoined, as where a man holds with his wife, or conversely, who are not called parceners because their rights and the property do not admit of division, for they are one flesh though different souls . . . [750]

§ 7.06(h). The Gage and the Mortgage.

Plucknett clarified the origins of the mortgage with the following

[749] Y.B. 14 Edw. 3 (Rolls Series), 198, 200 (1341); Y.B. 38 Edw. 3, Michaelmas Term, 26b (1364).

[750] *Bracton*, fol. 208.

explanation:

> The development of the mortgage is an interesting example of the interplay between legal doctrine and conveyancing custom. The gage, which is the root idea of the transaction, is really a relic of the days when credit was not yet in existence. It has been conjectured that in its oldest form the gage (in Latin *vadium*, and in modern English "pledge") was payment, subject only to the option of the purchaser to substitute at a later time payment in a different kind. Under this arrangement the handing over of the gage settled the debt; the creditor could not demand the substitution of a different kind of payment, and the debtor had no way of recovering any excess value in the gage over the price which he could substitute later.[751]

The gage, or something like it that made land available as security for a loan of money, appears in transactions described in Anglo-Saxon land charters. In one of its forms, the borrower turned the land over to a lender of money, who would satisfy the loan obligation out of the returns from the land, and then convey the land back to the borrower. Three entries in Domesday Book reveal land in the possession of persons to whom it was gaged.[752]

§ 7.06(h)(1). The Gage During Glanvill's Time.

In Glanvill's work, of the late 12th century, one may read lengthy provisions about the gage, but little is known of these gages outside those passages. The following excerpts are typical:

---

[751] Theodore F. T. Plucknett, *A Concise History of the Common Law* 603 (5th ed. 1956). In a footnote to the quote in the text, Plucknett added, "Remember that the mediaeval 'pledge' (*plegius*) is almost always a person, not a thing. The Teutonic *wed* has come down to us by various routes as 'gage', 'engagement', 'wage', 'wager', and 'wedding.'"

[752] *Domesday Book* 137, 141, 217.

> The loan for consumption may, however, be accompanied by the deposit of a gage; when this happens, sometimes movables such as chattels are deposited as gage, sometimes immovables such as lands and tenements and rents (which may consist of money or other things). When creditor and debtor agree to the deposit of a gage, whatever the nature of the gage, then the debtor, after he has received the loan, either immediately gives the creditor seisen of his gage or does not. Moreover, the gage may be for a fixed term, or with no fixed term. Furthermore, sometimes the gage is a dead gage (mortgage) and sometimes not; it is called mortgage when the fruits and rents accruing during its continuance do not count towards repayment of the loan . . .
>
> Furthermore, when anything is deposited as a gage for a fixed term, creditor and debtor either agree that if the debtor does not redeem his gage at the end of the term the gage shall become the property of the creditor who may deal with it as with his own property, or else there is no such agreement.[753]

Because under some mortgages the fruits and rents of the land, while held by the creditor, were not to be applied toward reducing the principle of debt,[754] these fruits and rents were effectively a form of interest for the creditor, and that interest under the religious doctrine of the time constituted a usurious transaction forbidden to Christians. As explained by Pollock and Maitland:

> Such a bargain is a kind of usury; but apparently it is a valid bargain, even though the creditor be a Christian. He

---

[753] *Glanvill,* X, 6.

[754] An alternative explanation for the "dead" gage is that if the debt is not paid, the land is dead as to the debtor; if the debt is paid, the land is dead to the creditor. The payment arrangement of a gage could also be gradually killing or "amortizing" the debt.

> sins by making it, and, if he dies in his sin, his chattels will be forfeited to the king; but to all seeming the debtor is bound by his contract. As to the Jew, he was not prohibited from taking usury from Christians; he took it openly. Even the Christian, if we are not much mistaken, was very willing to run such risk of sin and punishment as was involved in the covert usury of the mortgage. The plea rolls of the thirteenth century often show us a Christian gagee in possession of the gaged land, but we have come upon no instance in which he was called upon to account for the profits that he had received. We infer that the gagee was usually a mortgagee in Glanvill's sense of that term.[755]

Either an explicit agreement or a bargain that was reduced to a fixed term or left open-ended could produce the gage as outlined in Glanvill. If the gage was based on a fixed term, and the parties had agreed that the gagee could keep the property if the debt were not paid, then if the debt were not repaid by the end of the term, the gagee would simply keep the land without further action. If the gage were on a fixed term, but without an explicit agreement for the gagee to keep the property upon default, then at the end of the term, the gagee could obtain a judgment against the debtor, ordering payment of the debt within a reasonable time and declaring ownership of the gaged property in the gagee if the debt were not paid. If the gage was given without a specific term, then the gagee could call the loan at any time, obtain a judgment requiring payment within a reasonable time, and be declared the owner if payment were not made.[756] This arrangement unmistakably resembled later equity courts' foreclosure decrees.

Certain obstacles rooted in feudal relationships restricted the utility of the procedure outlined in Glanvill. First, the gagee had to be put in possession of the land, or protective remedies of the royal courts would not be available. Once in possession, the gagee had a form of seisin, but, again,

---

[755] 2 Frederick Pollock and Frederic William Maitland, *The History of English Law Before the Time of Edward I* 119 (2d ed. 1909).

[756] *Glanvill*, X, 8.

an unconventional seisin that was not protected by remedies usually available to those with seisin. For instance, if the gagee were ejected, only the gagor had the right to seek recovery of the land. Even if the gagor ousted the gagee, the gagee could not recover the land, only the debt.[757] Thus neither the gagor nor the gagee had legal protection for possession of the premises. Moreover, if the mortgagee died while the mortgage was still in effect, thus while still engaged in the sin of usury, the property could be forfeited to the monarch. These procedural limitations on the gagee's interest existed, because that interest did not fit neatly into the feudal tenurial system. Only if the gagee could be treated as a tenant for years, for life, or in fee could the available remedies be invoked.

§ 7.06(h)(2). The Gage During Bracton's Time.

By the time Bracton wrote a couple of generations later, the gagee's interest had been adjusted to the feudal tenurial system. The gagee lent the money and took from the gagor a term of years and a conditional fee in the land to be used a security. If the gagor timely paid the debt, the term of years expired, the condition for retaining the fee would not materialize, and the fee and seisin returned to the gagor. During the term of the gage, the gagee had a termor's seisin, while the gagor had the seisin in fee, all of which was in harmony with feudal rules and capable of being spelled out in the single document creating the gage.[758] Even this feudally consistent formula was eventually simplified to the conditional feoffment mortgage of the classical common law: an enfeoffment from the gagor/debtor/feoffer to the gagee/creditor/feofee and heirs upon condition that, if the debt is timely paid, the feoffer and heirs may re-enter and resume ownership of the land.[759]

---

[757] *Glanvill*, X, 11.

[758] *Bracton*, fols. 20, 268-269.

[759] *See, e.g.*, Rye v. Tumby, Y.B. 8 Edw. 2, Michaelmas Term, No. 9 (1314) (Year Books of Edward II, 8 Edward II (Selden Society vol. 37, Vol. 18 Year Book Series, 1920)); Walsham v. Walsham, Y.B. 8 Edw. 2, Michaelmas Term, No. 10 (1314) (Year Books of Edward II, 8 Edward II 52 (Selden Society Vol. 37, Vol. 18 Year Book Series, 1920)).

During this time, parties made various arrangements for possession of the gaged property. Most gagees probably took possession of the property. Sometimes the gagor conveyed the land to the gagee without rent, and the gagee reconveyed to the gagor with a rent, with a covenant that the gage would terminate when enough rent had been received to pay back the loan. While the Christian gagees most often took possession of the gaged properties, the Jewish gagees often left the debtors in possession of the property, prompting Pollock and Maitland to comment, "We may guess that, if the Jews had not been expelled from England, the clumsy mortgage by way of conditional conveyance would have given way before a simple method of securing debts, and would not still be encumbering our modern law."[760]

With the expulsion of the Jews in 1290, the royal courts tended to construe common law mortgages literally and strictly; such mortgages "suffered from the incurable defect that they employed formulas which contradicted the true nature of the operation (they spoke of feoffments in fee, and leases for years, when the transaction was really neither) and such forms inevitably attracted several doctrines of seisin and the derivation of estates, which tended to defeat their purpose."[761]

§ 7.06(h)(3). Rise of the Classical Common Law Mortgage.

At some time during the 15th or 16th century, the form of mortgage shifted from an enfeoffment on condition of defeasance or of re-entry to an enfeoffment with a covenant for reconveyance. Courts more readily enforced the covenant through the device of a writ of instrument, and both common law and equity courts during this period were willing to order reconveyance, if the gagee met the payment conditions. Eventually courts recognized the power of sale in mortgagees, so the mortgagees no longer needed to proceed in court to satisfy their rights. Despite the additional

[760] 2 Frederick Pollock and Frederic William Maitland, *The History of English Law Before the Time of Edward I* 124 (2d ed. 1909).

[761] Theodore F. T. Plucknett, *A Concise History of the Common Law* 606 (5th ed. 1956).

protections afforded mortgagees by these changes, mortgagees still frequently took possession of the property, even into the middle of the 17th century.

But courts also began to develop protections for the mortgagors. Equity courts became reluctant to enforce penalties, and, near the end of the 16th century, fashioned doctrines on the equity of redemption. The equity of redemption was the right of a mortgagor, even after default, to cure the default and satisfy the obligation within a reasonable time, and rescue the property from forfeiture. Implicit in this doctrine was the recognition that the mortgage was really a security, not a conveyance.

§ 7.06(h)(4). Other Security Devices.

In the towns, an alternative to gages and mortgages was afforded by the Statute of Merchants and the Statute of Staples. The Statute of Merchants[762] enabled creation of a creditor's estate as tenant by statute merchant until the debt was discharged. This security interest was created through a procedure that took place by the parties appearing before the chief magistrate of a trading town. These procedures were termed "recognizances" or "statutes," because they were entered into under the Statute of Merchants. It is worthy of note that this statute permitted executions (proceedings for using the debtor's property to satisfy indebtedness) that would today be considered drastic, apparently in response to complaints by merchants who experienced difficulty in debt collection under traditional common law remedies. Execution actually began with the imprisonment of the debtor, who then had three months to sell property to satisfy the debt; if the debtor was unsuccessful in thus satisfying the debt, the property would be turned over for sale by the creditor. If the security was in land, then it applied to all lands held by the debtor at the time of entering into the statutory procedure, even if the lands were later alienated.

[762] De Mercatoribus, 13 Edw. I (1285).

The later legislation, called the Statute of Staples,[763] similarly enabled creation of a creditor's estate or tenancy by statute staple until the debt was discharged. The estate was created in a procedure carried out before the mayor of the staple.[764]

Under both of these procedures, if a creditor obtained a judgment and then obtained the land in execution of the judgment, the creditor's possession was considered a freehold; the statutes authorized protection of such possession by the assize of novel disseisin.

§ 7.06(i). Conveyancing.

§ 7.06(i)(1). Early Conveyances by Charter Only.

The principal issue in the early history of English conveyancing is whether any of the various documentary forms in use were actually effective to convey real property interests, or merely memorialized a conveyance accomplished by other means. Anglo-Saxon landholders recorded transfers of bookland and laenland in written charters, but it is not known whether some other ceremony was also a necessary part of the conveyance. As to Anglo-Saxon folkland, apparently not even written documents were used. The early charters, and the hundreds of county court ceremonies used with them in transfers, were elaborate. Simpler documents took their place at the close of the Anglo-Saxon period. The only direct evidence of Anglo-Saxon conveyancing comes from bookland and laenland charters, and the wording of these charters suggests that the execution and delivery of those documents themselves effected the conveyances. To deliver the original deed to land that had once been booked seems to have been sufficient to transfer the property. It is not known what significance may have attached to the occasional reports of a turf being placed upon an

---

[763] Statute of Staples, 27 Edw. 3, c. 9 (1353).

[764] The mayor of the staple was the chief officer of the staple or great market at Westminster who took acknowledgements of estates created under statutes staple as security for debts.

altar in connection with a bookland transfer.

The charters used in England after the Norman Conquest invariably included such phrases as “I give and grant,” suggesting that the charter itself was the effective instrument of transfer. Gradually, however, conveyancers also adopted the phrasing “I have given and granted,” suggesting that the charter was not the conveyance, but was only recording an act that had already occurred. Often, parties delivered these charters together with other tangible symbols, such as a knife, rod, or helmet, and made the delivery in a church or a court. What is unclear in these early Anglo-Norman conveyances is whether the charter with its symbol constituted the actual conveyance, i.e., delivery of seisin, or some other conveyancing procedure was necessary to complete the transaction. Even in the latter event, the symbolic ceremony probably gave rise to a right to have the conveyance made.

§ 7.06(i)(2). Early Conveyances by Livery of Seisin.

Eventually, however, judges resolved the confusion and began imposing strict requirements that transfer of ownership be accomplished by ceremonies taking place on the land itself, if possible. Juries strengthened this notion by giving witness to such public ceremonies. However, a time of transition and confusion probably occurred, when delivery of a document sufficed to transfer, or when parties performed ceremonies on the land and execution of documents and other pertinent acts. Pollock and Maitland described the details of these transitional practices as follows:

> As a matter of fact, in the first half of the thirteenth century it was still common for the feoffor and the feoffee to attend the county or hundred courts, to have their charter read there and to procure its attestation by the sheriff and the leading men of the district. In addition to this, if the gift was to be made to a monastery, the charter would be read in the chapter house and then it would be carried into the church and offered upon the altar along with knife or rod. Beside this there would be a ceremony

> on the land, including sometimes a perambulation of boundaries in the presence of witnesses; and this was the more necessary because the charter rarely described the many small strips of land which made up that hide or virgate which had been bestowed. One could not be too careful; one could not have too many ceremonies. But what the king's court demanded was a real delivery of a real possession.[765]

The strict distinction drawn between charter and seisin was well illustrated by the conveyancing practices of the king: the monarch not only sent out a charter, but also sent a writ to the local sheriff ordering him to make livery of seisin. In case of conflicting charters, the earlier seisin prevailed.[766]

However, in all of these conveyances, whether by king or subject, it was not enough to speak only of livery of seisin. The grant of land consisted of two elements, the feoffment and the livery of seisin. The feoffment was the gift of a freehold estate, such as the fee or a life estate. The enfeoffment could be expressed either by a written document or orally.[767] Even into the thirteenth century, conveyances of freeholds without charter were common.[768] By that time and for some time earlier, however, when the charters were used, their language suggested only that they recorded a conveyance that had already occurred, not they were the instrument of conveyance. The livery of seisin accomplished the conveyance, described by Pollock and Maitland in the following terms:

> The donor and the donee in person or by attorney must

---

[765] 2 Frederick Pollock and Frederic William Maitland, *The History of English Law Before the Time of Edward I* 90 (2d ed. 1909). *See also Bracton's Note Book* pl. 375 (1230), pl. 754 (1233).

[766] *Bracton*, fol. 56b.

[767] *Bracton*, fol. 33b.

[768] *See, e.g.,* Y.B. 20 & 21 Edw. 1 (Rolls Series), 32 (1292) ; Statutes of Marlborough, 52 Hen. 3, c. 9 (1267).

> come upon the land. There the words of gift will be said or the charter, if there be one, will be read. It is usual, though perhaps not necessary, that there should be some further ceremony. If the subject of the gift is a house, the donor will put the hasp or ring of the door into the donee's hand . . . ; if there is no house, a rod will be transferred . . . or perhaps a glove. Such is the common and the safe practice; but it is not indispensable that the parties should actually stand on the land that is to be given. If that land was within their view when the ceremony was performed, and if the feoffee made an actual entry on it while the feoffer was yet alive, this was a sufficient feoffment. But a livery of seisin either on the land or "within the view" was necessary.[769]

Some of the more colorful elaborations of livery of seisin, often popularly ascribed to the English common law, were in fact practices of the continental Germanic tribes of an age before the Norman Conquest of England.[770]

If, as is believed, the livery of seisin practices on the continent had so far progressed that it was no longer necessary to go onto the land, and merely ceremonial passing of the symbols sufficed for the conveyance, then it is all the more surprising that in England of the thirteenth century the courts began to insist upon the literal elements of livery of seisin, the handing over of some part of the land, while on the land or within view of the land.

§ 7.06(i)(3). Quitclaim Without Livery of Seisin.

For two types of transfers the livery of seisin was not required. One type of transfer occurred when one party held as tenant for years or life,

---

[769] 2 Frederick Pollock and Frederic William Maitland, *The History of English Law Before the Time of Edward I* 83 (2d ed. 1909). *See Bracton*, fols. 40, 41; Y.B. 20 & 21 Edw. 1 (Rolls Series), 256 (1292).

[770] *Id.* at 85-86.

with the fee in another party, or one party held adversely to another, and the out-of-possession party wished to yield the property rights to the party in possession. A document sufficed for this; no ceremony of enfeoffment was necessary.[771] No standard terminology applied to such a document at first, although a quitclaim was commonly used to surrender adverse rights.[772] Later the document terminology became standardized with various kinds of releases.

§ 7.06(i)(4). Surrender Without Livery of Seisin.

The second type of transfer for which livery of seisin was not required arose when a tenant wished to surrender the tenancy to the lord. Because the lord was already seised (either in fee if the tenancy were for a term, or in service if the tenancy were for life or in fee) probably neither deed nor livery was necessary. Quite frequently, however, the tenant used a deed of surrender.

§ 7.06(i)(5). Transfers to Change the Type of Tenancy.

Those who wished to change the nature of their tenancy (for instance, from fee simple to fee tail) usually needed two enfeoffments: the first to a disinterested grantee, and the second from that grantee back to the original grantor with the proper tenancy incorporated into the second enfeoffment. Probably the grantee would have to actually take seisin before making the second enfeoffment.

§ 7.06(i)(6). Transfers Between Freeholders with Villeins in Occupancy.

When neither party to the conveyance was in actual occupancy, and the

---

[771] *See Bracton* fol. 41.

[772] "Quit-claim" derives from *quietum clamare*, to "cry quits."

occupant was a tenant of the grantor, the parties used another procedure for conveyancing. Of course, the occupancy rights would have to be taken into account when making the conveyance, but the method of doing that depended on whether the occupant was a freeholder or held in villeinage. If the tenancy was in villeinage, the grantor simply enfeoffed the grantee with livery of seisin. However, the parties could also direct that the villeins involved acknowledge the transfer of lordship. When Richard de Turville conveyed to the Abbot of Missenden, he sent letters patent to the villeins, and after the villeins had gathered, Richard delivered seisin of them and their tenements to the abbot. The abbot took their fealty and demanded rent; because no rent was due, the abbot lent some pennies to the villeins, who then each paid a penny for the right to remain in occupancy.[773]

§ 7.06(i)(7). Transfers Between Freeholders with Freeholders in Occupancy; Attornment to the Grantee.

If, on the other hand, a freeholder was in occupancy, a different procedure took place. The grantor in effect granted the incorporeal lordship (seignory) or reversion rather than the corporeal land itself, although there must still be some symbolic transfer of the land. This act conveyed the incorporeal right by a document that came to be called a deed of grant, and in addition the occupant attorned to the grantee.[774] To attorn meant to "turn over" the tenant to the new lord, the grantee. If the tenant in occupancy would not agree to attorn himself or herself to the new grantee, then the grantor could resort to the court; the court could compel the tenant to make an acknowledgment that the tenancy was held of the new lord. The court could hold that the new lord was seised of the tenant's service, but would not require the tenant to do homage to the new lord.[775]

---

[773] *Bracton's Note Book*, pl. 524 (1231).

[774] Throughout this chapter the terms grantor and grantee, rather than donor and donee, are used because of their meaning for the modern reader; however, as is explained in the text, the only proper medieval usage for the grant terminology is when transfer of lordship occurs while a freehold tenant is in occupancy.

[775] *Bracton*, fols. 80b, 81b; Y.B. 32 & 33 Edw. 1 (Rolls Series), 43 (1304).

§ 7.06(i)(8). Elements of the Charter or Deed.[776]

Even though the written charter or deed was merely evidence of a conveyance, rather than the conveyance itself, and even though much land was transferred without deed, there were still advantages to using a deed. In addition to using the deed for a grant, the grantor could use the deed form for a release and a surrender. Moreover, after it became settled that certain interests, such as reversions, rents and other incorporeal interests, could be granted even though livery of seisin was not possible, then the grantor had to use a deed to transfer those interests.

§ 7.06(i)(8)(A). Recitals in the Deed.

The early deeds were quite simple and uniform in format, and almost always were unilateral in the sense that they were given in the name of the grantor. As innovations in the form arose, such as inclusion of the word "assigns" or of a warranty clause, conveyancers rapidly and widely adopted those innovations. The standard form first recited that the grantor had given, and by charter confirmed, to the grantee and heirs and assigns forever, certain land, the boundaries of which the deed would describe with particularity. Then followed the habendum clause describing the nature of the interest taken by the grantee. Because subinfeudation was no longer possible after the Statute Quia Emptores, deeds thereafter had to recite that the grantee held of the grantor's lord by the services customarily due. The deed also described any rights reserved by the grantor (such as rent), or created for others (such as remainders).

In early times the deed usually concluded with a clause stating that the deed was sealed, in order that the grant "may remain forever good and valid." However, even though a seal remained a requirement for validity, by the fourteenth century conveyancers often omitted a recital of seal, and then replaced statements of sealing and of witnesses by a clause stating the time and place of the deed. Beginning in the fifteenth century, grantors endorsed on deeds a recital that livery of seisin had taken place. And they

---

[776] This section is based on Theodore F. T. Plucknett, *A Concise History of the Common Law* 610-613 (5th ed. 1956).

placed signatures on deeds beginning only in the sixteenth century, although not commonly until after the Statute of Frauds was enacted in the seventeenth century.

§ 7.06(i)(8)(B). Warranties in the Deed.

Perhaps the most important benefit of a deed in fee simple was the clause of warranty it typically included, by which the grantor and heirs and assigns warranted the land to the grantee and heirs and assigns "against all men forever." The warranty had a twofold purpose: (1) to compel a response from the grantor if the grantee's title was challenged (and to obtain compensation or equivalent land from the grantor, if the challenge was successful), and (2) to bar the grantor and grantor's heirs from later challenging the conveyance. The warranty undoubtedly helped establish the alienability of fee simple interests, even overcoming family restraints.

In transfers of interests other than in fee simple, the warranty was more troublesome. When a person holding a dower or curtesy interest enfeoffed another (tortiously) with warranty, even though the feoffor had a child, the warranty would usually bar the child as heir from claiming what would normally be the inheritance. A statute in 1278 partially removed this bar by warranty.[777] The statutory relief expressly applied only to warranties created by tenants in curtesy, but in 1306 the courts extended it to tenants in tail who had received no assets by descent.[778] Before this an enfeoffment or fine by a tenant in tail, with warranty, could bar the feoffer's heir, to whom the estate in tail was limited by descent. Attempts to bar claims from the heir through use of warranties continued for several centuries more. The courts generally recognized that warranties accomplished the bar, although the bar of certain "collateral" warranties was abolished by statute in 1706.[779]

Frequently, however, the bar of a warranty affected only the inheritance

---

[777] Statutes of Gloucester, 6 Edw., c. 3 (1278).

[778] Y.B. 33 & 35 Edw. (Rolls Series), 388 (1306).

[779] 4 & 5 Anne, c. 3, s. 21 (1706).

right, and not reversions and remainders. Fines more effectively barred reversions and remainders, and in the case of fee simple interests a fine barred all claims after a year and a day. In 1361, a statute completely abolished the bar effect of the fine.[780] Unhappiness with that state of affairs prompted a partial reversal in the next century, so that a fine could be a bar after five years and after fulfilling certain procedural requirements.[781] However, even with this change, the fine would bar only issue in tail, but not most remainders and reversions. Not until a later century would the procedure known as common recovery bar remainders and reversions.

§ 7.06(i)(8)(C). Physical Form of the Deed.

If a deed contained especially elaborate provisions, the parties might have it made in two copies on one page, with the page then divided by an indented cut that angled through the word "Chyrographum." The deed thus became an indenture or indented writing.

Conveyancers also enrolled many deeds in the courts, especially if the transfer itself took place in court. For a small charge a person could enter a deed on the pipe roll (a treasury account kept in the Exchequer), and they frequently enrolled such deeds on the backs of the close rolls (closed records of sealed letters or grants from the monarch to particular parties).

§ 7.06(i)(9). The Fine or Final Concord.

The impulse to improve the authority and security of deeds by invoking court proceedings and by making multiple copies, came together in the important procedure called the fine, or final concord, that was practiced from 1195 to 1833.

Much experimentation occurred before 1195. Conveyancers had copied charters onto the pipe rolls and the close rolls. Upon concluding a court case dealing with a conveyance, the parties could obtain charters from the

---

[780] 34 Edw. 3, c. 16 (1361).

[781] 1 Rich. 3, c. 7 (1484); 4 Hen. 7, c. 24 (1489).

court and other parties confirming the outcome. This made seisin determined by legal action especially secure. Parties might embark on a procedure of trial by battle and, at a prearranged moment, have the exchange stopped by friends, and present a peaceful accord for approval by the court. The effect was the same as if the battle had been carried to conclusion.[782] Not only did this procedure conclude the contest between the immediate parties with finality, but it barred any others who might have an interest or claim in the matter if they did not quickly come forward.[783] Most importantly, the parties could then use court action to enforce the terms of the concord. Lawyers developed a form for such agreements, and once the royal court adopted the form, they used it in lesser courts.[784]

The royal court then developed a form for recording the agreements on parchment, and some of the early chirographs, or indented writings, are these so called "final concords."[785] One such document dated July 15, 1195, proclaims itself to be the first chirographic final concord that was made in three parts, one of which was to remain as a record in the royal treasury.

The action to have a fine "levied" began with a writ, usually either a form of writ of covenant or writ of warranty. In imitation of the simulated battle trials, the parties would carry the litigation to some length before presenting their concord. Later, they would present the concord as soon as all parties had joined the action and were before the court. The parties had to request leave of court to compromise the action.

Court involvement was not merely cosmetic. The most important supervisory function exercised by the judges was to examine married women appearing before them as grantors, to be assured that the women

---

[782] *Bracton's Note Book*, pl. 101 (1220), 147 (1222), 168 (1222), 316 (1229), 363 (1229), 815 (1233), 851 (1234), 1035 (1225), 1619 (1223).

[783] Bracton declared the bar to be effective as soon as the chirograph was delivered to the parties, not less than fifteen days after the agreement was struck in court. *Bracton*, fol. 436. At other times the period may have been a year and a day.

[784] *See Bracton's Note Book*, pl. 992 (1224), 1223 (1238), 1616 (1223), 1619 (1223).

[785] *See Glanvill*, VIII.

understood what they were doing, that is, surrendering dower and other rights. Indeed, even by Bracton's time, the fine had become the conveyance of choice for married women.[786]

The fine was also advantageous for other kinds of conveyances. To convey a non-possessory interest such as a lordship (seignory) or a reversion, where it was uncertain whether the tenant would willingly attorn to the grantee, the fine action included a regular procedure for compelling the grantee's attornment or accomplishing attornment by the court. The fine served well in conveyances connected with family settlements. If a landholder wished to settle property on family members, that meant changing the grantor's own form of tenancy, normally accomplished by a two-step conveyance to a third person and then back to the family members, and the fine could help avoid the risks of that procedure. The fine enabled the entire settlement to be achieved in one step, with court approval.

These features of the fine did not come fully formed. Transfer of seisin and the land were at first still necessary, and could only be compelled when the fine was submitted to execution. In the typical family settlement, the fine recorded that the third party had been enfeoffed before granting back to various family members the specified interests, when in fact no enfeoffment had occurred. (The fine, after all, was in reality a collusive action and a feigned compromise.) The fine did not bind the settlor's heir[787] until a statute in 1299 removed the heir's plea.[788] Indeed, the statute went far toward making all aspects of the fine truly final.

---

[786] *Bracton*, fol. 321b.

[787] *Bracton*, fols. 242b, 262, 270; *Bracton's Note Book*, pl. 125 (1222), 778 (1233), 853 (1234); Y.B. 33 & 35 Edw. 1 (Rolls Series), 201, 435 (1306).

[788] Statute de Finibus Levatis, 27 Edw.,Stat. I (1299).

§ 7.07. Uses.

§ 7.07(a). Origins of Uses.

The term "use" in English law derives from the Latin "opus," signifying a benefit or "on behalf of." One person could give land or chattels to another, for the use or benefit of a third person. Knights embarking on crusades employed uses. One wishing to confer the benefit of land on a religious order not authorized to hold land could convey a use. Villeins could convey their land only by yielding it to the lord "for the use of" the intended grantee. When a wardship was taken from an unfaithful guardian and given to another, the new guardian held "to the use of" the ward.[789]

Uses had apparently become quite common during the fourteenth century, because several statutes of the latter part of that century deal with uses. One statute made lands held to the use of defrauding debtors subject to execution for their debts.[790] Another statute made uses for the benefit of religious houses and other corporations subject to the Statute of Mortmain,[791] meaning that no uses could be created for the benefit of such institutions, upon pain of forfeiture (except that mortmain practice permitted such conveyances after first obtaining a royal license).[792] A statute made uses and other property interests forfeitable for treason.[793]

---

[789] Statute of Westminster I, 3 Edw., c. 48 (1275).

[790] 50 Edw. 3, c. 6 (1376).

[791] 7 Edw., Stat. 2 (1279).

[792] 15 Rich. 2, c. 5(4) (1391).

[793] 21 Rich. 2, c. 3 (1397):

> And he for him and his heirs shall forfeit all the lands, tenements, and possessions, liberties and all other hereditaments, which he hath or *any other hath to his use*, or had the day of the treason done as well in fee tail as in fee simple to the King and his heirs, as well such lands holden of other as of himself forever; *and also such possession as other have to his use.* (Emphasis added.)

§ 7.07(b). Advantages and Disadvantages of Uses.

The beneficiary of the use, the "cestui que use," frequently benefitted from a collusive or fraudulent arrangement, and just as frequently that beneficiary could be victimized by an unfaithful feoffee who would not honor the terms of the use. Certainly wrongful employment of the use could work much mischief: "The purpose of such conveyances frequently was to enable the landowners to deal with their lands in a manner not countenanced by the common law or to evade the liabilities incident to legal ownership." [794] It was also the rule that dower and curtesy would not attach to uses, which significantly aided the free alienability of uses. Succumbing to the attractive features of the use, however, the landowner became very vulnerable to a false feoffee.[795]

§ 7.07(c). Equitable Intervention in the Development of Uses.

This situation naturally invited intervention by the Chancellor, acting on equitable principles to provide relief unavailable under the common law. So, early in the fifteenth century, the Court of Chancery began accepting cases in which feoffees were accused of not honoring their instructions on behalf of a *cestui que use*. The Chancery Court did not interfere with the feoffees' legal title, but did impose fines and imprisonment for misconduct of feoffees.

§ 7.07(d). Early Statutory Reform of Uses.

Legitimizing uses under equity jurisdiction did not successfully quell the abuses, and movements for statutory reform continued to gain momentum. One statute permitting a remedy against a person receiving the

---

[794] Sheldon F. Kurtz, *Moynihan's Introduction to the Law of Real Property* 229 (4th ed. 2005).

[795] *Id.* at 229-230.

profits of land,[796] and another statute enabling a cestui que use to convey a legal estate,[797] reflected a policy position that the *cestui que* use should be treated as a legal owner of the property, not merely as an equitable owner. Based on this same position, other statutes declared void certain trusts and uses of chattels to the use of a settlor (similar to a modern grantor trust),[798] declared that wardship and reliefs would be due from the *cestui que use* of military land,[799] and decreed that execution was a remedy that could be awarded against land held under a use, with the *cestui que use* permitted to wield the same defenses as were available to a legal owner.[800] When Richard III became king, after he had been enfeoffed to use by several of his associates, a statute required that such lands of which he was seised for the use of others were to vest in the *cestui que use*,[801] another example of treating the owner of the use as the legal owner. This long-emerging legislative policy of treating the equitable interest of the cestui que use as a legal interest culminated in the great Statute of Uses of 1536.

§ 7.07(e). Conveyancing of Uses.

Before the Statute of Uses, however, an extensive conveyancing practice involving uses had developed. At the time of an enfeoffment to use, the feoffer could include uses in a written document, state the uses orally, or declare the uses in the grantor's will. If the feoffer made the use known at the time of the enfeoffment, the grant was presumed to be for the use of the feoffer. A wide variety of flexible conveyancing techniques could raise a use.[802]

---

[796] 1 Hen. 7, c. 1 (1485).

[797] 1 Rich. 3, c. 1 (1484).

[798] 3 Hen. 7, c. 4 (1487).

[799] 4 Hen. 7, c. 17 (1489).

[800] 19 Hen. 7, c. 15 (1504).

[801] 1 Rich. 3, c. 5 (1484).

[802] Sheldon F. Kurtz, *Moynihan's Introduction to the Law of Real Property* 234 (4th ed. 2005).

Eventually, uses become so common that when a fee simple enfeoffment with no use was declared, with no consideration, a use was presumptively raised in the feoffor. This implied use in the feoffer was termed a "resulting use."

Grantors often conveyed uses to several persons as joint tenants; this arrangement offered some security against simultaneous dishonesty by all the feoffees and through operation of survivorship avoided questions of dower or feudal incidents when any of the joint tenants died.

Conveyancers also employed the bargain and sale to raise a use. By a conventional bargain and sale agreement, oral or written, an owner accepted monetary consideration in return for a promise to sell the land to the buyer. The promise alone effected no conveyance of the legal title, but the bargainee would be treated in equity as the beneficial owner and, by a suit in equity, the bargainee could compel the bargainor to convey legal title. This arrangement was also a natural vehicle for raising a use. By bargain and sale the owner could agree to hold the land for use or benefit of the buyer and the buyer's heirs. Again, the buyer could compel the seller to permit the buyer's use of the land, including its rents and profits. As early as the fifteenth century, a bargain and sale that had not proceeded to conveyance of the legal title was deemed to raise a use in the bargainee. For those who actually wanted no more than the use, the bargain and sale arrangement would thus be left in this suspended, uncompleted state, with the purchasers holding only equitable title in the form of a use. From the point of view of feudal tenurial doctrine, this circumstance was significant, because it meant, as mentioned above, that a grantor could raise a use without transferring seisin. Parties also found appealing the confidentiality of the transaction, because without conveyance of the legal title, there was no occasion to make a public record of the transaction.

§ 7.07(f). Enactment and Effects of the Statute of Uses (1536).

§ 7.07(f)(1). Circumstances Leading to the Enactment of the Statute of Uses.

Conveying land to uses spread widely and produced much abuse, complication, and fraud. The Statute of Uses peremptorily wiped most of this away. This, perhaps the most famous and significant English property law statute, became effective in 1536. The circumstances that finally prompted the monarchy to act against uses and force restrictive legislation through Parliament have been well-summarized by Moynihan: "The Statute of Uses is arguably the most important piece of legislation dealing with English land law, and its far-reaching consequences are still felt today. The causes which led to its enactment are to be found in an English King's need of money."[803] Maitland characterized the Statute of Uses as "forced upon an extremely unwilling Parliament by an extremely strong-willed king."[804]

§ 7.07(f)(2). The Operating Principle of the Statute of Uses.

The Statute's method was simple: it simply declared that whoever held the use would now also be deemed the holder of the legal title. Its arcane

---

[803] Sheldon F. Kurtz, *Moynihan's Introduction to the Law of Real Property* 236-237 (4th ed. 2005). A detailed discussion of the political causes leading to the Statute of Uses is in 4 William Holdsworth, *A History of English Law* 450-461 (3d ed. 1945).

[804] The quoted passage of Maitland is from Frederic William Maitland, *Equity, Also The Forms of Action at Common Law* 35 (1909), who added:

> It [the Statute of Uses] was very unpopular and was one of the excuses, if not one of the causes, of the great Catholic Rebellion known as the Pilgrimage of Grace. It at once seemed that it would deprive men of that testamentary power, that power of purchasing the repose of their souls, which they had long enjoyed. The king was the one person who had all to gain and nothing to lose by the abolition of uses.

but essential language was paraphrased by Maitland:

> Where any person or persons shall be seised of any lands or other hereditaments to the use, confidence, trust of any other person or persons, in every such case such person and persons that shall have any such use, confidence or trust in fee simple, fee tail, for term of life or for years or otherwise shall stand and be seised, deemed and adjudged in lawful seisin, estate and possession of and in the same lands and hereditaments in such like estates as they had or shall have in use.[805]

§ 7.07(f)(3). The Impact of the Statute of Uses on Conveyancing.

The Statute of Uses did not alter the traditional common law methods of conveying interests. Livery of seisin still effectively conveyed a freehold estate, a grant conveyed a vested remainder or a reversion, and an agreement and entry sufficed to convey a term of years. The common law rule that a conveyance could not create a freehold to commence at some time in the future remained in effect. The important impact of the Statute of Uses was to add several new possibilities for conveyancing.

§ 7.07(f)(3)(A). Feoffment to Uses.

The feoffment to use as practiced prior to the Statute of Uses was still a legitimate vehicle for conveyancing, but the Statute of Uses converted interests conveyed previously as uses into legal interests. This had its advantages. By a feoffment to uses before the Statute a man could convey a use directly to himself and his wife, a conveyance that, if applied to legal interests, was not permitted under common law. After the Statute of Uses, a man could convey a legal estate directly to himself and his wife by means of a feoffment to uses, which use the Statute converted into the equivalent

---

[805] Frederic William Maitland, *Equity, Also The Forms of Action at Common Law* 35 (1909).

legal interest.

§ 7.07(f)(3)(B). Resulting Uses.

Before the Statute of Uses, a resulting use in a grantor arose when a landowner conveyed to another with no consideration and no use declared. The Statute converted such a resulting use in the grantor into the equivalent legal interest, so the conveyance to uses became circular and meaningless. Conveyancers countered this result by including in conveyances an express declaration of use in the grantee, so the Statute would infer no executed use.

§ 7.07(f)(3)(C). Bargain and Sale.

Before the Statute of Uses, conveyancers employed a bargain and sale to raise a use. When the Statute converted this to a legal interest, it made the bargain and sale an appropriate method of creating a legal estate. Indeed, the Statute vested the seller's seisin in the buyer by operation of law. Because no livery of seisin was necessary after the Statute, conveyancers needed no writing for a bargain and sale, creating the possibility that oral, unrecorded, and therefore secret conveyances of freeholds could take place by bargain and sale. Such secret conveyances were deemed undesirable. Therefore, in the same year as the Statute of Uses Parliament also enacted the Statute of Enrolments,[806] requiring freehold conveyances by bargain and sale to be in writing, under seal, and to be entered or enrolled in certain public offices.

§ 7.07(f)(3)(D). Lease and Release.

To evade the public writing requirement of the Statute of Enrolments, conveyancers devised the lease and release. An owner of land would by bargain and sale convey the land to the grantee for a term of years (the lease), not required to be in writing or to be enrolled under the Statute of Enrolments, because it was not a conveyance of a freehold estate. This

---

[806] 27 Hen. 8, c. 16 (1536).

would also "release" the grantor's reversion by common law release to the termor, who thus obtained the entire estate. The Statute of Enrolments applied only to bargain and sale freehold transactions, and thus did not require the release to be in writing or be enrolled. Because the term for years was created by bargain and sale, the grantee obtained the term without entering into possession, and the interest was vested by operation of the Statute of Uses. Having not entered into possession, the grantee was eligible to accept the release of the reversion. "From approximately 1620 until 1845 the conveyance by lease and release was the most commonly used method of conveying land in England."[807]

§ 7.07(f)(3)(E). Covenant to Stand Seised.

Even after the Statute of Uses, a mere agreement by one person to hold land for the use of another did not create an enforceable use. Lacking was the element of consideration, which is why conveyances in the form of bargain and sale or feoffment to uses were enforced as raising uses that were "executed" or converted into legal interests by operation of the Statute of Uses. However, not long after enactment of the Statute, courts held that such an agreement, or covenant, to hold to the use of another, even without the traditional consideration, could be enforced as raising a use. They required the covenant to stand seised to be written, to be under seal, and to be supported by the consideration of natural love and affection (if to the use of a relative) or of marriage.[808] Once courts recognized that such a covenant to stand seised raised a use, the use was executed, or converted into a legal estate, by the Statute of Uses.

Conveyancers used the covenant to stand seised mostly to effect family settlements, or distributions, of land to other family members, because (under its particular consideration requirements) it was valid only as to parties who were related by blood or marriage. The covenant to stand seised could remain secret, because it, too, was not required to be enrolled

---

[807] Sheldon F. Kurtz, *Moynihan's Introduction to the Law of Real Property* 243-244 (4th ed. 2005).

[808] Sharrington v. Strotton, Plowden 298 (1566).

under the Statute of Enrolments.

§ 7.07(f)(3)(F). Executory Interests.

In addition to new conveyancing methods, the Statute of Uses also introduced several new types of future interests. Before the statute's enactment, the common law recognized only the future interests of reversions and remainders, and these (especially the remainders) were hedged about by limits linked to the logic of tenures and estates.[809] It was not permissible, for instance, for a grantor to convey a legal freehold estate at one moment in time, with the estate to commence as an interest until some time thereafter. Under the practice of uses prior to the Statute of Uses, however, such a conveyance was common: an owner might enfeoff land to a feoffee to the use of another, such use to not commence until the occurrence of some event in the future. The transaction was called a springing use, but when such a use was "executed" into a legal interest by the Statute of Uses, the springing use became a springing "executory" interest, such as was formerly forbidden under the common law. The feoffer, making such a conveyance after the Statute of Uses, would still hold the estate in fee simple (because the conveyance to a feoffee to use would have been ineffective), but the estate would be subject to an executory interest in the party that would formerly have held the springing use. After the Statute of Uses and upon the occurrence of the event that would have commenced the use, the executory interest would have become the fee simple interest, with no interest left in the feoffor. This conveyance could be created by means of a bargain and sale, an enfeoffment, or a covenant to stand seised.

Another future interest not possible under the common law was a conveyance of successive future interests with a gap in time between the end of one and the beginning of the next. Such a conveyance to use, however, was another variety of springing use and was possible before the Statute of Uses. An enfeoffment to the feoffee for the use of another for life, with the permanent use to go over to yet another party one year after the use for life ended, was valid. Such uses would have been "executed" by

---

[809] *See* Roe *ex dem.* Wilkinson v. Tranmer, 2 Wils. 75, 95 Eng. Rep. 694 (1757).

the Statute of Uses, so that the holder of the use for life would have a life estate, the feoffor would have a reversion for a year, and the holder of the permanent use would have an executory interest, to become a fee simple one year after the life estate ended. This conveyance could be created by means of a bargain and sale, an enfeoffment, or a covenant to stand seised.

Yet a third variety of springing use became a valid legal interest after the Statute of Uses. A conveyance in use, such as a bargain and sale, to one for a term of years and then to the heirs of another who was then living, created a contingent interest following a term of years. This is because the remaindermen could not be vested until the death of the ancestor and determination of heirship, which might be long after the end of the preceding term. Again, the Statute of Uses "executed" such springing uses into valid legal estates, so that the conveyance became an estate for years, a reversion in the grantor if necessary until heirship of another was determined, and then an executory interest in the nature of a springing use in those prospective heirs. This conveyance could be created by a bargain and sale or a covenant to stand seised.

In addition to the varieties of springing use described in the preceding paragraphs, the Statute of Uses also executed a type of "shifting" use into a valid executory interest. A conveyance to one, in use, with the use to go over to another upon the happening of a certain event, such as making a particular forbidden use of the property, was not possible under the common law. When the Statute of Uses executed the use, then the conveyance to the grantee became an estate in fee simple, subject to a shifting executory interest in another, that would ripen into a fee simple if the property were used in the forbidden way. This conveyance could be created by a bargain and sale, a covenant to stand seised, or an enfeoffment.

§ 7.07(f)(3)(G). Devises.

Before the Statute of Uses it had not been possible to devise a legal estate, except in some areas by local custom, but courts upheld a feoffment to uses declared in a will. When the Statute of Uses executed the feoffee's interest into a legal interest, that interest suddenly was no longer devisable. The Statute of Wills, enacted in 1540, placated the strong opposition to this state of affairs[810] by conferring limited powers of devise. Under these limitations, a landowner could devise any lands held under socage tenure, and up to two-thirds of lands held by knight tenure. Devisees became liable for feudal obligations as if the devisees had taken by descent. Because livery of seisin was not required for an effective devise, the common law restrictions on certain types of future interests were inapplicable; therefore, it was possible to devise springing and shifting future interests that would have been inappropriate as inter vivos conveyances of legal future interests. Such devises are executory devises and are included with inter vivos shifting and springing interests as executory interests.

§ 7.07(f)(3)(H). Contingent Remainders.

As already mentioned, common law contingent remainders were subject to destruction, if the supporting freehold estate were forfeited through tortious alienation. Under this rule of destructibility, if the holder of the life estate attempted to convey a fee simple, the attempted alienation would be treated as tortious and the life estate would be forfeited before the contingent remainder vested. Thereupon the contingent remainder was deemed destroyed.[811] When courts first recognized executory interests, judges considered those interests subject to the same rule of destructibility, but later reversed that position.[812] Common law contingent remainders, however, were still destructible, and the courts even extended the rule of destructibility to contingent remainders created by use and by devise.

§ 7.07(f)(3)(I). Uses Not Executed by the Statute of Uses.

The Statute of Uses did not convert several kinds of uses into legal estates. The Statute's wording executed into legal interests only uses derived from one who was seised of the land. Because seisin applied only

---

[810] 32 Hen. 8, c. 1 (1540).

[811] *See, e.g.*, Archer's Case, 1 Co. Rep. 66b, 76 Eng. Rep. 146 (1597).

[812] Pells v. Brown, Cro. Jac. 590 (1620).

to freehold estates, if one held a non-freehold estate to the use of another, that use was not executed. Uses raised on an estate held for a term of years, or on personal property such as chattels or a chose in action, remained unexecuted.

If a person was seised to the use of another, who held to the use of yet another (a so-called use limited on a use) the courts held the second use void even before the Statute of Uses was enacted. After the Statute of Uses, courts considered the second use unexecuted, and in equity void, so no interest at all passed under the second use. Sometime in the late seventeenth century,[813] after enactment of the statute abolishing tenures in 1660,[814] equity courts began to uphold a use upon a use.[815] This in turn once again enabled landholders to split their interests between legal and equitable titles, and the second use came to be commonly referred to as a trust. The holders of the first uses, executed into legal interests, became the trustees, not only holders of the legal title but bound to act in the interests of the trust owners or beneficiaries.

A few years after enactment of the Statute of Uses, courts held still another category of uses exempt from execution into legal interests. These were the so-called active uses, created by a conveyance to use with the grantee to perform affirmative duties on behalf of the *cestui que use*. Typically, such affirmative duties might consist of collecting and paying to the *cestui que use* the rents and profits from the property, or conveying the property to another at the direction of the *cestui que use*. This exemption for active uses is not in the wording of the Statute of Uses, but was invoked by judicial decision.

The equitable estates arising out of unexecuted active uses gradually merged with the unexecuted uses upon use and appeared in the 18th century as early forms of the modern trust.

---

[813] The earliest case acknowledging the validity of the second use is the 1676 case of Grubb v. Gwillim, 1 Lord Nottingham's Chancery Cases 347, No. 487 (Selden Society, Vol. 73, 1957).

[814] Tenures Abolition Act, 12 Car. 2, c. 24 (1660).

[815] A. W. B. Simpson, *A History of the Land Law* 198-207 (2d ed. 1986).

§ 7.08. Bibliography.

Books

Adams, Henry, et al., *Essays in Anglo-Saxon Law* (1905).
Amato, di Montecassino, History of the Normans. (Prescott N. Dunbar, trans., 2004).
Anderson, J. Stuart, *Lawyers and the Making of English Land Law, 1832-1940* (1992).
Attenborough, F. L., ed. & trans., *The Laws of the Earliest English Kings* (1922).
Baker, Timothy, *The Normans* (1966).
Barlow, Frank., *Edward the Confessor* (1970).
Barlow, Frank (ed. and trans.), *The Life of King Edward* (1962).
Bean, J.M.W., *The Decline of English Feudalism 1215-1540* (1968).
Bell, Andrew, *A History of Feudalism, British and Continental* (1863).
Bennett, Henry Stanley, *Life on the English Manor: a Study of Peasant Conditions 1150-1400* (1971).
Biancalana, Joseph, *The Fee Tail and Common Recovery in Medieval England* (2001).
Blair, John, *Early Medieval Surrey: Landholding, Church and Settlement Before 1300* (1991).
Blount, T., *Tenures of Land and Customs of Manors* (1679).
Brondsted, Johannes, *The Vikings.* (Kalle Skov, trans., 1965).
Brown, R. Allen, *Origins of English Feudalism* (1973).
Brown, R. Allen, *The Normans* (1984).
Brown, R. Allen, *The Normans and the Norman Conquest* (1969).
Brunner, Heinrich, *The Sources of English Law (*Ernst Freund, trans.) (1908).
Byrne, Joseph Patrick, *Daily Life During the Black Death* (2006).
Cairn, John W. and Grant McLeod, eds., *The Dearest Birth Right of the People of England: The Jury in the History of the Common Law* (2002).
Cecil, Evelyn, *Primogeniture* (2009).
Coulborn, Rushton, *Feudalism in History* (1965).
Dalrymple, John, Sir, *An Essay Towards a General History of Feudal Propertv in Great Britain* (1758).
Darby, H. C., *Domesday England* (1977).
de Coulanges, Fustel, *The Origin of Property in Land* (1927).
Digby, K.E., *An Introduction to the History of the Law of Real Property with Original Authorities* (1897).
Douglas, David C, *The Norman Achievement, 1050-1100* (1969).
Douglas, David C., *William the Conqueror: the Norman Impact upon England* (1964).
Erskine, R. W. H., and Ann Williams, *The Story of Domesday Book* (2003).
Fleming, Robin, *Domesday Book and the Law: Society and Legal Custom in Early Medieval England* (1998).
Ganshof, Francois Louis, *Feudalism* (Philip Grierson trans., 3d ed. 1996).
Green, Judith A., *The Aristocracy of Norman England* (1997).
Helmholz, R. H., *Marriage Litigation in Medieval England* (1974).
Holdsworth, William Searle, *A History of English Law (*3d ed. 1922).
Holdsworth, William Searle, *An Historical Introduction to the Land Law* (repr. 2004).
Hudson, John, *Land, Law and Lordship in Anglo-Norman England* (1997).

Hudson, John, *The Formation of the English Common Law: Law and Society in England from the Norman Conquest to Magna Carta* (1996).
Jessel, Christopher, *The Law of the Manor* (1998).
Jewell, Helen M., *Women in Late Medieval and Reformation Europe, 1200-1550* (2007).
John, E., *Land Tenure in Early England* (1960).
Kay, J. M., *Medieval English Conveyances* (2009).
Keeton, George W., *The Norman Conquest and the Common Law* (1966).
Larson, P. L., *Conflict and Compromise in the Late Medieval Countryside: Lords and Peasants in Durham, 1349-1400* (2006).
Kenny, C. S., and P. M. Laurence, *Two Essays on the Law of Primogeniture* (1878).
Klindt-Jensen, Ole, *The World of the Vikings* (1970).
Kurtz, Sheldon F., *Moynihan's Introduction to the Law of Real Property* (4th ed. 2005).
Le Patourel, John, *The Norman Empire* (1976).
Liebermann, F., *Die Gesetze der Angelsachsen* (1906).
Lindsay, Jack, *The Normans and their World* (1973).
Littleton, Thomas, Sir, *Lyttleton, His Treatise of Tenures* (1841).
Lobban, Michael, *The Common Law and English Jurisprudence, 1760-1850* (1991).
Maitland, F. W., *The Constitutional History of England* (1968).
Maitland, F. W., *Equity, Also: The Forms of Action at Common Law* (1909).
Marvin, William Perry, *Hunting Law and Ritual in Medieval English Literature* (2006).
McSheffrey, Shannon, *Marriage, Sex, and Civil Culture in Late Medieval London* (2006).
Milsom, S. F. C., *A Natural History of the Common Law* (2003).
Milsom, S. F. C., *The Legal Framework of English Feudalism* (1976).
Mulder-Bakker, Anneke B. and Jocelyn Wogan-Browne, eds., *Household, Women, and Christianities In Late Antiquity and the Middle Ages* (2006).
Munzer, Stephen R., *A Theory of Property* (1990).
Nasse, E., *On the Agricultural Community of the Middle Ages, and the Inclosures of the Sixteenth Century in England* (Henry Aim Ouvry, trans., 2d ed. 1872).
Nelson, William, *Lex Maneriorum: Or, the Law and Customs of England, Relating to Manors and Lords of Manors, Their Stewards, Deputies, Tenants, and Others the Whole Being a Methodical Collection of the Cases Dispersed in the Several Volumes of the Law Relating to Copyhold Estates, and to Every Thing Depending on That Tenure. To Which Is Added, an Appendix of All the Modern Entries of Declarations, Pleas, Demurrers, Issues, Special Verdicts, Writs of Recordari, Certiorari, C., Relating to the Said Cases* (1726).
Neveux, Francois, *A Brief history of the Normans : The Conquests That Changed the Face of Europe* (Howard Curtis, trans., 2008).
Noy, William, *The Principal Grounds and Maxims: with an Analysis; and a Dialogue and Treatise of the Laws of England; and on Tenures, Estates, Heriditaments, and Chattels, Real and Personal; and in What Manner They May Be Recovered and Conveyed* (1821).
Petersen, Craig A., *The Evolution of Tenures in England* (1983).
Pollock, Frederick, *The Expansion of the Common Law* (2009).
Pollock, Frederick, and Frederic William Maitland, *The History of English Law Before the Time of Edward I* (2d ed. 1909).
Plucknett, Theodore F. T., *A Concise History of the Common Law* (5th ed. 1956).
Plucknett, Theodore F. T., *Studies in English Legal History* (1983).
Raban, Sandra. *Mortmain Legislation and the English Church, 1279-1500* (1982).

Raftis, J. A., *Peasant Economic Development Within the English Manorial System* (1996).
Razi, Zvi, *Medieval Society and the Manor Court* (1996).
Robertson, Agnes Jane (ed. and trans.), *The Laws of the Kings of England from Edmund to Henry I* (1925).
Shetelig, Haakon, and Hjalmar Falk, *Scandinavian Archaeology* (Eric Valentine Gordon, trans., 1937).
Simpson, A. W. B., *A History of the Land Law* (2d ed. 1986).
Simpson, Stanhope Rowton, *Land Law and Registration* (1976).
Stephenson, Carl, *Mediaeval Feudalism* (1956).
Stenton, Doris M., ed., *Rolls of the Justices in Eyre for Gloucestershire, Warwickshire and Staffordshire 1221-1222* (1940).
Stenton, Frank Merry, *The First Century of English Feudalism, 1066-1166* (1961).
Stenton, Frank Merry, *Anglo-Saxon England* (1943).
Stubbs, William, *Lectures on Early English History* (Arthur Hassall, ed., 1906)
Stubbs, William, ed., *Select Charters and Other Illustrations of English Constitutional History* (1895).
Sturluson, Snorri, *The Heimskringla: A History of the Norse Kings* (1907).
Swanton, Michael (ed. and trans.), *The Anglo-Saxon Chronicle* (1996).
Tabuteau, Emily Zack, *Ralph v. Turner, Judges, Administrators and the Common Law in Angevin England* (1994).
Thorne, Samuel Edmund, *Essays in English Legal History* (1985).
Tiffany, Herbert Thorndike, *The Law of Real Property and Other Interests in Land* (1920).
Turner, Ralph V., *The English Judiciary in the Age of Glanvill and Bracton, C.1176-1239* (2008).
Van Caenegem, R. C., *The Birth of the English Common Law* (2d ed. 1988).
Vinogradoff, Paul, *The Growth of the Manor* (1920).
Vinogradoff, Paul, *English Society in the Eleventh Century: Essays in English Mediaeval History* (1908).
Vitalis, Ordericus, *Ecclesiastical History of Orderic Vitalis* (Marjorie Chibnal, ed. and trans., (1969).
Webb, Sidney, *The Manor and the Borough* (1963).
West, Francis, *The Justiciarship in England, 1066-1232* (1966).
William of Poitiers, *Gesta Guillelmi ducis Normannorum et regis Anglorum* (R. Foreville, ed. and trans., 1952).
Williams, Joshua, *The Seisin of the Freehold* (2008).
Whitelock, Dorothy, *The Beginnings of English Society* (1952).
Wright, Nancy E., Margaret W. Ferguson and A.R. Buck, eds., *Women, Property, and the Letters of the Law in Early Modern England* (2004).

Chapters in Books

Dudo, "De Moribus et Actis Primorum Normanniae Ducum," in Andreas Duchesnius, *Historiae Normannorum Scriptores Antiqui* (1619).
"Select Passages From the Annals Ascribed to Florence of Worcester," in D. C. Douglas and Andrew Browning, eds., *English Historical Documents* (1953).
"The Coronation Charter of Henry I (5 August 1100)," in D. C. Douglas and Andrew Browning, eds., *English Historical Documents* (1953).
"The Laws of William the Conqueror," in D. C. Douglas and Andrew Browning, eds., *English Historical Documents* (1953).
Thomas, David A., Ch. 4, "The Growth of the English Common Law of Real Property," in 1 David A. Thomas, *Thompson on Real Property, Second Thomas Edition* (2009).

Thomas, David A., Ch. 70, "Waste," in 8 David A. Thomas, *Thompson on Real Property, Second Thomas Edition* (2005).
Vinogradoff, Paul, "The Transfer of Land," in Paul Vinogradoff, *The Collected Papers: With a Memoir. Jurisprudence*, Vol. 2 (1928).
Williams, Ann, "The Land of the Conqueror," in *Domesday: 900 Years of England's Norman Heritage* (1986).
Wormald, Patrick, "The Burhs, in James Campbell et al., eds., *The Anglo-Saxons* (1982).
"Writ of William I Concerning Spiritual and Temporal Courts," in D. C. Douglas and Andrew Browning, eds., *English Historical Documents* (1953).
"XIII. Earl Simon's Charter introducing the law of Primogeniture into Leicester, instead of inheritance by the youngest son, in Mary Bateson, ed., *Records of the Borough of Leicester* (1899).

Articles

Adams, George Burton, "The Origin of the Common Law, 34 *Yale L.J.* 115 (Nov. 1924).
Becker, David M., "Eroding the Common Law Paradigm for Creation of Property Interests and the Hidden Cost of Law Reform," 83 *Wash. U. L.Q.* 773 (2005).
Bordwell, Percy, "The Common-Law Scheme of Estates and the Remainder," 34 *Iowa L. Rev.* 401 (March 1949).
Boyle, James, "The Second Enclosure Movement and the Construction of the Public Domain," 6 *Law & Contemp. Probs.* 33 (Winter/Spring 2003).
Brake, Merle E., "The Beginnings of Property Law-Part I: Feudalism's Contributions," 16 *U. Det. L.J.* 1 (Nov. 1952).
Briggs, Chris, "Manor Court Procedures, Debt Litigation Levels, and Rural Credit Provision in England, c. 1290-1380," 24 *Law & Hist. Rev.* 519 (Fall, 2006).
Bryan, Frederick C., "Origin of English Land Tenures," 40 *Am. L. Rev.* 9 (1906).
Brody, Burton F., "Anglo-Saxon Contract Law: A Social Analysis," 19 *DePaul L. Rev.* 270 (Autumn 1969).
Brown, Desmond H., "Historical Perspective on the Statute of Uses," 9 *Man. L.J.* 409 (1978)
Carnahan, Wendell, "Introduction to the Statute of Uses," 24 *Ky. L.J.* 172 (Nov. 1935).
Chaplin, H. W., "The Story of Mortgage Law," 4 *Harv. L. Rev.* 1 (April 1890).
Douglas, David C., "Rollo of Normandy," 57 *The English Historical Review* 417 (Oct. 1942).
Douglas, David C., "The Earliest Norman Counts, 61 *The English Historical Review* 129 (May 1946).
Douglas, David C., "The Rise of Normandy," 33 *Proceedings of the British Academy* 101 (1947).
Elton, Charles, "Early English Land Tenures," 4 *L. Q. Rev.* 276 (Jan. 1888).
English, Joseph F., "Concurrent Estates in Real Property I," 11 *Cath. U. L. Rev.* 63 (Jan. 1962).
English, Joseph F., "Concurrent Estates in Real Property II," 12 *Cath. U. L. Rev.* 1 (1963).
Gallanis, T. P., "The Future of Future Interests," 60 *Wash. & Lee L. Rev.* 513 (Spring 2003).
Haskins, George L., "Curtesy at Common Law: Historical Development," 29 *B.U. L. Rev.* 228 (Jan. 1949).
Haskins, George L., "The Development of Common Law Dower," 62 *Harv. L. Rev.* 42 (Nov. 1948).

Hazeltine, Harold D., "The Gage of Land in Medieval England," 18 *Harv. L. Rev.* 36 (Nov.1904).
Hazeltine, Harold D., "The Laws of the Anglo-Saxons," 29 *L. Q. Rev.* 387 (Jan. 1913).
Helmholz, R. H., "The Early Enforcement of Uses," 79 *Colum L. Rev. 1503* (Jan. 1979).
Higham, N. J., "The Domesday Survey: Context and Purpose," 78 *History* 7 (Feb. 1993).
Hollister, Warren C., "The Norman Conquest and the Genesis of English Feudalism," 66 *The American Historical Review* 641 (Apr., 1961).
Holmes, O. W., "Early English Equity," 1 *L. Q. Rev.* 162 (1885).
Holt, J. C., "Politics and Property in Early Medieval England: A Rejoinder," 65 *Past & Present*, 127 (Nov. 1974)
Hulsebosch, Daniel J., "The Ancient Constitution and the Expanding Empire: Sir Edward Coke's British Jurisprudence," 21 *Law & Hist. Rev.* 439 (Fall, 2003).
Hyams, Paul R., "The Origins of a Peasant Land Market in England, 23 *The Economic History Review, New Series*, No. 1 (Apr. 1970).
Lifshitz, Felice, "Dudo's Historical Narrative and the Norman Succession of 996," 20 *Journal of Medieval History* 101 (June 1994).
Lobingier, Charles Sumner, "The Rise and Fall of Feudal Law," 18 *Cornell L. Q.* 192 (1933).
Lund, Thomas, "Some Interesting Medieval Dower Cases," 37 *U. Tol. L. Rev.* 659 (Spring 2006).
Maitland, F. W., "The Materials for English Legal History," 4 *Political Science Quarterly* 496 (Sep. 1889).
Miles, Maria Funk, "The Value of a Woman: A Comparison of the Laws and the Traditions of Divorce in Medieval Europe and Modern America " 15 *UCLA Women's L.J.* 139 (Fall 2006).
Oosterhoff, A. H., "The Law of Mortmain: An Historical and Comparative Review," 27 *U. Toronto L.J.* 257 (1977).
Orth, John V., "Tenancy by the Entirety: The Strange Career of the Common-Law Marital Estate," 1997 *BYU L. Rev.* 35 (1997).
Orth John V., "The Mystery of the Rule in Shelley's Case," 7 *Green Bag 2d* 45 (Autumn, 2003).
Pollock, Frederick, "Anglo-Saxon Law," 8 *The English Historical Review* 239 (Apr. 1893).
Rabinowitz, Jacob J., "The Story of the Mortgage Retold, 94 *U. Pa. L. Rev. 94* (Oct. 1945).
Schecter, Frank I., "Popular Law and Common Law in Medieval England," 28 *Colum. L. Rev.* 269 (March 1928).
Senn, Mark A., "English Life and Law in the Time of the Black Death," 38 *Real Prop., Prob. and Trust J.* 507 (Fall, 2003).
Siedel, George J., "For Sale: The Manorial System," 68 *A.B.A. J.* 442 (1982).
Silberbogen, Rebecca E., "Does the Dissolution of Covenant Marriages Mirror Common Law England's Subordination of Women?" 5 *Wm. & Mary J. Women and the Law* 207 (Winter, 1998).
Smith, David T., "The Statute of Uses: A Look at Its Evolution and Demise," 18 *W. Res. L. Rev.* 40 (Nov. 1966).
Smith, Llinos Beverly, "The Gage and the Land Market in Late Medieval Wales," 29 *The Economic History Review (New Series)* 537 (Nov. 1976).
Spitzer, Ann L., "Joint Tenancy with Right of Survivorship: A Legacy of Thirteenth Century England," 16 *Tex. Tech L. Rev.* 629 (1985).
Stephenson, Carl, "The Origin and Significance of Feudalism," 46 *The American Historical Review* 788 (Jul. 1941).

Sweet, Charles, "Seisin," 12 *L. Q. Rev.* 239 (Jan. 1896).
Thomas, David A., "Anglo-American Land Law: Diverging Developments from a Shared History, Part 1: A Shared History," 34 *Real Prop. Prob. & Tr. J.* 143 (Spring 1999).
Thomas, David A., "Origins of the Common Law Part III: Common Law under the Early Normans," 1986 *BYU L. Rev.* 109.
Thorndike, J. L., "Contingent Remainders," 30 *Harv. L. Rev.* 226 (Nov. 1916).
Walsh, William F., "Development of the Title and Lien Theories of Mortgages," 9 *N.Y.U. L. Q.* Rev. 280 (Sept. 1931).
White, Stephen D., "English Feudalism and its Origins," 19 *Am. J. Legal Hist.* 138 (1975).
Williams, T. Cyprian, "History of English Law," 7 *Jurid. Rev.* 260 (1895).
Wormald, Patrick, "Frederic William Maitland and the Earliest English Law," 16 *Law & Hist. Rev.* 1 (Spring 1998).

Statutes

De Mercatoribus, 13 Edw. 1 (1285).
Statute de Finibus Levatis, 27 Edw. 1,Stat. I (1299).
Statutes of Gloucester.
Statute of Staples, 27 Edw. 3, c. 9 (1353).
Statute of Westminster I.
Statute of Westminster II.
Tenures Abolition Act, 12 Car. 2, c. 24 (1660).
1 Hen. 7, c. 1 (1485).
1 Rich. 3, c. 1 (1484).
1 Rich. 3, c. 5 (1484).
1 Rich. 3, c. 7 (1484).
3 Hen. 7, c. 4 (1487).
3 Edw. 1, c. 48 (1275).
4 Hen. 7, c. 17 (1489).
4 Hen. 7, c. 24 (1489).
4 & 5 Anne, c. 3, s. 21 (1706).
6 Edw. 1, c. 3 (1278).
7 Edw. 1, Stat. 2 (1279).
13 Edw. 1, c. 1 (1285).
13 Edw. 1, c. 3 (1285).
15 Rich. 2, c. 5(4) (1391).
19 Hen. 7, c. 15 (1504).
21 Rich. 2, c. 3 (1397).
27 Hen. 8, c. 16 (1536).
31 Hen. 8, c. 1 (1539).
32 Hen. 8, c. 1 (1540).
32 Hen. 8, c. 32 (1540).
34 Edw. 3, c. 16 (1361).
50 Edw. 3, c. 6 (1376).
52 Hen. 3, c. 6 (1267).

Cases

Archer's Case, 1 Co.Rep. 66b, 76 Eng.Rep. 146 (1597).
Belyng v. Anon., Y.B. 5 Edw. 2, Easter Term, No. 2 (1312).
Grubb v. Gwillim, 1 Lord Nottingham's Chancery Cases 347, No. 487 (Selden Society, Vol. 73, 1957).

Neuton v. Staynford, Y.B. 5 Edw. 2, Michaelmas Term, No. 24 (1311).
Pells v. Brown, Cro. Jac. 590 (1620).
Roe ex dem. Wilkinson v. Tranmer, 2 Wils. 75, 95 Eng. Rep. 694 (1757).
Sharrington v. Strotton, Plowden 298 (1566).
Y.B. 2 Edw. 2, 4 (1309).
Y.B. 5 Edw. 2, No. 78 (1311).
Y.B. 11 Rich. 2, 283 288 (1388).
Y.B. 14 & 15 Edw. 3 (Rolls Series), 34 (1341).
Y.B. 17 & 18 Edw. 3 (Rolls Series), 174 (1343).
Y.B. 18 & 19 Edw. 2 (Rolls Series), 378 (1345).
Y.B. 14 Edw. 3 (Rolls Series), 198, 200 (1341).
Y.B. 18 & 19 Edw. 2 (Rolls Series), 378 (1345).
Y.B. 20 & 21 Edw. 1 (Rolls Series), 32 (1292).
Y.B. 20 & 21 Edw. 1 (Rolls Series), 256 (1292).
Y.B. 32 & 33 Edw. 1 (Rolls Series), 328 (1304).
Y.B. 32 & 33 Edw. 1 (Rolls Series), 43 (1304).
Y.B. 33 & 35 Edw. 1 (Rolls Series), 388 (1306).
Y.B. 38 Edw. 3, Michaelmas Term, 26b (1364).

Other

Bracton, fol. 13.
Bracton, fol. 17.
Bracton, fol. 17b.
Bracton, fol. 18.
Bracton, fols. 20, 268 269.
Bracton, fol. 33b.
Bracton fol. 41.
Bracton, fol. 56b.
Bracton, fol. 68b.
Bracton, fol. 72.
Bracton, fols. 72, 77b.
Bracton, fol. 80.
Bracton, fol. 80b.
Bracton, fol. 81b.
Bracton, fol. 92.
Bracton, fol. 93.
Bracton, fols. 96, 97.
Glanvill, VI, 1.
Glanvill, VII, 1.
Glanvill, VII, 9 and 10
Glanvill, VII, 1.
Glanvill, VII, 18.
Glanvill, VIII.
Glanvill, IX, 4.
Glanvill, X, 6.
Glanvill, X, 8.
Glanvill, X, 11.
Glanvill, XII, 25.
Bracton, fol. 208.
Bracton, fols. 242b, 262, 270
Bracton, fol. 321b.
Bracton's Note Book, pl. 86 (1220).
Bracton's Note Book, pl. 101 (1220).

Bracton's Note Book, pl. 125 (1222).
Bracton's Note Book, pl. 147 (1222).
Bracton's Note Book, pl. 168 (1222).
Bracton's Note Book, pl. 316 (1229).
Bracton's Note Book, pl. 363 (1229).
Bracton's Note Book, pl. 524 (1231).
Bracton's Note Book, pl. 778 (1233).
Bracton's Note Book, pl. 815 (1233).
Bracton's Note Book, pl. 851 (1234).
Bracton's Note Book, pl. 853 (1234).
Bracton's Note Book, pl. 992 (1224).
Bracton's Note Book, pl. 1035 (1225).
Bracton's Note Book, pl. 1223 (1238).
Bracton's Note Book, pl. 1334 (1217).
Bracton's Note Book, pl. 1616 (1223).
Bracton's Note Book, pl. 1619 (1223).

Chapter 8

English Land Law After the Middle Ages[816]

SYNOPSIS

[816] The content of this chapter was originally written by the author, and some content was drawn or reprinted from Vol. 1 of Thompson on Real Property.

Chapter 8. English Land Law After the Middle Ages

§ 8.01. Introduction to the Chapter.

This chapter resumes the discussion of developments in English land law commenced in Chapter 7. In that chapter, those developments were described through the middle of the 16th century, after the principal effects of the Statute of Uses (1536) had been made manifest. This chapter describes how, throughout the 16th, 17th, and 18th centuries, landowners, lawyers and legislators in England struggled with the task of fitting the feudal framework of land law to the many new features of the emerging modern English state. The adaptations were piecemeal and tended to obscure and only partially correct the archaic aspects of land law, rather than reform or remove them. By the time of the really meaningful statutory reforms in the 19th century, land law, like other aspects of English law, had become exceedingly and unnecessarily complex, trying to respond to new elements in English society while perpetuating traditional rules from the ancient and honored past. This chapter concludes by relating how 19th- and 20th-century statutory reforms effectively transformed English land law, eradicating most vestiges of medievalism and creating a modern and model regime of land law for the original common law state.

§ 8.02. Summary of Early Developments in the Common Law of Land.

Although the elements of land law in England after the Norman Conquest were generally Anglo-Saxon in substance, the extent to which those elements entered into the *common* law was almost entirely a result of Norman activity. The Normans are sometimes credited with introducing feudalism into England, yet feudal characteristics of land law were present among the Anglo-Saxons, at least in incipient form. Likewise, the administration of law and custom regarding land was largely left to the local institutions of government, including the local courts, and these institutions were Anglo-Saxon in origin and character.

§ 8.02(a). Early Norman Influence on English Legal Developments.

The Norman impact, by contrast, struck at the apex of the feudal system. William the Conqueror assumed the position as the only allodial landowner in England, the only holder of land who did not hold of any superior lord, and simultaneously he was the ultimate lord of all other landholders in England. Although he carefully followed feudal strictures and observances, essential to his claim of royal legitimacy, during his lifetime he exercised the lord's power over the large majority of English land, often by declaring forfeitures of lands held by those Anglo-Saxon aristocrats who had unsuccessfully opposed him.[817] Near the end of his reign he reinforced his position at the peak of English feudalism by obtaining an oath of fealty from all landholders, whether or not they held directly of him.

The Norman monarchy early and directly asserted itself into local legal machinery through the office of the sheriff. The Anglo-Norman sheriff, more subordinate and responsive to the king than his Anglo-Saxon predecessor had been, acquired expanded judicial functions, both in bringing cases before royal courts and in sometimes even hearing and deciding cases.

In addition to influencing legal activity in the shires and villages through the sheriffs, the Norman monarchs also gradually developed legal functions for the royal court. Initially the royal court was simply a group of servants who occasionally performed ministerial functions of a judicial nature and sometimes witnessed royal writs. This group was augmented from time to time by the king's closest or most powerful tenants-in-chief, who would discuss important issues and, acting collectively, sometimes

---

[817] By the time of the Domesday Survey in 1086 only two Anglo-Saxon lords of high rank were left in England.

issue writs and judgments. At the three annual religious festivals all the available tenants-in-chief came together in the royal council to hear important cases.

Also, at the Easter and Michaelmas gatherings, the king's chief justiciar audited financial returns from local officers and resolved disputes connected with those accounts. William II (1087-1100) also appointed other justiciars to perform similar financial and judicial duties in the shires. These same local justiciars could also try cases in the shires between tenants-in-chief. A century after the conquest, during the reign of Henry II (1154-1189), the monarch replaced local justiciars with itinerant or traveling justices. With their broad jurisdiction and sometimes explicit instructions, these justices enlarged the influence of the monarchy in legal matters, and at the same time brought more consistency to the rules of law being applied in various localities.

Complaints about lack of restraint in some traveling justices exercising their broad jurisdiction led to the appointment of five judges to sit as a permanent royal court. At first this royal court was expected to travel with the king, but by the time of Magna Carta in 1215 (See Illustration 28) the court was required to remain at Westminster, and was eventually known as the Court of Common Pleas. When some matters were considered too weighty for this court, the cases were referred to a group of counselors close to the king, which group became a separate court known as the Court of King's Bench. During the reign of Edward I (1239-1307), the Court of King's Bench officially separated from the king's council.

The centralizing of judicial power in the monarchy and the consequent reduction of particularized local legal customs to broader, more uniform principles were key factors in the formation of the common law.

From the beginning the Normans, through a decree from William the Conqueror, promised the English that they could "have and hold the law of King Edward in respect of their lands and all their possessions, with the addition of those decrees I have ordained for the welfare of the English people."[818] After a time of disorder following the Conqueror's death, Henry I again promised to restore to the people "the law of King Edward together with such emendations to it as my father made with the counsel of his barons."[819]

Illustration 28. Originally issued in 1215, the Magna Carta was revised and reissued numerous times during the following decades, and one of the later editions is part of English statutory law. The version pictured here from the British Library is one of four of the 1215 version held in England. The document's enduring significance is its imposition of certain limits defined by law on the monarch's royal powers. Many of those restraints on royal power dealt directly with rights in land.

But even this foundation of Anglo-Saxon law and William's persistence in his claim to be the legitimate successor of Edward, the last Anglo-Saxon king, could not mask the profound changes the Normans imposed on English landholding practices. Under Edward, no doubt much land, especially bookland, had been held free of obligation to the monarch, subject only to the customary duties of military service, road building and fortress repair. At first William asserted ownership only over the lands of

[818] "The Laws of William the Conqueror," 2 *English Historical Documents* 399-400 (D. C. Douglas, ed., 1953).

[819] "The 'Coronation Charter' of Henry I (5 August 1100)," 2 *English Historical Documents* 400-02 (D. C. Douglas, ed., 1953).

those Anglo-Saxons who had actively opposed him, but after suppressing a series of rebellions beginning in 1069, he took huge additional tracts of land and asserted ownership over all English land; eventually he replaced almost all of the principal English landholders with Norman barons owing fealty directly to the monarch.

§ 8.02(b). Introduction of Feudal Tenures.

Those who held land directly of the king, called tenants in chief, almost always owed some sort of military service, so the rights of landholding they enjoyed could be referred to as military tenure. The characteristics of military tenure endured in Anglo-Norman land law long after this type of military service ceased to serve the monarch's needs. Leading landholders parceled out their obligations of knight service to others through subinfeudation, and basic units of land parcels sufficient to support a mounted warrior were referred to as knight's fees. The resulting hierarchy of landowners, under military and other forms of tenure, placed all landholders other than the king either in the relation of tenant to a lord, or lord to a tenant, or most commonly in both relationships simultaneously, and often in multiple dual relationships. These tenurial relationships imposed on both parties several rights and duties called incidents, and these feudal incidents eventually became the rights and duties that attached to the land itself.

As the land became the means of securing loyalty, protection and services between landholders, it also continued in its ancient role as the principal source of wealth. Land was the "glue" holding together family dynasties and political and social relationships, so landholding needed to be stabilized, assuring that feudal obligations would be met and that future generations of great families could continue their high status. However, as the main source of prosperity in an active economy, land also needed to be freely transferable if its full value were to be realized, even though such transferability could jeopardize the stability of feudal and family resources.

These conflicting impulses were the driving forces behind development of English land law in the Middle Ages. Feudal incidents institutionalized in the early law were constantly challenged by innovative conveyancing practices and new forms of landholding that threatened or even overtly evaded the most onerous feudal obligations. Many, if not most, of the feudal incidents represented sources of income and thus continued as part of the land law long after the society that spawned them had been succeeded by other relationships and values. Even after statutes finally abolished the most persistent feudal incidents, many of the incidents' underlying philosophical values and presumptions carried on into elements of modern land law that remained essentially feudal in origin and purpose.

§ 8.02(c). Incidents or Characteristics of Tenure.

In military tenures, the most important feudal incidents may be summarized as follows:

Homage: A tenant under homage was bound to do nothing that would injure the lord or the land, and likewise the lord was so obligated toward the tenant.

Wardship: In a Norman change from Anglo-Saxon practice, the lord, and not the mother, took custody of a minor tenant's land (a lucrative privilege, in most cases) until the ward came of age. The change was prompted by feudal values: the lord was bound by homage to act fairly; the mother was thought to be less reliable because she could presumably remarry and shift loyalty from the minor to the new husband.

Marriage: The lord had a right to grant or withhold approval for the remarriage of a widow or the marriage of a daughter. In practice, this approval was available for a price and thus also became a source of revenue.

Aids: A lord could require financial or other aid from a tenant on important or exigent occasions, typically to ransom the lord, to knight the lord's oldest son, or to celebrate the marriage of the lord's oldest daughter. The incident of aids invited abuse simply because it was always a potential source of revenue.

Relief: The lord's permission for the heir of a deceased tenant to continue the tenancy was called relief, was obtained by payment, and was also an important source of revenue. When custom fixed the amount of relief payments, inheritability of the tenancy was effectively assured.

From this brief summary it can be seen that feudal incidents of military tenures were economically significant and would not be lightly surrendered by their claimants, even if their original purposes no longer pertained. Conversely, those upon whom the incidents were imposed became all the more eager to escape them when the incidents became mere money charges without contemporary purpose or function.

Tenures other than military tenures developed their own lists of incidents, frequently quite similar to the incidents of military tenure. These other tenures included the serjeanty tenures, usually requiring a form of personal service to the royal court, tenure in burgage for some lands in the towns and boroughs, and tenure in free alms or frankalmoign, for some lands given to the church.

All lands not held under these tenures or military tenure were considered to be held in free socage tenure. Freed of the most burdensome incidents of military tenure, free socage tenure eventually became the great residual free tenure and the tenure of choice; usually the socage tenants were bound only to pay rent or perform labor services. If a substantial lord held in socage tenure, required labor services would be performed by the lord's own tenants on the land.

The large majority of the medieval English population consisted of "unfree" agricultural peasants, or villeins, who were more or less bound to their land and rendered agricultural labor services in return for their small landholdings. Their obligations were generally fixed by custom, but the precise work they would do from day to day remained uncertain, so these villein tenures were termed "unfree."[820] No strict correlation existed

---

[820] The relationship of unfree tenure to uncertainty of daily labor was explained by Pollock and Maitland as follows:

> If the labour services are "uncertain," the tenure is unfree; and it

between unfree tenure and unfree social status. As marks of unfree status many villein tenants were required to pay the merchet, the lord's leave for various activities, and the tallage, a form of tax on persons, in amounts and on occasions as defined variously by local custom. However, many villeins were not under those obligations.

§ 8.02(d). Duration of Tenures Under the System of Estates.

§ 8.02(d)(1). Duration Extended by Inheritability.

These free and unfree tenures, with their respective incidents and privileges, could be held under various arrangements as to duration, known as estates. Estates emerged from developing rules about whether any of the tenures could be freely inherited or alienated. Inheritability of certain tenures arose earliest, granted on payment of a fixed sum relief to obtain the lord's permission for a deceased tenant's heir to continue in the tenancy. Once it was recognized for military tenures, inheritability spread to other tenures.

§ 8.02(d)(2). Tension Between Inheritability and Alienability.

Recognition of inheritability necessarily implied rights in the heirs of

---

> is a test which condemns as unfree the great bulk of the tenures which obliged men to perform any considerable amount of agricultural labour for their lord, because, however minutely some particulars of those services may be defined, there is generally a spacious room left for the play of the lord's will. Thus the test roughly coincides with another: labour service is not necessarily unfree, but a service which consists of much labour, of labour to be done all year round, is almost of necessity unfree; for almost of necessity the tenant will be bound to obey, within wide limits, whatever commands the lord or the lord's bailiff may give him.

Frederick Pollock and Frederic William Maitland, *The History of English Law Before the Time of Edward I* 372 (2d ed. 1909).

a landholder, and such rights posed some obstacle to the free alienability of land. While land was not frequently bought and sold during the early Middle Ages, gift transfers to the church were common and often raised questions about residual rights in the donor's heirs. Consequently, before making gifts donors often obtained consents for such transfers from the donor's prospective heirs.

Eventually, the spreading practice of primogeniture (the rule that only the oldest son would inherit the patrimonial tenancy) mitigated the risks to fulfillment of feudal obligations posed by sharing of tenancies among multiple heirs. This in turn obviated the need to obtain consents for inter vivos transfers from other prospective heirs. Ultimately, it even became no longer necessary to obtain consent from the oldest son as prospective heir, and through transfers of land rights any prospective heirs could be completely disinherited by the father.

Another common form of transfer was subinfeudation, by which holders of military tenures transferred portions of their holdings to others in return for commitments to fulfill some part of the transferors' original feudal obligations. Until subinfeudation was prohibited by the Statute Quia Emptores in 1290, it was widely practiced and probably required the lord's consent, readily obtainable upon payment of a customary sum of money.

In some instances, a tenant desired to leave the tenancy altogether, and so would seek the lord's permission to turn the tenancy over to a substitute. This transfer, too, could be achieved by obtaining the lord's permission upon payment of a sum of money. The same Statute Quia Emptores that in 1290 prohibited subinfeudation also gave to all landholders except tenants in chief the right to substitute tenants without any payment of money to the lord.

One type of transfer that was very inimical to the feudal system was a grant in mortmain (signifying dead hand). These were transfers to the church or to other institutional or corporate donees whose members, because of their religious vows, were considered dead persons before the law and therefore incapable of fulfilling feudal obligations. Because such grants effectively nullified feudal obligations, some landholders would make grants in mortmain and then continue to occupy the land as tenants. So widespread was this abuse that it was specifically prohibited by the Magna Carta in 1215 and by the Statute of Mortmain in 1279.[821] Even then, a grantor could convey in mortmain after obtaining a royal license, which the monarch often readily granted upon payment of a sum of money.

§ 8.02(e). Types of Estates.

The property interest of an English landholder was thus partly defined by the type of tenancy under which the land was held, and the type of tenancy was characterized by whatever rights of inheritability and alienability were customary for that tenancy at any given time and place. The other major component of a landholder's property interest was the estate by which the tenancy was held. In its most simplistic form, the estate could be described as the duration of the tenancy. Eventually, the duration of the tenancy became the most important determinant of the various property rights associated with the tenancy; as the early distinctions between tenancies or tenures tended to meld and finally disappear, the estates became the chief distinguishing characteristics between different types of landholding.

The various types of estates that developed in medieval England may be summarized as follows:

Fee simple: The term "fee" signified an interest in land, and the term "simple" came to mean fully inheritable, that is, inheritable without restrictions, and therefore potentially endless in duration. A property interest granted to a person "and heirs" came to mean an inheritable estate and thus the estate of maximum duration. In addition to inheritability, after about 1200 the fee simple also came to be alienable without the consent of presumptive heirs; after the Statute Quia Emptores in 1290 it became alienable even without the consent of the lord. The fee simple estate has endured into the modern common law system of property rights, even though the various property rights pertaining to it have altered over time. As stated in a previous chapter:

---

[821] 7 Edw. 1 (1279).

> The fee simple of the thirteenth century was unlike the modern fee simple, mostly because the medieval estate consisted only of a set of feudal dues and responsibilities (all related to and burdening the land, of course), whereas the modern fee is simply full ownership subject to a less onerous set of sovereign prerogatives.[822]

Conditional fee and fee tail: Conditional fees were fee interests that were not necessarily fully inheritable. The most common conditions imposed upon these fee interests were that inheritability would arise only upon the birth of a live child of the landholder, or that only direct descendants could inherit from the landholder, or that a conveyance would be irrevocable only upon the birth of an heir of the third generation after the original grantee. Such conditions were considered important for keeping landholdings in the family, but they were also obstacles to alienability. When customs and court decisions affirming alienability despite such conditions prevailed, the Statute De Donis Conditionalibus in 1285 decreed that fees limited to inheritability by the heirs of the grantee's body, the so-called fee tail, would remain conditional, with a reversion in the grantor, as long as the possibility existed that the line of natural descendants could expire at some time in the indefinite future. This meant that the present holder of such an interest could effectively convey only the present possessory interest, and that the interests of prospective heirs were protected from disinheritance caused by alienation of land. In a later century it became possible rather easily to convert the fee tail into a fee simple.

Life estate: The life estate was not inheritable, but was limited in duration to the life of a specified person; upon the expiration of that life, the possession of the land reverted or went over to the tenant who held the fee interest. Life estates could either be created through conveyance or arise by operation of law, such as dower and curtesy interests. While a life tenant enjoyed broad rights of possession, a significant restriction was that the "inheritance" could not be damaged by depletion of, destruction of, or change to the land, according to the law of waste.

---

[822] Ch. 7, at § 7.06(a), *supra*.

Term of years: While the fee estates and life estates were considered "free" or "freeholds" because of the several judicial protections available to such estates, the term of years struggled for such recognition. One who held land as a lessee for a specified period of time, a so-called term of years, was at first regarded in the law as not even having an interest in the land; legal actions concerning the land were to be brought by or against the lessor, until in 1278 the Statute of Gloucester gave the lessee the right to intervene in such actions.[823] For one or more of several possible reasons, including the fact that tenancies for term could be held by either free or unfree persons, the estate of term of years was deemed an "unfree" tenure and was given little legal protection until the trespass action became available about the middle of the 13th century.

§ 8.02(f). Other Forms of Property Interests Within the System of Estates.

Whenever land was held as any estate other than a fee simple, some other person necessarily held the balance of total property interest, usually either a reversion or a remainder. When more than one person held an estate concurrently, such a concurrent estate would be a joint tenancy, tenancy in common, tenancy in coparcenary or tenancy by the entirety. If a person intended to make only a provisional conveyance in order to provide security for a loan, then the lender would hold the land by gage or mortgage. Other creditor's estates or tenancies were created by the Statute of Merchants[824] and the Statute of Staples.[825]

§ 8.02(g). Uses.

By the fourteenth century it had become common for a landholder to grant land to a grantee, to be held for the use of a third person. The third person was the intended beneficiary of the possessory rights in the land and

---

[823] 6 Edw. 1, cc. 11 (1278).

[824] 13 Edw. 1 (1285).

[825] 27 Edw. 3, cc. 9 (1353).

was said to hold a "use," a term derived from the Latin "*opus*," signifying a benefit. The purpose of such an arrangement frequently was to avoid feudal incidents;[826] however, the beneficiary of the use, or "*cestui que use*," who enjoyed possession of the land without its attendant feudal obligations, also risked being victimized by an unfaithful grantee who might deal with the land adversely to the rights of the use. The common law courts, wedded to the technicalities of seisin, were sometimes unable to protect such a victim, so early in the 15th century the Court of Chancery began to intervene in cases accusing unfaithful grantees and, under equity rules, to impose fines and imprisonment for misconduct. Even with this assistance from equity for holders of uses, abuses of feudal obligations by grantors to use were still left unchecked. Several statutes attempted to declare the *cestui que use* as the legal owner of the land, and therefore obligated to render the feudal dues, but not until the Statute of Uses[827] became effective in 1536 was such a policy position instituted for all uses.

By declaring that any person who held a use would be deemed the holder of the legal title, the Statute of Uses peremptorily eliminated the worst problems associated with uses. However, in the years and decades after 1536, a series of other significant impacts flowed from the Statute of Uses, impacts which, when fully felt, permanently transformed the law of land. For instance:

> (1) Several methods of conveyancing unique to uses became available for conveying legal title, including enfeoffment directly to the grantor and spouse, bargain and sale (which under the Statute of Enrolments was required to be in writing and to be enrolled in a public office), lease and release, and the covenant to stand seised used for effecting family settlements;

---

[826] The avoidance was achieved because the grantee who was technically bound to perform the feudal obligations did not have seisin or possession of the land and thus theoretically did not have the means to fulfill the obligations.

[827] 27 Hen. 8, c. 10 (1535).

> (2) new future interests were created when shifting and springing uses were "executed" or transformed into legal executory interests; and
>
> (3) a use on a use was at first held unexecuted under the statute and void in equity, but after the abolition of tenures in 1660 it gained recognition in equity as a trust; even earlier, judges had held "active" uses exempt from execution under the Statute of Uses, and the equitable interests of such unexecuted uses emerged in the 18th century as the early forms of the modern trust.

§ 8.03. The Impact of Changing Social Conditions on the Common Law of Land.

§ 8.03(a). The Rise and Decline of the Manorial System.

§ 8.03(a)(1). General Description of English Manors.

Pollock and Maitland ventured a very generalized description of medieval manors in England:

> Now speaking very generally we may say that a man who holds a manor has in the first place a house or homestead which is occupied by himself, his bailiffs or servants. Along with this he holds cultivable land, which is in the fullest sense (so far as feudal theory permits) his own; it is his demesne land. Then also, as part of the same complex of rights, he holds land which is holden of him by tenants, some of whom, it may be, are freeholders, holding in socage or by military service, while the remainder of them, usually the large majority of them, hold in villeinage, by

a merely customary tenure.[828]

The physical and legal organization of the manor was inextricably bound up with the economic and agricultural practices of the period, especially the common field system.[829]

§ 8.03(a)(2). Origins of English Manors.

According to Vinogradoff, the manorial system in England originated in two developments that occurred during the period of Anglo-Saxon dominance. One was the practice of voluntary patronage or commendation by which a person would enter into a formal and subservient but protective relationship with a socially and materially superior person. Although the relationships were voluntary, they were stabilized and prolonged, if satisfactory, and eventually expanded into numerous additional material obligations, such as loans, gifts, endowments, rents, and tenancies. Some commendations became involuntary: "a householder commended to a great

---

[828] Frederick Pollock and Frederic William Maitland, *The History of English Law Before the Time of Edward I* 363 (2d ed. 1909).

[829] "We have usually therefore in the manor lands of three kinds, (1) the demesne strictly so called, (2) the land of the lord's freehold tenants, (3) the *villenagium*, the land holden of the lord by villein or customary tenure. Now in the common case all these lands are bound together into a single whole by two economic bonds. In the first place, the demesne lands are cultivated wholly or in part by the labour of the tenants of the other lands, labour which they are bound to supply by reason of their tenure. A little labour in the way of ploughing and reaping is got out of the freehold tenants; much labour of many various kinds is obtained from the tenants in villeinage, so much in many cases that the lord has but small, if any, need to hire labourers. Then in the second place, these various tenements lie intermingled; neither the lord's demesne nor the tenant's tenement can be surrounded by one ring-fence. The lord has his house and homestead; each tenant has his house with more or less curtilage surrounding it; but the arable portions of the demesne and of the various other tenements lie mixed up together in the great open fields. There will be two or three or perhaps more great fields, and each tenement will consist of a number of small strips, of an acre or half-acre apiece, dissipated about in each of these fields. These fields are subjected to a common course of agriculture, a two-field system or a three-field system, so that a whole field will lie idle at one time, or be sown with winter seed or, as the case may be, with spring seed. After harvest and until the time for tilling comes, the lord and the tenants turn their beasts to graze over the whole field." *Id.* at 364. The authors cite one illustrative instance in which a holding of only five acres was scattered about in fourteen noncontiguous strips.

man had usually to stick to his patron, or to put it another way, patronage had a tendency to strike roots and to develop into a lasting lordship over free men and their land."[830]

Concurrent with the highly individualized relationships that grew out of commendation were frequent grants of private judicial jurisdiction, defined by territorial boundaries, made by Anglo-Saxon monarchs to their important allies among the landholding aristocracy. In their manorial courts, these lords imposed fines, composed local disputes and enforced obedience, relieving common people of expensive legal process.[831]

As the royal courts arose and defined their function, they determined that questions of villein tenure, as distinct from villein or unfree status, would be outside their powers and more appropriate for the manorial customary courts to consider.

Jurisdictional subjugation of the peasants eventually led to economic subjugation: the freeman who was required to appear and pay fines at a lord's court "came to be considered as a paying dependent, and indeed as a rent-paying tenant of the lord."[832] The powers over territorial districts granted with estates combined with the powers over individual persons created by commendation, shifting society into a system of subjection to local lords that was the essence of manorial economy. The lords themselves grew out of an increasingly important military class which, while not formalized until the Norman period, was quite fully formed before the Conquest:

---

[830] Paul Vinogradoff, *The Growth of the Manor* 213 (3d. ed. 1920).

[831] "Fines had to be imposed and levied, local means provided for the easy discharge of petty causes, and great men were considered the best local agents for enforcing obedience and taking up the settlement of local disputes. Small people were freed, on their side, from costly peregrinations and processes, while great people obtained new sources of income and influence. Many interests worked together in this way for the institution of aristocratic franchises on a territorial basis." *Id.* at 214.

[832] *Id.* at 215.

> [The thane's] estate was tending to become a unit of police and jurisdiction on the basis of governmental claims. In this way the political changes which followed the rise of the military class and the extension of commendation and franchise led in a considerable degree to the formation of a lordship as a superstructure of the township.[833]

Even in areas where the lord had not reserved certain lands for personal use and cultivation, the ancient tradition of progressive travel by lord or monarch through tenants' lands, with pauses to receive in kind tribute and rents and therewith to be hosted and feasted, eventually led to domainal holdings, surrounded by dependent holdings. The rise of these holdings required "a number of officers, servants and labourers, who have to take care of the lord's interests, to perform the special work of the demesne, to supervise the services and to exact the dues from the peasant population."[834]

More widespread, however, was the rise of requirements for services to be rendered for the lord's domain by the peasant population. Initially, the specific nature and extent of the work were not prescribed with precision, but customs formed to fix these firmly in tradition.

As to factors fostering the Anglo-Saxon origins of the manorial system, Vinogradoff thus concludes:

> On the whole we are, perhaps, warranted to conclude, firstly, that the manorial system arises at the end of the Old English period mainly in consequence of the subjection of a labouring class, and, secondly, that the personal authority of the lord of the manor is gradually gaining the mastery over a rural economy of ancient and independent growth.[835]

---

[833] *Id.* at 221.

[834] *Id.* at 227.

[835] *Id.* at 235.

It seems clear enough that by the time of the Conquest, a large majority of the English population lived and worked under some sort of manorial arrangement, although the individual details varied enormously. After the Conquest the Normans "found little difficulty in expressing the situation in tenurial terms," so that in a short time "the humble peasant class of cultivators had been fitted neatly into the universal tenurial system."[836]

The economic subservience of the manorial relationship was not always coincident with personal subservience. And even if a person were unfree in the relationship with the lord of the manor, such a person would still enjoy the rights of a free person with respect to the world outside the manor territory. One who was personally free could still hold the tenure characteristic of a person who was not free, the so-called villein tenure.

As pointed out earlier in this chapter,[837] villein tenures were under obligations fixed by custom, but the precise work to be done from day to day remained uncertain until the call actually went out from the reeve or bailiff. The duty to respond with personal service under circumstances of uncertainty, subordinating even the need to pursue one's own crucial agricultural tasks of the moment, was what characterized a tenure as unfree, and distinguished it from free tenures, for which often similar work was required, but whose type and extent were firmly fixed and limited by custom.

§ 8.03(a)(3). Decline of English Manors.

Villeinage as a matter of personal status steadily declined in England throughout the Middle Ages and had entirely disappeared by early in the 17th century. During the peasant revolt of 1381, one of whose underlying causes was the Black Death beginning in 1348-1349, many peasants sought out and destroyed manorial records in attempts to eliminate any evidence of servile status. Even as more and more villeins became personally free, they continued to hold their lands in unfree or villein tenure. This in turn

---

[836] A. W. B. Simpson, *A History of the Land Law* 156-57 (2d ed. 1986).

[837] *See,* § 8.02(c), *supra.*

prompted the common law courts finally to take cognizance of some cases dealing with the unfree tenures, but this did not occur until the end of the 15th century. Meanwhile, equity was available in many cases of villein tenures.

Beginning in the 14th century, an even more significant development was underway, the commuting of services in kind for money payments. With the money from such payments the lord of the manor would hire laborers, rather than rely on the work of the villein tenants. The process began with a succession of famines and then dramatically accelerated after the Black Death in 1348-1349 and a series of subsequent plagues; so many villein tenants died that the survivors could rather easily hire out for wages driven up by manpower shortages, despite statutory attempts to thwart such competition.[838] A century later, most villein tenants were paying a fixed sum of money in place of their tenurial services, and the natural progress of inflation made such monetary obligations ever lighter.

The breakdown in villeinage occasioned by judicial recognition of villein land rights and by gradual but massive personal emancipation of serfs combined with a third factor to destroy the medieval manorial system; this factor was the series of great enclosure movements in the 16th through the 18th centuries. Many landowners encouraged and carried out enclosures to reform the old open field strip-farming system and to enclose and allot portions of common land. By the time most of the enclosures were completed, the village community of the English Middle Ages, and the manorial system to which it was tied, had been completely transformed. Illustration 29 shows pasture land that was formerly a medieval open field in a strip-farming system.

---

[838] This process is more fully described in the following section, § 8.03(b).

Illustration 29. This pasture land near Berwick-upon-Tweed, close to the Scottish border in Northumberland, England, still shows the gentle curves and contours typical of the medieval open field strip farm of which it was once a part. Whether the fields were part of the manor lands or lands held by the peasants, this farming method required a coordinated effort by all the plough-teams and farm laborers.

§ 8.03(b). Changes in the Law of Land Coincident with the Decline of the Manorial System.

§ 8.03(b)(1). Copyhold Tenure and Judicial Recognition of Villeins' Land Rights.

Although originally a strong correlation existed between villein status and villein—or unfree—tenure, the determination of what constituted villein tenure derived only from characteristics of the tenure itself, without regard to the personal status of one who held such tenure. While the work owed by one in villein tenure might be very similar to the work owed by a free tenant, if the timing or precise nature of the work was uncertain, left somewhat in the discretion of the lord of the manor, then the tenure would usually be considered unfree. The royal common law courts took the position that legal issues arising from such tenures should be left to the jurisdiction of the manorial lords whose interests such tenures most closely served. Even if a free person held land under unfree tenure, the common law courts considered their jurisdiction determined by the nature of the tenure rather than by the status of the person.

This dichotomy between personal status and tenure among villeins had two consequences for legal developments. One was that the natural tendency of villeins to seek and obtain free status carried on without the need to transform the land interests they already held. This probably left the emancipation processes less restrained than they might otherwise have been, and the same royal courts that declined jurisdiction of villein tenures adopted legal rules that encouraged villein emancipation.

The other consequence of royal court rejection of jurisdiction over villein tenures was the way in which such tenures did finally achieve recognition in the law. The villein tenures did indeed have a unique characteristic of uncertainty about them, but their features that could be specified came to be firmly defined by local custom, considered to be binding on both lord and laborer. The manorial court, in its role as a court of custom, took cognizance of such local customs to confer a measure of protection on villeins who had no status in the royal courts.

The customs in some manors were reduced to writing, both because court rolls were kept for some manorial courts and because some manors were systematically surveyed as to tenurial obligations and the survey results were recorded. "Some manorial courts often modeled their procedure upon that of the royal courts, so that actions imitating novel disseisin and the other real actions were allowed in them. Some manors even went so far as to copy statutory law, the most notable instance of this being the recognition of a custom allowing entails in some manors, in imitation of the *Statute De Donis*."[839]

---

[839] A. W. B. Simpson, *A History of the Land Law* 159-60 (2d ed. 1986).

Perhaps the most common reason for making a written record of villeinage rights and obligations was to facilitate transfers of those tenures. Because the lord of the manor was theoretically all-powerful with respect to villein tenures, any transfer of tenure from one villein to another first required the transferor villein to grant or surrender the tenure to the lord (upon payment of the customary fee or fine, of course); then the lord re-granted the tenure to the transferee villein and admitted the transferee to the land. The parties entered a written record of the transaction in the manorial court rolls. Thus the court roll eventually became a record of villein "title," and a copy of the court roll was prepared to help resolve disputes over villein tenures without having to look up the information in the court rolls. The copy itself became authoritative evidence of title, so that it could be said a villein held "by copy of the court roll." Not all villein tenants were copyholders, but enough of them were that there developed an assumption that one who held by copy held in unfree tenure.

Late in the 15th century the common law courts began to extend some legal protection to copyholders. Up to this time, the common law courts recognized only the lords' rights in villein tenures, and the lord was considered as holding the freehold and seisin in those tenures. A villein tenant wishing to resolve some question over the tenancy that did not involve the lord could request that the lord pursue an action in one of the royal common law courts. An action between the tenant and the lord was relegated to the manorial court, which was obviously subject to some influence by the manorial lord. For at least those villeins who were copyholders, however, common law protection in disputes against the lords began to emerge. In one 1467 case a judge stated that a lord had no right to eject a copyholder who had defaulted in his services (even though the lord had a common law right to eject a tenant at will).[840] In a case from 1481 a judge declared that a lord who breached the manorial custom by ejecting a copyhold tenant could be sued in trespass and subjected to a judgment for damages.[841] These judicial holdings were included in a 1530 edition of Littleton's famous work on tenures.

---

840 Y.B. 7 Edw. 4, Michaelmas Term, f. 19, pl. 16 (1467).

841 Y.B. 21 Edw. 4, Michaelmas Term, f. 80, pl. 27 (1481).

If a third person ejected the copyholder, however, the common law courts still afforded no relief. The copyholder could either pursue the matter in the manorial court or ask the lord to take up the action in a law court. Late in the 16th century, first the Court of King's Bench[842] and then the Court of Common Pleas[843] permitted a copyholder to sue in ejectment for recovery of lands.

Equity protection for copyholders was slowly developing during this same period, and the steady stream of petitions to the Chancellor during the 15th century[844] may have influenced the law courts eventually to recognize some copyholder rights. By the first half of the 16th century it was established that the copyholder could have the Chancellor's assistance against various forms of misconduct by the lord of the manor:

> . . . and therefore if the lord will put out his copyholder that payeth his customs and services, or will not admit him to whose use a surrender is made, or will not hold his court for the benefit of his copyholder, or will exact fines arbitrary when they be customary and certain, the copyholder shall have a subpoena to restrain or compel him as the case shall require.[845]

The action in ejectment to recover land was permitted in the Exchequer court in 1596.[846]

---

[842] *See, e.g.*, Melwich v. Luter, 4 Co. Rep. 26a, 76 Eng. Rep. 935 (1588); Rumney v. Eves, 1 Leon. 100, 74 Eng. Rep. 93 (1588).

[843] *See, e.g.*, Petty v. Evans, 2 Brownl. 40, 123 Eng. Rep. 652 (1610); Ever v. Aston, Moo. K. B. 271, 72 Eng. Rep. 575 (1599); Stephens v. Eliot, Cro. Eliz. 484, 78 Eng. Rep. 735 *(1596)*.

[844] *The Reports of Sir John Spelman* 187-192 (J. H. Baker, ed., Selden Society, vol. 94, 1977); *Select Cases in Chancery* xxxix (William Paley Baildon, ed., Selden Society, vol. 10, 1896) ("465-1467; case 146. The plaintiff, a villein, had agreed with his lord, the defendant, for manumission, the deed of which was to be kept by A until the money was paid. This having been done, A has of malice given the deed back to the defendant, who refuses to deliver it to the plaintiff.").

[845] Cary 3 (1557).

[846] Goodwin v. Longhurst, Cro. Eliz. 535, 78 Eng. Rep. 782 (1596).

When the common law courts did extend jurisdiction to copyholders, it was under the theory that they were simply enforcing the custom of the manor, which, of course, varied widely from place to place and was not part of the *common* law. Copyholders, therefore, came into court with interests defined by local manorial custom rather than a set of standard legal rules. Thus a common law of copyholds never did develop; however, because copyholders' entry into common law courts was by means of an action in ejectment, copyholds obtained protection similar to that afforded freeholds and leaseholds, so some common rules did emerge. Also, courts tended to follow uniform procedures for determining and applying the varied manorial customs."[847]

The old theoretical notion that copyholders had no estate but were merely tenants at will was, as a practical matter, readily refuted by establishing the custom of the manor. However, the concept of tenancy at will was not completely extinguished, and the lord and copyholder were recognized as having concurrent rights in the land. The lord's rights in copyhold tenures included a limited right to exploit mines, minerals, and timber, the right to prohibit the waste by tenants, the right to prohibit leases longer than one year, and the right to collect old feudal exactions, such as heriot, rents and fines.[848]

Copyholders could hold essentially the same estates and interests as could freeholders, including entailed estates. Copyholders used common recoveries to bar entails (converting the entailed estate into a fee simple estate) until 1833, when the Fines and Recoveries Act[849] went into effect.

Despite the facts that copyholds remained mostly outside the common law, and that early copyholders were drawn from the humblest class of the English landholding population, Sir Edward Coke declared as early as 1584

[847] 7 William Holdsworth, *A History of English Law* 304 (2d ed. 1937).

[848] A.W.B. Simpson, *A History of the Land Law* 168-69 (2d ed. 1986).

[849] 3 & 4 Will. 4, ca. 74 (1833).

that the "great part of the land within the realm is in grant by copy."[850] Copyhold tenure was born and nurtured within the manorial system and proved flexible in adapting to new circumstances when that system became obsolete. It was a tenure that was held by large numbers of English landowners until formally abolished and converted into free and common socage on January 1, 1926, by the 1922 Law of Property Act.[851]

§ 8.03(b)(2). The Black Death and Emancipation of the Villeins.

The impact of the Black Death on the manorial system and unfree tenures has been succinctly summarized by Plucknett:

> The nation was already weakened by a series of famines when the arrival of the Black Death (1348-1349) from the East wrought a revolution in social and economic conditions. The terrible mortality from this plague completely disorganized the manorial system, which had hitherto depended upon a plentiful supply of labour born and bred within the manor. The plague accelerated and intensified forces which were already at work, and the result was a very serious depletion of the labour supply. Consequently lords began to compete among themselves for such free labour as was available. This tempted servile inhabitants of manors to leave their holdings and become

---

[850] Heydon's Case, 3 Co. Rep. 8b, 76 Eng. Rep. 640 (1584).

[851] Certain incidents of copyhold tenure were expressly preserved, unless the parties agreed to their abolition:

> (a) Any commonable rights to which the tenant is entitled.
> (b) Any right of the lord or the tenant to mines, minerals, gravel, pits or quarries, whether in or under the land.
> (c) Any rights of the lord in respect of fairs, markets or sporting.
> (d) Any liability for the construction, maintenance, cleansing or repair of any dykes, ditches, canals, sea or river walls, bridges, levels, ways, etc.

E. H. Burn, *Cheshire and Burn's Modern Law of Real Property* 84-85 (13th ed. 1982).

hired labourers.[852]

It would be easy to overstate the effect of the Black Death on villeins' status, because that effect was so dramatic. Less dramatic but equally effective were the general economic conditions that impelled manorial lords to commute their villeins' service duties into monetary obligations.[853]

Perhaps more revealing than the generalizations for the English nation as a whole are the anecdotal and local studies of conditions at these times. For instance, the tiny village of Landbeach, north of Cambridge, is likely typical of thousands of English villages in its experience, but is more fortunate in the richness of documentation available to modern researchers. In the following excerpt from *The Domesday Inheritance*, a history of Landbeach, it is possible to picture the profound stresses of the 14th century, the famines, floods, pestilence, looting and lawlessness that followed, and the new opportunities for personal and economic freedom:

> For a moment there is a glimpse of a half-ghost village, with looting where the plague had passed on. The court rolls tell more. Walls and fences had become ruinous from failure to make essential repairs. Animals were straying in the hay and growing corn. Bands of villeins failed to turn up for their harvest works. The lord did not find it possible to replace all his dead villein landholders with men prepared to accept the old conditions. Five tenements were let for life at a small cash rent with an obligation to provide one man for one day in hay harvest for lifting the crop. This was practically giving the land for nothing compared with the heavy labour services under the pre-plague terms. Too much had been lost through failure to cope with getting the harvest home to miss even one man's work for a single day. In any case, he was taking

[852] Theodore F. T. Plucknett, *A Concise History of the Common Law* 32 (5th ed. 1956).

[853] *See* H. S. Bennett, *Life on the English Manor* 280 (1937) (*see* especially the sources cited in n.1).

land that no one seemed to want.

Of nine cattle caught wandering and impounded as strays, not one was claimed.

Leases changed, and the main clauses of many were the obligation to inhabit and maintain the tenement. Desperate times called for desperate remedies. Peasants helped themselves to the lord's corn and turf for sale. At one court in 1356, nine peasants were presented for stealing the lord's corn and a further 32 for trespass in the lord's crops. By 1357 things were getting even more out of hand. John Emme went out into the fen by night, stealing the turves of several of his neighbours to sell in Cambridge. A woman and her daughter raided a villein's house for timber. Stealing from the lord had been one thing, although before the Pestilence it was not frequent, and stealing from fellow villagers very rare. Now the villeins seem to have learnt the habit of looting, and are prepared to steal from their fellows quite flagrantly . . .

In 1365 the most dramatic change in the manor of Chamberlains [the most prominent landholding in Landbeach] began. The demesne arable, all two hundred and six acres of it, was let to sixteen villeins in varying amounts for thirteen years at 18d. an acre . . .

Some of the old disabilities of villeinage were beginning to soften. In practice it was becoming harder to prevent a villein from leaving the manor. After the Second Pestilence flight becomes more frequent as the chances of escape seem to improve. In the old days, the need of a licence from the lord to marry a daughter had enabled the lord to charge what the traffic would bear; in the last quarter of the fourteenth century it would no longer bear very much.[854]

One can surmise that villein emancipation and the breakdown of manorial tenures would have eventually occurred even without the devastation of the Black Death. But there must be little doubt that the massive mortality among the land's laborers hastened and made irreversible the movement to modern conditions. In terms of land law, the decline of villein tenures infused with new importance the free tenures and leaseholds and contributed to the eventual demise and abolition of tenures altogether.

§ 8.03(b)(3). The Consequences of Enclosures.

As previously described, the common field or open field strip system characterized English agriculture from Anglo-Saxon times almost to the modern era. It was the system of agricultural organization out of which the common law of land and the manorial system arose. Despite the persistence of this system, discontent with it was of long standing and "denounced by all writers on agriculture from the sixteenth to the nineteenth century."[855]

The obvious but profoundly difficult solution was to implement what was referred to as the process of enclosure. Enclosure, or inclosure, actually consisted of two quite distinct activities, even the most benign of which could mean a traumatic adjustment for the inhabitants of a village or manor. This least offensive aspect of enclosure consisted simply of combining the individual field strips into contiguous plots of land which were then reassigned to individual ownership. Even this disruption brought about changes that "affected the whole structure of rural society."[856]

The other type of enclosure was far more odious, disruptive and unfair to the small farmer. These enclosures took over the areas of commons or waste, extinguishing the ancient and essential peasant rights in such lands and their resources; they also converted lands long used for tillage into

---

[854] Jack Ravensdale, *The Domesday Inheritance* 56-60 (1986).

[855] 2 William Holdsworth, *A History of English Law* 60 (4th ed. 1936).

[856] J. H. Plumb, *England in the Eighteenth Century* 18 (1963).

huge pasture areas, evicting the farmers and razing or forcing abandonment of their farmhouses and buildings. Even though enclosures generally meant important improvements in agricultural techniques and yields, much of this enclosure activity was illegal and utterly devastating to smaller landholders.[857]

Some enclosures took place in the 16th and 17th centuries, but most of the land remained unenclosed during that period; open field agriculture was still common enough then that emigrating farmers transplanted it to British colonies in New England.[858]

Beginning early in the Tudor period, enclosures became the subject of frequent Parliamentary enactment, with varying motives. One motive was to legitimize some enclosures in the face of unrest and disruption among the villein class. Another motive was to afford some protection to such small landholders against overly rapacious lords. Yet another was to give expression to official preferences for particular types of land use after enclosure became an accomplished fact. For instance, apparently the Tudor governments believed that enclosures to enhance productivity of tilled land was commendable: labor demand was not diminished and land yields increased. Enclosures in order to turn tilled land into pastures were condemned: families were evicted, buildings fell into ruin, and large tracts of land were left without any persons to provide a modicum of defense and security.

---

[857] 4 William Holdsworth, *A History of English Law* 364 (3d ed. 1945).

> Consequently the old cultivating community was broken up, many of the smaller owners were evicted from the land, and rights of common either in the open fields or in the waste disappeared . . . if by agreement, purchase, or eviction a whole manor was enclosed, existing rights of common disappeared with disappearance of those entitled to exercise them. That these enclosures raised the value of the property is clear. *Id.*

[858] W. Cunningham, *The Growth of English Industry and Commerce* 548 (4th ed. 1907) (*see* especially n.1, p. 548, noting examples of New England open field survivals described *in* 1 William B. Weeden, *Economic and Social History of New England, 1620-1789* 58-62 (1890)).

The first general act resulting from enclosures in 1489 operated to penalize large aggregations of pasture land; lessees with farms of twenty acres or more were required to maintain buildings serving tillage activities on that land or else pay half their profits to the Crown until the buildings were repaired.[859] Parliament passed a similar act a quarter-century later.[860] Two decades later an act prohibited and penalized keeping more than 2,000 sheep;[861] and still later a requirement issued that as much land should remain in tillage as was tilled at the beginning of Henry VIII's reign.[862]

The litany of complaints against these early enclosures was aptly expressed in the preamble to the act of 1533-1534:

> Forasmuch as divers and sundry persons of the King's subjects of this realm, to whom God of his goodness hath disposed great plenty and abundance of moveable substance, now of late within few years have daily studied, practised, and invented ways and means how they might accumulate and gather together into few hands, as well great multitude of farms as great plenty of cattle, and in especial sheep, putting such lands as they can get to pasture, and not to tillage, (2) whereby they have not only pulled down churches and towns, and inhanced the old rates of the rents of the possessions of this realm, or else brought it to such excessive fines that no poor man is able to meddle with it, but also have raised and enhanced the prices of all manner of corn, cattle, wool, pigs, geese, hens, chickens, eggs, and such other, almost double above the prices which have been accustomed; (3) by reason whereof a marvellous multitude and number of the people of this realm be not able to provide meat, drink and clothes

[859] 4 Hen. 8, c. 19 (1489).

[860] 6 Hen. 8, c. 5 (1514-1515).

[861] 25 Hen. 8., c. 13 (1533-1534).

[862] 5 & 6 Edw. 6, c. 5 (1551-1552).

> necessary for themselves, their wives and children, but be so discouraged with misery and poverty, they fall daily to theft, robbery and other inconveniences, or pitifully die for hunger and cold; (4) and as it is thought by the King's most humble and loving subjects, that one of the greatest occasions that moveth and provoketh those greedy and covetous people so to accumulate and keep in their hands such great portions and parts of the grounds and lands of this realm from the occupying of the poor husbandmen, and so to use in pasture, and not in tillage, is only the great profit that cometh of sheep; . . . (7) which things, thus used, be principally to the high displeasure of Almighty God, to the decay of the hospitality of this realm, to the diminishing of the King's people, and to the let of the cloth-making, whereby many poor people have been accustomed to be set on work; and in conclusion, if remedy be not found, it may turn to the utter destruction and desolation of this realm, which God defend . . . .[863]

The complexity of these acts, with their various exceptions and difficulties of enforcement, led in 1624 to the repeal of all of them, except the 1533-1534 act quoted above. None of this early Tudor legislation, however, directly prohibited all enclosures, but was intended mostly to prevent an imbalance from developing between land in tillage and land in pasturage. By the time enclosure acts were formally repealed in 1624, much enclosure had occurred, especially for tillage. Not only did enclosures other than for pasturage proceed essentially unhindered,[864] but even some statutory assistance was given.[865]

---

[863] 25 Hen. 8, c. 13 (preamble) (1533-1534).

[864] "No statute made it unlawful for a man to buy out his neighbours, or for all the inhabitants to agree to inclose their common fields." 4 William Holdsworth, *A History of English Law* 369 (3d ed. 1945).

[865] In 35 Hen. 8, cc. 17, § 6 (1543), was enacted a procedure by which justices of the peace could assist in enclosing and dividing wooded land, in which several persons had rights, when those persons could not reach agreement privately.

On the one hand, during the 16th and 17th centuries, enclosures dispossessed many defenseless folk, and enclosure riots did occur. Some lords applied improper pressure on their tenants and without compassion exercised rights to evict or to not renew leaseholds. On the other hand, many enclosures were consensually and equitably carried out. The Council and the Star Chamber gave special attention to redressing complaints from the dispossessed. But the government and the more ambitious, enterprising farmers could hardly ignore the economic reality that enclosures were immensely beneficial. With new wealth from commercial enterprises, and new land entering the market from forfeiture of church holdings, it was only natural that individual, self-contained farms let to individual, enterprising yeoman farmers would be by far the most sensible method of holding land and conducting agriculture.

By the end of the 17th century, the outcry against enclosures had somewhat diminished and Parliament attempted no comprehensive enclosure legislation for a century thereafter. Some acts sought to make consensual enclosures easier to achieve,[866] while others attempted to improve administration of the remaining open field operations. The failure of an act attempting to improve administration of open field farms probably led to the popularity of private legislation as the primary method of advancing enclosures during the 18th century.

The private acts were the source of much mischief in the progress of enclosures, leaving behind, as one historian commented, "a permanent legacy of bitterness."[867]

---

[866] For example, in 29 Geo. 2, c. 36 (1754), lords and tenants of common land were given a consensual procedure to enable them to plant timber on the land; in 13 Geo. 3, ca. 81 (1773), three-fourths of the occupants of a common field system were empowered to make rules for the entire holding (an act that proved to be ineffective probably because it was still very difficult to achieve even a three-fourths majority consent on many issues).

[867] "No doubt these Acts did make for the greater efficiency of all branches of the agricultural industry. But there is also no doubt that they were passed with too little regard for the rights of small owners and commoners; and that the elimination of their rights had grave social and economic effects, which . . . "left behind it a permanent legacy of bitterness." 11 William Holdsworth, *A History of English Law* 455 (1938).

The problem was not only that the enclosures directly dispossessed the poor; they also burdened the poor with "overhead" expenses. Usually the private legislation provided for not only division of the enclosed areas but also that each landholder bear a proportionate part of the heavy expenses incurred in obtaining the legislation and fencing the land. Such burdens were impossible for numerous small landholders and left them indebted and landless. Parliament remained unaware of and insensitive to these injustices, and was in any event more favorably disposed toward the larger landholders who made up a large share of its membership, and so failed to cure these defects with comprehensive legislation.

The heavy dominance of private enclosure acts at the end of this era may be seen in the numbers of private enclosure acts passed during successive monarchies of the 17th and 18th centuries:

Reign	Number of private enclosure acts
James I	1[868]
William and Mary	1[869]
Anne	2
George I	16
George II	276
George III	3360[870]

Statistics, of course, tell nothing of the individual lives disrupted or enriched by enclosures and their consequences. Turning again to the village of Landbeach, near Cambridge, as described with its rich historical documentation in *The Domesday Inheritance*,[871] readers in modern times are able to glimpse a moment or two of the medieval milieu in which enclosures operated. First, before enclosure became an issue, villein tenures

---

868 4 Jam., c. 11 (1606-1607).

869 3 & 4 W. & M., c. 31 (1693).

870 11 William Holdsworth, *A History of English Law* 624-625 (1938).

871 Jack Ravensdale, *The Domesday Inheritance* 65-88 (1986).

gradually turned into copyhold:

> Gradually the customary tenements or bondage holdings of the villeins turned into copyhold, customary tenure proved by copy of the court roll, with labour services replaced by cash rents, usually fixed by custom, and all taint of personal unfreedom gone. Where custom fixed the cash rent the inflations of the sixteenth century would reduce its value until it remained a mere nuisance and the peasants felt themselves full owners. Heriot [a requirement that upon the tenant's death the decedent's best beast or some equivalent thing be given over to the lord] often remained, but as a slighter nuisance.[872]

Already the lord of the principal manor in Landbeach had turned the entire manor into a cash enterprise. As early as 1352, just three years after the first attack of the Pestilence, no lord's demesne was retained by this manor, but all such land had been rented to others for cash rents. All labor services had been converted or commuted to cash:

> It followed hard on the heels of the great Pestilence, a very early example of a lord responding to that disaster by giving up cultivation, with all the problems of a desperate labour shortage, and attempting to live from rents.[873]

The manor then came into the ownership of Corpus Christi College in Cambridge, whose records for 1467-68 show that rent-paying peasants could take odd jobs with the lord in Cambridge and thus earn cash with which to pay their rents.

A century later, during the reign of Elizabeth I, the tenants of this manor had to unite in resisting the aggressions of Richard Kirby, lord of another manor in Landbeach, who seemed consumed by insatiable greed,

---

[872] *Id.* at 65.

[873] *Id.*

and who found enclosures and associated legal procedures as convenient means to serve his covetousness. When Kirby came into his lordship in 1521, rapid inflation was occurring in the English economy, and much blame for this was laid on enclosures that were converting tilled land into pasture land, especially for sheep. The Corpus Christi manor already had ample grasslands available and remained quite stable with respect to enclosures. But Kirby exemplified almost every abuse criticized in the anti-enclosure legislation of Henry VIII's reign, including having let his copyholders' houses fall into ruin, so that almost none were left. With empty houses and untilled arable lands, Kirby designed to turn those lands into pasture, especially suitable for lambing and winter care, because they were near the manor, rather than some distance out in the fens. He eventually enclosed 22 acres of arable land.

Once this conversion was accomplished, he encroached on and took over some of the field ways[874] and sought to further consolidate some contiguous holdings by exchanging some tenements with another owner. He then sought to take over the commons, but not by direct enclosure. Instead, "he tried to use his power as lord to impound strays, in a move to drive the peasants from the commons. For such animals as were straying on land belonging to *his* manor, and lawfully impounded, could be regained by their owners only on payment of a sum, called a 'replevin,' which the lord could fix, although it was supposed to be at a reasonable amount . . . . He needled the peasants by impounding their oxen straight from the ploughing when they were manifestly not straying, and so held up urgent work.:[875]

He brought vexatious but groundless lawsuits, used and wore out animals falsely impounded, and hired thugs to physically ambush and attack men and women on their way to the commons with their cattle. One peasant was wounded with a sword while Kirby's men were illegally enclosing a part of the commons. When the peasants finally collectively resisted, Kirby brought a petition in the Star Chamber, whose decision is

[874] Field ways were peasant paths through commons and waste, out to the common fields.

[875] Jack Ravensdale, *The Domesday Inheritance* 72 (1986).

not known, but after which the conflicts and violence in Landbeach apparently ceased.

Contemporaries of Kirby were also actively acquiring grazing lands in the nearby village of Cottenham. A man who eventually became the sheriff of Cambridgeshire and Huntingdonshire had, in 1488, let a house in Cottenham fall into ruin in order to claim the commons rights pertaining to the house. In the same area, another prominent person in 1560 claimed as his own 5,000 acres of fenland, including two large enclosures, but two men had broken into the enclosures and destroyed the fences. This enclosure activity was governed somewhat by private agreement:

> There had been agreements in the 1560s and 1580s giving the lord some right to enclose, but the final agreement came in 1596. This described in detail the enclosures in Longhill, Marehill and Tilling which the lord could keep for himself, yielding up in turn all his common rights. It listed all the tenants with common rights, detailing these. Most important of all in the long run, it was agreed that no more regulations of the fields should be made by the manor court. The commoners' meetings, with their ordermakers, fen reeves and other officers, took over power. Two of the orderbooks survive, recording variations made from time to time on the Articles, the statutes of a village parliament, one might say. On occasions even the voting for and against any change is recorded.
>
> Some of the lists of ordermakers suggest that the ordermakers were chosen as freeholders and copyholders, manor by manor . . .
>
> The Articles of Agreement of 1596 were of the greatest practical value to the peasants and farmers of Cottenham right up to enclosure in 1846, and many copies survive,

both printed and in manuscript.[876]

In Landbeach itself, the commoners did not begin to act in concert until much later, when in 1735 they reached an agreement on control of the open field agriculture and management of the fens. Later in that century a concerted propaganda effort by the national Board of Agriculture promoted enclosure and discouraged continuation of open fields, in order to improve agricultural productivity. Reports on the status of agriculture and productivity were provided to the Board on a county-by-county basis. In 1794 the report on Landbeach proclaimed:

> The enclosures in severalty contain about 150 acres and are rented at twenty shillings per acre. The commons contain about one thousand acres, all of which, except about sixty acres, are high and dry . . . .The common husbandry of two crops and a fallow is here the usual practice. An enclosure is greatly desired, under the encouragement of which very considerable improvements in the stock and husbandry of the parish would immediately take place . . . .[877]

A contemporaneous description by one Robert Masters, an enclosure enthusiast and the author of a description of the nearby village of Waterbeach, adopts a similar tone and was also given to one of the Board Commissioners:

> Landbeach is of a good natural soil: yet although cultivated by judicious farmers, its produce is unequal to that of some neighbouring parishes. The quantity of arable land is less than 1,000 acres, whilst that of the enclosed pastures does not greatly exceed 100. There is a fine common nearly equal in quantity to the arable fields, which enclosed and well cultivated would be superior to

---

[876] *Id.* at 80-81.

[877] *Id.* at 153-54.

> them in quality, and not less profitable than in its present state . . . .An enclosure of a very considerable part at the least of these commons would be highly beneficial, and will, I should hope, be soon adopted by those who are wise enough to discover their own true interest therein.[878]

Because the expense of buying out commons rights was prohibitive, the private enclosure act covering Landbeach was not enacted until 1807, and the Award was not signed until 1813. In time the allocations were made, the old common was taken from the villagers,[879] the old boundaries obliterated, and the new borders established. "Slowly, especially by steam ploughing between the two World Wars, the patched corduroy pattern of ridge and furrow in the furlongs was smoothed out. Straight fences, ditches, paths and roads replaced the organic pattern of the old field ways: access to the countryside began to be lost to all but the farmers . . . The complicated pattern of the ploughman's ridge and furrow began to disappear in time: the lawyers' tangle of strips in divers hands was disentangled."[880]

The mass of private enclosure acts waned in the 19th century; at the same time a series of public acts[881] promoted enclosures until 1876. These acts did not entirely eliminate the small landholders, but diminished their numbers.[882]

---

[878] *Id.* at 154.

[879] *Id.* at 64.

[880] *Id.* at 155.

[881] The first nineteenth-century public act facilitating enclosure was enacted in 1801, 41 Geo. 3, c. 109 (1801), and an act in 1845, 8 & 9 Vict., c. 118 (1845), established a Board of Inclosure Commissioners to regulate enclosure proposals presented to them; this act effectively eliminated the need for any further private enclosure acts.

[882] "In 1835 an Act was passed to facilitate the exchange of lands in the common fields; and in 1836 it was provided that such lands should be enclosed if two-thirds in the number and value of the persons having an interest in these lands consented . . . in 1845 an elaborate Act was passed under which, and its amending Acts, most of the remaining common fields were enclosed, and rights of common which prevented the profitable use of the land were got rid of. These Inclosure Acts did not eliminate the small holders, but they did materially diminish their number." 13 William Holdsworth, *A History of English Law* 353 (1952).

In 1876 a concern over diminishing open spaces prompted passage of the Commons Act of 1876,[883] which imposed the present strict limits on enclosure. By the time this act thus halted the progress of enclosures, the manorial structure of the villages had been almost completely altered. Today common rights remain significant only in those mountainous areas of the country used for grazing flocks of sheep.[884]

§ 8.04. Major Developments in English Land Law Before 1926.

§ 8.04(a). Abolition of Tenures.

The preceding chapter described the establishment of tenures during the Middle Ages[885] and their reinforcement by the Statute of Uses beginning in 1536.[886] For the most part, tenures had long ceased to be a useful means of providing the services for which they were originally intended. As with the scutage payments substituted for knight service, landholders commuted many other services into money payments; when the amounts became fixed by custom, continuing inflation drove them into insignificance. Homage and fealty also lapsed into unimportant formalities. Only a few generations after the Conquest, tenures were desirable principally for the income they generated through the incidents of marriage, wardship, aids, reliefs and fines. These impositions, however, remained burdensome irritants, the more so because in time they lost all relevance; the society which had spawned such incidents was one in which less powerful persons had relied heavily on the warrior class for protection and civil stability. The feudal tenurial incidents could be justified only as a form of individualized taxation for provisions of civil services and order. After the feudal order was replaced by a strong central government in

---

[883] 39 & 40 Vict., c. 56 (1876).

[884] A. W. B. Simpson, *A History of the Land Law* 261-62 (2d ed. 1986).

[885] § 7.05(b)(3)-(7), *supra*.

[886] § 7.07, *supra*.

England, the tenurial incidents became merely means of obtaining revenue, either for private landholders or for the government itself, as the greatest of feudal lords.

Quite naturally, landholders and their lawyers exhibited great ingenuity in evading the exactions of tenurial incidents. Perhaps the most conspicuous of these devices to escape tenurial impositions was the use. Through a conveyance to use, one person could give land to another, but specify that the grantor held the land only nominally, while a third person actually used or benefitted from the land. This beneficiary of the use was the so-called "*cestui que use*."

Early conveyances to uses were intended to strengthen tenurial relationships: a knight embarking on a crusade might convey land to another who could be responsible for feudal obligations, but would actually hold the land for the benefit of the knight's family. Through a use a landholder could confer the benefit of landholding on a religious order not authorized to actually hold land; a villein, not ordinarily authorized to convey land, could accomplish a conveyance by granting to the lord "for the use of" the intended grantee; and when a guardianship was transferred, the new guardian would hold "to the use of" the ward. "However, the potential for uses as means to avoid feudal obligations was not overlooked: The purpose of such conveyances frequently was to enable the landowners to deal with their lands in a manner not countenanced by the common law or to evade the liabilities incident to legal ownership, such as the rule of destructibility."[887]

The reaction of the government and major landholders to such developments was to protect and enforce the incidents, often by means of statute. Beginning late in the 15th century, a series of statutes initiated piecemeal reforms by declaring the *cestui que use* as holder of the legal title (and therefore the one responsible for performing feudal tenurial obligations) in certain, specific situations. However, comprehensive reform did not occur until the Statute of Uses in 1536, and that was prompted by

---

[887] Sheldon F. Kurtz, *Moynihan's Introduction to the Law of Real Property* 229 (4th ed. 2005).

the interests of the English government, as the greatest of feudal lords and the entity with the most to gain by preserving tenurial incidents. By the simple tactic of declaring holders of uses to be the holders of the legal title, the Statute of Uses solved a major problem in the feudal system and gave new life to the feudal tenures, which were actually otherwise no longer relevant in English society. "The causes which led to its enactment are to be found in the king's need of money. The Statute was primarily designed to restore to the Crown the feudal revenues that were lost because of the conveyance of lands to uses."[888]

Thus the Statute of Uses at bottom was a device to resuscitate tenurial incidents and give new life to a system that was already terminally ill. In the end, the Statute of Uses did little to revive the failing tenurial system, but it did lead to an enormous elaboration of land law in England. For instance, methods previously used to convey uses, not bound by common law conveyancing restrictions, became available to convey legal estates, such as a feoffment to uses, a resulting use, a bargain and sale, a lease and release, and a covenant to stand seised. Also, several uses incorporating future interests outside the common law rules, such as shifting and springing uses, were "executed" into legal interests and, as executory interests, became "new" future interests with new legal rules. The ability to transfer land interests by devise was expanded as a result of the Statute of Uses. When the courts began to treat certain uses as outside of and unexecuted by the Statute of Uses, new rules and new applications for such uses began to develop, including the entire law of trusts.

Henry VIII's eagerness to recover feudal dues by reforming land law governing uses was accompanied by a direct assault on one of England's largest class of landowners, the various religious houses, including the monasteries and abbeys. These he summarily dissolved beginning in the 1530s, and most were stripped of their wealth and sold or granted to private parties. Thereafter, as shown by Tintern Abbey pictured in Illustration 30, they fell into sometimes romanticized decay.

---

[888] *Id.* at 236.

Illustration 30. The ruins of Tintern Abbey, in Monmouthshire, Wales. The abbey was founded in 1131 and dissolved by action of Henry VIII in 1536. The abbey had, until dissolution, very extensive landholdings.

At first, the Statute of Uses achieved its avowed purpose of preserving and recovering tenurial revenues for the Crown and other major landholders. In 1540, four years after the Statute of Uses, Parliament established the Court of Wards and Liveries to oversee the collection of such tenurial charges.[889] The court was effective, and landowners chafed under the renewed exactions. Even the monarch became dependent upon such revenues, especially in the struggle between Crown and Parliament in the 17th century, when that income enabled the king for a time to function without Parliament and its taxing power. When the Long Parliament of that era was finally summoned by King Charles I, both the Commons and the Lords passed resolutions in 1645 calling for abolition of feudal dues, mostly as a means of weakening the monarch. An act of Parliament in 1656 confirmed the resolutions. After the Restoration, the tenures Abolition Act of 1660 confirmed the 1656 act. In connection with this legislation, the Crown received some compensatory revenue for the loss of feudal income.[890] "The effect of the Act of 1660, which is extraordinarily ill-drawn, was to abolish knight-service and grand serjeanty, and convert these tenures into free and common socage, that is into socage tenure where no services were due and no special customs applied . . . In effect, therefore, from 1645 onwards the only free tenure of any importance which remained was socage, and the preservation of the feudal revenues had ceased to be of any importance. The economic purpose of the Statute of Uses had disappeared."[891]

Tenures have had a fundamental impact on English land law in the sense that they stand in the place of outright ownership. Because of tenure, any occupier of land other than the monarch always "held" of someone else; absolute ownership rested only and completely with the sovereign. And it could perhaps be said that tenures, especially military tenures, were functionally important with respect to shaping land law for only the first one or two centuries of their 600-year existence; thereafter their effects were financial, and their chief influence on the law issued from the conflicts between those who wished to preserve tenures and those who sought to avoid them. By the time the major tenures were formally abolished in 1660, land law had moved on and remained essentially unaffected; the abolition merely removed a fiscal irritant.

---

889 32 Hen. 8, c. 46 (1540).

890 12 Car. 2, c. 24 (1660).

891 A. W. B. Simpson, *A History of the Land Law* 199 (2d ed. 1986).

Nevertheless, the doctrine of tenure still infuses the land law, in that even today one only holds the land, but does not own it outright. In their modern form tenures have undergone profound changes: English landholders now, for the most part, hold directly of the Crown, with all intermediate lordships having disappeared; feudal burdens attached to tenures have also been eliminated; all tenures except leasehold tenure have been converted into the single tenure of free and common socage.[892]

§ 8.04(b). Leaseholds.

The concept of tenure is still of significance in leaseholds. Because early feudal leaseholds were distinguished from freehold tenures, they were technically outside the laws governing real property and courts treated them as chattels, or personal property. Today leaseholds in English law are still technically chattels, although there is, of course, a tenurial relationship between the landlord and the tenant.

The preceding chapter pointed out that leaseholds—that is, tenancies for a term—may have been treated differently under the law because they performed a different function in medieval English society. If the land's main value was as a source of livelihood and sustenance for the population, then legal doctrines should encourage the more or less permanent settlement and cultivation of the land. Thus the rules regarding estates in land and the tenures by which landholding was governed were all oriented to the interests of the long-term occupant; they held the so-called "free tenements." The finite term for years, or leasehold, on the other hand, was often simply a device for raising revenue, land turned over to a

---

[892] "[T]he first thing to teach a student of land law is the doctrine of tenure, the second is that it has no importance. Unfortunately, it cannot be ignored completely because the ghost of tenure has left its imprint on the language of modern law. The language of possession is still used. Today, the student will find sometimes the language of possession, sometimes that of ownership. He will find both the expressions "freehold owner" and "freehold tenant."He will read both that a freeholder owns the land and that he holds it as tenant. Again a life tenant may be described as a limited owner. Theoretically, the language of possession is more correct; in practice the language of ownership is more apt." Michael Harwood, *Modern English Land Law* 7-8 (2d ed. 1982).

money-lender until the debt was repaid.[893]

The position of the leasehold tenant was indeed precarious under early English land law. If someone other than the lessor disturbed a tenant in occupancy, the tenant could bring only an action for breach of covenant against the lessor. Not until a trespass action became available in the mid-13th century could a lessee bring an action directly against such a third party.

By defaulting in an action against the land brought by a colluding third party, a lessor could extinguish the lessee's right of occupancy; the lessee could not intervene in such an action until enactment of the Statute of Gloucester in 1278.[894] By being excluded from the "free tenements," leaseholds were held not entitled to the protection of the petty assizes, a form of action for recovery and protection of the tenancy.

This deficiency was overcome when the trespass action was made available to lessees, including even a specialized writ. With the trespass action, a lessee could achieve direct protection against any person who disturbed occupancy, including a remedy either in damages, or much later, at the end of the 15th century, for actual recovery of possession.[895]

The need for greater protection arose from changes in the way leaseholds were used. Especially after the Black Death in the mid-14th century, leases for farming purposes, so-called husbandry leases, became common as lords sought new arrangements to bring workers back onto their manorial lands. Indeed, rather than being used as security for a disingenuous moneylending scheme, the lease was entered into "regularly by a freeman whose capital is insufficient to purchase much land, although

---

[893] Theodore F. T. Plucknett, *A Concise History of the Common Law* 573 (5th ed. 1956).

[894] 6 Edw., c. 11 (1278).

[895] Theodore F. T. Plucknett, *A Concise History of the Common Law* 574 (5th ed. 1956).

he is active and enterprising enough to work the land of other owners."[896]

This process at a very local level is well-illustrated from the post-Pestilence accounts for the medieval village of Landbeach, north of Cambridge. "The lord did not find it possible to replace all his dead villein landholders with men prepared to accept the old conditions. Five tenements were let for life at a small cash rent with an obligation to provide one man for one day in hay harvest for lifting the crop. This was practically giving the land for nothing compared with the heavy labour services under pre-plague terms . . .".[897]

After it became possible for the lessee through the trespass action to obtain actual recovery of the leasehold, additional legal protections arose. In the early 16th century, the old feudal rule permitting a lord as guardian to oust the lessee during the minority of the lessor was changed.[898] Then a statute in 1529 prohibited the practice by which a lessor could recover the leasehold by defaulting in a collusive action by a third party against the leasehold.[899] In 1540 another statute gave lessees some protection against ousters by landlords' successors.[900]

Improving security for the lessee's interest did not resolve the questions concerning what kind of interest the leasehold was in legal terms. Through the confusion of conflicting court decisions, it appeared that a leasehold was real property for purposes of tenures, but was not for purposes of estates. Because a lease was not real property in terms of estates, and chattels could not be the subjects of estates, the lessee could not create remainders in or entail the leasehold. Eventually, courts held this restriction applicable only to *inter vivos* transfers, and permitted devises of remainders

---

[896] *Id.*

[897] *Id.* at 57, 60, 62.

[898] *The Reports of Sir John Spelman* 182 (J. H. Baker, ed., Selden Society, vol. 94, 1977).

[899] 21 Hen. 8, c. 15 (1529).

[900] 32 Hen. 8, c. 28 (1540).

and entails.[901] But even though estates in leaseholds could be devised, they could not be created or limited through intestate inheritance. This was because chattels passed to executors or administrators, rather than to heirs. And because of the dual nature of a leasehold, part real property and part personal property, it came to be called a chattel real.

Courts determined that the length of lease terms was not limited, but it became common for some agricultural leases to be limited to 21 years and some building leases to 99 years. In the 15th century, a leasehold without a fixed duration usually left lessees as tenants at will. At first, courts treated periodic tenancies also as tenancies at will,[902] but after two centuries of judicial inconsistency, the courts finally agreed that a periodic lease created a tenancy for the initial term, followed by successive tenancies for each term during which the lease was continued.[903] Thereafter, courts usually construed tenancies whose nature was unclear as periodic tenancies rather than as tenancies at will.[904]

The law of leaseholds also intersected with the law of covenants. By the seventeenth century, covenant obligations of lessors included rights to demise, of quiet enjoyment, of freedom from encumbrances, and of further assurances. The lessee covenanted to pay rent. By analogy from earlier authority on restrictive covenants,[905] both the benefits and burdens of these covenants ran with the lease, and by statute the grantees of reversions were empowered to enforce lease covenants.[906] "With these changes, leaseholds, worked by tenant farmers in actual possession of the land, came to cover

[901] Lampet's Case, 10 Co. Rep. 46b, 77 Eng. Rep. 994 (1612); Manning's Case, 8 Co. Rep. 94b, 77 Eng. Rep. 618 (1609).

[902] *See, e.g.,* Y.B. 21 Hen. 7, Michaelmas Term, f. 38, pl. 47 (1506).

[903] Leighton v. Theed, 1 Ld. Raym. 707 (1702).

[904] William Blackstone, *Commentaries* Ch. 9, Sec. II. 145.

[905] Spencer's Case, 5 Co. Rep. 16a, 77 Eng. Rep. 72 (1583).

[906] 32 Hen. 8, c. 34 (1540).

a large portion of English lands.[907]

After the massive English property reform legislation of 1925, leases became estates and remained the only tenures of any significance. According to these acts, an estate is an interest in land of defined duration, and the only two types of *legal* estates now recognized are the fee simple absolute in possession and the term of years absolute. The term of years absolute is the right to possess land for a period of fixed and certain duration, even for less than a year, and can include periodic tenancies. It need not be a presently possessory interest, and can be created to commence at some time in the future less than 21 years from the time the lease was created.

Because of flexibility in duration, leases have achieved a unique utility in English land law. For instance, leases may be used to provide a form of security in certain conveyances. Typically, a mortgagor will give a long-term lease of 3,000 years to the mortgagee, with the term of years to cease when the loan is repaid. A building lease may also be exceptionally long.[908]

In addition to its function as a security device in a mortgage, the lease may also serve to secure trust payments to minor beneficiaries. Under such a trust settlement, the trustee would grant a long-term lease to the settlor,

---

907 "The landed gentry retained freehold interests, commonly under settlement, and exploited the land at one remove, and left a class of tenant farmers in actual occupation of the soil . . . .The landlord and tenant divided between them the burden of providing capital for agriculture, and a progressive landlord could do a great deal to encourage, and indeed insist upon, good husbandry . . . ." A. W. B. Simpson, *A History of the Land Law* 251 (2d ed. 1986).

908 "Under a building lease, for example, the land is let for a long term at a ground rent, the tenant puts up a building at his own expense, and at the end of the term this becomes the landlord's property; such a lease is therefore a valuable long-term investment for the landlord. Leases of anything up to 999 years, or even more, are sometimes granted for similar purposes; here the reversion is too remote to have any value, but the advantage to the landlord is that he can control the use of the land by means of covenants in the lease, and a greater variety of covenants are enforceable under a lease than under an outright conveyance of the fee simple. Such very long term leases may therefore be useful when a landlord is developing an estate and wishes to keep control over its appearance and character." R. E. Megarry and H. W. R. Wade, *The Law of Real Property* 620 (3d ed. 1966).

but neither the settlor nor the mortgagee lessee typically would take possession of the land.

Piecemeal legislation since the 19th century has brought much of leasehold law under statute. Reforms introduced by the Agricultural Holdings (England) Act of 1875, the Agricultural Holdings Act of 1923, the Agriculture Act of 1947, the Agricultural Holdings Act of 1948, and the Agriculture Act of 1958 have made agricultural tenancies more secure, requiring a year's notice to terminate in every instance, even after expiration of the regular term. Even those terminations operate in only narrowly specified circumstances. Otherwise, agricultural tenancies continue indefinitely until terminated according to the provisions of the applicable statute. More recent changes in these laws were made by the Agriculture Act of 1976 and the Agricultural Holdings Act of 1977.

Business tenants became more secure in their tenancies after the Landlord and Tenant Act of 1927. Tenants in occupancy for more than five years who could prove that business goodwill had become attached to the premises had a right to renew the lease. These rights were expanded and strengthened by the Landlord and Tenant Act of 1954.

Tenants of furnished dwellings first obtained statutory protection in 1920 and have since received the attention of numerous items of legislation.[909] Tenant rights, both as to security of tenure and as to rent limits, in both private and public housing, are protected under current legislation.

---

[909] These include the Rent and Mortgage Restrictions Acts of 1920-1939, the Furnished Houses Act of 1946, the Landlord and Tenant Act of 1949, the Housing Repairs and Rents Act of 1954, the Rent Act of 1957, the Rent Act of 1965, the Rent Act of 1968, the Housing Act of 1969, the Housing Finance Act of 1972, the Counter-Inflation Act of 1973, the Rent Act of 1974, the Rent Act of 1977, and the Housing Act of 1980 .

§ 8.04(c). Changes in Future Interests.

§ 8.04(c)(1). Reversions and Remainders.

§ 8.04(c)(1)(A). Reversions.

The early common law often interchanged the terminology of reversions and escheats, but after the Statute De Donis Conditionalibus in 1285, it became more clear that the interest of a fee simple holder who died without heirs would "escheat" to the lord; after the death of a life tenant, however, the land could "revert" to the grantor as holder of the fee.

§ 8.04(c)(1)(B). Remainders.

If the land did not revert upon the death of the life tenant, it might "remain" to some person other than the grantor who held the fee. Not all the features of these remainders were fully defined during this period. There is some evidence, for instance, that even in the late twelfth century conveyancers created remainders following conditional fees, conveyances that would be impermissible under modern law even if conditional fees were still recognized.[910]

§ 8.04(c)(1)(C). Contingent Remainders.

A contingent remainder was hesitatingly upheld in a case as early as 1304,[911] but, conscious of the feudal order, judges were troubled over who would do homage.[912] Common law contingent remainders were fragile interests, subject to destruction upon forfeiture for tortious alienation (an attempt by a life tenant to convey a fee simple was considered a tortious

---

[910] Under modern law, a remainder typically may follow only an interest that is less than a fee.

[911] Y.B. 32 & 33 Edw. (Rolls Series), 328 (1304).

[912] Y.B. 2 Edw. 2, 4 (1390).

alienation). The rule of destructibility had enough vitality to extend even to contingent remainders created by use or devise. Cases beginning as early as 1336 suggest that contingent remainders could be upheld if the remainders subsequently vested,[913] and that the death of a living person was the only contingency recognized at law. But in a 1550 case[914] a judge stated as settled law that a remainder could be based on any condition that was not illegal or repugnant.[915] Contingent remainders were also then considered destructible and were in fact destroyed if they could not take effect upon termination of the precedent estate, such as a contingent remainder to a posthumous son.[916] As noted before, an attempt by a life tenant to convey a fee (the so-called tortious alienation), as well as disseisin of the life tenant (thereby prematurely terminating the life estate), also resulted in destruction of a contingent remainder.[917]

Despite destructibility, contingent remainders had an alluring role to play in achieving disposition of family lands, so-called family settlements, in a way that would inhibit alienability by individual family members. In the 17th century, conveyancers who wished to create a life tenancy with contingent remainder as part of a family settlement began to insert a remainder in trust for the life of the life tenant, in case the life estate terminated prematurely, threatening the contingent remainder with destructibility. The vested nature of the remainder in trust was upheld in 1740.[918]

---

[913] Y.B. 10 Edw. 3, Michaelmas Term, No. 8 (1336).

[914] Colthirst v. Bejushin, 1 Plowden 20, 75 Eng. Rep. 33 (1550).

[915] An example of a repugnant condition would be a series of successive remainders with forfeiture by any remainderman who attempted to alienate the interest, but with the alienee also being the next or only remainderman.

[916] Reeve v. Long, 3 Lev. 408, 1 Salk. 227, 4 Mod. 282, 87 Eng. Rep. 395 (1695).

[917] Saltmarsh v. Redeness, Y.B. 11 Edw. 2, Michaelmas Term, pl. 8 (1317) in *Year Books 11 Edward II 1317-18* 12 (John P. Collas and William S. Holdsworth, eds., Selden Society Vol. 61, Year Book Series vol. 22, 1942).

[918] Dormer v. Packhurst, 6 Bro. P. C. 351 (1740), upholding Duncomb v. Duncomb, 3 Lev. 437, 83 Eng. Rep. 770 (1697).

§ 8.04(c)(1)(D). The Rule in *Shelley's Case.*

An important early gloss on the normal rules for creating and conveying remainders came to be known as the Rule in *Shelley's Case*, although that case in 1581 was only the culmination of more than two centuries of judicial development. The foundation of the rule, though obscure, was apparently deeply anchored in feudal formalism. Simply stated, this formalism required that if the heir of a certain landholder succeeded by inheritance to the seisin of the land, then the usual feudal payments would be due to the lord. No such feudal dues would be owed by a successor who entered by way of purchase, that is, by means other than inheritance. Thus grantors made early attempts to convey a life estate to a grantee, with remainder in the life tenant's heirs, so that those heirs would come into their interest by means of the conveyance rather than by normal inheritance from the life tenant. Accordingly, as early as 1350[919] and 1366[920] courts were agreeing that a remainder in fee to a life tenant's heirs should be treated as a fee in the life tenant; therefore, the life tenant's heirs would take, if at all, through inheritance and thus be liable for the usual feudal dues.

The rule has been labeled as the decision in *Shelley's Case* probably because that case gave the rule relatively succinct expression, even though by that time much of the feudal justification for the rule had dissipated:

> [I]t is a rule in law, when the ancestor by any gift or conveyance takes an estate of freehold, and in the same gift or conveyance an estate is limited either mediately or immediately to his heirs in fee or in tail; that always in such cases, "the heirs" are words of limitation of the estate, and not words of purchase.[921]

Thus a remainder to the life tenant's heirs was simply a remainder in

---

[919] Y.B. 24 Edw. 3, 70 no. 9 (1350).

[920] Y.B. 40 Edw. 3, f. 9 no. 18 (1366).

[921] Shelley's Case, 1 Co. Rep. 88b, 93b, 76 Eng. Rep. 199, 206 (1581).

fee, so indicated by the use of the word "heirs," and this remainder in fee was considered to belong to the life tenant and not to the heirs. Through operation of the principle of merger, the life tenant who obtained the remainder in fee pertaining to the land held in life tenancy, would have the fee simple absolute, if there was no intervening estate. "The Rule had such vitality that it survived in full force for many centuries after the conditions which gave it birth were only dimly discernible in history."[922]

The Rule in *Shelley's Case* survived in England until enactment of the Law of Property Act in 1925.[923]

§ 8.04(c)(1)(E). The Doctrine of Worthier Title.

A rule of law less well known than the Rule in *Shelley's Case* but born of the same impulse is the doctrine of worthier title. According to the doctrine of worthier title, a landholder could not convey or devise a remainder to his or her own heirs. The remainder would be considered void, leaving the fee in the grantor. The heirs who therefore could not obtain the fee by conveyance or devise were presumed to ultimately receive it by inheritance and, just as under the Rule in *Shelley's Case*, would also be liable for the payment of feudal dues. It was therefore "worthier" (and, it might be added, "worth" more to the feudal lord) for the heir to receive the ancestor's land by inheritance (as distinguished from devise) than by gift or purchase. Despite this feudal explanation for the expressions of this rule, the label of "worthier title" is American in origin.[924]

The first documentary manifestation of this rule was in the 13th-century Statute of Fraudulent Feoffments,[925] which voided a

---

[922] Sheldon F. Kurtz, *Moynihan's Introduction to the Law of Real Property* 189 (4th ed. 2005).

[923] 15 & 16 Geo. 5, c. 20, § 131 (1925).

[924] *See, e.g.*, Ellis v. Page, 61 Mass. (7 Cush.) 161 (1851).

[925] 52 Hen. 3, c. 6 (1267).

landholder's conveyance to his heir apparent. The earliest cases applying the rule did not appear in the case reports until the 16th century.[926]

As with the Rule in *Shelley's Case*, the courts applied the doctrine of worthier title long after its feudal justifications had disappeared. As applied to devises, the rule had to be frequently taken into account on behalf of certain creditors, who could reach assets held by a decedent's heirs, but not by the decedent's devisees. The rule was applied as a rule of law rather than as a discretionary rule of construction. While the rule tenuously lives on in American jurisprudence, it was statutorily abolished in England in 1833.[927]

§ 8.04(c)(2). Reversionary Interests.

§ 8.04(c)(2)(A). Possibilities of Reverter.

Even more obscure are the origins of the reversionary interests associated with defeasible fees. One of these types of defeasible fees, the determinable fee, was the subject of considerable controversy among legal scholars a century ago. The controversy concerned whether the Statute Quia Emptores in 1290 operated to prohibit the creation of determinable fee simple estates. Implicit in this controversy was the notion that interests like determinable fees had been possible before 1290,[928] and that interests like possibilities of reverter were derived from such limited fees and had likewise existed before 1290. The better view seems to be that the Statute Quia Emptores operated only on fee simple absolute interests, and that the determinable fees, while not especially common, were acceptable interests both before and after 1290. Some evidence for the existence and acceptability of determinable fees (and, by inference, for possibilities of reverter) emerges from case reports in the 15th, 16th and 17th centuries,

---

926 These cases are cited and summarized in Joseph W. Morris, "The Inter Vivos Branch of the Worthier Title Doctrine," 2 *Okla. L. Rev.* 133, 135-138 (1949).

927 3 & 4 Will. 4, c. 106, § 3 (1833).

928 *See* examples cited in Richard R. B. Powell, "Determinable Fees," 23 *Colum. L. Rev.* 207, 212 (1923).

during the reign of Elizabeth I and from the writings of Littleton and Coke. Except for the interest one might have in completing the historical record, the question has been mooted by modern developments–both English and American cases recognize determinable fees and possibilities of reverter.[929]

§ 8.04(c)(2)(B). Rights of Entry or Powers of Termination.

Another defeasible fee simple interest known in modern terminology as a fee simple subject to a condition subsequent also was connected to a reversionary interest, known either as a right of entry or a power of termination. Its origins, too, are obscure, but from early cases it seems certain that this type of estate and its accompanying future interests were being created and recognized perhaps as early as the 12th century.[930] In 1220 the grantor of such a fee on condition obtained a royal writ to recover the land following occurrence of the condition.[931] However, in the less certain terminology of the time, the future interest following a conditional fee was often called a remainder.

The rules regarding rights of entry for breach of condition were settled by the time Littleton wrote in the 15th century, and by the time of the Tudors, courts were holding the right of entry to arise implicitly in the creation of the condition, and did not need to be expressly included in the conveyance.[932] Also, "under the early common law, an actual entry was

---

[929] "But whatever one may think about historical arguments as to the existence of fees determinable, the short answer to the whole question is that there are no decisions denying their existence, and that one recent English case [1944] and numerous American cases have recognized them. It is too late now, in view of these numerous decisions, to say that there is no such thing as a determinable fee." 1 Lewis F. Simes and Allan F. Smith, *The Law of Future Interests* § 283, pp. 332-35 (1956).

[930] 2 Frederick Pollock and Frederic William Maitland, *The History of English Law Before the Time of Edward I* 17-19, 23-29 (2d ed. 1909).

[931] *Bracton's Note Book*, Nos. 61, 86 (1220).

[932] Mary Partington's Case, 10 Co. Rep. 35b (1613). "In the United States, however, courts have often held that words of condition or proviso, standing alone, are ambiguous and that the grantor who omits any express provision for re-entry,

generally necessary to effect a forfeiture of a condition subsequent annexed to a freehold estate,"[933] probably so the grantor could once again obtain the seisin. In modern times no formal entry is necessary to recover the estate, and because actual entry is infrequent, some prefer the technically more correct term of "power of termination" as the proper name for this future interest.

§ 8.04(c)(3). Executory Interests.

§ 8.04(c)(3)(A). Springing Interests.

The preceding chapter described how the Statute of Uses gave rise to new forms of future interests.[934] Certain uses were given as future interests in forms that were prohibited for legal interests under the common law. When the Statute of Uses in 1536 converted most use interests into legal interests, the future interest uses also became legal interests, but not subject to the traditional common law restrictions. For instance, a so-called springing use was created when one enfeoffed land to a feoffee to the use of another, such use to not commence until some time in the future. When "executed" by the Statute of Uses, this springing use became a legal springing executory interest: the feoffor held the estate in fee simple (the grant to the feoffee having been invalidated by the Statute of Uses), but the fee simple estate was subject to the executory interest. Other springing executory interests resulted from conveyances of successive uses with gaps of time in between. Also, a conveyance to one in use with remainder in use to the heirs of a person then living would create yet another variety of springing executory interest, because a gap of time might be required to determine heirship.

---

termination, or forfeiture may be found to have intended to create only a personal covenant, a real covenant, or equitable servitude, an easement, an equitable charge, or a trust rather than a defeasible estate." William B. Stoebuck and Dale A. Whitman, *The Law of Property* § 2.5, p. 41 (3d. ed. 2000).

[933] Lewis M. Simes and Allan F. Smith, *The Law of Future Interests* § 254, p. 294 (2d ed. 1956).

[934] § 7.07(f)(3), *supra*.

§ 8.04(c)(3)(B). Shifting Interests.

A shifting use resulted from a conveyance to one, in use, with the use to go over to another upon the occurrence of a specified event, a conveyancing sequence also forbidden for legal interests under the common law. After execution by the Statute of Uses, such shifting uses became legal shifting executory interests.

After passage of the Statute of Wills in 1540, it was also possible to devise springing and shifting interests, and these devises became known as executory devises.

§ 8.04(c)(4). Fees Tail.

With respect to all of these future interests, once their formative period was past, little change occurred in their inherent characteristics until modern times. However, several significant changes did occur in the availability and utility of these interests and their underlying estates. The career of the fee tail presents perhaps the most interesting example.

When in the 12th century it became common for landholders to give land to a grantee and the heirs of his or her body, the grantor was commonly considered to have a reversion if the grantee had no issue. By the mid-13th century it was common for holders of such conditional fee interests to transfer them to others free of the conditions. The Statute De Donis Conditionalibus in 1285 prohibited this practice, which required that the land be inherited by the grantee's issue, if there be any, or if not, that it revert to the grantor. With these new characteristics, the interest called the fee tail arose out of the statute.

While the statute on its face applied only to the first generation of issue, leaving such issue to alienate freely after they acquired the estate, some court decisions shortly after *Quia Emptores* insisted that the restrictions as to issue be observed until the fourth generation of issue. Even that extension of the statutory restriction was not stable, and by early in the 15th century courts held the restriction of the fee tail to possession by descendant issue, with reversion to the grantor if such descendants should fail, to be of indefinite duration. Parliament resisted petitions to ameliorate these restrictions, because of the fee tail's other advantages: after the tenant's lifetime the fee tail was not subject to attainder for felony or forfeiture for treason, nor could it be reached to satisfy debts of former tenants in tail. Not until Littleton's treatise at the end of the 15th century were some of these rules stabilized.

Meanwhile, persons who promoted such rules as aids to maintaining family dynastic landholdings were opposed by those who sought to realize the market value of their landholdings and therefore to lift or lighten the restrictions. This latter interest was most often aided by the courts. In a 1472 case,[935] the court acknowledged that the rights of issue could be barred by a collusive procedure known as a common recovery, described in detail in the footnote.[936]

---

[935] Taltarum's Case, Y.B. 12 Edw. 4, Michaelmas Term, f. 14, pl. 16, f. 19, pl. 25, 13 Edw. 4, Michaelmas Term, f. 1, pl. 1 (1472).

[936]

> The collusive common recovery worked in the following way. Suppose Smith to be tenant in tail in possession of Blackacre, which he wishes to sell for a fee simple to Jones. A collusive real action is brought by Jones against Smith on a feigned title, Jones having already paid or agreed to pay Smith for the land. In this action Jones claims a fee simple in the land. Smith appears in court and vouches one Brown to warranty. Brown does not dispute his obligation to warrant Smith's title, and the action then proceeds between Jones and Brown. Instead of putting up a defence Brown asks for 'leave to imparl,' that is, he asks the court for an adjournment whilst he talks the matter over with Jones in the hope of reaching a settlement, and he and Jones leave court to have their imparlance. Brown promptly disappears. This is a contempt of court, and when Jones arrives back before the Justices and tells them that Brown has absconded, they at once give judgment in favour of Jones. The judgment is that Jones recovers the land, and that Brown is to convey to Smith lands of equal value to those recovered. Unfortunately Brown, who has been carefully selected for this reason (and paid for his trouble), has no land, so that the judgment can never [be] satisfied. If it ever was satisfied, then the land conveyed would be held on the same terms as that lost to Jones; it would be subject to the entail and to any interest in remainder or reversion after Smith's estate . . . .A blind eye is turned to the fact that the whole procedure is an obvious fraud, and neither the issue nor the remaindermen are allowed to do anything about it.

Around the common recovery hangs a great mystery. In the first

The common recovery was probably practiced before *Taltarum's Case* in 1472, but probably was not fully developed until sometime afterward; indeed it seems that the judge in *Taltarum's Case* allowed the recovery only on the assumption that the vouchee really would provide lands of equal value. When Littleton was writing his treatise on tenures at about that same time, he did not consider the fee tail a barrable estate. Later judges did not rest on that optimistic assumption, and by the middle of the 16th century it is clear that any expectation that the vouchee could satisfy a judgment had been abandoned: the court crier became the standard vouchee.[937] Still later in that century courts decided that the common recovery would bar not only the issue but also any reversioners or remaindermen.[938] Much mystery surrounds the courts' motives for acceding to such devices.[939]

During the reign of Henry VIII courts accepted the notion that entails could be barred and considered the common recovery procedure, sometimes involving more than one vouchee, apparently too cumbersome; an already established procedure known as the fine, or final accord, was also allowed to bar entails. According to the fine procedure, participating parties would engage in litigation over rights in land, pause to ostensibly reach a compromise, and then have the court accept and record the terms of the compromise, which were actually the terms of the intended original conveyance. In its collusive aspects it was similar to the common recovery and no doubt seemed an appropriate alternative procedure for barring entails. A statute of 1490 suggested the availability of the fine for this

---

> place we do not really know when it was evolved, and in the second place there is no full understanding of the theoretical justification which allowed its entrance into the law.

A. W. B. Simpson, *A History of the Land Law* 130 (2d ed. 1986).

[937] The first reported case in which the court crier appears as the common vouchee is Anon (1538).

[938] Capell's Case, 1 Co. Rep. 54a, 61a, 76 Eng. Rep. 121, 134 (1581).

[939] A. W. B. Simpson, *A History of the Land Law* 134-35 (2d ed. 1986).

purpose,[940] courts accepted it in 1527,[941] and a statute in 1536 reinforced the decision.[942] Conveyancers used the fine procedure to convert the entailed estate into a fee simple until the Fines and Recoveries Act of 1833 abolished both fines and recoveries.[943] Thereafter the entailed estate could be "barred" or "docked" by means of a deed recorded with the Chancery Court.

§ 8.04(d). Family Settlements or Succession.

Estates in tail were a major factor in English family settlements. Land, as the principal form of wealth, was often "settled" on family members, especially younger siblings perhaps starting out with their own new family units. When trusts began to be fashionable for family settlements, the grantor of the trust was and still is frequently referred to as the settlor. From a modern perspective, the family settlement was simply a means of conferring on the children of a family their respective inheritances. Probably the main concern during the Middle Ages was to provide each new generation with appropriate lands, yet to keep the lands "within the family," so as to maintain large, dynastic landholdings. Thus a primary purpose in family settlements was to restrict grantees' abilities to alienate their lands outside the family, and no form of landholding more closely fit this purpose than the fee tail.

On the other hand, a younger family member in possession of settled lands frequently needed cash, or the more flexible wealth represented by land, so that the restrictions on alienation imposed through family settlements were obstructive and generally undesirable. Those who held entailed lands were the persons most likely to seek out some way to bar the entail, either through common recovery or fine or some other device.

---

[940] 4 Hen. 7, c. 24 (1490).

[941] Anon, Dyer 2b, 73 Eng. Rep. 7 (1527).

[942] 28 Hen. 8, c. 36 (1536).

[943] 3 & 4 Will. 4, c. 74, §§ 15, 40 (1833).

In response, settlors as early as the 14th century began using combinations of a life estate with entailed fee in remainder to the life tenant's oldest son and successive remainders to younger sons. If the oldest or other sons were not yet born, the settlor would simply confer the remainder in fee tail on the life tenant's heir, in an age before the Rule in *Shelley's Case* turned such a conveyance into a fee simple absolute for the erstwhile life tenant. The entailed remainders became less functional as settlement devices when the courts began removing obstacles to their alienability.

During the 16th century, settlors acquired new tools for working out family settlements. The Statute of Uses in 1536 and the Statute of Wills in 1540 provided broad new means for both *inter vivos* and testamentary dispositions of landed interests. Powers of appointment were created by the Statute of Uses: before the Statute of Uses a grantor could convey to a feoffee to such uses as the feoffee would declare; after the Statute of Uses, such a declaration resulted in a legal estate being conferred on the person named in the declaration. "Towards the end of the seventeenth century, however, the activities of a number of eminent conveyancers . . . produced some order by designing model conveyances which satisfied the desires of the landowners and kept within reasonably well settled doctrines of the law; there arose a conveyancing tradition, and in the courts a respect for that tradition, which has continued to this day."[944]

Out of this era of ingenuity came the so-called strict settlement, based on the notion that in family settlements only a life tenant should ever be in actual possession of the land, and that entailed interests should always be remainder interests. If the entailed remainderman ever came into actual possession, then the entailment could be barred by fine or common recovery and become freely alienable. In a typical strict settlement, usually worked out at the time of the child's marriage, the owner in fee would settle the land on his son for life, with remainder in tail to the son's unborn oldest son, and successive remainders to any other unborn younger grandsons, all such remainders being contingent. The settlement would be in trust with the trustee instructed to preserve the contingent remainders of the unborn

---

[944] A. W. B. Simpson, *A History of the Land Law* 235 (2d ed. 1986).

younger grandsons, and whose legal interest effectively blocked the settlor's son from destroying his own life estate. This made the life tenancy secure and this security is what made the settlement "strict" or inviolable.

Before the entailed remainderman took steps to bar the entail, the tenant in possession would agree to provide an attractive income based on the lands in return for the remainderman's agreement to resettle the lands on the same terms for another generation. Income provisions for the wife and the younger children would be secured by the land and raised by trustees accumulating profits from the land. Sometimes the oldest son paid these so-called "portions" in advance, in order to clear the charges against his land title. Through use of powers of appointment, a child more able than the oldest son might occasionally be chosen for the first remainder. By enlarging the normal rights of life tenants, those in possession could be protected against claims for waste, encouraged to invest in improving the land, and even empowered to lease, sell or exchange the land. This arcane procedure was in common use from the end of the 17th century to very modern times, made unpopular only by various forms of 20th-century taxation, especially death duties.

The strict settlement was particularly well-suited to meet the uncertainties of marriages involving two wealthy families.[945] With large tracts of settled land held in life tenancy, and not all such life tenants enjoying broadened powers of use and disposition, the prevalence of strict settlement came to be viewed as harmful, hindering the full utilization of land.

§ 8.04(e). The Rule Against Perpetuities.

A constant apprehension of many judges and lawyers who shaped English land law was that, through the connivance of the law, large portions of land would be held unalienable and not fully utilized. The rule against perpetuities and various other rules favoring alienability of land are expressions of this perspective, which, however, was always tempered by

[945] *Id.* at 238.

desires of those who obtained land to secure their holdings.[946]

Land whose alienability remained restricted indefinitely was a great irritant to many in English society, and the issue of perpetuities in family settlements and other contexts had troubled judges, landowners and conveyancers for centuries. The archetype of such restricted land was land held in fee tail, with the entailment not subject to being barred. Thus conveyancers created devices to enable barring of the fee tail estate in some circumstances, making of it in essence a fee simple absolute.

The modern rule against perpetuities went considerably beyond concerns for barring entailed land and has its genesis in *The Duke of Norfolk's Case* in 1681.[947] The judge in that case had to determine if vesting was too remote in a devise of leasehold property. Specifically, a leasehold was devised to trustees for the benefit of the settlor's second son, in tail, but if the oldest son were to die without male issue during the lifetime of the second son, or if the settlor's patrimony descended to the second son, then the leaseholds would go over to the third son. The interests were upheld on the conclusion that they would have to vest in the third son, if at all, not later than during the lifetime of the second son. On this occasion the judge also announced a new rule of remoteness, superseding previous perpetuities rules, that an interest, to be valid, must vest, if at all, during the lifetime of a person in being at the time of the settlement. Judges in subsequent decisions extended the time slightly to a period of a life in being plus twenty-one years. The rule against perpetuities remains an active element in English land law today.

---

[946] "The lawyers and judges who moulded the more modern rules upon perpetuities in the period between 1450 and 1700 were themselves great purchasers and settlors of land; it could thus be that the rules worked out in the courts represent an attempt to balance the conflicting desires of their authors, and produced a body of law which indulged to some extent both the desire for an active land market and the desire to retain land in the family." *Id.* at 209.

[947] Howard v. Henry Duke of Norfolk, 3 Cas. in Chan. 1, 2 Swans. 454, 36 Eng. Rep. 690 (1681).

§ 8.04(f). Emergence of Trusts.

Even though the 1536 Statute of Uses applied to conveyances of "use, confidence or trust," the term "trust" eventually came to signify those uses that were not considered to be executed by the Statute. Among those unexecuted uses were uses declared on a term of years, which term, of course, was not a freehold estate. While some equity courts were at first reluctant to enforce such uses, because they could be viewed as attempts to evade the effects of the Statute of Uses, the Statute of Uses itself lost its practical vitality after abolition of tenures in 1660 and leasehold uses, known as trusts, became common after that time.

Certain freehold uses were also treated as unexecuted by the Statute of Uses. If a use was active, such as a use requiring the feoffee to make a further conveyance or to collect rents and pay debts, the judges ruled them unexecuted by the Statute, and they, too, were termed trusts.

A use on a use was also not executed, although before the eighteenth century such conveyances were probably the result of mistake and inadvertence. In 1668 a court seemed to suggest that the first *cestui que use* would hold in trust for the second,[948] and in 1700 a trust was recognized in a use deliberately created on a use.[949] Gradually, and with much hesitation, courts began consistently to regard a use on a use as not executed, not recognized by the common law courts, and enforceable only as a trust in equity.[950]

Trusts, labeled by one and considered by many to be "a brilliant invention of English jurisprudence,"[951] play a huge role in the practical

---

[948] Ash v. Gallen, 1 Ch. Cases 114, 22 Eng. Rep. 720 (1668).

[949] Sympson v. Turner, 1 Eq. Cas. Abr. 383 (1700).

[950] A. W. B. Simpson, *A History of the Land Law* 206 (2d ed. 1986).

[951] Jesse Dukeminier and James E. Krier, Property 287 (5th ed. 2002).

aspects of modern English and American property law.

§ 8.04(g). Servitudes.

§ 8.04(g)(1). Relationship to Incorporeal Hereditaments.

The English law of servitudes arose from that branch of property law dealing with incorporeal hereditaments, by which term is meant rights that are treated as property. Corporeal hereditaments are the physical objects, such as land, buildings and fixtures, that are governed by property law. Incorporeal hereditaments, on the other hand, consist of a wide variety of *rights* considered to be property and also governed by property law. Bracton recognized the distinction between corporeal and incorporeal hereditaments, but questioned whether one could have seisin of incorporeal things.[952] In the almost contemporary treatise known as *Britton*, that writer conceded that livery of seisin was not possible for incorporeal hereditaments, which must instead be conveyed by a grant in deed.[953]

For Bracton, all incorporeal hereditaments were servitudes.[954] Of the incorporeal hereditaments listed later by Blackstone, all were either then accepted as servitudes or were analogous to servitudes. Today, easements and profits, as the incorporeal hereditaments that are still of some importance, are also considered servitudes.

Principal incorporeal hereditaments still recognized today are rentcharges, annuities and corodies, advowsons, tithes, easements, *profits a prendre*, titles of honour, offices, franchises, reversions, and

[952] *Bracton*, f. 7.

[953] *Britton*, II, 8 and 9. "In Britton's day the correct method of grant was delivery of a charter in view of the lands to which they related, which was about as near to livery of seisin as one could get. But the grantee, if he wanted to alienate, must acquire seisin by enjoying the right before he alienated, and until he did so his title was imperfect." A. W. B. Simpson, *A History of the Land Law* 106 (2d ed. 1986).

[954] *Bracton*, f. 53.

remainders.[955]

From the preceding, it can be seen that easements and profits are the servitudes currently considered incorporeal hereditaments. Easements, however, were not considered incorporeal hereditaments before the 18th century, because the only easements then recognized were appurtenant to a dominant tenement, so the easement was merely a "right" appurtenant to a corporeal hereditament, that is, to the dominant tenement. Profits, too, were often appurtenant, but they could also exist in gross, and to that extent were always considered incorporeal hereditaments. Since the 18th century, English land law no longer draws the distinction between incorporeal hereditaments and those rights considered to be merely appurtenances to other land, so now, all easements and profits, whether appurtenant or in gross, are treated as incorporeal hereditaments. Restrictive covenants arose later and are strictly equitable interests, and so are a type of servitude outside the doctrines of incorporeal hereditaments.

§ 8.04(g)(2). Profits.

In Bracton's time in the 13th century, profits were more prominent than easements. *Britton*'s description of servitudes included profits and easements, "granting that another who has nothing therein, shall have a right of pasturing or mowing or fishing or of driving cattle or of way or of carrying therein or by other servitudes, which may be infinite and numberless . . . ."[956] Profits were distinguished as being rights to take something of value *away* from the servient land.

The most numerous types of profits in the Middle Ages were rights to common, either created by grant from the lord to one of his freeholders, or arising by custom:

> These common rights were a necessary part of that common or open field system upon which most of the land

---

[955] Helpful explanations of each of these incorporeal hereditaments are found in R. E. Megarry and H. W. R. Wade, *The Law of Real Property* 786-787 (3d ed. 1966).

[956] *Britton*, II, 23, 3.

> of England was cultivated for many centuries. Thus we find common of turbary, or the right to cut turf for fuel; common of estovers, or the right to cut timber, underwood, furze, etc., for fuel or litter; common of piscary, or the right to fish in another's water; and, by far the most important of all, the right to common of pasture.[957]

Profits that were not appurtenant to lands within the manor, that benefited persons outside the manor and were therefore in gross, were created or acquired by grant, reservation or long use.[958]

The long use required to establish a profit was described by Bracton as:

> user for a long time with peaceful, continuous and uninterrupted enjoyment of the right, the lord knowing of it and neglecting to interfere; for this is regarded as equivalent to a legal transfer, provided that the enjoyment has not been by violence, or clandestinely or by request and permission . . . .[959]

The time requirement for long use became one of the most fanciful fictions of the common law. The common law early referred to the "time whereof the memory of man runneth not to the contrary," fixed by odd analogy with a period of limitation in a statute of 1275 as the year 1189.[960]

---

[957] 3 William Holdsworth, *A History of English Law* 143 (5th ed. 1942).

[958] *Bracton*, f. 222.

[959] *Id.*

[960] "The long user became the common law's 'time whereof the memory of man runneth not to the contrary', and until after the time of Littleton there were lawyers who were prepared to take this phrase sensibly and literally. Unhappily, the view which prevailed, and which is to be found in the early year books, required user to be shown since 1189, with the absurd results all know. The date was selected by analogy with the period of limitation fixed in 1275 for the writ of right; until the Prescription Act (1833) the only attempt to mitigate the resulting injustices was the judicial invention of the fiction of the lost grant." A. W. B. Simpson, *A History of the Land Law* 109-110 (2d ed. 1986).

Frequently a freehold tenant would claim a common of pasture profit in waste land of the manor as an incident of the freehold tenure. Rather than proving long use, the tenant needed only to prove the tenure and show that the tenure was created before the *Statute Quia Emptores* of 1290. This right of common pasture was the most frequent and most essential of the profits claimed by manorial tenants and even the early common law courts suggested that such appurtenant, appended or annexed rights arose by long use or ancient custom.[961]

In the 15th century a court held that all freeholders had a right of common pasture by operation of law, and this freeholder right was labeled appendant.[962] Appendant rights were limited to freeholders and to their animals considered commonable, such as cattle and horses.

Courts recognized rights of common pasture available to both free and villein tenants and categorized the rights as appurtenant, in gross, "*pur cause de vicinage*," and common of shack. Appurtenant rights were other profits attached to a dominant tenement that arose by prescription or grant, and pertained to animals not considered commonable, such as pigs, donkeys, goats and geese, or pertained to land not anciently arable, such as land recently drained or reclaimed from waste. A common of pasture in gross was not connected with any dominant tenement. A common "*pur cause de vicinage*" occurred when two waste land areas from adjoining manors ran against each other and tenants from either manor were permitted to use both areas. A common of shack existed in some areas over lands between the time of harvest and re-sowing.

Rights of common in waste lands were among the earliest victims of enclosures. Lords of manors claimed rights of approvement, the right to approve enclosure of manorial waste lands, subject to the limitation that

---

[961] *See* Statute of Westminster II, 13 Edw. 1, st. 1, c. 46 (1285); Solers v. Parson of Dorstone, Y.B. 11 Edw. 2, Michaelmas Term, pl. 8 (1317), in *Year Books 11 Edward II 1317-18* 91 (John P. Collas and William S. Holdsworth, eds., Selden Society Vol. 61, Year Book Series vol. 22, 1942); Y.B. 27 Edw. 3 (Rolls Series), 353 (1343).

[962] Y.B. 22 Hen. 6, Michaelmas Term, pl. 13, f. 9, at f. 10 (1462).

adequate land was left to serve common rights.[963] The approvement right applied only to waste lands and only against freehold tenants and against appendant and appurtenant common rights.

A series of cases in the late 16th and early 17th centuries stabilized the law as to profits,[964] and that law conceptually remains essentially unchanged today.[965] Statutory reforms affected creation and acquisition of profits by grant, reservation or prescription. Problems arising from the ancient and varied natures of profits prompted passage of the Commons Registration Act of 1965, to ascertain what commons rights are still claimed and to extinguish the others.

§ 8.04(g)(3). Easements.

When the law of profits was being clarified four centuries ago, the law of easements was still very new and was able to benefit from emerging rules for profits.[966]

---

[963] Statute of Merton, 20 Hen. 3, c. 4 (1235); Statute of Westminster II, 13 Edw., c. 46 (1285).

[964] Tyrringham's Case, 4 Co. Rep. 36b, 76 Eng. Rep. 973 (1584); Gateward's Case, 6 Co. Rep. 59b, 77 Eng. Rep. 344 (1607); Wyat Wyld's Case, 8 Co. Rep. 78b, 77 Eng. Rep. 593 (1610); Mellor v. Spateman, 1 Wms. Saund. 339, 343, 85 Eng. Rep. 489, 495 (1669); Weekly v. Wildman, 1 Ld. Raym. 405, 91 Eng. Rep. 1169 (1699).

[965] *See* R. E. Megarry and H. W. R. Wade, *The Law of Real Property* 818-23 (3d ed. 1966).

[966] "The definition of these various classes of incorporeal things helped to bring out into clearer relief the nature of easements, and customary rights in the nature of easements. We have seen that the nature of the classes of incorporeal things which have just been described, was fairly well ascertained in the Middle Ages; but that the law relating to easements was still in a very uncertain state. We shall see that, during the sixteenth and seventeenth centuries, their nature began to be better understood. But it is significant that Blackstone does not describe easements in general, and that the only easements which he mentions in his list of incorporeal things are various rights of way. As we shall now see, it is not till after Blackstone wrote, that the rules as to easements, which had been evolved during this period, were elaborated and combined into a definite body of legal doctrine, which defined the incidents, both of easements in general, and of particular kinds of easements." 7 William Holdsworth, *A History of English Law* 321 (2d ed. 1937).

Social conditions furthered the development of easement law. Urbanization and progressive enclosure of agricultural land required more precise identification of landowners' respective holdings and rights: "In the days of common fields there was for example no need for many of the rights of way which exist today, for the local population could wander where they wished through the unfenced countryside without causing annoyance or injury, and the modern desire for privacy was hardly known."[967]

However, Holdsworth was quick to assure that more law on easements existed than was revealed in Blackstone.[968] It is generally believed that easement law remained in a rudimentary state until early in the 19th century, when Charles James Gale wrote his *Treatise on the Law of Easements*. His depiction of the state of the law of easements has been accepted:

> The difficulties which arise from the abstruseness and refinements incident to the subject, have been increased by the comparatively small number of decided cases affording matter for defining and systematizing this branch of the law. Upon some points, indeed, there is no authority at all in the English law; of the decisions some depend upon the circumstances of the particular case, and some are irreconcilable with each other.
>
> Water-courses are the only class of Easements with regard to which the law has been settled with any degree of precision . . .
>
> As in many other branches of the Law of England, the earlier authorities upon the Law of Easements appear to be based upon the Civil Law, modified, in some degree, probably, by a recognition of customs which existed

---

[967] A. W. B. Simpson, *A History of the Land Law* 262 (2d ed. 1986).

[968] 7 William Holdsworth, *A History of English Law* 322 (2d ed. 1937), citing Peers v. Lucy, 4 Mod. 355, 362, 87 Eng. Rep. 441, 444 (1695).

among our Norman ancestors.[969]

Before Gale's treatise, easement law largely reflected of the law of profits. That an easement was the right to use the land of another and a profit the right to take something of value from the land of another required few distinctions in applying the pertinent rules of law. But during the 19th century some important principles of easement law were settled. In 1868 a court declared that no easement could be in gross.[970] An earlier court had held that an appurtenant easement could be used only for purposes connected with the dominant tenement.[971] Easements were considered perpetual, [972] but inasmuch as the rules against perpetuities were being refined in the 19th century, easements as perpetual charges or encumbrances on the land came to be sharply limited. Thus in 1833 an English judge announced that "incidents of a novel kind cannot be devised, and attached to property, at the fancy and caprice of the owner . . . ."[973]

This well-known reluctance of English judges to approve new kinds of easements was not directed at affirmative easements. In addition to rights of way, the most common of the affirmative easements, Gale's treatise lists 28 other varieties of affirmative easements that had been judicially approved.[974]

As to negative easements, however, he wrote only the following:

> The principal negative easements are:

---

[969] Charles James Gale, *A Treatise on the Law of Easements* vii ("Preface to the First Edition") (11th ed. by F. Graham Glover, 1931).

[970] Rangeley v. Midland Ry. Co., L. R. 3 Ch., App. 306 (1868).

[971] Ackroyd v. Smith, 10 C. B. 164, 138 Eng. Rep. 68 (1850).

[972] This principle was suggested as early as the 13th century, *Bracton*, f. 233a.

[973] Keppel v. Bailey, 3 My. & K. 517, 39 Eng. Rep. 1042 (1833).

[974] Charles James Gale, *A Treatise on the Law of Easements* 28-31 (11th ed. by F. Graham Glover, 1931).

> Right to receive light by ancient apertures.
>
> Right to receive air by a defined channel.
>
> Right to support for buildings from land; or from buildings.
>
> Right to receive a flow of water in an artificial stream.[975]

During the 19th century, English courts approved no new types of negative easements, and, indeed it is commonly believed that "the English law courts in the nineteenth century called a halt to the creation of negative easements other than the four traditional kinds."[976] A modern English property treatise proclaims that "the list of easements is not closed."[977] However, it also asserts that there are limits, expressed in

> the overriding principle that the various kinds of proprietary interests are fixed by law, and finite in number. Even though the list of easements is not closed, it is not open to interests which do not conform to the rules about the general nature of easements. For example, a right to an unspoilt view or a right to put out pleasure boats on a lake cannot exist as an easement. Nor can the right to have the wall of a house protected from weather by an adjoining house, as contrasted with a right of support which is a well-recognised easement and which often exists in favor of semi-detached houses.[978]

---

[975] *Id.* at 31.

[976] Jesse Dukeminier et al., *Property* 737 (6th ed. 2006).

[977] R. E. Megarry and H. W. R. Wade, *The Law of Real Property* 807 (3d ed. 1966).

[978] *Id.* at 807-08.

Indirectly, this passage of commentary on modern law suggests that no new negative easements are likely to be approved in English jurisprudence.

§ 8.04(g)(4). Licenses.

A license is by definition not a right in property[979] and was early defined as a revocable permission to commit some act that would otherwise be considered unlawful.[980] When, in the 19th century, the revocability of a license coupled with the grant of an interest was contested,[981] some licenses were held to be irrevocable. Courts in some cases then elevated licenses to property rights, binding not only on the immediate parties to the license, but also on their successors in interest.[982]

§ 8.04(g)(5). Covenants.

§ 8.04(g)(5)(A). Real Covenants.

A covenant has been traditionally distinguished from an easement as binding only the actual parties to the covenant, whereas an easement pertains to the party that owns the dominant and servient tenements. However, even in the Middle Ages courts recognized that some covenants were so annexed to the land that they could be enforced by anyone who held that estate in land, although the enforcing party had to hold the same estate as the original covenantee. These covenants, therefore, ran with the holder of the estate, and not with the land.[983]

Early covenants probably arose in connection with express warranties attached to medieval conveyances. A feoffee would include in the deed

---

[979] Y.B. 20 Edw. 4, Trinity Term, pl. 2, f. 4.

[980] Thomas v. Sorrel, Vaughan 330, 124 Eng. Rep. 1098 (1674).

[981] Wood v. Leadbitter, 13 M. & W. 838, 153 Eng. Rep. 351 (1845).

[982] *See, e.g.,* Errington v. Errington, 1 K. B. 290 (1952).

[983] 3 William Holdsworth, *A History of English Law* 158 (5th ed. 1942).

warranties that no claim would be made by heirs or others; such warranties were in effect covenants attached to the estate in land being conveyed. In the 16th and 17th centuries conveyancers transformed the warranties into covenants for title, and rules as to the running of covenant benefits and burdens were worked out.[984]

As to the running of covenant burdens, Bracton expressed the view that the burden of a warranty could pass to the grantee of the land,[985] but in fact the matter remained unsettled until almost modern times. In a 13th-century case the court stated that "No one can bind his assigns to warranty, because the burden of warranty always extends only to heirs who claim by succession, and not to those who claim by assignment."[986] Coke noted that covenant benefits could be annexed to land, but said nothing about covenant burdens being annexed to land. Finally, in 1885 the matter was settled in a decision that the burden of covenants relating to the land could not run with the land:

> I am not prepared to say that any covenant which imposes a burden upon land does run with the land, unless the covenant does, upon the true construction of the deed containing the covenant, amount to either a grant of an easement, or a rent charge, or some estate or interest in the

---

[984] "[A]s early as 1401 it was recognized that the assign [of the benefit] must, to enable him to sue, have the land to which the covenant was annexed . . . Hence we get the modern rule that the benefit of covenants made with the purchaser of land will, if they relate to land, run with that purchaser's estate in the land, that is they can be enforced by successive tenants of that estate. It was partly this settlement of modern rule as to the conditions under which the benefit of covenants will run with the estate in the land, and partly the convenience of the procedure available to enforce a warranty, which has led to the substitution of the modern covenants for title for the old warranties express or implied. In the course of the 16th and 17th centuries covenants for seisin, for the right to convey, for quiet enjoyment, for freedom from incumbrances, and for further assurance, became usual covenants on a conveyance of land. They are at the present day by far the commonest class of covenants, the benefit of which runs with the estate in land." *Id.* at 162-63.

[985] *Bracton*, ff. 382, 382b.

[986] Y.B. 32, 33 Ed. 1 (R.S.) 516.

land.[987]

One additional aspect of the question about whether covenant burdens would run with the land was whether covenant burdens would run to a reversioner. Very little medieval authority on the question is known, but what there is suggests that neither benefits nor burdens of covenants would run with the reversion. A statute of 1540 dealing with reversions following gifts for life or for years contained a preamble reciting an apparent common law prohibition against covenant benefits and burdens running:[988] "no stranger to any covenant . . . shall take any advantage or benefit of the same . . . ."[989] The effect of the statute itself, however, was to permit both

---

[987] Lindley, L.J., in Austerberry v. Corporation of Oldham, 29 C. D. 750, 781 (1885).

[988] The statute was passed on the occasion of the dissolution of the monasteries, which resulted in transfers of many reversionary interests. The words prohibiting running of covenants are found in the preamble, concerning which Holdsworth remarked,

> it is clear that some of the statements in the preamble are too wide, as they would negative the possibility of any covenant running, not only with the reversion, but also with the land; and, as we have seen from the preamble to the statute of Uses, we cannot place very much reliance on the preambles to the Tudor statutes.

7 William Holdsworth, *A History of English Law* 288 (2d ed. 1937).

[989] 32 Hen. 8, c. 34, preamble:

> Where before this time divers, as well temporal as ecclesiastical and religious persons, have made sundry leases, demises and grants to divers other persons, of sundry manors, lordships, ferms, meases, lands, tenements, meadows, pastures, or other hereditaments, for term of life or lives, or for term of years, by writing under their seal or seals, containing certain conditions, covenants and agreements to be performed, as well on the part and behalf of the said lessees and grantees, their executors and assigns, as on the behalf of the said lessors and grantors, their heirs and successors; (2) and forasmuch as by the common law of this realm, no stranger to any covenant, action or condition, shall take any advantage or benefit of the same, by any means or ways in the law, but only such as be parties or privies thereunto, by the reason whereof, as well all grantees of reversions . . . be excluded to have any entry or action against the said lessees and grantees, their executors or assigns, which the lessors before that

benefits and burdens to run with respect to reversions of leases for life or years arising from royal grants. Subsequent case authority was deeply split on the larger question of covenants running.[990]

Not until *Spencer's Case* in 1583[991] did a court clarify to which covenants the statute should apply. This was the first prominent expression of the requirement that the substance of the covenants must touch or concern the land.[992]

As subsequent cases continued to work out covenant law, courts held that the original lessee and covenantor would continue to be liable on the covenant even after assignment,[993] and that the liability of an assignee of the land is not personal, but ends when tenure of the land ends.[994]

> time might by the law have had against the same lessees for the breach of any condition, covenant or agreement comprised in the indenture of their said leases, demises and grants . . . .

[990] Holding that covenants did not run with reversions, *see* Barker v. Damer, 3 Mod. 336, 338, 87 Eng. Rep. 223, 224 (1691); Thursby v. Plant, 1 Wms. Saund. 230, 237, 85 Eng. Rep. 254, 268 (1669). To the contrary, *see* Attoe v. Mennings, 2 Bulstr. 281, 80 Eng. Rep. 1123 (1613); Harper v. Burgh, 2 Lev. 206, 83 Eng. Rep. 521 (1677); Vyvyan v. Arthur, 1 B. & C. 410, 107 Eng. Rep. 152 (1823).

[991] Spencer's Case, 5 Co. Rep. 16a, 77 Eng. Rep. 72 (1583).

[992] "If the covenant touched or concerned the estate in the land demised or something actually on it, not only the benefit, but also the burden of it, ran with that estate. Probably the rule that the burden ran with the estate in land as well as the benefit, was due to considerations of convenience, and was perhaps new law . . . If, however, the covenant related to something to be newly done on the land demised there was nothing in being to which the covenant could be annexed . . . the benefit and burden of such covenants would only run with the estate in the land if assigns were named; and, though this rule has been criticized, it is still the law . . . The same principles as were applied to covenants running with the land were applied to covenants running with the reversion, by the resolution that the statute of 1540 extended 'to covenants which touch or concern the thing demised and not to collateral covenants.'" 7 William Holdsworth, *A History of English Law* 289-90 (2d ed. 1937).

[993] Walker's Case, 3 Co. Rep. 22a, 76 Eng. Rep. 676 (1587); Thursby v. Plant, 1 Wms. Saund. 230, 237, 85 Eng. Rep. 254, 268 (1669); Barnard v. Goodschall, Cro. Jac. 309, 79 Eng. Rep. 264 (1613); Bachelour v. Gage, Cro. Car. 188, 79 Eng. Rep. 765 (1631); Brett v. Cumberland, Cro. Jac. 521, 79 Eng. Rep. 446 (1617).

[994] Pitcher v. Tovey, 1 Salk. 81, 91 Eng. Rep. 76 (1693).

§ 8.04(g)(5)(B). Equitable Servitudes.

The running of covenants in equity in English land law did not occur until the famous decision in the 1848 case of Tulk v. Moxhay.[995] By the time of that case it had been well established in English law that the running of covenants related to land ("real covenants") was significantly restricted and that burdens did not run at all in covenants that were part of a conveyance in fee. In just such a conveyance, the court in *Tulk* held that the burden of a covenant therefore unenforceable against an assignee at law could be enforced against the assignee in equity if the assignee had notice of the covenant. Eventually most English courts accepted the notion that such a covenant imposed an equitable servitude on the land itself, rather than merely on an owner with notice, under a contract theory.[996]

§ 8.04(h). Mortgages.

The preceding chapter pointed out[997] that during the 15th or 16th century, the form of mortgage shifted from an enfeoffment on condition of defeasance or of re-entry to an enfeoffment with a covenant for reconveyance upon timely repayment of the debt, the so-called classical common law mortgage. This form of mortgage increased greatly in popularity during the 16th century, when the Chancellor began specifically enforcing the covenant of reconveyance rather than just granting money damages for breach. In time, courts recognized a power of sale in the mortgagee who had not been paid, but even with this and other protections, mortgagees even into the mid-17th century were still frequently taking possession of the land.

An alternative to the classical common law mortgage, that eventually overtook it in popularity, was the grant of a long-term lease to the mortgagee. These long-term leaseholds had several variants. A mortgagor

---

[995] Tulk v. Moxhay, 2 Phil. 774, 41 Eng. Rep. 1143 (1848).

[996] London County Council v. Allen, 3 K. B. 642 (C.A.) (1914); David J. Hayton, "Restrictive Covenants as Property Interests," 87 *Law Q. Rev.* 539 (1971).

[997] At § 7.06(h)(3), *supra*.

might grant a leasehold of 500 years with a provision that the mortgagor could retain possession until default occurred, if at all. The lease would become void upon repayment. Or the mortgagee might grant a sublease back to the mortgagor with a provision that the sublease would be void if default occurred. During the 17th and 18th centuries mortgages by lease were perhaps more popular than the classical form of mortgage. Besides being applicable to both freeholds and leaseholds, they created a chattel interest in the mortgagee which upon death passed to the mortgagee's heirs, the persons most likely entitled to the debt repayment. However, the fee simple reversion left in the mortgagor, even after default, was inconvenient and few used this form of mortgage after the 18th century.[998]

Protections for mortgagors also emerged. At the beginning of the 17th century, equity courts began intervening to provide relief against remedies in the nature of a penalty and against terms that were usurious. If a mortgagee had been effectively repaid from the rents and profits of possession, the courts gave the mortgagor an equitable remedy.[999] Equity intervened if the mortgagor repaid the debt on time but the mortgagee refused to reconvey.[1000] The equity of redemption, allowing mortgagors who defaulted an opportunity to redeem the land upon payment of the debt and expenses, was allowed as early as 1594[1001] and is mentioned in a case in 1612.[1002] These early courts developed the rule that they would grant redemption upon special hardship, but by 1625 they dropped even the hardship requirement.[1003] The relief of equity of redemption produced a

---

[998] A. W. B. Simpson, *A History of the Land Law* 242-43 (2d ed. 1986).

[999] Holman v. Vaux, Tothill 133 (c. 1616); Bodenham v. Halle (1456), *in* Select Cases in Chancery A.D. 1364-1471 137 (William Paley Baildon, ed., Selden Society, Vol. 10 (1896)).

[1000] Y.B. 9 Edw. 4, Trinity Term, f. 25, pl. 34.

[1001] Langford v. Barnard, Tothill 134 (1594).

[1002] Hanmer v. Lochard, Tothill 132 (1612).

[1003] Emmanuel College v. Evans, 1 Ch. Rep. 18 (1625).

countering remedy of foreclosure[1004] for mortgagees, first mentioned in a case in 1629.[1005] The equity of redemption eventually took on a life of its own and became a separate species of property right, subject even to being entailed in equity.[1006]

> An equity of redemption is considered an estate in land; it will descend, may be granted, devised, entailed, and that equitable estate may be barred by a common recovery. This proves that it is not considered as a mere right, but as such an estate whereof, in the consideration of this court, there may be a seisin, for without such a seisin, a devise could not be good.[1007]

This was part of a larger movement to perceive the mortgage transaction in land as one for security rather than strictly as a conveyance. "By the end of the seventeenth century this new conception of the mortgage had become established, and a long line of cases begins, some defending it against attempts to "clog the equity," and others settling the rights of successive mortgagees, a complication which now became possible under the new view of the mortgage."[1008]

By that time mortgagors customarily remained in possession of the land until default,[1009] and mortgagees in possession became strictly accountable for profits of the land during their possession. Mortgages began to include express powers of sale in order to free land from the equity of

---

1004 "Foreclosure" is a shorthand expression for "foreclosure of the equity of redemption."

1005 How v. Vigures, 1 Ch. Rep. 32, 21 Eng. Rep. 499 (1629).

1006 Roscarrick v. Barton, 1 Ch. Cas. 217, 22 Eng. Rep. 767 (1673).

1007 Casborne v. Scarfe, 1 Atk. 598, 26 Eng. Rep. 377 (1737).

1008 Theodore F. T. Plucknett, *A Concise History of the Common Law* 690 (5th ed. 1956).

1009 Stone v. Grubham, 2 Bulstrode 225, 80 Eng. Rep. 1079 (1615).

redemption.[1010] These arrangements for mortgagors and mortgagees in England remained in effect until the reforms introduced by the massive property legislation of 1925.

§ 8.04(i). Statutory Reforms Up to the Nineteenth Century.

Statutory reform of archaic common law property doctrines was not significant until the 19th century. In the 17th century, the only two important pieces of property reform legislation were the Statute of Tenures in 1660[1011] and the Statute of Frauds in 1677.[1012] The Statute of Frauds, as it related to real property, required writings for conveyances of freeholds, for leaseholds of longer than three years, for devises of real property, for trusts of land, and for contracts to convey interests in land.[1013] The essence of the Statute of Frauds remains an integral part of Anglo-American land law today.

In the 18th century several attempts were made to establish registries for conveyances, either general or local. Only a few local registries resulted: the West Riding of Yorkshire in 1703,[1014] the East Riding of Yorkshire and Kingston-upon-Hull in 1707, Middlesex in 1708,[1015] and the North Riding of Yorkshire in 1735. Some defects in common recoveries procedure were corrected in a statute of 1741.[1016] The reluctance to embark on the more urgent matters of reform has been attributed to a combination

---

[1010] Tucker v. Wilson, 1 P. Wms. 261, 24 Eng. Rep. 379 (1714).

[1011] 12 Car. 2, c. 24 (1660).

[1012] 29 Car. 2, c. 23 (1677).

[1013] The requirement of a writing for real estate contracts was countered by the emergence of the equitable doctrine that part performance of the contract could overcome the absence of a writing.

[1014] 2 & 3 Anne, c. 4 (1703).

[1015] 7 Anne, c. 20 (1708).

[1016] 14 Geo. 2, ca. 20 (1741).

of vested interests in and ignorance of the English land law in effect during the 18th century.[1017]

In the early 19th century lawyers obtained a legislative monopoly over conveyancing for gain and thus intensified their special interest in maintaining the complex system of conveyances.

Reform momentum did increase in the 19th century, however, and in 1829 Real Property Commissioners were appointed to conduct studies and make recommendations. Their extremely significant reports generated a series of profoundly important legislative reforms. Their first report in 1829 covered inheritance, dower, curtesy, fines, recoveries, prescription, and limitations. The second, in 1830, covered proposals to establish a general registry of deeds and other instruments dealing with land. The third, in 1832, included recommendations for tenures, contingent remainders, future interests, perpetuities, covenants, and limitation of ecclesiastical land rights. The fourth report, in 1833, dealt with will and probate proceedings.

From these reports emerged the Inheritance Act of 1833,[1018] the Fines and Recoveries Act of 1833,[1019] the Real Property Limitation Act of 1833[1020] (abolishing all but three of the real actions), the Dower Act of 1833,[1021] the Wills Act of 1837,[1022] and the Prescription Act of 1832.[1023] The Real Property Act of 1845[1024] adopted some of the reform proposals omitted from legislation of the 1830s. Some procedural aspects of property-related

---

[1017] A. W. B. Simpson, *A History of the Land Law* 272-73 (2d ed. 1986).

[1018] 3 & 4 Will. 4, c. 106 (1833).

[1019] 3 & 4 Will. 4, c. 714 (1833).

[1020] 3 & 4 Will. 4, c. 27 (1833).

[1021] 3 & 4 Will. 4, c. 105 (1833).

[1022] 7 Will. 4 and 1 Vict., c. 26 (1837).

[1023] 2 & 3. Will. 4, c. 71 (1832).

[1024] 8 & 9 Vict., c. 106 (1845).

actions were altered by the Common Law Procedure Act of 1852,[1025] and some minor and incomplete reforms were embodied in the Contingent Remainders Act of 1877.[1026]

Agitation continued for a system of registration of deeds or titles. A system for voluntary registration of indefeasibly vested titles after examination was introduced by Lord Westbury's Act of 1862,[1027] but volunteers did not come forward. Then in 1875, Lord Cairns' Act[1028] permitted registration for mere possessory titles, but this act, too, was voluntary and generated little interest. Finally the Land Transfer Act of 1897[1029] introduced compulsory registration, but made it immediately applicable only to the County of London and, in 1902, to the City of London. Other localities could request extension of the system to their areas, but none did before legislation in 1925 set up a new but similar system. Solicitors consistently opposed compulsory title registration.

Because so many land occupants were only life tenants of lands held under strict settlement, it became important to expand the freedom of such tenants to deal with their land. A series of enactments made the position of such life tenants more comparable to that of a fee simple owner, "whilst providing that for the purposes of beneficial enjoyment the life tenant remained a limited owner, entitled only to the income of the settled estate, not the capital, and unable freely to alter the beneficial provisions of the settlement."[1030] These acts included drainage acts,[1031] the Improvement of

---

[1025] 15 & 16 Vict., c. 76 (1852).

[1026] 40 & 41 Vict., c. 33 (1877).

[1027] 25 & 26 Vict., c. 53 (1862).

[1028] 38 & 39 Vict., c. 87 (1875).

[1029] 60 & 61 Vict., c. 65 (1897).

[1030] .W.B. Simpson, *A History of the Land Law* 284 (2d ed. 1986).

[1031] Settled Lands Act, 3 & 4 Vict., c. 55 (1840); Settled Estates Act, 8 & 9 Vict., c. 56 (1845).

Land Act in 1864,[1032] the Settled Estates Act of 1858,[1033] the Settled Land Act of 1877,[1034] and the Settled Land Act of 1882.[1035]

The common law disabilities of married women in dealing with their land, which effectively required the husband's concurrence to make dispositions of the land, were removed by a series of statutes beginning with the Married Women's Property Act of 1882,[1036] and continuing with the Married Women's Property Act of 1907,[1037] the Law Reform (Married Women and Tortfeasors) Act of 1935[1038] and the Married Women (Restraint upon Anticipation) Act of 1949.[1039] Of this legislation, one historian commented, "If one excepts the Married Woman's Property Act of 1882, which belongs to the special history of family law, one cannot but be struck by the air of caution which characterizes the nineteenth-century reforming legislation. The legislation was indeed very tender to the rights of property, and there are only a few instances where anything which could be viewed as expropriation, or as direct attacks on freedom of contract, took place."[1040]

§ 8.05. Nineteenth Century Reforms in English Land Law.

Although a discussion of English land law in the 19th century is no

---

1032 27 & 28 Vict., c. 114 (1864).

1033 21 & 22 Vict., c. 77 (1858).

1034 40 & 41 Vict., c. 18 (1877).

1035 45 & 46 Vict., c. 38 (1882).

1036 45 & 46 Vict., c. 75 (1882).

1037 7 Edw. 7, c. 18 (1907).

1038 25 & 26 Geo. 6, c. 30 (1935).

1039 12, 13 & 14 Geo. 6, c. 78 (1949).

1040 5 William Holdsworth, *A History of English Law* 192 (1965).

longer directly connected to the shared history of American land law, it is interesting and instructive to consider briefly a summary of these unique and independent English activities.

A strong desire to reform English law resulted in parliamentary reform beginning in 1832, and this opened the way for land law reforms. Reform began in Parliament, and it gradually diminished the power of the landed class. These reforms, especially those that removed restrictions on alienability, helped England compete as a more powerful commercial and industrial nation.[1041]

Parliamentary reforms were prompted by major changes in the nature and location of the English population, prompted principally by massive effects of the Industrial Revolution. The three illustrations that follow depict important elements in this process. Illustration 31 shows a colliery in Wales; Illustration 32 shows an early iron works; and Illustration 33 represents manufacturing.

The four Real Property Commission Reports of 1829-1833 produced several reform recommendations.[1042] Parliament acted on those recommendations and passed the Inheritance Act of 1833,[1043] which implemented most of the reports' recommendations relating to inheritances, and the Fines and Recoveries Act of 1833,[1044] which abolished fines and recoveries. As noted in the preceding paragraphs, the Real Property Limitation Act of 1833[1045] abolished almost all real actions and established a twenty-year limitation for actions affecting real property. The Dower Act

[1041] *See generally* A.W.B. Simpson, *A History of the Land Law* 273 (2d ed. 1986) (stating that changes improved chances for reforming land law).

[1042] *See id.* at 274.

[1043] 3 & 4 Will. 4, ch. 106 (1833).

[1044] 3 & 4 Will. 4, ch. 74 (1833).

[1045] 3 & 4 Will. 4, ch. 27 (1833).

Illustration 31. Old colliery works in Porth, Rhondda Valley, Mid Glamorgan, Wales. These structures represent factors that brought enormous numbers of people away from occupying the land as farm laborers.

Illustration 32. Old iron works in Blaenavon, Monmouthshire, Wales. Although coal mining has had more attention as a product of the Industrial Revolution, iron mining was as essential and prevalent. All of the heavy industries tended to change the face of the land as well as draw much of the population from working the land.

Illustration 33. A restored and working Mule spinning machine at Quarry Bank Mill in Styal, Cheshire, England, one of the best preserved textile mills from the Industrial Revolution. These manufacturing enterprises, along with heavy industrial enterprises, drew enormous numbers of people from the land.

of 1833[1046] limited dower rights, and the Wills Act of 1837[1047] simplified the law of testamentary disposition. Together, the Real Property Act of 1845[1048] and the Real Property Limitation Act of 1833 effectively abolished the common law concerning seisin and simplified the law of future interests.

Parliament addressed the destructibility of contingent remainders in the Contingent Remainders Act of 1877.[1049] Another act introduced a system of compulsory title registration in 1897.[1050] Parliament also passed a series

---

[1046] 3 & 4 Will. 4, ch. 105 (1833).

[1047] 7 Will. 4 & 1 Vict., ch. 26 (1837).

[1048] 8 & 9 Vict., ch. 106 (1845).

[1049] 40 & 41 Vict., ch. 33 (1877).

[1050] *See* An Act to Establish a Real Representative, and to Amend the Land Transfers Act, 1875, 1897, 60 & 61 Vict., ch. 65 (1897).

of laws to break up strict settlement arrangements on large tracts of land, the most important of which passed in 1883.[1051] Those acts increased the management powers of life tenants and gave tenants broader powers to improve, lease, sell, exchange, and partition the land. Furthermore, a series of agricultural holdings acts gave relief to agricultural tenants, who had had no previous right to payment for improvements they had placed on the tenancy if the tenancy terminated. Parliament also gave farmers the right to shoot game animals that were considered pests.[1052]

These nineteenth-century land law reforms were relatively conservative. More fundamental changes followed World War I with the massive statutory reforms of the 1920s. Although Parliament had intended the early reforms to help simplify conveyancing practices, it recognized that simplifying conveyancing was not possible without simplifying the underlying substantive land law. As a result, the 1920s reforms did both.

§ 8.06. Twentieth-Century Reforms in English Land Law.

The spirit of reform mildly but persistently in evidence during the 19th century carried into and gained momentum during the 20th century. During the first quarter of the 20th century the English Parliament culminated an extensive period of law reform by enacting of the Property Acts of 1925, consisting of several statutory components: the unrepealed portions of earlier reform acts (especially of the Law of Property Act of 1922[1053] and the Law of Property (Amendment) Act of 1924),[1054] the Settled Land Act

---

[1051] *See* Settled Estates Act, 1877, 40 & 41 Vict., ch. 18 (1883); Limited Owners Residences Act, 1870, 33 & 34 Vict., ch. 56, *amended by* 34 & 35 Vict., ch. 84 (1871); Settled Estates Act, 1858, 21 & 22 Vict., ch. 77 (1858); Improvement of Lands Act, 1864, 27 & 28 Vict., ch. 114 (1864); Drainage Acts, 1840, 3 & 4 Vict., ch. 55, 8 & 9 Vict., ch. 56 (1840).

[1052] *See* Ground Game Act, 1880, 43 & 44 Vict., ch. 47 (1880).

[1053] 12 & 13 Geo. 5, c. 16; Law of Property (Amendment) Act, 15 & 16 Geo. 5, c. 5.

[1054] 15 & 16 Geo. 5, c. 5.

of 1925,[1055] the Trustee Act of 1925,[1056] the Law of Property Act of 1925,[1057] the Land Registration Act of 1925;[1058] the Land Charges Act of 1925,[1059] and the Administration of Estates Act of 1925.[1060] Since 1925, specific areas of land law have also been subject to reform statutes, including, among others, the Perpetuities and Accumulations Act,[1061] the Law of Property (Joint Tenants) Act,[1062] the Matrimonial Homes Act,[1063] the Leasehold Reform Act,[1064] another Law of Property Act,[1065] the Charging Orders Act,[1066] and the Limitation Act.[1067] Particularly during the twentieth century, English land law reforms have been characterized by increasing governmental regulation to achieve public benefits or protections at the expense of purely private interests. The following sections summarize the most important effects of this statutory revision of British land law.

[1055] 15 & 16 Geo. 5, c. 18.

[1056] 15 & 16 Geo. 5, c. 19.

[1057] 15 & 16 Geo. 5, c. 20.

[1058] 15 & 16 Geo. 5, c. 21.

[1059] 15 & 16 Geo. 5, c. 22, later replaced by the Land Charges Act of 1972, c. 61.

[1060] 15 & 16 Geo. 5, c. 23.

[1061] 1964, c. 55.

[1062] 1964, c. 63.

[1063] 1967, c. 75.

[1064] 1967, c. 88.

[1065] 1969, c. 59.

[1066] 1979, c. 53.

[1067] 1980, c. 24

§ 8.06(a). Simplifying British Land Law.

§ 8.06(a)(1). Tenures

The greatest change was in the law of tenures. The importance of this reform is surprising because the Tenures Abolition Act in 1660,[1068] which affirmed prior changes in English land law, supposedly rendered tenures unimportant. The following brief historical review of tenures places the modern changes in tenures in proper perspective.

During feudal times, tenure was the central premise of land law. Only the monarch owned land; others only had the right to occupy and use the land in return for rendering something of value to the monarch.[1069] The monarch permitted faithful followers to hold large tracts in return for their commitments to provide military services.[1070] The English called this practice "tenure by knight service."[1071] A few generations after the Norman Conquest in 1066, tenure by knight service had become obsolete as a method of raising and managing a military force.[1072] However, some incidental aspects of the knight's tenure, called reliefs, grew in financial importance.[1073] Other forms of tenure also arose among the monarchs' followers. One of these, the frankalmoign tenure, was a grant of land rights to an ecclesiastical official or body in return for spiritual services.[1074] Tenure by sergeanty gave land rights to followers who rendered personal

---

[1068] 12 Car. 2, ch. 24 (1660).

[1069] David J. Hayton, *Megarry's Manual of the Law of Real Property* (1982).

[1070] A.W.B. Simpson, *A History of the Land Law* 3-4 (2d ed. 1986).

[1071] *Id.*

[1072] Sheldon F. Kurtz, *Moynihan's Introduction to the Law of Real Property* 11 (4th ed. 2005).

[1073] *Id.* at 16-20.

[1074] *Id.* at 12.

services to the monarch.[1075] The English classified almost all other forms of landholding as socage tenures, or free tenures, because they applied to free persons.[1076] Non-free tenures applied to land that agricultural serfs held. Serfs were virtually bound to the land because their obligations to manorial lords were so oppressive.[1077]

For more than two centuries after the Norman Conquest, tenants who held by any of the free tenures could take on their own subtenants and share their holdings if the subtenants agreed to provide some of the obligatory services. This process, known as subinfeudation,[1078] greatly complicated English landholding relationships before the Statute Quia Emptores partially prohibited it in 1290.[1079] Quia Emptores applied only to land that tenants held in fee simple and did not apply to new tenancies that the monarch created. Thus, some subinfeudation continued, and free tenures continued to be a factor in English land law long after their original practical utility had disappeared.[1080]

Socage tenure eventually became an important part of English law. At first, socage tenure was a catch-all category, a residuary form of nonmilitary free tenure that was not frankalmoign, knight service, or sergeanty.[1081] A peasant farmer who was not a serf would usually hold land by a form of socage tenure that could adapt to innumerable formulations and combinations of required agricultural services. This form of tenure eventually began to appeal to those in higher social orders because socage

---

[1075] *Id.* at 11-12.

[1076] *Id.* at 13.

[1077] A.W.B. Simpson, *A History of the Land Law* 12-13 (2d ed. 1986).

[1078] *Id.* at 4-5.

[1079] Statute Quia Emptores, 1290, 18 Edw., ch. 1,2 (1290).

[1080] Sheldon F. Kurtz, *Moynihan's Introduction to the Law of Real Property* 23 (4th ed. 2005).

[1081] *Id.* at 13.

was free of the worst financial burdens attached to knight tenure.[1082] As successive monarchs substituted the services of socage tenure with fixed money payments, and inflation eroded the value of those fixed payments, socage attained even greater appeal as the favored tenure among all classes.[1083]

The ancient, pre-feudal land holding rights of the serfs, or villeins, eventually merged into the manorial system.[1084] As a result, serfs became obligated to perform the services necessary to cultivate their lords' lands.[1085] If the lord of the manor did not define the service obligations precisely, and the assignment of the villein's work remained at the lord's discretion, the villein's tenure was unfree.[1086] In time, the villeins paid their obligations in money rather than services, and lords used the money to hire laborers. Custom fixed the amount of payments, and inflation eventually eroded the value of the payments they received, similar to the socage tenure payments.[1087] Manorial courts recorded transactions of villein holdings and noted the services of the fixed payments.[1088] The courts made copies of pertinent portions of these records, or rolls, for the buyer of a villein tenant's interest. The buyer was the copyholder because he held by copy of the court roll.[1089] A villein's social status significantly improved when his interest changed from a servility subject to the lord's discretion to a firm, custom-fixed interest that was entitled to court protection. Tenants could

---

[1082] *Id.*

[1083] *Id.*.

[1084] A.W.B. Simpson, *A History of the Land Law* 156-57 (2d ed. 1986).

[1085] *Id.*

[1086] Sheldon F. Kurtz, *Moynihan's Introduction to the Law of Real Property* 13-16 (4th ed. 2005).

[1087] *Id.* at 14-15.

[1088] *Id.* at 15.

[1089] A.W.B. Simpson, *A History of the Land Law* 160-61 (2d ed. 1986).

convert copyhold tenure into socage tenure,[1090] and in 1926 the 1922 Law of Property Act converted all copyhold land into freehold land held by socage tenure.[1091] Occasionally, manorial court records were so obscure, and the mixing of socage and copyhold lands was so confused, that a sale required two conveyances—one in the form appropriate for copyhold, and one in the form appropriate for socage.[1092]

Through all this lengthy history of refining and reforming the land law in England, the judges and the lawyers who appeared before them were vital to the process. The best were often trained in the venerable Inns of Court, including Lincoln's Inn, shown in Illustration 34.

The theoretical existence of tenurial relationships in modern English landholding has no practical significance. The lord has no right of escheat, and legislation has abolished any other incident of tenure that might bring profit to a lord.[1093] No tenurial lord has any incentive to establish or exercise the lordship, and tenure restricts no tenant in the free enjoyment of land.

[1090] David J. Hayton, *Megarry's Manual of the Law of Real Property* 26-27 (1982).

[1091] Law of Property Act, 1922, 12 & 13 Geo. 5, ch. 16, §§ 128-137 (1922). Other customary tenures in English land law were gavelkind, which applied to socage land located in Kent; borough-English, which customarily descended only to the youngest son of the holder; and ancient demesne, which was freehold land that the crown owned at or about the time of the Norman Conquest, which was subject to certain limitations and immunities. Sheldon F. Kurtz, *Moynihan's Introduction to the Law of Real Property* 13 (4th ed. 2005).

[1092] A.W.B. Simpson, *A History of the Land Law* 171-172 (2d ed. 1986).

[1093] *Id.* at 23-24.

Illustration 34. One of the buildings of Lincoln's Inn, which is one of four Inns of Court in London that have trained barristers since the 15th century. The skilled barristers have heavily influenced the evolution of land law in England.

§ 8.06(a)(2). Estates.

While tenure describes the relationship between lord and tenant, a different term denotes the nature and extent of the interest held within that tenurial relationship. The term "seisin" best describes the concept in medieval English land law of rights emanating from possession of land.[1094] This emphasis on possession rather than ownership is a direct consequence of the persistence of tenure, a concept under which no private person has outright title to or ownership of the land. However, the possessory rights of seisin define the nature of the landowner's estate. The owner of an estate in land may exercise rights over that land for the period of time the particular estate describes and subject to any duties the estate owner's tenurial relationship prescribes.[1095] The differences in duration of estate ownership mean that owners can divide estates. For instance, two or more owners can hold rights in land simultaneously. Examples include tenancies in common, or future estates with firm rights to assume possession in the future.

Early English law categorized estates in land according to the holders' tenurial relationships. Originally, a freehold estate was a free tenure, such as tenure by knight service or socage.[1096] Later, freehold estates included estates that were of uncertain duration, such as a fee simple or life estates, and those estates in which a court action could restore the property rather than merely enable recovery of money damages. Eventually, freehold estates encompassed estates whose holders had rights similar to rights of those who held free tenures.[1097]

Persons such as villeins, who held estates subjecting them to servile

---

[1094] *Id.* at 88.

[1095] *Id.* at 88-89.

[1096] Sheldon F. Kurtz, *Moynihan's Introduction to the Law of Real Property* 13 (4th ed. 2005).

[1097] *Id.*; A.W.B. Simpson, *A History of the Land Law* 66 (2d ed. 1986).

requirements, held by non-free tenures.[1098] Paradoxically, the non-free tenures, which were distinguished by uncertainty in the types and timing of services required, later became distinguished by certainty in duration. A tenant who held under a lease for a definite period held by a non-free tenure.[1099] Even later, English courts determined that freehold estates, such as the fee simple, fee tail, and life estate, derived from seisin and therefore, should receive the aid and protection of certain court actions known as real actions.[1100] According to English law, persons who held nonfreehold estates possessed those estates, but were not seised of them. For a time, the law extended no legal protection, such as the real action, to nonfreehold estates.[1101] Indeed, the law did not even consider nonfreehold estates, such as leaseholds, as real property. Instead, the nonfreehold estate received the hybrid classification as a "chattel real," an interest that was partly real property and partly personal property.[1102]

The system of and governing rules for estates in English land law were vastly simplified in modern reform legislation.

A relatively small number of outstanding scholars and lawyers have strongly influenced the refining and ordering of English land law. One of the most important was Sir Thomas Littleton, a judge, who in the middle 1400s wrote an enduring treatise on tenures, which came to be known simply as Littleton on Tenures. It was the first textbook on English land law and the first to make a systematic statement of a very complex part of that law. In 1628 Sir Edward Coke (Illustration 35) wrote another important book commenting helpfully on Littleton's treatise. Coke was also highly influential as a barrister, judge and political figure.

[1098] *Id.* at 157.

[1099] *Id.*

[1100] *Id.* at 7.

[1101] *Id.* at 13.

[1102] *Id.* at 75-77.

Illustration 35. Bust of Sir Edward Coke, in the Squire Law Library, Cambridge University. As a barrister, judge, writer and political officer, Coke was one of the most influential persons in the refining of English land law in the 16th and 17th centuries.

§ 8.06(a)(3). Summary of Twentieth Century Tenures and Estates Reforms in England.

The reforms of English land law in the 1920s focused first on tenures and then on estates. Reformers converted copyhold tenures into freehold land held by socage tenure, and they abrogated all other tenures and local or customary forms of descent.[1103] Certain incidents of copyhold tenure that still held some money value to the lord or tenant survived either temporarily or indefinitely.

Reformers changed the law governing estates by merging a variety of personal property rules with real property rules. Consequently, the differences between freehold and nonfreehold estates largely disappeared.[1104] Reformers also abolished some anachronistic medieval rules,[1105] such as the rules in Shelley's Case[1106] and Dumpor's Case.[1107]

§ 8.06(b). Simplifying British Conveyancing.

§ 8.06(b)(1). Equitable Estates and Expanded Methods of Conveyancing.

Historically, a grantor could use a conveyance to place land beyond the reach of a creditor or to deprive a lord of important incidents, such as the

---

[1103] David J. Hayton, *Megarry's Manual of the Law of Real Property* 26-27 (1982).

[1104] *Id.*

[1105] *Id.* at 351.

[1106] 1 Coke 93b, 76 Eng. Rep. 206 (K.B. 1581).

[1107] 4 Coke 119b, 76 Eng. Rep. 110 (K.B. 1603).

monetary benefits flowing from wardship, marriage, and relief.[1108] Dower and curtesy rights did not attach to use interests, and this significantly aided the free alienability of uses. When someone was enfeoffed to the use of another, and then failed to honor the terms of the use, the Chancellor could provide a remedy in equity, which was not available under common law. These rulings recognized equitable estates that existed alongside the legal estates in land. The Chancellor protected the equitable interest of the use beneficiary, who was called the *cestui que use*.[1109]

In response to these rulings, early statutory reforms referred to such use beneficiaries as the legal owners of the land.[1110] These reforms culminated with the Statute of Uses,[1111] which converted the equitable interests of most use beneficiaries into legal interests. However, before the Statute of Uses passed, the English legal profession had developed an extensive and unique conveyancing practice in uses.[1112] Interestingly, the conveyancing practices that the early statutory reforms of uses helped to legitimize were the same practices that Parliament addressed in the statutory reforms of the twentieth century. At the time of an enfeoffment to use, the uses could be included in a written document, stated orally, or declared to be the uses included in the grantor's will. If uses were not made known at the time of the enfeoffment, the grant was presumed to be for the use of the feoffor.

Eventually, uses became so common that when a fee simple enfeoffment occurred and no use was declared, but the transaction was without consideration, a use was presumed in the feoffee. This implied use

---

[1108] David A. Thomas, "Anglo-American Land Law: Diverging Developments from a Shared History–Part I: The Shared History," 34 *Real Prop. Prob. & Tr. J.* 143, 179 (1999).

[1109] *Id.*

[1110] *Id.* at 179-80.

[1111] 27 Hen. 8, ch. 10 (1536) (Eng.).

[1112] For sources and additional information on conveyancing as discussed in the following paragraphs, *see* David A. Thomas, "Anglo-American Land Law: Diverging Developments from a Shared History–Part I: The Shared History," 34 *Real Prop. Prob. & Tr. J.* 143, 182 (1999).

in the feoffee was termed a "resulting use." Uses were often conveyed to several persons as joint tenants. This arrangement offered some security against simultaneous dishonesty by all the feoffees and, through operation of survivorship, avoided questions of dower or feudal incidents when any of the joint tenants died.

A use also was frequently raised by a bargain and sale. By an oral or written bargain and sale agreement, an owner accepted monetary consideration in return for a promise to sell the land to the buyer. The promise alone did not convey the legal title, but equity treated the bargainee as the beneficial owner who could sue in equity to compel the bargainor to convey legal title. This arrangement was also a natural vehicle for raising a use. By bargain and sale, the owner could agree to hold the land for the use or benefit of the buyer and the buyer's heirs. Again, the buyer could compel the seller to permit the buyer's use of the land, including its rents and profits. As early as the fifteenth century, a bargain and sale that had not proceeded to conveyance of the legal title was deemed to have raised a use in the bargainee. For those who actually wanted no more than the use, the bargain and sale arrangement would be left in a suspended, incomplete state in which the purchaser held only equitable title in the form of a use. According to feudal tenurial doctrine, this circumstance was significant because it meant, as mentioned above, that a use could be raised without a transfer of seisin. Parties also found appealing the confidentiality of the transaction because, without conveyance of the legal title, no occasion arose to make a public record or display the transaction.

The Statute of Uses had an immediate impact on many different conveyancing practices. For example, it permitted the direct conveyance of an estate to oneself and another. The Statute of Uses allowed the grantor to use a feoffment to uses also to convey a legal estate directly to himself and his wife.[1113]

Another practice was the bargain and sale without livery of seisin. Before 1536, people used the bargain and sale procedure to create a use.

[1113] Sheldon F. Kurtz, *Moynihan's Introduction to the Law of Real Land* 228-229 (4th ed. 2005).

After 1536, the bargain and sale procedure was also available to create a legal estate.[1114] This method vested the seller's title by operation of law without the necessity of livery of seisin.[1115] Initially, bargain and sale transactions did not need to be in writing, which raised the possibility of secret, oral transactions without the public event of livery of seisin. Consequently, Parliament adopted the Statute of Enrolments in 1536,[1116] which required freehold conveyances by bargain and sale to be in writing, under seal, and entered or enrolled in certain public offices.

A third conveyancing practice that the Statute of Uses affected was the lease and release. To avoid the writing requirement, conveyancers tried to convey lands in leaseholds. The Statute of Enrolments did not require writing or enrolling leaseholds, because leaseholds were not freeholds.[1117] After such a conveyance, the grantor would release the reversion to the lessee, who was still eligible to accept the reversion, having not yet entered into possession. This procedure allowed the lessee to obtain the entire estate. "From approximately 1620 until 1845 the conveyance by lease and release was the most commonly used method of conveying land in England."[1118]

The Statute of Uses also affected the covenant to stand seised. Before the Statute passed, the law did not require a party to enroll a covenant or agreement to hold land for the use of another.[1119] After the Statute of Uses, courts enforced such agreements if the agreement was for the use of a relative or for marriage and the consideration consisted of natural love and

---

[1114] *Id.* at 241-242.

[1115] *Id.*

[1116] 27 Hen. 8, ch. 16 (1536).

[1117] Sheldon F. Kurtz, *Moynihan's Introduction to the Law of Real Land* 242-244 (4th ed. 2005).

[1118] *Id.* at 243 (citing Lutwich v. Mitton, 79 Eng. Rep. 516 (1621)).

[1119] *Id.* at 244-245.

affection.[1120] Once the court established the validity of the agreement, the Statute of Uses converted the use into a legal interest. The covenant to stand seised was a popular tool in family settlements because it was mostly available to family members, and it was unenrolled and secret.[1121]

Additionally, the Statute of Uses converted executory interests into new future interests. Parties commonly conveyed a variety of springing and shifting uses as uses before 1536. After 1536, the Statute of Uses converted these uses into springing and shifting executory interests. Executory interests comprised a type of future interest that the common law had not previously recognized.[1122]

One other conveyancing practice that the Statute of Uses affected was the devise. Before 1536 a party could devise shifting and springing future interests. After the Statute of Uses curtailed this practice, the Statute of Wills introduced some corrective action in 1540.[1123]

Most of these conveyancing techniques were obsolete by the time land law reforms began in England in the nineteenth and twentieth centuries.[1124] However, the techniques all embodied the notion that land should be more freely alienable than was possible under traditional common law conveyancing rules.

§ 8.06(b)(2). Trust Estates and Conveyancing.

The Statute of Uses did not affect a use given for a term of years. Nor did it affect a use under which the feoffee to uses had active duties, such as

---

[1120] *Id.*

[1121] *Id.*

[1122] *Id.* at 245-247.

[1123] *Id.* at 247-248 (citing Statute of Wills, 32 Hen. 8, ch. 1 (1540)).

[1124] *Id.* at 270.

collection of rent.[1125] In both of these instances, the feoffee to uses had an affirmative duty on behalf of the beneficiary to restore possession at the end of the term and to remit the rents, in essence, a trust duty.[1126] Beneficiaries could enforce the trust only in equity in the Court of Chancery.[1127] Much later, a feoffee could become a passive trustee for a second beneficiary by accepting a use upon a use.[1128] Thus, O to A for the use of B for the use of C left A with nothing, B with the legal estate, and C with the equitable estate. In effect, B became a trustee for C, but without active duties to perform. Courts considered the beneficiaries' interests valid against all but those who purchased the legal estate in good faith and without notice of the equitable interest.[1129] The most common conveyancing application of these principles arose in the practices of settling land.

§ 8.06(b)(3). Settlements and Conveyancing.

For centuries, English families with substantial landholdings had sought to keep these properties in the family and prevent heirs or descendants from exchanging the land for other forms of wealth. The common law achieved this goal by permitting family members to convey the land to the oldest son, who would agree to do the same for his oldest son, and so on.[1130] This grant was a fee tail, an estate limited to the grantee and the heirs of his body.[1131] However, the legal devices available to "bar the entail" and confer on the entailed grantee a fee simple absolute prevented landowners from ensuring that their wishes would always be

---

[1125] *Id.* at 269-270.

[1126] A.W.B. Simpson, *A History of the Land Law* 189 (2d ed. 1986).

[1127] Sheldon F. Kurtz, *Moynihan's Introduction to the Law of Real Land* 267-269 (4th ed. 2005).

[1128] *Id.*

[1129] *Id.* at 265-269.

[1130] David J. Hayton, *Megarry's Manual of the Law of Real Land* 235 (1982).

[1131] *Id.*

carried out.

When the Statute of Uses made the conveyancing techniques of uses available to convey legal interests, families were able to achieve settlements by conveying highly restrictive uses. This flexibility increased when powers of appointment emerged and permitted dispositions after settlement to conform to the demands of developing circumstances.

As settlements restricted more and more land, people realized that the inability of occupants to alienate their land had serious financial consequences. This system removed large tracts of land from the stream of commerce, and landowners were less likely to develop and improve their land. The income rights of younger children often deprived the oldest child of any monetary benefit during that child's occupancy. Additionally, long leases of the land were not possible without authorization of the occupant.[1132] With a larger portion of English land under settlement in the nineteenth century, the situation became serious enough that statutory reforms, beginning with the Settled Land Act of 1882,[1133] put full management authority in the life tenants.[1134] This management authority included powers to sell, lease, mortgage, exchange, and partition.[1135] These powers permitted the tenant to overreach the rights of the beneficiaries by paying the purchase money to trustees or a court for distribution to the beneficiaries while enabling the tenant to convey the land free of the beneficial interests.[1136]

However, the popularity of sales into trust, which required two separate deeds, eclipsed these settlement conveyancing and sales procedures. The first deed conveyed land to trustees eventually to sell the land and hold the

---

[1132] *See*, Eileen Spring, "The Settlement of Land in Nineteenth Century England," 8 *Am J. Legal Hist.* 209, 211 (1964) and cases cited therein.

[1133] 45 & 46 Vict., ch. 38 (1882).

[1134] David J. Hayton, *Megarry's Manual of the Law of Real Property* 239 (1982).

[1135] *Id.*

[1136] Settled Land Act, 1882, 45 & 46 Vict., ch. 38, §§ 20, 22, 39 (1882).

purchase price, accrued rents, and profits according to one or more trusts declared in the deed.[1137] The second deed gave detailed instructions for the distribution of the money and often embodied former limitations on alienation of the land, but facilitated the transaction by use of appointive powers.[1138] The trust for sale was useful as an investment resource, while the settlement arrangements were useful to retain the land in the family.[1139] The utility of the trust for sale enabled British land law reformers to simplify both real property law and land conveyancing.

§ 8.06(b)(4). Conveyancing of Legal and Equitable Estates

§ 8.06(b)(4)(A). Legal Estates.

As a result of the 1925 property acts,[1140] English law now recognizes only two types of legal estates. These estates are the fee simple absolute in possession and the term of years absolute.[1141] Apart from these estates and the legal property interests in the lands of another, English law treats all other estates, interests, and charges relating to land as equitable interests.[1142]

The fee simple absolute, a present possessory estate, is the form of land ownership that is potentially infinite in duration and has the maximum cognizable interests of land ownership.[1143]

[1137] David J. Hayton, *Megarry's Manual of the Law of Real Property* 245 (1982).

[1138] *Id.*

[1139] *Id.* at 236.

[1140] Law of Property Act, 1925, 15 & 16 Geo. 5, ch. 20, § 1(1) (1925).

[1141] *Id.* § 1(1)(a)-(b).

[1142] *Id.* § 1(3).

[1143] David J. Hayton, *Megarry's Manual of the Law of Real Property* 87 (1982).

The term of years absolute means any right to possess land for a period of fixed and certain duration, including periods less than one year. This estate also can include periodic tenancies.[1144] It is not necessarily a present possessory interest, and it can commence at some time in the future less than 21 years from the time the lease was created.[1145]

If a conveyance is to tenants in common or multiple trustees, then the limit on the number of concurrent owners is four.[1146] The limitation on concurrent ownership is not as explicit in joint tenancies, but English law treats the two tenancies equally.[1147]

English law also recognizes five types of legal interests in another's land.[1148] The first of these is the easement, which is a right or privilege in land equivalent in duration to a legal estate. Easements include the right to use another's land in a certain way, to prevent another from using the land in a certain way, or to take something from another's land.[1149] Easements are legal interests if their specified duration is similar to one of the two legal estates, either perpetual or limited to a fixed and certain time.[1150]

The second type of interest is a rentcharge, which is the grantor's right to collect periodic payment from the occupant.[1151] For a rentcharge to be a legal interest, the party obligated to pay must possess the land, even if the charge commences at a future date.[1152] Furthermore, the rentcharge's

---

1144 Law of Property Act, 1925, 15 & 16 Geo. 5, ch. 20, § 205 (1)(xxxvi) (1925).

1145 David J. Hayton, *Megarry's Manual of the Law of Real Property* 88 (1982).

1146 Law of Property Act, 1925, 15 & 16 Geo. 5, ch. 20, § 34 (1925).

1147 David J. Hayton, *Megarry's Manual of the Law of Real Property* 310 (1982).

1148 Law of Property Act, 1925, 15 & 16 Geo. 5, ch. 20, § 1(2)(a)-(e) (1925).

1149 David J. Hayton, *Megarry's Manual of the Law of Real Property* 88 (1982).

1150 *Id.*

1151 *Id.*

1152 *Id.*

duration must be similar to the duration of one of the two legal estates.[1153] Since 1977, severe restrictions have hampered the creation of new rentcharges.[1154]

Another legal interest is the legal mortgage. The parties create this interest by (1) conveying a term of years absolute subject to defeat by redemption, or (2) having a deed create a charge by way of legal mortgage.[1155] The legal mortgage is often security for a debt, and repayment extinguishes the interest. If the debtor defaults, the mortgagee may exercise certain rights in the land to satisfy the debt.

The fourth interest in another's lands consists of obligations similar to the old land taxes and tithe rentcharges, which statutes have abolished.[1156] These legal interests involve periodic payments that arise by operation of law.[1157]

The last of these interests is a typical right of entry. Under this interest, the landlord has a right to enter the premises within a legal term of years absolute if the tenant fails to pay the rent or fails to observe other covenants of the term.[1158]

§ 8.06(b)(4)(B). Equitable Estates.

In modern English land law, all other interests in land are equitable interests.[1159] For example, a life estate or a fee tail is no longer a legal

---

[1153] Law of Property Act, 1925. 15 & 16 Geo. 5, ch. 20, § 122 (1925).

[1154] Rent Charges Act, 1977, 25 & 26 Eliz. 2, ch. 30, § 2 (1977).

[1155] Law of Property Act, 1925, 15 & 16 Geo. 5, ch. 20, § 85(1) (1925).

[1156] Finance Act, 1963, 11 &12 Eliz. 2, ch. 25, pt. VI, sched. 14 (1965); Tithe Act, 1936, 26 Geo. 5 & Edw. 8, ch. 43, sched. 9 (1936).

[1157] David J. Hayton, *Megarry's Manual of the Law of Real Property* 89 (1982).

[1158] *Id.* at 90.

[1159] Law of Property Act, 1925, 15 & 16 Geo. 5, ch. 20, § 1 (1925).

estate, but can exist within the framework of a trust. If the legal estate in fee simple vests in a trustee, then the beneficial or equitable interests that the trust instrument defines can take the form of a life estate, a fee tail, or a variant of those interests. Other interests that are no longer legal in nature, but still function as equitable interests, are restrictive covenants and other interests under trust.[1160]

Legal and equitable interests have one basic distinction. Legal interests are binding against all others, including bona fide purchasers without notice.[1161] Holders of equitable interests are not similarly protected.[1162]

Parliament addressed this distinction in the land law reforms of 1925. Lawmakers attempted to reduce the number of legal estates and interests to protect purchasers and holders of equitable interests.[1163] The Land Charges Act of 1925 also permits holders of equitable interests to protect themselves by registering their commercial interests.[1164] Registration of the equitable interest confers binding notice on all potential purchasers.[1165] If the holder fails to register the equitable interest, then the purchaser is not bound even if there is actual notice.[1166] The Land Charges Act does not specifically cover certain equitable interests, but those interests are still subject to the old doctrine of constructive notice.[1167] Apart from equitable interests registrable under the Land Charges Act, only legal estates and legal interests in the land of another are registrable under the Land

---

[1160] *Id.* § 4.

[1161] David J. Hayton, *Megarry's Manual of the Law of Real Property* 83 (1982).

[1162] Id.

[1163] *Id.*

[1164] Land Charges Act, 1925, 15 & 16 Geo. 5, ch. 22 (1925).

[1165] David J. Hayton, *Megarry's Manual of the Law of Real Property* 83 (1982).

[1166] *Id.*

[1167] *Id.* at 84.

Registration Act of 1925.[1168]

§ 8.06(b)(4)(C). Conveyancing and Title Registration.

The legal rules for registering land titles and for conducting transactions in unregistered land titles are aligned with the procedures for conveying real property. Registration is a system of certified titles that the government guarantees. This system replaces the routine of making a separate title investigation each time a transaction occurs involving that land.[1169] The traditional search was cumbersome because it involved inspecting the land and reviewing the abstract of the deed and encumbrances on the title.[1170] In a conveyance of registered land, the legal interest does not pass to the purchaser until the purchaser registers as the new proprietor of the title.[1171] About seventy-five percent of current conveyancing activity in England and Wales concerns registered land.[1172]

Whether or not the owner has registered the land, the conveyancing process requires preliminary negotiations and inquiries, the creation of a draft contract, the execution of a formal contract, and the exchange of consideration and title documents.[1173] In the typical sale of a fee simple interest, the purchaser should inspect the land and conduct a preliminary examination of the title before entering into any contract. The purchaser may note items that are not in order in a form called Inquiries before Contract. Also, the purchaser should review the registration records to discover local land charges, or public encumbrances, and submit a form to

---

[1168] Land Registration Act, 1925, 15 & 16 Geo. 5, ch. 21 (1925).

[1169] David J. Hayton, *Megarry's Manual of the Law of Real Property* 111 (1982).

[1170] *Id.* at 112.

[1171] Land Registration Rule 83(2), *cited in* David J. Hayton, *Megarry's Manual of the Law of Real Property* 156, n. 48 (1982).

[1172] David J. Hayton, *Megarry's Manual of the Law of Real Property* iii (1982).

[1173] *Id.* at 134-36.

the local authority to search for encumbrances that are not registrable.

Some areas of England and Wales are compulsory registration areas where the law requires sellers to register their title if they are selling a fee simple, or creating or assigning certain leases.[1174] Registration is optional for other transactions in the compulsory areas.[1175] The compulsory areas are expanding, especially in urban regions, and they now affect three-fourths of the population and cover well over half the area of England and Wales.[1176] The Land Charges Act of 1925[1177] and its successor, the Land Charges Act of 1972,[1178] greatly increased the types of rights that land holders can register, and thus protect against purchasers without notice.[1179]

If an owner properly registers an interest, the registration constitutes notice to all persons for all purposes.[1180] These protected interests include land charges (equitable interests that are valuable because of their effect on another's land),[1181] pending actions (both an ordinary lis pendens and an action in bankruptcy),[1182] writs and orders affecting land,[1183] and deeds of arrangement (similar to receiverships).[1184] The land charge is the most

[1174] Land Registration Act, 1925, 15 & 16 Geo. 5, ch. 21 § 123 (1925).

[1175] *Id.* §§ 4-8.

[1176] David J. Hayton, *Megarry's Manual of the Law of Real Property* 116 (1982).

[1177] 15 & 16 Geo. 5, ch. 22 (1925)

[1178] 20 & 21 Eliz. 2, ch. 61 (1972).

[1179] David J. Hayton, *Megarry's Manual of the Law of Real Property* 90 (1982).

[1180] *Id.*

[1181] Land Charges Act, 1972, 20 & 21 Eliza. 2, ch. 61, § 2 (1972)

[1182] *Id.* § 5.

[1183] *Id.* § 6.

[1184] *Id.* § 7.

comprehensive type of registrable interest.[1185] Land charges include interests or encumbrances that statutes impose on land; certain legal mortgages; obligations owed to a life tenant or statutory owner for discharging death duties or other liabilities; general equitable charges, such as unpaid vendor's liens; contracts to convey or create legal estates, including purchase options and preemptive rights; death duties, restrictive covenants, and certain equitable easements; certain annuities; and spousal rights to enter and occupy a house that the other spouse owns.[1186]

When parties have entered into a contract for the sale of registered land, the vendor gives the purchaser authorization to make a search of the Land Register,[1187] which is otherwise not open to public inspection.[1188] The vendor also must provide copies or abstracts of documents that the register refers to, such as those imposing encumbrances on the land.[1189] If any unfavorable or unexpected entries appear in the register, the parties negotiate the contract terms through a process of inquiries and responses known as requisitions.[1190] When both parties are satisfied with the contract terms, the purchaser completes a standard draft transfer form, includes any appropriate special clauses, and sends it to the vendor for approval.[1191] Upon approval, the purchaser prepares a clean copy and sends it to the vendor for execution.[1192] A few days before the closing date, the purchaser makes an official search of the register to discover any new entries against

---

[1185] *Id.* § 2.

[1186] *Id.*

[1187] The register provides an instant title, negating the need to search its history. *See* David J. Hayton, *Megarry's Manual of the Law of Real Property* 155 (1982).

[1188] Land Registration Act of 1925, 15 & 16 Geo. 5, ch. 21, § 112 (1925).

[1189] David J. Hayton, *Megarry's Manual of the Law of Real Property* 155 (1982).

[1190] *Id.*

[1191] *Id.*

[1192] *Id.*

the title.[1193] The official search begins the thirty-day priority period, which protects the title from other claims.[1194] Other potential claimants must either wait to register or subordinate to the purchaser's interest, provided the purchaser registers the title transfer within the priority period.[1195]

When parties enter into a contract for the conveyance of unregistered title, the vendor must deliver an abstract of title to the purchaser.[1196] The abstract includes a good "root of title" document, which summarizes the documents and events that have affected the title for at least the past fifteen years.[1197] A root of title is "a document which deals with the whole legal and equitable interest in the land, describes the land adequately, and contains nothing to throw any doubt on the title."[1198] As an alternative to the abstract, the vendor may prepare an epitome, which is a summary of the essential facts in the chain of title. The vendor also may attach photocopies of the actual documents for support.[1199]

As with conveyances of registered land, if the abstract or epitome raises questions about the title, the purchaser may submit requisitions on title to the vendor to request further information or corrective action."[1200] The

---

[1193] *Id.*

[1194] *Id.*

[1195] "Before expiry of the priority period afforded by the official search certificate, [the purchaser] will attend upon [the vendor] to receive the duly executed transfer and the land certificate in return for [the purchaser's] banker's draft for the moneys due under [the vendor's] completion statement. Unlike the unregistered land position, the legal title does not pass until [the purchaser] has lodged his application to register the transfer with the appropriate District Land Registry, and [the purchaser] must ensure that this is done before expiry of the priority period afforded by the official search certificate." *Id.* at 156.

[1196] *Id.*

[1197] Law of Property Act, 1969, ch. 59, § 23 (1969).

[1198] David J. Hayton, *Megarry's Manual of the Law of Real Property* 68 (1982).

[1199] *Id.* at 148.

[1200] *Id.* at 149.

vendor responds to the requisitions, and the parties negotiate until they have established mutually satisfactory terms.[1201]

The purchaser then prepares a standard draft conveyance form (deed)[1202] and sends it to the vendor for approval.[1203] After the parties add and approve any amendments, the purchaser prepares a new, formal copy and sends it to the vendor for signature. A few days before closing, the purchaser conducts an official search of the Land Charges Register, which begins the priority period and subordinates or postpones new entries of certain interests until the expiration of thirty working days.[1204] The closing should occur before the priority period expires.

At closing, the purchaser pays the amount shown on the "completion statement," which includes the agreed-upon price, plus taxes and other charges apportioned to the date of completion.[1205] The vendor then may deliver the title deed and signed conveyance to the purchaser.[1206] However, in some circumstances, the vendor might not deliver the title to the purchaser, such as when the deed relates to other land retained.[1207]

After the closing, the purchaser typically submits an application to

---

[1201] *Id.*

[1202] A conveyance of a legal estate must be by deed. Law of Property Act, 1925, 15 & 16 Geo. 5, ch. 20, § 52(1) (1925)

[1203] David J. Hayton, *Megarry's Manual of the Law of Real Property* 149 (1982).

[1204] *Id.*

[1205] *Id.* at 150.

[1206] The purchaser will sign the conveyance only if it contains some obligations, such as restrictive covenants, that the purchaser must observe. *Id.* at 149.

[1207] "[The vendor] may retain any deed which (i) relates to the other land retained . . . or (ii) creates a trust which is still subsisting; or (iii) relates to the apportionment or discharge of trustees of a subsisting trust. If [the vendor] retains any deeds, he must give [the purchaser] an acknowledgement of [the purchaser's] rights to production of the deeds and . . . an undertaking for their safe custody." *Id.* at 150. *See also* Law of Property Act, 1925, 15 & 16 Geo. 5, ch. 20, §§ 45, 64 (1925) (requiring safekeeping of documents retained by vendor).

register the conveyance with the Land Registry.

§ 8.06(c). Review of Principal Twentieth Century British Land Law Reforms.

Statutory reform of British law in the twentieth century technically began with the Law of Property Act of 1922.[1208] Parliament made more extensive amendments with the Law of Property (Amendment) Act of 1924.[1209] However, in 1925, lawmakers repealed these acts and converted most of their substance into the following six major laws: the Settled Land Act of 1925,[1210] the Trustee Act of 1925,[1211] the Law of Property Act of 1925,[1212] the Land Registration Act of 1925,[1213] the Land Charges Act of 1925,[1214] and the Administration of Estates Act of 1925.[1215] Later, Parliament enacted other reform laws to address individual areas of land law, including the Perpetuities and Accumulations Act,[1216] the Law of Property (Joint Tenants) Act,[1217] the Matrimonial Homes Act,[1218] the

---

[1208] 12 & 13 Geo. 5, ch. 15 (1922).

[1209] 15 & 16 Geo. 5, ch. 9 (1924).

[1210] 15 & 16 Geo. 5, ch. 18 (1925).

[1211] 15 & 16 Geo. 5, ch. 19 (1925).

[1212] 15 & 16 Geo. 5, ch. 20 (1925).

[1213] 15 & 16 Geo. 5, ch. 21 (1925).

[1214] 15 & 16 Geo. 5, ch. 22 (1925), *amended by* Land Charges Act, 1972, ch. 61 (1972).

[1215] 15 & 16 Geo. 5, ch. 23 (1925).

[1216] 1964, ch. 55.

[1217] 1964, ch. 63.

[1218] 1964, ch. 75.

Leasehold Reform Act,[1219] another Law of Property Act,[1220] the Charging Orders Act,[1221] and the Limitation Act.[1222] In contrast to nineteenth century reforms, English land law reforms of the twentieth century have increased governmental regulation to achieve public benefits at the expense of purely private interests in land.

§ 8.07. Bibliography.

Books

Bennett, H. S., *Life on the English Manor* 280 (1937).

Biancalana, Joseph, *The Fee Tail and the Common Recovery in Medieval England 1176-1502* (2001).

Bracton's Note Book (1220).

Burn, E. H., *Chesire and Burn's Modern Law of Real Property* (13th ed. 1982).

Cunningham, W., *The Growth of English Industry and Commerce* (4th ed. 1907).

Dukeminier, Jesse and James E. Krier, Property (6th ed. 2006).

Gale, Charles James, *A Treatise on the Law of Easements* (11th ed. by F. Graham Glover, 1931).

Harwood, Michael, *Modern English Land Law* (2d ed. 1982).

Hayton, David J., *Megarry's Manual of the Law of Real Property* (1982).

Holdsworth, William, *A History of English Law* (various dates and editions)

Hyams, Paul R., *King, Lords and Peasants in Medieval England: The Common Law of Villeinage in the Twelfth and Thirteenth Centuries* (1980).

Kurtz, Sheldon F., *Moynihan's Introduction to the Law of Real Property* (4th ed. 2005).

Megarry, R. E. and H. W. R. Wade, *The Law of Real Property* (3d ed. 1966).

Plucknett, Theodore F. T., *A Concise History of the Common Law* (5th ed. 1956).

Plumb, J. H., *England in the Eighteenth Century* (1963).

Pollock, Frederick and Frederic William Maitland, *The History of English Law Before the Time of Edward I* (2d ed. 1909).

Ravensdale, Jack, *The Domesday Inheritance* (1986).

Simes, Lewis F. and Allan F. Smith, *The Law of Future Interests* (2d ed. 1956).

Simpson, A. W. B., *A History of the Land Law* (2d ed. 1986).

Stoebuck, William B. and Dale A. Whitman, *The Law of Property* (3d ed. 2000).

Vinogradoff, Paul, *The Growth of the Manor* (3d ed. 1920).

[1219] 1967, ch. 88.

[1220] 1969, ch. 59.

[1221] 1979, ch. 53.

[1222] 1980, ch. 24.

Chapters in Books

"The 'Coronation Charter' of Henry I (5 August 1100)," in 2 *English Historical Documents* (D. C. Douglas, ed., 1953).
Blackstone, William, Ch. 9, Sec. II. in *Commentaries.*
Britton, II, 23, 3; II, 8 & 9.
"The Laws of William the Conqueror," in 2 *English Historical Documents* (D. C. Douglas, ed., 1953).

Articles

Banks, Taunya Lovell, "Dangerous Woman: Elizabeth Key's Freedom Suit, Subjecthood and Racialized Identity in Seventeenth Century Colonial Virginia," 41 *Akron L. Rev.* 799 (2008).
Barros, D. Benjamin, "Toward a Model Law of Estates and Future Interests," 66 *Wash & Lee L. Rev.* 3 (Winter 2009).
Hayton, David J., "Restrictive Covenants as Property Interests," 87 *Law Q. Rev.* 539 (1971).
Morris, Joseph W., "The Inter Vivos Branch of the Worthier Title Doctrine," 2 *Okla. L. Rev.* 133 (1949).
Powell, Richard R. B., "Determinable Fees," 23 *Colum. L. Rev.* 207, 212 (1923).
Spring, Eileen, "The Settlement of Land in Nineteenth Century England," 8 *Am J. Legal Hist.* 209 (1964).
Thomas, David A., "Anglo-American Land Law: Diverging Developments from a Shared History-Part I: The Shared History," 34 *Real Prop. Prob. & Tr. J.* 143 (1999).

Statutes

Administration of Estates Act, 15 & 16 Geo. 5, c. 23 (1925).
Charging Orders Act, 1979, c. 53.
Drainage Acts, 1840, 3 & 4 Vict., ch. 55, 8 & 9 Vict., ch. 56 (1840).
Finance Act, 1963, 11 & 12 Eliz. 2, ch. 25, pt. VI, sched. 14 (1963).
Ground Game Act, 1880, 43 & 44 Vict., ch. 47 (1880).
Land Charges Act, 15 & 16 Geo. 5, c. 22 (1925) replaced by Land Charges Act of 1972, c. 61.
Land Registration Act, 15 & 16 Geo. 5, 21 (1925).
Law of Property (Amendment) Act, 15 & 16 Geo. 5, c. 5 (1922).
Law of Property (Amendment) Act, 15 & 16 Geo. 5, c. 5. (1924).
Law of Property Act, 15 & 16 Geo. 5, c. 19-20 (1925).
Law of Property Act, 1969, c. 59.
Law of Property (Joint Tenants) Act, 1964, c. 63.
Leasehold Reform Act, 1967, c. 88.
Limitation Act, 1980, c. 24.
Limited Owners Residences Act, 1870, 33 & 34 Vict., ch. 56, amended by 34 & 35 Vict., ch. 84).
Matrimonial Homes Act, 1967, c. 75.
Perpetuities and Accumulations Act, 1964, c. 55.
Rent Charges Act, 1977, 25 & 26 Eliz. 2, ch. 30 (1977).
Settled Estates Act, 8 & 9 Vict., c. 56 (1845).
Settled Estates Act, 1858, 21 & 22 Vict., ch. 77 (1858).
Settled Land Act, 15 & 16 Geo. 5, c. 18 (1925).
Settled Land Act, 1882, 45 & 46 Vict., ch. 38, §§ 20, 22, 39 (1882).
Settled Lands Act, 3 & 4 Vict., c. 55 (1840).

Statute of Enrolments, 27 Hen. 8, ch. 16 (1536) (Eng. 1536).
Statute of Merton, 20 Hen. 3, c. 4 (1235).
Statute of Uses, 27 Hen. 8, ch. 10 (1536).
Statute of Westminister II, 13 Edw. 1, st. 1, c. 46 (1285).
Statute Quia Emptores, 1290, 18 Edw., ch. 1, 2 (1270).
Statute of Wills, 32 Hen. 8, ch. 1 (Eng. 1540).
Tenures Abolition Act, 12 Car. 2, ch. 24 (Eng. 1660).
Tithe Act, 1936, 26 Geo. 5 & Edw. 8, ch. 43, sched. 9 (1936).
Trustee Act, 15 & 16 Geo. 5, c. 19 (1925).
2 & 3 Anne, c. 4 (1703).
2 & 3 Will. 4, c. 71 (1832).
3 & 4 W. & M., c. 31 (1693).
3 & 4 Will. 4, c. 27 (1833).
3 & 4 Will. 4, c. 74, §§ 15, 40 (1833).
3 & 4 Will. 4, c. 105 (1833).
3 & 4 Will. 4, c. 106 (1833).
3 & 4 Will. 4, c. 714 (1833).
4 Hen. 7, c. 24 (1490).
4 Hen. 8, c. 19 (1489).
4 Jam., c. 11 (1606-1607).
5 & 6 Edw. 6, c. 5 (1551-1552).
6 Edw. 1, cc. 11 (1278).
6 Hen. 8, c. 5 (1514-1515).
7 Anne, c. 20 (1708).
7 Edw. 1 (1279).
7 Edw. 7, c. 18 (1907).
7 Will. 4 and 1 Vict., c. 26 (1837).
8 & 9 Vict., c. 106 (1845).
8 & 9 Vict., c. 118 (1845).
12 Car. 2, c. 24 (1660).
12 & 13 Geo. 5, c. 16 (Eng. 1922).
12, 13, & 14 Geo. 6, c. 78 (1949).
13 Edw. 1 (1285).
13 Geo. 3, ca. 81 (1773).
14 Geo. 2, ca. 20 (1741).
15 & 16 Geo. 5, c. 20 (1925).
15 & 16 Vict., c. 76 (1852).
21 Hen. 8, c. 15 (1529).
21 & 22 Vict., c. 77 (1858).
25 Hen. 8., c. 13 (1533-1534).
25 & 26 Geo. 6, c. 30 (1935).
25 & 26 Vict., c. 53 (1862).
27 Edw. 3, cc. 9 (1353).
27 Hen. 8, c. 10 (1535).
27 & 28 Vict., c. 114 (1864).
28 Hen. 8, c. 36 (1536).
29 Car. 2, c. 23 (1677).
29 Geo. 2, c. 36 (1754).
32 Hen. 8, c. 28 (1540).
32 Hen. 8, c. 34 (1540).
32 Hen. 8, c. 46 (1540).
35 Hen. 8, cc. 17 ° 6 (1543).
38 & 39 Vict., c. 87 (1875).
39 & 40 Vict., c. 56 (1876).

40 & 41 Vict., c. 18(1877).
40 & 41 Vict., c. 33 (1877).
41 Geo. 3, c. 109 (1801).
45 & 46 Vict., c. 38 (1882).
45 & 46 Vict., c. 75 (1882).
52 Hen. 3, c. 6 (1267).
60 & 61 Vict., c. 65 (1897).

Cases

Ackroyd v. Smith, 10 C. B. 164, 138 Eng. Rep. 68 (1850).
Anon, Dyer 2b, 73 Eng. Rep. 7 (1527).
Ash v. Gallen, 1 Ch. Cases 114, 22 Eng. Rep. 720 1668).
Attoe v. Mennings, 2 Bulstr. 281, 80 Eng. Rep. 1123 (1613).
Austerberry v. Corporation of Oldham, 29 C. D. 750, 781 (1885).
Bachelour v. Gage, Cro. Car. 188, 79 Eng. Rep. 765 (1631).
Barker v. Damer, 3 Mod. 336, 338, 87 Eng. Rep. 223, 224 (1691).
Barnard v. Goodschall, Cro. Jac. 309, 79 Eng. Rep. 264 (1613).
Bodenham v. Halle (1456), in Select Cases in Chancery A.D. 1364-1471, 137 (William Paley Baildon, ed., Selden Society, Vol. 10 (1896)).
Brett v. Cumberland, Cro. Jac. 521, 79 Eng. Rep. 446 (1617).
Capell's Case, 1 Co. Rep. 54a, 61a, 76 Eng. Rep. 121, 134 (1581).
Cary 3 (1557).
Casborne v. Scarfe, 1 Atk. 598, 26 Eng. Rep. 377 (1737).
Colthirst v. Bejushin, 1 Plowden 20, 75 Eng. Rep. 33 (1550).
Dormer v. Packhurst, 6 Bro. P. C. 351 (1740), upholding Duncomb v. Duncomb, 3 Lev. 437, 83.
Dumpor's Case, 4 Coke 119b, 76 Eng. Rep. 110 (K.B. 1603).
Ellis v. Page, 61 Mass. (7 Cush.) 161 (1851).
Emmanuel College v. Evans, 1 Ch. Rep. 18 (1625).
Errington v. Errington, 1 K. B. 290 (1952).
Ever v. Aston, Moo. K. B. 271, 72 Eng. Rep. 575 (1599).
Gateward's Case, 6 Co. Rep. 59b, 77 Eng. Rep. 344 (1607).
Goodwin v. Longhurst, Cro. Eliz. 535, 78 Eng. Rep. 782 (1596).
Hanmer v. Lochard, Tothill 132 (1612).
Harper v. Burgh, 2 Lev. 206, 83 Eng. Rep. 521 (1677).
Heydon's Case, 3 Co. Rep. 8b, 76 Eng. Rep. 640 (1584).
Holman v. Vaux, Tothill 133 (1616).
How v. Vigures, 1 Ch. Rep. 32, 21 Eng. Rep. 499 (1629).
Howard v. Henry Duke of Norfolk, 3 Cas. in Chan. 1, 2 Swans. 454, 36 Eng. Rep. 690 (1681).
Keppel v. Bailey, 3 My. & K. 517, 39 Eng. Rep. 1042 (1833).
Lampet's Case, 10 Co. Rep. 46b, 77 Eng. Rep. 994 (1612).
Langford v. Barnard, Tothill 134 (1594).
Leighton v. Theed, 1 ld. Raym. 707 (1702).
Lutwich v. Mitton, 79 Eng. Rep. 516 (1621).
London County Council v. Allen, 3 K. B. 642 (C.A.) (1914).
Manning's Case, 8 Co. Rep. 94b, 77 Eng. Rep. 618 (1609).
Mary Partington's Case, 10 Co. Rep. 35b (1613).
Mellor v. Spateman, 1 Wms. Saund. 339, 343, 85 Eng. Rep. 489, 495 (1669).
Melwich v. Luter, 4 Co. Rep. 26a, 76 Eng. Rep. 935 (1588).
Peers v. Lucy, 4 Mod. 355, 362, 87 Eng. Rep. 441, 444 (1695).
Petty v. Evans, 2 Brownl. 40, 123 Eng. Rep. 652 (1610).
Pitcher v. Tovey, 1 Salk. 81, 91 Eng. Rep. 76 (1693).

Rangeley v. Midland Ry. Co., L. R. 3 Ch., App. 306 (1868).
Reeve v. Long, 3 Lev. 408, 1 Salk. 227, 4 Mod. 282, 87 Eng. Rep. 395 (1695).
Roscarrick v. Barton, 1 Ch. Cas. 217, 22 Eng. Rep. 767 (1673).
Rumney v. Eves, 1 Leon. 100, 74 Eng. Rep. 93 (1588).
Saltmarsh v. Redeness, Y.B. 11 Edw. 2, Michaelmas Term, pl. 8 (1317) in Year Books 11 Edward II 1317-18 12 (John P. Collas and William S. Holdsworth, eds., Selden Society Vol. 61, Year Book Series vol. 22, 1942).
Shelley's Case, 1 Co. Rep. 88b, 93b, 76 Eng. Rep. 199, 206 (1581).
Solers v. Parson of Dorstone, Y.B. 11 Edw. 2, Michaelmas Term, pl. 8 (1317), in Year Books 11 Edward II 1317-18, 91 (John P. Collas and William S. Holdsworth, eds., Selden Society Vol. 61, Year Book Series vol. 22, 1942).
Spencer's Case, 5 Co. Rep. 16a, 77 Eng. Rep. 72 (1583).
Stephens v. Eliot, Cro. Eliz. 484, 78 Eng. Rep. 735 (1596).
Stone v. Grubham, 2 Bulstrode 225, 80 Eng. Rep. 1079 (1615).
Sympson v. Turner, 1 Eq. Cas. Abr. 383 (1700).
Taltarum's Case, Y.B. 12 Edw. 4, Michaelmas Term, f. 14, pl. 16, f. 19, pl. 25, 13 Edw. 4, Michaelmas Term, f. 1, pl. 1 (1472).
Thomas v. Sorrel, Vaughan 330, 124 Eng. Rep. 1098 (1674).
Thursby v. Plant, 1 Wms. Saund. 230, 237, 85 Eng. Rep. 254, 268 (1669).
Tucker v. Wilson, 1 P. Wms. 261, 24 Eng. Rep. 379. 379 (1714).
Tulk v. Moxhay, 2 Phil. 774, 41 Eng. Rep. 1143 (1848).
Tyrringham's Case, 4 Co. Rep. 36b, 76 Eng. Rep. 973 (1584).
Vyvyan v. Arthur, 1 B. & C. 410, 107 Eng. Rep. 152 (1823).
Walker's Case, 3 Co. Rep. 22a, 76 Eng. Rep. 676 (1587).
Weekly v. Wildman, 1 Ld. Raym. 405, 91 Eng. Rep. 1169 (1699).
Wood v. Leadbitter, 13 M. & W. 838, 153 Eng. Rep. 351 (1845).
Wyat Wyld's Case, 8 Co. Rep. 78b, 77 Eng. Rep. 593 (1610).
Y.B. 2 Edw. 2, 4 (1390).
Y.B. 7 Edw. 4, Michaelmas Term, f. 19, pl. 16 (1467).
Y.B. 9 Edw. 4, Trinity Term, f. 25, pl. 34.
Y.B. 10 Edw. 3, Michaelmas Term, No. 8 (1336).
Y.B. 20 Edw. 4, Trinity Term, pl. 2, f. 4.
Y.B. 21 Edw. 4, Michaelmas Term, f. 80, pl. 27 (1481).
Y.B. 21 Hen. 7, Michaelmas Term, f. 38, pl. 47 (1506).
Y.B. 22 Hen. 6, Michaelmas Term, pl. 13, f. 9, at f. 10 (1462).
Y.B. 24 Edw. 3, 70 no. 9 (1350).
Y.B. 27 Edw. 3 (Rolls Series), 353 (1343).
Y.B. 32 & 33 Edw. 1 (R.S.) 516.
Y.B. 32 & 33 Edw. 1 (Rolls Series), 328 (1304).
Y.B. 40 Edw. 3, f. 9 no. 18 (1366).

Chapter 9

Land Law in the Colonies of Virginia (from 1607), Massachusetts (from 1620), New Hampshire (from 1623) and New York (from 1624)[1223]

SYNOPSIS

[1223] The content of this chapter was originally written by the author, and some content was drawn or reprinted from Vol. 1 of Thompson on Real Property.

Chapter 9. Land Law in the Colonies of Virginia (from 1607), Massachusetts (from 1620), New Hampshire (from 1623) and New York (from 1624)

§ 9.01. Introduction to Chapters 9, 10 and 11.

In strict chronological sequence these three chapters should fall between Chapter 7 and Chapter 8. Chapter 7 traces the progress of English land law to roughly the middle of the 16th century, by which time many of the effects of the 1536 Statute of Uses had revealed themselves. Chapter 8 is a discussion of the significant subsequent changes in English land law up to modern times. At about the same time as the chronological division between these two chapters, the English exploration and colonization of North America was just getting underway, and early in the 17th century, the first permanent English settlements in North America were established. Therefore, the state of affairs in English land law as described in Chapter 7 provides an appropriate background for understanding the beginnings of property rights in England's earliest American colonies.

These three chapters examine the land law developments in each of the 13 English colonies, up to the time of national independence. Chapters 12-14 then cover basic American land law developments thereafter, including developments in each of the states.

The contents of Chapters 9, 10 and 11 consist of an independent section for each of the 13 colonies, beginning with the earliest to have permanent European settlements, and proceeding in the mostly chronological order of their first settlements. The transformation of land law described in these chapters parallels, and may be usefully compared with, the concurrent land law changes in England, as described in Chapter 8. It will, of course, be abundantly evident that developments unique to one country were prompted by forces and circumstances peculiar to that country, despite the shared historical origins of English and American law.

It is also noteworthy that, in the earliest of England's North American colonies, the acclaimed common law of England had little specific influence when the colonists actually had to create rules to govern their everyday affairs, such as working out rights in land. Property arrangements were often a combination of what the colonists had learned from limited firsthand experience in their homelands and of their aspirations for a better society. Only later would the colonists routinely hold up the common law of England as the protective shield for English citizens' most important personal and civic rights.

§ 9.02. Development of Land Law in Virginia (from 1607).

§ 9.02(a). The Charter of 1606.

The royal charter that led directly to establishment of Jamestown, Virginia, as the first permanent English settlement in North America was probably drafted in 1606 by the Lord Chief Justice of England, Sir John Popham. Popham's group, which included prominent merchants and other men from London, Bristol and Plymouth, then petitioned King James I for a patent to validate the charter, and letters patent were granted by the king on April 10, 1606.

The charter asserted English sovereignty over a huge area of North America, between 34 and 45 degrees north latitude from coast to coast and one hundred miles into each ocean, all called Virginia. The land granted included all land:

> along the sea coasts, between four and thirty degrees of Northerly latitude from the Equinoctial line, and five and forty degrees of the same latitude, and in the main land between the same four and thirty and five and forty degrees, and the Islands thereunto adjacent, or within one

> hundred miles of the coasts thereof.[1224]

With our modern knowledge of North American geography, it is hard to take seriously the magnanimous extent of this grant:

> This tremendous tract included, in addition to the area of the present state of Virginia, in part the states of Maine, Michigan, Wisconsin, Minnesota, South Dakota, Montana, Idaho, Oregon, North Carolina, South Carolina, Georgia, Alabama, Mississippi, Arkansas, Texas, New Mexico, and Arizona; and in their entirety or very nearly their entirety, the states of Maryland, Delaware, New Jersey, Pennsylvania, New York, Connecticut, Rhode Island, Massachusetts, New Hampshire, Vermont, Ohio, West Virginia, Kentucky, Tennessee, Indiana, Illinois, Missouri, Iowa, Oklahoma, Kansas, Nebraska, Wyoming, Colorado, Utah, Nevada, and California. In short, this vast virginal tract included all or part of each of forty-two of the present fifty states. The territory embraced as well Lake Ontario and Lake Erie and much of Lakes Huron and Michigan. In addition, its boundaries encompassed part of what is today the Canadian province of Ontario. This transcontinental grant stretched approximately two thousand five hundred miles in an eight hundred mile wide belt from the Atlantic to the Pacific. It also extended one hundred miles into each of those oceans . . . .[1225]

This swath, then, ran from Passamaquoddy Bay in Maine south to Cape Fear River in North Carolina, and extended from coast to coast. Even contemporaries realized it was a vast tract; witness the comment of Captain John Smith:

[1224] "Letters Patent to Sir Thomas Gates et al., April 10, 1606," art. I, *in* 1 *William Waller Hening, The Statutes at Large, Being a Collection of All the Laws of Virginia* 57-58 (1823).

[1225] Alf J. Mapp, Jr., *The Virginia Experiment* 11 (3d ed. 1987).

> This Virginia is a country in America between the degrees of 34 and 45, of the North latitude. The bounds thereof on the East side are the great Ocean: on the South lyeth Florida: on the North nova Francia: as for the West thereof, the limits are unknowne.[1226]

The patentees who were from London were authorized to establish a privately funded joint stock company in order to set up a colony anywhere on the coast between 34 and 41 degrees latitude, and to take jurisdiction of a tract 50 miles north and 50 miles south of the settlement and one hundred miles out to sea and one hundred miles inland. This London group was designated the "first colony," while the group from Plymouth and Bristol, called the "second colony," accepted similar instructions pertaining to a second joint stock company and a colony in the territory between the 38th and 45th parallels.[1227]

In each colony a council of thirteen persons was to govern "according to such laws, ordinances, and instructions, as shall be in that behalf, given and signed with our hand or sign manual, and pass under the privy seal of our realm of England."[1228] These two colonial councils were made subject to the direction of another council of thirteen, sitting in England, called the Council of Virginia.[1229]

The charter secured to all persons dwelling or born within the colonies the right of English citizens to ""have and enjoy all liberties, franchises, and immunities, within any of our other dominions, to all intents and purposes, as if they had been abiding and born, within this our realm of

---

1226 John Smith, *The General Historie of Virginia* 43 (1624).

1227 "Letters Patent to Sir Thomas Gates et al., April 10, 1606," arts. IV and V, *in* Hening, *supra* n. 1224 at 58-60.

1228 "Letters Patent to Sir Thomas Gates et al., April 10, 1606," art. VII, *in* Hening, *supra* n. 1224 at 60-61.

1229 "Letters Patent to Sir Thomas Gates et al., April 10, 1606," art. VIII, *in* 1 Hening, *supra* n. 1224 at 61.

England, or any other of our said dominions."[1230] Supplemental instructions drafted in November 1606, proclaimed that:

> for the good government of the people to be planted in those parts, and for the good ordering and disposing of all causes happening within the same, and the same to be done for the substance thereof, as neer to the common lawes of England, and the equity thereof, as may be . . . .[1231]

Thus was expressed from the outset a fundamental commitment to a rule of law based on the rules of common law and equity in the English jurisprudence of the time.

The provision for two colonies with potentially overlapping territories (between 38 and 41 degrees latitude), with the injunction that the colonial seats should be at least 100 miles apart, meant that the territory in the middle could be jointly settled, but that the "first colony" would effectively determine the land of joint occupation by selecting its colonial seat first.

For the power over the land itself, the 1606 letters patent, in which James I as grantor assumed the tone of the royal "We," proclaimed with respect to both colonies,:

> And do therefore, for us, our heirs, and successors, grant and agree . . . that the patentees shall have all the lands, woods, soil, grounds, havens, ports, rivers, mines, minerals, marshes, waters, fishings, commodities, and hereditaments, whatsoever, [within the boundaries of the colony] . . . and that no other of our subjects shall be permitted, or suffered to plant or inhabit behind, or on the backside of them, towards the main land, without the

---

[1230] "Letters Patent to Sir Thomas Gates et al., April 10, 1606," art. XV, *in* 1 Hening, *supra* n. 1224 at 64.

[1231] "'Articles, Instructions and Orders,' etc., Nov. 20, 1606," in 1 Hening, *supra* n. 1224 at 68.

> express licence or consent of the council of that colony, thereunto in writing first had and obtained.[1232]

The patentees were not, however, empowered to make outright grants of land to their settlers. Instead, the colonial council would petition the king for letters patent to individual settlers:

> And finally, we do, for us, our heirs, and successors, grant and agree, to and with the [patentees] . . . that we, our heirs, and successors, upon petition in that behalf to be made, shall, by letters, patent under the great seal of England, give and grant unto such persons, their heirs, and assigns, as the council of that colony, or the most part of them, shall, for the purpose nominate and assign, all the lands, tenements, and hereditaments, which shall be within the precincts limited for that colony, as is aforesaid, to be holden of us, our heirs, and successors as of our manor of East-Greenwich in the county of Kent, in free and common socage only, and not in capite . . . .
>
> All which lands, tenements, and hereditaments, so to be passed by the said several letters patent, shall be sufficient assurance from the said patentees . . . .[1233]

That this language invokes and relies upon the English common law of land is obvious. Nominees for land patents received them directly from the monarch, not as tenants in chief, or *in capite*, but in the tenure known as free and common socage (with the manorial holding of East Greenwich in Kent as a model). This tenure, evolved from earlier feudalism, has been described earlier in this work as follows:[1234] "Any tenure that on the one hand is free and on the other hand is not spiritual, nor military, nor

---

[1232] "Letters Patent to Sir Thomas Gates et al., April 10 1606," arts. IV and V, *in* 1 Hening, *supra* n. 1224 at 58-60.

[1233] "Letters Patent to Sir Thomas Gates et al., April 10, 1606," arts. XVIII, XIX and XX, *in* 1Hening, *supra* n. 1224 at 65-66.

[1234] *See* §7.05(b)(3)(D) in ch. 7, *supra*.

'serviential,' is called tenure in free socage.[1235]

Tenure in free socage eventually developed as the one great residual tenancy for almost every arrangement that was not military tenure. It also was free of the most burdensome incidents of military tenure, so that it became the tenancy of choice, even if holding it inferred a relatively lower social status.

The very wide variety of socage tenures arose from several types of circumstances. For instance, a tenant might be bound to render only nominal services or rents to the lord, either because the conveyance might be between related persons, or because the grantee had actually purchased the land: "to have put the purchaser in the vendor's place might have been difficult, perhaps impossible [given the restrictions on alienability at the time]; so the purchaser is made tenant to the vendor at an insignificant rent."[1236]

Some socage tenures demanded a more substantial rent in money or goods or produce, possibly the result of some bargaining by lords and tenants trying to strike the best deals that economic circumstances would allow. Other socage tenures imposed requirements of ordinary agricultural labor, even if the tenant was an important aristocrat. These duties would have been fulfilled by the socage tenant's undertenants and "seem to be the channel by which the term *socage* gradually spreads itself."[1237]

At times it might have been quite natural for a villein able to supply some needed labor services to step up into a socage tenure that was ordinarily open only to free persons. Indeed, some socage tenants were barely distinguishable from the unfree villeins.

At the time of the Virginia patents, the tenure of free and common

---

[1235] Frederick Pollock and Frederic William Maitland, *The History of English Law Before the Time of Edward I* 291 (2d ed. 1909).

[1236] *Id.*

[1237] *Id.* at 292.

socage was simply the almost universal "tenure" by which land was held. By this time most tenures themselves were unimportant; only certain revenue-producing tenurial incidents were still protected by their beneficiaries. Half a century later, legislation officially abolished tenures in England.[1238]

The supplemental instructions of November 20, 1606, added further confirmation that land rights rested on the established rights under the laws of England:

> . . . [A]nd moreover wee doe hereby ordaine and establish for us, our heires and successors, that all the lands, tenements, and hereditaments to be had and enjoyed by any of our subjects within the precincts aforesaid, shall be had and inherited and enjoyed, according as in the like estates they be had and enjoyed by the lawes within this realme of England . . . .[1239]

The instructions of November 1606, not only contained no express prohibition of private property in land, but indeed suggested that private land grants would be made in the future. However, the joint trading regulations and overall communal rules for the colony were not conducive to private land holdings. For persons other than the patentees, private property rights in Virginia lands did not appear until several years after the initial settlements.

As leaders of a proprietary form of colony, the Virginia patentees had control of the economic and commercial activities of their colonies, and the powers of government rested with the two resident councils subject to the overall direction of the Council of Virginia sitting in London. When the three vessels bearing the first, or London, company's complement of settlers arrived in Virginia in May 1607, they selected the Jamestown site and immediately began work on clearing land and constructing a protective

---

[1238] Tenures Abolition Act, 12 Car. 2, c. 24 (1660).

[1239] "'Articles, Instructions and Orders,' etc., Nov. 20, 1606," *in* 1 Hening, *supra* n. 1224 at 69.

fort and dwellings. The settlers of the second, or Plymouth, company did not arrive until the end of August 1607, and selected a site they called Sagadahoc near the mouth of the Kennebec River in present day Maine, at a latitude of 431/2 degrees. The corporate management of both settlements was identical:

> The colonies which were founded at Sagadahoc and Jamestown were both plantations, owned, officered, and managed by the proprietors or company. The colonists were servants of the company. They were freely transported to Virginia in its vessels, and there worked for the company under prescribed regulations. They were fed and housed out of the products of the total labor of the colony, supplemented by cargoes of provisions received from home. When, if ever, the colony became able to furnish a surplus product, - lumber, furs, tobacco, - it was sent home in the vessels of the company and sold for the benefit of the adventurers.[1240]

The settlement at Sagadahoc started badly and was abandoned a year later. The severe threats to Jamestown's existence, both from internal dissension and from external calamities, are well known and documented. Preoccupation with survival ensured that neither colony, especially under the governance arrangements of the 1606 charter, would expand its affairs beyond the enterprise of a single settlement. Despite the charter's assurance that English rights would be preserved, the corporate management form soon deteriorated into autocratic rule by a few or even by one, and individual property rights were not yet in existence.

[1240] 1 Herbert L. Osgood, *The American Colonies in the Seventeenth Century* 34 (1904).

§ 9.02(b). The Charter of 1609.[1241]

Early in 1609 the patentees drafted a new charter, which was approved by James I on May 23, 1609. The main objective of the new charter was to replace the old unworkable system of resident and London-based councils with a hierarchy of individual officers, such as governor and lieutenant governor. Most importantly, under the 1609 charter the king released all but nominal control over the Virginia colonies, leaving governing powers with the patentees of the company. A resident governor conducted the day-to-day rule, although he would exercise his powers only "according to such directions" as he received from the company in London.

The charter of 1609 required continuation of the plantation system, by which the colonists worked in groups under various officials as overseers. The workers were to live in common quarters and take their meals all together.

With respect to land rights, the 1609 charter reconfirmed that the patentees were authorized to acquire such rights after first obtaining royal permission:

> And that [the patentees] and their successors, shall be, from henceforth, forever enabled to take, acquire and purchase, by the name aforesaid (license for the same, from us, our heirs or successors, first had and obtained) any manner of lands, tenements, and hereditaments, goods and chattels, within our realm of England, and dominion of Wales.[1242]

The 1609 charter also confirmed that such land rights were the rights

---

[1241] In 1612 King James I issued a third charter for the Virginia Company, which extended the Virginia boundaries to include islands lying within 300 leagues of the continent between the 30th and 41st latitudes, and accepted numerous additional subscribers. *See* 2 Alexander Brown, *The Genesis of the United States* 540-553 (1890). *See* § 9.02(c), *infra*.

[1242] "The Second Charter to the Treasurer and Company, for Virginia," art. IV, *in* 1 Hening, *supra* n. 1224 at 88.

recognized under existing English law, although this time an additional form of consideration was exacted, one-fifth of the yield of any gold and silver mines:

> [The patentees] are to have and to hold, possess and enjoy, all and singular the said lands, countries and territories, with all and singular other premises, heretofore by these presents granted, or mentioned to be granted . . .; to the sole and proper use of [the patentees], their successors and assigns for ever; to be holden of us, our heirs, and successors, as of our manour of East Greenwich, in free and common socage, and not in capite; yielding and paying, therefore, to us, our heirs, and successors, the fifth part only of all ore of gold and silver, that from time to time, and at all times hereafter, shall be there gotten, had, or obtained for all manner of services.[1243]

The charter ratified land rights previously granted, except that the northern boundary of the territory open to Virginia Company colonization was shifted back from the 41st to the 40th parallel.[1244]

The new charter stimulated a new interest in Jamestown, and more colonists and supplies were shipped to succor the struggling settlement. By the time these arrived in the summer of 1609, however, Jamestown was nearly dead; fewer than one-third of all previous colonists there were still alive. Conditions grew even worse. The 100 survivors and 400 new arrivals were wracked by starvation and disease throughout the next winter, so that only about 60 of the 500 survived to the summer of 1610. On June 17, 1610, they had abandoned Jamestown and boarded ship back to England when they met the new governor upon his arrival, who had them disembark and start anew.

1243 "The Second Charter to the Treasurer and Company, for Virginia," art. VI, *in* 1 Hening, *supra* n. 1224 at 89.

1244 "The Second Charter to the Treasurer and Company, for Virginia," art. XXVII, *in* 1 Hening, *supra* n. 1224 at 97.

The new governing arrangements authorized by the 1609 charter were more fully installed in 1610 . The following year, in 1611, the colonists even prepared a law code, the "Lawes and Orders, Divine, Politique, and Martiall, for the Colony of Virginia,"[1245] for up to this time no written laws had existed in the colony. This code severely restricted personal freedom.[1246]

Under such a regimen, probably necessary for the colony's survival, the leaders hoped that their farmers could be soldiers too, with military obedience and diligence characterizing their efforts to conquer the land. The colony now had not only a governor, but also a marshal, who—according to a familiar model—was responsible for directing the activities and maintaining the discipline of the colonists. Sir Thomas Dale arrived at Jamestown on May 19, 1611, and assumed duties as deputy governor but was referred to as, and functioned as, marshal.

Under Dale the colonists quickly founded a new settlement, called Henrico, about 40 miles upriver from Jamestown, and in 1613 secured the entire peninsula from Indian attacks. Much of Jamestown's population relocated to the new site, and an unprecedented measure of health and prosperity began to emerge.

This success was marred by the severity of discipline imposed by Dale, especially after he became acting governor in 1614. During this time it could be said of the Virginia settlements that "a planned economy was placed in operation for the first time in American history. Supervision of crop production was the very least of the economic controls imposed . . . . Virginia's economy was essentially communistic. To the colony accrued the products of its lands. To the government fell the task of

---

[1245] This code was prepared in 1611 and codified and published in 1612.

[1246] "According to this code, freedom of action within the colony was to be reduced to a minimum. The colony was to be regarded and treated as an absolute unit. The traditional forces of military discipline, several penal enactments, and strict religious observance were brought to bear, to repress disorder and direct the productive energies of the settlement" in "The Second Charter to the Treasurer and Company, for Virginia," art. XXVII, *in* 1 Hening, *supra* n. 1224 at 70.

distribution."[1247]

§ 9.02(c). The Charter of 1612.

In the meantime, the patentees had sought and on March 12, 1612, the king had approved a third charter. This charter reaffirmed the grants of the earlier charters and extended the Virginia boundaries to include islands lying within 300 leagues (900 miles) of the continent between 30 and 41 degrees latitude, and it accepted numerous additional subscribers.[1248] No subscribers were permitted to join the company for less than £12 10s, an amount which entitled the purchaser to not less than 100 acres in Virginia.[1249]

The charter of 1612 reiterated the language of the two previous charters concerning the holding of lands in free and common socage, and of the 1609 charter concerning payment of one-fifth of the yield from any gold and silver mines.[1250] It also confirmed interests previously granted[1251] and declared that questions in construing or interpreting any of the charter provisions should be resolved in favor of the company.[1252]

[1247] Alf J. Mapp, Jr., *The Virginia Experiment* 34 (1987).

[1248] 2 Alexander Brown, *The Genesis of the United States* 540-553 (1890).

[1249] "This amount finally entitled the payer to a share of not less than 100 acres in Virginia. Of those who paid their subscriptions and took therefor bills of adventure, it may be stated, as approximately correct, that about one third came to Virginia themselves and settled on their lands; about one third sent over their agents, or finally their heirs, to occupy theirs; while the remaining third sold their shares to others, who generally settled on the lands. These classes were the landed gentry, and they brought, or sent, over another class as servants, etc." *Id.* at 549-550.

[1250] "A Third Charter of K. James I. to the Treasurer and Company, for Virginia," XXI, in vol. 1 Hening, *supra* n. 1224 at 109.

[1251] "A Third Charter of K. James I. to the Treasurer and Company, for Virginia," XXI, in vol. 1 Hening, *supra* n. 1224 at 109.

[1252] "A Third Charter of K. James I. to the Treasurer and Company, for Virginia," XX, in vol. 1 Hening, *supra* n. 1224 at 109.

§ 9.02(d). Introduction of Private Landholding.

Under the desperate circumstances of Jamestown's early years, of course, there could be little thought of private property interests in land for the individual colonists, yet the land was there in such unimaginable abundance. "The sheer quantity of land was a powerful attraction. So far as anyone knew in 1607 the amount was boundless, and for the English, whose homeland was a small island, that thought was mind-boggling."[1253]

But the dream of possessing one's own land was not yet the lot of the Virginia colonists because of the militaristic plantation system enforced with renewed vigor again after 1610, and especially after the introduction of the severe code of military rules in 1611. However, human nature soon asserted itself against the new communalism, as described in a contemporary account:

> When our people were fed out of the common store, and labored jointly together, glad was he who could slip from his labor, or slumber over his task he cared not how, nay, the most honest among them would hardly take so much true pains in a week, as now they themselves will do in a day: neither cared they for the increase, presuming that howsoever the harvest prospered, the general store must maintain them.[1254]

Dale was not oblivious to those sentiments, and as early as 1611 he had consulted the Council about allotting to each colonist a private garden. It was not until 1614, however, that he actually introduced a form of private property into the colonial economy. At that time, the leaders assigned to a large number of colonists private plots of three acres each, which they held under lease. The lessees, called farmers in accordance with contemporary

---

[1253] Warren M. Billings, John E. Selby and Thad W. Tate, *Colonial Virginia - A History* 25 (1986).

[1254] Reported in 1 Herbert L. Osgood, *The American Colonies in the Seventeenth Century* 72 (1904).

English land terminology,[1255] were to pay two and one half barrels of corn annually as rent and were declared exempt from community labor during eleven months of the year. Other arrangements were soon introduced to attract new settlers:

> In order further to encourage the development of tenant right, and the cultivation of commodities which were useful as food, Dale assured to every man with a family who came into the colony a house with four rooms, which he was permitted to occupy for at least a year without the payment of rent. Twelve acres fenced and adjacent to the house assigned for cultivation. With this went tools, live stock, and provisions adequate to the support of the family during a twelvemonth. After that time the newcomer was expected to maintain himself.[1256]

By the time Dale left in 1616, four settlements in addition to Jamestown and Henrico had been established, and the 381 surviving settlers appeared acclimated and fit to further the colony's development.

§ 9.02(e). The Spread of Private Landholding.

According to company regulations, the system of joint land management was to expire in 1616, and dividends on the stock issued in 1609 fell due. Because no cash profits had accumulated during the seven years since 1609, the company was able to pay the dividend only in land. The stockholders were therefore promised fifty acres for each share and told that an additional two hundred acres per share might be later given, but that in order to cover the costs of surveying, each was invited to contribute an additional £12 10s, in return for an additional fifty acres. The results of all of these promotions were inadequate, so in 1617 the company offered 50 acres for each person intending to settle in Virginia. This began the headright system, the main means of distributing land in Virginia for many

---

[1255] A farmer was a person who paid rent as a condition of his tenure.

[1256] 1 Herbert L. Osgood, *The American Colonies in the Seventeenth Century* 76 (1904).

decades thereafter.[1257]

In the colony itself, leaders made other preparations for division of the land near the settlements. In 1617 some indentured laborers, who in 1614 had been promised their freedom after three years' work, were actually emancipated and probably joined the ranks of the tenant farmers. In addition, some lands were most likely held in fee simple, having been so granted by former governors to some of the earlier colonists.[1258] When a new governor arrived in 1617, however, the land distributions ceased, and a new requirement was imposed on each tenant to plant at least two acres in grain, a hedge against the temptation to plant nothing but tobacco.

A new charter was issued in 1618 but was never delivered, because the new governor bringing it with him died while making the ocean crossing. Later that year, on November 18, 1618, the Virginia Company in London issued instructions that transferred governmental power to the colony in Virginia and mandated that the colony be governed by both appointed officers and an assembly consisting of colonists' representatives. These instructions, the so-called "Great Charter" of Virginia, were of greatest importance because they led to the swift assembling of the earliest representative legislative body in North America. The General Assembly, consisting of the governor, six councilors and twenty-two burgesses elected by the colonists, first met at Jamestown on July 30, 1619, shown in Illustration 36.[1259] In addition, a large part of the company instructions dealt with major changes in the management of land.'[1260]

[1257] Richard L. Morton, *Colonial Virginia* 46 (1960); 2 Alexander Brown, *The Genesis of the United States* 774-780 (1890).

[1258] 1 Philip Alexander Bruce, *Economic History of Virginia in the Seventeenth Century* 221 (1896).

[1259] Alf J. Mapp, Jr., *The Virginia Experiment* 44 (1987). According to the modern calendar, the date would have been designated August 9, 1619; according to older authority, the assembly was first called together near the end of June, 1619. 1 Hening, *supra* n. 1224 at 119-121.

[1260] Richard L. Morton, *Colonial Virginia* 52-53 (1960).

Illustration 36. First settled in 1607, Jamestown, Virginia, was the first permanent English settlement in North America. After prodigious struggles in the early years, the colonists were established enough in 1619 to conduct the colonies' first representative assembly in this Jamestown church. This and similar assemblies issued many laws and regulations relating to land.

Three thousand acres were set aside as land and residence for the governor, to be cultivated by the governor's guard and fifty tenants; an additional three thousand acres at each of the principal settlements were assigned to pay the expenses and salaries of councilors and public officers of the colony, and some of the later arriving settlers were placed on these under seven-year tenancies. "There were also provisions in these instructions . . . for the granting of one hundred acres of land (and more later) to each individual adventurer or planter who had already bought a share of £12 10s. in the Company's stock, or who had come over at his own expense and had died or had remained in the Colony for at least three years, or who had come over at the Company's expense before [the former governor] Dale's departure in 1616 and who had completed his term of service to the Company."[1261]

[1261] *Id.* at 54.

Embodied in these rules, therefore, was a liberal right to acquire fee simple in land. Even common laborers were able to become landholders under the farmers' tenure:

> Far more powerful was the influence of a fee simple title upon those who received this invaluable gift on account of their long connection with the Colony; it is stated [by Captain John Smith, *Works*, p. 542] that a strong rivalry at once sprang up among them as to which one should excel in building and planting.[1262]

As to the lands assigned for the support of public offices, it was necessary to also provide the means for making the lands productive. This was done by establishing a system of leases of lands held by public officials.[1263]

[1262] 1 Philip Alexander Bruce, *Economic History of Virginia in the Seventeenth Century* 227-228 (1896).

[1263] "The apportionments of land would have been worthless if no provision had been made for their cultivation. A system of leases in consequence was adopted. To the Governor one hundred tenants were allowed; to the Treasurer and Marshal, fifty each; to the superintendent of the Company's lands, forty; to the Secretary and Physician, twenty apiece; and to the Vice-admiral, twelve. Each one of these public officials, when his tenure ceased, was required to transmit to his successor the whole number of tenants who were by law attached to his office. It was the intention of the Company that each one should receive such an area of land and such a number of servants as would be sufficient to afford him an ample support as well as to sustain the dignity of his position. The plan was in large measure carried into practical effect." *Id.* at 229-30.

Illustration 37. Captain John Smith, third leader of the Jamestown colony, invoked discipline and leadership essential to the colony's survival. He oversaw some beneficial changes in the landholding arrangements.

§ 9.02(f). Tenancy in Land.

The tenancy attached to such lands at that time was a form of landholding resting somewhere in the middle of the progression from the medieval unfree villein tenure and the modern agriculture tenancy known today. The Jamestown tenants were not indefinitely bound to the soil and subject to the needs and directions of the lords of the manor, as their peasant forebears may have been; still, the farmer's seven year term was a form of servitude, requiring payment of half the annual crops and labor services for the entire seven years. Some abuse of the tenants' labor occurred.[1264]

[1264] "[It was] openly asserted that the officers of the Company made an improper use both of their tenants and the tenants' servants. The servants were taken away from their masters and removed by the officers to their private estates, while the tenants themselves were kept so constantly engaged in rowing the officers to and

Not more than three years after this system went into effect, the tenants obtained a change in the arrangements favorable to their situation. The rent was changed from one-half the crop (no rent if the crop failed) to 20 bushels of grain, sixty pounds of tobacco, and one pound of silk, plus six days' labor on public works. To ensure performance, no fewer than three tenants were required to live together, each being bound for the rent requirements.

§ 9.02(g). Land Grants to Private Societies.

Yet another form of land grant commenced in 1618, a type of sub-patent issued to private societies. Under this arrangement several prominent colonists banded together, combining their own shares and sometimes purchasing additional shares, and offered to form a plantation at their own expense. The result was the assigning of very large tracts of Virginia land for private plantations, which tended to quickly use up the available land.[1265]

Among the terms of the private plantation grants or patents was that the grantees could regulate their servants and business in ways not repugnant to the laws of England. This was tested when, at the time the first assembly

---

fro between Jamestown and the lands assigned to the different official positions . . . that it was not in their power to pay the rent expected of them . . . . The amount of rent exacted of the tenants was undoubtedly too large, being very much in excess of that which was required of the farmers during the administration of [former governor] Dale." *Id.* at 232-33.

[1265] "The first private plantation thus granted was Southampton or Smith's Hundred, consisting of two hundred thousand acres . . . . Within this some three hundred tenants were settled. Shortly after other grants were made to "Argall and his associates," "Hamor and his associates," "Martin and his associates." Of these the last, known as Martin's Plantation or Hundred, [was] the only one of the three to be developed . . . . The grantee was Captain John Martin, who had been connected with the fortunes of the colony from the outset. The grant contained eighty thousand acres." 1 Herbert L. Osgood, *The American Colonies in the Seventeenth Century* 84-85 (1904). A later writer distinguishes between Martin's Brandon (on the west bank of the James River) and Martin's Hundred or Plantation (on the peninsula, on the east bank of the James River), indicating that Martin's Hundred was settled by Richard Martin. Richard L. Morton, *Colonial Virginia* 62-65 (1960). Curiously, even Osgood, at page 91, recognized that the two settlements were in two different locations.

met, John Martin claimed the privileges of an English manorial lord over his plantation, but he was directed instead to submit to usual company regulations. Nevertheless, the grantees of private plantations were called commanders and seem to have had some semi-military powers of governance. When the company was eventually dissolved and Virginia became a royal province, the characteristics of local government that had grown up with private plantation settlements were preserved.

§ 9.02(h). Summary of How Private Landholding Progressed.

Thus, by several devices the vast lands of tidewater Virginia began to shift into private ownership. Farmers completing their tenancies might be in position to buy land outright; settlers could receive land for their work, and if they properly exploited their first grant, they could receive a second grant of equal size without further investment; likewise, investors received grants in recognition of their stock, with further grants to follow if the first were profitably developed; private societies obtained large "plantation" tracts; large tracts were reserved for public institutions and officials, which were worked by soldiers, servants and tenants; and under the headright system, those who sponsored and sent colonists received grants of land for every person they sent.

The significance of the headright system cannot be over-emphasized. To this system, which would result in a vast increase in private landholding one historian has attributed a remarkable increase in the colonists' energy and diligence.[1266]

[1266] "The system of head rights played a prominent part in the settlement of Virginia, and of the other provinces as well, for generations to come, and by it the supply of the colonies with a due proportion of servants was insured. As an additional inducement to private settlers it was ordered that those who received their bills of adventure before midsummer 1625, should be free from the payment of quitrents. Those issued later than this date were subject to that obligation. As the result of successive divisions and the multiplication of private grants, large and small, the unoccupied land of the province gradually became the property of the individual freeholders. Those who possessed the smaller estates worked them themselves with the aid of a few laborers or servants. The larger grantees employed many servants, - or later, slaves, - and in some cases leased their estates partly or wholly to tenants . . . .

§ 9.02(i). Changes in Governance Affecting Private Landholding.

The deaths of Pocahontas in 1617 in England and of her father, Powhatan, in Virginia the next year, eventually led to changed relations with the natives. On March 22, 1622, Powhatan's successor was able to coordinate a widespread surprise attack on numerous Virginia settlements, resulting in the massacre of about 350 men, women and children—a quarter of the colony's population at the time. An attack of plague only a few months earlier had been even more devastating.

The discouragement following these disasters prompted King James I, later in 1622, to involve himself more directly in the affairs of the company, fearing the conditions in the colony were fomenting too much independence and possible sedition. He submitted names of his own candidates in elections of company officers, but when they were rejected, he began planning for the destruction of the company. Following the contrived work of a royal investigative commission, James offered the company a guarantee that their land interests would be preserved if they would surrender their charter to royal control, which proposition the colonists also rejected. Then James had his attorney general issue a *quo warranto* against the company; when the matter came before the King's Bench on June 26, 1624, the court revoked the company's charter on a technicality—an alleged error in pleading.

Upon the return of the colony to royal governance, the king appointed a commission with the objective of reinstating the plan of government described in the 1606 charter. James died, however, before the commission could finish its work. His successor, Charles I, then officially proclaimed Virginia a royal colony, and in the end no major changes were made to the form of government that was in place in 1624. The Virginia assembly did not meet officially between 1624 and 1628; but following this hiatus, the members resumed meeting and legislating, albeit without formal sanction

---

"General indolence, of which John Smith and Dale complained, disappeared with the advent of the system of individual estates." 1 Herbert L. Osgood, *The American Colonies in the Seventeenth Century* 87 (1904).

from the king. Finally, in January 1639, Charles gave formal consent to the restoration of the assembly as a permanent institution of the colony. This was the first representative assembly in an English royal colony. During this period the settlement of land continued, impeded only by the presence of large abandoned tracts owned by those who had died or returned to England. In 1648. "[B]y authority of his instructions Governor Berkeley allowed colonists to settle in the James River Valley on lands previously granted to others but which either had been abandoned or never settled. Former owners who protested were given lands in unsettled regions elsewhere. This doubtless marked the end of many particular plantations on paper."[1267]

For defensive purposes, commanders were authorized to build forts at designated locations and to keep the forts and the land belonging to them so long as they maintained the garrison. Similarly, to encourage exploration, a 1652 act of the assembly authorized exploration projects under which the explorers could choose for themselves a portion of the land discovered. In 1653 the assembly established reservations for certain Indian tribes and required colonists within those areas to move. In 1656 the Indians were prohibited from selling or trading their land without assembly consent.

The huge territory of the colony was also destined for division. The issuance of the Maryland charter in 1632 hemmed in Virginia on the north. In 1663 eight persons received from King Charles II proprietary rights to the region between Virginia and Spanish Florida on the south. When Charles seized New Netherlands in 1664, he granted it to his brother, the Duke of York. Even before coming to power, Charles had made direct grants of Virginia land to several of his friends, although eventually they fully submitted to the authority of the colonial government. When Charles II in 1673 granted almost all of Virginia to two of his favorites, in disregard of established grants and governments already in place, the Virginians were able to undo most of his mischief. Thereupon they petitioned for a completely new charter, but the charter they received did little more than confirm titles to lands.

[1267] Richard L. Morton, *Colonial Virginia* 150 (1960).

§ 9.02(j). The Influence of English Common Law on Landholding.

§ 9.02(j)(1). Adoption of English Common Law in Virginia.

The adoption of English common law, as modified by local circumstances, appeared in early Virginia patents almost as an afterthought. The underlying assumption that the laws of England applied in colonial Virginia, except where local circumstances dictated otherwise, was made more explicit after the Stuart Restoration in 1660. It seemed appropriate to the assembly members at that time to confirm their allegiance to that rule of law. The assembly sorted through its past enactments and compiled those to be kept in a new code of laws adopted in March 1662. In this the assembly proclaimed that Virginians "have also endeavoured in all things (as neere as the capacity and constitution of this country would admitt) to addhere to those excellent and often refined laws of England, to which we profess and acknowledge all due obedience and reverence . . . ."[1268] These important acts were summarized by one scholar as follows:

> By the statutes of 1661-1662, procedure in the courts was regulated. At the time of the Restoration, Virginia seems to have been especially anxious to show herself loyal to England, and these enactments breathe a deep respect for the common law. In the preamble it is stated that the legislature has endeavored in all things to adhere to these "excellent and refined laws of England to which we profess to acknowledge all due obedience and reverence." As a reason for enacting laws at all they assign the vast volume of the English law from which courts would be unable to collect the necessary principles without the aid of such codification. The former laws are repealed and a new code is enacted. As some former laws restrained the trial by jury quite contrary to the laws of England, the law

[1268] Virginia Assembly of 1660-61, Preamble, in 2 Hening, *supra* n. 1224 at 43.

> of juries is restated with special carefulness and precision. It is interesting to note in this connection that the colonists express their regret that they are unable to comply with the requirement of the English jury system that the jurors shall come from the immediate neighborhood of the place where the fact was committed; but they state that they desire to approach as near as possible to compliance by enacting that six men of the ablest and nearest of the inhabitants of the county shall be on the jury . . . . In this code the period of prescription for land is limited to five years.[1269]

In 1666 the assembly appropriated money to purchase law books, in order to more faithfully adhere to English common law:

> Whereas for the better conformity of the proceedings of the courts of this country to the lawes of England, as appeares necessary for their better direction therein, all the former statutes at large and those made since the beginning of the raigne of his sacred majestie that now is and a few other approved books of law should be purchased, It is therefore by this grand assembly and the authority thereof enacted accordingly that all the aforesaid statute books, and Daltons justice of the peace, and office of a sherriffe, and Swinburnes book of Wills and Testaments may be sent for by the auditor for the use of the general courts and assembly, . . . and the like books be sent for by some of the commissioners of the severall county courts for the use of the respective counties, and paid for out of the county levy.[1270]

Given the background of colonial Virginia's early leaders, reliance on English common law was only natural. The colony's leaders were

[1269] Paul Samuel Reinsch, "The English Common Law in the Early American Colonies," in 1 *Select Essays in Anglo-American Legal History* 367, 405-406 (Association of American Law Schools, 1907).

[1270] "Virginia Assembly of 1666," Act XX in 2 Hening, *supra* n. 1224 at 246.

members of the English ruling class and had "been well schooled in English law and custom."[1271]

§ 9.02(j)(2). Regulation of Attorneys.

While the English legal system of the 17th century may have been only implicitly accepted as the rule of law in Virginia, the colonists seemed eager to act against defects in that system. Prominent among the defects was the conduct of attorneys, that is, of persons acting on behalf of others in litigation. In 1642 the Virginia Assembly commenced an amazing series of enactments regulating attorneys that knows no parallel for legislative schizophrenic paranoia.

The 1642 act provided for licensing attorneys and limiting their fees;[1272] in 1645 the assembly prohibited attorneys from collecting fees, labeling those who did as mercenary attorneys and, in effect, expelling them from office.[1273] In the session of 1645-1646, the 1642 act (for licensing attorneys) was repealed and the 1645 act (expelling attorneys) was confirmed in perpetuity.[1274] In 1647, the assembly further prohibited even

---

[1271] "Throughout the nearly two decades that the London Company managed Virginia, it recruited the colony's leaders from England's ruling classes. Those men were well schooled in English law and custom. They had been educated at the universities or Inns of Court; some knew martial law, and they all enjoyed ties to the court and Parliament. Despite such qualifications these men were to leave only a slight impression on colonial law. Few survived or stayed in Virginia long enough to make much of a mark. Furthermore, there was little agreement before 1625 as to which of England's legal traditions were most suitable to a struggling colony. The question of what law should prevail was only vaguely addressed before formulation of *The Lawes Divine, Morall and Martiall* [the very severe code adopted for Jamestown in 1611, and sometimes enforced]. The Charter of 1618 supplanted *The Lawes*, but that change merely introduced the possibility of adopting a more familiar form of law. Thus it was the members of the post-1625 general assemblies, together with their counterparts in local government, who assumed the greater role in grafting English common law to colonial needs." Warren M. Billings, John E. Selby, Thad W. Tate, *Colonial Virginia* 75 (1986).

[1272] "Virginia Assembly of 1642-1643," Act LXI, *in* 1 Hening, *supra* n. 1224 at 275.

[1273] "Virginia Assembly of 1645," Act VII, *in* 1 Hening, *supra* n. 1224 at 302.

[1274] "Virginia Assembly of 1645-1646," Act VIII, *in* 1 Hening, *supra* n. 1224 at 313.

any indirect compensation to those who functioned as attorneys but empowered the courts to chose from among the people someone who could help weaker litigants.[1275] In 1656, all acts against mercenary attorneys were repealed, and a licensing provision was once again put into place:

> And be it enacted that the Governour and Councill shall appoint and allow such as they shall find fitt and able to be attornies in the quarter courts, and the commissioners to do the like by nominateing attornies for the county courts, Provided that no attorney be admitted to practice or plead, before he have taken this oath following: [The oath is omitted from the extant manuscripts.]
>
> And if any controversies arise between attornie and his client about their fee, it shall be determined in the court where the cause is pleaded, Provided allwaies that those onely be called councellors at law, who have allreadie been qualified thereunder by the lawes of England, and those so qualified to enjoy all privilege those lawes give them.[1276]

Nevertheless, the assembly of 1657-1658 reversed itself again and reinstated the expulsion of attorneys.[1277]

[1275] "Virginia Assembly of 1647," Act XVI, *in* 1 Hening, *supra* n. 1224 at 349.

[1276] "Virginia Assembly of 1656," Act VI, *in* 1 Hening, *supra* n. 1224 at 419.

[1277] "Virginia Assembly of 1657-1658," Act CXII, *in* 1 Hening, *supra* n. 1224 at 482-483.

§ 9.02(k). Virginia Landholding During the Later Colonial Period.

§ 9.02(k)(1). Early Legislative Provisions Concerning Land.

Title to lands and numerous other rules regulating interests in real property were implicitly drawn from the common law of England. As to the management of lands, little changed after the form of government stabilized. During the 1620's and 1630's, the Virginia Assembly typically enacted provisions regulating the surveys of land, the settling of new lands, and the disposing of abandoned lands, and requiring homesteads to be palisaded in defense against Indian attacks. In general, the traditional English land law typically invoked by the earliest charters remained intact.

The occasional minor land regulation that was enacted gives a glimpse into everyday early colonial life, when land transactions were an ordinary activity. For instance, a provision enacted by the Assembly of 1639-40 declared that "A deed or mortgage made without delivery of possession [is] to be adjudged fraudulent unless entered in some court."[1278] Other examples of legislative provisions indicating that the colonists were conducting private land transactions include:

> a requirement that mortgages be registered in quarter or monthly courts, or be deemed fraudulent as to creditors;[1279]
>
> assignment of abandoned lots in Jamestown to others;[1280]
>
> prohibiting alienation of orphans' lands during their

[1278] "Virginia Assembly of 1639-1640," Act XVI, *in* 1 Hening, *supra* n. 1224 at 227.

[1279] "Virginia Assembly of 1642-1643," Act XII, *in* 1 Hening, *supra* n. 1224 at 248-249.

[1280] "Virginia Assembly of 1642-1643," Act XIX, *in* 1 Hening, *supra* n. 1224 at 252.

minority;[1281]

resolving settlers' rival claims to the same land;[1282]

confirming all former surveys of land;[1283]

the evidence and surveys required to claim patents by head rights;[1284]

prohibiting desertion of plantations that had already been seated;[1285]

granting proprietary forts and adjoining land, on condition that proprietors keep the forts garrisoned and supplied;[1286]

a five-year limitation on actions for claims and titles to land;[1287]

requiring fencing of cleared ground;[1288]

[1281] "Virginia Assembly of 1642-1643," Act XXXII, in 1 Hening, *supra* n. 1224 at 260.

[1282] "Virginia Assembly of 1642-1643," Act XXXIII, *in* 1 Hening, *supra* n. 1224 at 260.

[1283] "Virginia Assembly of 1642-1643," Act XXXVIII, *in* 1 Hening, *supra* n. 1224 at 262-263.

[1284] "Virginia Assembly of 1642-1643," Act LVIII, *in* 1 Hening, *supra* n. 1224 at 274.

[1285] "Virginia Assembly of 1644-1645," Act VII, *in* 1 Hening, *supra* n. 1224 at 291.

[1286] "Virginia Assembly of 1646," Act II, *in* 1 Hening, *supra* n. 1224 at 326-327.

[1287] "Virginia Assembly of 1646," Act XIII, *in* 1 Hening, *supra* n. 1224 at 331.

[1288] "Virginia Assembly of 1646," Act XV, *in* 1 Hening, *supra* n. 1224 at 332.

regulating surveyors;[1289]

abolishing property taxes in favor of taxes only upon persons;[1290]

prohibiting alienation of Indian lands without assembly approval;[1291]

a holding in litigation that a devise not using the words of fee simple, or heirs and assigns forever, passed only a life estate;[1292]

a holding in litigation describing how to assign dower lands (division into thirds, with the widow having first choice of the divided portions);[1293]

confirmation of Statute of Frauds provisions enacted in 1642 and 1643;[1294]

regulating the form of land patents;[1295]

confirmation of former patent rights, even if not recorded

1289 "Virginia Assembly of 1646," Act XXIV, *in* 1 Hening, *supra* n. 1224 at 335.

1290 "Virginia Assembly of 1648," Act VI, *in* 1 Hening, *supra* n. 1224 at 356.

1291 "Virginia Assembly of 1655-1656," Act I, *in* 1 Hening, *supra* n. 1224 at 396.

1292 "Bromfeild v. Crumpe, Virginia Assembly of 1655-56," *in* Hening, *supra* n. 1224 at 405.

1293 "In the matter of Burbage, Virginia Assembly of 1655-1656," *in* 1 Hening, *supra* n. 1224 at 405.

1294 "Virginia Assembly of 1656," Act IV, *in* 1 Hening, *supra* n. 1224 at 417-418.

1295" Virginia Assembly of 1657-1658," Act LXXXVII, in 1 Hening, *supra* n. 1224 at 472.

> or indexed in the records;[1296]
>
> condemnation of land;[1297]
>
> validating conveyances by husband and wife, if the wife conveyed freely, even though not done by fine and recovery;[1298] and
>
> validating a large entailed conveyance in trust with provisions for settlement upon family members.[1299]

In 1670, the colony restricted the franchise to freeholders who held at least fifty acres. The Council that assisted in the ministerial functions of government had the responsibility for "making grants, and passing all the patents for land," according to a report of 1705. The colonial secretary, chosen from the Council, was:

> to keep the public records of the [colony], and to take care that they be regularly and fairly made up; namely, all judgments of the General Court, as likewise all deeds and other writings there proved; and further to issue all writs, both ministerial and judicial, relating thereto; to make out and record all patents for land, to file the rights by which they issued, and to take the return of all inquests of escheat.[1300]

§ 9.02(k)(2). Quit Rents in Virginia.

In the assembly session of 1639-40, the issue of quit rents first

---

[1296] Virginia Assembly of 1666," Act XIX, *in* 2 Hening, *supra* n. 1224 at 245.

[1297] Virginia Assembly of 1667," Act I, *in* 2 Hening, *supra* n. 1224 at 256.

[1298] "Virginia Assembly of 1674," Act VII, *in* 2 Hening, *supra* n. 1224 at 374.

[1299] "Virginia Assembly of 1674," Act X, *in* 2 Hening, *supra* n. 1224 at 321-325.

[1300] Alf J. Mapp, Jr., *The Virginia Experiment* 212 (1987).

appeared as a matter of legislative concern: "Seven years after date of patents, 2s. per hundred acres quit rents to be paid yearly, at some convenient place to be appointed in each county."[1301] Quit rents are of more than passing interest, because they are an unequivocal indication that landholding was still considered tenurial rather than allodial. Enforcement, or even recognition, of quit rents was only patchy in the British colonies as a whole, but in Virginia, quit rents were more consistently and successfully collected than in any of the other colonies.

Quit rents were usually associated with the tenure of free and common socage and consisted of a typically small service or sum rendered to the grantor in recognition of a persisting but nominal tenurial relationship.[1302] As to quit rents during colonial times and beyond, some were granted in attempts to establish manorial systems and privileges.[1303]

Quit rents were not mentioned in the earliest Virginia charters, but the charter of 1609 was interpreted as reserving the right to reserve a quit rent.[1304] The quit rents in force in Virginia, subject to the provisions enacted during the 1639-40 Assembly, were not required to be paid until seven years after the patent was granted, and then they were in the standardized sum of 2s. per hundred acres. Additional early legislative enactments concerning quit rents were issued by the assemblies of

---

1301 "Virginia Assembly of 1939-40," Acts XXIV, V *in* 1 Hening, *supra* n. 1224 at 228.

1302 Sheldon F. Kurtz, *Moynihan's Introduction to the Law of Real Property* 24-25 (4th ed. 2005).

1303 "In the charters granted to Lord Baltimore and to Penn they were given the right to erect manors and to hold therein courts-baron and courts-leet. Perhaps the closest approach to a successful attempt to set up a manorial system took place in New York. Some of the grants made by Colonial governors to the great proprietors purported to confer manorial privileges. The proprietors in turn made to settlers numerous conveyances in fee reserving in the deeds a perpetual rent payable in wheat, "fat hens" and a day's service "with carriage and horses" and a fine for alienation. In the 1840s these perpetual rents resulted in resentment, rioting, litigation and legislation." *Id.* at 25, n.1.

1304 Beverly W. Bond, Jr., *The Quit-Rent System in the American Colonies* 32 (1919, reprint 1965).

1642-1643,[1305] of 1645,[1306] of 1647,[1307] of 1660-1661,[1308] and of 1661-1662.[1309]

The Virginia colony more successfully collected quit rents and applied them to various public works in Virginia than any other American colony. However, Virginians resisted when quit rent rights were granted to individual proprietors, rather than being exercised by the crown, because they feared the revenue would not be applied for public purposes. Quit rents as a source of revenue may have induced members of the English aristocracy to find both lands and feudal privileges in America.[1310]

Of all the seigniorial rights the collecting of a quit rent was the most important and the most controversial.[1311]

1305 Virginia Assembly Session of 1642-43," Act LXXII, *in* 1 Hening, *supra* n. 1224 at 280 (reiterating that quit rents need not be paid until seven years after the grant).

1306 "Virginia Assembly of 1645," Act XIV, *in* 1 Hening, *supra* n. 1224 at 316 (quit rents could be paid in tobacco at three pennies per pound).

1307 "Virginia Assembly of 1647," Act XX, *in* 1 Hening, *supra* n. 1224 at 351 (distraint upon the land available as a remedy for delinquency in payment of quit rents).

1308 "Virginia Assembly of 1660-1661," Act XXXVI, *in* 2 Hening, *supra* n. 1224 at 31 (quit rents payable in tobacco at two pennies per pound).

1309 "'Virginia Assembly of 1661-1662," Act LXXIV, *in* 2 Hening, *supra* n. 1224 at 99 (quit rents payable in tobacco at two pennies per pound).

1310 "[In the colonies generally] there is no doubt that the quit-rent as a source of revenue influenced the nobility of the seventeenth and early eighteenth centuries in seeking lands in America . . . . For more than a century and a half, lords and gentlemen of rank tried to obtain a footing on American soil and to introduce there the feudal rights and privileges which they exercised upon their own franchises at home. Had they succeeded they might have fastened upon the colonies feudal obligations that the New World would have found it difficult to shake off, as was the case with Canada under the French regime. In England these seignorial rights continued to exist because they had a financial value; and it was apparently easy for the manorial lord at home to believe that he could recoup his failing resources in a similar manner from lands granted to him in America." *See generally* Beverly W. Bond, Jr., *The Quit-Rent System in the American Colonies* (1919, reprint 1965).

1311 "The quit-rent in the domain of real property, like the royal prerogative in the field of government and the navigation acts in the field of commerce, was an obstacle to complete colonial independence, and a check upon the ability of people

§ 9.02(k)(3). Impact of Landholding Practices on Virginia Society.

The continuing availability of land ownership exercised a powerful effect on Virginia and, eventually, on American society. "[A] blurring of customary [social] distinctions occurred. For one thing, landownership was not restricted to a few. Land existed in abundance, and anyone could become a landowner; at least that was the promise if not always the practice."[1312]

Right on through the colonial period in Virginia, land distribution continued to be a central issue. Abuse of headrights was rife: ships' crews claimed headrights every time they entered Virginia, and captains claimed headrights for the same crews each time; no one followed up on whether the minimum improvements were installed on the acreage thus claimed, and unimproved land never reverted back to the government. Headrights were also claimed for imported slaves. This latter abuse was corrected in 1699, but none of the others was changed.

This laxness perhaps led more readily to a change in land distribution that was intended to encourage settlement of western lands. Beginning in the 1690's, settlers were granted their acreage before they actually arrived, under the assumption that they would achieve the "seating" of their lands within a specified period of time, but no reversions ever occurred for non-compliance. As part of this system, however, land speculators were able to amass huge holdings in the West, and eventually the plantation system of the tidewater country worked its way west.

By the end of the American Revolution, tax lists showed that half of adult white males in Virginia owned land, about a third were agricultural laborers, and the rest were tenants. Although the "bulk of the land was not

---

to utilize its own resources for its own benefit and advantage." Charles M. Andrews, "Introduction," in Beverly W. Bond, Jr., *The Quit-Rent System in the American Colonies* 18-19, 21-22 (1919, reprint 1965).

[1312] Warren M. Billings, John E. Selby, and Thad W. Tate, *Colonial Virginia* 56 (1986).

widely held . . . most white Virginians in the eighteenth century were small farmers . . .," and "[l]andholding was more widely distributed in Virginia than in the mother country, and two to three times as many persons by percentage of the population had the vote in the colony as in contemporary Britain."[1313]

§ 9.03. Development of Property Law in Massachusetts (from 1620).

§ 9.03(a). The Plymouth Colony.

§ 9.03(a)(1). Origins of the Pilgrims.

Massachusetts' first settlers were Puritans, and the first Puritans in Massachusetts included a particular variety called Separatists, later referred to as "Pilgrims" in William Bradford's history, written many years later. The Puritans in England were a faction, or movement, within the Church of England, that sought to purify doctrine and practice by returning to the original teachings, simplicity and, indeed, austerity of the Christian church. The Separatists agreed but believed that a complete separation from the Anglican church was essential. Though they were in congregations widely scattered throughout England, the Separatists were heavily persecuted by the English government. The congregation in Scrooby, Nottinghamshire, with which William Brewster and William Bradford affiliated, moved to Holland in 1608, settling first in Amsterdam and then in Leiden. Although enjoying religious freedom, they did not have citizenship and were thus limited in occupational possibilities; this kept their economic circumstances depressed. In addition, they felt that their children were being drawn from the faith by their worldly surroundings.[1314] The Separatists who came to Massachusetts in 1620 were made up of a portion of the Leiden congregation and additional Separatists from England; about sixty percent of this first Massachusetts group also consisted of those who were not

---

[1313] *Id.* at 209-212.

[1314] William Bradford, *Of Plymouth Plantation* 25 (Samuel Eliot Morison, ed., 1959).

Separatists and who were called "Strangers."

§ 9.03(a)(2). The Legal Beginnings of Plymouth Colony.

The legal origin of the Plymouth colony lies in the original Virginia charter of 1606, which extended from 34 to 45 degrees latitude. The group obtaining that first charter consisted of prominent merchants and others from London, Bristol and Plymouth. The charter authorized the London patentees to establish the "first colony" in the southern sector of that grant, while the group from Plymouth and Bristol was also authorized to form a joint stock company and establish a "second colony" in the northern sector. Accordingly, the Jamestown settlers of the first group landed in May 1607, and a second group of settlers attempted to found a northern colony in August 1607. Their site, which they named Sagadahoc, was located near the mouth of the Kennebec River in present-day Maine, but they abandoned it a year later:

> After the failure of the experiment at Sagadahoc, the Plymouth patentees limited their efforts to fishing voyages and to the detailed exploration of the coast of northern Virginia. The number of patentees was small and their resources were limited. They slumbered on while the London merchants procured two new charters, by which the extent of their domain was made more definite, and under the authority of which they successfully founded a colony on the James River.[1315]

In 1620 the Plymouth patentees successfully petitioned the king for a new charter for northern Virginia, now named New England, seeking rights to the territory between the 40th and 48th parallels from sea to sea. The king granted the charter on November 3, 1620—after the first group of settlers was already well on their way—and created a new corporation called The Council Established at Plymouth in the County of Devon for the

---

[1315] 1 Herbert L. Osgood, *The American Colonies in the Seventeenth Century* 98 (1904).

Planting, Ruling, Ordering and Governing of New-England in America, better known as the Council for New England. After reciting the granting of the Virginia charter of 1606 and the separation of the London and Plymouth companies under the Virginia charter of 1609, the provisions of this 1620 New England patent, which are important for the history of colonial land law, are as follows:

> [Various named persons] to be the first Councill, . . . [to receive, hold, and dispose of real and personal property] . . . .
>
> And Wee do further grant that it shall be lawfull for the said Councill, in their discretions to admitt such Persons . . . to have any Lands or Hereditaments in New-England, as they shall think fitt, according to the Laws, Orders, Constitutions, and Ordinances, by the said Councill and their Successors from time to time to be made and established by Virtue of, and according to the true Intent of these Presents, . . . and also to make all Manner of Orders, Laws, Directions, Instructions, Forms, and Ceremonies of Government and Magistracy fitt and necessary for any concerning the Government of said Collony and Plantation, so always as the same be not contrary to the Laws and Statutes of this our Realme of England . . . . And Wee do further absolutely give, grant, and confirm unto the said Councill all the aforesaid Lands together also, with the Firme Lands, Soyles, Grounds . . ., to be holden of Us as of our Manor of East-Greenwich, in our County of Kent, in free and common socage and not in Capite nor by Knight's Service . . . . [English settlers, and their children born in the colony, are to have the rights of natural-born Englishmen. Rights granted in previous charters are confirmed, except those altered by this charter].[1316]

[1316] *Select Charters and Other Documents Illustrative of American History (1606-1775)* 24-33 (William MacDonald, ed., 1914).

Illustration 38. This pavillion sheltering the small boulder in the grotto traditionally marks the so-called Plymouth Rock, where the Pilgrim settlers landed in December, 1620, to form the first permanent English settlement in New England. Half their number died that first winter, but they and other colonists set many useful precedents for distributing the huge tracts of available land.

Meanwhile, in February 1620, the London Company had granted a patent to a group of private adventurers, and one member of that group attempted to recruit the Separatists of the Leiden congregation as settlers. Articles of agreement were drawn up between the adventurers (those who were investing funds in the enterprise) and the settlers (principally, the Separatist congregation of Leiden) but, in fact, were never signed because of a dispute over some changes introduced to secure more investors. Specifically, one of the changes deleted provisions securing to the settlers the right to separate houses and home lots for themselves and their families, as well as the right to two days a week in which to work for themselves. Otherwise, the articles established a venture patterned after the arrangements in Virginia: the plantation would be managed as a joint stock company for seven years, with contributions to and withdrawals from a common stock, and with shareholders entitled to a division of land at the end of that time. In the end, the settlers from the Leiden congregation refused to sign the agreement without restoration of desired provisions.

The settlers' ship the *Mayflower* sailed apparently without specific instructions as to where to land, but the colonists probably intended to settle near present-day Manhattan. When they did ultimately land, farther north than planned, they were without any rights regarding the region they proposed to settle. They had not formally concluded an agreement with their sponsoring adventurers (who were acting on authority granted to the London Company), and in any event, during their sea crossing, a new royal patent had been issued giving authority over this area to the Plymouth Company. Realizing their ambivalent situation, they undertook the first steps toward self-government, as described by William Bradford:

> I shall a litle returne backe and begine with a combination [the *Mayflower Compact*] made by them before they came ashore, being the first foundation of their governmente in this place; . . . That when they came a shore they would use their own libertie; for none had power to command them, the patente they had being for Virginia, and not for New-england, which belong to an other Government, with which the Virginia Company had nothing to doe. And partly that such an acte by them done (this their condition considered) might be as firme as any patent, and in some respects more sure.[1317]

In this agreement, the *Mayflower Compact,* they made no mention of government according to the laws of England, but instead agreed to enact such laws as they thought best for the general good of the colony:

> We . . . covenant and combine our selves togeather into a civill body politick, for our better ordering and preservation and furtherance of the ends aforesaid; and by vertue hearof to enacte, constitute, and frame such just and

---

[1317] *Bradford's History of Plymouth Plantation* 106 (William T. Davis, ed., 1908).

> equall lawes, ordinances, acts, constitutions, and offices, from time to time, as shall be thought most meete and convenient for the generall good of the Colonie, unto which we promise all due submission and obedience.[1318]

§ 9.03(a)(3). Early Landholding in Plymouth.

Because the settlers had not signed the articles of agreement that omitted their right to establish separate houses and lots, they quickly created separate homesteads:

> We divided by lot the plot of ground whereon to build our town, after the proportion formerly allotted. We agreed that every man should build his own house, thinking by that course men would make more haste than working in common.[1319]

Of course, after the brutal hardships of that first winter of 1620-1621, when about half of the 102 original Pilgrims died of disease and exposure, the colonists established common fields adjacent to the settlement and worked them by their common labor. Indeed, late in 1621 the articles of agreement were finally signed, without the provisions for individual homesteads, so it is likely that no private labor occurred except around the private dwellings and garden plots already established.

In 1623, well before the division of land scheduled for 1627, the settlers introduced a serious departure from the system of common labor:

> So they began to thinke how they might raise as much corne as they could, and obtaine a beter crope then they had done, that they might not still thus languish in miserie. At length, after much debate of things, the Gov'r (with the advise of the cheefest amongest them) gave way that they

1318 *Id.* at 107.

1319 As reported in 1 Herbert L. Osgood, *The American Colonies in the Seventeenth Century* 110 (1904).

> should set corne every man for his own perticuler, and in that regard trust to them selves; in all other things to goe on in the general way as before. And so assigned to every family a parcell of land, according to the proportion of their number for that end, only for present use (but made no devission for inheritance), ranged all boys and youth under some familie. This had very good success; for it made all hands very industrious, so as much more corne was planted then other waise would have bene by any means the Gov'r or any other could use, and saved him a great deall of trouble and gave far better contente.[1320]

Governor Bradford devoted a lengthy comment in his history to the implications of this move toward private property:

> The experience that was had in this commone course and condition, tried sundrie years, and that amongst godly and sober men, may well evince the vanitie of that conceite of Platos and other ancients, applauded by some of later times; - that the taking away of propertie, and bring in communitie into a comone wealth, would make them happy and florishing; as if they were wiser then God. For this comunities (so far as it was) was found to breed much confusion and discontent, and retard much imployment that would have been to their benefite and comforte. For the yong-men that were most able and fitt for labour and service did repine that they would spend their time and streingth to worke for other mens wives and children, with out any recompence. The strong, or man of parts, had not more in devission of victails and cloaths, then he that was weake and not able to doe a quarter the other could; this was thought injuestice. The aged and graver men to be ranke and equalised in labours, and victails, cloaths, etc., with the meaner and yonger sort, thought it some indignite and disrespect unto them. And for mens wives to be

[1320] *Bradford's History of Plymouth Plantation* 146 (William T. Davis, ed., 1908).

> commanded to doe servise for other men, as dresing their meat, washing their cloaths, etc., they deemd it a kind of slaverie, neither could many husbands well brooke it. Upon the poynte all being to have alike, and all to doe alike, they thought themselves in the like condition, and one as good as another; and so, if it did not cut of those relations that God hath set amongest men, yet it did at least much diminish and take of the mutuall respects that should be preserved amongst them. And would have bene worse if they had been men of another condition. Let none object this is men's corruption, and nothing to the course it selfe. I answer, seeing all men have this corruption in them, God in his wisdome saw another course fiter for them.[1321]

Later that year additional colonists arrived, including a group known as the "Perticulers," accompanied by instructions that they should receive separate allotments of land but should remain under the colonial government. Their allotments were assigned within the town itself, and because they did not participate in the common labor, they were taxed.

Because of the success realized from the experiment of letting the settlers plant corn for themselves, the settlers each received in perpetuity an acre of land near the town.

By this time, the colony's "chain of title" problems had been partially resolved. As soon as it was realized that the colony was north of the 40th parallel, and therefore subject to the New England Council, the group that in 1620 had obtained a grant for New England lands from the London Company in June 1621, obtained a deed of grant from the New England Council. The grantees' original London grant had been rendered obsolete by the patent given the Plymouth Company in November 1620, and the June 1621 grant from the New England Council was based on the authority

[1321] *Id.* at 146-147.

of that patent. The new grant contained boundary descriptions.[1322]

Notwithstanding these provisions, in 1627 the settlers and their sponsoring adventurers/investors decided to part company. The settlers agreed to buy out the adventurers' interests for a specified sum of money, with eight of the most prosperous planters acting as sureties. About the time this agreement was reached, the period of required joint land tenure expired, and the heads of families and young men assembled to work out a division of the tillable land. A division of arable land near the town was worked out by lot, with the more remote land and meadow being left as common. In 1633 they also divided the meadow because of increasing numbers of livestock and the need for more hay. To pay off the debt, they continued to carry out the trade of the colony on a joint basis. The planters also obtained patents for other settlements, but only the satellite settlement on the Kennebec River continued for very long. When the colony's last debts were finally paid in 1646, it completed the process of change from a proprietary plantation to a corporate colony.

The Plymouth colony received another patent in 1629, the so-called "Warwick Patent," issued in the name of William Bradford, who, as governor, held the grant as trustee for the colony. The patent did not affect political development of the colony. Eventually, the colonists founded settlements which became towns with their own local officials and the power to grant land. The first of these was Scituate in 1636, followed by Duxbury in 1637, and others in close succession. These towns remained a part of Plymouth colony and were subject to colonial supervision in several important respects. In 1641 Bradford surrendered his trusteeship and

---

[1322] "[The new grant] contained simply a grant of land, in amount proportional to the number of permanent settlers . . . . No attempt was made to bound the grant or to specify its location otherwise than by the statement that the land taken up should not lie within ten miles of any other English settlement, unless the two were on opposite sides of some large navigable river. Provision was made for the payment to the council of a quitrent of two shillings per hundred acres. The patentees were temporarily granted the power to issue such ordinances as were necessary "for their better government," and to put them into execution through elected officers. They were also promised that, if after seven years the request was presented, the grantees should be incorporated with some fit name and received additional powers of government . . . ." Herbert L. Osgood, *The American Colonies in the Seventeenth Century* 116 (1904).

assigned the patent to the freemen of the colony.

§ 9.03(a)(4). The Foundation of English Land Law in Plymouth.

In addition to patents and charters, the colony also issued numerous decisions in legal disputes, as well as legislative pronouncements on specific issues. Periodically, the colonial administration gathered the laws in force into "codes," or compilations, that revealed the colonists' attitudes towards sources of law, and the efficacy of English law in general. Plymouth issued four compilations of its colonial laws during the 17th century, in 1636, 1658, 1671, and 1684. The significance of the 1636 code has been characterized "as the first comprehensive body of law to be enacted in North America.[1323]

Several passages of the 1636 code suggest that a comprehensive basis of English law existed even in Plymouth. In Act 1 the drafters declare:

1323 "The compilation of 1636 has been variously described as the first comprehensive body of law to be enacted in North America, as the first American code of laws, and as a simple model upon which subsequent bodies of American law were patterned. All of those claims can easily be defended, but from the point of view of the framers the compilation was regarded as the "ordering of a body politick" agreeable to the Mayflower Compact and the Warwick patent [issued in 1629]. Some of its clauses were based upon English law and custom, such as the regulation of inheritances according to the custom of East Greenwich, and the requirement that jury trials be conducted as nearly as possible to English practice. In other instances, such as the provision for civil marriage, equality of descent, liberal provisions for women and widows, and the institution of a recording system, all unknown in England, we find partly an attempt to fill the needs of a frontier society and partly the Puritan predilection to enact laws based upon scriptural authority. The discretionary power of Magistrates, for example, was based upon *Romans* 13, the division of lands upon *Deuteronomy* 21, civil marriage upon *Ruth* 4, and capital offenses upon various admonitions.

Two months after the compilation of 1636 was enacted, the General Court met in legislative session and passed six additional miscellaneous measures; it marked the beginning of a regular legislative process that was to continue unabated until the demise of the colony." *The Laws of the Pilgrims* xiv (John D. Cushing, ed., 1977) (a facsimile edition of *The Book of the General Laws of the Inhabitants of the Jurisdiction of New-Plimouth 1672 & 1685*, introduction by John D. Cushing).

> And finding that as freeborne subjects of the State of England we hither came indewed with all and singular the privilege belonging to such, in the first place we think good that it be established for an act That according to the . . . due priviledge of the subject aforesaid no imposicon of law or ordnance be made or imposed upon us by ourselves [or others at] present or to come but such as shall be made [or] imposed by consent according to the free liberties [of the] State and Kingdome of England and no otherwise.[1324]

Other provisions relating to reliance on English law or, specifically, to regulation of real property rights are as follows:

> That all trialls whether Capitall or between man and man be tryed by Jewryes according to the presidents of the law of England as neer as may be.[1325]
>
> That all sales exchanges gifts and morgages leases or other Conveyances of howses and land and the sale to be acknowledged before the Gov'r or any one of the Assistants and committed to publick Record and the fees to be payd.[1326]
>
> That Inheritance to descend according to the commendable custome of England and hold of East Greenwich.[1327]
>
> That If the husband died the wife shal have a third pt of his land during her life and a 3d of his goods to be at her owne

[1324] *Records of the Colony of New Plymouth in New England* 6 (David Pulsifer, ed., 1861).

[1325] *Id.* at 12.

[1326] *Id.*

[1327] *Id.*

disposing.[1328]

In 1658 a new compilation replaced that of 1636 and subsequent legislation. A lengthy preamble contained:

> a succinct summary of the puritan philosophy of law, which held essentially that the only true law was the law of God as revealed in His Holy Scriptures, and that laws made by man must be derived from them and conformable to them in all respects. The puritans found the divine origins of all civil authority in the thirteenth part of *Romans*, and the introduction to the 1658 compilation stressed that God had endowed man with right judgment and true laws (Scripture) as well as with a capacity to be guided by "good and wholesome lawes" derived from and agreeable to the "Ancient platforme of God's Lawe." The framers then went on to proclaim that they had been guided accordingly in the preparation of the new revision of the laws.[1329]

The code also declared that its drafters:

> "the Associates of New Plymouth coming hether as freeborne Subjects of the State of England [this impersonal reference to the government was used during the Commonwealth] Indowed with all and singular privilege belonging to such [do enact that law] which is according to the free liberties of the State of England."[1330]

The 1658 code served until the colony produced a new code in 1671,

---

[1328] *Id.* at 13.

[1329] *The Laws of the Pilgrims* xv (John D. Cushing, ed., 1977) (a facsimile edition of *The Book of the General Laws of the Inhabitants of the Jurisdiction of New-Plimouth 1672 & 1685*, introduction by John D. Cushing).

[1330] *Records of the Colony of New Plymouth in New England* 78 (David Pulsifer, ed., 1861).

which included an entire chapter (Chapter X) of five sections devoted to "Lands, Inheritances, and Wills." These sections covered the tenure of landholding, acknowledgment of conveyances, lands held in partnership, escheat of estates, and a statute of limitations. The chapter concludes with the statement, "It having been the usual manner and custome of this Court, as much as may be to have recourse to the commendable Laws of England in such case wherein there is no other Law by this Court provided more suitable to our condition."[1331]

The colony drew up a final code in 1684 and published it in 1685. This code, too, devoted a chapter (Chapter XII) to "Lands and Inheritances," that was substantially similar to the counterpart provisions of the 1671 code. It added one detail to specifically invoke English law in a matter of real property: "It is Ordered and Declared by this Court and the Authority thereof; That all Lands heretofore Intailed, and that shall be Intailed hereafter, shall descend and enure as by the Law of England the same ought to do."[1332]

However, signaling that no wholesale reception of English land law should be presumed, the very next section made an original modification of primogeniture:

> It is Ordered and Declared, etc. That all the Sons of any Person, having Lands in fee simple, shall be Heirs (paying and satisfying in case as is by Law provided) the Eldest Son shall have double to any of his Brethren; and all the younger equal Shares of the Land of their Ancestors; and where there is but one Sone, he shall be sole Heir, paying and satisfying, as aforesaid; And where there is no Son, all the Daughters shall Inherit alike."[1333]

Even taking full account of the Plymouth settlers' religious motivation,

---

[1331] *Id.*, 1671 Code at 34-35.

[1332] *Id.* 1685 Code at 42.

[1333] *Id.*

it must still be conceded that the availability of land was a powerful inducement for immigration, and that English land law was still the foundation of land rights. Eventually, the attraction of seemingly unlimited acreage helped weaken the cohesion of Plymouth colony.[1334]

The development of land law in Plymouth was inevitably similar to, and eventually was merged with, the counterpart land history in the Massachusetts Bay Colony. When the Massachusetts Colony resisted imposition of English trade controls, King Charles II revoked its charter in 1684. Charles' successor, King James II, began his rule in 1685 and established a royal government in Massachusetts in 1686, but James was overthrown in 1688. William and Mary granted the colony a new charter in 1691, which combined the Plymouth and Massachusetts Bay colonies.

[1334] "Bradford, to whom Plymouth was a Zion, deplored the trend of his friends, colleagues, and fellow settlers to desert Plymouth in favor of greater acres elsewhere . . . . "But yet seeking to keep the people together as much as might be," Bradford wrote, they agreed that the owners of the near acres would share their land with the owners of the far acres, and thus Plymouth could be kept as a compact community. . . .

> In his account of the year 1632, Bradford laments that "there was no longer holding them together, and they must of necessity go to their great lots . . . ." Still trying to keep Plymouth together as much as possible, Bradford records that "to prevent any further scattering from this place and weakening of the same, it was thought best to give out some good farms to special persons that would promise to live at Plymouth . . . ." These favored people would keep their cattle and farms there, maintained by servants, but would themselves continue living in Plymouth. "But, alas," cried Bradford, with the benefit of hindsight, "this remedy proved worse than the disease."
>
> . . . [T]he promise of land grants was an important inducement in attracting servants to Plymouth Colony, and some of these servants eventually acquired considerable land holdings. . . . In fact, a perusal of court records shows the court handing out grants [to servants and free persons] as if land were one of the world's cheaper commodities, a procedure which could not continue indefinitely. . . . The abandonment of primogeniture from the beginning guaranteed that holdings would on the average get smaller as a number of sons inherited from a father." Eugene Aubrey Stratton, *Plymouth Colony, Its History & People 1620-1691* 169-170, 176-177 (1986).

§ 9.03(b). The Massachusetts Bay Colony.

§ 9.03(b)(1). Events Leading to the First Charter.

The Plymouth colony's parent governing authority, the New England Council in England, made an attempt to recruit more investors by specifying the land they would receive for their investors' shares. On paper the colony was divided into vast tracts proposed for grants under feudal tenures, but the council made no effective efforts to take possession of or colonize such grants.[1335]

Several of these individual grants were made over the years, but few grantees perfected the grants and even fewer actually took seisin. The grants were not carefully drawn and often overlapped, conflicted with, or superseded other grants, even occasionally grants that were being actively settled. When the council made grants for private plantations, it specified that the tenants or freeholders should not alienate without prior council approval and that a certain number of people should be settled, with livestock and other possessions, within five years after the grant was issued. The product of the land and of related trade would typically be managed in common between the grantee who actually settled the land and the partners in England who helped underwrite the grant. At the end of the five-year period, the land and accumulated profits would be divided between the settler and the other partners, and the partnership would be dissolved. This pattern was typical of many smaller settlements in the area.

The New England Council also planned to make grants with governmental institutions in the nature of sub-fiefs. The Council conferred

---

[1335] "Since . . . no steps were taken by those adventurers who had received allotments in 1623 to improve them or even to take out patents for them, all that could be done by the council was to grant its domain in parcels to such as would undertake to found private or subordinate public plantations. It was too weak to directly colonize or govern. . . . It was . . . proposed that all patents should be called for, perused, and confirmed, if the council saw fit; that a surveyor should be sent over to set the bounds of every grant that had been made, and that other steps should be taken to uphold the monopoly of the council, and to regulate affairs within its domain. But no effective measures were taken to execute these plans." *Id.* at 122-123.

on these public plantations powers to call assemblies, make laws and appoint magistrates, even though it actually had no right to grant such powers without first obtaining the sanction of the monarch.

The number of grants that materialized into settlements was relatively small, but development was steady. In 1623 a group of adventurers from Dorchester, England, founded a fishing station at Cape Ann, after first securing a permit from Plymouth settlers who also occupied the area under an indenture from an English nobleman. The enterprise struggled, prompting the adventurers to abandon the enterprise in 1626, and thereafter the Dorchester settlers moved a short distance west to the area of modern Salem. Obtaining a patent from the New England Council for their new territory in 1628, the grantees, who were not incorporated, were granted the land for themselves, their heirs and their assigns, with no governmental powers. They became direct tenants of the monarch, because subinfeudation had not been permitted since the Statute *Quia Emptores* of 1290. In March 1629, after adding new associates, the group obtained a royal charter confirming the territorial grant and adding full powers of incorporation and of government, thus creating the company of Massachusetts Bay.

§ 9.03(b)(2). Early Landholding in Massachusetts Bay.

The charter of the Massachusetts Bay Company was patterned after the charter of the London Company from two decades earlier. The charter provided for quarter courts, elections, a governor and other officials, and associated powers. By way of noteworthy difference, the Massachusetts charter called for a quorum of six in order to conduct business and permitted its membership to be enlarged by the addition of "freemen." The charter instructed the plantation to acquire and extinguish Indian claims by purchase. While the settlers conducted fishing as a joint enterprise, they never practiced joint landholding at Salem (Illustration 39):

Illustration 39. Salem, neighboring Boston, was the first area settled by members of the robust Massachusetts Bay Colony beginning in 1630. The well-known Salem attraction House of Seven Gables, shown above, typified the colony's eventual prosperity, related to both land and commerce.

The planters were under no contract which required it, and in the summer of 1629 an instruction was sent to [Governor] Endicott to allot to the adventurers in the proportion of two acres for each sum of £50, or fraction or multiple thereof, which was invested in the enterprise. The grantees were given the liberty to build and improve where they pleased, except that a tract should be reserved for a town. A town lot one-half acre in extent should also be granted to each adventurer who desired it. Planters who had also purchased shares in the common stock should receive fifty acres for each person in their families, while persons other than adventurers who brought families at their own expense into the colony should receive fifty acres for the master of the family and such additional allotments as, "according to their charge and quality," might be provided through special agreement with the company or by the magistrates in the colony. Those who brought or at their own charge sent servants into the

> colony should receive fifty acres for each of them. No mention is made in the records of the requirement of a quitrent on any of the grants to adventurers, but those who were not such must annually render suit or service. . . . Provision was made in the scheme for private plantations. . . . [T]he company also had its plantations, which were cultivated by servants and managed by the governor under instructions from England. It thus appears that, before it had been in existence a year, the colony at Salem reached the stage of development which was inaugurated in Virginia by Governor Dale.[1336]

Of special significance in this early history of the Massachusetts Bay Colony is the omission from the charter of the usual clause requiring election of the governor and officers in England. The omission was probably intentional from the colonists' perspective; from the royal ministers' perspective, the omission was probably inadvertent, or at least undesired. Even without the English residency requirement, the colony's corporation still conducted its business in England for several months after the charter was granted. The removal to New England was effected in the spring of 1630, as virtually all the officers, and several patentees, together with their charter, made the Atlantic crossing. With this transfer, the company's direct involvement in colonial trading ceased; trade was carried on as private enterprise, subject to the regulations of the colonial government.

At this same time, the corporation, now resident in New England, no longer functioned as a land company and did not seek to profit from land transactions. Indeed, the company was not even able to cultivate its own lands because there was so much sickness when the immigrants of 1630 arrived that even the company's servants had to be released to engage in agriculture in their own behalf. The newcomers soon established seven small settlements around the bay. They moved the seat of government from Salem to Charlestown, and then to Boston. These settlements became towns, which as communities were the grantees of the company land. The

---

1336 *Id.* at 135-136.

towns' proprietors held the lands within their boundaries either in common or conveyed the lands to individual grantees. Monetary gain seemed to play no role in these grants: no quit rents were established, the land was seldom sold or leased, and rent was a rarity. It is also significant that as numerous persons applied as "freemen" for membership in the corporation later in 1630, an additional qualification was added, that they must be ""members of some of the churches within the lymitts [of the body politic]."

The fundamental form of land regulation in effect in the Massachusetts Bay Colony was, in most respects, identical to that of Plymouth:

> The form of group settlement which we have seen developing in Plymouth was reproduced throughout New England, and wherever New Englanders settled. The joint action of the settlers in locating dwellings and home lots, in laying out village streets, in subdividing the adjacent arable land, in subjecting the meadow and forest for a time to common management, resulted in the founding of the town of Plymouth. . . .
>
> That which occurred at Plymouth happened also at Salem, in each of the settlements about Massachusetts bay, in the towns of Plymouth colony, as one after another they came into existence, among the settlements of northern New England, in the towns which were founded on the shores of Narragansett bay and along the course of the Connecticut river. On Long Island, too, and wherever in New Jersey New Englanders found their abode, the same form of settlement was reproduced.[1337]

In none of the New England colonies were land sales intended to be a primary source of public profit. No colony established a land office; land was not sold directly by a colony and was rarely rented. Most land grants were to towns, which then re-granted to individual settlers, acting with

---

[1337] 1 Herbert L. Osgood, *The American Colonies in the Seventeenth Century* 424 (1904).

delegated authority from the colony. The colony imposed quite a high degree of regulation in both the founding and development of towns. As to those fields held in common, an 1643 act of Massachusetts colony gave typical direction:

> Whereas it is found by experience that there hath bene much trouble and difference in severall townes about the manner of planting, sowing, and feeding of common corne fields, & that upon serious consideration wee finde no generall order can provide for the best improvement of every such common field, by reason that some consists onely of plowing ground, some haveing a great part fit only for planting, some of meadowe & feeding ground; also so that such an order as may bee very wholesome and good for one field may be exceeding preiudiciall & inconvenient for another, it is therefore ordered, that, where the commoners cannot agree about the manner of improvement of their field, either concerning the kind of graine that shall be sowen or set therein, or concerning the time or manner of feeding the herbage thereof, that three such persons in the several townes that are deputed to order the prudential affairs thereof, shall order the same, or in case where no such are, then the maior part of the freemen, who are hereby enioyned with what convenient speed they may to determine any such difference as may arise upon any information given them by said commissioners.

"Thus, throughout New England there was substantial similarity in the system followed by those colonies in the establishment of plantations, the recognition of them as towns, the fixing and maintenance of their bounds, the regulation of the granting of lands, of common fields, fences, herds, the punishment of trespass, the admission of inhabitants and freeholders, the requirement that fence-viewers and pound-keepers should be appointed, [and] that records of land titles should be kept. . . ."[1338]

[1338] *Id.* at 435.

§ 9.03(b)(3). The Role of Towns in New England Private Landholding.

The conspicuous role of the New England towns in bringing about a broad base of private landownership has been well summarized by Osgood:

> The most prominent feature of the New England land system was the town grant, which in every case became the territorial basis of a group settlement. Though grants were made by the general court to individuals, they were the exception rather than the rule. The result was that the landed estate of nearly every individual in New England was located in one or more towns, and was subject to the regulations which were made by the town for the management of land. The territorial affairs of the colony were largely administered through the towns as agencies. Land passed from joint control to individual ownership chiefly by means of town allotments. The towns came nearer to performing the function of proprietors than did any other administrative bodies in New England.
>
> In the corporate colonies, moreover, the characteristic elements of the fief were lacking. The quitrent does not appear as a distinct form of income, and land was not extensively leased. The result was that the tenement or holding, which was so characteristic of English land law, was practically obliterated, and an allodial system was substituted. Had the New England governments sought revenue from the land in the form of rents, this result could not have followed. A system of tenure would have been perpetuated, and the general court would have acted as proprietor. As it was, the court avoided the private legal attitude toward land, and kept itself well within the range of public law. The only revenue which it sought from land was in the form of taxes. This is one of the most notable consequences which resulted from the founding of the

corporate colonies of New England.[1339]

§ 9.03(b)(4). Land Regulation and Codification of Laws in Massachusetts Bay.

A more general influence on the development of land law in the Massachusetts Bay Colony was the adoption of a code of laws. The drafting process actually began in 1635, but the long delay in accepting a draft resulted from the colonists' reluctance to frame laws in anticipation of conditions that might require imposition of those laws. Colonists also resisted limiting colonial laws to those that were consistent with laws of England, as required by the charter. Nevertheless, in 1641 the colony's General Court accepted a code that was styled "A Coppie of the Liberties of the Massachusets Collonie in New England." This original code was never printed, but it was officially adopted in 1644, so manuscript copies could be made. The colony cumulated revisions into a collection published in 1648 as the famous *Book of the General Lauues and Libertyes Concerning the Inhabitants of the Massachusets*. Provisions relating to real property are as follows:

> It is therfore ordered by this Court, & Authority therof, That no mans life shall be taken away; no mans honour or good name shall be stayned; no mans person shall be arrested, restrained, bannished, dismembred nor any wayes punished; no man shall be deprived of his wife or children; no mans goods or estate shall be taken away from him; nor any wayes indammaged under colour of Law or countenance of Authoritie unles it be by the vertue or equity or some expresse of law of the Country warranting the same established by a General Court & sufficiently published; or in case of the defect of a law in any particular case by the word of God. And in capital cases, or in cases concerning dismembring or banishment, according to that word to be judged by the General Court.

[1339] 2 Herbert L. Osgood, *The American Colonies in the Seventeenth Century* 16 (1904).

Abilitie. All persons the age of twenty-one years, and of right understanding & meamorie whether excommunicate, condemned or other, shall have full power and libertie to make their Wills & Testaments & other lawfull Alienations of their lands and estates.[1340]

Age. It is ordered by this Court & the Authoritie therof, that the age for passing away of lands, or such kinde of hereditaments, or for giving of votes, verdicts or sentences in any civil courts or causes, shall be twenty and one years: but in case of chusing of Guardions, fourteen years.

Conveyances fraudulent. It is ordered by this Court and the Authoritie therof, That all covenons or fraudulent alienations or conveyances of lands, tenements or any hereditaments shall be of no validitie to defeat any man from due debts or legacyes, or from any just title, claim or possession of that which is so fraudulently conveyed.

For avoiding all fraudulent conveyances and that every man may know that estate or interest other man have in any houses, lands or other hereditaments they are to deal in, it is therefore ordered by the authoritie of this Court;

That after the end of October 1640 no mortgage, bargain, sale, or graunt made of any houses, lands, rents or other hereditaments where the Graunter remains in possession, shall be of force against other persons except the Graunter and his Heirs, unles the same be acknowledged before

---

[1340] In the 1641 laws, a disability status was attached to married women, but this had apparently been repealed by the time of the 1648 code:

> Any Conveyance or Alienation of land or other estaite what so ever, made by any woman that is married, any childe under age, Ideott, or distracted person, shall be good, if it be passed and ratified by the consent of a generall Court.

Select Charters and Other Documents Illustrative of American History 1606-1775 72, 75 (William MacDonald, ed., 1914).

some Magistrate & recorded as is heerafter expressed: and that no such bargain, sale or graunt already made, in way of mortgage, where the Graunter remains in possession shall be of force against other but the Graunter or his Heirs, except the same shall be entred as is heerafter expressed within one month after the date aforementioned: if the partie be within this Jurisdiction or else within three months after he shal return. . . .

Deeds and writings. It is ordered by this court and Authoritie thereof; That no conveyance, deed or promise whatsoever shall be of validitie, if it be gotten by illegal violance, imprisonment, threatening or any kinde of forcible compulson, called Dures.

Dowries. Forasmuch as no provision have yet been made for any certain maintainance for Wives after the death of their Husbands, be it ordered and enacted by this present Court and Authoritie therof;

That every married Woman (living with her Husband in this Jurisdiction or other where absent from him with his consent or through his meer default, or inevitable providence, or in case of divorce where she is the innocent partie) that shall not before marriage be estated by way of joynture in some houses, lands, tenements or other hereditaments for term of her life, shall immediately after the death of her Husband have right and interest by way of *dower*, in, and to one third part of all such houses, lands, tenements, rents and hereditaments as her said Husband was seized of, to his own use, either in possession, reversion or remainder in any estate of inheritance . . . at any time during the marriage to have and injoy for term of her natural life according to the estate of such Husband free, and freely discharged of and from all titles, debts, rents, charges, judgements, executions and other incumbrances. . . .

Escheats. It is ordered by this Court and Authoritie therof, That where no Heir or Owner of houses, lands, tenements, goods or chattels can be found: they shall be seized to the publick Treasurie till such Heirs or owner shall make due claim therto, unto whom they shall be restored upon just and reasonable terms.

Indians. It is ordered by Authoritie of this Court; that no person whatsoever shall henceforth buy land of any Indian, without licence first had & obtained of the General Court: and if any shall offend heerin, such land so bought shall be forfeited to the Countrie.

Lands, Free lands. It is ordered, and by this Court declared; that all our Lands and Heritages shall be free from all Fines and Licenses upon alienations, and from all Hariots, Wardships, Liveries, Primerseizins, year, day and wast, Escheats and forfeitures, upon the death of Parents or Ancesters, be they natural, unnatural, casual, or judicial and that for ever.

Liberties Common. It is ordered by this Court, decreed and declared. . . .

Every Inhabitant who is an hous-holder shall have free fishing and fowling, in any great Ponds, Bayes, Coves and Rivers so far as the Sea ebs and flows, within the precincts of the town where they dwell, unles the Free-men of the same town, or the General Court have otherwise appropriated them. Provided that no town shall appropriate to any particular person or persons, any great Pond conteining more then ten acres of land: and that no man shall come upon anothers proprietie without their leave otherwise then as heerafter expressed; the which clearly to determin, it is declared that in all creeks, coves and other places, about and upon salt water where the Sea ebs and flows, the Proprietor of the land adjoyning shall have

> proprietie to the low water mark where the Sea doeth not ebb above a hundred rods, and not more wheresoever it ebs farther. . . .
>
> *Wills intestate.* It is ordered, and by this Court declared; that when Parents dye intestate, the eldest son shall have a double portion of his whole estate, reall, and personall unles the General Court upon just cause alledged shall Judge otherwise. And when parents dye intestate, having no Heirs males of their bodyes, their daughters shall inherit as copartners, unles the General Court upon just reason shall judge otherwise.[1341]

The colony issued additional compilations of Massachusetts laws in 1660 and 1672. A revision begun in 1679 became moot when the colony's charter was revoked in 1684. In 1692 Massachusetts merged with Plymouth, Maine, Nova Scotia, Nantucket, Martha's Vineyard and the Elizabeth Islands into the Royal Province of Massachusetts Bay in New-England, and legislative activity resumed. A new compilation of laws was then issued in 1699. Occupying 158 printed pages in its published form, this 1699 code provided much more detailed enactments for the various activities relating to land, but it introduced no matters that would have been unfamiliar to one acquainted with English law of the time.[1342]

§ 9.04. Development of Property Law in New Hampshire (from 1623).

§ 9.04(a). Legal Origins of the Earliest Settlements.

Englishmen explored the territory of present-day New Hampshire perhaps as early as 1583. In 1614 Captain John Smith sailed north from

---

[1341] 1 *The Laws and Liberties of Massachusetts* 1641-1691, 3-61 (John D. Cushing, ed., 1976).

[1342] *See Massachusetts Province Laws 1692-1699*, 17-178 (John D. Cushing, ed., 1978).

Virginia and perused the coast, reporting his pleasure at the prospect of fine land free of feudal restraints and available in abundance:

> Here should be no hard landlords to rack us with high rents, or extorted fines to consume us; here every man may be master and owner of his own labor and land in a short time. . . ."[1343]

He would have been disappointed that the two English aristocrats principally responsible for New Hampshire's earliest settlements had a different view of land rights:

> Smith's dream of a colony where landlords and quitrents should be unknown was far enough from the plans of [Captain John] Mason or [Sir Ferdinando] Gorges. They believed fully in the patents and monopolies which excited popular and parliamentary hostility in the Stuart reigns, and they aimed at baronies and lordships in New England similar to those of England and Scotland. They were ready to spend money in colonizing, but the colonists were to be their tenants, governed by their kindred and friends as a ruling class. . . .
>
> Mason and Gorges preferred a colony resembling what Virginia soon became, an aristocracy closely depended on the crown, and supplied with a loyal clergy selected by careful English bishops, who should preach passive obedience, so far as the turbulence of new colonies would permit that servile doctrine.[1344]

In what is now the state of New Hampshire, the first permanent European settlements were not coincident with status as a separate colony. Two of the first four New Hampshire settlements, Dover and Portsmouth,

---

[1343] Frank B. Sanborn, *New Hampshire, An Epitome of Popular Government* 7 (1904).

[1344] *Id.* at 8-9.

had their legal origins in the 1620 charter that created the corporation known as the Council for New England and which exercised jurisdiction over all of New England.

By a grant in 1621 the council had validated the settlement at Plymouth and later would authorize the grants for the Massachusetts Bay Colony. To boost its flagging efforts in recruiting investors for colonization, the council began to grant its domain to individual "adventurers" who would undertake to settle and cultivate the land. Only a few of these grants ever materialized into settlements or private plantations, but two of them were in New Hampshire, at Hilton's Point, later known as Dover, and at Strawbery Banke, later known as Portsmouth. Edward Hilton obtained an informal council grant for Dover and built up the settlement between 1623 and 1628. The grant was formalized in March of 1630. Of these grants, it was stated earlier in this chapter that:

> The grants were not carefully drawn and often overlapped, conflicted with, or superseded other grants, even occasionally grants that were being actively settled. When the council made grants for private plantations, it specified that the tenants or freeholders should not alienate without prior council approval and that a certain number of people should be settled, with livestock and other possessions, within five years after the grant was issued. The product of the land and of related trade would typically be managed in common between the grantee who actually settled the land and the partners in England who helped underwrite the grant. At the end of the five year period, the land and accumulated profits would be divided between the settler and the other partners, and the partnership would be dissolved. This pattern was typical of many smaller settlements in the area.[1345]

Among the other individual grants made by the New England Council was a patent issued in March 1622, to Captain John Mason for lands lying

---

[1345] § 9.03(b), *supra*.

between the Salem and Merrimac Rivers in present-day northern Massachusetts. In August 1622, Mason and Gorges obtained a joint grant of lands between the Merrimac and Kennebec Rivers, covering part of present-day New Hampshire and southern Maine, and designated as the province of Maine.

Then on November 7, 1629, the council regranted the part of the joint grant to Mason and Gorges lying between the Piscataqua and Merrimac Rivers to John Mason, individually, to be called New Hampshire. Ten days later, a group styling itself the "Laconia Company"—including Mason, Gorges and others–acquired a large, vague grant of land in the region, for the exploiting of which the group established settlements on both sides of the mouth of the Piscataqua River, the southern settlement being known as Strawbery Banke. The Laconia Company in November 1631 obtained a patent to the Piscataqua lands being settled. In 1634 Mason and Gorges, the two principal investors, purchased the lands of the Laconia Company on the northeast bank of the Piscataqua River from others who withdrew from the company, while other company lands southwest of the river remained in common ownership. In 1635, however, Mason acquired from the New England Council a grant, called New Hampshire, confirming all his previous grants, but he died before that latest grant could be confirmed.

§ 9.04(b). Landholding Rights in the Earliest Settlements.

The language of this unconfirmed charter tells much about the assumptions underlying landholding rights in these colonial ventures: Mason was to have "power over the land and water, forests, mines, and fisheries, according to the right and powers "had, used and enjoyed by the now or any former Bishop of Duresme within the County Palatine of Duresme."'[1346] The people of New Hampshire and their descendants:

> were to be "holden, reputed and had as the faithful liege people of Us [the crown], our heirs and successors,

---

[1346] Frank B. Sanborn, *New Hampshire, An Eitome of Popular Government* 13 (1904).

> originally springing up within our Realm of England." And they were to take by descent or purchase, and freely possess, property in the three kingdoms, as if living therein; and to have "all the liberties, franchises and privileges of this our realm of England, without any impediment whatsoever, any statute to the contrary notwithstanding . . . .
>
> . . . Power also was given to Mason and his heirs, "lest the way to honor and renown might seem difficult and hard to find in so remote and far distant a country," to create and bestow titles, "so they be such as in England now are in use," and "to create villages and into boroughs, and boroughs into cities . . . . We do declare and ordain, that the said Province of New Hampshire shall be immediately subject to our Crown of England, and dependent upon the same for ever."[1347]

These provisions were never confirmed and thus remained only expressions of intent and assumption. After Mason's death the Laconia Company went bankrupt, and the New England Council also dissolved, leaving the Hilton and Strawbery Banke settlers without governing authority. The various grants just described could be, and occasionally were, interpreted to overlap, and there was also a competing claim of the Massachusetts Bay Company to the entire area, so the potential for conflict over governance and over land titles was great.

As to landholding itself, the patents were quite consistent in conferring full ownership on the patentees. According to the 1622 grant of "Maine" from the New England Council to Gorges and Mason:

> Now this Indenture witnesseth that the said President and Councill . . . doe give grant . . . and confirme unto the said Sir Ferdinando Gorges & Captain John Mason their heirs and assignes all that part of the maine land in New

[1347] *Id.* at 14-15.

> England . . . .[1348]

Likewise, the grant to Mason called "New Hampshire" in 1629 was in terms of full ownership: ". . . the said President and Council . . . do give, grant . . . and confirm unto the said Captain John Mason, his Heires and Assigns, all that Part of the main Land in New-England [description of grant] . . . which said Portions of Lands with the Appurtenances, the said Captain John Mason, with the Consent of the President and Council intends to name *New-Hampshire:* . . . ."[1349] Both the 1622 and 1629 grants cited the 1620 grants to the New England Council as the source of their rights to make grants.

A third source of New Hampshire settlement emerged in 1638, when religious dissenter John Wheelwright, under sentence of banishment from Massachusetts, purchased lands in the Piscataqua region from the Indians. In 1639 the 35 families in this settlement entered into a civil compact that acknowledged loyalty to the English monarch, but only ""according to the libertys of our English Colony of Massachusetts."[1350]

A fourth area of settlement in New Hampshire was opened directly by Massachusetts, which in 1636 directed the establishment of a plantation at Hampton. The settlement obtained town status in 1639, so that:

> by 1640, there were four separate and unrelated settlements in New Hampshire, each originating from England (Dover and Strawbery Banke, or Portsmouth) or Massachusetts (Exeter and Hampton). All faced a generally similar frontier environment but reacted to it according to their own needs and interests as they

---

[1348] *Select Charters and Other Documents Illustrative of American History 1606-1775* 36-37 (William MacDonald, ed., 1914).

[1349] *Id.* at 50-51.

[1350] David E. Van Deventer, *The Emergence of Provincial New Hampshire 1623-1741* 8 (1976).

interpreted them.[1351]

At this key point in the history of New Hampshire colony, it could be said that:

> The confusion of patents and grants, whether made by the king, by the New England Council, by the towns of Massachusetts before 1642, or by Massachusetts afterwards, was very great at first, and continued to be a source of litigation for nearly a century and a half. The patents of the Hiltons on the Piscataqua, and of Thomas Wiggin in what is now Stratham, though conflicting with the general grants made to Mason and Gorges, were sustained by the local courts; and in Wiggin's case he was finally taxed in the town of Hampton, though never residing within its proper limits. The Hiltons, opposing the claim of Mrs. Mason to the ownership of their land, which at one time was allotted to her, finally recovered it. . . .[1352]

§ 9.04(c). Landholding Rights After Massachusetts Assumed Control.

In 1640 the Dover settlers, fearing a takeover by Massachusetts, entered into a civil compact known as the Dover Combination, by which they pledged loyalty to the laws of England "together with all such orders as shall be concluded by a major part of the freemen of our Society."[1353] However, for various reasons the inhabitants of all four early New Hampshire settlements by 1643 had acquiesced in Massachusetts' assertion of jurisdiction over their territories. Massachusetts' hegemony in New Hampshire prevailed until 1679, when the crown ordered Massachusetts to

---

[1351] *Id.* at 9.

[1352] Frank B. Sanborn, *New Hampshire, An Epitome of Popular Government* 24-25 (1904).

[1353] David E. Van Deventer, *The Emergence of Provincial New Hampshire 1623-1741* 14 (1976).

withdraw from the New Hampshire communities and appointed a royal governor. Throughout this period and extending until 1746, land titles and incidents were in a constant state of tension because heirs and successors of the Mason grants persisted in asserting their claims against the actual occupants of the land. From time to time, these claims were instrumental in the long effort to bring about the withdrawal of Massachusetts from New Hampshire.

> [Mason's] grandiose plans for founding a hereditary principality in American might even then have been realized had he not suddenly died in 1635. . . . The validity of Mason's claims to his vast holdings, and their subsequent disposition, were to be the source of endless altercation and political confusion, typing up hundreds of acres of land for almost 125 years. The litigations, changes of ownership, sales, claims, counterclaims, comings and goings of Mason descendants trying to secure their inheritance and the boundary and border disputes that resulted are an inextricable part of New Hampshire history.[1354]

§ 9.04(d). Landholding Rights After Becoming a Royal Province.

After appointment of the royal governor in 1679, events moved quickly. Shortly before his death in 1684, King Charles II revoked Massachusetts' charter and proposed to unite Massachusetts, Maine, New Hampshire, Rhode Island and Connecticut into one province. James II took the throne in 1685 and carried out this plan by creating the Dominion of New England. Governor Edmund Andros arrived in Boston in December 1685, and soon began to exercise his powers of government, including the power to inject further confusion into already turbulent landholding arrangements:

> By this commission, the governor with his council, five of

[1354] Elizabeth Forbes Morison and Elting E. Morison, *New Hampshire, A Bicentennial History* 11-12 (1976).

> whom were a quorum, were impowered to make such laws, impose such taxes, and apply them to such purposes as they should think proper. They were also empowered to grant lands on such terms and subject to such quitrents, as should be appointed by the king. Invested with such powers, these men were capable of the most extravagant actions. Though Androsse, like his master, began his administration with the fairest professions, yet like him, he soon violated them, and proved himself a fit instrument for accomplishing the most execrable designs . . . . Let it suffice to observe that the press was restrained; liberty of conscience infringed; exorbitant fees and taxes demanded, without the voice or consent of the people, who had no privilege of representation. The charter being vacated, it was pretended that all titles to land were annulled; and as to Indian deeds, Androsse declared them no better than "the scratch of a bear's paw." Landholders were obliged to take out patents for their estates which they had possessed forty or fifty years; for these patents extravagant fees were exacted, and those who would not submit to this imposition had writs of intrusion brought against them, and their land was patented to others.[1355]

These oppressions ended suddenly in 1688 when James II was overthrown, but the turbulent times had made it impossible for a stable government to form in New Hampshire. Therefore, the colony rejoined Massachusetts for a short time, until William and Mary designated it a royal province in 1691.

§ 9.04(e). Land Distribution Practices in the Local Communities.

The preceding discussion has shown on what basis the rule of law and the laws for landholding took form in colonial New Hampshire. To a

---

[1355] 1 Jeremy Belknap, *The History of New-Hampshire* 232-234 (1792).

certain extent, these foundational legal features remained theoretical and not quite consonant with landholding practices actually in force within the early settlements of New Hampshire. Moreover, the presumptive application of English land law implied in the charters was at best a generality and gave no instruction about specific practices of land distribution. For such information, one must look to the histories of individual early communities in New Hampshire.

Regular land distribution in New Hampshire occurred more frequently after the colony came under the jurisdiction of Massachusetts in the 1640's. Following Massachusetts' well-established pattern for setting up towns whose governments' primary function was to distribute land, orderly settlement proceeded much more rapidly.[1356] Generally, the original settlers received generous grants of land and then imposed some restrictions on those who came later. During the 1650's they relaxed such restrictions as the settlements competed for recruits. By the 1660's usable land had became scarce, and grants of land were ended; newcomers were required to purchase lands in established communities. Where grants were given, their size often depended on the means and abilities of the grantees to offer needed assistance to the community.

By way of example, Hampton's first land grants to its founders varied from 80 to 300 acres. In the second land grant, in 1640, grants of 10 acres each for house lots were made to numerous non-freemen, and one grant of 100 acres was made to a freeman. In 1645, 200 acres of land were set aside as a cow commons to be shared in various proportions by 58 people.

In Exeter,

> all meadows were divided into four equal parts, with the first three parts apportioned according to the number of cattle owned by each inhabitant and the fourth part divided into equal lots for those who had no cattle; the "upland lots for planting" were given on the basis of the

[1356] *See* § 9.03(b)(3), describing the role of New England towns in bringing about the private ownership of land.

> number of persons and cattle in each family; and the marshes were divided among all the inhabitants, with those owning cattle receiving proportionately larger shares. Family size and herd size - the practical needs and agricultural potential of each family - guided Exeter's approach to land policy.
>
> Other values also entered into Exeter land policy. When new marsh lands were found in 1643, the town rewarded individual initiative by voting that marshes of less than twenty acres belonged to the finder "forever," but marshlands of twenty acres or more became town property with the finder receiving a double portion.
>
> . . . The town exemplified its strong community cohesiveness by granting the sons of inhabitants at least thirty acres of land within the town when they were ready to set up for themselves.
>
> When it came to granting the common lands or new areas to the town inhabitants, the principal basis for division was the proportion of tax each individual paid in support of the minister; this proportion was in turn based upon his taxable property or "ratable estate."[1357]

In Dover, the earliest recorded land grants, in 1642, were of twenty-acre lots to twenty-three persons. Between 1642 and 1655, 42 grants were given, ranging between 3 and 500 acres in size.

The New Hampshire government also granted townships, which, in turn, had authority to make local land grants. The townships were similar to those of Massachusetts, with one twist:

[1357] David E. Van Deventer, *The Emergence of Provincial New Hampshire 1623-1741* 23-24 (1976).

> The New Hampshire government required the payment of a nominal quitrent from each new township: an ear of Indian corn, a pound of hemp, a pint of turpentine, a pound of flax, or a peck of potatoes served this function. Although these quitrents were payable only if demanded by the government, an action which seldom if ever occurred, nevertheless, the inclusion of quitrents in New Hampshire land grants originated from the colony's royal status and from the uncertain legality of the Masonian proprietary claims to the land of the colony.[1358]

After New Hampshire became a royal colony it typically imposed requirements on individual proprietors in its township grants, usually requiring of each proprietor certain minimum land improvements, a certain number of acres under cultivation, and assistance in obtaining and supporting a minister. Proprietors who failed to meet the requirements forfeited their shares to the others. Once the township was officially established, however, its proprietors assumed all power over land grants within their jurisdiction.

§ 9.04(f). New Hampshire's Earliest Published Laws Affecting Land Rights.

Despite the early date of its first settlement (1623), New Hampshire was very late in developing its own law:

> In contrast to Massachusetts and Plymouth, New Hampshire was settled by a number of commercial companies, each operating under the terms of its own charter, and interested primarily in extracting profits from the natural resources of the area. Most of the settlers were nothing more than employees of the proprietors; they clustered near the site of their operations and those settlements soon became towns. They appear to have had

[1358] *Id.* at 39.

> no strong desire to establish a well-ordered state governed according to precepts derived from scriptural law, as was the case in Massachusetts. Moreover, there was no clear-cut charter authority to establish a system of civil government and thus the earliest laws of the area were orders of the proprietors' agents and the self-generated regulatory measures adopted by the people assembled in town meeting. In short, for many years each town was an entity unto itself.[1359]

While New Hampshire was officially under the governance of Massachusetts Bay, between approximately 1641 and 1679, the laws of Massachusetts applied in New Hampshire. Under independent New Hampshire's first president, John Cutt, the colony compiled a code of laws, based largely on laws of Plymouth and Massachusetts, and the colony also made some use of a compilation of English statutes that had been sent. This Cutt Code invoked the laws of England to decide questions of real property. The president and council were established as a "constant and setled Court of record," to hear pleas in civil suits and actions:

> whether ye same do concern ye realty, and relate to a right of freehold and inheritance, or whether ye same do concern ye personalty, and relate to some matter of debt, contract, damage, or other person, iniury, and also in all mixt actions wch may concern both realty and person . . .: so always yt ye forms of proceeding in such cases and ye judgment thereupon to be given, be as consonant and agreeable to ye Laws and Statutes of this Our Realm of Engd, as ye prent state and condition of our subjects inhabiting within ye limits aforesaid, and ye circumstances of ye place will admit.[1360]

1359 *Acts and Laws of New Hampshire 1680-1726* vii (John D. Cushing, ed., 1978).

1360 *Id.* at 197-198.

The Cutt Code confirmed existing land rights and made provisions for the continued adjudication of the claims of Mason heirs. Its sparse provisions relating to landholding are adequately summarized by recitation of the headings: forcible detaining possession; burning fences; breaking down fences; defacing landmarks; townships, & c, confirmed; controversies of land to be tried by a jury; former laws to stand;[1361] province rate [of tax, upon persons and estates]; and age to make a valid act [21].[1362]

The colony also issued a short code in 1682 under the brief and unpopular regime of the second president, Edward Cranfield. The few land-related provisions of this code also deal with burning fences, defacing landmarks, and property tax rates.[1363] After Cranfield's departure in 1685, New Hampshire was part of the Dominion of New England until the dominion fell and New Hampshire temporarily reunited with Massachusetts. In 1691 New Hampshire resumed status as an individual colony with its own governor, and in 1699 printed a short compilation of laws. No provisions of this compilation deal directly with land.

The colony authorized a printing of a comprehensive compilation of New Hampshire laws in 1701 but did not complete the work until 1716. This much more extensive collection contains numerous provisions dealing with real property: prohibition of unfettered horses on the commons; prohibition against fencing the commons; recording deeds and conveyances, and validating all former deeds and conveyances; property tax collection; preventing trespass; regulating cutting of mast trees; preventing encroachments on highways; dealing with property interests of persons under disability; regulating dower; proceeding against forcible entry and detainer; partition of lands; regulating executors and administrators; regulating bankrupts and insolvent estates; preventing common nuisances; repairing highways; preventing the trespass of cutting down trees on unfenced land; regulating strays and lost goods; regulating

[1361] ". . . soe far as they will sute our constitution and be not repugnante to ye Laws of England . . . ." *Id.* at 219.

[1362] *Id.* at 195-229.

[1363] *Id.* at 231-248.

mills; making lands and tenements liable for payment of debts; preventing concealment of estates from assessors; settling and distributing estates of intestate decedents; enabling towns, villages and proprietors in common and undivided lands to sue and be sued; regulating powers of towns; preventing illegal purchase of Indian lands; preventing encroachments and encumbrances on highways; enacting a statute of frauds; redeeming mortgaged land; and prohibiting trespassing on the town commons.

Compared with contemporary colonial laws, this 1716 compilation from New Hampshire promulgates one of the most extensive regimes of real property regulation during the colonial period.

§ 9.05. Development of Land Law in New York (from 1624).

§ 9.05(a). The Dutch West India Company Charter of 1623.

In the service of the Dutch in 1609, Henry Hudson sailed up the river which now bears his name, almost as far as Albany. Although disappointed in his objective of finding the mythical Northwest Passage, he passed on to his employers descriptions of a fruitful land. The Dutch eventually formed a new venture, called the West India Company, to colonize the territory which they claimed and named "New Netherland." The Dutch government issued the company's charter in 1621. In 1623 New Netherland was officially designated as a province of the Company, and in 1624 the first settlers arrived.

§ 9.05(b). The Charter of Privileges to Patroons of 1629.

The charter of June 3, 1621, conferred on the company a monopoly over trade and traffic to the New World for a period of 24 years. Conspicuously absent from the charter is any mention of power in the company to deal with land.[1364] Nevertheless, the company exercised such power, and no stronger example of that may be found than in the Charter of Privileges to Patroons, adopted in 1629. The background and significance of this charter has been explained as follows:

> The government of the Dutch West India Company, chartered in 1621, was vested in five chambers, or boards, established in as many Dutch cities, with a board of nineteen for the exercise of general executive powers. Of the chambers, that of Amsterdam was the most important. The region known as New Netherland was not named in the charter, but was included within the jurisdiction of the Company. On the final organization of the Company under the charter, in 1623, New Netherland was made a province, and placed under the immediate control of the Amsterdam chamber. The continued unprofitableness, however, of the trade of New Netherland, except for the fur trade, led to a change of policy; and the Charter of Privileges to patroons, drafted in March, 1628, but not adopted by the board of nineteen until June, 1629, was intended to encourage private individuals to establish settlements at various points on the Hudson and Delaware, or North and South, rivers. Numerous grievances, occasioned by friction between the patroons and the Company, were partially allayed by a new charter in 1640, restricting the area of the grants, and encouraging independent settlement; but the feudal privileges of the patroons were not interfered with. "Many of the old patroon estates long remained undivided, and the heirs of the founders claimed some semi-feudal privileges well into the nineteenth century."[1365]

[1364] 1 E.B. O'Callaghan, *History of New Netherland* 399-407 (1845).

[1365] *Select Charters and Other Documents Illustrative of American History 1606-1775* 43 (William MacDonald, ed., 1914).

The somewhat vague boundaries of the province supposedly extended from the Delaware River to the Connecticut River. The first settlers were mostly Walloons, the French-speaking Huguenots who had fled France into what is now part of Belgium. Of the four settlements commenced by this first group, one was located a little south of Albany, another on Governor's Island off the southern tip of Manhattan, a third just south of present-day Philadelphia, Pennsylvania, and the fourth near present-day Hartford, Connecticut.

The policy of encouraging settlement by patroons imparted significant consequences for landholding in New Netherlands. Patroons can be described as the Dutch equivalents of English manorial lords. A patroon who held land held it according to a feudal system of land rights, which included the rights to require services as well as rents from tenants who were occupying the patroon's lands, and the right to exercise judicial and other governmental powers over the patroon's holdings. Only the patroon held the land outright; others could only be tenants of the patroon. The patroons of New Netherlands obligated themselves to commence a colony with at least 50 persons during a four-year period of time, in return for which each patroon received manorial and proprietary rights to sixteen miles of Hudson River shoreline and the lands behind the shoreline.

The following excerpts from the 1629 Charter of Privileges to Patroons amply illustrate this explicit introduction of feudalism into North America:

> III. All such [members of said Company as may be inclined to settle a Colonie in New Netherland] shall be acknowledged Patroons of New Netherland who shall, within the space of four years next after they have given notice to any of the Chambers of the Company here, or to the Commander or Council there, undertake to plant a Colonie there of fifty souls, upwards of fifteen years old; one-fourth part within one year, and within three years after the sending of the first, making together four years, the remainder, to the full number of fifty persons, to be shipped from hence, on pain, in case of wilful neglect, of being deprived of the privileges obtained . . . .

IV. They shall, from the time they make known the situation of the places where they propose to settle Colonies, have the preference to all others of the absolute property of such lands as they have there chosen . . . .

VI. They shall forever possess and enjoy all the lands lying within the aforesaid limits, together with the fruits, rights, minerals, rivers and fountains thereof; as also the chief command and lower jurisdictions, fishing, fowling and grinding, to the exclusion of all others, to be holden from the Company as a perpetual inheritance, without it ever devolving again to the Company . . .; and further, no person or persons whatsoever shall be privileged to fish and hunt but the Patroons and such as they shall permit. And in case any one should in time prospere so much as to found one or more cities, he shall have power and authority to establish officers and magistrates there, and to make use of the title of his Colonie, according to his pleasure and to the quality of the persons.

VII. There shall likewise be granted to all Patroons who shall desire the same, . . . liberty to dispose of their aforesaid heritage by testament.

VIII. The Patroons may, if they think proper, make use of all lands, rivers and woods lying contiguous to them, for and during so long a time as this Company shall grant them to other Patroons or private persons. . . .

XIX. [The Company] will not take from the service of the Patroons any of their colonists, either man or woman, son or daughter, manservant or maid-servant; and, though any of these should desire the same, they will not receive them, much less permit them to leave their Patroons, and enter into the service of another, unless on consent obtained from their Patroons in writing, and this for and during so many years as they are bound to their Patroons. . . .

> XX. From all judgments given by the Courts of the Patroons for upwards of fifty guilders, there may be an appeal to the Company's Commander and Council in New Netherland.
>
> XXI. In regard to such private persons as on their own account, or others in the service of their masters here (not enjoying the same privileges as the Patroons), shall be inclined to go thither and settle, they shall, with the approbation of the Director and Council there, be at liberty to take up and take possession of as much land as they shall be able properly to improve, and shall enjoy the same in full property either for themselves or masters.[1366]

In the end, only one patroonship ever succeeded, that of Kiliaen Van Rensselaer. Over lands covering present-day Albany and Columbia and Rensselaer counties in New York, he established a feudal tenant system that persisted until tenants rebelled early in the 19th century. The patent to Van Rensselaer, dated August 13, 1630, contained the following language describing the land rights conveyed:

> We, the Director and Council of New England, . . . [do hereby convey and make over] to the Mr. Kiliaen van Rensselaer . . . the respective parcels of land hereinbefore specified, with the timber, appendencies and dependencies thereof, together with all the action, right and jurisdiction to them the grantors conjointly or severally belonging, . . . real and actual possession thereof, and at the same time giving him full, absolute and irrevocable power, authority and special command to hold, in quiet possession, cultivation, occupancy and use, . . . the land aforesaid . . . .[1367]

[1366] *Select Charters and Other Documents Illustrative of American History 1606-1775* 43-50 (William MacDonald, ed., 1914).

[1367] 1 *Documents Relative to the Colonial History of the State of New York* 44 (E.B. O'Callaghan, ed., 1856).

A nearly contemporary patent of land, dated July 15, 1630, used similar language in the grant, conveying the lands "with all the action, right and jurisdiction to them" and giving "full and irrevocable authority, power and special command, to hold in quiet possession, occupancy and use . . . ."[1368]

As a feudal lord, the patroon enjoyed several traditional privileges relating to the land and labor of the patroonship's tenants, as described not many years after the last patroonships disappeared:

> At the close of the harvest, the farmer was bound to hand in a return of the amount of grain which he had for sale, after deducting what was due to the landlord by the lease, and offer to him or his commissary the preemption of such produce. In case he refused to buy it, then the farmer was at liberty to sell the same elsewhere. The like rule obtained in regard to cattle. When these were to be sold, the first offer was also to be made to the Patroon, in order, we presume, that he should have an opportunity of retaining the stock within the colonie. Every settler was, likewise, obligated to grind his corn at the Patroon's mill, and the latter was equally obligated to erect, and keep such mill in repair, at his own expense, for the accommodation of his colonists. No person could hunt or fish within the limits of the colonie, without license from the Patroon, who, on the exchange, sale, and purchase of real estate within his jurisdiction, was entitled to the first offer of such property; or if he declined to resume it, to a certain portion of the purchase money, except such mutation occurred in the natural line of descent. Finally, it was his right, as "lord of the manor," to succeed to the estate and property of all persons who might die intestate within his colonie.[1369]

[1368] *Id.* at 43.

[1369] 1 E.B. O'Callaghan, *History of New Netherland* 325-326 (1845).

Patroons also granted leaseholds, and typical provisions of leaseholds are the following from a lease dated September 7, 1646:

> This day . . . the presiding officers of the Colonie Rensselhaerswyck on one side, and Thomas Chamber on the other, have agreed and consented about a certain parcel of land . . . [described], which land he, Thomas aforesaid, shall occupy as a bouwerie [farm] for the term of five successive years, commencing the 15th of November, anno 1647, on the following conditions:
>
> [The lessee agreed to build houses, barns and fences, and turn the improvements over to the lessor at the end of five years; "the said houses, barns, and fences, shall be the Patroon's rent for the aforesaid five years]."[1370]

§ 9.05(c). Conflicts Between Company and Patroon Landholding.

Inevitably, the institutions of colonial government clashed from time to time with the feudalistic independence of the patroons. The monopolistic powers exercised by the Dutch West India Company as colonial proprietor were very extensive. Even when its monopoly was abolished in 1640, its director and council remained the principal organs of government in the province.[1371] The director and council exercised legislative power, especially in the absence of any popular legislative assembly similar to those appearing in contemporary English colonies. Their power over

---

1370 *Id.* at 473-474.

1371 "Few formal instructions [from the company] appear, but orders were transmitted in the letters concerning grants of land, recall of grants, duties and all the minutia of trade relations, claims and suits against the company, dealings with the Indians, relations with the English on the north and the south and with the Swedes, the appointment and removal of officials, and the claims of patroons." 2 Herbert L. Osgood, *The American Colonies in the Seventeenth Century* 99 (1904).

management of the land was almost total.[1372]

When the company revised its rules of settlement in 1640, under a grant entitled Freedoms and Exemptions for New Netherland,[1373] it surrendered its colonial monopoly and opened the possibility of colonies being founded by private persons. If settlements in such private colonies grew into towns or villages, the company was required to grant to such villages powers of local government; eventually, village magistrates exercised authority to pass ordinances regulating land, fences, highways, schools, and churches. Even during the Dutch era, a large proportion of the villages were populated by English settlers, so it is not surprising that the first bestowal of village rights was on English towns within Dutch territory on Long Island in 1644. Other bestowals of village rights on Dutch communities followed quickly and continued right up to the time of the English takeover in 1664. In addition to these developments, officials in the patroonships sought to exclude completely any exercise of provincial government within the patroon holdings; these conflicts also continued unresolved right up to the end of Dutch rule in New Netherland.

§ 9.05(d). Early Incursions by English Settlers.

The English represented another fertile source of conflict. It may be recalled that the original grant of Virginia land to the London Company included coastal and inland territory extending northward to and including most of New England. Indeed, the Plymouth Company that had been organized in connection with the London Company had planted a settlement at Sagadahoc, near present-day Salem, Massachusetts, in August 1607, only to abandon the project a year later. Clearly, the Dutch colony of

---

[1372] "By ordinances concerning land, provisions were made for the extinguishment of Indian claims, for issue of patents, for the annulment of extravagant and unimproved grants, for the fencing of land, for the levying of tenths and other taxes upon it, for the collection of rents, and the prevention of trespass. Courts were established under the authority of these ordinances; their jurisdiction was prescribed, and provision was made for their officials. Provisions for land grants and for courts, when combined, led to the origin of local government within New Netherland." *Id.* at 104.

[1373] 1 *Documents Relative to the Colonial History of the State of New-York* 118-123 (E.B. O'Callaghan, ed., 1856).

New Netherland was a technical intrusion into lands already claimed by the English, although not settled or in any way occupied by the English. The first overt outbreak of strife occurred in the spring of 1632, when a Dutch ship returning to Holland was forced by weather to put into Plymouth, where the vessel and its passengers were detained while the governments at home bickered over their respective claims. The ship was released in May, but the English asserted the release was "without any prejudice to his majesty's rights."[1374]

Further contentions followed in 1633. The Dutch obstructed English trade with the Indians; colonists from Plymouth began a settlement in territory along the Connecticut River claimed by the Dutch, and by 1635 numerous families from Massachusetts Bay had followed. By 1639 migration into New Netherlands was originating from both New England and Virginia. From as many English settlers as possible, the Dutch colonial government obtained an oath of fidelity:

> to their High Mightinesses the Lords States General, his Highness of Orange, and the Noble Director and Council of New Netherland; to follow the Director or any of his Council, wherever they shall lead; faithfully to give instant warning of any treason, or other detriment to this country that shall come to their knowledge; to assist to the utmost of their power in defending and protecting with their blood and treasure, the inhabitants thereof against all its enemies.[1375]

The English soon commenced a settlement at New Haven and purchased Indian land in all the surrounding areas. As for Long Island, "the Plymouth Company had taken upon itself to grant, at the request of Charles I, in 1635, the whole of Long Island to William Alexander, Earl of Stirling, who, in the early part of the following year, appointed an agent to dispose

---

[1374] 1 E.B. O'Callaghan, *History of New Netherland* 130-136 (1845).

[1375] *Id.* at 298.

of the lands thus conveyed to him, to all who were desirous to purchase and settle them."[1376] While the English were settling the eastern end of Long Island, the Dutch were purchasing and settling the western lands of the island. A series of isolated confrontations led, in 1641, to negotiations between the Dutch and English, which resulted in an agreement that the English could settle in territory claimed by the Dutch according to the provisions of the 1640 charter revising the Freedoms and Exemptions for New Netherland. Several families which had been considering a move from Massachusetts to Long Island then declined to do so, for the new arrangement tacitly conceded the Dutch rights to colonize.

Nevertheless, the provisions of the 1640 charter "formed the basis of all future grants from the Dutch to the English."[1377] According to those provisions, English settling in Dutch territory took an oath of allegiance to the Dutch authorities and enjoyed limited discretion in religious conduct and judicial administration.[1378]

In March 1642, several families from Massachusetts, under the leadership of the Rev. Francis Doughty, a dissenting minister, obtained a patent for 13,342 acres on Long Island and resettled there. Families from Lynn had obtained a similar patent in June 1641. Under both patents, the English settlers had the usual privileges of free manors, including free exercise of religion and powers to establish towns, churches, and systems

---

[1376] *Id.* at 209-210.

[1377] *Id.* at 237.

[1378] "[The English] were to take the oath of allegiance to their High Mightinesses the States General and the West India Company, and in return, to enjoy free exercise of religion, and if they desired to have a magistracy from among themselves, they were to be allowed to nominate three or more persons from the most respectable among them, from which the Director-general would select one or more schepens, or magistrates . . . . In criminal cases, they might proceed to, but not inflict capital punishment. They were empowered to erect towns, but could not construct forts except by special leave. Lands were to be shown to them free of expense, and whatever ground they might select, they were to hold free of rent or taxes for ten years; at the expiration of which time, they should be holden to pay the tenths of the produce. They were, in addition, to enjoy free hunting and fishing, and unshackled commerce, conformably to the privileges granted to New Netherland, but they were bound, in return, to make use of the weights and measures of the country." *Id.*

of civil and criminal justice, all according to the charter of 1640. The patent to Francis Doughty and associates, dated March 28, 1642, used the following language to confer these land rights and privileges:

> We, [the Director-general and the council of New Netherland] . . . do give and grant, unto Francis Doughty and associates, their heirs and assigns, in real, actual, and perpetual possession, all and every parcel of land situate on Long Island [boundaries described] . . . . .
>
> With power to establish, in the aforesaid tract, a town or towns; to erect a church or churches; to exercise the Reformed Christian Religion and church discipline, which they profess; also, to administer, of right, high, low, and middle jurisdiction; to decide civil suits not exceeding fifty Dutch florins; to impose definitively and without appeal in criminal matters, fines to an equal amount; to pronounce the first sentence in other criminal actions of greater moment, and to execute the same . . .: together with the right of hunting, fowling, fishing, and of trading, according to the immunities granted, and to be granted to the colonists of this province, without any exception:
>
> Wherefore the aforesaid F. Doughty and his associates, their heirs and assigns, shall be obligated, so long as they are in possession of the above-mentioned lands, to acknowledge the aforesaid lords for their sovereign Lords and Patroons; to pay, after the lapse of ten years, the tenth part of the produce of the land, whether cultivated with the plough, hoe, or otherwise, orchards and kitchen-gardens, not exceeding one Dutch acre, excepted.[1379]

[1379] 2 E.B. O'Callaghan, *History of New Netherland* 425-425 (1845).

§ 9.05(e). Landholding After the English Takeover in 1664.

§ 9.05(e)(1). The 1664 Patent to the Duke of York.

The English, who had never officially acknowledged Dutch claims to the territory of New Netherlands, took over the colonial government by force, but without much violence, in 1664. By means of a royal charter dated March 12, 1664, and despite King James I having included the same lands in the 1606 patent for the Virginia colony, the English King Charles II granted full rights over the province to his brother the Duke of York—the future King James II. The patent was expressed in terms of the fullest land rights consistent with the feudal incidents still connected with the tenure of free and common socage, including a nominal annual rent of 40 beaver skins:

> And by these presents for us our heires and Successors Doe give and Graunt unto our dearest Brother James Duke of Yorke his heires and Assignes [boundaries described], Together with all the lands Islands Soyles Rivers Harbours Mynes Mineralls Quarries Woods Marishes Waters Lakes fishings hawking hunting and fowleing and all other Royalities proffitts Comodities and hereditaments to the said several Island lands and premises belonging and appertaineing with their and every of their apurtennes AND all our Estate right title interest benefitt advantage Clayme and demaund of in or (to) the said lands and premises . . . together with the yearely and other the Rents Revenues and proffitts of all and singuler the said premisses and of every part and parcell thereof to HAVE AND TO HOLD ALL and singuler the said lands Islands hereditaments and premisses with their and every of their appurtenncs hereby given and Graunted (or hereinbefore menconed to bee given and granted) unto our said dearest Brother James Duke of Yorke his heirs and Assignes for

> ever To the only proper use and behoofe of the said James Duke of Yorke his heires and Assignes for ever To bee holden of us our Heires and Successors as of our Manor of East Greenwich in our County of Kent in ffree and Comon Soccage and not in Capite or by Knights Service YEILDING AND RENDERING And the same James Duke of Yorke Doth for himselfe his heirs and Assignes covenant and promise to yeild and Render unto us our heires and Successors of and for the same yearely and every yeare ffortie Beaver Skynns when they shall be demanded or within Nynety days after . . . .[1380]

The patent gave the grantee, as a feudal lord, extensive powers of government and court jurisdiction. The laws to be administered in the granted lands were to be not contrary to and as near "as conveniently may bee" to the laws of England, and judicial judgments and sentences were subject to a right of appeal in England:

> AND WE DOE FURTHER of our speciall grace certaine knowledge and meere mocon for us our heires and Successors give and Graunt unto our said dearest Brother James Duke of Yorke his heires Deputyes Agents Commissioners and Assignes by these presents full and absolute power and authority to Correct punish Pardon Governe and Rule all such the Subjects of us our heires and Successors as shall from tyme to tyme Adventure themselves into any the parts or Places aforesaid . . . according to such Lawes Orders Ordinances direccons and Instruments as by our said dearest Brother or his Assignes shall bee established . . . as well in all Causes and matters Capitall and Criminall as Civill both Marine and others SOE ALLWAYES as the said Statutes Ordinances and Proceedings bee not contrary to but as neare as conveniently may bee agreeable to the Lawes Statutes and

---

[1380] *The Earliest Printed Laws of New York 1665-1693* 103-104 (John D. Cushing, ed., 1978).

> Governement of this our Realme of England AND SAVEING and reserveing to us our heirs and Successors the receiving heareing and determineing of the Appeale and Appeales of all or any Person or Persons of in or belonging to the Territories or Islands aforesaid in or touching any Judgment or Sentence to bee there made or given . . . .[1381]

The terms of this patent appear to have been designed to expressly supersede any previous and conflicting grants of the same lands:

> AND LASTLY OUR WILL and pleasure is and wee doe hereby declare and Graunt that these our Letters Pattents or the Inrollment thereof shall bee good and effectuall in the Law to all intents and purposes whatsoever NOTWITHSTANDING the not reciteing or menconing of the premisses or any part thereof or the Meets or Bounds thereof or of any former or other Letters Patents or Graunts heretofore made or Graunted of the premisses or of any part thereof by us or of any of our Progenitors unto any other Person or Persons whatsoever Bodyes Politique or Corporate or any Act Lawe or other Restraint incertainty or ymperfeccon whatsoever to the contrary in any wise notwithstanding . . . .[1382]

§ 9.05(e)(2). The "Duke's Law" of 1665.

These powers were implemented in 1665, when the Duke appointed a governor who promulgated a simple code known as the "Duke's Law." This law eventually governed the Duke's vast American grant, which included (along with New York) Delaware, New Jersey, and Pennsylvania. With the exception of New York City, the settlers in the Dutch areas were permitted to be governed by their traditional laws, especially as to landholding. A

[1381] *Id.* at 104-105.

[1382] *Id.* at 106-107.

brief of revival of Dutch rule in 1673 and 1674 resulted in the Duke's Law replacing even these traditional Dutch laws after English rule was restored in 1674.

The Duke's Law has been described as rudimentary, probably because it was patched together from laws of other English colonies in America. Nevertheless, it is a lengthy code, occupying almost 100 pages in its most recent printing.[1383]

The provisions of the Duke's Laws dealing with land matters cover the following topics, in terms typical of English laws adapted to the frontier environment:

> Bounds (of towns, requiring marks to be renewed every three years)
> Cattle, corn, fields, fences
> Conveyances, deeds and writings
> Dowries
> Purchase of Indian lands
> Laws (to be ""not Contrary to the known Lawes of England")
> Orphans
> Possession (persons holding for the past four years without interruption, shall be confirmed in their holdings.)
> Records (of bargain and sale or other conveyances)
> Townships
> Lands, affirming rights of present occupants, and quoted in full as follows (and probably reflecting the statutory abolition of feudal tenures that had occurred in England only five years earlier):

1383 "The Duke of York's Laws for the government of the Colony of New York were compiled from the statutes for the government of the other English colonies in America, under the direction of Nicolls, the first English Governor. They were promulgated at Hempstead, on Long Island, March 1, 1665, and copies were transmitted to the several ridings, constituting the shire of Yorkshire." *Id.* at 110.

All Lands and heritages within this Goverment shall be free from all fines and Licenses, upon Alienation and from all Heriotts, Wardships liveryes Primier Seizins year day and wast, Escheats, and forfeitures upon the Death of Parents or Auncestors Natural, unnatural, Casuall, or judiciall, and that for ever (Cases of high treason only Excepted.)

To the end all former Purchasers may be ascertained to the present possessor or right owner They shall bring in their former Grants, and take our new pattents for the same from the present Gouvernoure in the behalfe of his Royall Highness the Duke of Yorke.

All Purchasers of implanted Lands shall of their Cost and Charge, Cause a Survey and Draught thereof to be made within one yeare after such Purchases and deliver the same into the Office of Records, whereby the bounds and Limits thereof may bee justly distinguished, and if the purchasors shall not within three years after the Survey plant Seat or Inhabit upon the said purchasse they shall forfeit their Right, Title, and Interest therein.

Every Purchaser in acknowledgment of the propriety of such Lands belonging to his Royal Highness James Duke of Yorke, shall upon Sealing of the Pattent Pay unto the Governoure So much as they shall agree upon; Not exceeding for every hundred Acres.

And upon the Seating of a Towne two Towne Lotts shall be reserved by the Purchaser to the use of the Gouvernoure (Gratis) to dispose of to such as he shall thinke fitt.[1384]

[1384] *Id.* at 148.

§ 9.05(e)(3). The Second Grant to the Duke of York in 1674.

When the English retook the lands from the Dutch in 1674, Charles II issued a second grant to the Duke of York, specifying certain territories in addition to those described in the first grant, but describing the rights in those lands in terms essentially identical to the wording of the first grant.[1385] These grants and laws remained formally in effect even after the "Glorious Revolution" in England in 1688, when the Stuart monarchy was ejected. A provincial assembly met in 1690 and temporarily kept in force the existing laws; however, eventually it enacted sufficient legislation to replace the "Duke's Law."[1386]

§ 9.05(e)(4). Additional Land Legislation After 1691.

In 1693 a legislative committee began reviewing all legislation enacted since 1691 and preparing it for printing. It became the first printed collection of laws for New York.

The enactments relating to land included in this collection are as follows:

> An Act for the Settling, Quieting and Confirming unto the Cities, Towns, Mannours and Freeholders within this Province, their several Grants, Patents and Rights respectively ("Rights and Privilege formerly held by and granted . . . should be now ratified and confirmed . . . .")

[1385] *Id.* at 109.

[1386] "With the "Duke's Law" still in effect, the earliest work of the new legislature was directed toward proclaiming and defining the new political authority, establishing courts, adjusting municipal boundaries, establishing a body of liberties, repairing the damage done by the [Leisler] rebellion, and establishing the law of England as the basis of all provincial legislation. Thereafter, as in all other jurisdictions, the assembly confined itself to meeting the current and ever-changing needs of the province, and its enactments eventually became sufficiently extensive to replace the 'Duke's Law.'" *Id.* at viii.

> An Act for the Regulating the Buildings, Streets, Lanes, Wharffs, Docks and Alleys of the City of New-York
>
> An Act for the supervising Intestates Estates, and Regulating the Probate of Wills, & granting Letters of Administration
>
> An Act declaring what are the Rights & Privilege of Their Majesties Subjects inhabiting within Their Province of New-York.

Pertinent land law provisions of this important "body of liberties" enactment are quoted in full, revealing their heavy reliance on Magna Carta, among other sources:

> That no Free-man shall be taken or imprisoned, or be deprived of his Free-hold or Liberty, or free Customs, or Out-Lawed, or Exiled, or any other wayes destroyed; nor shall be passed upon, adjudged or condemned, but by the lawful Judgment of his Peers, and by the Law of this Province.
>
> Justice nor Right shall be neither Sold, Denyed or Delayed to any Person within this Province.
>
> That no Aid, Tax, Talliage or Custom, Loan, Benevolence, Gift, Excise, Duty or Imposition whatsoever shall be laid, assessed, imposed, levied or required of or on any of Their Majesties Subjects within this Province, &c. or their Estates, upon any manner of Colour or Pretence whatsoever, but by the Act and Consent of the Governour and Council, and Representatives of the People in General Assembly met and convened.
>
> That no Man, of what Estate or Condition soever, shall be put out of his Lands, Tenements, nor taken, imprisoned, nor disinherited, nor banished, nor any ways destroyed or

molested, without first being brought to answer by due court of Law.

That a Free-man shall not be amerced for a small Fault, but after the manner of his Fault, and for a great Fault after the greatness thereof, saving to him his Free-hold; and a Husband-man, saving to him his Wainage . . . and none of these Amercements shall be assessed, but by the Oath of Twelve Honest and Lawful men of the Vicinage . . . .

That no Free-man shall be compelled to receive any Souldiers or Marriners, except Inholders, and other Houses of publick Entertainment, who are to quarter for ready Money into his House, and there suffer them to sojourn again their Wills; provided it be not in time of actual War within this Province . . . .

That all the Lands within this Province shall be esteemed and accounted Lands of Free-hold, and Inheritance in free and common Soccage, according to the Tenor of East-Greenwich in their Majesties Realm of England.

That no Estate of a Feme-Covert shall be sold or conveyed, but by Deed acknowledged by her in some Court of Record, the Woman being secretly examined, if she doth it freely, without threats or compulsion of her Husband . . . .

That all Lands and Heritages within this Province and Dependencies shall be free from all Fines, Lisences upon Alienations, and from all Heriots, Wardships, Liveries, Primiers, Seizins, Year and Day, and Waste, Escheat and Forfeiture upon the Death of Parents and Ancestors, Natural, Unnatural, Casual or Judicial, and that forever, Cases of High-Treason only excepted . . . .[1387]

[1387] *Id.* at 19-23.

The thoroughness of common law adoption in New York after 1700 can be illustrated by the fact that it was only in 1782, after the Revolution and after adoption of a state constitution, that the state legislature acted to abolish primogeniture, reestablish partible inheritance, and eliminate further entails.[1388]

§ 9.05(f). Summary of Landholding Arrangements in Colonial New York.

§ 9.05(f)(1). Land Grants.

At the top of the landholding hierarchy in colonial New York were those who received their proprietary grants directly from the European government, whether Dutch or English. These grants were estates of inheritance, descending to heirs, and the grantees were landlords. Because they also obtained powers of government, they in effect functioned as territorial lords in the feudal sense. They could sell, mortgage, lease, devise or convey in trust any portion of their holding. Because the prohibitions of the English Statute *Quia Emptores* forbidding subinfeudation were not enforced in New York, a proprietor could make further grants "on such conditions as he chose limited by the nature of his own patent, to erect or permit the erection of manors, to devise the machinery necessary for surveying, issuing, and recording grants and collecting rents."[1389]

When the proprietors were preparing for colonization, they issued documents containing "concessions," "conditions of plantation," or "instructions" that stated the terms under which the land would be granted to the colonists. Although this was the model among the English provinces, the pattern of Dutch administration over New Netherland did not significantly differ. The patroonships and other settlements were commenced under the authority of the 1629 charter of Freedoms and

---

[1388] New York Laws of 1782, ch. 2.

[1389] 2 Herbert L. Osgood, *The American Colonies in the Seventeenth Century* 20 (1904).

Exemptions, which charter constituted a sort of "conditions of plantation." When the English administration was substituted for the Dutch in 1664, and again in 1674, Dutch titles were confirmed, and there was a general renewal of patents, accompanied by the requirement of an oath of allegiance to the English monarch.

Since the English had taken the entire estate of the Dutch West India Company, unoccupied land in New York became subject to their administration. The English governor in New York prescribed regulations for the settlement of those lands, including making purchases from the Indians, extending temporary exemptions from taxes, and establishing towns. In New York, many such rules were drawn from well-established regulations in both New England and Maryland. The size of individual holdings was also affected by this system, with the result that those holdings tended to be much larger in New York than in New England.[1390]

Among all the English colonies in America, only in New York did any fully developed manors come into existence, and these originated in the patroonship system introduced by the Dutch, exhibiting many features of continental feudalism. Ultimately, however, only the patroonship of the Van Rensselaer family survived the vicissitudes of frontier life to become an enduring fixture in New York landholding arrangements. The decline of the manorial influence of the old Dutch patroonships was revived in part by huge grants of land to private families made by Peter Stuyvesant and early English governors.[1391]

1390 "In general, estates were much larger in the provinces [such as New York] than they were in the corporate colonies. The few scores of acres which, as the result of a series of town allotments, ordinarily came into the possession of a New England farmer, were almost insignificant when compared with the princely estates of the Dutch patroons . . . ." *Id.* at 24.

1391 "Owing to these events, toward the close of the period of Dutch rule the manorial influence declined and ceased practically to exist in the southern part of the province. From time to time, however, both by Stuyvesant and by the early English governors, grants of considerable size were made. Some of these, notably Fordham, Pelham, and Phillipsburg in Westchester, assumed the name and to an extent the organization of manors. Toward the close of the Dutch period the Van Cortlandt family began to build up its large estate. During the administration of Governor Dongan the first grants were made which resulted in the development of the Livingston manor. By these events the manorial system began again to assume

Small grants, most under 1,000 acres in size, were also made under the Dutch charter of Freedoms and Exemptions of 1629, and these were encouraged even more under the amended version of the charter issued in 1640. These smaller grants were nominally organized as manors, with regulations for leases and rents, but were often left unsettled and neglected. Because land was so frequently in need of settlers, usually it was simply granted under conditions of settlement and, in New York, only rarely sold for money, except at the highest proprietary level.

Certain English settlements in which the grant was made collectively to a group arose during the period of Dutch rule, especially on Long Island and in the area of Westchester County, and these settlements shared characteristics with New England towns, from whence their founders had migrated.

Throughout the period of Dutch rule, as an alternative to settlement under manorial patroonships, individual settlers ventured into unoccupied land, purchased rights from the Indians, and had their purchases confirmed by the colonial government. Eventually, these settlements or groups of them received patents as towns and thereby obtained rights of local governments. After issuance of the town patent, the town itself made grants of land to individual persons. Common rights also arose within the towns, eventually to be divided by lot.[1392]

---

a prominence in New York like that from which, since the dissolution of the early association of patroons, it had declined. The social and political development of New York has been deeply affected by the family alliances and the system of tenant rights which, as the result of these grants, extended so widely within its borders." *Id.* at 31-32.

1392 "Within towns thus organized unoccupied land was treated as commons, and the system of common fields, pastures and woods, with town herds and common fences, appears, much as in New England. As time progressed the towns divided their commons by lot, as they did in New England. A genuine village community system existed among the Dutch, as it did among the New Englanders, but in the two sections it come into existence in a somewhat different way. In New England, as a rule, the group of settlers was original, and secured the town grant and managed it from the first. Among the Dutch, as a rule, the villages originated from aggregations of farms, and attained their corporate life in consequence of such preexistent aggregation. When the Dutch village community had once been formed, it exhibited most of the characteristics of the New England village, though it was always subject to certain limitations which did not attach to the latter. Moreover, in

With the eventual elimination of all but one patroonship, the towns and villages played a large role in establishing the patterns of landholding in New York.

§ 9.05(f)(2). Leases and Quit Rents.

The quit rents that figured prominently in some of the proprietary English provinces were not a consistent part of the Dutch landholding arrangements in New Netherland.[1393]

The articles of capitulation guaranteed that the Dutch could "enjoy their own customs concerning their inheritances" and that land records would be preserved. The oath of allegiance required by the English effectively broke the tenure of landholding under the Dutch and re-established it under the English tenure of free and common socage.

Those who held land rights under the Dutch were directed by the Duke's Law of 1665 to turn in their old grants and receive new patents from the English; in most of these confirmations no mention was made of a quit rent, especially with respect to lots in New York City. However, the confirmation of Indian deeds and the bestowal of new grants were usually

---

New Netherland the village was by no means the only form of settlement, and it did not determine the form of society to the extent which was true of the villages in New England." *Id.* at 50.

[1393] "In the Dutch ground briefs no definite provision was made for the payment of a rent. In some of the patents the payment of a tenth of the products of the soil was required. In many only the general obligation of submission and allegiance was enforced, with some special duty, such as that of fencing the land. The West India company owned six boweries, which were situated on the east side of Manhattan island outside the limits of the Dutch town. They were furnished with buildings and with cattle, and were leased for short periods, with the stock and other outfit, on such terms as were customary throughout the province. The farms of the colony of Rennselaerswyck were managed according to the same system of stock leases. Some were let at a fixed rent, payable in grain, beaver, or wampum, while others were let at halves or thirds, including one-half of the increase of the stock and a few pounds of butter as a recognition. The tenant was bound to keep the buildings and tools in good repair.

The English Conquest in 1664 resulted in no immediate change in the land law of the province." *Id.* at 39-40.

conditioned on payment of the customary rent for new plantations; this nominal rent was usually in kind, such as a bushel of wheat, a lamb, or a barrel of fish. When English rule was interrupted and then re-established in 1673-1674, and old grants were again asked to be renewed, quit rents were more prominent, but hardly universal.[1394]

The inhabitants of the English towns that arose during the period of Dutch rule eventually became subject to quit rents, even though quit rents were completely absent from the New England traditions from which the settlers of these communities had issued.

No separate land office existed in New York, so the chief provincial officials were responsible for making surveys, issuing patents, and collecting rents. New York laws provided that a registry be established for leases, mortgages, conveyances, and wills.

§ 9.06. Bibliography.

Books

Allen, David Grayson, *In English Ways: The Movement of Societies and the Transferal of English Local Law and Customs to Massachusetts Bay in the Seventeenth Century* (1981).

[1394] "In 1686 Governor Dongan reported that the quitrents, at his arrival in the province, were very inconsiderable, the larger part coming from the Delaware region under the terms of the patents granted by Andros. But Andros even had renewed Indian purchases and township grants with the former reservation of a lamb only as a quitrent. Dongan, however, insisted that all patents or deeds which were recorded during his administration should contain provision for a quitrent. No exception was made even in the case of city lots.

Rent in the city was made payable in money, but in the country it was payable in wheat, fish, or other commodities. Albany was made the place of payment for the northern part, and New York for the southern part, of the province. At first rents were payable to the duke, but later, after his accession, to the king. Dongan himself explains how he succeeded in increasing the quitrent in some of the towns. He found that certain tracts of land within their limits had not been purchased from the Indians and were at the disposal of the government. By threatening to grant them to outside parties, he induced the proprietors of the town to submit to an increase of rent. By these measures the system of quitrents was extended throughout New York, and its practice in this respect was brought into conformity with that of the other English provinces." *Id.* at 41-42.

Andrews, Charles L., *The Colonial Period* (1912).
Andrews, Matthew Page, *Virginia, The Old Dominion* (1949).
Batchelor, Albert S., ed., *Laws of New Hampshire: Province Period* (1904).
Belknap, Jeremy, *The History of New Hampshire* (1792).
Biemer, Linda, *Women and Property in Colonial New York* (1983).
Billings, Warren M., *A Little Parliament: The Virginia General Assembly in the Seventeenth Century* (2004).
Billings, Warren M., ed., *The Old Dominion in the Seventeenth Century* (1975).
Billings, Warren M., John E. Selby, and Thad W. Tate, *Colonial Virginia: A History* (1986).
Bodin, Jean, *The Six Books of a Commonweale* (Kenneth D. McRae, ed., (1962).
Bond Jr., Beverly W., *The Quit-Rent System in the American Colonies* (1919, reprint 1965).
Bradford, William, *Of Plymouth Plantation* (Samuel Eliot Morison, ed., 1959).
Brigham, William, ed., *The Compact, Charter and Laws of the Colony of New Plymouth* (1836).
Brodhead, John R. et al., *Documents Relative to the Colonial History of the State of New York* (1857).
Brown, Alexander, *The First Republic in America* (1898).
Brown, Alexander, *The Genesis of the United States* (1890).
Bruce, Philip Alexander, *Economic History of Virginia in the Seventeenth Century* (1896).
Campbell, Charles, *History of the Colony and Ancient Dominion of Virginia* (1860).
Craven, Frank, *The Southern Colonies in the Seventeenth Century, 1607-1689* (1970).
Cushing, John D., ed., *Acts and Laws of New Hampshire 1680-1726* (1978).
Cushing, John D., ed., *Massachusetts Province Laws 1692-1699* (1978).
Cushing, John D., ed., *Colony Laws of Virginia, 1619-1660* (1978).
Cushing, John D., ed., *The Earliest Printed Laws of New York 1665-1693* (1978).
Cushing, John D., ed., *The Laws and Liberties of Massachusetts 1641-1691* (1976).
Cushing, John D., ed., *The Laws of the Pilgrims* (1977).
Daniell, Jere R., *Colonial New Hampshire* (1981).
Davis, William T., ed., *Bradford's History of Plymouth Plantation* (1908).
Ely, James W., Jr., ed., *Property Rights in the Colonial Era and Early Republic* (1997).
Engerman, Stanley L. and Robert E. Gallman, eds., *The Cambridge Economic History of the United States* (1996).
Fry, William Henry, *New Hampshire as a Royal Province* (1908).
Hening, William Waller, ed., *The Statutes at Large, Being a Collection of All the Laws of Virginia* (1823).
Hilkey, Charles J., *Legal Development in Colonial Massachusetts 1630-1686* (2005).
Hoffer, Peter Charles, *Law and People in Colonial America* (1998).
Horn, James, *Adapting to a New World: English Society in the Seventeenth-Century Chesapeake* (1994).
Hughes, Sarah S., *Surveyors and Statesmen: Land Measuring in Colonial Virginia* (1979).
Kammen, Michael, *Colonial New York* (1975).
Kim, Sung Bok, *Landlord and Tenant in Colonial New York* (1978).
Kurtz, Sheldon F., *Moynihan's Introduction to the Law of Real Property* (4th ed. 2005).

Langdon, George D., *Pilgrim Colony: A History of New Plymouth 1620-1691* (1966).
Lincoln, Charles Z. et al., *The Colonial Laws of New York from the Year 1664 to the Revolution* (repr. 2006).
MacDonald, William, ed., *Select Charters and Other Documents Illustrative of American History (1606-1775)* (1914).
Maitland, Frederic and William Frederick Pollock, *The History of English Law Before the Time of Edward I* (2d ed. 1909).
Mapp, Alf J., Jr., *The Virginia Experiment* (3d ed. 1987).
Mark, Irving, *Agrarian Conflicts in Colonial New York* (1940).
Morison, Elizabeth Forbes and Elting E. Morison, *New Hampshire, A Bicentennial History* (1976).
Morton, Richard L., *Colonial Virginia* (1960).
Narrett, David E., *Inheritance and Family Life in Colonial New York City* (1992).
Nelson, William E., *The Common Law in Colonial America* (2008).
O'Callaghan, E. B., ed., *Documents Relative to the Colonial History of the State of New York* (1856).
O'Callaghan, E.B., *History of New Netherland* (1845).
Osgood, Herbert L., *The American Colonies in the Seventeenth Century* (1904).
Price, Edward T., *Dividing the Land: Early American Beginnings of Our Private Property Mosaic* (1995).
Pulsipher, David, ed., *Records of the Colony of New Plymouth in New England,* (1861).
Salmon, Marylynn, *Women and the Law of Property in Early America* (1986).
Sanborn, Frank B., *New Hampshire, An Epitome of Popular Government* (1904).
Smith, John, *The General Historie of Virginia* (1624).
Spencer, Charles W., *The Land System of Colonial New York* (1917).
Stackpole, Everett S., *History of New Hampshire* (1916).
Stratton, Eugene Aubrey, *Plymouth Colony, Its History and People* (1986).
Taylor, Alan, *American Colonies* (2002).
Van Deventer, David E., *The Emergence of Provincial New Hampshire 1623-1741* (1976).
Vickers, Daniel, *A Companion to Colonial America* (2006).
Wertenbaker, Thomas J., *The Shaping of Colonial Virginia* (1958).
West, Willis Mason, *A Source Book in American History to 1787* (1913).

Chapters in Books

Andrews, Charles M., "Introduction," in Beverly W. Bond, Jr., *The Quit Rent System in the American Colonies* (1919, reprint 1965).
Bethell, Tom, Ch. 3, "Plato's Conceit: Property at Jamestown and Plymouth," in Tom Bethell, *The Noblest Triumph* (1998).
Ely, James W., Ch. 1, "The Origins of Property Rights: The Colonial Period," in James W. Ely, *The Guardian of Every Other Right: A Constitutional History of Property Rights* (2007).
Hone, E. Wade, Ch. 2, "British Possession," in E. Wade Hone, *Land and Property Research in the United States* (1997).
Lemon, James T., "Spatial Order: Households in Local Communities and Regions," in Jack P. Greene and J. R. Pole, eds., *Colonial British America, Essays in the New History of the Early Modern Era* (1984).
Reinsch, Paul Samuel, "The English Common Law in the Early American Colonies," in 1 *Select Essays in Anglo-American Legal History (*Association of American Law Schools , 1907).

Articles

Dayton, Cornelia H., "Turning Points and the Relevance of Colonial Legal History," 50 *Wm. & Mary Q.* 7 (1993).

Hart, John F., "Colonial Land Use Law and Its Significance for Modern Takings Doctrine," 109 *Harv. L. Rev.* 1252 (1996).

Keim, C. Ray, "Primogeniture and Entail in Colonial Virginia," 25 *Wm. & Mary Q.* 545 (Oct. 1968).

Main, Gloria L., "The Standard of Living in Colonial Massachusetts," 43 *J. Econ. Hist.* 101 (1983).

Mensch, Elizabeth V., "The Colonial Origins of Liberal Property Rights, 31 *Buff. L. Rev.* 635 (1982).

Priest, Claire, Creating an American Property Law: Alienability and Its Limits in American History, 120 *Harv. L. Rev. 385* (2006).

Rosen, Deborah A., Women and Property across Colonial America, 60 *Wm. & Mary Q.* 355 (2003).

Seiler, William H., "Land Processioning in Colonial Virginia," 6 *Wm. & Mary Q.* 416 (July 1949).

Springer, James Warren, "American Indians and the Law of Real Property in Colonial New England," 30 *Am. J. Legal Hist.* 25 (1986).

Chapter 10

Land Law in the Colonies of Connecticut (from 1633), Maryland (from 1634), Rhode Island (from 1636), Delaware (from 1638) and New Jersey (from 1638)[1395]

[1395] The content of this chapter was originally written by the author, and some content was drawn or reprinted from Vol. 1 of Thompson on Real Property.

SYNOPSIS

Chapter 10. Land Law in the Colonies of Connecticut (from 1633), Maryland (from 1634), Rhode Island (from 1636), Delaware (from 1638) and New Jersey (from 1638)

§ 10.01. Introduction to Chapters 9, 10 and 11.

In strict chronological sequence these three chapters should fall between Chapter 7 and Chapter 8. Chapter 7 traces the progress of English land law to roughly the middle of the 16th century, by which time many of the effects of the 1536 Statute of Uses had revealed themselves. Chapter 8 is a discussion of the significant subsequent changes in English land law up to modern times. At about the same time as the chronological division between these two chapters, the English exploration and colonization of North America was just getting underway, and early in the 17th century, the first permanent English settlements in North America were established.

Therefore, the state of affairs in English land law as described in Chapter 7 provides an appropriate background for understanding the beginnings of land rights in England's earliest American colonies.

These three chapters examine the land law developments in each of the 13 English colonies, up to the time of national independence. Chapters 12-14 then cover basic American land law developments thereafter, including developments in each of the states.

The contents of Chapters 9, 10 and 11 consist of an independent section for each of the 13 colonies, beginning with the earliest to have permanent European settlements, and proceeding in the mostly chronological order of their first settlements. The transformation of land law described in these chapters parallels, and may be usefully compared with, the concurrent land law changes in England, as described in Chapter 8. It will, of course, be abundantly evident that developments unique to one country were prompted by forces and circumstances peculiar to that country, despite the shared historical origins of English and American law.

It is also noteworthy that, in the earliest of England's North American colonies, the acclaimed common law of England had little specific influence when the colonists actually had to create rules to govern their everyday affairs, such as working out rights in land. Land arrangements were often a combination of what the colonists had learned from limited firsthand experience in their homelands and of their aspirations for a better society. Only later would the colonists routinely hold up the common law of England as the protective shield for English citizens' most important personal and civic rights.

§ 10.02. Development of Land Law in Connecticut (from 1633).

§ 10.02(a). The Founding of the Connecticut River Towns.

§ 10.02(a)(1). Settlement from Massachusetts.

A congregation of Puritans under the leadership of the Rev. John Warham immigrated to the Massachusetts colony in 1630 and eventually began a settlement that became the town of Dorchester. A few years later they moved to the Connecticut River and founded the town of Windsor. Another congregation, under the Rev. George Phillips and a magistrate named Sir Richard Saltonstall, settled at Watertown, and also later moved to the Connecticut River to found the town of Weathersfield. The Rev. Thomas Hooker, a well-known but persecuted non-conformist minister from Chelmsford, England, fled to Holland in 1632 and thence to Boston in 1633. Many of his followers had settled earlier in Weymouth and in Newtown (Cambridge). Upon Hooker's arrival, they congregated in Newtown. This congregation later founded a third settlement on the Connecticut River: Hartford. All three of these first Connecticut settlements, Weathersfield, Windsor, and Hartford, were founded between 1634 and 1635.

§ 10.02(a)(2). Warwick Patent of 1631.

Meanwhile, in 1630 the Plymouth Company in England had granted to Robert, Earl of Warwick, an aristocratic friend of Hooker and president of the Council of Plymouth, a large tract of land including most of present-day Connecticut. The grant was confirmed by a patent from King Charles I. On March 19, 1631, Warwick granted the same Connecticut territory to eleven persons, including Sir Richard Saltonstall, whose subsequent patentees were the settlers of the Connecticut River and New Haven colonies. The validity of the grant to Warwick was questioned, especially after the Plymouth Company re-granted the same lands to the Marquis of Hamilton in 1635, but Hamilton's claim was later held barred by prescription.[1396]

§ 10.02(a)(3). Confrontation with the Dutch.

In 1632 members of the Plymouth Colony selected a site for a trading post at Windsor, which they began to construct in earnest in 1633, after purchasing the land from the Indians. Meanwhile, the Dutch were asserting a claim to Connecticut by commencing a settlement at the site of Hartford, a few acres of which they also purchased from Indians. The Dutch even launched a military assault on the Plymouth trading house, but they were repulsed; afterwards, the settlement groups lived in uneasy peace.

§ 10.02(a)(4). Migration Under Massachusetts' Jurisdiction.

In 1634 settlers at Newtown with their pastor Thomas Hooker, complaining about unavailability of land, petitioned the Massachusetts General Court for permission to migrate to Connecticut, but they were denied. In 1635, however, people from Watertown, Dorchester and Roxbury were permitted to migrate on the condition that they agreed to continue to be governed by Massachusetts. It is believed that Newtown settlers were allowed to leave under the same condition later in the year. Because the Connecticut River settlements were outside the Massachusetts territory, this condition was quite unusual and could not be a permanent arrangement for governmental organization. At first, the Massachusetts General Court in 1636 appointed a commission of eight persons to regulate affairs in the Connecticut settlements for a period of one year. The commission had power to control trade, grant land lots, and regulate building, military discipline, defensive war, and the conduct of judicial proceedings. Undoubtedly, distribution of land took place, and landholding arrangements were fashioned, exactly as was then occurring in the Massachusetts settlement, and has been described in the preceding chapter, § 9.03(a)(3) and § 9.03(b)(2), *supra*.

[1396] Benjamin Trumbull, *A Complete History of Connecticut* 10 (1898).

§ 10.02(a)(5). Self-government Under the 1639 Fundamental Orders.

When the year's term expired in 1637, a general court of Connecticut settlers met in Hartford and began to function as an independent, indigenous colonial government. The settlers conferred with Massachusetts leaders about uniting the colonies in 1638 but talks broke down. So, late in 1638 Connecticut leaders drafted a frame of government, the Fundamental Orders, which they adopted in January 1639. This document has been described as "the first written constitution known to history that created a government."[1397] The Fundamental Orders included detailed provisions for the establishment of a general assembly or court and the appointment or election of various public officials. In the general court reposed the basic governing power:

> In which said Generall Courts shall consist the supreme power of the Commonwelth, and they only shall have power to make lawes or repeale them, to graunt levys, to admitt of Freemen, dispose of lands undisposed of, to severall Townes or persons, and also shall have power to call ether Courte or Magestrate or any other person whatsoever into question for any misdemeanour, and may for just causes displace or deale otherwise according to the nature of the offence; and also may deale in any other matter that concerns the good of this commonwelth, excepte election of Magestrats, which shall be done by the whole boddy of Freemen.[1398]

The legislative powers of this Connecticut General Court were essentially the same as in Massachusetts.

[1397] *Select Charters and Other Documents Illustrative of American History 1606-1775* 60 (William MacDonald, ed., 1914).

[1398] *Id.* 64-65.

More than the substantive provisions, the preamble of the Fundamental Orders has attracted attention. It has been depicted as a more striking expression of independence than even the Mayflower Compact.[1399]

Among its other extensive powers, the general court had comprehensive control over land distribution and management.[1400]

This colony of Connecticut River towns thus proceeded to develop in an orderly way, even though it had no royal charter. In a short time it expanded by absorbing two other colonies. One was the settlement that colonists acting under the terms of the Warwick patent had founded at Saybrook, although that patent did not extend to the Saybrook area. This colony was added to the river towns by purchase in 1644. The second colony, New Haven, had been settled by strict Puritans who had first landed

---

[1399] "If marked originality is to be found anywhere in the Fundamental Orders, it must appear in the preamble. This is, in fact, the part of the document which has chiefly attracted the attention and awakened the imagination of historians. The frank declaration of independence which is there made, and the announcement of the fact that in the opinion of the framers an original compact was being formed, has given to this document most of its interest. The preamble has been dwelt on at greater length and with much greater enthusiasm than have the provisions of the constitution concerning government. It has been made to signify much more than the Mayflower Compact, and its adoption has been regarded as the initial act in the development of American democracy. But really there is nothing in the preamble, or in the body of the Fundamental Orders, to indicate that, if the settlers of Connecticut had possessed a royal charter, they would have proceeded in a manner essentially different from that of the colonists of Massachusetts." 1 Herbert L. Osgood, *The American Colonies in the Seventeenth Century* 312 (1904).

[1400] "The business of the general court was very extensive. Besides its two regular sessions, many extra sessions were held. In 1645 it met seven times; in 1658 it met twice in March and once in May, in August and in October; in many years it met as often as in these. As in the other corporate colonies, its work was legislative, administrative, and judicial; while the character and volume of its product in each of these lines were not materially different from that which appears elsewhere in New England. Its most important legislation . . . had reference to towns, military affairs, moral and ecclesiastical relations, the levy of rates, Indian relations, crimes and their penalties. Not only did the general court legislate comprehensively, as in October, 1639, for the establishment and regulation of towns, but by special orders it provided for the enforcement of this legislation, and controlled the action of towns in many ways. As a result of these acts and a series of land grants, a town system similar to that of Massachusetts and Plymouth was developed; and by means of this system the territory of the colony was extended eastward to include the Pequot country, southward to the mouth of the river, and westward till it was met by the counter claims of the Dutch." *Id.* at 317.

in Boston, remained for only a few months, and had then chosen New Haven as a permanent location.

§ 10.02(b). The Founding of the New Haven Colony.

This New Haven group was remarkably independent from colonial regulation imposed either by English or by Massachusetts authorities. Consistent with the efforts in Hartford to form a government, the New Haven settlers held a "general meeting" in June 1639, and reached agreement upon the fundamental rules for self-government, called the Fundamental Articles of New Haven.[1401] The first public assembly or court held thereafter, of which there is record, took place in October 1639, and at that meeting the colonists acted to exclude English statutory and common law from their settlement. They resolved "thatt the worde of God shall be the onely rule to be attended unto in ordering the affayres of government in this plantation."[1402]

Several other plantations and settlements grew up in the general vicinity of New Haven, and some of these were as independent of New Haven as New Haven was of England or Massachusetts; others, such as Stamford and Branford, for instance, were settled by seceders from Weathersfield, one of the river towns, and they obtained land grants directly from New Haven. In 1643 New Haven along with the colonies in Connecticut, Plymouth and Massachusetts Bay formed the United Colonies of New England in order to achieve concerted action in matters of warfare, boundary dispute resolutions, division of conquered Indian territory, and taxation of goods moving between colonies.[1403]

[1401] *Select Charters and Other Documents Illustrative of American History, 1606-1775* 67-72 (William MacDonald, ed., 1914).

[1402] 1 Herbert L. Osgood, *The American Colonies in the Seventeenth Century* 323 (1904).

[1403] *See* the "Articles of Confederation betwixt the Plantations. . ." printed as part of New Haven colony's first printed compilation of laws in *The Earliest Laws of the New Haven and Connecticut Colonies, 1739-1673* 4-8 (John D. Cushing, ed., 1977).

§ 10.02(c). Land-related Legislation in Early Connecticut.

§ 10.02(c)(1). Connecticut Code of 1650.

Both New Haven and Connecticut colonies were active in legislating. Connecticut produced a code in 1650, the third code produced in New England (after Plymouth in 1636 and Massachusetts in 1648), but did not print the code, instead distributing it in manuscript form to various settlements in the colony. Provisions of the 1650 Connecticut code relating to land are quoted or summarized as follows:

> . . . no mans goods or estate shall bee taken away from him, nor any wayes in damages, under colour of Law or countenance of Authority, unless it bee by the vertue or equity of some express Law of the Country warranting the same, established by a Generall Courte, and sufficiently published, or in case of the defect of a Law in any perticular case, by the word of God.
>
> Ability
>
> Age
>
> Bounds of Townes and Perticular Lands
>
> Cattle, Cornefeilds, Fences
>
> Common Fields
>
> Caveats Entred [recording of creditors' claims against debtors' lands]
>
> Conveyances Fraudulent
>
> Escheats

Fences

Forgerie

Highe Wayes

Lands; Free Lands: It is ordered, and by this Courte declared, that oure Lands and Heritages shall bee free from all fynes and lycenses uppon Alienations, and from all Harriots, Wardships, Liveries, Primer seizins, yeare, day and waste, escheats and forfeitures uppon the death of parents or ancestors, bee they naturall, unnaturall, casuall or juditiall, and that for ever.

Rates [of property taxation]

Records

Timber

Trespasses

Home Lotts: Whereas there is creeping in, in severall Townes and plantations within this Jurissdiction, a great abuse of buying and purchasing Home Lotts and laying them together, by meanes whereof great depopulations are like to follow. It is ordered that all dwelling or mansion houwses that are or shall bee allowed in any plantation or Towne within this Jurissdiction, shall bee upheld, repaired and meinteined sufficiently in a comely way: As allso, whosoever shall possess and injoye any homelotts within any such plantation or Towne, that is not yet built uppon, shall, within twelve months after the making of this order, erect and build a howse there, fitt for an inhabitant to dwell in, unless the Courte, uppon knowledge of the case, finde cause to abate, give longer time for building.[1404]

§ 10.02(c)(2). New Haven Laws of 1656.

New Haven Colony actually preceded the Connecticut river towns in producing a printed compilation of its legislation in force. A work entitled *New Haven's Settling in New England*, published in London in 1656, "included the text of the New England Confederation, the fundamental agreement of 1639, and a remarkably sophisticated code of laws based upon the Massachusetts code of 1648, and presumably the supplements of 1650 and 1654 as well."[1405] Provisions of this compilation relating to land are quoted or summarized as follows:

> . . . no mans goods, or estate shall be taken from him, under colour of Law, or Countenance of authority, unlesse it be by vertue, or equity of some expresse Law of this Jurisdiction, established by the Generall Court, and sufficiently published, or for want of a Law in any particular case, by the word of God. . . .
>
> Age
>
> Cattell, Corn, Fields, Fences
>
> Charges publick [taxes on property]
>
> Conveyances fraudulent
>
> Distresse
>
> Dowryes

[1404] 1 J. Hammond Trumbull, *The Public Records of the Colony of Connecticut* 509-563 (1950).

[1405] John D. Cushing, ed., *The Earliest Laws of the New Haven and Connecticut Colonies 1639-1673* viii (1977).

Escheates

Forgery, or Falsifying

Plantations

Records

Wills, Inventories, and the Estates of such as dye intestate

No provisions relate to the public authority or private power to convey lands in this compilation, undoubtedly because these practices had been well-established and orderly, on the Massachusetts model, from the beginning.

§ 10.02(c)(3). The Royal Charter of 1662 and Unification of Connecticut and New Haven Colonies.

The Stuart Restoration in England, in 1660, once again exposed the Connecticut colonies' lack of charter or patent, so colonial governor John Winthrop was delegated to go to England and seek a charter. He succeeded in obtaining a very favorable charter, dated April 23, 1662, which also included the New Haven settlements, and over much objection by some New Haven colonists, Connecticut absorbed that colony during the two years following issuance of the charter. This charter of 1662 remained of fundamental importance for Connecticut until well after statehood and the adoption of a new state constitution in 1818.[1406]

[1406] "The delay [of New Haven] in proclaiming Charles II, and its tender treatment of the regicides, had brought it into disfavor with the king; and it now . . . resisted annexation, and appealed to the Commissioners of the United Colonies. But the conquest of New Netherland by the English, in 1664, and the grant to the Duke of York of territory as far east as the Connecticut River, hastened submission; and in December of the latter year a committee was appointed to arrange for the union. A *quo warranto* was issued against the Connecticut charter in 1684, but judgment was not entered. When Andros demanded the charter, in 1687, it was secreted, and remained hidden until 1689, when, upon the deposition of Andros, government under the charter was resumed. The State constitution of 1776 continued the charter

Important excerpts from this charter establishing the rule of English law and the power of the colonial government over land affairs are as follows:

> [The Colony of Connecticut] to have, take, possess, acquire, and purchase lands, tenements, or hereditaments, or any goods, or chattles, and the same to lease, grant, demise, alien, bargain, sell, and dispose of, as other our liege people of this our realm of England. . . .
>
> . . . that all, and every the subjects of us, our heirs, or successors, which shall go to inhabit within the said colony, and every of their children which shall happen to be born there, or on the sea in going thither, or returning from thence, shall have and enjoy all liberties, and immunities of free, and natural subjects within any the dominions of us, our heirs, or successors, to all intents, constructions, and purposes whatsoever, as if they, and every of them were born within the realm of England. . . .
>
> . . . and also from time to time to make, ordain, and establish all manner of wholesome, and reasonable laws, statutes, ordinances, directions, and instructions, not contrary to the laws of this realm, of England. . . .
>
> . . . And know ye further, that we of our abundant grace, certain knowledge, and meer motion, have given, granted, and confirmed, and by these presents for us, our heirs, and successors, do give, grant, and confirm unto the said governour, and company, and their successors, all that part of our dominions in New England [boundaries described], with the islands thereunto adjoyning, together with all firm lands, soyles, grounds, havens, ports, rivers, waters,

---

in force, with a few changes, and it remained the fundamental law of Connecticut until the adoption of a new constitution in 1818." *Select Charters and Other Documents Illustrative of American History, 1606-1775* 116 (William MacDonald, ed., 1914).

> fishings, mines, minerals, precious stones, quarreys, & all & singular other commodities, jurisdictions, royalties, privileges, franchises, prehiminences, and hereditaments whatsoever, within the said tract, bounds, lands, and island aforesaid, or to them, or any of them belonging. To have and to hold the same unto the said Governour & Company, their successors, and assigns for ever, upon trust, and for the use, and benefit of themselves, and their associates, freemen of the said colony, their heirs, and assigns, to be holden of us, our heirs, and successors, as of our mannor of East-Greenwich, in free, and common socage, and not in capita, nor by knights service, yielding, and paying therefore to us, our heirs, and successors, only the fifth part of all the oar of gold, and silver, which from time to time, and at all times hereafter, shall be there gotten, had, or obtained, in lieu of all services, duties, and demands whatsoever, to be to us, our heirs, or successors therefore, or there out rendered, made, or paid. . . .[1407]

§ 10.02(c)(4). Connecticut Laws of 1673.

After Connecticut obtained its charter, it replaced the 1650 code by a new, printed compilation in 1673. Provisions of the 1673 Connecticut code relating to land are quoted or summarized as follows:

> . . . No mans Goods or Estate shall be taken from him, nor any wayes undamaged under colour of Law, or countenance of Authority, unless it be by the vertue or equity of some express Law of this Colony warranting the same, established by the General Court, and sufficiently published; or in case of the defects of a Law in any particular case by some clear and plain Rule of the word of God, in which the whole Court shall concorde.

[1407] John D. Cushing, ed., *The Earliest Laws of the New Haven and Connecticut Colonies, 1639-1673* 65-70 (1977).

Ability

Age

Bounds of Towns and particular Lands

Cattle, Corn-fields

Caveats Entred

Common-Fields and Fences

Commons to be cleared

Conveyance fraudulent

Distresse

Dowries

Escheats

Farms [militia manpower requirements for farms remote from towns]

Fences

Forgery

Gates, Bars, and Fences

High-Wayes

Home Lotts: Whereas there hath been a great abuse in several Towns, and Plantations in this Colony, of buying and purchasing Home lots, and laying them together, by means whereof great depopulation may follow, for the prevention whereof: It is Ordered by the Authority of this Court; That all dwelling or mansion houses, that are or shall be allowed in any Plantation or Town within this Jurisdiction, shall be upheld, repaired and maintained sufficiently in a comely way, as also, whosoever shall possess and enjoy any Home-lots within any such Plantation or Town that is not yet built upon, he shall within twelve months after the publication hereof, erect and build a house there fit for an Inhabitant to dwell in, if his Lot be one Acre and half, unless the Court upon knowledge of the case, find cause to abate or give longer time for building, upon the penalty of twenty shillings per year, for every breach of this order, to be paid to the Town Treasury.

Houses and Lands to be tendered to the Town before sold

Houses and Lands to be Secured for Heirs.

Housing to be kept in repair for Legatees.

Lands the tenour [tenure] of our Lands: It is Ordered by the Authority of this Court; that whatsoever Lands have or shall be granted by the Court to the respective Townships, or to any particular persons either by the Court or particular Town ships, shall be held to them, their Heirs, Successors and Assignes for ever, according to the most free Tenour of East Green-wich in the County of Kent in the Realm of England, according to our Charter Grant.

Lands not to be purchased by particular persons of the Indians

Mines and Minerals

Possession [confirming titles based on long possession]

Rates [of property taxation]

Records

Timber

Town-ships

Trespass

Trespasses

§ 10.02(d). Land Distribution and Management in Connecticut.

The methods for distributing and managing land were similar throughout New England: the settlers acted jointly to locate lots for houses, lay out streets in the villages, subdivide the arable land, and manage the common lands and forests.[1408]

The huge role of the towns in land distribution and management produced a land system among New England settlers that differed

---

[1408] "The form of group settlement which we have seen developing in Plymouth was reproduced throughout New England and wherever New Englanders settled. The joint action of the settlers in locating dwellings and home lots, in laying out village streets, in subdividing the adjacent arable land, in subjecting the meadow and forest for a time to common management, resulted in the founding of the town of Plymouth. The agrarian policy of the settlers constituted the most characteristic element in the town organization. . . .

That which occurred at Plymouth happened also at Salem, in each of the settlements about Massachusetts bay, in the towns of Plymouth colony, as one after another they came into existence, among the settlements of northern New England, in the towns which were founded on the shores of Narragansett bay and along the course of the Connecticut river. . . .

. . . The town has been likened to the manor, and the analogy to an extent is justified. . . . The manor, especially in its later and customary form, was a democratic group with a monarchical head. The New England town was a democratic group without a monarchical head." 1 Herbert L. Osgood, *The American Colonies in the Seventeenth Century* 424-426 (1904).

fundamentally from the land systems in the private proprietary colonies. The New England colonies did not distribute their lands for profit, but rather to meet needs.[1409]

Because the founding of towns and allotment of land was usually a group process at the beginning, the transformation of landholding to individual interests was evolutionary. However gradual, the result of the process was to produce a system of individual ownership in place of the original joint ownership and management.[1410]

[1409] "The Puritan colonies as such did not seek to profit from their land, but granted it freely to actual settlers and in such amounts as suited their immediate and prospective needs. No distinct land office was established by any New England colony. Land was not sold by the colony; neither, except in the case of certain islands and very rarely of some other tract, was it leased. Rent formed no appreciable part of the colony revenue . . . . By far the greater part of the land in the New England colonies was granted to towns, that is, to groups or communities of settlers by whom it was allotted to individuals. The grants to towns were made in large tracts, six miles square or more, the grant often being described in the most general terms, without even a specification of its bounds. . . .

. . . From the existing hive swarms might be sent off in any direction, and might establish a new hive at any point. . . . It is clear that circumstances of climate and soil were more favorable to the extension of settlement in the northern than in the southern colonies. But the process of settlement itself was more effective and vital in New England than was that which obtained under the proprietary regime in the south." *Id.* at 428-432.

[1410] "The settlement of a town normally began with the laying out of the village plot and the assignment of home lots. . . . The idea of a home lot was a plot of ground for a dwelling-house and outbuildings, for a dooryard and garden, and usually also an enclosure for feeding cattle and raising corn. . . . At Hartford some contained two acres and others only half an acre each. . . .

The assignment of the first home lots was accompanied or immediately followed by the earliest allotments of arable land and meadow. This process steadily progressed with the increase of population in the towns and with the clearing of forests. By means of it the settlers secured planting land, and the process advanced through various stages until the available land of the towns was approximately or entirely occupied. When the process was completed the township had been entirely laid out, and settlement within it had assumed a relatively permanent form. This was accomplished in part by the granting of lots to individuals and in part by the laying out of common fields. The common fields, too, in their turn were later subdivided among their proprietors. As the result of this process a system of individual ownership gradually took the place of a system of joint ownership and management . . . . *Id.* at 438-440. More detailed descriptions for allotments of individual land parcels in Connecticut settlements are found in *Id.* at 445-447, 449-450, 453-454, 463-465.

As has been noted with respect to other New England colonies, the government only rarely imposed and collected quit rents.[1411]

§ 10.03. Development of Land Law in Maryland (from 1634).

§ 10.03(a). The Charter of 1632.

After much importuning, George Calvert, who seven years earlier had been raised to the peerage as the first Baron of Baltimore, obtained in 1632 the king's assent for a grant of the land known as Maryland. This first Lord Baltimore died on April 15, 1632, so the charter for Maryland issued on June 20, 1632, named as grantee George's son Cecilius, the second Baron of Baltimore. The Maryland grant included lands that had been earlier granted to the Virginia Company in their charter of 1609, but, according to one legal theory, unoccupied parts of Virginia became subject to re-grants when the Virginia province changed from proprietary to royal status in 1624.

The Maryland charter was distinctly feudal in tone and has been described as conferring "on the grantee probably the most extensive political privileges ever enjoyed by an English subject, since the great houses had bowed before the successive oppression of Yorkist and Tudor rule."[1412] These extensive rights applied both to powers of government and to rights of holding and granting land:

> IV . . . . We do Grant, and likewise confirm unto the said Baron of Baltimore, . . . [the lands previously described] . . . with all, and singular such, and as ample Rights, Jurisdictions, Privileges, Prerogatives, Royalties, Liberties, Immunities, and royal Rights, and temporal Franchises whatsoever, as well by Sea as by Land, within the Region

---

[1411] *See* §§ 9.03(b)(2) and 9.03(b)(3), *supra*.

[1412] *Select Charters and Other Documents Illustrative of American History, 1606-1775* 53 (William MacDonald, ed., 1914).

. . . aforesaid, to be had, exercised, used, and enjoyed, as any Bishop of Durham, within the Bishoprick or County Palatine of Durham, in our Kingdom of England, ever heretofore hath had, held, used, or enjoyed, or of Right could, or ought to have, hold, use, or enjoy.

V. And We do by these Presents. . . Make, create and constitute Him, the now Baron of Baltimore, and his Heirs, the True and Absolute Lords and Proprietaries of the Region aforesaid, and of all other the Premises . . .; to hold of us . . . as of our Castle of Windsor, in our County of Berks, in free and common Soccage, by Fealty only for all Services, and not in capita, nor by Knight's Service, Yielding therefore unto Us . . . two Indian arrows of those Parts, to be delivered at the said Castle of Windsor, every Year. . .: And also the fifth Part of all Gold and Silver Ore, which shall happen from Time to Time, to be found within the aforesaid limits . . . .

VII . . . . We . . . do grant unto the said now Baron, . . . and to his Heirs, for the good and happy Government of the said province, free, full, and absolute Power, by the tenor of these Presents, to Ordain, Make, and Enact Laws, of what kind soever, according to their sound Discretions, whether relating to the Public State of the said Province, or the private Utility of Individuals, of and with the Advice, Assent, and Approbation of the Free-Men of the same Province. . . . So Nevertheless, that the Laws aforesaid be consonant to Reason and be not repugnant or contrary, but (so far as conveniently may be) agreeable to the Laws, Statutes, Customs and Rights of this Our Kingdom of England . . . .

XVIII. . . . We . . . do give . . . unto the aforesaid now Baron of Baltimore, his Heirs and Assigns, full and absolute Licence, Power, and Authority . . . [to] assign, alien, grant, demise, or enfeoff so many, such, and

> proportionate Parts and Parcels of the Premises, to any Person or Persons willing to purchase the same, as they shall think convenient, to have and to hold . . . in Fee-Simple, or Fee-tail, or for Term of Life, Lives, or Years; to hold of the aforesaid now Baron of Baltimore, his Heirs and Assigns, by . . . such . . . Services, Customs and Rents of this kind, as to the same now Baron of Baltimore, his Heirs and Assigns, shall seem fit and agreeable, and not immediately of Us . . . .

The charter thus not only secured feudal rights and jurisdictions to the proprietors, but also guaranteed to the settlers the rights of Englishmen.[1413]

The feudalistic powers of Lord Baltimore were far-ranging indeed, and their significance was long felt in Maryland. "As Lord Proprietor, Baltimore answered only to the king for his government of Maryland; while the settlers were to enjoy the rights of Englishmen, Calvert owned all the territory within the boundaries of this grant, expected to receive traditional rents, taxes, and fees, appointed all officials necessary to enforce the law, and exercised final political and judicial authority in his domain."[1414]

§ 10.03(b). The Proprietor's "Conditions of Plantation."

As the actual process of land distribution was about to begin, Lord Baltimore issued "conditions of plantation" describing the terms on which land would be granted to colonists. Such statements were issued in 1633, 1636, 1642 and 1648.[1415] The earliest of these, issued even before the settlers left England, became a contract between the individual colonists

---

[1413] "The Settlement, in The Old Line State," in *A History of Maryland* 4 (Morris L. Radoff, ed., 1971).

[1414] Robert J. Brugger, *Maryland, A Middle Temperament, 1634-1980* 12 (1988).

[1415] According to one authority, new statements of conditions of plantation, superseding all previous statements of conditions, were issued in 1641, 1648, 1649, and 1658. Newton D. Mereness, *Maryland as a Proprietary Province* 50 (1901).

and the proprietor, requiring each free planter to pay the cost of outfit and transportation. New versions of the conditions were issued, changing or revoking the previous conditions, and ultimately they provided for establishment of manors.[1416]

§ 10.03(c). Later Land Distribution.

This method of land distribution, an example of the headright system intended to encourage colonists, was abolished in 1683, and thereafter land was obtained only by purchase or other conveyance from someone who already held land. A settler who obtained land under the headright system received a warrant which authorized the services of a surveyor to lay out the specified acreage wherever vacant land was available. When the certificate of the surveyor was returned, showing the boundaries of the parcel, a patent issued under the provincial seal conveyed title, subject to a usually modest quit rent.[1417] Because lands were selected according to the subjective choice of individual settlers, who sought the most fertile lands, a haphazard pattern of settlement resulted.[1418]

[1416] "[The earliest contracts provided] that each free planter should pay the cost of his outfit and transportation, which amounted to about £20. To every married man who thus provided for the voyage, and for that of his family, the proprietor promised one hundred acres of land for himself, and one hundred for his wife, if she accompanied him; one hundred acres also for each adult servant, and fifty for each child under sixteen years of age. Two thousand acres of land should also be given to each adventurer who, in the year 1633, should take into the province, for the purpose of settlement, five men between the ages of sixteen and fifty. . . . By each new issue [of conditions of plantation] former conditions were amended or revoked. . . . The conditions of 1648 were especially elaborate, and provided at length for the erection of manors, the reserve of one-sixth of each manor as demesne, and the grant of the remainder by the lord to tenants under such terms as should not infringe on the jurisdiction of the proprietor or prevent his collecting the rents reserved in the original patents. These privileges were to obtain in every grant of two thousand acres, though under earlier conditions grants of one thousand acres might carry with them manorial rights." 2 Herbert L. Osgood, *The American Colonies in the Seventeenth Century* 20-21 (1904). The text of a possible version of "conditions" from 1636 is published in 2 John Leeds Bozman, *The History of Maryland* 35-38 (1837).

[1417] Quit rents in Maryland were not formally abolished until 1780.

[1418] "Lands from which grants were made according to the conditions of plantation became known as vacant land, and were left uncultivated. A considerable quantity of this remained in nearly all parts of the province down to the final overthrow of

Persons who could not afford passage or outfit could exchange those costs for service. A servant might accompany his or her master, or an aspiring colonist might enter into an obligation with the sea captain, who would sell the rights to the services upon arrival. Upon completion of the term of service, usually four or five years, the master was obligated to provide the servant with a set of clothes, a year's provision of corn, and the right to fifty acres of land.[1419]

§ 10.03(d). Creation and Administration of Manors.

In addition to such individual grants, it was possible for manorial holdings to be conveyed. "It is clear that Lord Baltimore desired to establish as a support for his palatine dominion a landholding aristocracy after the pattern of feudal England. He offered the courts leet and baron to regulate the numerous tenantry that was expected to settle as retainers of the manorial lords. Some few manors were actually laid out, and from two of these records of the feudal courts have survived as an indication that the manorial system was tried in colonial Maryland."[1420]

Indeed, after 1670, possession of a 50-acre freehold (or a tangible estate of £40) was added to "free" personal status as a qualification for voting, so colonists had even more incentive to avoid the manorial tenancies. Ultimately, only a few manors with feudal institutions of courts leet and baron succeeded in functioning for even a few years.[1421]

---

the proprietary government. But it had been the practice to locate under land warrants by selecting the most rich and fertile land without regard to the regularity of its area or making it in any way coincide with the boundary of land previously granted. Therefore, especially in the older counties, the most of what came to be left of this vacant land was not only the poorest in quality, but it lay in such small irregular parcels as to be of but little value." Newton D. Mereness, *Maryland as a Proprietary Province* 54-55 (1901).

[1419] Robert J. Brugger, *Maryland, A Middle Temperament, 1634-1980* 16 (1988).

[1420] "Aubrey C. Land, "The Colonial Period," in *The Old Line State, A History of Maryland* 14 (Morris L. Radoff, ed., 1971).

[1421] *Id.* at 17.

While some aristocratic landowners with very large holdings appeared in early colonial Maryland, it is clear that the majority of land was held by small freeholders. By 1676 about 60 manors had been established in Maryland, averaging about 3,000 acres each,[1422] but only on a few of those manors were the feudalistic proprietary rights exercised, so most "manors" were, in reality, simply very large freeholds. Of the ordinary freeholds granted before 1663, 60 were of 1,000 acres or more, 241 of between 500 and 1,000 acres, 778 of between 200 and 400 acres, and 389 grants were of less than 200 acres each.

While the Maryland manors did not achieve the importance in the colony the proprietors had hoped for, they represented the most intriguing and anomalous throwback to English feudalism to be practiced in the American colonies. An earlier historian has given the following summary of the manorial practices in early Maryland:

> A manor differed from a mere freehold in that it was given a name, and in that the grantee was allowed to hold court-baron and court-leet, and have all fines and profits belonging thereto. Further, the early grants of manor gave the grantee the advowsons of churches and unrestricted privileges of hunting for any game. The court-baron was given jurisdiction over civil cases in which the damages did not exceed a fine of forty shillings, while the court-leet took cognizance of criminal offenses committed within the precincts of the manor. To what extent such courts were held, there remains no evidence except the records of a court-baron held on St. Gabriel's Manor in the year 1656, and the records of a few sessions of both court-baron and court-leet held on St. Clement's Manor between the years 1659-72. The records of the latter manor show that it had its steward, constable, and bailiff, and that a jury of twelve men, after hearing the charges or complaints, made its presentments, often fixing the fines, and occasionally referring the matter to the governor of the province. If the

---

[1422] Newton D. Mereness, *Maryland as a Proprietary Province* 52 (1901).

fine imposed by the jury was thought to be too excessive, it might be revised by affeerors sworn for that purpose.

Only in the grants of the first three manors was any portion of the land set apart as demesne land, that is, land which was not to be granted out in tenancy nor in any way severed or aliened from the said manor. The grant of a manor, like that of a freehold, subjected the grantee to the payment to the proprietor of the annual rent, and the fine for every alienation.

In 1665 the proprietor issued instructions directing that in every county at least two manors, containing not less than six thousand acres each, be surveyed and set apart for his private use. Each of these proprietary manors was placed in charge of a steward, who leased it in parcels to tenants usually for three lives, or for a long term of years, at a rent seldom exceeding ten shillings per hundred acres. Owing to failure to preserve the bounds of them, these manors much dwindled in size or, in some cases, entirely vanished; while such portions of them as were preserved suffered from shameful neglect by poorly paid and incompetent stewards. As a consequence, the bounds between tenements could not be found, leases were lost, and the rents not paid.

In addition to the proprietary manors, the proprietor made several other reserves for the purpose of confining surveys and settlements to those parts of the province in which it was desired that they should be made, or because of the appearance of copper or other ore, the extraordinary fertility of the soil, or the contiguity to towns. Although portions of such reserves were leased, yet none of them were surveyed, laid out, and named as the manors were.

In 1766 the proprietor appointed a commission to sell his manors and reserves; and although the sale of them was

> somewhat slow, yet nearly fifty thousand acres were sold in seven years, and this meant that the proprietary lands corresponding to those of the lord's demesne in the medieval fief were to disappear.[1423]

In at least one respect, landholding according to fundamental precepts of English law had a substantial impact, and that was in the matter of escheat. Because all land was held by the tenure of free and common socage, it was subject to escheat, which under the broad interpretation adhered to by the proprietor could occur in several ways. The most common circumstances for escheat were nonpayment of the quit rent or death of the landholder with no surviving heirs . In the early years of the province, a person who suspected land was subject to escheat could petition for a legal action, always with a jury, to make that determination. If the jury decided that the land was escheated, the successful petitioner could apply for a resurvey and eventually obtain the land.

By the early 18th century, the feudalistic proprietary claims had all been fatally weakened.[1424]

§ 10.03(e). Restriction of Church Rights in Land.

The strong representation of Catholics among Maryland's settlers led to another unique element of Maryland land law. The presence and activity of Catholic priests, especially Jesuits, created situations in which it was possible to obtain grants of land rights from Indians and other sources for the Roman church. But a proclamation from the proprietor in 1648 forbade any person from alienating lands to a church or other society for uses forbidden by the statutes of mortmain, without permission from the

---

[1423] *Id.* at 53-54.

[1424] "The proprietor was unable, after 1738, to enforce his claim to surplus land, while his benefit from the disputed right to escheated land was doubtful. The attempt to erect manors for the largest tenants, and thereby to create a nobility on which he might rely for support, was given up before the close of the seventeenth century. Everything was, therefore, nearly levelled to the simple freehold from which the proprietor continued to receive his rents and some alienation fines." *Id. at 58.*

proprietor. The mortmain statutes of England generally operated against conveyances to charitable organizations, which were deemed uneconomic uses of the land. "In no other British-American colony was such a precaution necessary, but it kept the land law of Maryland in harmony with that of the mother country and of the other colonies."[1425]

§ 10.03(f). Local Legislative Regulation of Provincial Land Law.

§ 10.03(f)(1). Achievement of Legislative Initiative.

The activities of Maryland's legislative body, or Assembly, also played a role in shaping early land law. At the outset of this colony's history, the proprietor assumed, with the support of the charter, that all legislation would be initiated by the proprietor and that the representative assembly's function was simply to confirm or deny the propositions. This was stoutly resisted by the legislators, however, and in 1638, after four years and two sessions of the Assembly, the Lord Proprietor conceded that the colonists themselves could initiate legislation.

This concession resulted partly from the Assembly's refusal to approve several propositions that would have vastly strengthened the feudal and medieval character of the province, such as maintaining trained soldiers at the ready on each manor.[1426]

[1425] 2 Herbert L. Osgood, *The American Colonies in the Seventeenth Century* 33 (1904).

[1426] "Had the freemen acknowledged that right [of the Proprietor alone to initiate legislation] to be vested solely in him, it is highly probable that the sale of manors would have been forbidden by law. It is equally probable that the laws of the province would have required that on every manor there should be at least twenty freemen, that fifteen of them should be trained as soldiers and kept ready for the service of the country, and that the lord of the manor should maintain them in time of such service. But instead of succeeding in thus providing the land system with the military features of a fief, the bills containing those requirements failed to become laws, and in August, 1638, the lord proprietor conceded to the Assembly the right of initiating legislation." *Id.* at 96-97.

§ 10.03(f)(2). Reception of English Law.

This early legislative deadlock left in doubt just how fully the law of England applied in the colony. In the opinion of one scholar, "The common law of England seems here rather to be looked upon as a system useful for illustration and guidance than a subsidiary law; equity and good conscience was considered to afford proper rules to fill the omissions of the positive law."[1427]

Accordingly, in 1662 the Assembly enacted a provision declaring that in the absence of provincial law, justice would be sought according to the laws and statutes of England and "that all courts shall judge of the right pleading and the inconsistency of the said laws with the good of the province according to the best of their judgment."[1428] Though in force for only a short time, this Maryland provision has been described as "the first definite recognition in America of the power of the courts to apply the common law of England to colonial conditions, and to reject provisions deemed unsuitable."[1429] Still unsettled for many decades thereafter was the extent to which English statutes were considered adopted in the colony. Not until an enactment in 1732 was the controversy neutralized by the equivocal provisions that the colony could call upon "the laws and statutes and reasonable customs of England, as used and practiced within the province."[1430]

§ 10.03(f)(3). Compilation of Legislative Enactments.

The earliest Maryland legislation was not printed, but kept in

---

[1427] Paul Samuel Reinsch, "The English Common Law in the Early American Colonies, in Association of American Law Schools," in *Select Essays in Anglo-American Legal History* 401 (1907).

[1428] *Id.*

[1429] *Id.* at 402.

[1430] *Id.* at 402-403.

manuscript form and circulated as needed. Even when Maryland became a royal province in 1692, shortly after the accession of William and Mary, no printed version of the laws appeared until 1700. A second compilation was issued in 1707 and a third in 1718, in the midst of the controversy over how extensively English statutes were received into the colony's jurisprudence. The topics relating to land law found in the 1718 compilation are summarized below, illustrating the extent to which the Assembly had attempted to regulate landholding, even though landholding was fundamentally based on English common law:

> Changing communities designated as towns into ports and towns
> Marking highways and making waterways passable
> Confirming titles of land given to churches
> Conferring right of action of trespass on those with lands lying within Indian land
> Ascertaining boundaries of Indian land
> Preserving harbors and landing places
> Empowering justices to regulate parish boundaries
> Ascertaining the height of fences
> Quieting possessions, enrolling conveyances and securing the estates of purchasers
> Securing persons' rights to own lands
> For better administration of justice in testamentary affairs, granting administrations, recovery of legacies, securing filial portions, and distribution of intestates' estates
> Encouraging settlements by ascertaining the manner of paying alienation fines and quit-rents
> Ascertaining land boundaries[1431]

[1431] According to Osgood, "fines on alienation were actually enforced only in Maryland." In the conditions of plantation issued in 1658, the alienation fine was set at the equivalent of one year's rent, due within one month after sale. 2 Herbert L. Osgood, *The American Colonies in the Seventeenth Century* 34 (1904).

§ 10.03(g). Land Management in Colonial Maryland.

Maryland's character as a proprietary colony shaped the management of land in Maryland. During the colony's early years, the governor and council and secretary took charge of issuing patents for lands claimed by headrights, and collecting rents and other land-based income. Sheriffs, as agents of the colonial government, did the work of collecting the rents. In 1680 the government organized a land office, and in 1684 the proprietor commissioned a land council consisting of four members from the council of state to take over most ministerial duties relating to land. "Thus the business of granting land, collecting revenue therefrom, and keeping the land records was organized under one distinct office, which continued in existence until 1689, and after a suspension of five years was reopened and remained in activity, with certain administrative changes, as long as Maryland was a province."[1432]

Land arrangements were also effected from time to time with various Indian tribes, but eventually, the encroaching white settlement rendered most of these agreements unworkable. A treaty typically terminated in obsolescence by the colony throwing open Indian lands for white settlement and inviting Indians to submit claims of wrongs[1433] to certain designated colonial officials. Weaker tribes sought the protection of the colonists against more aggressive tribes and were given lands as a permanent refuge, within which white settlement would be prohibited. Such was the arrangement extended to the Pascataway Indians in 1668.

§ 10.04. Development of Land Law in Rhode Island (from 1636).

Unlike the other New England colonies of Plymouth, Massachusetts, and Connecticut, the colony of Rhode Island did not originate as a

---

[1432] 2 Herbert L. Osgood, *The American Colonies in the Seventeenth Century* 44 (1904).

[1433] A typical trespass might be caused by livestock of white settlers breaking through fences and trampling Indians' cornfields.

conscious project of settlement. The colony's genesis lay in the settlements at Providence, Portsmouth and Newport founded independently of one another and of any of the other colonies between 1636 and 1639. Later, the town of Warwick joined with the other three. In 1647, acting with the authority of a charter obtained from the revolutionary English government, they combined into a colony. Before that time, Rhode Island had been independent of any superior government authority or authorization and, "[more] than an other American colony, the settlement of Rhode Island was the result of unforeseen conditions, for which immediate provision had to be made."[1434]

§ 10.04(a). The Settlement at Providence.

Roger Williams, a refugee from Massachusetts Bay Colony, with a few companions, settled the area that is now Providence and, as was his practice, procured a "deed" to the land from local Indian chiefs. The grant extended from the Pawtuxet River on the west to the Pawtucket River on the east, although the inland extent of the grant was left indefinite.

Whether Williams actually obtained a document of gift at the time of first settlement is not known; however, about two years later a "memorandum" describing the grant was signed by the two chiefs,

---

[1434] "More than any other American colony, the settlement of Rhode Island was the result of unforeseen conditions, for which immediate provision had to be made. No man was its founder; that appellation belongs to no single group of men. It was settled by bands of fugitives, who came from different quarters and at different times. Their movement was not the result of concerted action, though they removed thither to escape oppression in the strictly Puritan colonies or conditions there which to them had become intolerable. With the exception of the few who came from Salem, none were disciples of Roger Williams, nor did they go into exile in order to testify to the truth of his beliefs, or to their loyalty to him as a man. And yet common opposition to Massachusetts and the policy of which it was the leading representative, brought them into practical harmony with him. As time passed and the dangers which continued to surround them became evident, this was generalized into a principle, that of the exclusively secular community. It was declared first among the orders of Providence, later among those of the plantations on Aquedneck and in the legislation of the colony. But this action was occasioned by the relations that existed between the inhabitants of all those settlements and by the struggle in which they were all engaged, rather than by the personality or direct influence of Roger Williams." 1 Herbert L. Osgood, *The American Colonies in the Seventeenth Century* 334 (1904).

Miantunnomi and Cannonnicus. The memorandum described the terms of the original deed and, in a separate paragraph, extended the grant to the "grass and meadows" along the Pawtuxet River, which was well beyond the original grant. Thus, the settlers were given the right to graze their livestock as far up the river as they wished:

> Memorandum, that we Cannaunicus and Miantonomi, the two chief sachems of Nanhiggansick, having two yeares since sold unto Roger Williams, ye lands and meadows upon the two fresh rivers, called Mooshausick and Wanasqutucket, doe now by these presents, establish and confirme ye bounds of those lands, from ye river and fields at Pautuckqut, ye great hill of Notquonckanet, on ye northwest, and the two of Maushapogue on ye west.
>
> As also, in consideration of the many kindnesses and services he hath continually done for us, both with our friends at Massachusetts, as also at Quinickicutt and Apaum or Plymouth, we doe freely give unto him all that land from those rivers reaching to Pawtuxet river; as also the grass and meadows upon ye said Pawtuxet river.[1435]

Although this "deed" has been characterized as Williams' attempt "to extinguish the claims of the Indians to the land of the plantation,"[1436] in fact the Indians, about 5,000 Narragansetts and about 1,500 Wampanoags, continued to roam in the granted area as before. The more limited grant of grazing and water privileges along the full extent of the named streams was "understood by Williams to concede to the English by 'courtesy,' joint use of the lands with the Indians."[1437]

Williams and those who accompanied him began holding town

[1435] 1 *Records of the Colony of Rhode Island and Providence Plantations* 18 (John Russell Bartlett, ed., 1856).

[1436] Herbert L. Osgood, *The American Colonies in the Seventeenth Century* 335 (1904).

[1437] *Id.* at 236.

meetings in 1636, under a form a government that was memorialized the next year in a written covenant:

> We whose names are hereunder, desirous to inhabit in the town of Providence, do promise to subject ourselves in active and passive obedience to all such orders or agreements as shall be made for public good of the body in an orderly way, by the major consent of the present inhabitants, masters of families incorporated together in a Towne fellowship, and others whom they shall admit unto them only in civil things.[1438]

With this form of government in place and theoretically able to promulgate all laws thought necessary by the settlers, including those related to landholding, these first Providence folk then determined the qualifications for one to become an inhabitant of the town. As stated later by Roger Williams:

> it was agreed between us, that every person that should be admitted into the fellowship of injoying landes and disposing of the purchase, should pay thirtye shillinges into the public stock; and ffirst about thirtye poundes should be paid unto myselfe by thirty shillings a person, as they were admitted.[1439]

Thereafter, Williams apparently obtained his thirty pounds, so in 1638 he made out a deed to himself and twelve associates. A memorandum of the deed recited:

> Memorandum, that I Roger Williams having formerly purchased of Conanicus and Miantonomi, this our situation or Plantation of New Providence, . . . in consideration of thirty pounds, received from the

---

[1438] 1 *Records of the Colony of Rhode Island and Providence Plantations* 14 (John Russell Bartlett, ed., 1856).

[1439] *Id.* at 23.

> inhabitants of the said place, do freely and fully pass grant and make over equal right and power of enjoying and disposing the same ground and lands unto my loving friends and neighbors . . . and such others as the major part of us shall admit unto the same fellowship with of vote us.[1440]

"The effect of the document was to transfer the land to the thirteen of whom Williams was one as an association or quasi-corporation, to be held temporarily in trust by them for the rising town."[1441] Also in 1638, Williams and the others entered into an agreement dividing up certain meadowlands:

> . . . all the meadow ground at Pawtuxet, bounding upon the fresh river upon both sides, is to be impropriated unto these thirteen persons, . . . and to be equally divided among them, and every man to pay an equal proportion to raise up the sum of twenty pounds for the same, and if it shall come to pass, that some or any of these thirteen persons abovesaid do not pay or give satisfaction . . . that they or he, shall leave their or his proportion of meadow ground unto the rest of those thirteen persons.[1442]

Even before these documents were executed, apparently the town government had exercised the power of distributing land to the inhabitants. Minutes of a town meeting held on June 10, 1637, record that "portions of grass and meadow . . . were confirmed [to several named persons] as their proper right and inheritance to them and theirs . . . ."[1443]

[1440] *Id.* at 19-20.

[1441] Herbert L. Osgood, *The American Colonies in the Seventeenth Century* 338 (1904).

[1442] 1 *Records of the Colony of Rhode Island and Providence Plantations* 20-21 (John Russell Bartlett, ed., 1856).

[1443] *Id.* at 17.

After the agreement and declaration of 1638, differences between Williams and some of the other twelve began to develop. Apparently Williams conceived of an ever expanding democratic community, with inhabitants admitted to town membership and granted land ownership on an equal footing with the original thirteen. Some of the other twelve, however, were striving to establish a narrow, exclusive town proprietorship, with themselves and their designated successors as the perpetual proprietors. For a time, this group succeeded in conducting the affairs of Providence according to their proprietary notions. "They consolidated the board of proprietors, controlled the town meeting, and through that the granting of land and the admission of freemen."[1444]

Despite this control, controversies over land increased. In 1640, a "board of five arbitrators or 'disposers' was chosen by the town meeting, not only to settle disputes, but to dispose of town lands, fix their bounds, and act as an executive board for the town."[1445] A major controversy developed around one Samuel Gorton, who twice tried unsuccessfully to be admitted to town privileges, and who then joined other disaffected persons who also had not been admitted to the town or given access to the common land. They were aware that Providence had no proper authority from England to conduct itself as a colony. The tumult caused by these dissidents was such that some of the proprietors appealed to neighboring Massachusetts for protection. The immediate problem dissolved when Gorton moved, but the need for a colony charter was made clear.

§ 10.04(b). The Settlement at Portsmouth.

Other refugees banished from Massachusetts because of religious nonconformance settled the island of Aquedneck. Through Roger Williams' assistance, they obtained a deed to the land from the Indian chiefs Cannonicus and Miantunnomu, the same two who had made the

---

[1444] Herbert L. Osgood, *The American Colonies in the Seventeenth Century* 339 (1904).

[1445] *Id.* at 340. Osgood further noted, "This cumbersome machinery furnished a weak substitute for government in a plantation of squatters, that was rent by internal strife and was adjacent to two colonies which were ready to absorb it." *Id.*

Providence grant, and the chiefs also secured the removal of twenty Narragensett Indians from the island in preparation for the immigration of the English settlers. The deed recited

> That we Cannonnicus and Miantunnomu . . . have sold unto Mr. Coddington and his friends . . . the great Island of Acquednecke . . .; allso the grasse upon the rivers . . . for the full payment of forty fathom of white beads. . . .
>
> That by giveinge by Miantunnomus' ten coates and twenty howes to the present inhabitants, they shall remove themselves from off the Island before next winter. . . .[1446]

Even before obtaining the deed, eighteen of the prospective original proprietors of this settlement and one other person met at Providence in March 1638, and entered into a plantation covenant. The covenant stated nothing specific about land, but it declared that the covenantors "incorporate ourselves into a Bodie Politick and . . . submit our persons . . . to all those perfect and most absolute laws of [Jesus Christ] given us in his holy word of truth, to be guided and judged thereby."[1447] Coddington was chosen as judge, and he covenanted "to do justice and Judgment impartially according to the lawes of God, and to maintaine the Fundamentall Rights and Privileges of this Bodie Poliltick . . . ."[1448] The town assembly also was an incipient colony, with those at the town meetings "passing orders like that at Providence or elsewhere, about the laying out and sale of lots, care of the unimproved land, locating the meeting-house, repairing highways, building a mill, local police, and other similar affairs. It controlled its own membership under an order reserving to "the body the right to receive inhabitants or freemen."[1449] According to

---

[1446] 1 *Records of the Colony of Rhode Island and Providence Plantations* 45-46 (John Russell Bartlett, ed., 1856).

[1447] *Id.* at 52.

[1448] *Id.* at 53.

[1449] Herbert L. Osgood, *The American Colonies in the Seventeenth Century* 342 (1904).

minutes of a general meeting on May 13, 1638, persons were to be admitted as "inhabitants or Freemen, to build or plant upon the Island" upon the consent of the proprietors and agreeing to submit to the island's government.[1450]

The land distribution and landholding practices in Portsmouth differed markedly from those at Providence. Most importantly, the Portsmouth grants were apportioned according to the wealth and social rank of the settlers.[1451] Whether because of or in spite of these land distribution patterns, the island settlement of Portsmouth prospered and grew faster than Providence.[1452]

When several of the leading men of Portsmouth moved to a better site, now known as Newport, the remaining members adopted a new covenant on April 30, 1639. A striking change from the first covenant is that the signers departed from their earlier position of recognizing no earthly superior governing authority. They agreed that they "[doe acknowledge] ourselves the legall subjects of [his Majestie] King Charles, and in his name [doe hereby binde] ourselves into a civill body politicke, unto his

---

1450 1 *Records of the Colony of Rhode Island and Providence Plantations* 53 (John Russell Bartlett, ed., 1856).

1451 "Unlike Williams's group, who tried to give equal plots of land to all respectable settlers, Coddington's government allocated land in proportion to the wealth and social rank of each settler. "Gentlemen" received larger grants than millers or coopers; and they, in turn, had larger shares than common laborers. Moreover, land was given sparingly to newcomers, at first; hence, only a minority of the inhabitants were entitled to vote." William C. McLoughlin, *Rhode Island, A Bicentennial History* 21 (1978).

1452 "The community at Portsmouth took shape . . . as an agricultural one, with a common field or pasture at the north end of the island just beyond the cluster of houses. Allocation of land, and soon the placement of dwellings, spread around the coast, drawn by the need for water transportation. Apart from lingering preference for living in a compact village, only the ferry to the mainland and the original common field preserved a geographical focal point. The community at Portsmouth took shape . . . as an agricultural one, with a common field or pasture at the north end of the island just beyond the cluster of houses. Allocation of land, and soon the placement of dwellings, spread around the coast, drawn by the need for water transportation. Apart from lingering preference for living in a compact village, only the ferry to the mainland and the original common field preserved a geographical focal point." Sydney V. James, *Colonial Rhode Island, A History* 26 (1975).

lawes according to matters of justice."[1453] They designated seven men to "lay out lands as they shall be disposed."[1454]

§ 10.04(c). The Settlement at Newport.

As noted above, only four months after settling at Portsmouth, Coddington and others removed to a better harbor at the southwest end of the island, the site of the present-day Newport. Ten men, exhibiting a definite aristocratic spirit, including Coddington as judge, entered into a compact, dated April 28, 1639:

> [We] doe engage ourselves to bear equall charges, answerable to our strength and estates in common; and that our determinations shall be by major voice of judge and elders; the Judge to have a double voice.[1455]

In Newport, land distribution patterns followed closely those of Portsmouth:

> [T]he apportionment of land provided many farms of middling size and gave the leading men enormous estates which they generally put in the hands of tenants for development . . . . The new town from the start had its center around the brook running into the harbor, with buildings slowly extending south by the water's edge and northeast inland. The first settlers gave themselves allotments of various sizes, but each man's grant ordinarily included a house lot by the harbor, a meadow lot, and a much larger tract of arable land.[1456]

[1453] Herbert L. Osgood, *The American Colonies in the Seventeenth Century* 70 (1904).

[1454] *Id.* at 71.

[1455] 1 *Records of the Colony of Rhode Island and Providence Plantations* 87 (John Russell Bartlett, ed., 1856).

[1456] Sydney V. James, *Colonial Rhode Island, A History* 27-28 (1875).

§ 10.04(d). Newport and Portsmouth United.

The Newport colonists in 1640 acknowledged King Charles as their sovereign and made overtures of union toward Portsmouth. The union was amicably achieved; five men were chosen for laying out Portsmouth lands, and three men were selected for laying out Newport lands.[1457] Further, as to land distribution:

> It is ordered, that Libertie is granted for the Major parte of the Freemen of each Towne to select certaine men from among themselves to proportion forth to each man his propriety of Land, and then having it layd forth orderly, it shall be recorded at the General Court.[1458]

A general court, or assembly, held at Newport on May 6, 1640, gave further instructions for land management:

> It is ordered, that all such who shall have a Howse lott granted unto them within any of our Townes, shall build a Howse thereon within a yeare after the Grant thereof, or else it shall be forfeited to the Towns use. Repealed . . . .
>
> It is ordered, that Commission be directed to the Treasurers to make demands of all such monies as are due to the Treasury for the Lands assigned forth to particular men, and to make returns of all such who shall be therein remiss, at the next particular Courte who are to be ordered thereby according to Law . . . .[1459]

Another general court of March 16-19, 1641, attempted once again to identify and confirm the source of governmental authority:

[1457] 1 *Records of the Colony of Rhode Island and Providence Plantations* 100-102 (John Russell Bartlett, ed., 1856).

[1458] *Id.* at 102.

[1459] *Id.* at 103.

> It is ordered and unanimously agreed upon, that the Government which this Bodie Politick doth attend unto in this Island, and the Jurisdiction thereof, in favour of our Prince is a Democracie, or Popular Government; that is to say, It is in the Powre of the Body of Freemen orderly assembled, or the major part of them, to make or constitute Just Lawes, by which they will be regulated, and to depute from among themselves such Ministers as shall see them faithfully executed between Man and Man.[1460]

At this same assembly, an order to establish systematic land records was also given:

> It is ordered, that each Towne shall provide a Towne Book, wherein they shall Record the Evidences of the Lands by them impropriated; and shall also have Powre to give forth a Coppie thereof, which shall be a clear evidence for them and theirs, to whom it is so granted.[1461]

A form of land tenure conferring nearly absolute ownership was declared for the two settlements:

> It is ordered, Established and Decreed, unanimouslie, that all men's Properties in their Lands of the Island, and the Jurisdiction thereof, shall be such, and soe free, that neyther the State nor any Person or Persons shall intrude into it, molest him in it, to deprive him of anything whatsoever that is, or shall be within that, or any of the bounds thereof; and this Tenure and Propriety of his therein shall be continued to him, or his; or to whomsoever he shall assign it for Ever.[1462]

[1460] *Id.* at 112.

[1461] *Id.* at 114.

[1462] *Id.* at 116.

In a general court held September 19, 1642, an order described the power of town freemen to appoint juries, affirming "that they shall have powre as well to appoint the Inhabitants, as Freemen for that service, by virtue of the Tenure and grant of their lands which is freehold . . . ."[1463] Also, the court prohibited all persons from making "any sale of his lands (in or belonging to our Jurisdiction) to any other Jurisdiction, or person therein, unless that Jurisdiction or person shall be subject to the Government here established, upon paine of forfeiture of the said lands so proferred."[1464]

At a general court held on March 13, 1644, the court acknowledged that many land transactions had occurred without being recorded, and invited persons holding such lands to come forward with documentary or testimonial evidence so that a proper recording could be made. When the transaction was thereupon recorded by the secretary, the record would be "authentick to [the landholder] or them, their Heirs, Executors or Assigns, as if the said Lands had been originally granted, and according to that Tract in all points observed."[1465]

§ 10.04(e). The Settlement at Warwick.

During this period Samuel Gorton, previously mentioned in connection with the settlement at Providence, achieved notoriety throughout the Massachusetts and Rhode Island settlements for his refusal to submit to most forms of government (except as properly authorized by England) and to most exercises of governmental authority. The misadventures of him and his associates led him to purchase from the Indians a large tract of land running twenty miles west from Narragansett Bay, south of Providence. Local Indians and other settlers objected to the colonization and sought the aid of Massachusetts in bringing it to a halt. Meanwhile, the settlers conceded that they had no authority to govern themselves but also denied that any of the other Rhode Island towns had any such authority.

[1463] *Id.* at 124.

[1464] *Id.* at 126.

[1465] *Id.* at 128.

Nevertheless, they did not combine together as a corporation or attempt to exercise any powers of government. Massachusetts then acted to claim power over the Warwick tract, arrested Gorton and others, and eventually sentenced them to hard labor and banishment from the Warwick area.

While political machinations proceeded, the settlement grew slowly, with landholding practices similar to those of its sister settlements.[1466]

§ 10.04(f). The First Charter for the Rhode Island Settlements in 1644.

All four settlements in the Rhode Island area shared the common characteristic of being utterly without a superior governing authority; they were, therefore, necessarily without any authority to formally colonize or conduct governmental activities, except such authority as they agreed to exercise among themselves. That this left the settlements vulnerable to larger, more legitimate and acquisitive neighbor colonies was punctuated in 1643, when Massachusetts, Plymouth, Connecticut and New Haven formed a federation specifically excluding the Rhode Island settlements. The federation not only belabored lack of legal title in the Rhode Island settlers, but asserted its own claims, based on conquests of and treaties and alliances with the Indians. In addition, settlers in Providence had submitted to Massachusetts' authority in an attempt to obtain assistance.

Roger Williams therefore traveled to England and obtained a patent in 1644. The timing of his arrival was fortunate, inasmuch as King Charles had fled from London in 1642, and governmental power was in the hands of the Puritans, giving Williams early access to persons with power. While the patent ostensibly applied to all the Rhode Island settlements, it was not

---

[1466] "The little town there grew slowly, requiring two or three decades to reach fifty families. The house lots at the head of the Cove made a town center. Newcomers who did not acquire a stake in the Shawomet Purchase [the original tract purchased from the Indians] lived on the west side on the edge of a large tract. Warwick Neck to the east of the Cove was for the purchasers and their successors. There they created common fields and pastures, taking advantage of the many geographical features that facilitated fencing out predators and closing in livestock, and set about providing themselves with the necessities of life." Sydney V. James, *Colonial Rhode Island, A History* 31-32 (1975).

readily accepted because the Newport and Portsmouth settlers had not requested Williams to act as their agent in obtaining a patent, and the Warwick settlers decided to seek their own patent. On behalf of this latter group, Samuel Gorton obtained a confirmation of his original purchase from the Indians in 1646, but by the time he returned to Rhode Island in 1648, delegates from all four colonies had met to establish laws for a centralized government.

The patent of 1644, obtained by Roger Williams, declared the basic authority for law and governance, and confirmed the rights to the land: The Earl of Warwick, as governor in chief of the plantations, and a majority of commissioners by the authority of Parliament:

> do . . . give, grant, and confirm, to the aforesaid Inhabitants of the Towns of Providence, Portsmouth, and Newport, a free and absolute Charter of Incorporation . . . Together with full Power and Authority to rule themselves, and such others as shall hereafter inhabit within any Part of the said Tract of land, by such a Form of Civil Government, as by voluntary consent of all, or the greater Part of them, they shall find most suitable to their Estate and Condition . . . Provided, nevertheless, that the said Laws, Constitutions, and Punishments, for the Civil Government of the said Plantations, be conformable to the Laws of England, so far as the Nature and Constitution of the place will admit.[1467]

§ 10.04(g). The Code of 1647.

The meetings with representatives from all four colonies culminated in May, 1647, with the "Code of Laws" adopted by the First General Assembly of "The Incorporation of Providence Plantations." This legislation has been described as the "first body of American law to permit

---

[1467] 1 *Records of the Colony of Rhode Island and Providence Plantations* 143-146 (John Russell Bartlett, ed.,1856).

absolute and unqualified religious freedom throughout the colony."[1468]

The provisions of the 1647 Code relating to governance of landholding are summarized as follows:

> The delegates consent to be governed by the laws of England, "together with the way of the Administration of them, soe far as the nature and constitution of this Plantation will admit . . . ."
>
> For the Province of Providence:
>
> . . . the form of Government established in Providence Plantations is Democraticall; that is to say, a Government held by ye free and voluntarie consent of all, or the greater parte of the free Inhabitants.
>
> Touching Laws [with language drawn from the Magna Carta]:
>
> That no person, in this Colonie, shall be taken or imprisoned, or be disseized of his Lands or Liberties, or be Exiled, or any other otherwise molested or destroyed, but by the Lawfull judgment of his Peeres, or by some known Law, and according to the Letter of it, Ratified and confirmed by the major part of the Generall Assembly lawfully met and orderly managed.
>
> Burning of houses is prohibited.
>
> Forcible entry and detainer are defined, described, and penalized.

[1468] *The Earliest Acts and Laws of the Colony of Rhode Island and Providence Plantations, 1647-1719* vii (John D. Cushing, ed., 1977).

Various trespasses are prohibited, and punished with double damages.

Fraudulent Dealing.

Various transactions are to be in writing.

Fraudulent, Deceitfull and Fained Deeds, Bonds and Gifts made by Debtors to avoid their Creditors . . . shall be void . . . And the parties to such fraudulent Deeds, not made in good faith and upon good consideration, shall forfeit one yeare's rent of the Lands and Tenements; the whole value of the Goods and Chattells, and so much money as shall be conteyned in the Bond, the one moytie wherof is the King's Custome, the other goes to the party grieved.

No Lands, Tenements, or other Hereditaments, shall pass, alter or change from one to another, whereby any state of inheritance or Freehold shall be made or take effect in any person or persons, or any use thereof to be made by reasons only of any bargaine and sale thereof, except the same bargaine and sale be made by writing, indented, sealed and enrolled in a Meeting of the Towne, where such Lands, or Tenements soe bargained doth lye . . . .

Forging of deeds and records is prohibited and remedies are prescribed.

Probate of wills is provided for and regulated in detail.

Provision is made for a general recorder.

In court actions, a person may plead his or her own case, may use an attorney, or may use one of the two attorneys assigned to the court.[1469]

[1469] *Id.* at 3-56.

The prescriptions of this "code" remained the basic law of the Rhode Island settlements for some decades to come, even though the colony remained entangled in political controversy for yet many years.[1470]

§ 10.04(h). The Royal Charter of 1663.

A reconfirmation of the original patent was obtained and brought back to the colony in 1652, but it was not until 1658 that the various factional interests receded and a single government exercised authority over all four settlements. With the restoration of the Stuart monarchy in England in 1660, a new peril arose, for the 1644 patent had not been issued as a royal grant. Rhode Island as a colony thus quickly professed allegiance to Charles II and acted to obtain a royal charter, which was finally issued in 1663.

The charter finally gave authoritative guarantees of fundamental rights, such as rights to travel, carry on business with other English colonies, and fish in the New England coastal waters.[1471]

In the matter of land rights, the charter offered the same specifics that applied in the other New England colonies and established fundamental law for the colony, conforming in most essentials to English law.[1472]

[1470] Sydney V. James, *Colonial Rhode Island, A History* 63 (1975).

[1471] "Unlike the first patent, the royal charter of 1663 prescribed a form of government. It differed from the constitution worked out in 1647 and 1648 primarily by enhancing the powers of magistrates. The rights to operate a government and dispose of the colony's land were given to the governor and company as a corporation that is, to the freemen . . . . Under the charter, Rhode Islanders received welcome assurances of good standing among the English Americans. They were guaranteed rights to travel and carry on business in the other English colonies, regardless of old sentences of banishment. They were given rights to fish off the New England coast. They could engage in commerce with other ports in the king's dominions. The monarch declared that the territory of Rhode Island should not be invaded by armed men from neighboring colonies without consent of local officials. . . ." *Id.* at 68-69.

[1472] "The charter also laid down a few fundamentals of law for Rhode Island. Existing statutes and practices were to continue in force until changed. As before, any new colonial legislation was required to conform to English law as nearly as

In the royal charter, the named patentees and others thereafter admitted to their number, were constituted "a Body Corporate and Politick in Fact and Name" and "They and their Successors, shall and may have Perpetual Succession . . . And also to have, Take, Possess, Acquire, and Purchase Lands, Tenaments and Hereditaments, or any Goods or Chattels; and the same to Lease, Grant, Demise, Aliene, Bargain, Sell and dispose of, at their own will and Pleasures, as other our Leige People of this Our Realm of England . . . ."[1473]

§ 10.04(i). Land-Related Legislation of the Rhode Island Assembly.

Both before and after the royal charter of 1663, the various colonial assemblies of Rhode Island met and enacted statutes related to landholding and land rights. The subjects of these provisions may be summarized as follows:

> No person to be disseised of lands except by the lawful judgment of peers or by some known law.
>
> Burning of dwellings or of barns
>
> Forcible entry and detainer
>
> Trespass
>
> Fraudulent deeds
>
> Forged records and writs

---

circumstances would permit. The terms of land ownership were to be the same as in the king's manor of East Greenwich, thus providing the colony with the most attractive variety of land tenure in English law, attractive because it was the kind with fewest medieval features. Somewhat loosely, it was said that Rhode Island land was held in "fee simple" that is, full ownership subject only to paying taxes." *Id.* at 69.

[1473] *The Earliest Acts and Laws of the Colony of Rhode Island and Providence Plantations 1647-1719* 128 (John D. Cushing, ed., 1977).

Probate of wills and granting of administrations

Laying out the township of East Greenwich

Intruders on lands

Regulating fences

Prohibiting the recorder from being an attorney

Requiring assembly consent for land purchases from Indians

Requiring a writing for certain bargains and deeds

Regulating execution proceedings and distraints on goods and chattels

Preventing inhabitants from subjecting their lands to any other government

Preventing excessive riding [speeding] on streets and highways

Establishing townships

Confirming land grants made in Newport, Providence, Portsmouth, Warwick and Westerly prior to the royal charter of 1663:

Be it therefore Enacted . . . That all the Lands Lying and being, with the Limits of each and every of the aforesaid Towns, . . . Be and hereby is Allowed of, Ratified and Confirmed, to the Proprietors of each of the aforesaid Towns . . . their Heirs and Assigns for ever . . .; and whereas there is within several of the Towns within this Colony, considerable of Lands, Lying yet Uncommon or Undivided; And for the more orderly way and manner of the several proprietors . . . and that the Exact Boundaries of each and every Mans Allotments, when Laid to him may be kept in perpetuam . . . That it shall and may be lawful for the Proprietors, to chuse and appoint a Clerk, and a Surveyor . . . as they shall judge needful and convenient, for the orderly carrying on and management of the whole affairs on such Community . . . .

Regulating ferries

Preventing unauthorized settlements

Invoking the law of England where no law of the colony provides a remedy

Regulating assessments for and collecting of taxes

Preventing forest fires

Regulating deer hunting

Quieting possession (confirming old grants and confirming title upon twenty years' possession):

> Whereas at the first settling of this Colony, and for sundry Years afterwards, Lands were of little or no Value, and Skilful Men in the Law were much wanted, whereby many Deeds, Grants and Conveyances were weakly made, which may Occasion Great Contests in Law, if not timely prevented.
>
> Be it therefore Enacted . . . That all Grants, Charters, Profits, Rights and Priviledges, heretofore Granted and Given by the General Assembly . . . hereby are Ratified and Confirmed

> to be Good and Effectual . . . to the Persons therein Mentioned, and their Heirs and Assigns for ever.
>
> . . . where any Person . . . shall by the space of Twenty Years, be in the Uninterrupted, Quiet, Peacable and Actual Seisin and Possession of any Land or Hereditaments within this Colony, for and during the said time, Claiming the same as his, her or their proper, sole and Rightful Estate in Fee Simple, such Actual Seisin and Possession, shall be allowed to give and make a Good and Rightful Title to such person or persons, their Heirs and Assigns for ever . . . .

Preventing purchase of Indian lands without governmental consent

Recording deeds and conveyances

Laying out highways and roads in the towns

Appointing overseers to lease out lands in behalf of Ninigret the Indian chief

Distributing and settling intestates' estates.[1474]

§ 10.04(j). Summary of Land Rights in Colonial Rhode Island.

One of the most distinctive features of Rhode Island's early colonial history is the absence of any effective jurisdiction exercised by a superior governmental authority. The first settlers were entirely on their own, wholly without authority or restraint from any other English colony or,

---

[1474] *Id.* at 57-120, 135-236.

indeed, from England itself. Their very immigration to the Rhode Island area was an attempt to escape or avoid such authority. This absolute independence of action, coupled with their own background of New England colonial experience in which land was held virtually free of any feudal burdens, led directly to landholding in the form of absolute ownership. At first, the absolute ownership rested with the original proprietors of each township, but they eventually sold or gave their rights in individual land parcels to others. Rights retained by the proprietors consisted mostly of the usual rights of government, while the conveyance and possession of land carried full rights of seisin. What controversies did surround landholding in Rhode Island were usually associated with disputed rights of government, conforming the size of land grants to the grantees' social status, and difficulties in tracing title. The historian Herbert Osgood provided enlightening details on these land-related issues:

> In the Narragansett [Rhode Island] settlements the towns were always much more independent of colony action than they were elsewhere . . . . The colony laws make no important reference either to that, or to the regulation of town lands and herds . . . . [I]n the management of their lands, as in everything else, the towns of Rhode Island pursued a more independent course than did those in the other New England colonies. A comparison, however, of their internal history with that of the towns in the adjacent colonies will show that in all essential particulars they conformed to the New England model. The original Narragansett towns were themselves offshoots of Salem, Boston, and other pre-existing towns, and their founders remained true to the polity with which they were familiar . . . .
>
> . . . [I]n those colonies there was no *land system* apart from the towns . . . . The management of land throughout those colonies was left to the towns . . . .
>
> In nearly all cases the settlements which were made prior to 1660 were located on arms of the sea or on the banks of

streams within the tide-water area. The land which was subject of grant, when cleared, consisted of upland, meadow, salt marsh, and fresh marsh or swamp. In many cases the upland which was first utilized was an Indian corn-field or clearing . . . .

The settlers made use of the upland for home lots and planting fields. The meadow was generally utilized for hay and pasturage. From the marshes and swamps hay and thatch were also procured. In the remote uncleared or only partially cleared tracts, swine, sheep, and young cattle were pastured. Oxen, horses, and milch cows were pastured upon land nearer the village . . . .

Several of the towns . . . which later formed the colony of Rhode Island . . . were established by the spontaneous act of their settlers and upon land which they had occupied in most cases after the extinguishment of Indian claims . . . .

The settlement of a town normally began with the laying out of the village plot and the assignment of home lots. This to an extent determined the location of highways, of the village common, and of some of the outlying fields. On or near the common the church was built, and in not a few cases the site that was chosen for this building went far toward determining the entire lay-out of the town. The ideal of a home lot was a plot of ground for a dwelling house and outbuildings, for a dooryard and garden, and usually also an enclosure for feeding cattle and raising corn . . . . In Providence [home lots] contained five acres.

The assignment of the first home lots was accompanied or immediately followed by the earliest allotments of arable land and meadow. The process steadily progressed with the increase of population in the towns and with the clearing of the forests. By means of it the settlers secured planting land, and the process advanced through various

> stages until the available land of the towns was approximately or entirely occupied. When the process was completed the township had been entirely laid out, and settlement within it had assumed a relatively permanent form. This was accomplished in part by the granting of lots to individuals and in part by the laying out of common fields. The common fields, too, in their turn were later subdivided among their proprietors. As the result of this process a system of individual ownership gradually took the place of a system of joint ownership and management; a settled and cultivated township came to exist where previously there had been only an unappropriated forest and waste.[1475]

Osgood's excellent work also provides specific commentary on the evolution of individual landholdings through the early decades of Rhode Island settlement and of New England colonization, in general:

> A necessary consequence of the method of allotting land . . . was, that the estate of each individual would consist of a number of small tracts located in different parts of the town plot . . . .
>
> . . . But before the towns had long been settled, a tendency toward consolidation of estates appears. Many exchanges of land were effected which had this as their object. Purchases and sales often had a similar effect. So did intermarriages and inheritance. The result of this process, operating through generations, has been to substitute for the early system of parcelled estates the consolidated farms of the present day.
>
> Common fences and herds were characteristic accompaniments of the system of common fields and joint

[1475] Herbert L. Osgood, *The American Colonies in the Seventeenth Century* 435-440 (1904).

cultivation which were the basis of the town economy . . . . As a rule, instead of fencing off by itself the allotment of each individual in a field or meadow, the entire field was surrounded by a common fence, and this was furnished with gates and approached by paths or highways. All grants of land were made subject to the right of the community to open highways through them . . . . Of the common fences, each shareholder was bound to build and keep in repair the part which was adjacent to his lot or lots . . . .

In Warwick, Rhode Island, the "front fence" which separated the homesteads from the large common that lay west of the village marked a most important line of division. Orders for its repair continually recur, and it was maintained both summer and winter . . . .

In the assignment of town lots and the drafting of regulations for the use of common lands a rigid numerical equality was occasionally maintained; each individual received just so many acres and just as much accommodation as any other, no more and no less. But in most instances an effort is discernible to make the grants proportional to what might be called the investment of the individual settler in the enterprise of founding the town. This assumed two forms, that of the expense or cost to which he was subjected and that of the ability which he contributed to the undertaking . . . . In the case of the early towns . . . on Narragensett Bay (Rhode Island), the cost, small though it was, of extinguishing the claims of the Indians had to be borne by the towns rather than the colony . . . . Those who met those [and other expenses, such as surveying and building a common house] were proprietors and received their dividends in the form of lands . . . .

The original contribution to the founding of a town by a

natural transition developed into the town rate . . . .

The colonists possessed the elements [for making contributions] in varying proportion . . . . Some had served out their indentures as servants, and in consequence of a small grant from their former masters or from the town had found a place among the class of cottagers. On the outskirts of the settlement, in the tracts which had early lain common as pasture, provision was usually made for families of this class . . . .

. . . In 1652 Warwick, in Rhode Island, laid out its meadow near the town, for the inhabitants who, as yet, had not been provided for . . . .

. . . Town records also abound in references to grants, the purpose of which was to equalize inequalities which had resulted from earlier allotments. Individual allotments were frequently eked out and inconveniences of location were removed in this way . . . .

. . . The land of the towns, their herds and fences, were subject to joint management. But the question arises, To what extent did this originate with the town meetings or how far did it proceed from distinct boards of proprietors?

. . . The town meeting was at the same time a meeting of proprietors, or might easily become such. In the early history of towns a very important part of the business of the town meetings consisted in making grants of land . . . .

. . . In Rhode Island . . . boards of proprietors of common lands appear at an early date in the towns of Providence and Warwick, though in Portsmouth the town lands were directly controlled by the town meeting.

> But in all towns, even from the outset, there were certain grantees of land who were not admitted to the body of proprietors. They might become freemen of the town and thus have a voice in town meeting, or even be freemen of the colony, and yet not find admission with the circle of proprietors. The idea of freemanship was political in its nature, that of proprietorship was territorial . . . .
>
> In every towne there were also certain cottagers who, in the language of the Hartford records, "were granted lotts to have onely at the towne's courtesie, with liberty to fetch woode and keepe swine or cowes on the Common." These were not even freemen, and their admission to the town was safeguarded in such as, if possible, to prevent their adding to the number of the town poor. They were simply inhabitants . . . .
>
> . . . As the supply from which allotments could be made grew less, land became an increased object of desire, both to those who controlled it and to those who were seeking to possess it . . . . [I]n towns where the number of non-commoners came to equal that of the proprietors, struggles over the management of the town lands were very likely to occur . . . .
>
> . . . [T]he earliest controversy of this kind developed in Providence . . . .[1476]

Not only in Providence, but in other Rhode Island towns the controversies over land distribution flared up persistently.[1477]

[1476] *Id.* at 448-467.

[1477] "On Aquidneck (Portsmouth and Newport) the founders planned communities with traditional gradations from gentleman to servant. The levels were initially marked out by the amounts of land given to the various settlers from several hundred acres to none at all. Those in the upper half of the spectrum were to have political rights, the rest would not. The levels were assigned roughly in accord with rank held previously in other places, but a few men, selected mainly on the basis of

Shortly after Williams' death in 1683, Providence began granting small lots, 400 to 600 square feet, along the waterfront for use as wharves or warehouses, and at that time the town's rise to commercial prominence began.[1478]

In the early years of the 18th century, the colonial government became much more assertive in resolving long-standing land disputes based on the perceived inequities in early allotments. To end disputes over common land in the few places where any remained after 1715 the government parcelled out almost all common land to individual grantees. The power of proprietors, especially of the Narragansett proprietors, gradually weakened, and more of their lands opened for settlement, with consequent economic progress for the colony. Also, with new lands more freely available, some were able to add to their already large holdings.

§ 10.05. Development of Land Law in Delaware (from 1638).

§ 10.05(a). Land Rights in Early Dutch Settlements.

European exploration of the territory that was to become the colony of

---

wealth, were to be lifted to the status of gentlemen and rulers. There were no settlers of genuinely high birth to begin with . . . . In Portsmouth some of the men given little land and no political rights clamored for higher positions and brazenly set up their own meeting to seek their goals . . . . In Providence, by contrast, the conflict seemed to begin over religious liberty, but came to rest on land. Williams wanted to keep the town open for victims of religious persecution. To do this he espoused an egalitarian social policy: let everyone who was admitted have the same shares of land a package of allocations including a house lot, meadow, crop land, and privileges to use the commons. His earliest companions, however, wanted special consideration. After heated exchanges with them, Williams agreed that part of the town should be set aside for them (and himself), leaving the rest to be divided up among the first settlers plus a growing number of other people. Still the townsfolk were not satisfied. Some newcomers were admitted only to quarter-share rights; ultimately admissions with full land allocations were stopped after about one hundred had been made." Sydney V. James, *Colonial Rhode Island, A History* 78-79 (1975). *See also* Charles Wyman Hopkins, *The Home Lots of the Early Settlers of the Providence Plantations* (1886).

[1478] *Id.* at 262.

Delaware commenced in August 1609, when Henry Hudson, in the employ of the Dutch, entered Delaware Bay and later reported his observations to his Dutch employers. As a result of his reports, Dutch trading vessels made frequent visits to both the Hudson and Delaware Rivers in attempts to develop a profitable fur trade. In 1610 the English sailor Samuel Argall entered Delaware Bay seeking protection from a storm while on a voyage from Virginia, and he named the area for the then governor of Virginia, Lord de la Warr. The English later extended the name to the entire bay, the river, and the land on the western shore.

As early as 1624, the Dutch settled a few Walloon families along the Delaware River, but then removed them to Manhattan in 1628; thereafter the Dutch kept only a small vessel at the river site to facilitate the fur trade. Then in 1629, some of the wealthy members of the company's Amsterdam chamber secured the Charter of Exemptions and Privileges, authorizing creation of the feudalistic patroonships in New Netherland. Two persons who were among the first to act under this Charter, Samuel Blommaert and Samuel Godwyn, in 1629 sent two agents to buy lands from the Indians. The purchases, the first within the area of modern Delaware, were recognized by the company by means of a "deed" issued on the island of Manhattan and dated July 15, 1630, with granting language as follows:

> We, the Directors and Council of New Netherlands . . . hereby acknowledge and declare, that on this day, the date underwritten, came and appeared before us in their proper persons, Queskacous and Entquet, Siconesius and the inhabitants of the village, situate at the South Cape of the bay of South [Delaware] River, and freely and voluntarily declared by special authority of the rulers, and consent of the commonality there, that they already on the first day of June, of the past year 1629, for, and on account of certain parcels of cargoes, have transferred, ceded, given over, and conveyed, in just, true, and free property, as they hereby transport, cede, give over, and convey to, and for the behoof of Messrs. Samuel Godwyn and Samuel

Blommaert absent . . . .[1479]

Although it was typical—indeed, even essential—to secure a surrender of native rights in land already obtained under a grant from a European authority, the patroons and others undoubtedly realized that the Indian "deeds" had only limited value, that the Indians believed that they were agreeing only to let the settlers "share" the land.[1480]

The first Dutch settlers for this land arrived in April 1631, and founded Zwaanendael. Thus, the first European settlement in Delaware was one of the first patroonships authorized under the 1629 Charter and was, therefore, under the same regime of land rights as described for the New Netherland patroonships in § 9.05(b). However, even before the next supply ship arrived in 1632, a misunderstanding with the Indians resulted in the Indians massacring the entire Zwaanendael settlement in Delaware.

§ 10.05(b). Land Rights in Early Swedish Settlements.

No further Europcan settlement was attempted in Delaware until Swedish and Finnish settlers arrived near the site of present-day Wilmington in 1638 and founded a colony they called New Sweden. Unable to base claims to land on rights of discovery or conquest, the Swedes "purchased" lands from the Indians. The purchaser was nominally

---

1479 J. Thomas Scharf, *History of Delaware 1609-1888* 31 (1888).

1480 "The European concept of land-holding was unknown to the Indians, . . . and incompatible with their culture. It did not occur to the natives that the Europeans might demand that the Indians quit some or all of their lands along the river and move elsewhere; they understood that the "purchase" conferred on the [European purchasers] the right to share the land with them to hunt, fish, plant crops, and build houses, but not to *own* it in the sense that a man owned his bows and arrows. In the Indians' way of thinking, land was comparable to water and air it was free for the use of all. That concept, an important part of the Indians' belief that man was part of nature, led to numerous misunderstandings between natives and newcomers, especially when the wily Dutch, more used to dealing with the natives, made haste to "buy" the same land for themselves to undermine [the] tenuous claim [of Sweden's earlier purchasers]. The Indians, of course, understood only that they had agreed, for the price of some foreign artifacts, to share their land with yet another European nation. To the Swedes, the Indians' action was proof of a despicable lack of integrity." Carol E. Hoffecker, *Delaware, A Bicentennial History* 14 (1977).

the Swedish South Sea Company, which had received its first letters patent from King Gustavus Adolphus in 1624, and an essentially similar second charter in 1626. No settlement activity occurred at that time because Sweden had become distracted by a long war with Spain, but by 1637 the Swedes were once again ready to consider colonization in America.

In 1640 the Swedish West India Company granted to certain Dutch investors a charter effectively creating a patroonship so that they could found another settlement in New Sweden. The grantees held their land under the protection of Sweden as hereditary property, with the feudalistic high and low jurisdiction. Meanwhile, contention over concurrent Swedish and Dutch claims to the same land in Delaware continued, and even an English settlement had arisen nearby. For those who agreed to recognize Swedish jurisdiction in the colony and were not bound as servants, "they were at liberty to build and settle themselves where they thought proper and to return home when they pleased."[1481] For his zeal in protecting Swedish interests in the colony the Swedish government in about 1645 awarded governor Johan Printz a grant of land as a perpetual possession for himself and his heirs forever.[1482] For the most part, however, the rival Dutch and Swedish colonies competed in "purchasing" lands from the Indians. The rivalry erupted into open hostilities, resulting in a surrender of the Swedish settlements to Dutch jurisdiction in 1655. The Dutch agreed to respect the customs, religion, and private property claims of Swedish settlers who wished to remain. When the Dutch took up possession of this territory, they also introduced their land management practices, including an annual payment for land occupancy.[1483]

[1481] J. Thomas Scharf, *History of Delaware 1609-1888* 48 (1888).

[1482] *Id.* at 49.

[1483] "In the settlement of the country, the colonists were to concentrate themselves in families of sixteen to twenty in number, and were to pay annually for their lands twelve stivers a morgen [approximately two acres] in lieu of tenths. The town lots [in what is today's New Castle] were forty feet by fifty, and the streets from four to five rods in breadth. The Swedes were to be closely watched, and if any should be found disaffected, they were to be sent away . . . and, if possible, induced to come to Manhattan." *Id.* at 62.

§ 10.05(c). Land Rights in Delaware After the English Conquest of 1664.

Events elsewhere in America soon overtook the struggling Delaware settlements. In 1664 the English king Charles II granted to his brother the Duke of York lands that included much of what the Dutch claimed in America; this led directly to the English takeover of New Amsterdam, quickly renamed New York. An English fleet then approached the Delaware settlements and obtained the acquiescence of the Swedish colonists and, after a brief battle, the surrender of the Dutch. The English also took some territory of the Dutch that was not included in the grant to the Duke of York, but had, in fact, been included in the 1632 grant of Maryland to Lord Baltimore.

From 1664 to 1682, the English ruled Delaware as part of New York, so that New York laws pertaining to land also applied in Delaware.[1484] During one brief interlude, the Dutch reconquered New Netherland in 1673 and reoccupied Delaware without resistance, but they lost it all again in 1674. The"Duke's Law" of 1665 was supposedly in effect in Delaware, but over a decade passed before even a copy of the laws reached the Delaware settlements. Meanwhile, a brisk land business was carried on, and a court was established to register deeds, probate wills and settle land disputes.[1485]

[1484] *See* § 9.05(e), *supra*.

[1485] "New lands were being taken up in a rather haphazard fashion, with the government seeking an income from land, both by fees to confirm possession and by quitrents, modest annual charges upon landowners (usually one bushel of wheat per hundred acres) in lieu, theoretically, of services that might have been demanded of them. Old Swedish, Finnish, and Dutch settlers moving westward up the Christina [River] or southward from New Castle took up some of the new lands. Of the English settlers, some came from Maryland, bringing slaves with them. The government sought to attract settlers on terms as favorable as in neighboring Maryland or in New England. In theory, a tract of fifty acres was assigned to each member of a family, but in actuality the grants seem to have been larger, varying from under two hundred to over one thousand acres. As central Delaware was gradually settled, farmers on the St. Jones River appealed to the governor for their own court so they would not need to go to Lewes or New Castle to register deeds, probate wills, or settle disputes over land. . . . [I]n 1680 the governor approved their request, appointing justices of the peace and thereby creating the third Delaware county, called St. Jones." John A. Munroe, *History of Delaware* 33-34 (2d ed. 1984). *See also* John A. Munroe, *Colonial Delaware, A History* 74-75

§ 10.05(d). Land Rights in Delaware After Coming Under the Governance of Pennsylvania.

§ 10.05(d)(1). Land Grants and Sales.

Delaware's relative isolation permitted localities to develop their own customs and practices with respect to landholding, but important changes began to take place in the 1680's. By a royal patent dated March 4, 1680, William Penn received a patent for lands and governmental authority in the province of Pennsylvania from King Charles II. By deed of feoffment dated August 4, 1682, the Duke of York granted to Penn all the lands in the New York provincial territory covered by the royal patent to Penn, which meant conveyance of title to the Delaware lands.[1486] In contrast to the previous colonial practice of simply giving land to settlers willing to come and stay,

(1978).

[1486] The interesting peculiarities of this conveyance, with strong overtones of medieval English land law, have been explained as follows:

> There were actually four legal documents involved in these grants, an absolute deed (called a "deed of feoffment") and a lease for ten thousand years for New Castle and the circle around it, and another deed and a similar lease for the land from twelve miles south of New Castle to Cape Henlopen . . . Probably the division is explained by the duke's desire to get some revenue from these territories . . . but not to interfere with Penn's use of New Castle or with his revenues from it . . . Perhaps both deed and lease were used because of the uncertainty of the duke's legal rights to Delaware . . .
>
> Then on October 28 [the day after Penn's arrival on October 27, 1682], in a ceremony called "livery of seisin," Penn formally took possession of New Castle and the territory within twelve miles about it, except on the east side of the Delaware. After the deeds from the Duke of York were read, Penn took the key to the New Castle fort, entered and locked himself in alone, then came out and received a piece of turf with a twig upon it and a porringer with river water and soil as symbols of his new possession. John A. Munroe, *Colonial Delaware, A History 83-84* (1978).

Penn began selling land as soon as he secured his title.[1487]

Landholdings in at least two of Delaware's counties tended to be quite large. According to surviving rent rolls, "55 percent of the landowners in Kent and Sussex owned five hundred acres or more."[1488] This was three times larger than the average holding in contemporary Pennsylvania counties.

§ 10.05(d)(2). Quit Rents.

In the matter of quit rents, the experience in Delaware was typical of most American colonies and, indeed, after 1684, was identical to Pennsylvania's experience. In Delaware's early colonial history under the Dutch, however, quit rent was seldom a factor, and this changed only gradually after the English took over in 1664.[1489] By the time Governor Dongan of New York was reporting quit rent payments from Delaware, the colony had passed over to the jurisdiction of Pennsylvania. In Pennsylvania and its territories, including Delaware, quit rents were actively pursued, and so the various issues and controversies surrounding colonial quit rents became important in Delaware.[1490]

[1487] "In New Netherland and New York . . . during the [early] period . . ., a price seems never to have been put upon the land. Land was sold in Pennsylvania from the very first. As soon as he had secured his title, Penn offered for sale shares of five thousand acres at £100 each. After 1684 this land was also to be liable to a quitrent. The practice of selling land was steadily continued, the prices varying with the period of time which had elapsed since the settlement of the province, with the character and location of the land, and with such other conditions as might affect a bargain. After 1732 prices become more permanent. For thirty years from that date the price was £15, 10s. per hundred acres. Prices were always fixed by the proprietor and his officials . . . . Escheated land, with such improvements as had been made upon it, was sold at auction, and the larger part of the purchase money went to the proprietor. It was a requirement in all the provinces that land should be settled within a brief period often designated as three years after the issue of the patent. Squatters' rights, as evidenced by 'improvment," were as a rule generously enforced." Herbert L. Osgood, *The American Colonies in the Seventeenth Century* 34-35 (1904).

[1488] John A. Munroe, *Colonial Delaware, A History* 94 (1978).

[1489] *Id.* at 39-42.

[1490] *Id.* at 36-37.

§ 10.05(d)(3). Administration of Land Affairs.

Both the sales of land and the administration of quit rents under the Pennsylvania's rule of Delaware required creation of a rudimentary bureaucracy. "Not until 1741 was the care of these matters intrusted to the governors. Instead, a commission or board of property was from time to time designated, which acted as the special agent of the proprietor. The board consisted of a secretary, who was at the same time secretary of the province, the surveyor-general, and from three to five special commissioners."[1491]

In the view of one important historian, the land systems in the proprietary colonies were kept strictly within the control of the executive and away from legislative regulation. "In all the provinces the land system was kept as free as possible from the control of the legislature. It was organized and regulated under instructions and proclamations of the proprietors and their appointees. Any attempt to regulate it by legislation was resented and opposed. It was regarded as the private concern of the proprietor and its administration as distinctly as an executive function . . . ."[1492]

However, legislation in matters touching land was both common and comprehensive in Delaware under Pennsylvania administration.

§ 10.05(d)(4). Legislation Relating to Landholding.

Soon after the 1682 conveyance from the Duke of York, Penn issued the Frame of Government of the Province of Pennsylvania, consisting of a bill of rights and other laws that would become effective when ratified by the colonists in the province, including Delaware. In 1683, Penn issued a Charter of Privileges, which was revised in 1701, and which added further governing provisions applicable to Delaware as well as to Pennsylvania and

---

[1491] *Id.* at 46.

[1492] *Id.* at 46-47.

Penn's other territories. Meanwhile, the Duke's Law of 1665 also remained in force in Delaware. For Delaware then, the Duke's Law of 1665 and Penn's 1682 Frame of Government and 1683 Charter of Privileges were all potential sources of laws governing landholding. The fundamental legal rules for land were lodged in the Duke's Law and are described in the context of colonial New York in §§9.05(e) and 9.05(f), supra. The land provisions of the 1682 Frame of Government and the Charter of Privileges of 1683 and 1701 are summarized in the following paragraphs.

§ 10.05(d)(4)(A). Penn's Frame of Government of 1682.

In his 1682 Frame of Government, Penn granted to "the freemen, planters and adventurers, of . . . the . . . province, these liberties, franchises, and properties [as granted to Penn], to be held, enjoyed and kept by the freemen, planters and inhabitants of the said province of Pennsylvania for ever."[1493] In addition to this conferral of rights, the other singular feature of the Frame of Government was the establishment of representative government in the form of the Provincial Council and General Assembly. The Provincial Council was directed to divide itself into four standing committees, the first of which would be "a committee of plantations, to situate and settle cities, ports, market-towns and high-ways, and to hear and decide all suits and controversies relating to plantations."[1494] Laws proposed by the Provincial Council were subject to rejection or ratification by the General Assembly. In April 1683, a new frame of government was drawn up, taking into account the incorporation of the Delaware settlements and providing for a reorganization of the council and general assembly.[1495]

[1493] *The Earliest Printed Laws of Pennsylvania 1681-1713* 200 (John D. Cushing, ed., 1978).

[1494] *Id.* at 196.

[1495] *See* No. 41. "Pennsylvania and Delaware Frame," in *Select Charters and Other Documents Illustrative of American History, 1606-1775* 199-204 (William MacDonald, ed., 1914).

§ 10.05(d)(4)(B). Laws for the Colony Agreed upon in England.

Even before the earliest legislative assembly met, certain laws for Pennsylvania were proposed and agreed to by the colonial leaders while they were still in England, subject to ratification by the colonists in America. Those provisions pertaining to landholding were as follows:

> First. That the charter of liberties [Frame of Government] . . . is hereby declared and approved, and shall be for ever held for fundamental in the government thereof, according to the limitations mentioned in the said charter.
>
> Second. That every Inhabitant in the said province, that is or shall be a purchaser of one hundred acres of land or upwards, his heirs and assigns, and every person who shall have paid his passage, and taken up one hundred acres of land, at a penny an acre, and have cultivated ten acres thereof, and every person that hath been a servant or bondsman, and is free by his service, that shall have taken up his fifty acres of land, and cultivated twenty thereof, and every inhabitant, artificer, or other resident in the said province, that pays scot and lot[1496] to the government, shall be deemed and accounted a freeman of the said province . . . .
>
> Fourteenth. That all lands and goods shall be liable to pay debts, except where there is legal issue, and then all the goods, and one third of the land only.

[1496] In English law scot was a form of tax on one's share of a customary contribution. Scot and lot was a particular customary contribution imposed upon subjects according to their ability to pay. In certain English boroughs, persons retained their franchise only by paying the scot and lot. A reference to scot and lot in Delaware appears in Frieszleben v. Shallcross, 19 A. 576 (1890), and is defined as "customary contribution laid upon all subjects according to their ability." 19 A. at 578.

Fifteenth. That all wills and writing attested by two witnesses, shall be of the same force, as to lands and other conveyances, being legally proved within forty days, either within or without the said province.

Sixteenth. That seven years quiet possession shall give an unquestionable right, except in cases of infants, lunaticks, married women, or persons beyond the seas . . . .

Twentieth. And to prevent frauds and vexatious suits within the said province, that all charters, gifts, grants and conveyances of land, (except leases for a year or under) and all bills, bonds, and specialties have five pounds, and not under three months, made in the said province, shall be enrolled or registered in the public enrolment office of the said province within the space of two months next after the making thereof, else to be void in law. And all deeds, grants, and conveyances of land (except as aforesaid) within the said province, and made out of the said province, shall be inrolled or registered as aforesaid, within six months next after the making thereof, and settling and constituting an enrolment office or registry within the said province, else to be void in law against all persons whatsoever . . . .

Thirty-first. That for the encouragement of the plants and traders in this province, who are incorporated into a society, the patent granted to them by William Penn, Governor of the said province, is hereby ratified and confirmed . . . .[1497]

[1497] *The Earliest Printed Laws of Pennsylvania 1681-1713* 201-205 (John D. Cushing, ed., 1978).

§ 10.05(d)(4)(C). The Charter of Privileges of 1683 and 1701.

The Charter of Privileges, issued in 1683 and revised in 1701, gave specific instructions for choosing members of the General Assembly but contained only one additional provision touching upon land rights:

> Eighthly: If any person, through Temptation or melancholly, shall Destroy himself, his Estate, Real & Personal, shall, notwithstanding, Descend to his wife and Children or Relations as if he had Died a natural Death; and if any person shall be Destroyed or kill'd by Casualty or accident, there shall be no forfeiture to the Governour by Reason thereof . . . .[1498]

§ 10.05(d)(4)(D). Delaware Legislation After 1704.

When the legislature established by William Penn first met, colonists in the Delaware region, known as the Three Lower Counties, had the same number of representatives as colonists in the Pennsylvania region. As Pennsylvania thereafter embarked on much more rapid growth, the Delaware colonists soon feared becoming outnumbered in the legislature. Thus, in 1701 they refused to meet with the Pennsylvania legislators and requested from William Penn the privilege of establishing their own legislature, which was granted. As a result, from 1704 Delaware had its separate legislature, although the region was still under the jurisdiction of the Pennsylvania governor, who had the power to approve or disallow all enactments of the Delaware legislature. This arrangement continued until 1777, when Delaware voters elected their own chief executive.

The earliest compilation and arrangement of these Delaware legislative enactments was not completed and printed until 1741 or 1742. The topics

---

[1498] *The Earliest Printed Laws of Delaware 1704-1741* 1-8 (John D. Cushing, ed., 1978).

of those provisions dealing with land rights are noted as follows:

> Orphans' courts
>
> Settling intestates' estates
>
> Building mills
>
> Establishing courts of law and equity (to "hear and determine all . . . actions . . . real, personal and mixt, according to the Laws and Constitutions of this Government, as fully and amply to all Intents and Purposes, as the Justices of the King's-Bench, Common-Pleas and Exchequer in England, or any of them may or can do.")
>
> Taking lands in execution for payment of debts
>
> Against removing landmarks
>
> For better confirmation of the owners of lands and their just rights and possessions
>
> Regulating fences
>
> Against unseasonable firing of woodlands and marshes
>
> For preventing accidental fires in towns and villages
>
> Partitioning land into 200-acre lots for sale to the public
>
> Constructing roads, bridges, highways and causeways
>
> Against forcible entry, barratry, maintenance, champerty and embracery
>
> Acknowledging and recording deeds

Preventing destruction of timber and other trees

Limitations of actions

Probate of estates.[1499]

From this review of Delaware's colonial history, it is clear that despite early settlements from several European nations, the colony eventually adopted English law as the basis of its legal system and regime of land rights.

§ 10.06. Development of Land Law in New Jersey (from 1638).

§ 10.06(a). Early English Grants of New Jersey Land.

The land that ultimately became the colony of New Jersey was first the subject of English land grants in late 16th century conveyances to Sir Humphrey Gilbert and to Sir Walter Raleigh. Next, the land was included in the letters patent granted on April 10, 1607, by King James I for the colonization of Virginia. Patentees from London were authorized to establish a privately funded joint stock company to colonize the southern half of the territory included in the patent, between the 34th and 41st parallels, roughly from southern North Carolina to southern Pennsylvania. Other patentees, principally from Plymouth, were authorized to similarly found a second colony somewhere in the northern part of the patent, between the 38th and 45th parallels, extending from northern Virginia to the middle of Maine.

The area in the middle of both patented territories, between 38 and 41 degrees latitude, which could be settled by either the Virginia Company or the Plymouth Company, included most of present-day New Jersey. When the Virginia Company obtained a second patent in 1609, this overlapping area was reduced by the southern half being shifted back to 40 degrees

---

[1499] *Id.* at 9-290.

latitude, and thus, most of New Jersey was assigned unequivocally to the Plymouth Company's northern part of the Virginia patent. While haphazard exploration by the English occurred after this time, no meaningful attempt at colonization took place until the Dutch began to arrive several years later.

§ 10.06(b). First Settlements by the Dutch.

In the absence of English settlers during the early years of the 17th century, Dutch colonists founded the first permanent European settlement in New Jersey. The precursors of Dutch settlers on New Jersey land were members of Henry Hudson's *Half Moon* crew in 1609, and these may indeed have been the first Europeans to set foot on New Jersey soil. No further Dutch activity occurred until 1610, when Amsterdam merchants sent a ship to the area to open trade with the Indians. In 1611 the Dutch government licensed two ships to proceed to the Bay of New York.

In 1614 the Dutch government issued an edict by which Dutch citizens were invited to explore the territory and thus obtain exclusive privileges of settlement. Pursuant to the edict, explorers for the newly formed United Netherland Company reached the American coast, made extensive investigations, and returned and reported. In October 1614, this United New Netherland Company obtained an exclusive right to visit and navigate in New Netherland, lying between the 40th and 45th parallels. During the years to follow, the company began to form a small trading settlement on Manhattan Island and undoubtedly explored the lands west of the Hudson River.

Their first settlement, on an island in the Hudson called Fort Orange (near Albany), they abandoned for the more favorable Fort Amsterdam site on Manhattan Island. In 1615, they established a small fortification opposite the Manhattan settlement on New Jersey territory. Sometime between 1617 and 1620, they may have established another settlement at Bergen.[1500] It is believed that sometime in 1614, the Dutch at Manhattan were visited by a Captain Argall of the English colony at Jamestown, who

[1500] Isaac S. Mulford, *A Civil and Political History of New Jersey* 41 (1851).

forced them to submit themselves and their settlement to the English monarch. Then in November 1620, the old Plymouth Company was revived with a grant of all lands between 40 and 48 degrees latitude (roughly between southern Pennsylvania and northern Maine) to Sir Ferdinando Gorges and others, naturally in complete disregard of any Dutch claims.

While the Dutch settlers were threatened with conflicting claims from the English, their original company license expired. In 1621 the Dutch government granted a new charter to the West India Company with much broader governmental powers and stronger participation by the government. The 1621 charter gave the company a monopoly over trade and traffic to the New World for a period of twenty-four years but contained no mention of any company power to deal with land. Nevertheless, the company did exercise power over land transactions.[1501]

In 1624 the first Dutch settlers in New Jersey, consisting of two families and eight single men, took up residence on what is now called Burlington Island, in the Delaware River, but they abandoned it by 1630. They then set up a small trading post at Fort Nassau, in the present city of Gloucester, but occupied it only intermittently. No permanent settlement in New Jersey arose until after the Charter of Privileges to Patroons was announced in 1629.

The patroonships constituted an attempt by the company to completely delegate responsibility for colonization to affluent and interested adventurers. The owner of a patroonship was vested with certain manorial rights, as described in Chapter 9:

> The policy of encouraging settlement by patroons imparted significant consequences for landholding in New Netherlands. Patroons can be best described as the Dutch equivalents of English manorial lords. A patroon who held land held it according to a feudal system of land rights, which included the rights to require services as well as rents from tenants who were occupying the patroon's

---

[1501] *See* § 9.05(b), *supra*.

> lands, and the right to exercise judicial and other governmental powers over the patroon's holdings. Only the patroon held the land outright; others could only be tenants of the patroon. The patroons of New Netherlands obligated themselves to commence a colony with at least 50 persons during a four-year period of time, in return for which each patroon received manorial and proprietary rights to sixteen miles of Hudson River shoreline and the lands behind the shoreline.[1502]

The following excerpts from the 1629 Charter of Privileges to Patroons amply illustrate this explicit introduction of feudalism to North America:

> III. All such [members of said Company as may be inclined to settle a Colonie in New Netherland] shall be acknowledged Patroons of New Netherland who shall, within the space of four years next after they have given notice to any of the Chambers of the Company here, or to the Commander or Council there, undertake to plant a Colonie there of fifty souls, upwards of fifteen years old; one-fourth part within one year, and within three years after the sending of the first, making together four years, the remainder, to the full number of fifty persons, to be shipped from hence, on pain, in case of wilful neglect, of being deprived of the privileges obtained . . . .
>
> IV. They shall, from the time they make known the situation of the places where they propose to settle Colonies, have the preference to all others of the absolute property of such lands as they have there chosen . . . .
>
> VI. They shall forever possess and enjoy all the lands lying within the aforesaid limits, together with the fruits, rights, minerals, rivers and fountains thereof; as also the chief command and lower jurisdictions, fishing, fowling

[1502] *Id.*

and grinding, to the exclusion of all others, to be holden from the Company as a perpetual inheritance, without it ever devolving again to the Company . . .; and further, no person or persons whatsoever shall be privileged to fish and hunt but the Patroons and such as they shall permit. And in case any one should in time prospere so much as to found one or more cities, he shall have power and authority to establish officers and magistrates there, and to make use of the title of his Colonie, according to his pleasure and to the quality of the persons.

VII. There shall likewise be granted to all Patroons who shall desire the same, . . . liberty to dispose of their aforesaid heritage by testament.

VIII. The Patroons may, if they think proper, make use of all lands, rivers and woods lying contiguous to them, for and during so long a time as this Company shall grant them to other Patroons or private persons . . . .

XIX. [The Company] will not take from the service of the Patroons any of their colonists, either man or woman, son or daughter, manservant or maid-servant; and, though any of these should desire the same, they will not receive them, much less permit them to leave their Patroons, and enter into the service of another, unless on consent obtained from their Patroons in writing, and this for and during so many years as they are bound to their Patroons . . . .

XX. From all judgments given by the Courts of the Patroons for upwards of fifty guilders, there may be an appeal to the Company's Commander and Council in New Netherland.

XXI. In regard to such private persons as on their own account, or others in the service of their masters here (not enjoying the same privileges as the Patroons), shall be

> inclined to go thither and settle, they shall, with the approbation of the Director and Council there, be at liberty to take up and take possession of as much land as they shall be able properly to improve, and shall enjoy the same in full property either for themselves or masters.[1503]

None of the patroonships in New Jersey were ultimately successful. Patroonship rights were either never claimed by actual settlement or were abandoned or were sold back to the company. However, even without official patroonship administration, some of the lands designated as patroonships remained undivided and at least nominally under feudal obligations.[1504]

The first permanent settlement in New Jersey originated with a patroonship, the Manor of Pavonia, which was registered in 1630 and included most of the modern shoreline of Jersey City and Hoboken. The settlement struggled, and by about 1634, the patroonship rights had been sold back to the company. By 1638, however, the settlement had become permanent.

Even though the patroonships failed, the principles announced in the patroonship charter remained as permanent characteristics of Dutch governance and land arrangements, which envisioned feudal or manorial rule and a class of American serfs.[1505]

[1503] *Select Charters and Other Documents Illustrative of American History 1606-1775* 43-50 (William MacDonald, ed., 1914).

[1504] . . . [T]he Charter of Privileges to patroons . . . was intended to encourage private individuals to establish settlements at various points on the Hudson and Delaware, or North and South, rivers. Numerous grievances, occasioned by friction between patroons and the Company, were partially allayed by a new charter in 1640, restricting the area of the grants, and encouraging independent settlement; but the feudal privileges of the patroons were not interfered with. Many of the old patroon estates long remained undivided, and the heirs of the founders claimed some semi-feudal privileges well into the nineteenth century. *Id.* at 43.

[1505] "This charter formed the principal basis upon which the civil institutions of New Netherland came to be placed . . . . The principal directors of the plan were ready to seize for themselves the advantages offered; in the character as Patroons, they secured acquisitions in the province which almost gave them a monopoly in land, and thus they were able to retain, in their own hands, some of the most

When Willem Kieft arrived as the new governor of New Netherland in 1638, there were only one bowery (farm) and four plantations in the New Jersey portion of the province.[1506] Upon Kieft's arrival, colonists founded settlements at present-day Hoboken, Ridgefield Park (Old Hackensack), and Old Tappan.[1507] Typical of them all was the landholding arrangement at Hoboken, where on January 1, 1641, a settler named Aert Teunissen leased a bowery within the bounds of the old Pavonia patroonship for a term of ten years, during which time he cleared the land, fenced the fields, and built a house.[1508] Indian attacks devastated the Pavonia settlements in 1643-1645 and 1655-1658. Finally, in 1660 settlers founded the Town of Bergen, New Jersey's first town, on the site, allotted families town plots, and permitted the town to have a court and local government powers. They strengthened the nearby settlement of Communipaw. By 1664, after half a century of Dutch colonizing, Bergen and Communipaw were the only two villages in New Jersey.

§ 10.06(c). Attempted Colonization by Swedes.

Meanwhile, a feeble Swedish attempt at colonization began with a settlement at Wilmington, on the Delaware side of the Delaware River, in 1638, followed by a settlement on the New Jersey side in 1643. This latter site they abandoned after a few years, but the Swedes sought to extend their control of the river all the way to Trenton, building forts and blockhouses

---

important privileges yielded in the charter. To the mass of actual settlers nothing whatever was given. The charter contemplated or allowed, the establishment of a kind of feudal or manorial rule, by which the colonists would be held in a state of complete independence. No provision was made for the division of lands, either present or prospective. The people to be sent by the Patroons, were regarded, and were to be controlled by the owners of the soil, as a servile class. They were to become American serfs . . . . By a wiser provision, the charter gave liberty to private adventurers to make a selection of lands and to enjoy the same by personal right." Isaac S. Mulford, *A Civil and Political History of New Jersey* 57 (1851).

[1506] If the farmer and family resided at the site, the site was called a bowery; if they resided elsewhere, the site was called a plantation.

[1507] Adrian C. Leiby, *The Early Dutch and Swedish Settlers of New Jersey* 14-17 (1964).

[1508] *Id.* at 17.

along the way. A show of Dutch force in 1655 convinced the Swedes to retreat. While some Swedish settlers left the area, others remained, but beyond the auspices of their government.

§ 10.06(d). English Take-Over in 1664.

During none of these decades did the English show any sign of relinquishing their claims to New Jersey land, which claims ultimately rested on John Cabot's 1497 discovery voyage. English claims to New Jersey land had been further based on the Elizabethan grant to Raleigh and Humphries, King James I's Virginia grants in 1606 and 1609, the Argall visit of 1614, and the Plymouth Company grant of 1620; nevertheless, in 1634 King Charles I granted New Jersey land to Sir Edmund Plowden and his associates, who called their grant New Albion.[1509] Beginning in 1642 and continuing thereafter, English colonists from New Haven made short-lived attempts to claim New Jersey lands along the Delaware River near present-day Salem. Finally, in 1664 King Charles II made his famous grant to his brother, the Duke of York (the future King James II), of the lands which encompassed the future states of New York, New Jersey, Delaware and Pennsylvania.

The royal charter of 1664 is discussed in detail in §9.05(e)(1). Here it is necessary only to reiterate that ""the patent was expressed in terms of the fullest property rights consistent with the feudal incidents still connected with the tenure of free and common socage"; that "the grantee, as a feudal lord, was given extensive powers of government and court jurisdiction"; that "the laws to be administered in the granted lands were to be not contrary to and as near "as conveniently may bee' to the laws of England, [with] judicial judgments and sentences . . . subject to a right of appeal in England"; and that "the terms of this patent appeared designed to expressly supersede any previous and conflicting grants of the same lands."[1510]

[1509] Plowden visited New Jersey settlements on the Delaware River in 1642, but had no success in establishing his right to conduct government, so he eventually returned to England. Richard P. McCormick, *New Jersey from Colony to State* 14 (1964).

[1510] *See* § 9.05(e)(1), *supra*.

§ 10.06(e). Landholding Rights Under the English Proprietors.

§ 10.06(e)(1). Application of The Duke's Law in 1665.

The "Duke's Law" of 1665 implemented the powers of the 1664 charter, although, at first, settlers in the former Dutch areas were permitted to govern themselves by their traditional laws. Even this changed when English rule resumed after a brief Dutch interlude in 1673-1674. The provisions of the "Duke's Law" related to landholding, typical of English laws adapted to the frontier environment, are summarized in §9.05(e)(2), *supra*.

§ 10.06(e)(2). Berkeley and Carteret's 1665 "Concessions and Agreement."

The Duke of York also had to subdue the Dutch of New Amsterdam in order to make good his claim to his vast American grant, but so sure was he of success, that even while his fleet was underway to attempt the task, by deed of lease and release he re-granted a large portion of his land, an area encompassing most of New Jersey, to John Lord Berkeley and Sir George Carteret.

Because the Duke of York had been granted governmental rights over his grant, Berkeley and Carteret assumed that their grant from the Duke also included rights of government, as if it were a feudal fief. In fact, the New Jersey patent of 1664 included only rights to the soil, for only the king could grant rights of government directly. These nearly feudal proprietorships typically included features annoying to individual colonists, such as requiring an oath of loyalty to the proprietor and the payment of quit rents.

To offset such objections, in 1665 the proprietors Berkeley and Carteret issued a set of "Concessions and Agreement of the Lords Proprietors of the

Province of New Caesarea or New-Jersey" to induce settlers into New Jersey. This document was the first explicit expression of fundamental law in New Jersey, and this law was to be "consonant" with the laws of England as much as "conveniently agreeable."[1511]

The specific provisions of the "Concessions" relating to land rights may be summarized as follows:

General Provisions:

> Item 3: The chief secretary shall record all grants, conveyances, leases (of more than one year) of land and houses, which shall be witnessed, acknowledged, and attested.
>
> Item 4: A surveyor general shall be appointed to lay out and bound all lands granted within the province.
>
> Item 6: All persons who swear allegiance to the King of England shall be admitted to plant and become freemen of the province.

[1511] "This instrument of government possessed the nature of a constitution even though, being handed down by a superior claiming both the right of territory and the right of government, it differs from the modern concept of an organic law as one created by the sovereign power residing in the people. It provided for a governor representing the proprietors, a council appointed by him and other officials designated by the proprietors or by him, and a general assembly consisting of the governor, members of the council, and elected representatives. The franchise was limited to freeholders and annual elections for the twelve representatives of the lower house were authorized. The legislature had authority to create courts of law, to levy taxes, to raise a militia, to establish local units of government, and to enact all other necessary laws provided they were 'consonant to reason and, as neare as may be conveniently agreeable to the Lawes and Customes of his Majesties Kingdom of England' and not against the interest of the proprietors or their heirs. The proprietors reserved the right to give their assent or refusal to such legislation. Certain private rights were assured, among them the guarantee of liberty of conscience. No taxes were to be levied without the consent of the representatives. Possession of land for seven years operated as a proscription against review or resurvey." *Fundamental Laws and Constitutions of New Jersey 1664-1964* 9-10 (Julian P. Boyd, ed., 1964).

Powers of the Assembly:

> To make necessary laws "as neere as may be conveniently agreeable to the Lawes and Customes of this Majesties Kingdom of England."
>
> To lay equal taxes and assessments upon lands.
>
> To create as many manors in the province as seems "meet and convenient."
>
> To prescribe the quantities of land to be allotted to each person, to make rules for casting of lots for land.
>
> To make provision for collecting quitrents.

Powers of the Governor and Council:

> To make warrants and to seal grants of land.
>
> For the Security of the Proprietors and Inhabitants:
>
> Lands quietly held, planted and possessed for seven years after survey shall not be subject to review or survey or alteration of bounds.
>
> No one whose cattle stray on public land within the province is liable for trespass, provided custom of commons is not claimed nor any person hindered from taking up and appropriating land so grazed upon, and the cattle are not intentionally grazed upon such lands.

For More Speedily Settling the Province [the following head rights apply]:

> Persons already in the province before January 1, 1665
> Freemen with arms and provisions - 150 acres

For servants with arms and provision - 150 acres
For weaker servants, slaves over 14 years of age /- 75 acres
For Christian servants, upon completion of service /- 75 acres
Persons who shall go to the province before January 1, 1665
Masters and mistresses /- 120 acres
For able-bodied male servants /- 120 acres
For weaker servants or for slaves over 14 years of age /- 60 acres
Christian servants, for their own use /- 60 acres
Persons who arrive during 1665
acres for each free person and able-bodied servant
acres for each weaker servant, slave over 14, Christian servant
Persons who arrive during 1666
acres for each free person and able-bodied servant
acres for each weaker servant, slave over 14, Christian servant
Various occupancy requirements

To Provide that Lands be More Regularly Laid Out and Titles and Possession Better Ascertained:

i. Lands shall be divided into lots of not less than 2,100 acres nor more than 21,000 acres.

ii & iii. The Governor or his deputy shall sign and seal warrants, and other provisions to survey, certify and record conveyances, with grants of land to be in approximately the following form:

The Lords Propriators of the Province of New Cesaria or New Jersey doe hereby Grannt unto A B of the Province aforesaid A plantation conteyning acres English measure bounding (as in the Certificates) To

> hold to him (or her) his (or her) heires and assignes for ever, Yeilding and payeing yearely to the said Lord Propriators their heires or assignes every 25th day of March according to the English account, One halfe penny or One penny of lawfull money of England for every of the said acres To be holden of the Manor of in free and common Soccage, the first payment of which Rent to begin the 25th day of March which shall be in the yeare of our Lord according to the English account 1670 . . . .
>
> iv. Convenient portions of lands are granted for highways and streets not more than 100 feet wide, and 200 acres for parish churches.
>
> Lands laid out for streets and churches are exempt from rents and taxes.
>
> vi. Quitrent of one half penny per acre paid yearly.
>
> vii. Inhabitants have "free passage through or by any Seas, bounds creeks rivers rivuletts &c. in the said Province through or by which they must necessarilie passe to come from the maine Ocean to any part of the Province aforesaid."[1512]

Meanwhile, even before the 1665 "Concessions and Agreement," the governor of New York in 1664 purchased large tracts of New Jersey lands from Indians and made grants of those lands to settlers from Long Island wishing to establish a town. The grants conferred the usual rights and required the payment of quit rents, but they remitted the quit rent payments until 1670. These settlers moved in under the New York grants and then took the oath of loyalty to the proprietary governor of New Jersey. The New York governor subsequently made another large grant of New Jersey land in 1665, this one deferring quit rent payments until 1672. Again the

---

[1512] *Id.* at 51-66.

settlers swore loyalty to the New Jersey governor, who issued confirmatory deeds of subsequent grants and, when he issued a town charter, required payment of the town quit rent.

The towns founded during this period were each planned before settlement. The typical town settler obtained by purchase a home lot with some meadow and upland acreage as well, distributed either by assignment or by lot. The town quit rents were also accorded a period of grace, but when that period ended, the towns objected to the quit rents; their objections rested on the theory that their land rights actually derived from the earlier grant to Berkeley and Carteret rather than from the New York governor's grant. The Berkeley and Carteret grant had not specified quit rent and had preceded the ""Concessions and Agreement". One town even based nonpayment on the theory that its land was obtained from the Indians.

Finally, in 1672 in England, the Duke of York responded angrily to the situation by revoking all grants from the New York governor and requiring obedience from all. To follow up with this retrenchment, on December 6, 1672, the proprietor Carteret issued changes in the government and land rules in a document styled "A Declaration of the True Intent and Meaning of the Concessions and Agreement."

§ 10.06(e)(3). Clarification of Land Rights in 1672.

The 1672 order of the proprietors called "A Declaration of the True Intent and Meaning of us Lords Proprietors, and Explanation of their Concessions made to the Adventurers and Planters of New-Caesarea or New-Jersey," among other provisions, required that no person could be considered a freeholder and able to vote unless already holding lands by patent, that is, by proprietary title.[1513] "All landowners must obtain proprietary patents lest their lands be forfeited, and the constables were ordered to collect quitrents by action of distraint . . . . Henceforth the

[1513] *Id.* at 67-70.

governor and council alone would qualify freemen, establish courts, charter town corporations, appoint provincial officers, and allot lands. They alone would decide what measures would be introduced in the assembly. Those participating in the rebellion must yield submission, and all individuals and towns must pay their quitrent arrears immediately. Though the revolt was put down, the grievances that were engendered festered until the end of the proprietary period in 1702." [1514]

§ 10.06(f). Division of the Province into East New Jersey and West New Jersey.

Berkeley sold his interest in New Jersey in 1674, but the buyer went bankrupt in 1676. One of the trustees managing his affairs was William Penn, and in 1676, Penn and the other trustees persuaded Carteret to permit a division of New Jersey into East New Jersey (3,000 square miles) and West New Jersey (4,600 square miles), with the western portion coming under the stewardship of Penn and the other trustees. This division of New Jersey would last until 1702.

§ 10.06(f)(1). Landholding in East New Jersey.

In East New Jersey, the basic law that had been adopted earlier by the first assembly of the whole province, in a five-day session held at Elizabethtown in 1668, was continued in force. After the division, the East New Jersey assembly met sporadically and adopted, with minor modifications, portions of the "Duke's Law."

The pattern of landholding differed between East and West Jersey. "In the eastern division the holdings were smaller, except probably among the Dutch, the land being more intensely cultivated. This was due somewhat to the nature of the soil, and the fact that a commercial spirit was more prevalent than in West Jersey."[1515]

[1514] John E. Pomfret, *Colonial New Jersey, a History* 31 (1973).

[1515] Francis Bazley Lee, *New Jersey As a Colony and As a State* 193-194 (1902).

In East New Jersey the discontent among the settlers continued over the issue of how much power rested with the proprietors. Finally, in 1682 the Carteret heirs sold their proprietorship over East New Jersey to a group headed by William Penn (who was already immersed in the affairs of West New Jersey). The conveyance was accomplished by a deed of lease and release, dated February 1-2, 1682, reciting that the purchasers had bought the soil, all arrears of quit rents, and the right of government. These new proprietors, along with others added to their number shortly thereafter, drew up "Fundamental Constitutions" for East New Jersey, revealing the proprietors' strong feudal orientation, but the assembly never adopted the provisions.

Upon the arrival of a new deputy governor (the chief official in residence in the province) in 1684, the proprietors instructed him to continue land purchases from the Indians, to resurvey patents in dispute, to collect quit rents in arrears, and to review the validity of disputed land titles. In 1685 the proprietors created the Board of Proprietors of the Eastern Division of New Jersey with broad powers. The Board could settle land issues between proprietors and settler, but the system of conveyancing was becoming very confused.[1516] Therefore, the Board was instructed to refine the land distribution procedures.[1517]

[1516] "[The Board] could approve acts of the assembly until reviewed by the British proprietors; it could settle matters at issue between the proprietors and the inhabitants, especially pretenses to land, arrears of quitrents, and the validity of titles; it could lease proprietors' lands, purchase land from the Indians, and determine the boundary lines with West New Jersey and New York . . . . Because East New Jersey land was held by twenty-four proprietors, conveyances were expressed as fractional shares of a proprietorship. . . By now the system of land conveyancing was causing untold confusion in both Jerseys. For instance, the transfer of 1/32 of 1/16 of ½ share (of 24) by Nicholas Brown of Shrewsbury to Stephen West of New England is a prime example of the process in East Jersey . . . ." *Id.* at 58.

[1517] "As instructed, the board strove to perfect the orderly laying out of the proprietors' lands. They would be sold at not less than £10 per acre. To prevent engrossing, no one might buy or lease more than 1,000 acres on one site. On individual holdings the quitrent was reduced to 1d. per acre. When huge tracts were purchased from the Indians, such as the 24,000-acre holding at Barnegat, they would be divided into twenty-four parts, and small purchases would be assigned in rotation to a few proprietors in turn. Assessments of £5 and £10 were levied from time to time for land development on all proprietors." John E. Pomfret, *Colonial New Jersey, A History* 58-59 (1973).

A dispute over quit rent payments was finally settled by a test case in the provincial court, following which the towns capitulated and paid their quit rents.

§ 10.06(f)(2). Landholding in West New Jersey.

In West New Jersey, Penn and his associates prepared the famous "Concessions and Agreements of the Proprietors, Freeholders, and Inhabitants of the Province of West New Jersey," written in 1676 (probably by Edward Byllynge, the chief proprietor) and issued in 1677. These "concessions and agreements" conferred substantial rights of self-government and liberal land provisions.[1518]

Over time the "medium-sized farm" evolved into a larger holding in West Jersey:

> In the western division the settlers took up large tracts, and through the consolidation of estates, owing to intermarriages of members of the Society of Friends and a general observance of the rule of primogeniture, acre

---

[1518] "The Concessions of 1677 provided for an elected assembly with power to enact laws providing they were in conformity with the laws of England and the Concessions themselves. All adult males, with few exceptions, were entitled to vote on measures of the assembly. The first duty of an assemblyman was to present the recommendations or grievances of his constituents, and should he fail to do so he could be challenged by the other members of his district. All bills could be amended, and a two-thirds vote was required for passage. Until the assembly met (the first meeting was scheduled for March 25, 1681, the beginning of the year, old style) the province would be governed by appointed commissioners who would also serve as magistrates. The Concessions also contained a carefully prepared code of law, embodying Quaker notions of justice which were adopted with little change. Since the trustees expected to dispose of all 100 shares, there could be no proprietary system of overlordship. The commissioners were instructed to purchase large tracts of land from the Indians and to divide each purchase into 100 parts. The first dividend of land was stipulated at 5,000 acres per full share, with the fractioner receiving land in proportion [by 1714 each full proprietary share had yielded its owner 16,500 acres in four dividends]. The quitrent system did not take root in West Jersey, because the shareholder imposing quitrents would have had little chance of selling his lands. The unit of settlement became a medium-sized farm cultivated by the owner and his family. The Concessions provided a headright system, and liberal terms - 50 acres and freedom dues were offered indentured servants at the expiration of a three or four-year term." *Id.* at 41-42 (1973).

was laid to acre, until West Jersey passed under the control of comparatively few families. Consequently the growth of a landed aristocracy was a logical conclusion. While many of West Jersey's landed proprietors, by their interests in timber and in trade, were enabled to maintain their estates, others were plunged hopelessly in debt, as the result of improvident and expensive methods of cultivation. This condition became apparent long before the outbreak of the Revolutionary War, and caused young men in such families to "clear" less desirable but cheaper land in the "Pines," or to engage in business in Philadelphia.[1519]

§ 10.06(f)(2)(A). The 1677 "Concessions and Agreements" for West New Jersey.

The provisions of the 1677 "Concessions and Agreements of the Proprietors Freeholders and Inhabitants of the Province of West New Jersey in America" relating to landholding are listed or summarized as follows:

Chapter 1: Commissioners to be appointed to obtain land and distribute it to shareholders, and to keep a registry; commissioners also to set out towns and establish boundaries.

Chapter 2: Commissioners to ensure that lands are properly surveyed and registered.

Chapter 4: Headright system established: during the first year, 70 acres per able-bodied person and 50 acres for each younger or weaker person; small acreages in subsequent years. Quitrents set at one penny per acre for

---

[1519] Francis Bazley Lee, *New Jersey As a Colony and As a State* 193-194 (1902).

town land and one-half penny per acre for other land, with declining amounts for land acquired later. Conditions of settlement and improvements set out for maintaining land grants; upon failure of an owner to meet the conditions, the commissioners may lease the land for a term of up to twenty years.

Chapter 5: Regulations for surveying and registering the land.

Chapter 6: Lands allotted for public facilities such as highways and streets, harbors and public houses. Rights in public lands described:

That all inhabitants within the said Province of West Jersey have the Liberty of Fishing in Delaware River or on the sea coast and the Liberty of Hunting and Killing any Deer or other wild beasts the Liberty to Shoot or Take any wild Fowles within the said Province provided alwaies that they doe not Hunt Kill Shoot or Take any such Deer wild Beasts or Fowles upon the Lands that is or shall be surveyed taken up inclosed sowen and planted except the owners of the sd lands or their assignes.

Chapter 7: Title to lands held at least seven years after survey and registration shall be secure.

Chapter 8: Custom of commons affirmed, and the owner of stray cattle on such land shall not be liable to trespass.

Chapter 11: No tax to be imposed on the inhabitants without their consent.

Chapter 17: No freeholder or inhabitant "shall be deprived or condemned of Life limb Liberty estate Property or any wayes hurt in his or their Priveledges Freedoms or Franchises . . . without a due tryall and Judgement passed by twelve good and Lawfull men of his neighborhood first had . . . ."

Chapter 24: Registers of "all deeds evidences and conveyances of land" to be kept both in England and in the province of West Jersey. Instructions for execution and registration given for such documents, including leases and mortgages.

Chapter 26: Grants of Indian lands to be made in writing.

Chapter 29: Administration of decedents' estates and care of orphans.

Chapter 43: Taxes and assessments levied on lands shall be imposed equally.[1520]

§ 10.06(f)(2)(B). The Ten "Fundamentals" of 1681.

The commissioners governed until the assembly first met in 1681. When the assembly did meet, its first act was to adopt ten "fundamentals" whose purpose was to keep governing power in the hands of the inhabitants. None of the ten ""fundamentals" dealt directly with land rights, except number six, prohibiting the levying of any tax without authority of the assembly[1521]

§ 10.06(f)(2)(C). Later Land Regulations.

During the ensuing years, other laws and regulations dealing with land

---

[1520] *Fundamental Laws and Constitutions of New Jersey, 1664-1964* 71-104 (Julian P. Boyd, ed., 1964).

[1521] "The Fundamental Agreements of the Governor, Proprietors, Freeholders, and Inhabitants of the Province of West New Jersey, November 25, 1681," *Id.* at 105-108.

were adopted. The colony appointed and gave broad powers to Commissioners for the Settling and Regulation of Lands. Among other tasks they marked the bounds of tenths, laying out 64,000 acres in each tenth intended for distribution to the proprietors or their designees. By 1693, with the full establishment of the county system of local government, the system of tenths gradually fell into disuse. [1522]

As in East New Jersey, the system of conveyancing had become complex and confusing. With the proprietor Fenwick holding 10 of the 100 shares and disposing of them independently, a typical West New Jersey conveyance would be the "sale of shares by George Hutcheson to Anthony Woodhouse."[1523]

Among the West New Jersey proprietors, a Dr. Daniel Coxe purchased the holdings of the Byllynge heirs in 1687. In that same year, the West New Jersey assembly "requested the resident proprietors to assume management of all proprietary lands. A group of fifty-nine resident proprietors, each owning a share, organized as the Council of Proprietors of West Jersey in September 1688. From their number they elected nine commissioners, five from Burlington and four from Gloucester County. The principal responsibilities of the council were to record all proprietary rights, supervise the distribution of dividends of land, issue warrants of survey, and administer unappropriated lands."[1524]

As a sop to Coxe, the West Jersey Council refrained from enforcing its restriction on the formation of great estates. Coxe's agents proceeded to buy up huge tracts, so that by 1692 Coxe owned probably twenty proprieties amounting to more than one million acres. He even attempted to establish a manor, called Coxe's Hall, with servants, feudal services, and quit rents. Worried about interference with the province by Governor Andros of New York, however, Coxe sold his holdings in 1693.

[1522] John E. Pomfret, *Colonial New Jersey, A History* 47-48 (1973).

[1523] *Id.* at 58.

[1524] *Id.* at 48.

§ 10.06(g). Transforming the Proprietary Colonies into a Royal Province.

Proprietors of both New Jersey divisions were ready to transfer rights of government to the English crown in 1701. King William III approved the commission and instructions to the royal governor in November, 1702, but his death delayed the approval and execution of the Act of Surrender by Queen Anne until April 1703. The commission and instructions to the royal governor, with occasional enlargements and renewals, comprised the basic law of New Jersey until 1776.

§ 10.06(h). Instructions to the Royal Governor Pertaining to Land.

The provisions of the first royal governor's commission and instructions that related to landholding in the reunified New Jersey colony are listed or summarized as follows:

> One general assembly for both East New Jersey and West New Jersey should be formed and called.
>
> An assembly member must have a freehold interest in at least 1,000 acres situated in the division for which the member is elected; voters must have a freehold estate of at least 100 acres.
>
> The governor is to collect, revise, correct and enact all previous laws of New Jersey as "shall be judged proper, and conducive to Our service and the Welfare of Our said Province, that they may be transmitted unto Us in Authentick Form, for our Approbation or Disallowance.
>
> Our Will and Pleasure is that for the better quieting the minds of Our Good Subjects Inhabitants of Our said Province, and for settling the Properties and Possessions of all Persons concerned therein, either as General

Proprietors of the Soyle under the first Original Grant of the said Province made by the late King Charles the Second to the late Duke of Yorke, Or as particular Purchasers of any Parcells of Land from the said General Proprietors, You shall propose to the General Assembly of Our Said Province the passing of such Act, or Acts, whereby the Right and Property of the said General Proprietors, to the Soyle of Our said Province may be confirmed to them according to their respective Rights and Titles; together with all such Quit-Rents as have been reserved or are or shall become due to the said General Proprietors from the Inhabitants of our said Province, and all such Priviledges as are exprest in the Conveyances made by the said Duke of Yorke; Excepting only the Right of Government, which remains in Us; And You are further to take care that by the said Act or Acts so to be passed the particular Titles and Estates of all the Inhabitants of that Province and other Purchasers claiming under the said General Proprietors be confirmed and Settled as of Right does appertain, under such obligations as shall tend to the best and speediest Improvement or Cultivation of the same. Provided always that you do not consent to any Act or Acts to lay any Tax upon Lands that lye unprofitable.

You shall not permit any other Person or Persons, beside the said General Proprietors, or their Agents to purchase any land whatsoever from the Indians within the Limits of their Grant.

You are to permit the Surveyors and other Person appointed by the aforementioned General Proprietors of the Soile of that Province, for Surveying and recording the Surveys of Land granted by, and held of them, to Execute accordingly their respective Trusts, And You are likewise to permit and, if need be, aid and Assist such other Agent or Agents, as shall be appointed by the said Proprietors for that End, To Collect and Receive the Quit-Rents which are

> or shall be due unto them, from the particular Possessors of any parcells or Tracts of Land from time to time . . . .
>
> You are to take care that no Mans life, Member, Freehold or Goods be taken away or harmed in Our said Province, otherwise than by Established and known Laws, not repugnant to, but as much as may be agreeable to the Laws of England.
>
> [¶ 34 of instructions following the numbered paragraphs]:
>
> You are for the better Administration of Justice to Endeavour to get a Law passed (if not already done) wherein shall be set the Value of Mens Estates either in Good or Lands, under which they shall not be capable of Serving as Jurors.[1525]

The assembly of the now united province of New Jersey began to sit on a regular basis in 1703, issuing its session laws in printed form a few pages at a time. A collection of laws passed between 1703-1717 was published in 1717, with supplemented versions reprinted up through 1722. The laws relating to landholding in that legislation are listed or summarized as follows:

> Ch. I (1703): Regulating the purchasing of land from the Indians.
>
> Ch. XII (1709): Explaining grants and patents for land executed by Phillip Cartert and Council in the Eastern Division, "according to the true intent and meaning of the Grantor and Grantee."
>
> Ch. XXIII (1709): Dividing and ascertaining the boundaries of all the counties of the province.

[1525] "The Instructions from the Queen in Council to the Governor of the Province of New Jersey, November 16, 1702," in *Fundamental Laws and Constitutions of New Jersey, 1664-1964,* 126-154 (Julian P. Boyd, ed., 1964).

Ch. XXXIX (1713): Preventing waste of timber, pine and cedar trees and poles within the province.

Ch. XLVI (1713): Confirming letters of administration granted within the province.

Ch. XLVIII (1713): Regulating fences.

Ch. LI (1713): "An Act for Confirming of Conveyances of Lands made and to be made by Wills and Powers of Attorney, and declaring what Exemplifications of Records and other Things shall be holden and received for good Evidence of Estates of Inheritance, and for Transfering Uses into Possession." Included within this legislation is an intriguing section essentially reenacting the Statute of Uses, which had been in effect in England for 177 years and for 71 years before the first permanent English settlement in North America:

And be it enacted by the Authority aforesaid, That all and every Person or Persons to whom the use or uses of any Tract or Tracts of Land within this Province have been Sold, Given, Limited, Granted, Released or Conveyed by Deed, Grant or any other Legal Conveyance whatsoever, or that shall hereafter be granted by any Deed or Conveyance whatsoever, such Grantees, their Heirs and Assigns shall be Deemed, Taken and Esteemed to be in as Full and Ample Possession of such Lands, Tenements and Hereditaments, to all Intents, Constructions and Purposes as if such Grantees, their Heirs and Assigns were possessed thereof by solemn Livery of Seisin and Possession, and Usage or Custom to the contrary notwithstanding.

Ch. LII (1713): Shortening of law suits, and regulating the practice of law.

> Ch. LV (1713): Acknowledging and recording of deeds and conveyances of land within each county.
>
> Ch. LXVI (1713): Enforcing the observation of the ordinance for establishing fees within the province [including a schedule of attorney's fees for drafting of specific documents].

Among the private acts from this 1713 session of the assembly were several relating to testamentary conveyances of land and authorizing owners of meadow and marshland to take measures on both their own lands and adjoining lands to stop tides from overflowing their lands.

> An act of 1716 establishing a fee schedule for documents concerning titles to land.
>
> An act of 1718 "for Running and Ascertaining the Line of Partition or Division between the Eastern and Western Divisions of the Province of New-Jersey, and for preventing Disputes for the Future concerning the same; and for securing to the general Proprietors of the Soil of each of the Divisions, and Persons claiming under them their several and respective Possessions, Rights and Just Claims."
>
> An act of 1720 to prevent the multiplicity of lawsuits.[1526]

§ 10.06. Bibliography.

Books

Bartlett, John Russell, ed., *Records of the Colony of Rhode Island and Providence Plantations in New England* (1856).

Boyd, Julian P., ed., *Fundamental Laws and Constitutions of New Jersey 1664-1964* (1964).

Bozman, John Leeds, *The History of Maryland, From Its First Settlement, in 1633, to the Restoration, in 1660* (1837).

Brugger, Robert J., *Maryland, A Middle Temperament: 1634-1980* (1988).

[1526] *The Earliest Printed Laws of New Jersey, 1703-1722* 1-145 (John D. Cushing, ed., 1978).

Brumbaugh, Martin Grove, and Joseph Solomon Walton, eds., *Penn's Frame of Government and Privileges and Concessions of 1701* (1898).

Clark, George Larkin, *A History of Connecticut: Its People and Institutions* (1914).

Cushing, John D., ed., *The Earliest Acts and Laws of the Colony of Rhode Island and Providence Plantations, 1647-1719* (1977).

Cushing, John D., ed., *The Earliest Laws of the New Haven and Connecticut Colonies, 1639-1673* (1977).

Cushing, John D., ed., *The Earliest Printed Laws of Delaware 1704-1741* (1978).

Cushing, John D., ed., *The Earliest Printed Laws of New Jersey 1703-1722* (1978).

Cushing, John D., ed., *The Earliest Printed Laws of Pennsylvania 1681-1713* (1978).

Eaton, Amasa M., *The Development of the Judicial System in Rhode Island* (1904).

Fisher, Edgar Jacob, *New Jersey as a Royal Province, 1738-1776* (1911).

Friedman, Lawrence M., *A History of American Law* (3d ed. 2005).

Gordon, Thomas F., *The History of New Jersey, From its Founding by Europeans to the Adoption of the Federal Constitution* (1834).

Gould, Clarence P., *The Land System in Maryland, 1720-1765* (1913).

Hall, Clayton Colman, *The Lords Baltimore and the Maryland Palatinate: Six Lectures on Maryland Colonial History Delivered Before The Johns Hopkins University in the Year 1902* (1902).

Hoffecker, Carol E., *Delaware, A Bicentennial History* (1977).

Hood, John, *Index of Colonial and State Laws Between the Years of 1663 and 1877 Inclusive* (1877).

Hopkins, Charles Wyman, *The Home Lots of the Early Settlers of the Providence Plantations, with Notes and Plats* (1886).

Horle, Craig W., ed., *Records of the Courts of Sussex County, Delaware, 1677-1710* (1991).

James, Sydney V., *Colonial Rhode Island: A History* (1975).

Land, Aubrey C., *Colonial Maryland: A History* (1981).

Leaming, Aaron, and Jacob Spicer, *The Grants, Concessions, and Original Constitutions of the Province of New Jersey* (2002).

Lee, Francis Bazley, *New Jersey as a Colony and as a State* (1903).

Leiby, Adrian C., *The Early Dutch and Swedish Settlers of New Jersey* (1964).

MacDonald, William, ed., *Select Charters and Other Documents Illustrative of American History, 1606-1775* (1914).

McCormick, Richard P., *New Jersey from Colony to State* (1964).

McLoughlin, William C., *Rhode Island, A Bicentennial History* (1978).

Mereness, Newton D., *Maryland as a Proprietary Province* (1901).

Moyer, Timothy C., *A Survey of Land Use and Acquisition Laws in Colonial New Jersey* (1977).

Mulford, Isaac S., *A Civil and Political History of New Jersey* (1851).

Munroe, John A., *Colonial Delaware, A History* (1978).

Munroe, John A., *History of Delaware* (2d ed. 1984).

Osgood, Herbert L., *The American Colonies in the Seventeenth Century* (1904).

Pomfret, John E., *Colonial New Jersey, A History* (1973).

Pomfret, John E., *The Province of East New Jersey, 1609-1702: The Rebellious Proprietary* (1981).

Pomfret, John E., *The Province of West New Jersey, 1609-1702: A History of the Origins of an American Colony* (1956).

Price, Edward T., *Dividing the Land: Early American Beginnings of Our Private Property Mosaic* (1995).

Rairigh, William Nelson, *The English Law in Maryland, 1634-1689* (1939).

Reinsch, Paul Samuel, *English Common Law in the Early American Colonies* (1899).

Scharf, J. Thomas, *History of Delaware 1609-1888* (1888).
Shepherd, William Robert, *History of Proprietary Government in Pennsylvania* (2009).
Soderlind, Arthur E., *Colonial Connecticut* (1976).
Steiner, Bernard C., *Beginnings of Maryland, 1631-1639* (1903).
Taylor, Robert J., *Colonial Connecticut: A History* (1979).
Trumbull, Benjamin, *A Complete History of Connecticut, Civil and Ecclesiastical* (1898).
Trumbull, James Hammond, *The Public Records of the Colony of Connecticut* (2009).
Weslager, C. A., *Dutch Explorers, Traders and Settlers in the Delaware Valley, 1609-1664* (1961).
Whitehead, John, *The Judicial and Civil History of New Jersey* (1897).

Chapters in Books

Land, Aubrey C., "The Colonial Period," in Radoff, Morris L., ed., *The Old Line State, A History of Maryland* (1971).
"Pennsylvania and Delaware Frame," in MacDonald, William, ed., *Select Charters and Other Documents Illustrative of American History, 1606-1775* (1914).
Reinsch, Samuel Paul, "The English Common Law in the Early American Colonies," in American Association of Law Schools, *Select Essays in Anglo-American Legal History* (1907).
"The Fundamental Agreements of the Governor, Proprietors, Freeholders, and Inhabitants of the Province of West New Jersey, November 25, 1681," in Boyd, Julian P., ed., *Fundamental Laws and Constitutions of New Jersey 1664-1964* (1964).
"The Instructions from the Queen in Council to the Governor of the Province of New Jersey, November 16, 1702," in Boyd, Julian P., ed., *Fundamental Laws and Constitutions of New Jersey 1664-1964* (1964).
"The Settlement," in Radoff, Morris L., ed., *The Old Line State, A History of Maryland* (1971).

Articles

Collier, Christopher, "Why the First Law School in The United States Was Founded in Connecticut," 31 *Int'l J. Legal Information* 205 (2003).
Dayton, Cornelia Hughes, "Turning Points and the Relevance of Colonial Legal History," 50 *The William and Mary Quarterly, Third Series* 7 (Jan., 1993).
Fogarty, Gerald P., "Property and Religious Liberty in Colonial Maryland Catholic Thought," 72 *The Catholic Historical Review* 573 (Oct., 1986).
Goodman, Leonard S., "Mandamus in the Colonies - The Rise of the Superintending Power of American Courts - Part 2," 2 *Am. J. Legal Hist.* 1 (1958).
Haskins, George L., "Influences of New England Law on the Middle Colonies," 1 *Law & Hist. Rev.* 238 (Spring 1983).
Haskins, George L., and Samuel E. Ewing III, "The Spread of Massachusetts Law in the Seventeenth Century," 106 *U. Pa. L. Rev.* 413 (Nov. 1957).
Lurie, Maxine N., "New Jersey: The Unique Proprietary," 111 *The Pennsylvania Magazine of History and Biography* 77 (Jan., 1987).
Mayo, Ernest G., "Rhode Island's Reception of the Common Law," 31 *Suffolk U. L. Rev.* 609 (1997).

Menard, Russell R., "From Servant to Freeholder: Status Mobility and Property Accumulation in Seventeenth-Century Maryland," 30 *The William and Mary Quarterly, Third Series* 37 (Jan., 1973).

Pomfret, John E., "The Problem of the West Jersey Concessions of 1676/7," 5 *The William and Mary Quarterly, Third Series* 95 (Jan., 1948).

Pope, Herbert, "The English Common Law in The United States," 24 *Harv. L. Rev.* 6 (Nov. 1910).

Presser, Stephen B., "An Introduction to the Legal History of Colonial New Jersey," 7 *Rutgers-Cam L.J.* 262 (1975-1976).

Steiner, Bernard C., "Adoption of English Law in Maryland," 8 *Yale L.J.* 353 (October 1898 - June 1899).

Stoebuck, William B., "Reception of English Common Law in the American Colonies," 10 *Wm. & Mary L. Rev.* 393 (Fall 1968).

Thomas, David A., "Anglo-American Land Law: Diverging Developments from a Shared History—Part II: How Anglo-American Land Law Diverged after American Colonization and Independence," 34 *Real Prop. Prob. & Tr. J.* 295 (Spring 1999).

Woodward, Carl R., "Agricultural Legislation in Colonial New Jersey," 3 *Agricultural History* 15 (Jan., 1929).

Cases

Frieszleben v. Shallcross, 19 A. 576 (Del. 1890).

Chapter 11

Land Law in the Colonies of Pennsylvania (from 1643), North Carolina (from 1650), South Carolina (from 1670) and Georgia (from 1732)[1527]

SYNOPSIS

[1527] The content of this chapter was originally written by the author, and some content was drawn or reprinted from Vol. 1 of Thompson on Real Property.

Chapter 11. Land Law in the Colonies of Pennsylvania (from 1643), North Carolina (from 1650), South Carolina (from 1670) and Georgia (from 1732)

§ 11.01. Development of Land Law in Pennsylvania (from 1643).

§ 11.01(a). Early Settlement Activity.

Entry of Europeans into the region that is now Pennsylvania began in 1609, when Henry Hudson sailed into Delaware Bay, soon to be followed by other Dutch parties exploring the Delaware River. In 1633 an employee of the Dutch West India Company purchased from the Indians a parcel of land near the Schuylkill River, to be used for establishing a trading post. Because the predominant Dutch interest was fur trading, large real estate holdings were not important.

In 1638 Swedish and Finnish settlers, under the leadership of the Dutchman Peter Minuit and the auspices of the New Sweden Company, purchased more land on the Pennsylvania side of the Delaware River, below the Schuylkill River, which they then divided into farms. As in their concurrent settlement activity in Delaware, the Swedes were unable to base claims to land on rights of discovery or conquest, so they "purchased" lands from the Indians. The purchaser was nominally the Swedish South Sea Company, which had received its first letters patent from King Gustavus Adolphus in 1624, and an essentially similar second charter in 1626.

In 1640 the Swedish West India Company granted to certain Dutch investors a charter effectively creating a patroonship, in order that they could found another settlement in New Sweden. The grantees held their land under the protection of Sweden as hereditary property, with the feudalistic high and low jurisdiction. For the most part, however, the rival Dutch and Swedish colonies competed in "purchasing" lands from the Indians.

§ 11.01(b). The Commencement of English Rule in 1664.

In 1664 the English King Charles II granted to his brother, the Duke of York, lands that included much of what the Dutch claimed in America; this led directly to the English takeover of New Amsterdam, which they quickly renamed New York. An English fleet then approached the Delaware settlements, obtaining the acquiescence of the Swedish colonists and the surrender of the Dutch after a brief battle. The lands included in this famous grant encompassed the future states of New York, New Jersey, Delaware and Pennsylvania. The English also took some territory of the Dutch that was not included in the grant to the Duke of York but had, in fact, been included in the 1632 grant of Maryland to Lord Baltimore.

The royal charter of 1664 is discussed in detail in §9.05(e)(1), and here it is necessary only to reiterate that "the patent was expressed in terms of the fullest property rights consistent with the feudal incidents still connected with the tenure of free and common socage"; that "the grantee, as a feudal lord, was given extensive powers of government and court jurisdiction"; that "the laws to be administered in the granted lands were to be not contrary to and as near "as conveniently may bee' to the laws of England, [with] judicial judgments and sentences . . . subject to a right of appeal in England"; and that "the terms of this patent appeared designed to expressly supersede any previous and conflicting grants of the same lands."[1528]

§ 11.01(b)(1). Application of The Duke's Law in 1665.

The "Duke's Law" of 1665 implemented the powers of the 1664

[1528] *See* § 9.05(e)(1).

charter, although at first, settlers in the former Dutch areas governed themselves by their traditional laws. Even this changed, however, when English rule resumed after a brief Dutch interlude in 1673-1674. The provisions of the "Duke's Law" relating to landholding, typical of English laws adapted to the frontier environment, are summarized in §9.05(e)(2).

§ 11.01(b)(2). Landholding in Pennsylvania Settlements Incident to Growth in Other Colonies.

In addition to the handful of Swedish, Finnish and Dutch settlers who remained on Pennsylvania soil after the English took over in 1664, a few English settlers moved in because the Pennsylvania land was near to settlement activity taking place in adjacent English provinces. For instance, while most of the English in the lower Delaware Valley were establishing themselves in West New Jersey by 1680, a few took up land across the river in Pennsylvania. Likewise, farther south, some settlers with land patents obtained from the Duke of York during the 1670's, moved in from Maryland; these Marylanders were tobacco farmers who brought slaves with them.

Virtually all of this settlement activity was confined to the Delaware Valley, or the valley of the Delaware River. While the east bank of the river was clearly in New Jersey Territory, the west bank, the so-called Three Lower Counties, was rather tenuously claimed by Maryland. In fact, this area had been included in the 1632 grant to Maryland's proprietor, Lord Baltimore, but the actual settlers had been mostly Dutch, initially under the governance of New Netherland and then under New York, but not under Maryland.

Landholding practices among these early settlers followed various patterns. In the Dutch communities, the basic assumptions underlying the patroonship system prevailed, even though patroonships themselves were not successful. Some lands designated as patroonships, even without official patroonship administration, remained undivided and at least nominally under feudal obligations.[1529]

Even though the patroonships failed, the principles announced in the patroonship charter remained as permanent characteristics of Dutch governance and land arrangements.[1530]

After the Dutch assumed nominal control of the Swedish settlements in 1655, they agreed to respect the customs, religion, and private property claims of Swedish settlers who wished to remain. When the Dutch took up possession of this territory, they also introduced their land management practices.[1531]

At the same time, a few English colonists from the New England

---

[1529] "[T]he Charter of Privileges to patroons . . . was intended to encourage private individuals to establish settlements at various points on the Hudson and Delaware, or North and South, rivers. Numerous grievances, occasioned by friction between patroons and the Company, were partially allayed by a new charter in 1640, restricting the area of the grants, and encouraging independent settlement; but the feudal privileges of the patroons were not interfered with. Many of the old patroon estates long remained undivided, and the heirs of the founders claimed some semi-feudal privileges well into the nineteenth century." William MacDonald, *Select Charters and Other Documents Illustrative of American History 1606-1775* 43 (1914).

[1530] "This charter formed the principal basis upon which the civil institutions of New Netherland came to be placed . . . . The principal directors of the plan were ready to seize for themselves the advantages offered; in the character as Patroons, they secured acquisitions in the province which almost gave them a monopoly in land, and thus they were able to retain, in their own hands, some of the most important privileges yielded in the charter. To the mass of actual settlers nothing whatever was given. The charter contemplated or allowed, the establishment of a kind of feudal or manorial rule, by which the colonists would be held in a state of complete dependence. No provision was made for the division of lands, either present or prospective. The people to be sent by the Patroons, were regarded, and were to be controlled by the owners of the soil, as a servile class. They were to become American serfs . . . . By a wiser provision, the charter gave liberty to private adventurers, to make a selection of lands, and to enjoy the same by personal right." Isaac S. Mulford, *A Civil and Political History of New Jersey* 57 (1851).

[1531] "In the settlement of the country, the colonists were to concentrate themselves in families of sixteen to twenty in number, and were to pay annually for their lands twelve stivers a morgen [approximately two acres] in lieu of tenths. The town lots were forty feet by fifty, and the streets from four to five rods in breadth. The Swedes were to be closely watched, and if any should be found disaffected, they were to be sent away . . . and, if possible, induced to come to Manhattan." J. Thomas Scharf, History of Delaware 1609-1888 62 (1888).

settlements migrated into the Pennsylvania region, bringing with them their notions of essentially democratic towns and absolute ownership of land. When England "conquered" the Dutch in 1664, assuming control over all Dutch territory in North America, little immediate increase of English immigration into the area followed.

§ 11.01(c). The Proprietorship of William Penn.

By a royal patent dated March 4, 1680, William Penn received from King Charles II a patent for lands and a grant of governmental authority in the province of Pennsylvania. By deed of feoffment dated August 4, 1682, the Duke of York granted to Penn all the lands in the New York provincial territory covered by the royal patent to Penn from the king, which meant conveyance of title to the Pennsylvania lands.[1532]

[1532] The interesting peculiarities of this conveyance, with strong overtones of medieval English land law, have been explained as follows, in connection with Penn's assumption of title to land in Delaware:

> There were actually four legal documents involved in these grants, an absolute deed (called a "deed of feoffment") and a lease for ten thousand years for New Castle and the circle around it, and another deed and a similar lease for the land from twelve miles south of New Castle to Cape Henlopen . . . Probably the division is explained by the duke's desire to get some revenue from these territories . . . but not to interfere with Penn's use of New Castle or with his revenues from it . . . Perhaps both deed and lease were used because of the uncertainty of the duke's legal rights to Delaware . . .
>
> Then on October 28 [the day after Penn's arrival on October 27, 1682], in a ceremony called "livery of seisin," Penn formally took possession of New Castle and the territory within twelve miles about it, except on the east side of the Delaware. After the deeds from the Duke of York were read, Penn took the key to the New Castle fort, entered and locked himself in alone, then came out and received a piece of turf with a twig upon it and a porringer with river water and soil as symbols of his new possession. John A. Munroe, Colonial Delaware, A History 83-84 (1978).

§ 11.01(c)(1). Charter Provisions Relating to Land.

The charter of January 26, 1682, from King Charles II to William Penn, came late enough in the English experience with North American colonies that provisions could be included for virtually every major source of concern that had arisen in the previous 75 years. It is a long and detailed document, exhibiting thoughtfulness about both Penn's desire to conduct a benevolent experiment in Pennsylvania and England's greater assertiveness on matters of empire. The charter formed the basic law of the colony, and its provisions relating to land, excerpted below, were of fundamental importance:

> The grant:
>
> . . . [W]ee . . . Have given and granted . . . unto the said William Penn, his heires and assignes all that tract or parte of land in America, with all the Islands therein conteyned [boundaries and hereditaments described] . . . .
>
> The statement of proprietary ownership and the requirement of allegiance to England:
>
> Wee Doe . . . make, create and constitute the true and absolute proprietaries of the Countrey aforesaid, and of all other, the premises, saving alwayes to us, our heires and successors, the faith and allegiance of the said William Penn, his heires and assignes, and of all other, the proprietaries, tenants and Inhabitants that are, or shall be within the precincts aforesaid . . . .
>
> The habendum, to the "use and behoofe" of Penn, and declaration of tenure in free and common socage, with annual payment of two beaver skins:

> To Have, hold and possesse and enjoy the said tract of Land . . . unto the said William Penn, his heires and assigns, to the only proper use and behoofe of the said William Penn, his heires and assignes forever. To be holden of us, our heires and successors, Kings of England, as of our Castle of Windsor, in our County of Berks, in free and common socage by fealty only for all services, and not in Capite or by Knights service, Yeelding and paying therfore to us, our heires and Successors, two Beaver skins to bee delivered att our said Castle of Windsor, on the first day of January, in every yeare . . . .

The declaration that the province is a seignory, or lordship:

> . . . [W]ee do hereby Erect the aforesaid Country and Islands, into a province and Seigniorie, and doe call it Pensilvania . . . and we have already made and ordeyned the aforesaid William Penn, his heires and assignes, the true and absolute Proprietaries of all the Lands and Dominions aforesaid.

The grant of governmental powers, consistent with the laws of England:

> . . . [W]ee . . . doe grant free, full and absolute power, by vertue of these presents to him and his heirs . . . for the good and happy government of the said Countrey, to ordeyne, make, enact and under his and their Seals to publish any Lawes whatsoever . . . by and with the advice, assent and approbacon of the freemen of the said Countrey, or the greater part of them . . . Provided; Nevertheless, that the said Lawes bee consonant to reason, and bee not repugnant or contrarie, but as neere as conveniently may bee agreeable to the Lawes, statutes and rights of this our Kingdome of England . . . .

The continuation of previously-established land rights:

> . . . [A]nd our further will and pleasure is, that the Lawes for regulateing and governing of propertie, within the said Province, as well for the descent and enioyment of lands, . . . shall be and continue the same as shall bee for the time being . . . .

The power to create municipalities:

> . . . And Wee Doe further . . . give and grant unto the said William Penn . . . free and absolute power to Divide the said Countrey, and Islands, into Townes, Hundreds and Counties, and to erect and incorporate Townes into Borroughs, and Borroughs into Citties . . . .

The power to sell and grant real property interests, by any estate, and suspending the operation of the Statute Quia Emptores with respect to conveyances from Penn:

> . . . Wee have given and granted . . . unto the said William Penn . . . full and absolute power, licence and authoritie, That he . . . from time to time hereafter forever, att his . . . will or pleasure, may assigne, alien, grant, demis or infeoffe of the premises, soe many, and such partes and parcells to him or them, that shall be willing to purchase the same, as they shall think fitt. To Have And To Hold to them, the said person and persons willing to take or purchase . . . in fee simple or fee taile, or for the term of life, or liues, or yeares, to be held of the said William Penn . . . as of the seigniory of Windsor, by such services, customes and rents, as shall seeme fitt to the said William Penn, and not imediately of us . . . the Statute Quia Emptores terrarum . . . in any wise notwithstanding . . . .

The power to create manors, hold a court baron, and to hold view of frankpledge, and reinstating the operation of Quia Emptores with respect to conveyances from Penn's successors in interest:

> . . . Wee give and grant licence unto the said William Penn . . . to erect any parcells of Land . . . into mannors, . . . to have and to hold a Court Baron . . . and to have and to hold view of frankpledge . . .; and Wee doe further grant licence and authoritie that every such person . . . who shall erect any such mannor . . . shall or may grant all or any parte of his said lands to any person . . . in fee simple or any other estate of inheritance, to be held of the said mannors respectively, soe as noe further tenures shall be created, but that upon all further and other alienacons thereafter, to be made the said lands so aliened, shall be held of the same Lord and his heires, of whom the alien did then before hold, and by the like rents and services, which were before due and accustomed.[1533]

The overall effect of these charter provisions was to give Penn the full extent of feudal powers still recognized in his day, while still preserving all the prerogatives of the monarchy.[1534]

[1533] The Earliest Printed Laws of Pennsylvania 1681-1713 181-190 (John D. Cushing, ed., 1978).

[1534] "By the charter Penn became the proprietor of a vast but loosely bounded domain . . . . Of this vast area Penn was made the true and absolute proprietor, to hold the land in free and common socage, as of the royal castle of Windsor, paying therefor fealty and allegiance and two beaver skins on the first of January in each year. Though all reference to the palatinate of Durham was carefully omitted, Penn was given almost equivalent authority in the complete control he could exercise over the soil, in his right to determine the form of government, in his extensive privileges of local appointment, and in his ability to issue ordinances of his own in time of need. He could initiate and promulgate laws, but only with the advice, assent, and approbation of the freemen in assembly, that is, as later shown, by the freeholders. In all its main features the charter followed the standard type, differing, however, from the charters of the earlier period in that it reduced considerably the proprietary prerogatives, toned down the strictly feudal aspects so as to render them as innocuous as possible, and reserved to the king all his sovereign powers. In this respect Penn's charter, compared with that of Lord Baltimore, issued fifty years before, or even with that of the Duke of York, issued in 1664, represents the changes which had come over the mind of the English government since the king had been restored to his throne." Charles M. Andrews, *The Colonial Period of American History* 282 (1937).

§ 11.01(c)(2). Land Distribution Practices.

In contrast to the previous colonial practice of simply giving land to settlers willing to come and stay, Penn began selling land as soon as he secured his title.[1535]

§ 11.01(c)(3). Quit Rents.

In Pennsylvania quit rents were actively pursued, and, therefore, the various issues and controversies surrounding colonial quit rents became important.[1536]

1535 "In New Netherland and New York . . . during the [early] period . . ., a price seems never to have been put upon the land. Land was sold in Pennsylvania from the very first. As soon as he had secured his title, Penn offered for sale shares of five thousand acres at £100 each. After 1684 this land was also to be liable to a quitrent. The practice of selling land was steadily continued, the prices varying with the period of time which had elapsed since the settlement of the province, with the character and location of the land, and with such other conditions as might affect a bargain. After 1732 prices become more permanent. For thirty years from that date the price was £15, 10s. per hundred acres. Prices were always fixed by the proprietor and his officials . . . . Escheated land, with such improvements as had been made upon it, was sold at auction, and the larger part of the purchase money went to the proprietor. It was a requirement in all the provinces that land should be settled within a brief period often designated as three years after the issue of the patent. Squatters' rights, as evidenced by "improvment," were as a rule generously enforced." Herbert L. Osgood, *The American Colonies in the Seventeenth Century* 34-35 (1904).

1536 "The most characteristic form of territorial revenue was the quitrent, paid annually at a rate prescribed by the proprietor and received in lieu of all services. It appears in all the provinces . . . . In all transactions, and in all the colonies, the form of payment was a matter of importance to the people. So scanty was their supply of money, that payment in kind was always strongly their preference. The proprietors, and afterward the crown, always found their interest in securing money payments whenever it was possible. This in many cases gave rise to controversies over quit rents, which in turn occasioned the interference of the assembly in a matter which the proprietors claimed as exclusively their own . . . . In all the provinces quit rents were an object of aversion. They were continually falling into arrears. Payment was avoided whenever it was possible; and it was not infrequently resisted. In the last resort payment could be enforced by distress, the assistance of the sheriff being called in for the purpose. In Pennsylvania, as in other provinces, these conditions were ever and anon recurring. . . ." *Id.* at 36-37.

§ 11.01(c)(4). Administration of Land Affairs.

Both the sales of land and the administration of quit rents in Pennsylvania required the creation of a rudimentary bureaucracy.[1537]

In the view of one important historian, the land systems in the proprietary colonies were kept strictly within the control of the executive, away from legislative regulation.[1538]

As will be shown in the next section, however, legislation in matters touching land was both common and comprehensive in Pennsylvania.

[1537] ". . . Pennsylvania had a land office, though until after 1732 its affairs were very much in confusion . . . . The long absences of Penn from his province made it impossible for him to attend in person to the details of selling and letting land and collecting rents. Not until 1741 was the care of these matters intrusted to the governors. Instead, a commission or board of property was from time to time designated, which acted as the special agent of the proprietor. The board consisted of a secretary, who was at the same time secretary of the province, the surveyor-general, and from three to five special commissioners. Closely associated with the board was the receiver-general, the keeper of the seal, and master of the rolls. The special duties of the commissioners related to the granting of lands, but, as their powers developed, they also became concerned with the collection of rents. After 1741 the governors became members of this board, but their authority to act with it was conveyed through a special commission . . . ." *Id.* at 46.

[1538] "In all the provinces the land system was kept as free as possible from the control of the legislature. It was organized and regulated under instructions and proclamations of the proprietors and their appointees. Any attempt to regulate it by legislation was resented and opposed. It was regarded as the private concern of the proprietor and its administration as distinctly as an executive function. . . . In the absence of a legislature [such as in New Netherland and proprietary New York] such an issue could not arise. But in the Carolinas, the Jerseys, and Pennsylvania it arose, and the occasion which usually brought it to the front was some dispute over the payment of quit rents. It was at this point that the territorial regulations of the proprietor touched the pocket of the colonist. Like a tax, the rent was a constantly recurring burden. Over its amount and the form of its payment the individual desired in some way to secure such control as had been effected in the case of taxation. Efforts to secure this helped to initiate the process of legislation related to territorial affairs." *Id.* at 46-47.

§ 11.01(c)(5). Legislation Relating to Landholding.

Soon after the 1682 conveyance from the Duke of York, Penn issued the Frame of Government of the Province of Pennsylvania, consisting of a bill of rights and other laws that would become effective when ratified by the colonists in the province. In 1683, Penn issued a Charter of Privileges, which was revised in 1701, and which added further governing provisions applicable to Pennsylvania and Penn's other territories. Meanwhile, the Duke's Law also remained in force in Pennsylvania. Therefore, the Duke's Law of 1665, and Penn's 1682 Frame of Government and 1683 Charter of Privileges were all potential sources of laws governing landholding.

The fundamental legal rules for land were lodged in the Duke's Law and are described in the context of colonial New York in §§9.05(e) and 9.05(f). The land provisions of the 1682 Frame of Government and the Charter of Privileges of 1683 and 1701 are summarized in the following paragraphs.

§ 11.01(c)(5)(A). Penn's Frame of Government of 1682.

In his 1682 Frame of Government, Penn granted to "the freemen, planters and adventurers, of . . . the . . . province, these liberties, franchises, and properties [as granted to Penn], to be held, enjoyed and kept by the freemen, planters and inhabitants of the said province of Pennsylvania for ever."[1539] In addition to this conferral of rights, the other singular feature of the Frame of Government was the establishment of representative government, in the form of the Provincial Council and General Assembly. The Provincial Council was directed to divide itself into four standing committees, the first of which would be "a committee of plantations, to situate and settle cities, ports, market-towns and high-ways, and to hear and

---

1539 *The Earliest Printed Laws of Pennsylvania 1681-1713* 200 (John D. Cushing, ed., 1978).

decide all suits and controversies relating to plantations."[1540] Laws proposed by the Provincial Council were subject to rejection or ratification by the General Assembly. In April 1683, a new frame of government was drawn up, taking into account the incorporation of the Delaware settlements and providing for a reorganization of the council and general assembly.[1541]

§ 11.01(c)(5)(B). Laws for the Colony Agreed upon in England.

Even before the earliest legislative assembly met, certain laws for Pennsylvania were proposed and agreed to by the colonial leaders while they were still in England, subject to ratification by the colonists in America. Those provisions pertaining to landholding are as follows:

> First. That the charter of liberties [Frame of Government] . . . is hereby declared and approved, and shall be for ever held for fundamental in the government thereof, according to the limitations mentioned in the said charter.
>
> Second. That every Inhabitant in the said province, that is or shall be a purchaser of one hundred acres of land or upwards, his heirs and assigns, and every person who shall have paid his passage, and taken up one hundred acres of land, at a penny an acre, and have cultivated ten acres thereof, and every person that hath been a servant or bondsman, and is free by his service, that shall have taken up his fifty acres of land, and cultivated twenty thereof, and every inhabitant, artificer, or other resident in the said province, that pays scot and lot[1542] to the government, shall

---

[1540] *Id.* at 196.

[1541] *See* "No. 41. Pennsylvania and Delaware Frame," in *Select Charters and Other Documents Illustrative of American History, 1606-1775* 199-204 (William MacDonald, ed., 1914).

[1542] In English law scot was a form of tax of one's share of a customary contribution. Scot and lot was a particular customary contribution imposed upon subjects according to their ability to pay. In certain English boroughs, persons retained their

be deemed and accounted a freeman of the said province . . . .

Fourteenth. That all lands and goods shall be liable to pay debts, except where there is legal issue, and then all the goods, and one third of the land only.

Fifteenth. That all wills and writing attested by two witnesses, shall be of the same force, as to lands and other conveyances, being legally proved within forty days, either within or without the said province.

Sixteenth. That seven years quiet possession shall give an unquestionable right, except in cases of infants, lunaticks, married women, or persons beyond the seas . . . .

Twentieth. And to prevent frauds and vexatious suits within the said province, that all charters, gifts, grants and conveyances of land, (except leases for a year or under) and all bills, bonds, and specialties have five pounds, and not under three months, made in the said province, shall be enrolled or registered in the public enrolment office of the said province within the space of two months next after the making thereof, else to be void in law. And all deeds, grants, and conveyances of land (except as aforesaid) within the said province, and made out of the said province, shall be inrolled or registered as aforesaid, within six months next after the making thereof, and settling and constituting an enrolment office or registry within the said province, else to be void in law against all persons whatsoever . . . .

Thirty-first. That for the encouragement of the plants and traders in this province, who are incorporated into a society, the patent granted to them by William Penn,

franchise only by paying the scot and lot.

> Governor of the said province, is hereby ratified and confirmed. . . .[1543]

§ 11.01(c)(5)(C). The Charter of Privileges of 1683 and 1701.

The Charter of Privileges, issued in 1683 and revised in 1701, gave specific instructions for choosing members of the General Assembly but contained only one additional provision touching upon land rights:

> Eighthly: If any person, through Temptation or melancholly, shall Destroy himself, his Estate, Real & Personal, shall, notwithstanding, Descend to his wife and Children or Relations as if he had Died a natural Death; and if any person shall be Destroyed or kill'd by Casualty or accident, there shall be no forfeiture to the Governour by Reason thereof. . . .[1544]

§ 11.01(c)(5)(D). Pennsylvania Landholding Legislation After Circa 1700.

Penn's long absences from England and the persisting conflict between the Pennsylvania governors and assemblies hampered the development of constructive legislation, even though the "Duke's Law" remained as a foundation. Thus, before 1700 there was no systematic and comprehensive compilation of provincial legislation, and no printed compilation until 1714. The 1714 printing "was the first compilation of Pennsylvania laws and purported to contain the text of all laws then in force, with repealed or obsolete statutes reported by title only." Summarized below are the provisions related to landholding found in the 1714 compilation:

[1543] *The Earliest Printed Laws of Pennsylvania 1681-1713* 201-205 (John D. Cushing, ed., 1978).

[1544] *The Earliest Printed Laws of Delaware 1704-1741* 1-8 (John D. Cushing, ed., 1978).

Forcible entry
Removing of landmarks
Defacers of charters
Buying land of the natives
Taking lands in execution for the payment of debts
Regulating and maintaining of fences
Erecting of bridges and maintaining highways
Cutting timber
Burning of houses
Better confirmation of the owners of lands, in their just rights and possessions
Probates of wills and confirming devises of lands
Settling of intestates' estates
Collecting of quit rents
Attachments
Seven years' quiet possession
Confirming sales of lands by attorneys or agents, and ascertaining the proof of instruments or writings
Better enabling inhabitants of the province to hold and enjoy lands, tenements and plantations
Acknowledging and recording of deeds
Privileges to a freeman:

> [N]o Free-man of this Province shall be taken or imprisoned, disseised of his Free-hold or Liberties, or to be Outlawed or Exiled, or any other ways hurt, damnified or destroyed, nor be tryed nor condemned but by the Lawful Judgement of his Twelve Equals, or by the Laws of this Province.

Preventing disputes that may arise about the dates of conveyances and other instruments and writings (affirming that March is considered the first month)

Regulating party walls and buildings in Philadelphia
Confirming patents and grants
Empowering religious societies to buy, hold and enjoy lands, tenements and hereditaments
Limitation of actions.[1545]

§ 11.01(d). Summary of Landholding Practices in Colonial Pennsylvania.

The grant to Penn was a proprietary grant, an estate of inheritance with as many feudal prerogatives as were still extant in that era. The province was literally Penn's private estate, and he was both owner and landlord. A proprietor such as William Penn might be an idealist, but he and the other proprietors were also investors in land, and:

> this, when combined with powers of government, made them territorial lords, and in order to collect their quit rents and fines on alienation, they had to institute a system of territorial administration.[1546]

Despite these extensive feudal prerogatives, the management of land in Pennsylvania was little affected by them. "Before Penn left England he disposed of large tracts of land to those known later as 'first purchasers,' a part of whose land was to lie in the 'country" and a part in the city that he was planning to build. But when he found that in order to carry out the terms of such sales (the allotment of ten acres in the city for every five hundred in the country) he would have to enlarge his city beyond the capacity of any available site, he ordered an area to be set off adjoining the city proper to be known as the 'liberties," for the purpose of taking up the excess."[1547]

[1545] *The Earliest Printed Laws of Pennsylvania 1681-1713* 1-178 (John D. Cushing, ed., 1978).

[1546] Herbert L. Osgood, *The American Colonies in the Seventeenth Century* 17 (1904).

[1547] Charles M. Andrews, *The Colonial Period of American History* 291 (1937).

Penn's seigniorial rights are well illustrated by his financial dealings with the rights in his provincial land during the years before his death. In 1708 he mortgaged Pennsylvania to nine persons in England.[1548] He died ten years later, and in his will, he devised the governmental powers to three named aristocrats, in trust, to dispose of to the queen or to any other person, as they determined. He devised his lands, rents and profits in Pennsylvania to his widow and eleven others, in trust, with instructions to pay off his debts. He made other dispositions of Pennsylvania lands entirely, as if they were his private estate, as they legally were.

In most of the proprietary colonies, land was usually granted gratis, rather than sold, in order to draw in the maximum number of settlers. Pennsylvania was an exception:

> Land was sold in Pennsylvania from the very first. As soon as he had secured his title, Penn offered for sale shares of five thousand acres at £100 each. After 1684 this land was also to be liable to a quitrent. The practice of selling land was steadily continued, the prices varying with the period of time which had elapsed since the settlement of the province, with the character and location of the land, and with such other conditions as might affect a bargain. After 1732 prices became more permanent. For thirty years from that date the price was £15, 10s. per hundred acres. Prices were always fixed by the proprietor and his officials.[1549]

Contrasted with the enormous importance of the towns in governing the New England colonies, villages and towns had less involvement in Pennsylvania affairs. The more common form of settlement was the isolated farm or plantation.

Whether land allotments were made in the country, in the towns, or in the city of Philadelphia, quit rents were reserved, payable directly to Penn.

[1548] When he died ten years later, the mortgage was still not fully paid off.

[1549] Herbert L. Osgood, *The American Colonies in the Seventeenth Century* 34 (1904).

While Philadelphia allotments were made to individual grantees, Germantown arose as a group settlement.

§ 11.02. Development of Land Law in North Carolina (from 1650).

§ 11.02(a). Land Rights in the Early Colonization Efforts.

§ 11.02(a)(1). Sir Humphrey Gilbert's Charter of 1578.

Almost nothing is known about the earliest settlers of North Carolina, and no regular government existed there until sometime after the first proprietary charter for the region was granted in 1663.[1550]

Most well-known of the early North Carolina settlement efforts is Sir Walter Raleigh's "lost colony" of the late 16th century. This settlement project actually had its genesis in a charter granted by Queen Elizabeth I to Sir Humphrey Gilbert on June 11, 1578, which, by its terms, gave rights to colonize virtually any unoccupied lands in the New World. On the condition that a settlement be commenced within six years after the granting of the charter, the charter conferred on Sir Humphrey, and his heirs and assigns forever, the right to discover "such remote heathen and barbarous lands, Countries, and territories, not actually possessed of any Christian Prince or people":

> And the same to have, hold, occupy, and enjoy, to him, his heirs and Assigns, forever, with all commodities, jurisdictions, and royalties, both by sea and land.[1551]

[1550] "Editorial Note" in *The Earliest Printed Laws of North Carolina* (John D. Cushing, ed., 1977).

[1551] *North Carolina Charters and Constitutions, 1578-1698* 5 (Mattie Erma Edwards Parker, ed., 1963).

Gilbert thus obtained the rights to "all the soil of all such lands . . . to be had or used with full power to dispose thereof, and of every part thereof, in fee simple or otherwise, according to the laws of England, as near as the same conveniently may be," reserving to the crown "for all services, duties, and demands, the fifth part of all the ore of gold and silver" discovered in those lands.[1552] The charter granted to Gilbert and all his fellow colonists that they "shall and may have and enjoy all the privileges of free denizens[1553] and persons native of England and within our allegiance . . . ."[1554] Powers of government, including the administration of justice, were also included in the charter, "so always, that the said statutes, laws, and ordinances may be, as near as conveniently may, agreeable to the form of the laws and policy of England. . . ."[1555]

§ 11.02(a)(2). Sir Walter Raleigh's Charter and the "Lost Colony" at Roanoke Island.

Gilbert's short-lived 1583 settlement in Newfoundland and his death during the voyage back to England resulted in the renewal of Gilbert's charter in Raleigh's name, on March 25, 1584. Issued shortly before Gilbert's charter was to expire, Raleigh's charter was, in effect, a six-year extension and was virtually identical to Gilbert's charter in its grants of land rights and governing power. Raleigh's unsuccessful efforts to commence a colony in North Carolina and the intrigue of the lost colony were still significant for all subsequent British American colonies.[1556]

[1552] *Id.* at 6.

[1553] "Denizen" ordinarily means an inhabitant or resident, although in British usage it may also mean a foreigner who is permitted certain rights of citizenship.

[1554] *North Carolina Charters and Constitutions, 1578-1698* 7 (Mattie Erma Edwards Parker, ed., 1963).

[1555] *Id.* at 8.

[1556] "In 1585, Raleigh sent out a colony . . . which settled on Roanoke Island. This was the first English colony to settle in America. About a year later, the colonists returned to England, for they had not received needed supplies and reinforcements. A supply ship arrived only a few weeks after the colonists' departure, and soon

Thereafter Raleigh's activities in the New World reflected only commercial interest. In 1602 he sent ships to trade with the Indians and obtain a cargo of timber and medicinal plants. In 1603 he sent ships to the Chesapeake region. Even before these ships returned, Raleigh had been imprisoned on charges of high treason. Upon his conviction, his charter rights were forfeited to the crown. Thus, "Virginia" became available for re-granting by King James I.

It is not known what land rights individual settlers in Raleigh's colonies enjoyed during their time of occupancy. If the pattern of the later Jamestown colony in Virginia was used, then these first North Carolina settlers commenced their colony by holding and working their lands as a community. Once they achieved stability, then they would have to form a plan for conveying some type of individual landholdings.

§ 11.02(a)(3). The Early Influence of Virginia.

When King James I took the throne after Queen Elizabeth's death in 1603, several influential and wealthy men were still interested in colonizing ventures. Hoping to resume what Raleigh had not finished, they approached James about another charter, and this was granted to the Virginia Company on April 10, 1606. The Virginia Company charter, obtained only three

---

afterward a relief expedition under Richard Grenville arrived. Grenville left a small garrison to hold possession and retain Raleigh's rights, but the garrison left the island and disappeared, after an attack by Indians. In late July, 1587, another colony sent by Raleigh arrived off Hatteras and settled on Roanoke Island. [They] had expected to settle in the Chesapeake region, . . . but they were forced to remain at Roanoke Island, for Simon Fernandez, master of the largest ship in the expedition, refused to take them farther . . . .

"At the urging of the other colonists, [Governor] White returned to England in late August to expedite the shipping of supplies, with the understanding that the colonists would move to the mainland and would leave at Roanoke Island directions for finding them. War with Spain prevented White's return until 1590, when he found Roanoke Island deserted; the only clues to the colonists' location were the letters CRO carved on a tree and the word CROATOAN carved at the entrance to the colonists' fort. Further search by White was prevented by damage to the ships in the expedition and by an unfavorable wind. No other immediate effort to find the lost colony is recorded, and later attempts, which appear to have been desultory, were unsuccessful. The fate of the colonists has never been learned. For many years, however, the colony was presumed in England to be in existence, and Raleigh's rights in "Virginia" were considered established." *Id.* at 11-12.

years after the last of Raleigh's expeditions, was a continuation of the Gilbert and Raleigh projects and included among its principals several men who had participated in those earlier enterprises. The charter divided the land into northern and southern sectors and assigned these to two different groups within the company; the charter's southern territory encompassed most of the coastal sector of North Carolina. Nevertheless, this charter was not as generous as the earlier charters given to Gilbert and Raleigh.[1557]

This charter is discussed in greater detail in connection with the Virginia Colony, in §9.02(a). The charter of 1606, of course, laid the foundation for the colony at Jamestown, the first permanent English settlement in North America. Members of the Jamestown colony explored the area of North Carolina and tried to locate the missing members of Raleigh's colonies. About 50 years after Jamestown was settled, colonists from there and other Virginia settlements moved into the region near Raleigh's original colonies and became the first permanent settlers in North Carolina.

As explained in §9.02(b), unsatisfactory aspects of the 1606 charter led to requests for a new charter, which was granted on May 23, 1609.[1558] Driven principally by the desire to extend jurisdiction over the Bermuda Islands, the company obtained yet another charter on March 12, 1612,

---

[1557] "The territory involved in the new charter was restricted to a prescribed region. The company was not given the right to own land, although it could parcel out land among settlers, to be granted to them by patents from the king. Governmental authority over colonies was reserved by the crown, to be exercised by a council resident in London, appointed and instructed by the king. The authority of the company chiefly consisted of recruiting, transporting, and supplying colonists, conducting trade, and handling other financial matters. Colonists were guaranteed the rights of Englishmen at home, such as trial by jury, habeas corpus, and the right to own and inherit land, but they were not given right to participate in government." *Id.* at 19-20.

[1558] "The new charter granted additional territory and conferred upon the company rights of ownership over this and the territory formerly assigned to the London [southern] group; it also gave the company the right to sub-grant land to settlers and shareholders." *Id.* at 30.

described in detail in §9.02(c).[1559]

Because of factional disputes within the colony, a court decision revoked this charter in 1624, and the land and rights of the Virginia Company reverted to the crown. No permanent settlement had yet been established in North Carolina, so that land was available for re-granting by the crown.

§ 11.02(b). Land Rights under the Heath Charter of 1629.

Such a re-grant occurred five years later, when King Charles I granted most of present-day North Carolina to his attorney general, Sir Robert Heath. Heath was unable to assemble the resources needed to commence colonization, so in the 1630's he disposed of his interest in the tract. Several of Heath's assignees continued to promote a colony in North Carolina, but no settlement materialized. Eventually, the crown considered the grant lapsed because no colonies had been established, and because of this, King Charles II re-granted the Heath tract to eight other persons in 1663.

The Heath Charter, however, did not remain a dead letter. First, despite the royal grant of 1663, persons holding rights under the Heath Charter of 1629 began to press their claims to North Carolina territory. Those claims were rejected by an order in council of August 12, 1663, but the claimants and their heirs and successors persisted, finally obtaining a court judgment in 1668 that awarded them a settlement of 100,000 acres in New York. Second, the Heath Charter of 1629 was the model for the new royal charter of 1663, and the essential provisions of 1629 reappeared in the proprietors' charters of 1663 and beyond. It is useful, therefore, to examine the provisions of the 1629 Heath Charter relating to colonial land rights in

---

1559 "The democratic element introduced into the control of the company was the most significant provision of the new charter. The organization of the company as thus established appears to have served as a model when the government of the Virginia colony was reorganized in 1618. An important feature of the reorganization of the colony was the establishment of a popular assembly, which held its first meeting on July 30, 1619. This assembly became a precedent for other English colonies in America, and provision for such a body was included in all the later charters involving the North Carolina area." *Id.* at 48.

North Carolina.

The charter states that "we . . . have Given, Granted, and confirmed . . . to the said Sir Robert Heath, Knight, his heirs and assigns, for ever, . . . all the lands, Tenements, and Hereditaments [in the described tract] . . . ."[1560] This grant of land was accompanied by a very broad grant of governmental authority that was as thoroughly feudal as was consistent with the times:

> Together with all . . . Rights, Jurisdictions, privileges, prerogatives, Royalties, liberties, and immunities . . .
>
> To have, exercise, use, and enjoy, in like manner as any Bishop of Durham within the Bishopric, or County Palatine, of Durham, in our Kingdom of England, ever heretofore had, held, used, or enjoyed, or of right ought or could have, hold, use, or enjoy.
>
> And, by these presents, we make, create, and constitute the same Sir Robert Heath, his Heirs and assigns, true and absolute Lords and Proprietors of the Region and Territory aforesaid, and all other the premises, for us, our heirs and successors;
>
> Saving always, the faith and allegiance due to us, our heirs and Successors . . . [1561]

The feudal nature of this proprietary grant was emphasized in the provision that described tenure as knight's service of a tenant-in-chief:

[1560] *Id.* at 64-65.

[1561] *Id.* at 65. The "Bishop of Durham" clause refers to the traditional expectation held of the bishop of Durham, located on the Scottish border, to help protect English land from foreign enemies who intruded on English land. To fulfill these expectations, the bishop enjoyed almost regal powers, including rights to enact laws, impose taxes, prepare for and conduct warfare, among others.

> To be held of Us, our Heirs and Successors, Kings of England, in chief, by Knight's service; and by paying for it, to us, our Heirs and successors, one Circle of Gold, formed in the fashion of a crown, of the weight of twenty Ounces, with this inscription engraved upon it, DEUS CORONET OPUS SUUM ["God crowns His work"], whensoever, and as often as it shall happen, that we, Our Heirs or Successors, shall enter the said Region . . . .[1562]

The proprietor Heath was granted a very broad lawmaking power, but with provision for a legislative body, and as consistently as possible with English law:

> . . . [W]e . . . do give Power to the said Sir Robert . . . and to his Heirs and assigns, for the good and happy Government of the said Province, to form, make, and enact, and Publish under the Seal of the said Sir Robert . . . what Laws soever may concern the public state of the said province, or the private profit of all, according to the wholesome directions of and with the counsel, assent, and approbation of the Freeholders of the same Province, or the Major part of them . . . .
>
> Yet, so that the foresaid laws and ordinances be consonant to Reason, and not repugnant or contrary but, as conveniently as may be done, consonant to the Laws, Statutes, Customs, and rights of our Realm of England.[1563]

Any person born into or coming into the colony would be considered an English subject or citizen, and their land rights would be the same as those of English subjects:

[1562] *Id.* at 66.

[1563] *Id.* at 66-67.

> And also, that they shall possess lands, Tenements, Rents, services, and Hereditaments whatsoever with our Kingdom of England and of our Dominions, to purchase, receive, take, have, hold, buy, and possess, and them to use and enjoy, and also, them to give, sell, alienate, and bequeath; and also, all liberties, franchises, and privileges of this our Realm to have and possess freely, quietly, and peacably; and that they may use and enjoy them as our lieges born or to be born within our Kingdom of England . . . .[1564]

The charter also contained a somewhat unique provision giving the proprietor the right to create titles of nobility:

> Furthermore, lest the way to Honours and Dignities may seem to be shut and altogether barred up to men honestly born, and who are willing to undertake this present expedition, . . . [we] Give full and free power to the aforesaid Sir Robert Heath, Knight, his heirs and assigns, to confer favours, graces, and honours upon those well-deserving Citizens that inhabit within the foresaid province, and the same with whatever Titles and dignities, provided they be not the same as are now used in England, to adorn at his pleasure . . . .[1565]

The charter also gave explicit power to the proprietor to create local municipalities, "with privileges and befitting immunities to be erected and incorporated . . . ."[1566]

Thus, the 1629 charter differed from earlier charters in that it conferred the extensive "bishop-of-Durham" feudal powers on the proprietors, authorized the proprietors to create a local nobility, and required that a representative lawmaking body have a role in the legislative process.

[1564] *Id.* at 68-69.

[1565] *Id.* at 70.

[1566] *Id.*

§ 11.02(c). Assertion of Virginia Authority in 1662.

Beginning in the early 1650's, settlers from Virginia began moving into lands located south of the present southern boundary of Virginia. By 1653, a trader named Nathaniel Batts had built a house and started to carry on trade with the Indians. He was still there in 1672 and was locally referred to as the "governor" of Roan-oak; "Roanoke" or "Old Virginia" were early labels sometimes attached to North Carolina territory to distinguish it from the territory of colonial Virginia. Other settlers from Virginia followed Batts, but without any regulation of landholding rights except for those with which they had become familiar in Virginia. Accordingly, they purchased land from the Indians and, out of caution, recorded these purchases and further conveyances in Virginia. Deeds as early as 1660 have been discovered.[1567]

As a result of these settlement activities, the council of Virginia decided to assert governmental authority. On October 9, 1662, the council appointed one Samuel Stephens as "commander of the southern plantation" and authorized him to appoint a sheriff, who would keep order and collect taxes. Although this is the beginning of governmental authority over settlers in North Carolina, nothing further is known about the activities of either commander or sheriff.[1568]

§ 11.02(d). The Royal Grant of 1663.

On March 24, 1663, shortly after Virginia appointed its "commander," King Charles II granted the old Heath tract to eight prominent men who had given important support toward the restoration of the Stuart monarchy. The tract did not actually include the area settled by the Virginians, but the omission was not immediately realized. In time, the eight new North Carolina proprietors authorized William Berkeley, one of their number who was also then governor of Virginia, to exercise governmental authority over

---

[1567] William S. Powell, *North Carolina, A Bicentennial History* 21-22 (1977).

[1568] *Id.* at 22; "Introduction," in *North Carolina Higher-Court Records 1670-1696* xv (Mattie Erma Edwards Parker, ed., 1968).

the settlement of Virginians in the area. North Carolina's legal authority over the settlement and other omitted territory was finally established in 1665, when a second North Carolina charter was issued expanding on the original grant.

The 1663 charter followed the 1629 Heath charter in important particulars, especially in its provision for representative government, the feudal powers resting in the proprietors, and the right of the proprietors to create a colonial nobility.

As in the 1629 charter, the feudal powers of the proprietors were expressed in the "bishop-of-Durham" clause, "To have, use, exercise, and enjoy, and in as ample manner as any Bishop of Durham, in our Kingdom of England, ever heretofore have held, used, or enjoyed, or of right ought or could have, use, or enjoy."[1569] This 1663 charter departed from the 1629 charter, however, in declaring the tenure by which the proprietors held. The earlier document had described Heath's tenure as "in chief, by Knight's service," with a somewhat nominal payment obligation (a gold crown to be given over each time the monarch visited the province). The new charter abandoned this outmoded formula and adopted the new tenurial language commonly found in other colonies' charters: the free and common socage of East Greenwich royal manor: "To be held of us, our heirs and successors, as of our Manor of East Greenwich, in our County of Kent, in Free and Common Soccage, and not in Capite nor by knight's Service.[1570]

Again, the lawmaking power was subject to the requirement "that the said laws be consonant to reason and, as near as may be convenient, agreeable to the laws and Customs of this our Kingdom of England," and that ordinances "do not extend to the binding, charging, or taking away of the right or interest of any Person or Persons in their freehold, goods, or Chattels whatsoever."[1571]

[1569] *North Carolina Charters and Constitutions, 1578-1698* 77 (Mattie Erma Edwards Parker, ed., 1963).

[1570] *Id.* at 78. Most tenures in England were statutorily abolished in 1660.

[1571] *Id.* at 80.

Of course, like all colonial charters, the central feature of this 1663 charter was the right to make grants of land. The charter gave proprietors "full and absolute licence, power, and authority [to] Assign, Alien, Grant, Demise, or enfeoff the premises, or any part or parcels thereof, to him or them that shall be willing to purchase the same, and to such Person or Persons as they shall think fit."[1572] In making such grants, the proprietors and, indeed, any grantors, could convey "in Fee simple or fee tail, or for term of life or years," to be held of the proprietors under feudal conditions, if they desired, "by such Rents, Services, and Customs as shall seem meet to [them]." Landholders could grant or hold by any estate that seemed expedient to the proprietors, even in ways contrary to the Statute Quia Emptores and other important property statutes:

> We do give and Grant . . . Licence, authority, and power That such Person or Persons may have or take the premises, or any parcel thereof, of [any of the proprietors] . . .; and the same to hold to themselves, their heirs and Assigns; in what estate of Inheritance soever, in Fee simple or Fee tail or otherwise . . .; The Statute made in the Parliament of Edward, Son of King Henry, heretofore King of England, our Predecessor, commonly called the Statute of *Quia Emptores Terrarum*, or any other Statute, Act, or Ordinance, use, Law, Custom, or any other matter, Cause, or thing heretofore published or provided to the contrary in any wise notwithstanding.[1573]

As in the 1629 Heath charter, the 1663 charter continued the unusual provision permitting the proprietors to give titles of nobility:

> . . . We do . . . Give and Grant unto the [proprietors] full Power and Authority to give and Confer, unto and upon such of the Inhabitants of the said Province as they shall think do or shall merit the same, such marks of favour and

---

[1572] *Id.* at 84.

[1573] *Id.* at 84-85.

> Titles of Honour as they shall think fit; so as those Titles or honours be not the same as are enjoyed by or Conferred upon any the Subjects of this our Kingdom of England.[1574]

As if to ensure that there would be no mistake about the extent of feudal powers granted to the proprietors (though this was made clear in other provisions), the charter also gave specific authority to establish manors and to conduct the uniquely manorial courts baron and leet:

> . . . We do . . . give and grant Licence to [the proprietors ...
>
> . . . to Erect and make in the Province . . . so many Manors as to them shall seem meet and convenient; and in every of the same Manors to have and to hold a Court Baron, with all things whatsoever which to a Court Baron do belong; And to have and to hold Views of Frankpledge and Courts Leet . . . .[1575]

Appearing for the first time in the 1663 charter was a religious toleration provision, giving the proprietors "Licence, liberty, and Authority" to grant "Indulgencies and Dispensations" to those who in good conscience could not conform to the ceremonies and tenets of the Church of England. This may be instructively contrasted with practice in the early New England colonies, in which admission to a town and obtaining a town lot often required the grantee to be a member of the dominant church in the area.

[1574] *Id.* at 85.

[1575] *Id.* at 86.

§ 11.02(e). The Proprietors' Concessions and Agreements of 1665.

§ 11.02(e)(1). Introduction of the Concessions into the Settlements.

A few months after receiving the 1663 charter, the proprietors authorized one of their number, William Berkeley, who was then serving as governor of Virginia, to exercise governmental authority over the only settlers then in the North Carolina territory, who had almost all come from Virginia. In October 1664, Berkeley selected William Drummond as governor. Both before and after this appointment, however, exercise of governmental authority in North Carolina consisted only of the proprietors' provisional instructions and authorizations.

Earlier, in 1663, the proprietors had approved a formal document of governmental regulations, called "A Declaration and Proposals to All That Will Plant in Carolina," but the document applied only to new settlements, and none were ever established while the document remained in effect.

On January 7, 1665, the proprietors adopted another, more formal, plan of government, known as the "Concessions and Agreement between the Lords Proprietors and Major William Yeamans and Others", and this was the first constitution or frame of government actually used in North Carolina. These "Concessions" were applicable not only to new settlements, but also to any existing settlements, such as that of the Virginians. It is not known when the "Concessions" were actually introduced into the Virginia settlement, but they were in effect by October 1667.

Also, in the spring of 1665, acting under of the 1663 charters, the proprietors convened a legislative assembly. This assembly had been specifically authorized by the charter of 1663, and was given broad powers under the 1665 "Concessions and Agreement," but its powers were later reduced.

§ 11.02(e)(2). The Effect of the Concessions on Landholding.

The provisions of the 1665 "Concessions and Agreement" relating to land rights and landholding may be summarized as follows:

> Certain settlers from Barbados were to have granted to them 500 acres of land for every 1,000 pounds of sugar they paid, the land to be taken up and settled within five years of the grant. To the leader was given a "head right" of 150 acres of land for himself, and between 150 and 50 acres for servants he would bring with him, with a quitrent of one half penny per acre annually, payable to the proprietors.
>
> Grants and conveyances of land to be recorded, and certain conveyances and leases must be in writing and in a certain prescribed format.
>
> A surveyor shall lay out and bound all lands granted.
>
> Procedures and powers of the legislative assembly are detailed. Among the assemblies' powers and duties are to establish and collect taxes on all lands and goods, to lay out rules for granting lands by "head right" (except on the unsettled lands of the proprietors), and to establish the standard quitrent at one half penny per acre.
>
> The governor is empowered to issue warrants for land entries and to seal grants of land.
>
> Land held and planted for seven years after being surveyed may be claimed without objection from the government.
>
> No trespass liability for cattle straying on unappropriated land; no "custom of commons" prevents any person from

claiming and appropriating "any Lands so grazed upon ...."

Headrights are announced for persons already in the colony.

Counties are to be between 40 and 1,600 square miles.

Lots other than in or near cities are to be from 200 to 20,000 acres in size.

Detailed instructions for issuing land grants are given, including a form providing for payment of quitrent and tenure in free and common socage.

A register or record of instruments and grants is to be kept.[1576]

It appears that these arrangements were actually implemented among the Virginia settlers in North Carolina and that their assembly and court began meeting in 1665. These settlers suffered many natural calamities and burdens in their attempts to work the land, such as yearly hurricanes, excessive rain alternating with frequent droughts, sickness among the animals and people, and depredations of wild animals. Perhaps even worse than these, however, were the unnecessarily burdensome land policies pursued by the proprietors over these earliest settlers.[1577]

[1576] *Id.* at 107-127.

[1577] "Before issuance of the charter of 1663, settlers had obtained land by purchase from Indians or by patent from the Virginia government. Some held a thousand acres or more. The first Carolina charter contained a saving clause to protect such settlers, but the proprietors ignored the clause. In their instructions to Berkeley, in September, 1663, the London proprietors directed Berkeley to "persuade and compell" settlers with large holdings to give up the large tracts and be content "with such proportions as we allot to others." Those proportions, as directed in 1665, were eighty acres or less for each person brought into the colony. The second charter contained no clause protecting the titles of early settlers. In addition to reducing the amounts of land allowed, the proprietors increased the quitrent and introduced other policies which worked hardship on Albemarle [early Virginia] inhabitants. Thus the colonists of the 1660's had reason for discouragement despite their achievements." "Introduction" in *North Carolina Higher-Court Records,*

The land distribution system was also complicated. The so-called "General Lots" of 2,200 to 22,000 acres in size were divided so that one-eleventh of each lot was assigned to the proprietors, and settlers' parcels were determined by time of arrival and casting of lots. The rent of one half penny per acre was double that charged in Virginia or earlier in Albemarle. For each 100 acres held by a colonist in excess of the original allotment, one servant had to be kept on the land, with forfeiture of the land as the penalty for failure to do so. No allotments for children of settlers were provided.[1578]

§ 11.02(e)(3). The Great Deed of Grant.

In about 1666, Albemarle allotments were increased, and in 1668 the proprietors directed the settlement's governor to grant land on the same terms as in Virginia and to abandon the system of land division and lot allocation. These proprietors' instructions came to be known as the "Great Deed of Grant." The key provision of the Great Deed stated:

> [W]e have appointed, to such Persons as shall come into our said County to plant or inhabit; to be held of us, our Heirs and Assigns, upon the same Terms and Conditions, that Land is at present usually Granted in Virginia; any thing in our Instructions and Concessions aforesaid to the contrary, notwithstanding . . . ."[1579]

Unfortunately, the proprietors simultaneously directed the governor to obtain action from the Albemarle assembly that would reinstate some of the objectionable land policies ostensibly abandoned by the Great Deed.[1580]

1670-1696 xx-xxi (Mattie Erma Edwards Parker, ed., 1968).

[1578] *Id.* at xxxiii-xxxiv.

[1579] *The Earliest Printed Laws of North Carolina, 1669-1751* following p. 353 (John D. Cushing, ed., 1977).

[1580] "By some means [the governor] induced the Albemarle Assembly to enact laws designed to achieve the proprietors' objectives. One act prohibited for five years the issuance of grants of more than 660 acres to anyone but a proprietor, a landgrave,

In 1672, after the government had been reorganized under the Fundamental Constitutions, the odious policies were still in effect, and additional objectionable policies had indeed been introduced by the Fundamental Constitutions; therefore, the governor, council and assembly petitioned the proprietors for changes.

Despite the detailed provisions for exercising power and organizing the government, no clause of charter or concessions suggested any means for resolving differences between the people and the proprietors. The Virginia settlers resented the impositions of the proprietors. Nevertheless, Berkeley began issuing land grants. Then the proprietors in London directed the establishment of three counties, to be named after proprietors. Albemarle took in the already established Virginia settlers. Clarendon County was settled briefly between 1662 and 1663 by New Englanders, and from 1664 to 1667 by Barbadians, but they all eventually abandoned the enterprise. Craven County eventually became part of South Carolina.

Meanwhile, in 1665, the Albemarle settlers had been "given" an appointed governor, an elected assembly, and courts. A quit rent on their lands had been announced, but deferred for several years to encourage more settlers to come in.

§ 11.02(f). The Charter of 1665.

The proprietors sought and obtained a new charter on June 30, 1665, ostensibly to correct the potential problem resulting from the 1663 charter having been granted before the Heath charter of 1629 had been declared void by an order in council. The new charter was very similar to the 1663

---

or a cacique without express permission from the proprietors. It further limited the amount of land allowed in one warrant to that set forth in the proprietors' instructions of "forme of government." Another act provided that land on which improvements had been made but which was not lived on was to escheat to the proprietors if the grantee did not move to the land and live on it within six months after publication of the act. A third law prohibited sale of headrights by any person who had not lived in the county at least two years. Thus, by legislation of the Albemarle Assembly, some of the concessions made in the Great Deed of Grant were nullified. The chief concession left was the reduction in quitrent." *North Carolina Higher-Court Records, 1670-1696* xxxvi (Mattie Erma Edwards Parker, ed., 1968).

charter, but it did include a few amendments. These changes included a slightly different wording for the religious toleration provision and a new clause in which the proprietors were given "full power and authority to erect, Constitute, and make several Counties, Baronies and Colonies" and to make for them "laws and Constitutions . . . according to their best discretion . . . ."[1581]

§ 11.02(g). The Fundamental Constitutions of 1669.

§ 11.02(g)(1). The Feudal Scheme of the Fundamental Constitutions.

In 1669 the proprietors were ready to implement a plan of government that more nearly reflected the enormous feudal powers they had obtained through their charters, even though it meant reducing the rights of the settlers. On July 21, 1669, they adopted their "Fundamental Constitutions of Carolina," which they often referred to as their Grand Model:

> The Fundamental Constitutions were never implemented in their entirety, but they shaped the early history of the North Carolina colony. For two decades the government of the colony was a modified form of the system provided in the Grand Model. For many decades the governmental institutions of the colony bore the imprint of the Constitutions. In fact, certain features of North Carolina courts today, such as the method of selecting jurors, were provided in the Fundamental Constitutions. Furthermore, events in the colony, such as the so-called rebellions, were due in part to the way in which the colony was governed.[1582]

Even though never fully implemented, the scheme of the Fundamental

---

[1581] *Id.* at 94.

[1582] *Id.* at xxiii.

Constitutions as it related to landholding could be described as feudal holdings belonging to an hereditary nobility.[1583]

According to the arrangement linking governmental power with one's land tenure, the proprietors and hereditary nobility were to have control of the provincial government, with only limited participation by freeholders; in the local agencies of government, on the other hand, the freeholders were to be dominant; "serfs" or "leetmen" had no governmental role but were to be completely within the jurisdiction of the manorial courts, in accordance with their medieval models; slaves were to be entirely within the control of their masters.

Even from the beginning, the system of government described in the Fundamental Constitutions was not implemented. The proprietors apparently realized that differing circumstances in individual settlements required modification, so they abandoned the plan of a centralized provincial government at the very outset. Instead, they "temporarily" customized the scheme of the Fundamental Constitutions for each colony, first for the Virginia settlement in Albemarle County, and then for another settlement that had arisen at Port Royal, in territory that was to become part of South Carolina.

§ 11.02(g)(2). Landholding Under the Fundamental Constitutions.

Sometime in 1670 the Albemarle government was reorganized along the lines of the Fundamental Constitutions, but scarcity of early records makes it difficult to determine whether these changes had any important impact on the settlement or its landholding practices. In 1671 the colony's

---

1583 "The Fundamental Constitutions provided for the entire province of Carolina, instead of each county, to be a palatinate. The counties were to be the chief divisions of the province. Members of an hereditary nobility, who were to be feudal lords, were to be distributed equally among the counties. Land in each county was to be distributed systematically among feudal lords and freeholders, and governmental power was to be allocated according to modes of land tenure. By those means the proprietors undertook to establish and maintain in Carolina a "balance of Government" which would institute and perpetuate a feudal society and aristocratic control." *Id.*

governor complained to the proprietors that a revised version of the Constitutions reinstated certain land policies offensive to the settlers that the proprietors had earlier agreed to withdraw. The proprietors made no response to any of the complaints and questions raised by the settlers over the next several years. Disorder arose over uncertainty about the legitimacy and competency of officials exercising governmental authority. As already mentioned, a central source of discontent and disorder in Albemarle was the land policy of the proprietors.[1584]

It thus appears that the proprietors were relentless in pursuing their objective to create a feudal colony in North Carolina. Their instructions to the Albemarle governor in 1667, the offensive Albemarle legislation in 1668 and 1669, and the Fundamental Constitutions sent to Albemarle in 1670 all tended to negate land rights which the settlers had obtained in the past (land titles obtained from the Virginia Council or from Indians were nullified) and to abandon the policies of the Great Deed of Grant that had been favorable to the small settlers. Moreover, the proprietors almost never responded to the written petitions and protests, and they failed to reconstitute or reorganize the government as appointments expired or vacancies arose.

A long period of violence and disorder followed, with various local

[1584] "The disturbances in Albemarle expressed a constant dissatisfaction which at times became desperation. The causes of discontent were many. Not only were the colonists confused regarding the legality of their government, dissatisfied with the form and conduct of the government, and frustrated by the seeming indifference of the proprietors, but they also were burdened with discouragement due to policies and conditions that made it impossible for them to prosper financially.

"One obstacle to prosperity was the land policy of the proprietors. Albemarle settlers sought large tracts of good land, for they wanted plantations similar to those in Virginia. The proprietors, on the other hand, visualized a province composed in large measure of compact settlements; they reserved large land-holdings for themselves, the nobility, and a few lords of manors. Consequently, their policies were designed to prevent colonists from obtaining large plantations. Furthermore, to attain their ideal of a systematically distributed population, the proprietors developed a method of land distribution that took no account of geographical realities, and they imposed conditions for retaining land which kept the colonists in perpetual danger of forfeiture. Under the proprietors' early policies, a settler could not be certain that even his small allotment would consist of good land; he might find that most or all of it was swamp. If he did get good land, he was in constant danger of losing it because of inability to meet the proprietors' conditions for retaining it." *Id.* at xxxi-xxxii.

settlers vying for political leadership positions and with the proprietors refusing to take any action at all. At length, in 1679, a new governor was appointed, and he was given instructions and a formal document containing a plan for reinstituting stable government in Albemarle. The instructions for Albemarle were contained in a document called "Temporary Laws," adopted on February 5, 1679; they remained in effect until the plan of the Fundamental Constitutions as a whole was suspended in 1691. In these instructions the proprietors apparently tried to adopt land policies more acceptable to the settlers: the governor and the council issued patents confirming pre-1663 land grants from Virginia at a quit rent of one farthing per acre; new grants were issued for land obtained after 1663 at a quit rent of a half penny per acre. For new arrivals, however, the quit rent on their allotments remained at one penny per acre.[1585]

In 1680, Virginia, which had reasserted a claim to the Albemarle region, sent tax collectors to the settlements there in attempts to collect taxes and quit rents.

Even though the land policies embodied in the Fundamental Constitutions were occasionally modified to meet settlers' objections, the basic land regulations and practices embodied in that document remained in effect until the government was reorganized in 1691. The provisions of the Fundamental Constitutions of 1669 dealing with land management practices or property rights not previously discussed in this section may be summarized as follows:

> Only a freeholder with at least 50 acres could be a juror in a precinct court.
>
> "It shall be a base and vile thing to Plead for money or Reward . . . ."
>
> "Since multiplicity of Comments, as well as of laws, have great inconveniences, and Serve only to obscure and perplex, all manner of comments and expositions on any

[1585] *Id.* at lv.

part of these fundamental constitutions, or on any part of the Common or Statute law of Carolina, are absolutely prohibited."

A registrar in every precinct shall enroll deeds, leases and judgments.

"No person above seventeen years of Age shall have any benefit or protection of the law, or be capable of any place of profit or honor, who is not a member of Some church or profession, having his name recorded in Some one, and but one Religion Record at once."

Whoever possesses a freehold shall, after 1689, pay an annual rent of one penny per acre.

§ 11.02(g)(3). The Demise of the Fundamental Constitutions.

As disorder and dissent under the Fundamental Constitutions continued, the proprietors attempted to make adjustments. Two revisions in 1682 were intended to meet objections from groups proposing to settle in the colony. Finally, in 1691 the proprietors informally and in 1693 officially suspended the Fundamental Constitutions. A new version in 1698 was never fully implemented. For all the controversy, it should be said that neither a landed nobility nor serfdom ever developed in North Carolina. Many of the large grants were never located or surveyed, and their legality was later denied; the feudal seigniories usually declined into ordinary proprietary holdings and eventually into plantations.[1586] The rough and disorderly early history of this colony can be traced to not only the unrealistic land and other policies, but also to greed, gross neglect and mismanagement by the proprietors and their appointees.

Despite the inadequacies and anachronisms of the Fundamental

[1586] Herbert L. Osgood, *The American Colonies in the Seventeenth Century* 26 (1904).

Constitutions, they did help to establish a system of representative government that eventually led to the demise of the proprietary system in North Carolina. Between 1689 and 1713, the administration of Carolina was formally divided between North Carolina and South Carolina; thereafter, the crown took over the colonies and in 1729 created the royal provinces of North and South Carolina.

§ 11.02(h). Other Laws of Colonial North Carolina Related to Landholding.

Until 1751, the laws of the colony were prepared and circulated only in manuscript form. The first printing in 1751 gave the full text of only the laws then in force, while obsolete or repealed acts were indicated by title only. The land-related legislation from the 1751 edition of North Carolina laws is summarized below, to help indicate that the North Carolina colonists were dealing with the same everyday real property issues as their contemporaries in other colonies:

1715:

Ch. XX: disposal of goods taken for execution; and for better regulation of distresses, for levies and quit rents.

Ch. XXVII: old titles of lands; limitation of actions.

Ch. XXVIII: passing of lands when the estate is in a feme covert.

Ch. XXIX: preventing disputes concerning lands already surveyed.

Ch. XXX: escheat lands and escheators.

Ch. XXXIII: regulating abuses in taking up lands; the method of taking up and surveying lands.

Ch. XXXVI: roads and ferries.

Ch. XXXVIII: appointment of public registers; method for conveying lands, goods, and chattels and for preventing fraudulent deeds and mortgages.

Ch. XLV: fences.

Ch. XLVIII: proving wills, granting letters of administration, and managing intestates' estates.

Ch. XLIX: orphans.

Ch. LIX: securing to Indians the right and property of their own lands.

Ch. LXIV [an example of private legislation related to landholding]: "An Act, impowering Johanna Peterson, Widow of Thomas Peterson, late of Albemarle County, Esq; to make Sale of Certain Lands, late belonging to the said Thomas Peterson; and to make other Provision for Ann, the Daughter of the said Thomas Peterson, to whom the said Lands do descend."

Ch. LXV [another example of private legislation related to landholding]: "An Act, Confirming the Titles of sundry Persons who have, or hereafter may, purchase Lands of Col. Thomas Cary, in Bath County."

1723:

Ch. IV: settling titles and bounds of lands.

Ch. X: additional act on proving wills, granting letters of administration, and preventing fraud in managing intestates' estates.

1729:

Ch. II: for more quiet settling the bounds of certain Indian lands.

Ch. VI: for more effectual and speedy administration of the act for settling the titles and bounds of lands.

Ch. VII: confirming the Bath-Town common.

1740:

Ch. I [an example of granting municipal privileges]: "An Act, for Confirming Titles to the Town Lands of Edenton, for securing the Privileges heretofore granted to the said Town, and for further Encouragement and better Regulation thereof."

Ch. IX: exempting inhabitants of Bath from working on the public roads, and obliging them to clear and keep the town streets clear and in good order.

Ch. X: quit rents payable to the crown.

1741:

Ch. XXI: for relief of persons who have suffered from official neglect in recording deeds or who through ignorance have not had their deeds or conveyances acknowledged or recorded.

1743:

Ch. IV: regulating attorney fees.

1748 [second session]:

Ch. III: ascertaining bounds of certain Indian lands, and preventing settling or taking of such lands, by purchase or otherwise, so long as they are occupied by the Indians.

Ch. IV: forming a rent-roll of all lands in the province; quieting possession, and directing payment of quit rents.

1749:

Ch. IV: directing the method for cutting or docking entails of small estates.

1749 [second session]:

Ch. I: putting in force in the province certain enumerated statutes of England.

1749 [third session]:

Ch. IV: enabling justices to obtain law books for county courts.

1751:

Ch. III: additional act on feme coverts conveying their estates in land.[1587]

[1587] *The Earliest Printed Laws of North Carolina, 1669-1751* 1-353 (John D. Cushing, ed., 1977).

§ 11.03. Development of Land Law in South Carolina (from 1670).

§ 11.03(a). Summary of South Carolina's Early Settlement History Shared with North Carolina.

South Carolina holds most of its earliest colonial history, and the foundation of its land rights, in common with North Carolina. These shared beginnings are discussed in detail in § 11.02. The beginnings lie late in the 16th century, when the English monarchy granted a charter to Sir Humphrey Gilbert in 1578, giving property and governmental rights to unoccupied North American lands, on condition he commence settlement within six years. A settlement was commenced within that time but survived only a few months, so the crown conferred a similar grant on Sir Walter Raleigh in 1584. Raleigh's ill-fated colony on Roanoke Island had entirely disappeared by the time a delayed supply ship was able to reach the site in 1590. Landholding was probably exercised communally during these colonizing ventures.

South Carolina territory next came under the jurisdiction of the Virginia Company according to its charter of 1606. The focal point of this company's colonial efforts in Jamestown did not have any direct effect on the Carolina territory until about 50 years after Jamestown was founded, when Virginia settlers moved into what is now northeastern North Carolina. The Virginia colonial regulations were revised by a new charter in 1609, and again by a third charter in 1612. All the charters were revoked in 1624, when Virginia Colony reverted to the English crown. By that time, still no permanent colony had arisen in Carolina territory.

With rights to the territory back in the hands of the monarch, King Charles I granted to his attorney general Robert Heath a huge tract that included virtually all of North and South Carolina. The grant extended from Virginia to Spanish Florida, and from the Atlantic Ocean to the Pacific Ocean, and is discussed in connection with North Carolina settlement in §11.02(b). Neither Heath nor any of his assignees were able to commence a colonization effort, so eventually the crown considered the grant lapsed and re-granted the territory in 1663. Claimants and their successors in interest under the Heath tract, after a long battle, were later able to establish their rights to some land and were awarded a compensatory tract in New York. More pertinent to South Carolina, however, was the fact that the 1629 charter set the pattern for the 1663 charter in defining the land rights of the Carolina colonists. The most noteworthy features of the 1663 charter, as explained in §11.02(d), were its provisions for representative government, for broad feudal powers resting in the private proprietors, and for authority in the proprietors to create a colonial nobility. The grant under the 1663 charter was revised and expanded under an additional charter in 1665 to extend north to southern Virginia and south to St. Augustine, in present-day Florida.

§ 11.03(b). The Earliest Settlements in South Carolina.

Early in 1663 a group of colonists from Massachusetts tried to establish a settlement in South Carolina territory, but they abandoned the attempt after only a few months. Then, in 1665, Barbadians settled at the same site and planned a second community, but they had abandoned both the actual and the planned settlements by 1667. A short time later, in 1669, a detailed set of rules for colonial government and land rights called the Fundamental Constitutions was announced by the Carolina proprietors, and this is discussed in detail in §11.02(g). It was under the auspices of this frame of government and of a separate governor appointed for South Carolina in 1669 that the founders of the first permanent settlement in South Carolina established their site in March 1670, at the site of present-day Charleston. More precisely, the Fundamental Constitutions were actually suspended until the new colony obtained a greater population. In their place, the proprietors directed that executive and judicial powers be exercised by a Grand Council, composed of proprietors' deputies, freemen, and the governor.

Dissent arose over this form of government, and two dissenters protested that their land rights could not be secured until a regular parliamentary assembly was chosen, which would then confirm their past land grants. A parliament *was* held in July 1670. In August 1671, the proprietors issued a set of temporary laws for this first South Carolina colony, clearly intended to impose provisions of the Fundamental Constitutions.[1588]

The colony failed to progress satisfactorily, and the proprietors were required to make additional investments; they had also agreed to forego quit rents for a period of twenty years (1669-1689). A systematic survey of lands proved too difficult because of the numerous inland waterways and the irregular coastline; and "after the very early days the settlers refused to establish themselves in compact townships, but spread out in isolated plantations along the rivers."[1589]

In 1682 several hundred English Presbyterians and other dissenters and a smaller body of Scottish Presbyterians immigrated to the province. The Scots were induced by the prospect of an extended quit rent exemption but also bound themselves to swear submission to the Fundamental Constitution as a condition of receiving land allotments they settled at Port Royal, which was wiped out by the Spanish only three years later.

[1588] "These [temporary laws] reveal anew the fact that the board intended to force upon the province the most important provisions of the [Fundamental] Constitutions. These temporary laws provided for an elaborate official system like that of England, for the development as rapidly as possible of the provincial nobility and its incorporation with the council, and for the exercise by the council of the right of initiation and the other powers prescribed for the grand council in the Constitutions. Parliaments were to be called biennially. The creation of landgraves also began at this time, and the governor and council were ordered to have their baronies surveyed when any of the provincial nobility should desire it." Herbert L. Osgood, *The American Colonies in the Seventeenth Century* 215 (1904).

[1589] "Only the city of Charles Town itself, to which the settlers moved in 1680, met some of the proprietors' expectations. Laid out on the neck of land between the Ashley and Cooper rivers with streets intersecting at right angles according to their instructions, it was one of the first planned cities in North America. Contemporaries were convinced that these arrangements would enable them to 'avoid the undecent and incommodious irregularities which other Inglish Collonies are fallen into for want of any early care in laying out the Townes.'" Robert M. Weir, *Colonial South Carolina, A History* 61 (1983).

§ 11.03(c). Political Turmoil Centered on Land Issues.

Before the Spanish massacre, authorities ordered the colony divided into three counties, but at first only one of them, Berkeley County, was even partially organized for its local government functions. The proprietors directed that future land grants must include a re-entry clause enabling the proprietors to recover the land if quit rents were not timely paid, and requiring payment in coin. Meanwhile, the proprietors also stepped up their efforts to have the Fundamental Constitutions fully accepted by the colonists. The 1669 version was repudiated for the 1682 version, but the legislators rejected that, too, with a unanimous declaration that the province should be governed solely by the terms of its charter. No new laws were passed, and the temporary laws expired in 1690; by that time, no statute at all was in force in South Carolina.

A five-year period of persistent political disturbance followed, unrelieved by any generally accepted source of law for the colony. When a new governor was appointed in 1695, he carried new powers from the proprietors that were used to reach accords. Because most of the unrest was over land issues, settlement of those issues was also essential in stabilizing the government.[1590]

The province nevertheless produced more problems than benefits for the proprietors. South Carolina formally separated from North Carolina in 1710; the proprietors, however, managed to retain actual title to the land and it was not until 1729 that the title was changed by purchase, the land reverted to the crown, and the royal provinces of North and South Carolina were established.

§ 11.03(d). Landholding Issues in the Later Colonial Period.

After takeover of the colony by the crown, governing officials in the 1730s promoted township arrangements similar to those that were so

---

[1590] *Id.* at 69-70.

common in New England. In the South Carolina scheme, townships of 20,000 acres, or squares approximately six miles in each dimension, were reserved for new settlers who would agree to locate in close proximity to one another. Each family would be allotted a town lot, fifty acres of outlying land, and an attractive package of other benefits: exemption from quit rents for ten years; cost of conveyance and surveying paid by the government; and public assistance with costs of tools, food and transportation. These so-called land bounties were available not only to new immigrants but also to indentured servants who were finishing their time. By the 1760's thirteen such townships had been established, and by 1770 these inducements had led to a population with three-quarters of the inhabitants living outside the older settlements.

By holding out hope of better frontier security, the township scheme was one of several factors that dramatically increased the demand for South Carolina land in the 1730's. Also, since the proprietors had closed the land office more than a decade earlier, much demand had become pent up during that time. Improved market conditions for rice also increased interest in acquiring acreage for rice lands. Before new grants of land could be made to meet this demand, however, a long and serious controversy over quit rents had to be resolved. "There was no difficulty in working out the basic terms of a new [1731] quit rent act with the legislature: in return for remission of arrears in payment, all who held land from the proprietors would be required to register it with the appropriate officials and receive new grants. Thus the crown would presumably have an accurate roll of all lands on which it would be collecting quit rents."[1591]

Many speculators and planters resorted to unscrupulous devices to obtain grants to large tracts of land, despite the authority of the 1731 Quit Rent Act and the official policy encouraging smallholders. Moreover, the act did not require registration of lands acquired by private conveyance or by royal grant in the future. Even though the legislature corrected these omissions in 1744, the collection of quit rents was lax, amounting to less than 20% of the total due by the time of the Revolution.

[1591] *Id.* at 113.

The early acquisition of land in South Carolina was remarkably easy, especially for those induced to come "under the bounty". "All an individual had to do was to petition the governor and council, who then issued a warrant authorizing the surveyor to stake out a tract of so many acres (during most of the colonial period, fifty or 100 for each member of the petitioner's family). The recipient or his surveyor chose an unoccupied site, made a survey, and returned the surveyor's map or plat to the proper office. In turn, a grant was issued in the name of the proprietors or the crown . . . . [F]or most of the colonial period, grants provided a way for men and women of modest means to acquire land, and most grants were in fact made to them."[1592]

Eventually, it became clear that most of the low land fell into the hands of large landholders, while small farmers concentrated in the back country on farms averaging about 175 acres in size.

§ 11.03(e). Colonial Statutes Relating to Landholding.

In 1736, a mere seven years after South Carolina became a royal province, the colony published a retrospective collection of South Carolina laws, covering the period from the time of the earliest settlement to when the crown took over the province. A review of the laws then in force relating to landholding gives additional insight into the real property issues faced by South Carolina colonists. Following is a summary of the subjects of that early legislation relating to property rights and landholding, with the year of enactment indicated:

Prevention of nuisances (1692).

Escheat for nonpayment of quit rents (1694).

Fences (1694).

Payment of arrears in rents (1695).

[1592] *Id.* at 148.

Forms of purchase grants (1696).

Prevention of double mortgages and conveyances (1698).

Encouraging immigration (1712).

"An Act to put in Force in this Province the several Statutes of the kingdom of England, or South-Britain. . ." (1712).

Limitation of actions (1712).

Collecting back taxes (1721).

Quit rents (1731).

Making effectual wills (1734).[1593]

§ 11.04. Development of Land Law in Georgia (from 1732).

§ 11.04(a). The Charter of 1732.

Georgia was the last of the thirteen English colonies in America to be formed and the only colony of the thirteen to be governed by trustees. England's desire to bring more settlers into the frontier areas of its South Carolina colony came together with the philanthropic motives of James Oglethorpe to produce the youngest of the American colonies.[1594]

[1593] *The Earliest Printed Laws of South Carolina, 1692-1734* vol. 1, 67-541; vol. II, 23-141 (John D. Cushing, ed.,1978).

[1594] "The plan for the colony originated with James Edward Oglethorpe, an English gentleman of good family, who had served with distinction under Prince Eugene of Savoy, and later had entered the House of Commons. Oglethorpe's sympathies having been enlisted on behalf of imprisoned debtors and discharged prisoners, he conceived the idea of establishing in America a colony where worthy persons of those classes could get a new start in life. The charter granted to trustees certain territory south of the Savannah river, which had originally formed part of South

The provisions of the 1732 Charter from George II to Oglethorpe and the other trustees relating to property rights and landholding are as follows:

Reasons for the Charter:

> Whereas we are credibly informed, that many of our poor subjects are, through misfortunes and want of employment, reduced to great necessity, insomuch as by their labor they are not able to provide a maintenance for themselves and families; and if they had means to defray their charges of passage, and other expences, incident to new settlements, they would be glad to settle in any of our provinces in America where by cultivating the lands, at present waste and desolate, they might not only gain a comfortable subsistence for themselves and families, but also strengthen our colonies and increase the trade, navigation and wealth of these our realms.

The Grant:

> [W]e have . . . willed, ordained, constituted and appointed . . . for us, our heirs and successors, . . . that our right trusty and well-beloved [trustees] . . . be, and shall be one body politic and corporate . . . and that they and their successors . . . shall and may forever hereafter, be persons able and capable in the law, to purchase, have, take, receive [etc.] . . . any manors, messuages, lands, tenements, rents, advowsons, liberties, privileges, jurisdictions, franchises, and other hereditaments . . . in fee and in perpetuity, . . . also estates for lives, and for years . . . .

Carolina, but had been retained by the Crown when the Carolinas were surrendered by the proprietors in 1729. To this was added the one-eighth interest retained by Carteret at the time of the surrender, and which he now conveyed to the trustees. The charter was surrendered in 1752, and Georgia became a royal province." *Select Charters and Other Documents Illustrative of American History, 1606-1775* 235 (William MacDonald, ed., 1914).

The Tenure and the Quit Rent:

> [T]o be holden of us, our heirs and successors as of our honour of Hampton-court, in our county of Middlesex in free and common soccage, and not in capite, yielding, and paying therefor to us, our heirs and successors yearly forever, the sum of four shillings for every hundred acres of said lands, which the corporation shall grant, demise, plant, or settle . . . .

Legislative Power:

> And we do hereby ordain . . . that for and during the term of twenty-one years, to commence from the date of these our letters patent, the said corporation assembled for that purpose, shall and may form and prepare, laws, statutes and ordinances, fit and necessary for and concerning the government of the said colony, and not repugnant to the laws and statutes of England . . . .
>
> * * * * *
>
> [I]t shall and may be lawful for the said common council . . . to distribute, convey, assign and set over such particular portions of lands, tenements and hereditaments . . . unto such of our . . . subjects . . . upon such terms, and for such estates, and upon such rents, reservations and conditions as the same may be lawfully granted . . . .

No Land Grants for Trustees:

> Provided always that no grants shall be made of any part of the said lands unto any person, being a member of said corporation, or to any other person in trust, for the benefit of any member of said corporation; and that no person having any estate or interest, in law or equity, in any part of the said lands, shall be capable of being a member of

> the said corporation, during the continuance of such estate or interest.

Land Grants Limited to 500 Acres:

> Provided also, that no greater quantity of lands be granted, either entirely or in parcels, to or for the use, or in trust for any one person, than five hundred acres; and that all grants made contrary to the true intent and meaning hereof, shall be absolutely null and void.

Corporate Duration of 21 Years:

> And we do . . . ordain . . . that the said corporation and their successors, shall have full power and authority, for and during the term of twenty-one years . . . .

Requirement to Register Property Interests:

> And our further will and pleasure is, that the said corporation and their successors, do from time to time, and at all times hereafter, register or cause to be registered, all such leases, grants, plantings, conveyances, settlements, and improvements whatsoever, as shall at any time hereafter be made by, or in the name of said corporation, of any lands, tenements or hereditaments within the said province; and shall yearly send and transmit, or cause to be sent or transmitted, authentic accounts of such leases, grants, conveyances, settlements and improvements respectively, unto the auditor of the plantations for the time being, and also to our surveyor for the time being of our said province of South-Carolina . . . .
>
> Provided always . . ., that all leases, grants and conveyances made by or in the name of said corporation, of any lands within the said province, or a memorial containing the substance and effect thereof, shall be

> registered with the auditor of the said plantations . . . within the space of one year, to be computed from the date thereof, otherwise the same shall be void . . . .

Survey and Inspection for Quit Rents:

> [To the auditor and surveyor] we do hereby grant full power and authority from time to time, as often as need shall require, to inspect and survey, such of the said lands and premises, as shall be demised, granted and settled as aforesaid: which said survey and inspection, we do hereby declare, to be intended to ascertain the quit rents which shall from time to time become due to us . . . .[1595]

§ 11.04(b). The Character of the Earliest Georgia Settlers.

Although it has long been the popular belief that Georgia was populated principally by paupers and imprisoned debtors, more recent research has yielded other information. Debtors were not sought from the prisons, and probably fewer than a dozen convicted debtors ever came to Georgia during the settlement period. Instead, the trustees sought out poor people from the English towns, who, as charity colonists, were then enabled to travel to Georgia at the expense of the trustees. Most were small tradespersons and artisans; sailors and soldiers were considered unfit; farmers were generally considered to be productive and therefore needed in England.

[1595] *Id.* at 236-248. By-laws of the trustee corporation are published in Allen D. Candler, *The Colonial Records of the State of Georgia* 31-42 (1904).

§ 11.04(c). The First Settlement at Savannah.

§ 11.04(c)(1). Securing Land Rights from the Indians.

When Oglethorpe selected the site for the first settlement, he conferred with the Indians there and received their permission for settlement. This led to more extensive negotiations with other tribes of the Creek Confederacy; in May 1733, they entered into a treaty ceding lands they were no longer using.[1596]

§ 11.04(c)(2). Laying Out the Town.

After an uneventful crossing, the site of modern Savannah was chosen for the first settlement. In a letter of February 10, 1733, to the trustees back in London, Oglethorpe described the first steps toward land allotment and distribution:

> Upon the River-side, in the Centre of this Plain, I have laid out the Town, opposite to which is an Island of very rich Pasturage, which I think should be kept for the Trustees Cattle . . . . I have marked out the Town and Common; half of the former is already cleared, and the first House was begun Yesterday in the Afternoon. A little Indian Nation, the only one within Fifty Miles, is not only at Amity, but desirous to be Subjects to his Majesty King George, to have Lands given them among us, and to breed their Children at our Schools.[1597]

The town layout at Savannah set the pattern for other Georgia towns during the trustee period and was itself probably derived from South Carolina's 1730 township plan. Each block, called a tithing, consisted of

---

[1596] Kenneth Coleman, ed., *A History of Georgia* 18-19 (2d. ed. 1991).

[1597] *Id.* at 27.

ten house lots sixty by ninety feet. Four tithings made up a ward, and each ward had a public square in the middle. Trustee lots were reserved for churches, markets and stores. Eventually, the Savannah township consisted of 24 square miles, or 15,360 acres. Twelve thousand of those acres were intended for private grants (240 grants of 50 acres each), with the balance reserved for roads, streets, commons, and other trustee reserves. "Immediately beyond the area of the town were the triangular shaped garden lots, which with the building lots, made up five acres to each grantee. Here settlers were supposed to raise vegetables and other garden truck for their tables. Beyond the garden lots were the forty-five acre farm lots where mulberry trees, corn, and other crops were to be planted. Beyond these farm lots, and outside the planned township area, were to be the larger grants of adventurers."[1598]

The main motivation for this plan was to keep the settlers in fairly close proximity with one another, as a defense against aggression by the Spanish or French. The contiguous settlement pattern did not, however, take into account the varying quality of farm land in the outlying grants. Many settlers complained bitterly about the poor quality of the farm land grants assigned to them in such systematic fashion and a few were allowed to exchange lands, but only after months of struggle on the unfit farmland. Another difficulty with land grants in the townships was that the colony's surveyor could not keep up with the needs of the settlers.

§ 11.04(d). Conflict Over the Tenure of Early Land Grants.

Formal land grant regulations were not announced by the trustees until 1735, but even before that time the land grants probably conformed to the pattern expressed in the regulations. The regulations included:

A limited grant of fifty acres for each head of a family,

[1598] *Id.* at 123.

> A restriction against alienation except by special permission from the trustees,
>
> A requirement that granted land be cleared and cultivated within ten years from the grant, or else the grant would revert,
>
> In order to commence silk production, a requirement that 100 mulberry trees be planted for every ten acres cleared, and
>
> Inheritance, or tenure, by fee tail-male only.

This latter limitation gave the most significant cause for colonists' concerns. From the beginning the colonists complained that the grants were not in fee simple, but rather in fee tail-male, meaning that the land could descend only to male heirs and only so long as the line of male heirs continued. "The tail-male provision applied to charity and adventurer grants and was designed to insure a soldier upon each fifty acres. This provision undoubtedly kept many prospective settlers from coming to Georgia, but it was never rigidly enforced. If there was no male heir, women were freely allowed to inherit land upon special application of the Trustees."[1599]

The restriction on alienation of lands held by the charity settlers was intended effectively to prevent them from divesting their landholdings in return for some more temporary or ephemeral form of wealth, or to prevent their lands from falling into the hands of creditors. More realistic, however, were the complaints from the colonists that tail-male tenure was of questionable validity under current English law, and that they were unable to lease, mortgage or sell their lands, unless they obtained special permission from the trustees.

In 1738, three years after the 1735 trustee regulations were announced, 119 freeholders of Savannah petitioned the trustees to allow fee simple

---

[1599] *Id.* at 122-123.

grants. After an investigation, the trustees denied the petition. Thereupon, Georgia settlers sent an even broader petition the next year, "asking that land might be granted where it was convenient to the settlers, that excessive quit rents be relaxed, that constables and tithingmen be under the order of the Trustees and the magistrates only, and that the people be allowed to choose their own bailiffs."[1600]

Eventually, beginning in 1739, the trustees worked out extensive revisions in the land grant policies and included them in a complete land regulation which was adopted by Parliament in 1742 (but never given royal approval).[1601]

In 1750 the trustees abolished tail-male, some quit rents, and limitations on land ownership.[1602]

§ 11.04(e). Controversy Over Quit Rents.

Under the 1732 charter, quit rents were set at four shillings per hundred acres, would not be payable until ten years after the land grants were made, and although paid to the trustees were ultimately to be given to the crown. In 1735 the trustees introduced a five-fold increase in quit rents on grants to adventurers. At the time, this new rate was the highest quit rent anywhere in the American colonies. The trustees suggested various reforms in 1741 and 1742, but the Privy Council approved none of them. Thus, in 1745 the trustees directed that rent rolls be prepared so collection could

---

[1600] *Id.* at 99.

[1601] "Inheritance of land was now allowed to wives, daughters, other relatives, and any heirs at law when there was no member of the immediate family to inherit. Widows were guaranteed all the rights of inheritance they had in England. Colonists could now acquire through inheritance or marriage up to two thousand acres and could lease their lands for not over twenty-one years. White mulberry planting for cleared land was reduced to a hundred trees for every fifty acres, and land did not need to be cleared and cultivated on as rapid a schedule as originally specified. These changes did not affect the basic land policy of the trustees, which required colonists to hold land in tail-male, except that adequate inheritance provisions were made where there was no male heir. Lands still could not be bought and sold freely." *Id.* at 124-125.

[1602] Harold H. Martin, *Georgia, A Bicentennial History* 24-25 (1977).

begin; in the end, however, no rent rolls were prepared, and no collection took place during the trustee period, which ended in 1752.

§ 11.04(f). Changes in Landholding Patterns.

Not all landholding was controlled by the trustees and their officials. Some grants were abandoned and then taken up by others, without any form of permission or legality. Some ungranted lands were simply taken over, especially by those who entered the colony in some capacity other than settlers under the trustees. By 1742 the process of consolidating small landholdings into larger plantations had already begun. The earliest consolidations probably resulted from remarriages of widows, who obtained trustee permission to join their landholdings with those of their new husbands.

§ 11.04(g). Landholding in Colonial Georgia Under Royal Administration.

When the trusteeship of George reverted to the crown in 1752, most landholding arrangements remained as they were, but several important changes in official land policy took place. Land was still granted free of charge, with the exception of surveying and land office fees. Headright grants were still available, at the rate of 100 acres for the head of the family and fifty acres for each other family member, and additional land for new family members. Larger headright grants could be obtained if the grantee could show an ability to use the additional land.

Coastal lands, of course, were the first to be granted, and by 1760 almost all good coastal land up to the boundary of Indian lands had been taken up. By the Treaty of Augusta of November 10, 1763, the Creeks ceded an additional 2,400,000 acres of land, which opened significant new territory and high quality land to Georgians. By 1772, most of the desirable land from this Indian cession had been granted. Another Indian cession occurred in 1773, but this time it was agreed that the Indians would be paid, so the land was sold (for sixpence an acre) rather than given to settlers, and sale proceeds were to be given to the Indians.

Consolidation of holdings, well under way during the trusteeship, accelerated during the crown colony years, but, with the earlier emphasis on small holdings, never reached the extent of large holdings in neighboring South Carolina.

To meet the growing problem of abandoned lands, the new royal governor was instructed to make records for all trustee grants that were inadequately documented and then to issue new grants. Later, a local rule gave absentee owners three years to either record their trustee grant or forfeit it to the colony.

The rather onerous clearing and cultivating requirements were originally set at 5% annually, but in 1758 this was relaxed in several ways. Although records are inconclusive, quit rents were probably never collected even during the crown colony period. Nevertheless, some Georgians raised a protest against quit rents on the eve of the Revolution.[1603]

§ 11.04(h). Georgia Colonial Statutes Related to Landholding.

In 1762 a printer was commissioned to print Georgia colonial legislation then in force which, in published form, amounted to 35 separate acts passed between 1755 and 1763. The provisions of those laws and of subsequent legislation that relate to property rights and landholding in colonial Georgia are summarized below:

> Confirming sales of land by attorneys or agents, and ascertaining the proof of instruments or writings (1757).
>
> Preventing private persons from purchasing lands from the Indians (1758, 1765).
>
> Limiting the time for persons claiming lands by virtue of warrants of surveys, allotments, nominal titles, or

[1603] Kenneth Coleman, ed., *A History of Georgia* 64 (2d ed. 1991).

possession, derived from the late trustees or from others acting under their authority (1758).

Regulating fences (1759).

Preventing the building of wooden chimneys in Savannah; providing against accidental fires (1759, 1763).

Enabling feme coverts (married women) to convey their estates and validating prior conveyances and acknowledgements (1760).

Subjecting to attachment real and personal estates of debtors (1761).

Ascertaining the commons land of Savannah (1761, 1766, 1770).

Preventing fraudulent mortgages and conveyances, and validating prior deeds and conveyances (1763, 1768).

Preventing the throwing of ballast, rubbish or falling trees into rivers and creeks (1763, 1765).

Empowering the General Court of Pleas to grant writs of partition of lands and tenements held in coparcenary, joint tenancy and tenancy in common, and prescribing procedures (1763, 1767).

Preventing damage from dams or banks used to reserve or stop water (1763).

Empowering surveyors to lay out public roads (1764, 1766, 1767).

Preventing trespass on lands of the crown or on Indian lands (1764).

Directing executors and administrators in returning inventories and accounts of estates, and permitting commissions therefor (1764).

Preventing frauds and abuses in laying out crown lands (1765).

Cultivating and improving lands; regulating surveying and marking of lines (1765).

Raising quit rent rates (1765).

Encouraging settlers [by granting township lots] (1766).

Limitation of actions (1767).

§ 11.05. Bibliography.

Books:

Andrews, Charles M., *The Colonial Period of American History* (1937).
Candler, Allen D., *The Colonial Records of the State of Georgia* (1904).
Coleman, Kenneth, ed., *A History of Georgia* (2d. ed. 1991).
Cushing, John D., ed., *The Earliest Printed Laws of Pennsylvania 1681-1713* (1978).
Cushing, John D., ed., *The Earliest Printed Laws of South Carolina, 1692-1734* (1978).
Harper, Steven Craig, *Promised Land: Penn's Holy Experiment, the Walking Purchase, and the Dispossession of Delawares, 1600–1763* (2006).
MacDonald, William, ed., *Select Charters and Other Documents Illustrative of American History 1606-1775* (1914).
Martin, Harold H., *Georgia: A Bicentennial History 24-25* (1977).
McIlvenna, Noeleen, *A Very Mutinous People: The Struggle for North Carolina, 1660–1713* (2009).
Miller, Randall M. and William Pencak, eds., *Pennsylvania: A History of the Commonwealth* (2002).
Moretta, John A., *William Penn and the Quaker Legacy* (2007).
Mulford, Isaac S., *A Civil and Political History of New Jersey* (1851).
Oatis, Steven J., *A Colonial Complex: South Carolina's Frontiers in the Era of the Yamasee War, 1680–1730* (2004).
Osgood, Herbert L., *The American Colonies in the Seventeenth Century* (1904).
Parker, Mattie Erma Edwards, ed., *North Carolina Charters and Constitutions, 1578-1698* (1963).
Parker, Mattie Erma Edwards, ed., *North Carolina Higher-Court Records, 1670-1696* (1968).

Powell, William S., *North Carolina, A Bicentennial History* (1977).
Ready, Milton, *The Tar Heel State: A History of North Carolina* (2005).
Roper, L.H., *Conceiving Carolina: Proprietors, Planters, and Plots, 1662-1729* (2004).
Scharf, J. Thomas, *History of Delaware 1609-1888* (1888).
Watson, Alan D., ed., *Society in Early North Carolina: A Documentary History* (2000).
Weir, Robert M., *Colonial South Carolina: A History* (1983).

www.ingramcontent.com/pod-product-compliance
Lightning Source LLC
LaVergne TN
LVHW062202200926
848484LV00006B/1299
* 9 7 8 1 6 0 0 4 2 2 0 5 8 *